# Esquire's Big Book *of* Great WRITING

# Esquire's Big Book *of* Great WRITING

MORE THAN 70 YEARS OF CELEBRATED JOURNALISM

EDITED BY **ADRIENNE MILLER**

HEARST BOOKS / A Division of Sterling Publishing Co., Inc., New York

Library of Congress Cataloging-in-Publication Data

Esquire's big book of great writing : more than 70 years of celebrated journalism/edited by Adrienne Miller.
p. cm.
ISBN 1-58816-298-2
I. Miller, Adrienne.
PN4726.E87 2003
814'.508—dc21

2003008985

10 9 8 7 6 5 4 3 2 1

*Cover design by Celia Fuller*
*Book design by Barbara Sturman*

Published by Hearst Books
A Division of Sterling Publishing Co., Inc.
387 Park Avenue South, New York, NY 10016



www.esquire.com

Distributed in Canada by Sterling Publishing
c/o Canadian Manda Group, One Atlantic Avenue, Suite 105
Toronto, Ontario, Canada M6K 3E7

Distributed in Australia by Capricorn Link (Australia) Pty. Ltd.
P.O. Box 704, Windsor, NSW 2756 Australia

Manufactured in China

ISBN: 1-58816-298-2

CONTENTS



## ESSAYS

## FEATURES

# PROFILES

# FOREWORD

I remember stories. Not every story, of course. But I remember stories my grandfather told me and stories I read as a child. I remember stories I read in textbooks and stories I read when I started reading this magazine in 1978. Storytelling is as basic a human impulse as eating. It's necessary and, when done effectively, elevating. Story is how we learn, it's how we communicate. There is no more intriguing conversation starter than, "I gotta tell you about this thing that happened to me." Stories are the bases of religion and the keepers of communal knowledge. They are essential.

For seventy years, *Esquire* magazine has been telling stories. Thousands and thousands of stories in nearly 900 issues of the magazine. Many of them have been made up—fiction written by virtually every one of the great American writers of the last seven decades. We collected the most memorable of those stories in *Esquire's Big Book of Fiction*.

This book is devoted to stories born of the actual lives and central events that *Esquire* reporters and writers have covered since the magazine's founding in 1933. Non-fiction takes many forms—essay, humor, war reporting, personality profile, investigation, opinion, reviews, feature writing. They're all in here. In many cases, *Esquire* invented the forms.

Two examples.

Nobody knew how to write a personality profile before Gay Talese taught them in the late 50s and early 60s. Prior to Talese, writing about famous people took the form of fawning transcription. With just one story, Talese taught at least three generations how to deal with fame—and it's often disappointing how little progress has been made since then. With "Frank Sinatra Has a Cold," Talese demonstrated that a writer doesn't even need his subject's cooperation to create a revealing, penetrating portrait. When you read the story now, you might be disappointed by its familiarity. But that is not the story's problem—it's because writers for the last forty years have been co-opting the techniques Talese invented.

I also have to look back at the groundbreaking work of John Sack. Our second Iraqi war brought the term "embedded reporter" into the public consciousness. The term was created by the Defense Department to describe the work John Sack wanted to do. He embedded himself with a group of soldiers—not as was done in the second Iraqi war, but from the beginning, from basic training on through months of fighting in Vietnam. The experience led to the extraordinary "M Company," which comprised nearly the entire issue of *Esquire* when it was published. Sack has covered every war and conflict since Korea, nearly always for *Esquire*. Because of the incredible ambition of "M Company," the story runs to a length that made its inclusion in this collection impossible. But Sack was one of the founding writers of what came to be called New Journalism, and his work, like Talese's, created a genre. He's a true original.

In the six years I've been the editor of *Esquire*, we have published many ambitious stories. We have occasionally broken new journalistic ground. Some of the stories have been mere tours de force in their nonfiction genre. Like Sean Flynn's "The Perfect Fire," one of the finest pieces of reporting ever published and the winner of The National Magazine Award in 2000. Like many pieces by Tom Junod, who is the primary setter of the new rules of magazine writing and who is represented in this collection by a profile of a man who was, at the time of the story's publication, an entirely unlikely subject: Mr. Rogers. We published a story by Dave Eggers, an editor at *Esquire* at the time, "Long Live the Career Smoker," that was a warm-up for his memoir/sensation *A Breathtaking Work of Staggering Genius*. One of our most prolific writers, and one who combines a barely-sheathed fury with cutting humor, is Scott Raab, whose profile of baseball demi-legend Don Zimmer is the kind of story that makes one wish he could love the game of baseball.

There are a hundred other people whose work deserves mention. It's the great joy of stewarding a great magazine like *Esquire* that writers want to do their best work for us, they want to expand the possibilities of the written word as part of the terms of their assignment. They labor in the shadow of the greatest magazine writers in American history—Tom Wolfe, Norman Mailer, Ernest Hemingway, Richard Ben Cramer, and so many others—and seek to free themselves from those shadows and create their own legacies.

This collection is an inspiration, as much for the stories contained within, as for the belief that the written word can change and enlighten the world, one story at a time.

—David Granger, Editor in Chief

# ESSAYS

# The Crack-Up

## F. SCOTT FITZGERALD

Of course all life is a process of breaking down, but the blows that do the dramatic side of the work—the big sudden blows that come, or seem to come, from outside—the ones you remember and blame things on and, in moments of weakness, tell your friends about, don't show their effect all at once. There is another sort of blow that comes from within—that you don't feel until it's too late to do anything about it, until you realize with finality that in some regard you will never be as good a man again. The first sort of breakage seems to happen quick—the second kind happens almost without your knowing it but is realized suddenly indeed.

Before I go on with this short history, let me make a general observation—the test of a first-rate intelligence is the ability to hold two opposed ideas in the mind at the same time, and still retain the ability to function. One should, for example, be able to see that things are hopeless and yet be determined to make them otherwise. This philosophy fitted on to my early adult life, when I saw the improbable, the implausible, often the "impossible," come true. Life was something you dominated if you were any good. Life yielded easily to intelligence and effort, or to what proportion could be mustered of both. It seemed a romantic business to be a successful literary man—you were not ever going to be as famous as a movie star but what note you had was probably longer-lived; you were never going to have the power of a man of strong political or religious convictions but you were certainly more independent. Of course within the practice of your trade you were forever unsatisfied—but I, for one, would not have chosen any other.

As the Twenties passed, with my own twenties marching a little ahead of them, my two juvenile regrets—at not being big enough (or good enough) to play football in college, and at not getting overseas during the war—resolved themselves into childish waking dreams of imaginary heroism that were good enough to go to sleep on in restless nights. The big problems of life seemed to solve themselves, and if the business of fixing them was difficult, it made one too tired to think of more general problems.

Life, ten years ago, was largely a personal matter. I must hold in balance the sense of futility of effort and the sense of the necessity to struggle; the conviction of the inevitability of failure and still the determination to "succeed"—and, more than these, the contradiction between the dead hand of the past and the high intentions of the future. If I could do this through the common ills—domestic, professional, and personal—then the ego would continue as an arrow shot from nothingness to nothingness with such force that only gravity would bring it to earth at last.

For seventeen years, with a year of deliberate loafing and resting out in the center—things went on like that, with a new chore only a nice prospect for the next day. I was living hard, too, but: "Up to forty-nine it'll be all right," I said. "I can count on that. For a man who's lived as I have, that's all you could ask."

—And then, ten years this side of forty-nine, I suddenly realized that I had prematurely cracked.

Now a man can crack in many ways—can crack in the head, in which case the power of decision is taken from you by others; or in the body, when one can but submit to the white hospital world; or in the nerves. William Seabrook in an unsympathetic book tells, with some pride and a movie ending, of how he became a public charge. What led to his alcoholism, or was bound up with it, was a collapse of his nervous system. Though the present writer was not so entangled—having at the time not tasted so much as a glass of beer for six months—it was his nervous reflexes that were giving way—too much anger and too many tears.

Moreover, to go back to my thesis that life has a varying offensive, the realization of having cracked was not simultaneous with a blow, but with a reprieve.

Not long before, I had sat in the office of a great doctor and listened to a grave sentence. With what, in retrospect, seems some equanimity, I had gone on about my affairs in the city where I was then living, not caring much, not thinking how much had been left undone, or what would become of this and that responsibility, like people do in books; I was well insured and anyhow I had been only a mediocre caretaker of most of the things left in my hands, even of my talent.

But I had a strong sudden instinct that I must be alone. I didn't want to see any people at all. I had seen so many people all my life—I was an average mixer, but more than average in a tendency to identify myself, my ideas, my destiny, with those of all classes that I came in contact with. I was always saving or being saved—in a single morning I would go through the emotions ascribable to Wellington at Waterloo. I lived in a world of inscrutable hostiles and inalienable friends and supporters.

But now I wanted to be absolutely alone and so arranged a certain insulation from ordinary cares.

It was not an unhappy time. I went away and there were fewer people. I found I was good-and-tired. I could lie around and was glad to, sleeping or dozing sometimes twenty hours a day and in the intervals trying resolutely not to think—instead I made lists—made lists and tore them up, hundreds of lists: of cavalry leaders and football players and cities, and popular tunes and pitchers, and happy times, and hobbies and houses lived in and how many suits since I left the army and how many pairs of shoes (I didn't count the suit I bought in Sorrento that shrank, nor the pumps and dress shirt and collar that I carried around for years and never wore, because the pumps got damp and grainy and the shirt and collar got yellow and starch-rotted). And lists of women I'd liked, and of the times I had let myself be snubbed by people who had not been my betters in character or ability.

—And then suddenly, surprisingly, I got better.

—And cracked like an old plate as soon as I heard the news.

That is the real end of this story. What was to be done about it will have to rest in what used to be called the "womb of time." Suffice it to say that after about an hour of solitary pillow-hugging, I began to realize that for two years my life had been a drawing on resources that I did not possess, that I had been mortgaging myself physically and spiritually up to the hilt. What was the small gift of life given back in comparison to that?—when there had once been a pride of direction and a confidence in enduring independence.

I realized that in those two years, in order to preserve something—an inner hush maybe, maybe not—I had weaned myself from all the things I used to love—that every act of life from the morning toothbrush to the friend at dinner had become an effort. I saw that for a long time I had not liked people and things, but only followed the rickety old pretense of liking. I saw that even my love for those closest to me had become only an attempt to love, that my casual relations—with an editor, a tobacco seller, the child of a friend, were only what I remembered I *should* do, from other days. All in the same month I became bitter about such things as the sound of the radio, the advertisements in the magazines, the screech of tracks, the dead silence of the country—contemptuous at human softness, immediately (if secretively) quarrelsome toward hardness—hating the night when I couldn't sleep and hating the day because it went toward night. I slept on the heart side now because I knew that the sooner I could tire that out, even a little, the sooner would come that blessed hour of nightmare which, like a catharsis, would enable me to better meet the new day.

There were certain spots, certain faces I could look at. Like most midwesterners, I have never had any but the vaguest race prejudices—I always had a secret yen for the lovely Scandinavian blondes who sat on porches in St. Paul but hadn't emerged enough economically to be part of what was then society. They were too nice to be "chickens" and too quickly off the farmlands to seize a place in the sun, but I remember going round blocks to catch a single glimpse of shining hair—the bright shock of a girl I'd never know. This is urban, unpopular talk. It strays afield from the fact that in these latter days I couldn't stand the sight of Celts, English, Politicians, Strangers, Virginians, Negroes (light or dark), Hunting People, or retail clerks, and middlemen in general, all writers (I avoided writers very carefully because they can perpetuate trouble as no one else can)—and all the classes as classes and most of them as members of their class . . .

Trying to cling to something, I liked doctors and girl children up to the age of about thirteen and well-brought-up boy children from about eight years old on. I could have peace and happiness with these few categories of people. I forgot to add that I liked old men—men over seventy, sometimes over sixty if their faces looked seasoned. I liked Katharine Hepburn's face on the screen, no matter what was said about her pretentiousness, and Miriam Hopkins's face, and old friends if I only saw them once a year and could remember their ghosts.

All rather inhuman and undernourished, isn't it? Well, that, children, is the true sign of cracking up.

It is not a pretty picture. Inevitably it was carted here and there within its frame and exposed to various critics. One of them can only be described as a person whose life makes other people's lives seem like death—even this time when she was cast in the usually unappealing role of Job's comforter. In spite of the fact that this story is over, let me append our conversation as a sort of postscript:

"Instead of being so sorry for yourself, listen—" she said. (She always says "Listen," because she thinks while she talks—*really* thinks.) So she said: "Listen. Suppose this wasn't a crack in you—suppose it was a crack in the Grand Canyon."

"The crack's in me," I said heroically.

"Listen! The world only exists in your eyes—your conception of it. You can make it as big or as small as you want to. And you're trying to be a little puny individual. By God, if I ever cracked, I'd try to make the world crack with me. Listen! The world only exists through your apprehension of it, and so it's much better to say that it's not you that's cracked—it's the Grand Canyon."

"Baby, et up all her Spinoza?"

"I don't know anything about Spinoza. I know—" She spoke, then, of old woes of her own, that seemed, in the telling, to have been more dolorous than mine, and how she had met them, overidden them, beaten them.

I felt a certain reaction to what she said, but I am a slow-thinking man, and it occurred to me simultaneously that of all natural forces, vitality is the incommunicable one. In days when juice came into one as an article without duty, one tried to distribute it—but always without success; to further mix metaphors, vitality never "takes." You have it or you haven't it, like health or brown eyes or honor or a baritone voice. I might have asked some of it from her, neatly wrapped and ready for home cooking and digestion, but I could never have got it—not if I'd waited around for a thousand hours with the tin cup of self-pity. I could walk from her door, holding myself very carefully like cracked crockery, and go away into the world of bitterness, where I was making a home with such materials as are found there—and quote to myself after I left her door:

*"Ye are the salt of the earth. But if the salt hath lost its savour, wherewith shall it be salted?"*

Matthew 5:13.

In a previous article this writer told about his realization that what he had before him was not the dish that he had ordered for his forties. In fact—since he and the dish were one, he described himself as a cracked plate, the kind that one wonders whether it is worth preserving. Your editor thought that the article suggested too many aspects without regarding them closely, and probably many readers felt the same way—and there are always those to whom all self-revelation is contemptible, unless it ends with a noble thanks to the gods for the Unconquerable Soul.

But I had been thanking the gods too long, and thanking them for nothing. I wanted to put a lament in my record, without even the background of the Euganean Hills to give it color. There weren't any Euganean Hills that I could see.

Sometimes, though, the cracked plate has to be retained in the pantry, has to be kept in service as a household necessity. It can never again be warmed on the stove nor shuffled with the other plates in the dishpan; it will not be brought out for company, but it will do to hold crackers late at night or to go into the icebox under leftovers . . .

Hence this sequel—a cracked plate's further history.

Now the standard cure for one who is sunk is to consider those in actual destitution or physical suffering—this is an all-weather beatitude for gloom in general and fairly salutory daytime advice for everyone. But at three o'clock in the morning, a forgotten package has the same tragic importance as a death sentence, and the cure doesn't work—and in a real dark night of the soul it is always three o'clock in the morning, day after day. At that hour the tendency is to refuse to face things as long as possible by retiring into an infantile dream—but one is continually startled out of this by various contacts with the world. One meets these occasions as quickly and carelessly as possible and retires once more back into the dream, hoping that things will adjust themselves by some great material or spiritual bonanza. But as the withdrawal persists there is less and less chance of the bonanza—one is not waiting for the fade-out of a single sorrow, but rather being an unwilling witness of an execution, the disintegration of one's own personality . . .

Unless madness or drugs or drink come into it, this phase comes to a dead end, eventually, and is succeeded by a vacuous quiet. In this you can try to estimate what has been sheared away and what is left. Only when this quiet came to me did I realize that I had gone through two parallel experiences.

The first time was twenty years ago, when I left Princeton in junior year with a complaint diagnosed as malaria. It transpired, through an X-ray taken a dozen years later, that it had been tuberculosis—a mild case, and after a few months of rest I went back to college. But I had lost certain offices, the chief one was the presidency of the Triangle Club, a musical comedy idea, and also I dropped back a class. To me college would never be the same. There were to be no badges of pride, no medals, after all. It seemed on one March afternoon that I had lost every single thing I wanted—and that night was the first time that I hunted down the specter of womanhood that, for a little while, makes everything else seem unimportant.

Years later I realized that my failure as a big shot in college was all right—instead of serving on committees, I took a beating on English poetry; when I got the idea of what it was all about, I set about learning how to write. On Shaw's principle that "if you don't get what you like, you better like what you get," it was a lucky break—at the moment it was a harsh and bitter business to know that my career as a leader of men was over.

Since that day I have not been able to fire a bad servant, and I am astonished and impressed by people who can. Some old desire for personal dominance was broken and gone. Life around me was a solemn dream, and I lived on the letters I wrote to a girl in another city. A man does not recover from such jolts—he becomes a different person and, eventually, the new person finds new things to care about.

The other episode parallel to my current situation took place after the war, when I had again overextended my flank. It was one of those tragic loves doomed for lack of money, and one day the girl closed it out on the basis of common sense. During a long summer of despair I wrote a novel instead of letters, so it came out all right, but it came out all right for a different reason. The man with the jingle of money in his pocket who married the girl a year later would always cherish an abiding distrust, an animosity, toward the leisure class—not the conviction of a revolutionist but the smoldering hatred of a peasant. In the years since then I have never been able to stop wondering where my friends' money came from, nor to stop thinking that at one time a sort of *droit du seigneur* might have been exercised to give one of them my girl.

For sixteen years I lived pretty much as this latter person, distrusting the rich, yet working for money with which to share their mobility and the grace that some of them brought into their lives. During this time I had plenty of the usual horses shot from under me—I remember some of their names—*Punctured Pride, Thwarted Expectation, Faithless, Show-off, Hard Hit, Never Again.* And after a while I wasn't twenty-five, then not even thirty-five, and nothing was quite as good. But in all these years I don't remember a moment of discouragement. I saw honest men through moods of suicidal gloom—some of them gave up and died; others adjusted themselves and went on to a larger success than mine; but my morale never sank below the level of self-disgust when I had put on some unsightly personal show. Trouble has no necessary connection with discouragement—discouragement has a germ of its own, as different from trouble as arthritis is different from a stiff joint.

When a new sky cut off the sun last spring, I didn't at first relate it to what had happened fifteen or twenty years ago. Only gradually did a certain family resemblance come through—an overextension of the flank, a burning of the candle at both ends; a call upon physical resources that I did not command, like a man overdrawing at his bank. In its impact this blow was more violent than the other two but it was the same in kind—a feeling that I was standing at twilight on a deserted range, with an empty rifle in my hands and the targets down. No problem set—simply a silence with only the sound of my own breathing.

In this silence there was a vast irresponsibility toward every obligation, a deflation of all my values. A passionate belief in order, a disregard of motives or consequences in favor of guesswork and prophecy, a feeling that craft and industry would have a place in any world—one by one, these and other convictions were swept away. I saw that the novel, which at my maturity was the strongest and supplest medium for conveying thought and emotion from one human being to another, was becoming subordinated to a mechanical and communal art that, whether in the hands of Hollywood merchants or Russian idealists, was capable of reflecting only the tritest thought, the most obvious emotion. It was an art in which words were subordinate to images, where personality was worn down to the inevitable low gear of collaboration. As long past as 1930, I had a hunch that the talkies would make even the best selling novelist as archaic as silent pictures. People still read, if only Professor Canby's book of the month—curious children nosed at the slime of Mr. Tiffany Thayer in the drugstore libraries—but there was a rankling indignity, that to me had become almost an obsession, in seeing the power of the written word subordinated to another power, a more glittering, a grosser power . . .

I set that down as an example of what haunted me during the long night—this was something I could neither accept nor struggle against, something which tended to make my efforts obsolescent, as the chain stores have crippled the small merchant, an exterior force, unbeatable—

(I have the sense of lecturing now, looking at a watch on the desk before me and seeing how many more minutes—)

Well, when I had reached this period of silence, I was forced into a measure that no one ever adopts voluntarily: I was impelled to think. God, was it difficult! The moving about of great secret trunks. In the first exhausted halt, I wondered whether I had ever thought. After a long time I came to these conclusions, just as I write them here:

(1) That I had done very little thinking, save within the problems of my craft. For twenty years a certain man had been my intellectual conscience. That was Edmund Wilson.

(2) That another man represented my sense of the "good life," though I saw him once in a decade, and since then he might have been hung. He is in the fur business in the Northwest and wouldn't like his name set down here. But in difficult situations I have tried to think what *he* would have thought, how *he* would have acted.

(3) That a third contemporary had been an artistic conscience to me—I had not imitated his infectious style, because my own style, such as it is, was formed before he published anything, but there was an awful pull toward him when I was on a spot.

(4) That a fourth man had come to dictate my relations with other people when these relations were successful: how to do, what to say. How to make people at least momentarily happy (in opposition to Mrs. Post's theories of how to make everyone thoroughly uncomfortable with a sort of systematized vulgarity). This always confused me and made me want to go out and get drunk, but this man had seen the game, analyzed it, and beaten it, and his word was good enough for me.

(5) That my political conscience had scarcely existed for ten years save as an element of irony in my stuff. When I became again concerned with the system I should function under, it was a man much

younger than myself who brought it to me, with a mixture of passion and fresh air.

So there was not an "I" anymore—not a basis on which I could organize my self-respect—save my limitless capacity for toil that it seemed I possessed no more. It was strange to have no self—to be like a little boy left alone in a big house, who knew that now he could do anything he wanted to do, but found that there was nothing that he wanted to do—

(The watch is past the hour and I have barely reached my thesis. I have some doubts as to whether this is of general interest, but if anyone wants more, there is plenty left, and your editor will tell me. If you've had enough, say so—but not too loud, because I have the feeling that someone, I'm not sure who, is sound asleep—someone who could have helped me to keep my shop open. It wasn't Lenin, and it wasn't God.)

I have spoken in these pages of how an exceptionally optimistic young man experienced a crack-up of all values, a crack-up that he scarcely knew of until long after it occurred. I told of the succeeding period of desolation and of the necessity of going on, but without benefit of Henley's familiar heroics, "my head is bloody but unbowed." For a checkup of my spiritual liabilities indicated that I had no particular head to be bowed or unbowed. Once I had had a heart but that was about all I was sure of.

This was at least a starting place out of the morass in which I floundered: "I felt—therefore I was." At one time or another there had been many people who had leaned on me, come to me in difficulties or written me from afar, believed implicitly in my advice and my attitude toward life. The dullest platitude monger or the most unscrupulous Rasputin who can influence the destinies of many people must have some individuality, so the question became one of finding why and where I had changed, where was the leak through which, unknown to myself, my enthusiasm and my vitality had been steadily and prematurely trickling away.

One harassed and despairing night I packed a briefcase and went off a thousand miles to think it over. I took a dollar room in a drab little town where I knew no one and sunk all the money I had with me in a stock of potted meat, crackers, and apples. But don't let me suggest that the change from a rather overstuffed world to a comparative asceticism was any Research Magnificent—I only wanted absolute quiet to think out why I had developed a sad attitude toward sadness, a melancholy attitude toward melancholy, and a tragic attitude toward tragedy—*why I had become identified with the objects of my horror or compassion.*

Does this seem a fine distinction? It isn't: identification such as this spells the death of accomplishment. It is something like this that keeps sane people from working. Lenin did not willingly endure the sufferings of his proletariat, nor Washington of his troops, nor Dickens of his London poor. And when Tolstoy tried some such merging of himself with the objects of his attention, it was a fake and a failure. I mention these because they are the men best known to us all.

It was dangerous mist. When Wordsworth decided that "there hath passed away a glory from the earth," he felt no compulsion to pass away with it, and the Fiery Particle Keats never ceased his struggle against T.B. nor in his last moments relinquished his hope of being among the English poets.

My self-immolation was something sodden-dark. It was very distinctly not modern—yet I saw it in others, saw it in a dozen men of honor and industry since the war. (I heard you, but that's too easy—there were Marxians among these men.) I had stood by while one famous contemporary of mine played with the idea of the Big Out for half a year; I had watched when another, equally eminent, spent months in an asylum unable to endure any contact with his fellowmen. And of those who had given up and passed on I could list a score.

This led me to the idea that the ones who had survived had made some sort of clean break. This is a big word and is no parallel to a jailbreak when one is probably headed for a new jail or will be forced back to the old one. The famous "Escape" or "Run away from it all" is an excursion in a trap even if the trap includes the South Seas, which are only for those who want to paint them or sail them. A clean break is something you cannot come back from; that is irretrievable because it makes the past cease to exist. So, since I could no longer fulfill the obligations that life had set for me or that I had set for myself, why not slay the empty shell who had been posturing at it for four years? I must continue to be a writer because that was my only way of life, but I would cease any attempts to be a person—to be kind, just, or generous. There were plenty of counterfeit coins around that would pass instead of these and I knew where I could get them at a nickel on the dollar. In thirty-nine years an observant eye has learned to detect where the milk is watered and the sugar is sanded, the rhinestone passed for diamond and the stucco for stone. There was to be no more giving of myself—all giving was to be outlawed henceforth under a new name, and that name was Waste.

The decision made me rather exuberant, like anything that is both real and new. As a sort of beginning there was a whole shaft of letters to be tipped into the wastebasket when I went home, letters that wanted something for nothing—to read this man's manuscript, market this man's poem, speak free on the radio, indite notes of introduction, give this interview, help with the plot of this play, with this domestic situation, perform this act of thoughtfulness or charity.

The conjurer's hat was empty. To draw things out of it had long been a sort of sleight of hand, and now, to change the metaphor, I was off the dispensing end of the relief roll forever.

The heady villainous feeling continued.

I felt like the beady-eyed men I used to see on the commuting train from Great Neck fifteen years back—men who didn't care whether the world tumbled into chaos tomorrow if it spared their houses. I was one with them now, one with the smooth articles who said:

*"I'm sorry but business is business."*

Or:

*"You ought to have thought of that before you got into this trouble."*

Or:

*"I'm not the person to see about that."*

And a smile—ah, I would get me a smile. I'm still working on that smile. It is to combine the best qualities of a hotel manager, an experienced old social weasel, a headmaster on visitors' day, a colored elevator man, a pansy pulling a profile, a producer getting stuff at half its market value, a trained nurse coming on a new job, a body-vender in her first rotogravure, a hopeful extra swept near the camera, a ballet dancer with an infected toe, and of course the great beam of loving kindness common to all those from Washington to Beverly Hills who must exist by virtue of the contorted pan.

The voice too—I am working with a teacher on the voice. When I have perfected it the larynx will show no ring of conviction except the conviction of the person I am talking to. Since it will be largely called upon for the elicitation of the word "Yes," my teacher (a lawyer) and I are concentrating on that, but in extra hours. I am learning to bring into it that polite acerbity that makes people feel that far from being welcome they are not even tolerated and are under continual and scathing analysis at every moment. These times will of course not coincide with the smile. This will be reserved exclusively for those from whom I have nothing to gain, old worn-out people or young struggling people. They won't mind—what the hell, they get it most of the time anyhow.

But enough. It is not a matter of levity. If you are young and you should write asking to see me and learn how to be a somber literary man writing pieces upon the state of emotional exhaustion that often overtakes writers in their prime—if you should be so young and fatuous as to do this, I would not do so much as acknowledge your letter, unless you were related to someone very rich and important indeed. And if you were dying of starvation outside my window, I would go out quickly and give you the smile and the voice (if no longer the hand) and stick around till somebody raised a nickel to phone for the ambulance, that is if I thought there would be any copy in it for me.

I have now at last become a writer only. The man I had persistently tried to be became such a burden that I have "cut him loose" with as little compunction as a Negro lady cuts loose a rival on Saturday night. Let the good people function as such—let the overworked doctors die in harness, with one week's "vacation" a year that they can devote to straightening out their family affairs, and let the underworked doctors scramble for cases at one dollar a throw; let the soldiers be killed and enter immediately into the Valhalla of their profession. That is their contract with the gods. A writer need have no such ideals unless he makes them for himself, and this one has quit. The old dream of being an entire man in the Goethe-Byron-Shaw tradition, with an opulent American touch, a sort of combination of J. P. Morgan, Topham Beauclerk, and St. Francis of Assisi, has been relegated to the junk heap of the shoulder pads worn for one day on the Princeton freshman football field and the overseas cap never worn overseas.

So what? This is what I think now: that the natural state of the sentient adult is a qualified unhappiness. I think also that in an adult the desire to be finer in grain than you are, "a constant striving" (as those people say who gain their bread by saying it), only adds to this unhappiness in the end—that end that comes to our youth and hope. My own happiness in the past often approached such an ecstasy that I could not share it even with the person dearest to me but had to walk it away in quiet streets and lanes with only fragments of it to distill into little lines in books—and I think that my happiness, or talent for self-delusion or what you will, was an exception. It was not the natural thing but the unnatural—unnatural as the Boom; and my recent experience parallels the wave of despair that swept the nation when the Boom was over.

I shall manage to live with the new dispensation, though it has taken some months to be certain of the fact. And just as the laughing stoicism which has enabled the American Negro to endure the intolerable conditions of his existence has cost him his sense of the truth—so in my case there is a price to pay. I do not any longer like the postman, nor the grocer, nor the editor, nor the cousin's husband, and he in turn will come to dislike me, so that life will never be very pleasant again, and the sign *Cave Canem* is hung permanently just above my door. I will try to be a correct animal though, and if you throw me a bone with enough meat on it I may even lick your hand.

—FEBRUARY, MARCH, AND APRIL 1936

# Sam

ALEC WILKINSON

My father held himself aloof from our family in a way that was common for the period, the 1950s and '60s. We lived in the suburbs of New York City and he had a job in Manhattan; he was the art director of the magazine *Woman's Day*. He was a charming, bluff, and somewhat insensitive man, and he was a philanderer, too, so a part of his attention was always somewhere other than in his household. I held him, though, in high regard, as children tend to do, and imitated his example, which was only intermittently appropriate, and so I had a lot of flawed experiences, and when enough of them had piled up, I sat in a leather chair in the office of a Jungian analyst once or twice a week for a number of years and, staring just to the left or right of him or at the row of small fetishes on the bookcase above his head, described my difficulties with my mother, while he replied, "I think you have more issues with your father." Son of a bitch isn't even listening to me, I thought, until I had a dream in which I was a teenager about to take the ice in a hockey game and discovered that my father had put me in skates with broken blades. After that I began to carry him a little bit less glamorously in my mind and eventually some kind of balance within me shifted, and somewhat unexpectedly and a little bit late—I was forty-two—I arrived at a point where I felt that I was prepared to raise a child. Prepared in the sense that I imagine the poor holy loser who died in the bus in Alaska felt that he was prepared, with his rifle, his books, and his bag of rice, to wait out the weather.

Before we leave Confession Gulch, I would like to add that I have been married twice. The first time, my wife and I both picked wrong and the marriage ended sadly after seven years. In truth, it had been over for some time, so it also took a few sessions in the leather chair to see why I had made such a piece of bad judgment, why both of us had engaged in it, and what I could do to make sure I would marry again happily, if I was lucky. When I did, I used sometimes to wake in the middle of the night and think, Please, God, let me live out my natural life in the company of this woman I love. My son was born six years ago, and it is not that my feelings for my wife ever changed, except to deepen, but I was aware that when he had been in the world only a short time, I had begun thinking, Please, God, let me live to see as much of his life as I can.

What has followed between us could not truly be described as a love affair, unless your version of one includes tests and dismissals and reversals and forbearance and an awareness that whatever you had thought the affair might be, had hoped or imagined it might be, is precisely what it won't, or even can't (apparently), ever be.

I did not expect to cry when my son was born—it seemed a silly and conventional and trivial thing to do, weep for joy, like a figure in an advertisement—but I did, quite suddenly and without warning, as if it were a reflex. He was delivered in the morning by a midwife in a hospital in Manhattan and I felt embarrassed, slightly, to be weeping among women, to be weeping when no one else was, as if trying to emphasize that the strength and capacity to bear pain that my wife had demonstrated were laudable, but I was *sensitive*, so I looked toward the floor and wiped away the tears. When his face had appeared, I had seen his eyes, and the instant in which consciousness lit them. He was examined briefly by a doctor and then lay with his mother and I watched them for a while, then went to get some coffee and bagels for our breakfast. When I got back, Sara, my wife, was in her room with Sam, our son, wrapped up—a small bundle with a cap on, a face about the size of a softball—and she handed him to me, and I held him for the first time. He felt like a piece of china in my hands. I held him the way you would hold a fragile and tiny creature whose existence depended entirely on the lightness of your touch. There was a nurse with us in the room. She said, "You'll scare him if you don't hold him tighter. They need to know they're being supported."

I spoke his name. I looked into his eyes, which had the luminance of polished stone. What I felt mainly was the absence of what I expected to feel—that is, I thought his arriving in my arms would somehow stimulate an awareness I had never felt toward anything before, a resonance that was primitive and universal and private, a code shared between us that couldn't possibly be stirred by any other form of contact, the kind of experience that would appear in a movie. Instead I heard a voice in my mind saying things such as, This is my son—my son. Yes, this is my son. And at the same time asking, Shouldn't something else, something more, be happening? Pay closer attention.

I have never asked any other man if he had an experience such as mine, but I don't think mine is singular. How could it be? I can imagine men holding their son or daughter for the first time and having feelings regarding the child's destiny or place in the family and among his or her ancestors or the traits he or she appears to display, but such feelings are sentimental, and sentimental feelings are a lie concocted to cover the feelings you might more straightforwardly have. You hate your brother who tormented you, but persist in feeling that your upbringing with him as your comrade and sergeant at arms was fortunate; it made you tougher. I am capable of insensitivity, as my father was, but I am not an insensitive person. I would mistrust the account of any man who told me that the first time he held his child he felt profoundly attached to him. Attached to what, really? Someone you're meeting for the first time, who is incapable of returning your feelings, who has only a peripheral awareness of you and none really of who you are, or of his relation to you, or that you might intend for him or her to be a fireman as you have been or a union man or a doctor or preside over a commercial empire or replace Wayne Gretzky or Willie Mays or James Taylor or John Coltrane or Billie Holiday? I do not mean that the moment of first embrace is not significantly charged, only that its import is elusive, and the elusiveness is the first signal that the process of caring for a child is fraught with ambiguity and things you can't know. A child is a territory, a landscape, a region, an outpost, a republic and island of worry.

You forget a lot of it. The first year is hell, I remember that. You don't sleep. The fatigue accumulates. Your child goes to bed, you have a little bit of fun, then you realize he has a two-hour head start on you. You see in your wife's face a concern, a preoccupation even, that you never saw before. The carefree look is gone, anyway. The emotional balance of your household is altered. Your wife and child have formed an alliance that at times excludes you. They spend so much time together and are so intimate with each other that it was bound to happen. My sense of my son as an enigma was reinforced during the first year because there was little I could provide for him. So far as I could tell, he liked dimly lit rooms, tranquil surroundings, breast milk, and the company of his mother. Because I had read about studies concluding that an infant prefers to his father's voice the higher, softer tones of his mother's speech, I tried for a while talking to Sam in a womanly voice, then worried that I had confused him in some essential way about the properties of masculine life, so went back to my own voice, to which he seemed only occasionally to respond. Sometimes he appeared to enjoy himself when I whistled.

A child's personality hardly emerges before he is seven or eight months old. During most of his or her first year, what you are aware of really is the child's temperament: his capacity for frustration, whether he is cautious or extends himself toward the world. It is easy to imagine who he is—that is, to make up an identity for him, as if he were a screen on which to display the images you have always intended for your son or daughter—and to persuade yourself that he or she is moving toward becoming some version of those images, and to do it all without really even being aware of it, to think that really you are occupied simply with his development, with his becoming, say, someone who will be accomplished at math because you played Mozart for him as he lay in his crib, overlooking that probably what you were doing was making it difficult for him to sleep, overstimulating him, making him nervous, and depriving him of rest. You meant well, and you can tell him that thirty years down the road when he confronts you, although it is very difficult to know what will prey on the minds of the adults who are small children now—certainly not what bothered us, it was a different time, the fifties and sixties and seventies, and people behaved differently and felt differently about what was proper in the way of raising a child. In any case, the slow appearance of his character has perhaps to do with the design of childhood. (Certainly in the past, and in cultures where women were not sufficiently valued and babies were killed for being of the wrong sex, a boy who disappointed his father might also be left in the forest.) So they emerge slowly. You become attached to them and to your version of them, and then they begin perilously to become themselves, someone different from your idea. This calls for a great deal of restraint, to let a child develop according to his nature. To give him sufficient guidance that he becomes equipped with the virtues and judgment he needs to preserve himself and to flourish but not so much that you cause him to repress parts of himself out of fear that they will not be accepted.

Children are utterly dependent. If they meet with disapproval, they will assume that something is wrong with them. Their security, their lives, depend on keeping their mothers and fathers interested in them. If a mom is taken with the bottle or drugs, or the dad is emotionally withdrawn or hostile to the child's well-being, the child will build an explanation for why he has brought such an existence on himself. The alternative—mother or father is unreliable—is a story by Stephen King, your well-being in the hands of people who are capricious about your welfare, who have their own plans for your future, who reward you for certain behavior that might make you uncomfortable and punish you for behavior you find fulfilling. Making a mess, for example.

We are only a few generations removed from the Victorian idea of the child as a little adult, which gave way to the child as a small being with instincts for sex, a devious and slothful package, which gave way to the child as a being engaged in behaviors and activities designed for his pleasure to oppose and thwart the interests of his parents, one who needs to be subdued, to be broken the way a horse might require it—spare the rod and spoil the child, and the advice current in my parents' generation of letting a child put down for the night lie in his crib crying; if you pick him up you'll only give him the impression that the world is a compassionate place interested in seeing him protected. Then he'll manipulate you mercilessly the rest of your life.

My wife and I haven't been to a movie since my son was born, in 1993. I have seen movies on airplanes and I have rented them, but none longer than an hour and a half, because that would keep us up too late. A year ago, I walked past a restaurant on Broadway that has a big window facing the street and saw the people at the tables and in the instant before my mind focused I thought, So how does that work, you go in there and ask for food and they prepare it and you pay them; how do you know what you can ask for?

Before I had a child, I had no interest in children; I had thought it was possible I might never have one. I didn't think children were amusing, sometimes I thought they were scary, and I was always on the side of the people on the airplane who crane their necks to stare at the mother unable to calm her child's crying.

I was not aware before Sam was born of the circumstance of feeling hostage to the unfolding of the universe, to the things that lie in wait for your child, the torments and hardships and assaults. I now know that there are disasters lurking everywhere for a child, many of them simple and commonplace. The threat of dehydration for the infant who throws up for too long—a day without water is all it seems to take—so that his eyes may roll back into his head, even while you are waiting in the doctor's anteroom, and you will have to be rushed to the hospital, carrying your child in your arms with people ahead of you kicking doors open, as on TV. Then the children's ward and children walking around with eyes that seem to have no light in them.

I am convinced that one needs to live beside one's children with the feeling that they might not be there at the end of the day, or that you won't, or your wife won't. There are accidents and illnesses, there are divorces. The cemetery is always waiting.

I should probably announce that I have an eccentric child, and that his eccentricities have influenced my feelings about childhood and being a father. What afflicts him, his mother and I only partly know. He appears, from tests and the opinions of various people with diplomas on their walls, to have great difficulty with sensations. Sounds are too loud, touch is often too abrasive or hard or ticklish or startling, something impedes his speech, he has no peripheral vision, and he has trouble organizing the elements of visual images—photographs and paintings and the movements on a television screen. I am not sure exactly how he views images, but it puts me in mind of the natives of whatever territory it was who were shown photographs of their faces and saw in them only areas of black and white.

My son began crawling when he was supposed to, but he dragged one leg. The world, though, has an abundance of people who tell you when your child has trouble, say, speaking, that their great-uncle so-and-so didn't say a word until he was four and then he framed perfect sentences, or in our case they say, "Did you ever meet anyone who didn't learn how to walk?" so you think, Well, that's unusual, the leg dragging, but they're right, and there isn't much you can do with the diagnosis of a child that young anyway, unless the difficulties are severe. So my son has grown into a radiant child who is a little clumsy and has a list of experiences he can't tolerate. My friend William Maxwell, the novelist, says, "Don't worry about him, he has the soul of a poet." Like a lot of poets, then, he isn't much socialized, because his excitement at the appearance of other children overrides what social patterns he might have collected by observing the way other children act, and instead of restraining himself, he races up to them and stands too close and waves his arms while he talks loudly, and this scares them. Some children it doesn't bother at all, but the majority don't cotton to it. Moreover, he doesn't have an older brother or sister whose manners he can imitate. If your attention is distracted by the imminence and immensity of the world and its lights and textures and sounds, if you are constantly alert to voices from the other side of the room or the movements of other children and adults in order to assess whether they contain some threat to you and so that you can keep some distance between yourself and them, your mind is occupied and hasn't got time to address the muscular patterns necessary for speech or movements. You fall behind. And once you are behind, what is measured is how far behind you are and whether you have fallen so far behind that you might not catch up. If you are a five-year-old with the capacities of a four-year-old, do you become a twenty-year-old with the capacities of a sixteen-year-old, or does the equation change? No one knows.

If you are father or mother to such a child, you might think that you have been wronged. You might, as I have occasionally done, feel resentful of the simple commonness, the uncomplicatedness, on display in the lives of garden-variety children, and then something, the sight in the newspaper of a child separated from his parents in Kosovo, say, might cause you to reflect that if this is the worst thing that happens to you and your child, among the catalog of grievances and disappointments and tragedies and unfair happenings in life, you will be lucky and you should probably shut up about it so that the Almighty doesn't hear you and send something else your way with the note, *You thought that was bad.*

A child such as my wife and I have needs extra care. You know what he doesn't like—loud places, places where there is a great deal of activity, especially chaotic places, especially loud, chaotic places, and you avoid taking him to any such places. You try to give him what he likes. The seashore, the wide-open beach, with no avenues of ambush for any adversary, with room for everyone, with the sounds of the waves and the games of running from them and into them and having them tumble you over and the dunes to climb and the sand to dig tunnels in and build cities on that you can destroy. You try to make him happy, to make his life, since it includes so much torment, a pleasure. The longer I can make him happy, the better I feel. The world with its thousand and one things is always waiting there to disappoint him, to bruise his feelings, to exclude him, and I figure that the more capital my wife and I give him in the form of solid fun, the more likely he is to spin off from the distasteful experience into another that pleases him and not to become stuck brooding on the insufficiencies that have made him a figure of sport or rejection for the moment.

One important thing a parent can do for a child, I think, is provide him with a sense of safety.

An irony of raising such children is that, if you are like me, you spend your life trying to get away from the small-minded and conventional people, the gym teachers and guidance counselors and spinster penmanship instructors who have a hold over you when you are young, and finally you're shed of them and then you have a child and they get their claws into you all over again. In order to obtain from the state the money to help pay for a portion of some of the therapies my son receives, he had to submit to examinations conducted by people who work for the government. The most indignant I have ever been made as an adult was when I learned that one of them, a psychologist, had asked my son, my heartbeat, my household angel, who was then four, "Have you ever wanted to kill yourself? Have you ever wanted to kill anyone else?"

Then it becomes time to get your child into school, which, if you intend it to be a private school, is not simple. When we went for an interview at one school, a woman with a clipboard said, "Is yours the child who also speaks Russian?" No three-year-old speaks Russian as a second language, a few words of Russian, some phrases perhaps, but a couple desperate enough to place their child had had the nerve to describe their three-year-old as a speaker of a complicated foreign language. I wasn't so surprised at that; people are always willing to make fools of themselves. What surprised me was that, so far as I could tell, the school had taken them seriously.

Schools do not like an eccentric or lively child. Schools—any school, a public school, the most prestigious private school, the school with the reputation for having great concern for the inner life of the child—are all interested in the same thing: tractability. None of them want a child who does not do what he is told. It is nice if your three-year-old plays the cello or speaks Hebrew or can ride a horse, but if he can't perform according to commands, if he is willful or resistant, you will have difficulty placing him in the school you might most wish he would attend, unless of course you are fortunate enough to have sound public schools in your neighborhood. Such a child makes the lives of everyone involved, the teachers and the administrators, more difficult. Other parents resent an obstreperous child. A child who is aggressive. During the interviews of three-year-olds, which are enveloped in mystery, only one assessment is taking place. Absent the variables of whether yours is a child of minority parents or not, prosperous or not, absent the consideration of how many spaces are available for siblings and boys and girls, only one judgment is taking place, indeed only one is possible, since the range of behaviors for children that age is so limited. Your child arrives and plays with two or three other children, then, having been told to, he puts the toys away and sits down for juice and a cookie, perhaps while a story is read. If your child plays nicely, fine, that's nice, nice child. The only gesture that matters is whether, when he is instructed to, he puts away the toys and sits down with the others. If he decides that he is having fun playing with the toys and wants to continue and resists, if he cries in frustration, he has failed his interview and has no chance of being accepted. He has displayed what the school will regard as difficulty with transitions, or, in the language of bureaucracy, he will be said to have difficulty transitioning. They will thank you for coming and you will receive in the mail a letter saying that the school is disappointed not to be able to admit your child, but that there were an unusual number of siblings this year. His future at that school is likely hopeless, unless you are in the position to make a donation of astonishing proportions.

For a couple of years, before I knew anything in my son was compromised, I thought that he was more interesting than the boys I saw in his classroom, more able to concentrate, more diverse in his reactions to play, more inventive, and more avid in his joy. The other boys seemed ordinary, a little mean, a little sneaky, a little quick to gang up and exclude, a little taken with aggression. The first time I began to feel something was amiss with Sam, I was watching him in his classroom and noticed that when he was moved toward an aggressive gesture, when another boy, say, had taken a toy he was playing with, Sam tried to get the toy back. There was a struggle. Once the matter was handled, he let it drop. If he had a conflict, he pushed or pulled in plain view. The other boys, I noticed, usually waited until the teachers were looking the other way and pushed or pinched or slapped the other child and impersonated innocence when the teacher looked in their direction. This, I thought, was cowardly. Because my son was open in his behavior, he was more often caught at it. I told one of the teachers that I was proud of him for not misbehaving behind their backs, that the other boys often struck me as angry and mean-spirited and were rarely brought to account because they were sneaky about it. The teacher was nearly as fond of Sam as I was. It pained her to say, "Yes, and you wonder why they have learned not to get caught and Sam hasn't."

My son's difficulties make simple coordination a problem for him. He could not ride a tricycle as a toddler because he could not alternate the actions of his feet without thinking about it. Among my own meager accomplishments are the kind of tennis game and skating style you can have only if you began these activities very early in life and practiced them intensely, so I had imagined that my son and I would go skating together and play tennis, but his difficulty controlling his excitement, which gives him at tranquil times the air of an ecstatic, means that he can't really yet concentrate on an activity as intricate as a tennis swing, or as relaying to his brain the myriad signals involved in maintaining your balance on ice skates. He is a terrific climber, and although he often looks as if he is about to lose his balance, he never does. I was pleased to realize that I would not likely be spending his adolescence in a car traveling between Providence and Boston and Philadelphia to take him to hockey tournaments, but I was concerned that he would not have the protective coloration of an athlete—being accomplished at tennis and captain of the hockey team had gotten me a lot of free passes.

I have no interest in being the kind of parent whose child takes lessons at cello and horseback riding and French and modern dance. Too great an involvement in these activities suggests parents who are social climbers or who have too little time to spend with their children. What I didn't realize was that there is an alternative version of this circuit of activities in which you have a child who takes speech therapy twice a week and has occupational therapy on the other three days.

Children are made uncomfortable by eccentricity, because it suggests mysteries they know intuitively they are not equal to. They will set upon children who are sufficiently different from them, or who seem to be made for their sport, to cause them anxiety. I have no idea how my son will do as an adolescent, whether he will escape harassment or be the object of it, but if he is a target of it I will tell him to try to find ways to avoid the person who bullies him, or to talk his way out of a confrontation, to outsmart his adversaries and leave them looking for easier marks. If he is unable to do one of these things, or if the schoolyard constantly throws him and the bully together, if the bully can't be escaped and he is making my son unhappy, I might also try to tell my son that the world is not built for our happiness and that we have to accommodate some degree of misery and ride it out the best we can.

If I feel that the bully might harm my son, I plan to visit the bully. I will pretend to be interested in something he is engaged in, perhaps. I am Sam's father, I might say. How are you? Those are terrific arms you have, you must lift weights, wonderful. Listen, are you busy, could we go sit over on that bench and talk for a moment? All right, here's fine, sure, listen, what I have to say is, I understand from Sam that you make him unhappy, you seem to like to tease him, and I just wanted to suggest that you find someone else, would that be hard? A little? All right, that's fair. Well, here's what I'm thinking: I'm thinking, if you don't quit, I will find you somewhere, when you really aren't thinking about me or Sam, of course, and I or someone representing my interests will beat you within an inch of your miserable, worthless little life, you understand? One more time I hear from Sam that he had any trouble from you of any kind, and those are the consequences for you. Everything in your life at one moment will be as good as it ever has been, and the next moment you will wake up in a hospital room, with double vision and your head hurting and you unable to take solid food. If you think I am not serious about this, try me. Go ahead, tell your father.

When the father calls me, I will say that his son, who makes things up, might need psychiatric help. If you think that this behavior is discreditable of me, I would suggest that we are all immortal in our souls, not in our characters.

The physical pleasure, the intimacy, the smell of their hair, their bodies, their closeness, their acceptance of you as their sheltering presence, the way they look when they sleep, their breathing in the night, the light in their eyes, is intoxicating to the point of exquisiteness. Throughout my son's life I have now and then thought of him as a household divinity—that is, as an uncorrupted presence of joy. Like any idol, he is susceptible to vanity and solipsistic behavior, he is interested in his acceptance as a majestic being, jealous and intolerant of the attention of his subjects being divided. Sometimes he hurts me so deeply by what appears to be indifference that I think I will refuse to look at him for the rest of his life, I will give him up. I hope that he will have none of my smaller and undesirable qualities and all of my better ones. I want him to grow into a man who is unplagued, regarded affectionately for his sensitivity and intelligence and candor and steadfastness and a tranquillity at the heart of his being that comes from knowing that he has been loved, that he has no obligation to carry forth a family myth, that he is unencumbered. And that he will value the company of his mother and father because he feels it is uncomplicated by our insistence that he abandon his identity for one we need him to embrace.

Perhaps nearly every observation I've made applies only in my case. I know one thing: A moment arrives when your child leaves your lap and you realize he isn't coming back.

—JUNE 2000

# Fifth Avenue, Uptown

JAMES BALDWIN

There is a housing project standing now where the house in which we grew up once stood, and one of those stunted city trees is snarling where our doorway used to be. This is on the rehabilitated side of the avenue. The other side of the avenue—for progress takes time—has not been rehabilitated yet and it looks exactly as it looked in the days when we sat with our noses pressed against the windowpane, longing to be allowed to go "across the street." The grocery store which gave us credit is still there, and there can be no doubt that it is still giving credit. The people in the project certainly need it—far more, indeed, than they ever needed the project. The last time I passed by, the Jewish proprietor was still standing among his shelves, looking sadder and heavier but scarcely any older. Further down the block stands the shoe-repair store in which our shoes were repaired until reparation became impossible and in which, then, we bought all our "new" ones. The Negro proprietor is still in the window, head down, working at the leather.

These two, I imagine, could tell a long tale if they would (perhaps they would be glad to if they could), having watched so many, for so long, struggling in the fishhooks, the barbed wire, of this avenue.

The avenue is elsewhere the renowned and elegant Fifth. The area I am describing, which, in today's gang parlance, would be called "the turf," is bounded by Lenox Avenue on the west, the Harlem River on the east, 135th Street on the north, and 130th Street on the south. We never lived beyond these boundaries; this is where we grew up. Walking along 145th Street—for example—familiar as it is, and similar, does not have the same impact because I do not know any of the people on the block. But when I turn east on 131st Street and Lenox Avenue, there is first a soda-pop joint, then a shoeshine "parlor," then a grocery store, then a dry cleaners', then the houses. All along the street there are people who watched me grow up, people who grew up with me, people I watched grow up along with my brothers and sisters; and, sometimes in my arms, sometimes underfoot, sometimes at my shoulder—or on it—their children, a riot, a forest of children, who include my nieces and nephews.

When we reach the end of this long block, we find ourselves on wide, filthy, hostile Fifth Avenue, facing that project which hangs over the avenue like a monument to the folly, and the cowardice, of good intentions. All along the block, for anyone who knows it, are immense human gaps, like craters. These gaps are not created merely by those who have moved away, inevitably into some other ghetto; or by those who have risen, almost always into a greater capacity for self-loathing and self-delusion; or yet by those who, by whatever means—War II, the Korean war, a policeman's gun or billy, a gang war, a brawl, madness, an overdose of heroin, or, simply, unnatural exhaustion—are dead. I am talking about those who are left, and I am talking principally about the young. What are they doing? Well, some, a minority, are fanatical churchgoers, members of the more extreme of the Holy Roller sects. Many, many more are "moslems," by affiliation or sympathy, that is to say that they are united by nothing more—and nothing less—than a hatred of the white world and all its works. They are present, for example, at every Buy Black street-corner meeting—meetings in which the speaker urges his hearers to cease trading with white men and establish a separate economy. Neither the speaker nor his hearers can possibly do this, of course, since Negroes do not own General Motors or RCA or the A&P, nor, indeed, do they own more than a wholly insufficient fraction of anything else in Harlem (those who *do* own anything are more interested in their profits than in their fellows). But these meetings nevertheless keep alive in the participators a certain pride of bitterness without which, however futile this bitterness may be, they could scarcely remain alive at all. Many have given up. They stay home and watch the TV screen, living on the earnings of their parents, cousins, brothers, or uncles, and only leave the house to go to the movies or to the nearest bar. "How're you making it?" one may ask, running into them along the block, or in the bar. "Oh, I'm TV-ing it"; with the saddest, sweetest, most shamefaced of smiles, and from a great distance. This distance one is compelled to respect; anyone who has traveled so far will not easily be dragged again into the world. There are further retreats, of course, than the TV screen or the bar. There are those who are simply sitting on their stoops, "stoned," animated for a moment only, and hideously, by the approach of someone who may lend them the money for a "fix." Or by the approach of someone from whom they can purchase it, one of the shrewd ones, on the way to prison or just coming out.

And the others, who have avoided all of these deaths, get up in the morning and go downtown to meet "the man." They work in the white man's world all day and come home in the evening to this fetid block. They struggle to instill in their children some private sense of honor or dignity which will help the child to survive. This means, of course, that they must struggle, stolidly, incessantly, to keep this sense alive in themselves, in spite of the insults, the indifference, and the cruelty they are certain to encounter in their working day. They patiently browbeat the landlord into fixing the heat, the plaster, the plumbing; this demands prodigious patience; nor is patience usually enough. In trying to make their hovels habitable, they are perpetually throwing good money after bad. Such frustration, so long endured, is driving many strong, admirable men and women whose only crime is color to the very gates of paranoia.

One remembers them from another time—playing handball in the playground, going to church, wondering if they were going to be promoted at school. One remembers them going off to war—gladly, to escape this block. One remembers their return. Perhaps one remembers their wedding day. And one sees where the girl is now—vainly looking for salvation from some other embittered, trussed, and struggling boy—and sees the all-but-abandoned children in the streets.

Now I am perfectly aware that there are other slums in which white men are fighting for their lives, and mainly losing. I know that blood is also flowing through those streets and that the human damage there is incalculable. People are continually pointing out to me the wretchedness of white people in order to console me for the wretchedness of blacks. But an itemized account of the American failure does not console me and it should not console anyone else. That hundreds of thousands of white people are living, in effect, no better than the "niggers" is not a fact to be regarded with complacency. The social and moral bankruptcy suggested by this fact is of the bitterest, most terrifying kind.

The people, however, who believe that this democratic anguish has some consoling value are always pointing out that So-and-So, white, and So-and-So, black, rose from the slums into the big time. The existence—the public existence—of, say, Frank Sinatra and Sammy Davis, Jr. proves to them that America is still the land of opportunity and that inequalities vanish before the determined will. It proves nothing of the sort. The determined will is rare—at the moment, in this country, it is unspeakably rare—and the inequalities suffered by the many are in no way justified by the rise of a few. A few have always risen—in every country, every era, and in the teeth of regimes which can by no stretch of the imagination be thought of as free. Not all of these people, it is worth remembering, left the world better than they found it. The determined will is rare, but it is not invariably benevolent. Furthermore, the American equation of success with the big time reveals an awful disrespect for human life and human achievement. This equation has placed our cities among the most dangerous in the world and has placed our youth among the most empty and most bewildered. The situation of our youth is not mysterious. Children have never been very good at listening to their elders, but they have never failed to imitate them. They must, they have no other models. That is exactly what our children are doing. They are imitating our immorality, our disrespect for the pain of others.

All other slum dwellers, when the bank account permits it, can move out of the slum and vanish altogether from the eye of persecution. No Negro in this country has ever made that much money and it will be a long time before any Negro does. The Negroes in Harlem, who have no money, spend what they have on such gimcracks as they are sold. These include "wider" TV screens, more "faithful" hi-fi sets, more "powerful" cars, all of which, of course, are obsolete long before they are paid for. Anyone who has ever struggled with poverty knows how extremely expensive it is to be poor; and if one is a member of a captive population, economically speaking, one's feet have simply been placed on the treadmill forever. One is victimized, economically, in a thousand ways—rent, for example, or car insurance. Go shopping one day in Harlem—for anything—and compare Harlem prices and quality with those downtown.

The people who have managed to get off this block have only got as far as a more respectable ghetto. This respectable ghetto does not even have the advantages of the disreputable one, friends, neighbors, a familiar church, and friendly tradesmen; and it is not, moreover, in the nature of any ghetto to remain respectable long. Every Sunday, people who have left the block take the lonely ride back, dragging their increasingly discontented children with them. They spend the day talking, not always with words, about the trouble they've seen and the trouble—one must watch their eyes as they watch their children—they are only too likely to see. For children do not like ghettos. It takes them nearly no time to discover exactly why they are there.

The projects in Harlem are hated. They are hated almost as much as policemen, and this is saying a great deal. And they are hated for the same reason: both reveal, unbearably, the real attitude of the white world, no matter how many liberal speeches are made, no matter how many lofty editorials are written, no matter how many civil-rights commissions are set up.

The projects are hideous, of course, there being a law, apparently respected throughout the world, that popular housing shall be as cheerless as a prison. They are lumped all over Harlem, colorless, bleak, high, and revolting. The wide windows look out on Harlem's invincible and indescribable squalor: the Park Avenue railroad tracks, around which, about forty years ago, the present dark community began; the unrehabilitated houses, bowed down, it would seem, under the great weight of frustration and bitterness they contain; the dark, the ominous schoolhouses, from which the child may emerge maimed, blinded, hooked, or enraged for life; and the churches, churches, block upon block of churches, niched in the walls like cannon in the walls of a fortress. Even if the administration of the projects were not so insanely humiliating (for example: one must report raises in salary to the management, which will then eat up the profit by raising one's rent; the management has the right to know who is staying in your apartment; the management can ask you to leave, at their discretion), the projects would still be hated because they are an insult to the meanest intelligence.

Harlem got its first private project, Riverton—which is now, naturally, a slum—about twelve years ago because at that time Negroes were not allowed to live in Stuyvesant Town. Harlem watched Riverton go up, therefore, in the most violent bitterness of spirit, and hated it long before the builders arrived. They began hating it at about the time people began moving out of their condemned houses to make room for this additional proof of how thoroughly the white world despised them. And they had scarcely moved in, naturally, before they began smashing windows, defacing walls, urinating in the elevators, and fornicating in the playgrounds. Liberals, both white and black, were appalled at the spectacle. I was appalled by the liberal innocence—or cynicism, which comes out in practice as much the same thing. Other people were delighted to be able to point to proof positive that nothing could be done to better the lot of the colored people. They were, and are, right in one respect: that nothing can be done as long as they are treated like colored people. The people in Harlem know they are living there because white people do not think they are good enough to live anywhere else. No amount of "improvement" can sweeten this fact. Whatever money is now being earmarked to improve this, or any other ghetto, might as well be burnt. A ghetto can be improved in one way only: out of existence.

Similarly, the only way to police a ghetto is to be oppressive. None of Commissioner Kennedy's policemen, even with the best will in the world, have any way of understanding the lives led by the people they swagger about in two's and three's controlling. Their very presence is an insult, and it would be, even if they spent their entire day feeding gumdrops to children. They represent the force of the white world, and that world's real intentions are, simply, for that world's criminal profit and ease, to keep the black man corraled up here, in his place. The badge, the gun in the holster, and the swinging club make vivid what will happen should his rebellion become overt. Rare, indeed, is the Harlem citizen, from the most circumspect church member to the most shiftless adolescent, who does not have a long tale to tell of police incompetence, injustice, or brutality. I myself have witnessed and endured it more than once. The businessmen and racketeers also have a story. And so do the prostitutes. (And this is not, perhaps, the place to discuss Harlem's very complex attitude towards black policemen, nor the reasons, according to Harlem, that they are nearly all downtown.)

It is hard, on the other hand, to blame the policeman, blank, good-natured, thoughtless, and insuperably innocent, for being such a perfect representative of the people he serves. He, too, believes in good intentions and is astounded and offended when they are not taken for the deed. He has never, himself, done anything for which to be hated—which of us has?—and yet he is facing, daily and nightly, people who would gladly see him dead, and he knows it. There is no way for him not to know it: there are few things under heaven more unnerving than the silent, accumulating contempt and hatred of a people. He moves through Harlem, therefore, like an occupying soldier in a bitterly hostile country; which is precisely what, and where, he is, and is the reason he walks in two's and three's. And he is not the only one who knows why he is always in company: the people who are watching him know why, too. Any street meeting, sacred or secular, which he and his colleagues uneasily cover has as its explicit or implicit burden the cruelty and injustice of the white domination. And these days, of course, in terms increasingly vivid and jubilant, it speaks of the end of that domination. The white policeman, standing on a Harlem street corner, finds himself at the very center of the revolution now occurring in the world. He is not prepared for it—naturally, nobody is—and, what is possibly much more to the point, he is exposed, as few white people are, to the anguish of the black people around him. Even if he is gifted with the merest mustard grain of imagination, something must seep in. He cannot avoid observing that some of the children, in spite of their color, remind him of children he has known and loved, perhaps even of his own children. He knows that he certainly does not want *his* children living this way. He can retreat from his uneasiness in only one direction: into a callousness which very shortly becomes second nature. He becomes more callous, the population becomes more hostile, the situation grows more tense, and the police force is increased. One day, to everyone's astonishment, someone drops a match in the powder keg and everything blows up. Before the dust has settled or the blood congealed, editorials, speeches, and civil-rights commissions are loud in the land, demanding to know what happened. What happened is that Negroes want to be treated like men.

*Negroes want to be treated like men:* a perfectly straightforward statement, containing only seven words. People who have mastered Kant, Hegel, Shakespeare, Marx, Freud, and the Bible find this statement utterly impenetrable. The idea seems to threaten profound, barely conscious assumptions. A kind of panic paralyzes their features, as though they found themselves trapped on the edge of a steep place. I once tried to describe to a very-well-known American intellectual the conditions among Negroes in the South. My recital disturbed him and made him indignant; and he asked me in perfect innocence, "Why don't all the Negroes in the South move North?" I tried to explain what *has* happened, unfailingly, whenever a significant body of Negroes move North. They do not escape jim-crow: they merely encounter another, not-less-deadly variety. They do not move to Chicago, they move to the South Side; they do not move to New York, they move to Harlem. The pressure within the ghetto causes the ghetto walls to expand, and this expansion is always violent. White people hold the line as long as they can, and in as many ways as they can, from verbal intimidation to physical violence. But inevitably the border which has divided the ghetto from the rest of the world falls into the hands of the ghetto. The white people fall back bitterly before the black horde; the landlords make a tidy profit by raising the rent, chopping up the rooms, and all but dispensing with the upkeep; and what has once been a neighborhood turns into a "turf." This is precisely what happened when the Puerto Ricans arrived in their thousands—and the bitterness thus caused is, as I write, being fought out all up and down those streets.

Northerners indulge in an extremely dangerous luxury. They seem to feel that because they fought on the right side during the Civil War, and won, that they have earned the right merely to deplore what is going on in the South, without taking any responsibility for it; and that they can ignore what is happening in Northern cities because what is happening in Little Rock or Birmingham is worse. Well, in the first place, it is not possible for anyone who has not endured both to know which is "worse." I know Negroes who prefer the South and white Southerners, because "At least there, you haven't got to play any guessing games!" The guessing games referred to have driven more than one Negro into the narcotics ward, the madhouse, or the river. I know another Negro, a man very dear to me, who says, with conviction and with truth, "The spirit of the South is the spirit of America." He was born in the North and did his military training in the South. He did not, as far as I can gather, find the South "worse"; he found it, if anything, all too familiar. In the second place, though, even if Birmingham *is* worse, no doubt Johannesburg, South Africa, beats it by several miles, and Buchenwald was one of the worst things that ever happened in the entire history of the world. The world has never lacked for horrifying examples; but I do not believe that these examples are meant to be used as justification for our own crimes. This perpetual justification empties the heart of all human feeling. The emptier our hearts become, the greater will be our crimes. Thirdly, the South is not merely an embarrassingly backward region, but a part of this country, and what happens there concerns every one of us.

As far as the color problem is concerned, there is but one great difference between the Southern white and the Northerner: the Southerner remembers, historically, and in his own psyche, a kind of Eden in which he loved black people and they loved him. Historically, the flaming sword laid across this Eden is the Civil War. Personally, it is the Southerner's sexual coming of age, when, without any warning, unbreakable taboos are set up between himself and his past. Everything, thereafter, is permitted him except the love he remembers and has never ceased to need. The resulting, indescribable torment affects every Southern mind and is the basis of the Southern hysteria.

None of this is true for the Northerner. Negroes represent nothing to him personally, except, perhaps, the dangers of carnality. He never sees Negroes. Southerners see them all the time. Northerners never think about them whereas Southerners are never really thinking of anything else. Negroes are, therefore, ignored in the North and are under surveillance in the South, and suffer hideously in both places. Neither the Southerner nor the Northerner is able to look on the Negro simply as a man. It seems to be indispensable to the national self-esteem that the Negro be considered either as a kind of ward (in which case we are told how many Negroes, comparatively, bought Cadillacs last year and how few, comparatively, were lynched), or as a victim (in which case we are promised that he will never vote in our assemblies or go to school with our kids). They are two sides of the same coin and the South will not change—*cannot* change—until the North changes. The country will not change until it re-examines itself and discovers what it really means by freedom. In the meantime, generations keep being born, bitterness is increased by incompetence, pride, and folly, and the world shrinks around us.

It is a terrible, an inexorable, law that one cannot deny the humanity of another without diminishing one's own: in the face of one's victim, one sees oneself. Walk through the streets of Harlem and see what we, this nation, have become.

—JULY 1960

# And Now Let's Hear It for the Ed Sullivan Show!

DONALD BARTHELME

The Ed Sullivan Show. Sunday night. Church of the unchurched. Ed stands there. He looks great. Not unlike an older, heavier Paul Newman. Sways a little from side to side. Gary Lewis and the Playboys have just got off. Very strong act. Ed clasps hands together. He's introducing somebody in the audience. Who is it? Ed points with his left arm. "Broken every house record at the Copa," Ed says of the man he's introducing. Who is it? It's . . . Don Rickles! Rickles stands up. Eyes glint. Applause. "I'm gonna make a big man outa you!" Ed says. Rickles hunches a shoulder combatively. Eyes glint. Applause. Jerry Vale introduced. Wives introduced. Applause. "When Mrs. Sullivan and I were in Monte Carlo" (pause, neatly suppressed belch), "we saw them" (pause, he's talking about the next act), "for the first time and signed them instantly! The Kuban Cossacks! Named after the River Kuban!"

Three dancers appear in white fur hats, fur boots, what appear to be velvet jump suits. They're great. Terrific Cossack stuff in front of onion-dome flats. Kuban not the U.S.S.R.'s most imposing river (512 miles, shorter than the Ob, shorter than the Bug) but the dancers are remarkable. Sword dance of some sort with the band playing galops. Front dancer balancing on one hand and doing things with his feet. Great, terrific. Dancers support selves with one hand, don and doff hats with other hand. XOPOWÓ! (Non-Cyrillic approximation of Russian for "neat.") Double-XOPOWÓ! Ed enters from left. Makes enthusiastic gesture with hand. Triple-XOPOWÓ! Applause dies. Camera on Ed who has hands knit before him. "Highlighting this past week in New York . . ." Something at the Garden. Can't make it out, a fight probably. Ed introduces somebody in audience. Can't see who, he's standing up behind a fat lady who's also standing up for purposes of her own. Applause.

Pigmeat Markham comes on with cap and gown and gavel. His tag line, "Here come de jedge," is pronounced and the crowd roars but not so great a roar as you might expect. The line's wearing out. Still, Pigmeat looks good, working with two or three stooges. Stooge asks Pigmeat why, if he's honest, he's acquired two Cadillacs, etc. Pigmeat says: "Because I'm very *frugal,*" and whacks stooge on head with bladder. Lots of bladder work in sketch, old-timey comedy. Stooge says: "Jedge, you got to know me." Pigmeat: "Who are you? Stooge: "I'm the man that introduced you to your wife." Pigmeat shouts, "*Life!*" and whacks the stooge on the head with the bladder. Very funny stuff, audience roars. Then a fast commercial with Jo Anne Worley from Rowan and Martin singing about Bold. Funny girl. Good commercial.

Ed brings on Doodletown Pipers, singing group. Great-looking girls in tiny skirts. Great-looking legs on girls. They sing something about "I hear the laughter" and "the sound of the future." Phrasing is excellent, attack excellent. Camera goes to atmospheric shot of a park, kids playing, mothers and fathers lounging about, a Sunday feeling. Shot of boys throwing the ball around. Shot of black baby in swing. Shot of young mother's ass, very nice. Shot of blonde mother cuddling kid. Shot of black father swinging kid. Shot of a guy who looks like Rod McKuen lounging against a . . . a what? A play sculpture. But it's not Rod McKuen. The Doodletown Pipers segue into another song. Something about hate and fear, "You've got to be taught . . . hate and fear." They sound great. Shot of integrated group sitting on play equipment. Shot of young bespectacled father. Shot of young black man with young white child. He looks into camera. Thoughtful gaze. Young mother with daughter, absorbed. Nice-looking mother. Camera in tight on mother and daughter. One more mother, a medium shot. Out on shot of tiny black child asleep in swing. Wow!

Sullivan enters from left applauding. Makes gesture toward Pipers, toward audience, toward Pipers. Applause. Everybody's having a good time! "I want you to welcome . . . George Carlin!" Carlin is a comic. Carlin says he hates to look at the news. News is depressing. Sample headlines: "Welcome Wagon Runs Over Newcomer." Audience roars. "Pediatrician Dies of Childhood Disease." Audience roars but a weaker roar. Carlin is wearing a white turtleneck, dark sideburns. Joke about youth asking father if he can use the car. Youth says he's got a heavy date. Pa says, then why don't you take the pickup? Joke about the difference between organized crime and unorganized crime. Unorganized crime is when a guy holds you up on the street. Organized crime is when two guys hold you up on the street. Carlin is great, terrific, but his material is not so funny. A Central Park joke. Cops going into the park dressed as women to provoke molesters. Three hundred molesters arrested and two cops got engaged. More cop jokes. Carlin holds hands clasped together at waist. Says people wonder why the cops don't catch the Mafia. Says have you ever tried to catch a guy in a silk suit? Weak roar from audience. Carlin says do you suffer from nagging crime? Try the Police Department with new improved GL-70. No roar at all. A whicker, rather. Ed facing camera. "Coming up next . . . right after this important word." Commercial for Royal Electric Jetstar Typewriter. "She's typing faster and neater now." Capable-looking woman says to camera, "I have a Jetstar now that helps me at home where I have a business raising St. Bernards." Behind her a St. Bernard looks admiringly at Jetstar.

Ed's back. "England's famous Beatles" (pause, neatly capped belch) "first appeared on our shew . . . Mary Hopkin . . . Paul McCartney told her she must appear on our shew . . . the world-famous . . . Mary Hopkin!" Mary enters holding guitar. Sings something about "the morning of my life . . . ceiling in my room. . . ." Camera in tight on Mary. Pretty blonde, slightly plump face. Heavy applause for Mary. Camera goes to black, then Mary walking away in very short skirt, fine legs, a little heavy maybe. Mary in some sort of nightclub set for her big song, "Those Were the Days." Song is ersatz Kurt Weill but nevertheless a very nice song, very nostalgic, days gone by, tears rush into eyes (mine). In the background, period stills. Shot of some sort of Edwardian group activity, possible lawn party, possible egg roll. Shot of biplane. Shot of racecourse. Camera on Mary's face. "Those were the days, my friends. . . ." Shot of fox hunting, shot of tea dance. Mary is bouncing a little with the song, just barely bouncing. Shot of what appears to be a French 75 firing. Shot of lady kissing dog on nose. Shot of horse. Camera in tight on Mary's mouth. Looks like huge wad of chewing gum in her mouth but that can't be right, must be her tongue. Still of balloon ascension in background. Live girl sitting in left foreground gazing up at Mary, rapt. Mary in chaste high-collar dress with that short skirt. Effective. Mary finishes song. A real roar. Ed appears in three-quarter view turned toward the right, toward Mary. "Terrific!" Ed says. "Terrific!" Mary adjusts her breasts. "Terrific. And now, sitting out in the audience is the famous . . . Perle Mesta!" Perle stands, a contented-looking middle-aged lady. Perle bows. Applause.

Ed stares (enthralled) into camera. "Before we introduce singing Ed Ames and the first lady of the American theatre, Helen Hayes. . . ." A Pizza Spins commercial fades into a Tareyton Charcoal Filter commercial. Then Ed comes back to plug Helen Hayes's new book, *On Reflection*. Miss Hayes is the first lady of the American theatre, he says. "We're very honored to. . . ." Miss Hayes sitting at a desk, Louis-something. She looks marvelous. Begins reading from the book. Great voice. Tons of dignity. "My dear Grandchildren. At this writing, it is no longer fashionable to have Faith; but your grandmother has never been famous for her chic, so she isn't bothered by the intellectual hemlines. I have always been concerned with the whole, not the fragments; the positive, not the negative; the words, not the spaces between them. . . ." Miss Hayes pauses. Hand on what appears to be a small silver teapot. "What can a grandmother offer. . . ." *She speaks very well!* "With the feast of millennia set before you, the saga of all mankind on your bookshelf . . . what could I give you? And then I knew. Of course. My own small footnote. The homemade bread at the banquet. The private joke in the divine comedy. Your roots." Head and shoulders shot of Miss Hayes. She looks up into the lighting grid. Music up softly on, "So my grandchildren . . . in highlights and shadows . . . bits and pieces . . . in recalled moments, mad scenes and acts of folly. . . ." Miss Hayes removes glasses, looks misty. "What are little grandchildren made of . . . some good and some bad from Mother and Dad . . . and laughs and wails from Grandmother's tales . . . I love you." She gazes down at book. Holds it. Camera pulls back. Music up. Applause.

Ed puts arm around Miss Hayes. Squeezes Miss Hayes. Applause. *Heavy* applause. Ed pats hands together joining applause. Waves hands toward Miss Hayes. More applause. It's a triumph! Ed seizes Miss Hayes's hands in his hands. Applause dies, reluctantly. Ed says ". . . but first, listen to this." Shot of building, cathedral of some kind. Organ music. Camera pans down facade past stained-glass windows, etc. Down a winding staircase. Music changes to rock. Shot of organ keyboard. Close shot of maker's nameplate, HAMMOND. Shot of grinning organist. Shot of hands on keyboard. "The sound of Hammond starts at $599.95." Ed introduces singer Ed Ames. Ames is wearing a long-skirted coat, holding hand mike. Good eyes, good eyebrows, muttonchop sideburns. Lace at his cuffs. Real riverboat-looking. He strolls about the set singing a Tom Jones-Harvey Schmidt number, something about the morning, sometimes in the morning, something. Then another song, "it takes my breath away," "how long have I waited," something something. Chorus comes in under him. Good song. Ames blinks in a sincere way. Introduces a new song from the upcoming show *Dear World*. "A lovely new song," he says. "Kiss her now, while she's yours." Set behind him looks like one-by-two's nailed vertically four inches on centers. The song is sub-lovely but Ames's delivery is very comfortable, easy. Chorus comes in. Ah ah ah ah ah. Ames closes his eyes, sings something something something something; the song is sub-memorable. (Something memorable: early on Sunday morning a pornographic exhibition appeared mysteriously for eight minutes on television-station KPLM, Palm Springs, California. A naked man and woman did vile and imaginative things to each other for that length of time, then disappeared into the history of electricity. Unfortunately, the exhibition wasn't on a network. What we really want in this world, we can't have.)

Ed enters from left (what's over there? a bar? a Barcalounger? a book? stock ticker? model railroad?), shakes hands with Ames. Ames much taller, but amiable. Both back out of shot, in different directions. Camera straight ahead on Ed. "Before I tell you about next week's . . . show . . . please listen to this." Commercial for Silva Thins. Then a shot of old man with ship model, commercial for Total, the vitamin cereal. Then Ed. "Next week . . . a segment from . . . the new Beatles film . . . The Beatles were brought over here by us . . . in the beginning. . . . Good night!" Chopping gesture with hands to the left, to the right.

Music comes up. The crawl containing the credits is rolled over shots of Russian dancers dancing (XOPOWÓ!). Produced by Bob Precht. Directed by Tim Kiley. Music by Ray Bloch. Associate Producer Jack McGeehan. Settings Designed by Bill Bohnert. Production Manager Tony Jordan. Associate Director Bob Schwarz. Assistant to the Producer Ken Campbell. Program Coordinator Russ Petranto. Technical Director Charles Grenier. Audio Art Shine. Lighting Director Bill Greenfield. Production Supervisor Herb Benton. Stage Managers Ed Brinkman, Don Mayo. Set Director Ed Pasternak. Costumes Leslie Renfield. Graphic Arts Sam Cecere. Talent Coordinator Vince Calandra. Music Coordinator Bob Arthur. The Ed Sullivan Show is over. It has stopped.

—APRIL 1969

# Long Live the Career Smoker

DAVE EGGERS

My father was a lawyer who dealt exclusively with commodities—oranges, pork bellies, gold—representing, from a paper-choked office on Chicago's Wacker Drive, people who had been beguiled by brokers out of their money. It was simple stuff for him; he knew the applicable laws inside and out, it was fairly easy to prove who was at fault, and he was, particularly when he started in the sixties, one of a handful of lawyers in the country practicing such law. Thus, without ever really having to go to court, he never lost.

As children, the three of us (and, much later, four of us) would, in most cases to fulfill this or that homework assignment, ask him to explain his work; we were yearning for details with which to piece something together, to get an idea of what he did with his days. *What was a future? How could you trade one?* We knew of some of his clients. There was the Cuban, who insisted on being met in Miami. There was the Widow, who had been bilked for half a million or so by her young broker, the Weasel. But we were hungry for more detail, a better understanding. Did he pace back and forth before juries, full of righteous indignation? We had seen TV, movies—*Inherit the Wind, To Kill a Mockingbird*. Was it like that? Did he pound his fist, make impassioned demands of the jurors? We knew nothing except what he said, vaguely and occasionally, about his legal successes. He would come home after a case had wrapped and, after changing into his khakis and claiming his spot on the couch, would, with a flourish, clasp his hands together behind his head and say, cocky smile spread wide, "All right, everybody, come here and congratulate your brilliant dad, who's never lost a case!" We would ever so briefly turn away from the television and toward him and would roll our eyes.

We pretended he was not cool, because on weekends he wore madras pants and leather sandals. Still, he seemed so satisfied with his achievements, the fruits of his labors, that we couldn't help bask in it, too. He would sit there with his hands behind his head, his legs stretched out on the coffee table, and that crooked grin of his was sort of contagious.

Death certificates are generally the same size as birth certificates, eight-and-a-half- by eleven-inch pages turned on their sides, and have on them roughly the same amount of data. Though birth certificates are typically a bit more decorative, the two documents are strikingly similar, despite the considerable difference in the volume of information available. The piece of paper that summarizes and makes official my father's death I have in a small box that holds what little about him I was able to salvage from the house we sold shortly after he died: some papers from his induction into the Army, a high school yearbook, a curiously extravagant cache of receipts from a summer in Cape Cod shortly after he married my mother.

He died of lung and brain cancer in 1991. After feeling dizzy for weeks and collapsing five or six times while standing or walking or working, he let himself be taken to the emergency room and, after a few tests, was diagnosed with advanced cancer of the everywhere. He was given a year on the outside. For reasons that only a man who wore madras pants and watched *ALF* religiously—and he did, he did, never missed it—would understand, when he got home from the hospital, he picked up as if nothing much had changed. He still went to work each day, driving his gray car and wearing his gray suits, sending memos and taking calls for cases he could scarcely have hoped to finish. At the same time, he flirted briefly with radiation and chemotherapy, vomited prodigiously, lost his hair, felt generally terrible for a month or so, and then, when it became clear that the treatments were doing little to slow his decline, he quietly quit the therapy altogether. Soon after, things progressed with pitiless speed. When other, similarly cancer-addled people might be in bed, he was defiant, unperturbed, coolly dismissive, still smoking and drinking and going to work—and thus he continued to fall while standing or walking or working, and then, after maybe a month, he quit whatever fighting he had been doing. And he slipped away one afternoon in November.

He was a smoker. A heavy smoker, a chain smoker, someone who bought cigarettes two cartons at a time. A career smoker. His skin was gray, his teeth yellow, the first two fingers on his right hand jaundiced from the rub of cigarette filters. He was a smokers' smoker. A smoke machine.

He had built most aspects of his life around the habit. He had an ashtray in each part of the house he frequented: one by the couch, one by the bed, one for the kitchen, one he could take into the backyard. He was particularly proud of the special ashtray—"*Check it out,*" he said to me in the garage one Sunday—he had installed in the door panel of his car so he could smoke with his left hand and drive with his right, instead of vice versa, which was apparently too awkward.

His smoking was, as indeed smoking becomes for many people, less a habit and more a defining characteristic, and, truthfully, smoking, his commitment to the near-constant smoking of cigarettes, is one of the two or three chief things I remember about him. I realize that seems sad and strange. It always seemed sad and strange to me, too.

As a lawyer's son—and, I should mention, the son of a lawyer who did not take cases that were not compatible with his sense of right and wrong—I look for blame. And responsibility for his death, the death of a father of four, cut down at fifty-five with presumably so much to live for, is what this is about.

It's early fall in Chicago, it's warm and clear, and we're at the glassy, faux-elegant Fairmont Hotel overlooking Lake Michigan's popsicle blue, and Woody Wilner is the belle of the ball. About 150 lawyers have gathered at this, Mealey's Tobacco Conference: Settlement and Beyond, to strategize, meet and mingle, and hear about the recently proposed global legal settlement (the Global, as it's called) engineered between forty state attorneys general and the country's major makers of cigarettes, collectively (and in almost all cases pejoratively) known as the Tobacco Industry.

Despite mediocre food and the grating presence of the convention emcee—who starts each seminar by asking, "How are we all feeling?" and then scolding, "I can't hear you!"—I'm having a great time. I like lawyers, and I am endlessly fascinated by this, the suing of tobacco companies, and by the alternately brilliant and clumsy legal dancing the tobacco companies do in response.

Announced last June, the global tobacco settlement would force the tobacco industry to create a fund of at least $368.5 billion, paid over twenty-five years, to cover states' medical costs for those who have smoking-related diseases, and for various cessation and anti-smoking-education efforts. In return, the industry would be inoculated against all current and future class-action liability lawsuits and punitive damages in individual suits, in turn giving them some predictability of future profits. The general consensus at the convention is that the settlement, albeit with a ream of modifications, will likely pass in the spring, when Congress resumes. And so naturally, there are all kinds of legal celebrities here to stand before the cameras and take credit. At the head of the pack, as always, is Mike Moore, the colorful but often sanctimonious Mississippi attorney general who in 1994 gave birth to the then-outlandish idea of suing the tobacco industry to recoup Medicaid costs incurred from smoking-related illnesses. The American Lung Association is here, Smith Barney's tobacco-industry analyst—a young man actually named Marty Feldman—is here, CNN is here. But the real star among this herd of competitive, self-righteous personalities is the guy who single-handedly scared the living shit out of the multibillion-dollar cigarette industry and its legions of lawyers: Norwood "Woody" Wilner.

He is chubby and disheveled, balding, and with a seeming inability to keep what hair he does have from looking as if he's been jogging in heavy winds. Still, the guy has presence. He glides through the Fairmont's carpeted halls like a titan, radiating a casual confidence, knowing, probably, that every lawyer there wants to be him, imitate him, learn from him, shake his goddamn tobacco-industry-crushing hand.

Groups gather around him, and his name is mentioned in virtually every speech and conversation. He is called a "pioneer," a "hero," and, twice, a "warrior." Why? Because Norwood "Woody" Wilner is the Guy Who Won.

He beat the tobacco-industry bastards, and on his first try. The victory had been long in coming. Since the 1950s, when the connection between cancer and cigarettes was first demonstrated, thousands of dying smokers, and thousands of their survivors, had been trying to sue, or at least thinking about suing, the tobacco industry, with the vast majority of them running out of money or patience long before getting to court. Until August 1996, of the at least nineteen cases that had made it to trial, only one had ever been awarded a judgment, and even that was overturned on appeal.

But then, in August 1996, completely out of nowhere came Woody Wilner, partner in a tiny practice in Jacksonville, Florida, a guy who had made his career, fifteen years' worth, defending the asbestos industry, oddly enough. Wilner then takes this client, Grady Carter—a sixty-six-year-old air-traffic controller who had smoked for forty-three years and then contracted lung cancer—sues Brown & Williamson, stuns everyone with some new and staggeringly incriminating industry documents, and wins a $750,000 judgment. Boom. Unbelievable.

On the day of the verdict, tobacco stocks tumbled. The industry lost $14.5 billion in a day. All because of this one guy, Wilner! And minutes later, the sensitive ears of the American legal profession had pricked up, and a whisper burned through the ears of every savvy trial lawyer in America, and the content of that whisper was this: It can be done.

So at the Fairmont, you can feel the momentum. The lawyers gathered are spirited and cheerful. All of a sudden, it's good to be an antitobacco lawyer. After so many years of frustration, so many years of being scorned (at least by their opponents) as moneygrubbing, ambulance-chasing communists, they finally have a reason to feel good about their work, because of the turning tide, because of the possibility of the largest legal payday in history, and because, when you think about it, for a trial lawyer, taking a bite out of the tobacco companies can scarcely be beat: They are menaces to the health of the populace, richer than the pope, and perfectly unapologetic about their complicity in the deaths of tens of millions.

The Chicago convention has more than a dozen seminars, but none are as popular as Wilner's "Standing Alone: Suits by Individual Smokers." It's the second day of the affair, and during his spiel, he's not only laying out the play-by-play of how he beat Brown & Williamson, he's got the crowd rolling in the aisles. What's so funny? A deposition. A few months before, Wilner had gone up to Louisville to depose Irwin Tucker, Brown & Williamson's director of research from 1953 to 1960. Now Wilner's got the deposition transcribed and on the overhead and is reading it aloud. A sample:

WILNER: As you sit here today, do you believe that cigarette smoke causes lung cancer in human beings?
TUCKER: No, I don't.
WILNER: Do you believe that air pollution causes lung cancer in human beings?
TUCKER: No.
WILNER: Do you believe that asbestos causes cancer in human beings?
TUCKER: Definitely not.
WILNER: What are the causes of human lung cancer, in your opinion?
TUCKER: I'd say the inhalation of very particular substances.
WILNER: Like what?
TUCKER: Like tar.
WILNER: Tar? What kind of tar?
TUCKER: From a—a bucket of boiling tar.

People are literally falling off their chairs. Wilner's got the crowd by the balls—they love him more now that they've seen him, heard him—because he's both very funny and he knows, as much as or more than anyone, about where the tobacco industry is hiding every last body.

The Tucker deposition and the ever-growing pile of incriminating internal documents and testimony that continue to turn up are part of the reason why so many lawyers are reluctant to embrace the global settlement now and why it's pretty easy to laugh at the aging, seemingly senile and delusional Irwin Tucker, despite the fact that we're talking about obfuscation on a level that seems implausible, almost science fictional. Then again, when evil at its most banal intersects with stupidity at its most pure, well, that's entertainment.

Entertainment. As an example, I would now like to relate, for the record, the Furry Oven Mitt Episode.

My mother was dying of cancer at the same time as my father, and there was a period when they were both doing the chemo and the radiation at the same time and had each come to the point where the hair starts coming out in clumps, making the use of wigs necessary, or at least prudent.

My mother had had cancer for years, so she already had a small assortment of hair simulations. Her favorite one was much like her own hair, full and curly, and didn't look all that wiggy, allowing her to carry it off somewhat convincingly.

Dad, though . . . well, he was never a vain man, yet had long prided himself on having, at forty, at fifty and beyond, a full head of wavy silver hair. Which made it all the more surprising to see him for the first time wearing the wig.

We were at home, and I was sitting across the room. He was watching *ALF*, chuckling, but there was something on his head that commanded attention. Now, it's important to keep in mind that he had already worn this wig to work and that he had, he smugly announced, gone to his barber, Pino, the day before to have it "styled." And I knew he was very sick, but I could not help myself from issuing comment. The wig was too short, too short the way a hat can be too small, leaving too much of the head, that which is to be covered, uncovered. And it really didn't look like hair at all—it was too soft, fuzzy even. And he was wearing it sort of . . . tilted. (Or was it on backward?) He was sitting there, smoking and having a vodka and tonic, blissfully unaware of the fact that on his head was not a wig styled by a man named Pino, was not a wig at all. It was a furry oven mitt.

Furry oven mitts were popular back then. I was sure that I had seen something like it that day at the hardware store, and told him so. I also commented on the personal-style element he had added: The tilted aspect reminded one of the way many youths of the day were wearing their baseball hats—30 degrees of calculated nonchalance. So I complimented him on both his fashion sense and his frugality. Why shell out the $200 for a real wig when a furry oven mitt from True Value would do?

My mother, sitting catercorner in her regular chair, wearing her own wig, laughed in agreement.

"John, it does look pretty dumb," she said.

Oblivious, he kept his attention on *ALF*. I turned toward the TV.

And that's when they must have plotted the counterattack. They knew I didn't much like seeing their bare heads, splotchy with hair clumps—even though it was less comfortable for them, I had begged them to keep the wigs on at home—so the next time I looked up from *ALF*, I found them both staring at me, wigs on their laps, their bald, spotty pates sitting open-aired and triumphant above their wild eyes and malicious grins.

Funny.

As I ran from the room, looking for a pillow to bury my head in, their shrieks of laughter followed me through halls and doors.

JoAnn Karbiwnyk has a severe kind of look about her. She is fifty-eight, with a sort of bouffant of white-blond hair that shoots from her face, straight and wispy like cotton candy. It is three weeks after the Chicago conference, and we are in Jacksonville, where Wilner is taking a whack at his third tobacco case. It's the first day of jury selection, and Karbiwnyk sits front and center, perhaps eight feet from the pool of twenty-five potential jurors, wearing a pink suit with shoes to match. Karbiwnyk is suing R. J. Reynolds for $400,000 in compensatory damages for the company's part in causing her cancer, first lung and then brain.

At the Fairmont lounge in Chicago, I had asked Wilner who would constitute a perfect client, one most likely to bring in a victory against a tobacco company. He took a sip of his drink, leaned back in his chair, and demurred, "We don't really pick and choose our clients."

Maybe, but there are things that one would obviously hope for in a client. First, a plaintiff who is suffering from cancer but is alive to testify is preferable to one whose survivors have to stand in and recount the suffering and loss. Second, if it can be reasonably proved that the plaintiff's cancer was caused solely by cigarettes—someone without a strong family history of cancer, someone who doesn't work around other carcinogens—it helps deflect the tobacco company's inevitable argument that genetics or "environmental factors" contributed to the disease. Third, a smoker who was loyal to one brand is preferable to one who switched; it makes it easier to single out one company. Last, the plaintiff should be able to prove that he or she was absolutely addicted to cigarettes, powerless to quit. If you can prove that the plaintiff tried the gum and the patches and therapy and hypnotism, that he or she desperately wanted to quit but always failed because, simply, the tobacco companies had engineered a deliberately addictive product, then you're getting somewhere.

But any casual observer could see that with Karbiwnyk, Wilner was at a disadvantage from the beginning. Considering that with his reputation he could have had virtually any case he wanted—and he has hundreds of tobacco plaintiffs awaiting his attention—Karbiwnyk's case seems at best an odd choice for Wilner to take to court. Karbiwnyk's case departs meaningfully from almost every one of the basic conditions mentioned above. Yes, she had cancer, but eleven years passed between the time she quit smoking and the diagnosis of her illness, making causation not impossible to prove but certainly more difficult. Worse, Karbiwnyk switched brands more than a few times. Thus, it's debatable that her addiction to nicotine happened with Reynolds's cigarettes. And the addiction question, in Karbiwnyk's case, was perhaps the biggest problem of all: When it eventually occurred to her to quit—in 1984, she began dating an avid jogger, who urged her to give up the habit—she quit on her first try, cold turkey. How does one claim addiction when the plaintiff can drop the habit the moment her head is turned by a new boyfriend?

And once jury selection started, everything got worse.

R. J. Reynolds's lawyer, Ted Grossman, is massaging the jury pool in a way that's almost pornographic. Grossman confounds the slick, Armani-clad image of a tobacco lawyer that might come to mind. A wonderfully unassuming-looking man, he is short and slight and has a slouchy sort of posture; his eyes are sad, pleading eyes, his voice raspy, and his suit is too small. But he has a way with these people. One by one, he interviews the potential jurors, chatting them up about their lives, their jobs, asking about their attitudes about smoking, how they get their news, but also, here and there, casually asking about their families, hobbies, and even their taste in music. When an older black woman mentions that she listens to gospel music on the radio, he takes off his glasses, puts one end in his mouth, and ventures thoughtfully, "It helps you through the day, doesn't it?" When she nods, he says, "That's nice," and then pauses for a moment that makes clear that he means it. He's calming and down-to-earth, conveying the impression that instead of being in this stuffy courtroom, he'd much rather be sitting on the front porch with these good people, sipping ice-cold lemonade and listening to their music.

And whether the prospective jurors want to please Ted Grossman or they simply are, from the perspective of someone hoping to sue the tobacco industry, the worst possible assemblage of people in Jacksonville or the world, they proceed to eviscerate Wilner's case before it even begins.

Seven of them used to smoke, and most say they quit with ease. There is one woman who has managed, over a number of years, to smoke only occasionally—a casual indulgence. There is one woman who quit when she became pregnant—"It wasn't hard," she says—and then picked it up again afterward. "With open eyes?" asks Grossman, meaning aware of the risks. "Yes," she says, nodding forcefully.

When Grossman asks if anyone would object to working for a tobacco company, only one raises his hand.

The only potential bright spot seems to be that no less than two thirds of the pool have lost loved ones to smoking. Fathers, mothers, grandparents, uncles, friends. But even this doesn't help.

Grossman turns to a woman whose mother smoked and died of cancer. "Do you blame the tobacco companies for your mother's death?"

"No," she says.

To a woman with two relatives dead from tobacco-related cancer: "Do you hold the tobacco companies responsible?"

"No. They were told to quit, and they didn't."

It gets worse. When asked if any of them would be unable to serve as objective jurors, three say they could not.

"Sounds like a fishy thing to me," says one man.

"Sounds like she's in it for the money," says another, who has just told a story about how, when he was a child, his father threatened to make him eat a pack of cigarettes if he was caught smoking.

"If I can quit," says the third objector, "why can't everyone else?"

Wilner is playing with his hair, a few fingers twirling among the thicket on the back of his head. At the same time that it becomes clear why these cases are so seldom won, I suddenly realize why Woody Wilner's hair is perpetually unkempt.

My father and I talked about drugs a few times, and each time he encouraged me to do them.

The conversations took place in high school and usually started when I was being harangued for something—leaving the garage door open at night, spilling something on the carpet—that I deemed unworthy of a harangue, and I would tell him so, and in doing so I would mention, by the way, that for a kid like me, a kid with good grades and no criminal record, a kid who had never known any trouble with anyone, a kid who had been, yes, given a citizenship award by the American Legion, to be harangued about spilled garbage was completely ridiculous. "This is completely ridiculous," I would say. "I could be drinking. I could be doing drugs like everyone else! You should be happy to have me. I'm a dream teenager!"

He sipped his vodka.

"Do drugs," he said. "Do drugs, and drink all you want, and get arrested—do it all."

I would stare blankly. Then he'd finish me off:

"You think you're hurting me if you do drugs? It's not my life, it's yours."

JoAnn Karbiwnyk has a taste for mirrors and chrome. Her one-bedroom apartment has the look of a vacation condominium—beveled glass, flowers, pastels, wall-to-wall carpeting. On a chrome shelf near the dining-room table, there is a stuffed-animal horse, white with a blue mane. Karbiwnyk is divorced and lives alone about thirty miles from downtown Jacksonville. I am visiting her at home because I have drawn the obvious parallels between her habit and her cancer and my father's. I have a vague hope that she can shed some light on my father, on the workings of his brain.

Karbiwnyk started smoking on a dare when she was about sixteen. By the time she was eighteen, in 1956, she was hooked. She says that she did not truly realize the dangers of her smoking until new warnings came out in 1984. The old warning, which read, warning: the surgeon general has determined that cigarette smoking is dangerous to your health, was replaced by a rotating foursome of labels, the most to the point of which was surgeon general's warning: smoking causes lung cancer, heart disease, emphysema, and may complicate pregnancy. About this time, she started jogging with her new boyfriend, and she quit.

I ask her what it was like every day to face the pressures of those around her urging her to quit. Her ex-husband needled her; her daughter hounded her. She accepted it as a condition of her habit, she says. When they insisted that she smoke outside, she smoked outside.

For my father, a preposterous idea. Driven from his own home? No. So we worked around it. As children, we were so repelled by the smell that even casual interaction was a struggle. When needing help on homework, for instance, we would attempt to fit entire conversations in the two to three minutes he tended to allot between cigarettes, requiring us to plan our thoughts, edit our words, and then talk as quickly as possible. All the while, we would be anxiously eyeing his right hand for signs of movement. When he reached for the cigarettes on the end table, the conversation was over, with us literally jumping from the room before he blew his first cloud to the ceiling. As we got older, we became more intolerant—*Jesus, Dad*—and soon stopped spending much time in his company at all. When our youngest brother was a baby, we kept him from the smoke entirely, forgoing the first floor for the smoke-free comforts of the basement. Thus, with a wife and four children in the house, my father often spent evenings alone, in the family room.

I ask if Karbiwnyk believes she bears any responsibility for contracting cancer after smoking for thirty years.

"No."

None?

"No."

I ask her to elaborate.

"Well, I didn't know it was dangerous. If I knew it was dangerous, I wouldn't have started smoking in the first place. It's pretty silly to start smoking when you know it can kill you."

Her daughter, Amanda, is twenty and has been smoking since she was fourteen. "She lived with me during chemotherapy and my hair falling out," says Karbiwnyk.

I mention that my brother is fourteen now, and, as I'm genuinely curious, parent to parent (after my mother died, I became his guardian), I ask what she did when she found out her fourteen-year-old daughter was smoking.

"I said to her, 'I can't stop you, but I wish you wouldn't do it,'" Karbiwnyk says. "I said, 'Don't expect me to buy you a pack of cigarettes.' " She pauses dramatically.

*"And I have never bought her a pack of cigarettes."*

I nod, then gently ask why she thinks her daughter smokes, considering that she not only had the benefit of strong warning labels and ubiquitous antismoking messages but also had been witness, in the form of her cancer-ridden mother, to the gory results of the habit.

She is not exactly sure.

I know the sounds. I know the sound of the kitchen cabinet opening and closing as he retrieved another pack from one of the cartons he would keep high above the counter. I know the *thwack thwack thwack* as he packed the cigarettes against his palm. I know the sound of his eight steps back to the living room, the slow *shhh* of him sinking into his spot on the couch, the soft thumps of his feet finding their place on the coffee table close to my head as I lay stomach-down on the floor, doing my homework. I know the crinkle as he removed the plastic from the package, the tap of a cigarette twice on the table. I know the click of metal on glass as he picked his silver lighter off the side table, the *phit phit phit* of metal striking flint. Then the squeak of the lighter's top swinging back and clacking closed. Then a pause. A kiss. Then the first exhale, deep with relief.

But I don't get much of a picture. I never watched.

Wilner and Karbiwnyk lost. And it wasn't because Wilner did not show that the tobacco industry has lied to the public for many, many decades. He did, and he also established, beyond a shadow of a doubt, that cigarettes cause cancer and that they are, for many people, extremely addictive.

Meanwhile, Ted Grossman's case was a marvel of blurry contradictions. The standard industry defense, the one it's been using since it started getting sued regularly, is startlingly circular, and, when you really think about it, either perfectly brilliant or perfectly stupid. They lay it out like this:

(1) We are not responsible for this person's cancer, because no one has definitively proved that cigarettes cause cancer.

(2) Even if cigarettes have ever, in a few rare instances, caused cancer, they did not cause cancer in this person, because this person (a) has relatives who have had cancer and is therefore genetically predisposed toward the disease; (b) lived near power lines or a factory or in or near a city where, as we all know, there is cancer-causing pollution.

(3) And even if cigarettes did cause this person's cancer, they should have known better because, as everyone knows . . .

(4) Smoking is bad for your health.

Ludicrous, yes, but come to think of it, so is Wilner's argument, which goes something like this:

(1) My client contracted cancer from smoking cigarettes.

(2) My client was addicted to cigarettes because cigarettes are as addictive as heroin or crack.

(3) Though most of the country was well aware, from the 1960s forward, that cigarettes were addictive and dangerous, my client was not. She did not know that they were dangerous until, in 1966, the labels said they were hazardous to your health.

(4) She smoked for eighteen more years because the labels were not sufficient until 1984, when they said that smoking causes lung cancer.

(5) At which time my client quit using the substance to which she was addicted . . .

On her first try.

After the verdict, the tobacco industry had reason to gloat, and suddenly its claims that the Grady Carter case was "an aberration" became more convincing. Wilner, however, was unfazed and immediately announced plans to be in court again in February. JoAnn Karbiwnyk was disappointed but had no plans to appeal and went back to her job as a loan processor. Meanwhile, California banned smoking in all bars and restaurants, Texas's case was settled for $15.3 billion, a handful of individual suits, most of which were benefiting from Wilner's consulting help, were headed to trial, the global settlement was awaiting the attention of Congress, and the tobacco industry was gazing longingly toward Asia.

There was a point in the Karbiwnyk trial, on maybe the third day, when the essence of what troubled me about these cases became clear. Wilner had his expert witness on the stand, an esteemed pulmonary pathologist from Duke University, and the two were laboriously detailing how the carcinogens in cigarette smoke invade the cells in lung tissue, causing mutations and thus cancer. Wilner offhandedly asked the doctor how long it usually took for a regular smoker to contract lung cancer.

"Thirty to forty years," the doctor said.

Wilner continued his questioning, on to the causation of Karbiwnyk's particular cancer, but my head had stopped short. Thirty to forty years. Wilner's case, if it wasn't doomed because of Karbiwnyk, was lost right there—*thirty to forty years*—and along with it I came to a point of understanding in the case of my own father.

Let's do the math:

My father smoked about two and a half packs of cigarettes a day. Fifty cigarettes a day. Three hundred and fifty a week. More than eighteen thousand a year. Six hundred and thirty thousand over thirty-five years. And that's the easy part. Now, let's acknowledge that, like Karbiwnyk, each time he opened a package, he was faced with a warning. By period, those warnings were:

1966–70. CAUTION: cigarette smoking may be hazardous to your health.

1970–84. WARNING: the surgeon general has determined that cigarette smoking is dangerous to your health.

1984. SURGEON GENERAL'S WARNING: smoking causes lung cancer, heart disease, emphysema, and may complicate pregnancy.

Now, depending on which side he set the package of cigarettes, he might have to see the warning just once while he was using its contents or each time he retrieved another cigarette. So let's say he could be seeing the warning anywhere from one to twenty times per pack. Now, considering the fact that he probably seldom read or at all acknowledged the existence of the warning—Karbiwnyk said, "I just ignored it"—let's say he saw the warning, and that it registered in some capacity, twice a day.

Okay, so twice a day from the package. Add in at least once from the warnings in cigarette ads in magazines and newspapers. So three times a day. Add to that at least once a day from a member of his family, which, coming from a child or a wife, should count for three. So six stern warnings a day. That's forty-two a week, 2,184 a year. Over thirty years, that's 65,520 warnings that the habit will kill you.

Then there's the scorn of one's family and much of the world at large. Every day, nonsmoking people, forced to inhale the acrid, ephemeral product of the habit, give dirty looks to smokers. Every day, a smoker like my father had to endure complaints and condescending comments from his children. People who smoke outside buildings must tolerate passersby who walk around them, glare at them: *You poor, desperate person*. So let's consider that each smoker might have to deal with perhaps five to ten instances, daily, of being treated like, and thus feeling hideous, self-enslaved. That's about twenty-five hundred times a year and about seventy-five thousand over the career of a typical smoker.

Now let's look at the math for a person who really lives the examined life, who contemplates his every decision. Let's say that someone thinks, with each and every puff, I shouldn't be doing this. Ten puffs per cigarette, twenty cigarettes per pack, two packs a day: 400 puffs a day; 2,800 a week; 145,600 a year; 4,368,000 over thirty years.

For so long, I considered my father's contraction of cancer a result of his indifference. Indifference to risk, to the consequences of that risk, to the effects his habit and inevitable death would have on his family. But dying from smoking is work. It takes concerted effort. It is simply, unequivocally, the most diffcult way to leave this world. My father's achievement was not accidental or tangential to another goal. It was the result of his continually facing a simple equation illustrating the clear relationship between action and consequence—and thus with little effort seeing a progression toward a black and miserable early death, with long and permanent shadows cast over every one of his family members. It was seeing all these things a million times and, more than likely, doing the intellectual equivalent of shrugging.

When Wilner says in conversation and in court that smokers are "weak," he is of course right, but he also couldn't be more wrong. Smokers are the most stalwart and persevering people there are. Who but someone with a will of iron could bear such pressure—the sneers of strangers, the glares of his sons and daughters, the bitter, seething comments of the people who are forced to tolerate him and his aura—such decades-long opprobrium? Who else would be willing to leave his office twice an hour to stand in the cold or rain to suck smoke from a paper tube? Who else would be willing to forgo going out to dinner, to movies, to any public place where smoking is not permitted, for fear that the urge will strike and not be quenchable?

Who but a giant could look at a dying wife, a pleading family, and a young son who will soon lose his mother and whose fate you hold in your yellowed fingers—will this boy lose *one* parent or *two?*—and yet still continue? Who but a man of outrageous fortitude, a will of steel, a mind of golden labyrinths?

A tobacco death requires years of meticulous attention and constant, obsessive care; it is perhaps a marvel of mortal achievement. When you die from smoking, your death is yours.

But by all means, let the tobacco companies settle; let them throw the billions at kids and the IVs and beds needed to ease the exit of smokers from this world. What are the chances that juries will, as Wilner and others hope, punish the industry for the decades-long suicides of hundreds of thousands of smokers? Painfully slim. There is a reason why one juror was sleeping through the Karbiwnyk trial, and there is a reason why I was one of only two members of the media at the trial, and that is that most people simply don't care—because really, as long as it stays out of public places, as long as it's just a habit for people who need a habit, it really cannot be an issue of concern for the public at large. Claiming that we all have to pay for the Medicaid costs, the costs of lost labor, of those dying of smoking-related illnesses, sounds convincing until one considers that the burden is actually lifted—*lifted*—by these smoking-related deaths, relieving, because these smokers die on average twelve years earlier than nonsmokers, the nation from the obligation to provide for them into their old age. We actually save, according to Harvard economist W. Kip Viscusi, $30 billion a year, or an average of $69,654.05 per dead smoker. But fine, let's take the money from the tobacco companies, if they are silly enough to offer it. We can take it, and maybe a few children who consider the smoking life will decide against it, and the other people, the people who have chosen the life, thirty years later and cancer-engulfed, will have clean hospital sheets as they fade away.

I did not know that the last time I saw my father would be the last time I would see my father. He was in intensive care, having been unable to lift himself from his knees after collapsing in the shower. I had come up from college to visit, but because it had been so soon after his diagnosis, I didn't make much of it. He was expected to undergo some tests and treatment, get his strength back, and return home in a few days.

I had come to the hospital with my mother, my sister, and my brother Toph, then eight. We came upon the door to my father's room, and it was closed. We pushed open the heavy door and were struck, immediately, by the fact that . . . that he was smoking! In intensive care! The windows were closed and the haze was thick, the stench unbelievable, and in the midst of it all was my father, looking happy to see us.

No one talked much. We stayed for maybe ten minutes, huddled on the far side of the room, attempting as best we could to stay away from the smoke. Chris was hiding behind me, scared. Two green lights on the machine next to my father blinked, alternately, on, off, on, off. A red light stayed steady, red.

My father was reclining on the bed, his back propped against two pillows. His legs were crossed casually, and he had his hands clasped behind his head. Again the deserving recipient of the fruits of his labors, he was relaxed, self-satisfied. And he was grinning his grin, for the world was his.

—APRIL 1998

# What Is the Difference Between This Photograph and a Real Frozen TV Dinner?

M. F. K. FISHER

Rich is the family with, at least every generation or so, its own newspaper or magazine! It appears two or three times, on the average, and seldom is the advance subscription price held to. (Once when I was going on ten I asked for one cent a copy, or six issues for a nickel, and I should be ashamed to admit here that I brought out only two, and never refunded a penny to my four subscribers. . . .) Jewels of inadvertent wit and even wisdom lurk in the hand-printed pages of such journals, and if a doctoral thesis has not yet been written on the subject, with prime examples, it is probably because in almost every case the paper has long since been lost. Hearsay is left. I cannot remember the sound of any of my own pearls, of course, but forever in my mind is one from another family.

A brother and sister wrote and published a weekly for the comparatively long time of about three months, and for the Christmas issue each editor contributed not only fiction, poetry, news, and an editorial, with of course the usual riddles, gossip items, and other such classical fillers, but a full-page illustration. The little boy drew something like a wreath or a *tannenbaum*, but his little sister's picture was so odd, when he appraised it, that he submitted it to the cold eyes of their mother. She, as bluntly as almost any grownup, asked at once and no matter how gently, "What is it?" The artist said patiently, "This is the Christmas edition. So that is the Virgin and Child."

The drawing, as I have been told about it, consisted of the two ovoids, one half the size of the other and below it a little, to the right. It was plain that the small egg was looking up at the big egg. The big egg was looking down with infinite tenderness at the little egg. They tilted together, and were filled only with space. The artist's mother perhaps suggested some eyes, a smile. . . . The little girl took back her picture and left with dignity, and when the family paper came out on Christmas Eve the drawing was called, in firm ornamented printing, *Different People Have Different Ideas of Madonnas, and This Is Mine.*

The phrase sounds familiar, as if somebody like Orwell had said it, but of course it was new in the mind of the innocent coeditor. It is a useful one. It applies to some of our most basic puzzlements and their satisfactions . . . the TV dinner, for instance.

This is not all things to all men, certainly, but it can be everything from an exotic or neurotic adventure to the lifesaver for countless Americans, and it is bound to become more so . . . a probability which is perhaps its most frightening promise. In different words, TV meals are not my own idea of how to survive, but they apparently are to myriad others of us.

Newcomers to our country find the flat rectangular packets, frozen stiff in every grocery store from the biggest supermarket to the smallest crossroads "general," an amusing thing to play with, and gradually to depend on. They seem, and too often they prove to be, unreal, unbelievable . . . and then routine. On the outside is a brilliant fakey picture in full color of the gastronomical bliss within. The directions for attaining it are in basic language, with the required oven temperature often in blacker, larger type for those of us who can read numbers but not words.

The process of hopefully turning the flat block of ugly, lumpy grey ice back into an appetizing collection of nourishing tidbits for human consumption is kept as simple as possible. After the final chef of a long series of them sees how hot the oven should be and how long the meal will take to emerge at its peak of perfection, the foil top is left alone or loosened or partly removed, according to what will finally emerge (French fries and rolls are "exposed" while their accompaniments steam along under cover), and presumably one's taste buds ready themselves as the tray with its neat compartments turns into exactly what the pretty picture promised: a "juicy tender all-sirloin chopped steak with gravy, fluffy whipped potatoes with extra pat of butter, peas-n-carrots just like Mom's. . . ." Yummy Eatin, one nationally distributed brand calls it.

Another popular purveyor offers, of course in its own little depression in the foil tray, what it calls an exclusive feature as well as "an extra 'home style' touch": a *muffin*! A full-page color ad in national magazines directed at Togetherness in the Home suggests that this bonus can turn any meal into a festive birthday treat by having a little candle stuck into it. Such whimsy contradicts the original and always preferred practice of eating TV meals in the half-dark in almost any position, but preferably on the floor or on the southernmost tip of the spine if in a chair: the bright cartoon shows a cretin-like little boy actually sitting at the table, probably because it is a Special Occasion. He is grinning, perhaps with anticipation. Mom, rushing in from right, is grinning with self-satisfaction of how loving and generous she is, to stick the candle in the fluffy free muffin which in turn has soothed her last-minute qualms about forgetting Junior's birthday . . . and all this thanks to the benevolent thoughtful home-style chefs who watch over our national diet in their sanitized factories.

Behind the grinning child and his harried but so happy grinning mother sits a grinning cat. Perhaps he thinks there is something he too can savor on that dimpled tray . . . although during my own clinical pursuit of the Really Delicious TV dinner I have yet to find a cat, my own pampered one or any of the otherwise omnivorous neighborhood bums, who will give the food more than a sniff. This in itself seemed ominous, but I think that the actual victuals are harmless enough but that felines rightly mistrust the excessive use of monosodium glutamate in every frozen dinner I have thus far baked, especially ones with *fish*! It makes their tongues and throats burn. (Mine too.) It makes them fiercely thirsty. (Me too.)

Mexicans who came to our western states for work, usually migratory, find TV meals not only handy but glamorous. Living conditions are seldom more than rudimentary, but somehow a way to heat an oven to 450 degrees for half an hour is generally procurable, and people who live in every seasonal-crop area along our border have told me that often one stove will run twenty-four hours a day, while families wait their turns. No pots and pans, no plates, no garbage: all are real problems to people who live in cramped cabins or tents and must follow the harvests in whatever beat-up car will hold the most children and cousins.

My grocer, by now one of the last small-town holdouts against supermarkets (which he knows tacitly that I go to for things he cannot possibly afford to stock), worries every summer when pickers move into our California valley for the prune and grape crops. Exhausted men will come into his store and buy twelve or fifteen frozen meals every night after work, he says. He hates to take most of what they have earned that day in the blazing sun, stooping over the vines and stretching into the trees. But they tell him their children love the surprise of the exciting dishes, and will eat every crumb. He sometimes reminds them in his anxiety that he carries good dried beans and fresh chili powder and that they can feed a hell of a lot of kids for what one frozen meal will cost them. They laugh happily and say they can eat beans in Jalisco. This is vacation, they say. "We take it easy in your country," they say, and they keep right on laughing, so that my friend is not sure what the joke might really be.

They buy without regard to price, but by the pictures on the packages, and they pay from an occasional 39 cents or "today's special smash bargain 3 for $1.19" to the rarer 79 cents, as do perhaps a hundred million other visitors and residents of America. The choice is wide, and while most combinations of food are straight Yankee (Swiss steak in beef and tomato gravy, French fries, mixed vegetables in seasoned sauce, vanilla pudding with macaroon crumbs), there are available dinners called Italian (spaghetti and meatballs), Chinese (chicken chow mein), and even "Continental" (beef Burgundian).

One production our spendthrift stoop-laborers never seem to buy is called Mexican Style. There are several versions of this, depending on the distributor and perhaps the locality, but a typical one (59 cents on sale) will include in its three compartments two cheese-stuffed enchiladas in a mild chili gravy, some pinto beans, and a portion of corn with bits of red and green pepper in it. The package will give some sensible hints on adding tomato soup, a salad of avocado and grapefruit, a custard of some kind for dessert.

Not too coincidentally, a costlier version of the same feast, grandly specifying three courses, has almost exactly that menu in its dimples, except for the salad, which would not survive too gracefully a half hour in a hot oven. (Neither does the pudding, unless one really likes one's custard bubbling. . . .) This "typical Mexican feast," still costing less than a dollar, has five places in its foil tray, filled with good bland tomato soup with bits of toasted tortillas floating limply in it, a bean enchilada and a beef tamale in chili-flavored gravy, "Spanish-type" rice, refried beans with grated cheese and, for a special surprise, an apple-custard pudding. Even gringos, whose palates are abashed by most seasoning south of the border, admit that such so-called Mexican frozen meals are almost tasteless, but that the quality of the food is somewhat above the usual level, for some reason. They are popular . . . unless you come from Jalisco.

Pressed-foil trays are as standard as the ubiquitous "fresh peas in seasoned sauce" which in eight out of ten menus fill the top right-hand compartments, and an aficionado will know exactly where to put his fork or spoon if he stares at the television or the wall, and exactly what will go into his mouth, and how it will taste, depending upon which brand his girl patronizes (or oftener, which one the nearest supermarket stocks).

It is perhaps of some historical interest that hostesses, as opposed to day-to-day cooks, are now urged in national advertising to be guests at their own parties and use plastic-coated disposable paper refills, pressed of course into four neat compartments, which will fit into stylishly designed metal trays for countless gastronomical gatherings. No fuss, no muss! No dishes! These timesavers are promised as "the ultimate in serving ease and dining elegance," and, to misquote a childhood joke, would be handy things to have on a picnic. I would not spurn them, *loudly* anyway, under a redwood tree on a sunny day, but am afraid I might behave coldly if I were expected to use one at a decent buffet supper. Tourist class on a transcontinental jet: yes, for how can one argue at thirty-three-thousand feet? Section D at the Medical Center: yes, for there are twelve beds jammed into a six-bed room and the nurses are going crazy and what more can one expect at only $79.50 a day, with free aspirin? At home, with aloneness or togetherness: *no*. Frozen dinners come already divided into compartments if they are required at all (once, in my whole culinary experience, I served something like twenty in three days to two little boys who had spent their lives in Africa and wanted to be American in a hurry), and small trays with sturdy plates and bowls on them are much more fun if one wants a chair-side meal: more *appetizing* to diehards like me, and no messier than those fancy foil things with soup splashing around in them!

Another household design which may possibly be a permanent part of our future dining habits is a plastic tray inverted to hold exactly one TV dinner, which in turn will fit into it on its little molded legs without any damage as it comes sizzling from the oven, for the gadget is made throughout of heat-resistant, machine-washable "Hi-Impact Styrene," whatever that might be. It looks a little like polished wood carved in Australia, and is "decorator-designed and Space-age engineered," to speed from the kitchen to one's easy chair, and once more there will be no fuss, no muss . . . and of course the kitchen will be immaculate, because nothing has gone on in it except turning the oven to 450 and then off. . . .

Although most of the pressed-foil trays have up to five compartments brimming with yummy eatin, there are a few with only two, like a Chinese dinner which is supposed to be augmented with fried rice (also procurable frozen). A typical one costs about 65 cents, and even without a starch it can make a good simple meal for one hungry person. It should: there are some thirty-five ingredients listed in the almost invisible print required legally for the contents of any such package. Of course they include monosodium glutamate, even more ubiquitous than green peas in TV meals, and then there are such banalities as caramel coloring and egg white and such exotics as hydrolyzed plant protein and sodium alginate (generously identified as a vegetable stabilizer).

A four-compartment banquet which somewhat surprisingly costs only 79 cents is the opposite of this two-section presentation of a harmless but almost meaningless mixture of would-be Oriental delicacies (guaranteed to leave you hungry in an hour, in the best tradition). It is a Yank's version of the good old Limey fish and chips, except of course that the label makes the word "and" a bit homier by spelling it "n." Under the strangely revolting picture on the lid it states that it is made of breaded filets of ocean haddock, apparently sliced from a fish shaped exactly to fit the largest compartment. This convenience, probably the result of special genetical research in the company's laboratories, is less astonishing than the statement, repeated at least three times, that the fish is from the *ocean*. Dictionaries say without quibble that the haddock is a small prolific food fish found in coastal salt waters. If the word "ocean" must be used to convey freshness and even authenticity, why not splurge even further and call the flat triangles something really tempting like "honest-to-Pete genuine Atlantic haddock"?

In one such production, the fish turns out to be chopped, seasoned, breaded, and shaped into position, although the word "filet" is used shamelessly. . . . This man-made wonder is accompanied by Krinkle-Kut deep-fried potatoes and ah yes, *mais oui*, "peas in seasoned sauce." (One reason for this gratuitous addition of MSG, salt, a pinch of marjoram, is so that the diner need not be bothered nor menaced by having to add condiments in the obscurity of his flickering room.) The little vegetables are very green, as if that matters in the dark, and they are round and uniformly meaningless. In the upper-middle compartment, usually reserved for the "extra festive touch" of a roll or muffin in this brand of meal, there is something called tartar sauce. What happens to it when it has been heated for twenty-five minutes at 450 should not happen to anything meant to be made of fresh and correctly chilled mayonnaise and its crisp additions. It is, flatly, a hot sour pickly custard, very disgusting. Peculiar, these Yanks! In London or Plymouth or Penzance we just douses a little vinegar over the fish in the newspaper twist if we feels like it.

• • •

There seem to be three main levels of dining on frozen meals. The first one is mass-produced and mass-distributed, all over the nation, mostly by reputable companies which are often local subsidiaries of huge firms like Campbell's and General Foods. (For this reason I use the word "reputable," in spite of some personal qualms, but with legal approval.) The locations of their production plants are strategically near main distribution centers for vegetables and meats, and are as awesome in their combining of the mechanical and the computer ages as a secret missile site. Words like "countless" and "untold" and "myriad" are ridiculous in describing the daily output of these plants, for not only every completed foil tray, correctly labeled, but every milligram of food it holds has been computerized. Precision is of the essence in the enormous vats that do their controlled simmerings and blanchings in the sterilized air-conditioned laboratories, and then the tons of seasoned nutritives shoot down to their separators, and when they fall at a blinding speed into exactly their right compartments on each tray as it whizzes along the belts, they will all look like the labels that are finally stuck on their sealed covers. They will vary a little in content, according to local and ethnic appetites, but usually one can buy the same meal in Vermont as in California or Wisconsin, and its additives will follow exactly the electronic decision: this much MSG and that much riboflavin per serving . . . and precisely the same number of those round green things in the upper right-hand compartment.

The second level of frozen foodery is comparatively amorphous. Its practitioners or disciples or victims usually live (usually alone) in small apartments. "Our junior executives," one serious and youthful manager of the frozen-food department of a stylishly located store assured me, "are real gourmets. They ignore the complete dinners, and don't seem to care how much they spend on the fancy stuff in small packages . . . frozen canapés, maybe stuffed Cornish hen with wild rice and the special sauce in a little bag inside, and then green beans in butter with fresh mushrooms. They go wild! This is when they entertain, you understand. At home, like. They always get a good bottle of wine, too. If it's for a girl they get some frozen pastry. They just don't care about the cost . . . and they love to cook, gourmet-style. They have little kitchenettes, mostly." (The young man sounded wistful. I asked him if he liked cooking too, and he said almost apologetically, "Well, you see I'm of Italian descent. So what I like is to start a good sauce on my day off . . . my girl grows basil and parsley like crazy in her window box . . . and then I pick up some fresh capellini . . ." and we were off, while the frozen gourmet stuff lay stiffly in his counters.)

A less extravagant side to this middle level of buying is maintained by people who are literally too housebound, too fragile or convalescent, too old to prepare decent meals for themselves, but who for one reason or another are still free from the hypnotic bonds of the enclaves built to receive them, the Rest Havens, the Golden Years Villages.

Much as I dislike TV dinners for my own self, at least now when I can still choose, I have often introduced them to gallant older friends, and have shown how to cope with the almost idiot-proof modes of preparing them. Even after half an hour in a hot oven, one of those pressed-foil trays is not actively dangerous in the wobbling grasp of an older man in his one-room flat, and there is usually pap-like food in the tidy compartments that will not need strenuous mastication, in either the mouth or the belly.

I know one Sprat-like couple who share a TV platter once a day, not from economy but because Jack cannot eat meat and his wife cannot tolerate vegetables. . . . And so, between them both, you see, they lick the aluminum clean! I know another old lady who manages to feed her equally ancient dog and herself from one so-called dinner: he likes the meat, and she munches slowly on the bright peas, carrot-colored but otherwise unrecognizable carrots, the occasional treat of a picked crab apple or a glazed slice of yam.

Such maneuverings as the Junior Executive goes through, needing pots and casseroles and plates for his Lucullan and wily tidbits, are impossible for the very weak, the elderly. They often find real succor in the makeshift but attainable food provided by an average frozen meal, and I am glad for that.

The third level of patrons of the galloping ready-to-heat food industry is strictly high-cost luxury living, with no heed for the bills but with an often finicky palate. It is made up of people who are used to good restaurants in many countries, to good chefs in the classical European attempts at *la haute cuisine*. They know something about sauces, either innately or by forced sophistication as their incomes have burgeoned. They pay for, and usually get, the best there is to be had and, much as I begrudge admitting it, that can be very good.

They are furnished by small outfits, usually headed by a noted and retired chef. They learn the lists of packaged foods they can choose from, as well as their own and their guests' tastes, and they stock their yacht reefers twice a year or oftener, and send hundreds of pounds of fine precooked frozen courses to their mountain lodges. When they recognize their own brand in First Class on a jet to Paris or Teheran, lusciously bubbling from the stewardess' infrared oven, they smile possessively, for they know that they are indeed flying high. Sure, it would cost little more to hire a good chef of their own. But fifty carefully wrapped packages of breaded breast of chicken with prosciutto don't have tantrums. They don't quit in the middle of dinner. They sit there in the fridge, waiting silently, worth every ounce of gold they cost. . . .

There are small, quiet top-drawer freezing kitchens all over the country . . . near affluent centers, that is. I know one north of San Francisco that does nothing but make entrées for a single airline noted for its worldly meals. A famous chef-emeritus from one of the very great restaurants in Paris supervises the immaculate kitchen. The packaging is done without any outward splash in colored advertising and so on, since the whole operation is discreetly under wraps . . . committed . . . pledged.

Another small factory south of Los Angeles takes care of a certain amount of summer Carriage Trade when there is anything to spare, but is tacitly devoted to provisioning the yachts which rest between cruises in Newport Beach or San Diego or Santa Barbara. Its list is fairly simple, and its quality apparently unwavering. Of course it is run by a former chef, and he keeps his tidy light kitchen humming quietly in the hands of a mixed batch of French, Italian, Swiss cooks, in a fascinating ballet of puff paste here, puree of abalones there, sauce for a wild-rice stuffing at the big range, cheese sticks being cut at a long corner table. . . . As in all small successful operations like this one, the setup is basically uncomplicated, with one man at the head, perhaps a couple of moneybags in the background, and a carefully chosen and dedicated crew to watch everything from the deep-freeze room to the temperature of a pot of sauce on the stove. (It will be poured into a big flat pan, on crushed ice, to cool on a kitchen table, and then moved directly to the flash-freeze room kept at 50 below zero. Once well frozen, it will go to the deep freezer kept at 10 to 20 below, depending upon its ingredients and purposes.)

Food poisoning is Brother Nightmare to professional freezer cooks who refuse to use some of the preservative tricks of their bigger colleagues. Once I ate a stuffed chicken breast from a careless and pretentious company, and was very sick indeed, because I knew almost at once that the rice had been put into the fowl while it was still warm, and that then the whole had been quick-frozen without pre-chilling. This can be death in the pot.

There is comparatively little demand, even in specialty shops, for this third and most elegant type of "TV" food. It needs careful attention, and proper serving utensils in the kitchens it is prepared for. And it can be good, for it is fastidiously prepared from the best procurable ingredients, and by knowing cooks. It costs a lot. A single portion of Chicken Burgundy, for instance, costs about $2.50, and if one likes that type of food it would be hard to equal it in a fine restaurant. On the other hand, a box of a hundred artfully fabricated canapés, correctly frozen according to their ingredients and flavors, can cost a moderate $11. Or there will be things like an excellent baked chicken-liver pâté for about $2 a pound, and a fancy sweet tart to serve eight people for $3. No fuss, no muss, *again* . . . and who could duplicate them for less?

The trouble with all such small, dewy-eyed, and idealistic ventures is that Expansion is almost bound to take over. I am sure that is why I was sick after eating the stuffed chicken from the little place where deep-freezing had started before the food was properly chilled. And once I could focus my bilious eyes I read the tiny print on the label, and was astonished as well as further nauseated to learn that the sauce contained pork, lard, MSG, and soy! There is no need for any of these in a proper stuffing made of rice and mushrooms, and the label spelled doom to whatever dreams were left in the head chef's heart. His was neither a huge mass production, able to market a "gourmet delicacy" for 79 cents, nor was it a ruthlessly small operation selling packages for $2.50. His stamped price was $1.29 . . . and there are cheaper and easier ways to die. . . .

At the little factory near Laguna Beach in Southern California, I sensed danger too: there was an air of controlled panic in the corners, for on a recent trip in Chicago the boss had rashly been flattered-cajoled-conned into promising to send back five hundred boxes of one hundred each of his really exceptional little hors d'oeuvres. He was scared, but still beaming at the memory of the praises he'd been heaped with. Several daily operations in his fine, quietly buzzing kitchen had been pushed aside for this basically egocentric caper, and I felt dismay. When I asked if I could take away a few of his deservedly famous chicken wings to grill for a cocktail nibble, he said in a carefully bland way that three tubs full of them would have to wait until the damned canapés were out of the way, but that extra marinating would not hurt the wings too much. Again I felt a cool whiff of apprehension, for in such evasions can lie disaster. Where will the quality go? When? What does it matter about those casual gluttons in Chicago? The boss will grow much harried, and his backers (and perhaps he) will be richer, and then they will sell out to a big company and nobody will bother to make those delicious silly chicken nibbles . . . and his once-fine sole stuffed with lobster mousse will sell for 69 cents instead of $1.50, and I won't be around to eat it. . . .

Actually I am not around to eat frozen food on any level, except perforce when it is served to me on a plane or at an otherwise trusted friend's table. I think it is fine to buy top quality whenever one can afford to . . . but I would rather cook it myself, now and then, for a luxurious spree. I think it is fine that eager Junior Executives can splash around in a fairly decent Hollandaise which comes in a little plastic bag with frozen asparagus spears . . . but I would rather forgo the whole thing, much as I admire both the vegetable and its stylish ointment. (I use several frozen vegetables, which are often much better than the fresh, but I like to play with them according to my own whims, and not have them swimming in some computerized version of "a special butter sauce.") I think it is truly fine that frail and old people, and families without decent pots and dishes, and even lonely little boys on their birthdays can spoon fairly decent nourishment from the compartments of millions of pressed-foil trays every day. I just wish that I did not feel so dismal about it.

Frozen packaged food is an increasingly important part of our culture. Its rapid adoption will give much thought to future historians, if there are any left to think, by the end of this century. One slightly macabre comfort is that by then the additives so calmly if tinily noted on every package, including such current dreads as the cyclamates and others possibly as dangerous, will probably have killed any semblance of healthy clean hunger in us, and we will welcome the predicted diet of the future, all tasteless pills and capsules. What such a regime will do to our two other basic needs, for warmth and for love, has had less study devoted to it, and in that lapse may lie our salvation, even gastronomically.

It is no longer a startling theory that the machine age is over and that we are now well into one called electronic, for a better term. Mechanization did take command of all our senses for a surprisingly long time, while artists from Leonardo to Calder tried to show us how to fly, both bodily and in the mind, and Alexis Soyer proved that natural gas would cook food better than a hearth fire. Now the computer is in control, or so it seems. Human beings continue to satisfy their three needs, but their ways of doing so are not those of a hundred or even five years ago, and science fiction is perhaps the best guide to our immediate future and its possible sensory rewards.

It is increasingly unnecessary to light a flame and even to push a button, to make food palatably warm when it is supposed to be, and of course chimney spits have been obsolete for generations. When my family moved into a house in Whittier, California, in 1911, we were considered strangers, outlanders truly, because the first thing we did was to take out the gas log that stood dustily on a small "status" hearth and have a large fireplace built, with room for an almost undying blaze to chuckle and whisper in. We never cooked anything there except an occasional marshmallow on a long twig, but in the kitchen there was a big gas range, and later we added a newfangled electric stove which our halting flow of skullery drabs mistrusted heartily, but which led me to prefer it to this day for many kitchen tricks. We even had a toaster which plugged into a switch under the dining-room table at breakfast, and which took the constant attention of at least two people. Probably the peak of our active mechanization was the gift by the local citrus growers' association to my father, the town's newspaper editor, of a gigantic orange juicer, as I think it was called. It sounded like an armada of outboard motors when the cook revved it before breakfast, and my room above the kitchen vibrated promisingly for at least 3650 mornings as I dressed to face the ritualistic glass of thick pungent juice, which half an hour before had been hanging in globes from our backyard trees. Perhaps I drank too much of it in my pleasure. Perhaps my palate was formed then to find our present frozen concentrates, no matter how honorable, a sad substitute. Is it the water we add which in turn pollutes what used to be thought of as "freshly squoze"? The miserable truth may be that I am one of the few Americans of my age and class and indeed almost any age and class who cannot accept mediocrity as best.

There used to be degrees of excellence. This, as such, is almost nonexistent today. Mediocrity has taken command, and I think it is much more a part of our cultural pattern than mechanization, or even automation and the electronic control of our media of existence.

If it is possible to limit our needs to three, sex (or "love" in the old-fashioned sense) is perhaps the most dominant, the least easily persuaded to calm down, lie low. It is of course impossible to practice, much less enjoy, unless food and warmth can enter at times into the scene, and all three necessities have been twisted nearly beyond recognition by, say, a Greek philosopher, an Elizabethan architect, a French cook. The act of reproduction of our earth-planet species has become so ambiguous that many polls and census takers now list several categories of us, including the unisex. In the same way, warmth and protection have no more to do with a Neanderthal cave blaze than they do with Sherlock Holmes's cozy coal grate on Baker Street, and for life itself we must depend increasingly upon the diffused heat and antipollution of air conditioning and thermostatic temperature control. As for what we eat in order to stay warm enough to cohabit and procreate, it is perhaps adapted to our present and future environments, but it is frightening in its almost cosmic mediocrity.

No longer can we find what once was thought passably good if not actually excellent: sweet butter, for instance, made from the unpasteurized milk of a cow who has spent all her days in a meadow which has never absorbed any fertilizer but her own occasional warm turds, and all her nights in a clean stall which has never stunk subtly of pesticides, germicides, insecticides. The skies have been unpolluted above her slow munchings, matings, and lactatings. The water she drinks has been clean, with no effluents and active wastes sullying it. The air she breathes is the kind that filled the lungs of Thoreau and mounted to his head. . . .

All this sounds like the mutterings of a hapless conservationist, which it obviously is. The fact remains that today, now, this minute, I do not know where to find a pat of *good* butter, even if I still know a good cow. She is not what her grandmother was . . . nor am I, perhaps the more unfortunate of us, because I can remember less mediocre days. . . . But I will settle perforce for something called "Golden Meadow First Quality Sweet Unsalted Butter Made from Fresh Sweet Pasteurized Cream No Salt Added Vegetable Coloring All Golden Meadow Products Unconditionally Guaranteed." I buy it. I use it. I know it is mediocre (a chemist has told me that one cube of it in a diesel or airplane engine would foul things forever). But the mediocre *is* the best, so therefore everything less than mediocre is not at all bad: we have accepted this reasoning in the United States, and are rapidly spreading our desperate doctrine to other less-advanced areas of the planet.

My own theory about this gradual substitution of mediocrity, for the simple lack of anything better to compare it with, holds water for *me*, of course. But there is another explanation of why we are accepting with such docility the drastic changes in our eating habits and our desires for good taste and textures in what we continue to ingest in order to exist: we are fast losing what used to be thought of as a sense of responsibility.

We want to stop planning and thinking and inventing. We are relieved and pleased when a big magazine ad tells us to put a candle in a thawed muffin for Junior's birthday surprise, instead of baking a cake and going to the extra emotional and physical bother of inviting four friends to eat it with him. We feel acceptive and even grateful that Junior's dad will down without question a 25-min-at-450 plate of tidily separated Swiss steak with brown gravy, mashed potatoes, peas-and-carrots, and apple Betty after he gets home from his day's work . . . and the no-fuss no-muss syndrome in his case covers no marketing, no preparing of vegetables and apples, no cooking while everybody else relaxes with TV . . . no *responsibility*! If the dinner is bad, it is not Mom's fault, but some invisible cook's. If Dad gets paunchy from all the beer he drinks to add some meaning to his TV food, is it her doing? If Junior gets cavities from his own hyper-sweetened digestive booze, plus a Psychiatric Referral from his teacher, can she help it? And do they kick? They *like* her meals (i.e., they have nothing to compare them to).

This irresponsibility carries over into every phase of our three-way urgency to continue breathing in and out. It is abetted by, unsurprisingly, the computers. Those Things know exactly how many people in northern Minnesota will want frozen dinners containing corned beef hash in 1974, and how many (and *why*) will whimsically settle for either chicken curry Calcutta-style or spinach soufflé with grilled liver Delight . . . all of course with fresh green peas in a special sauce and fluffy whipped potatoes for a Balanced Diet, and on the more expensive trays a moon of orange-flavored dessert called something like Lunar Surprise. They also know how much warmth any given human body needs to sustain and perhaps enjoy life, so that municipal furnaces are controlled to that practical end from a central thermostat. And They know exactly what to do to be able to dictate, but not too harshly, the reproductive urges in all seemingly sentient citizens, so that there need be no concern about such matters as food-heat-love *anywhere*, any*more*.

I subscribe more to my own theory of our general mediocritization (or would if the word itself were less unwieldy). People who are led to feel that it is basically desirable to let mass-produced precooked frozen foods nourish their families are perhaps the general run, or will be in a few years. But I prefer to believe that there remain many stalwarts, and of every age, in the quite unflagging protest against such flabby irresponsibility, such carelessness about the levels of decent quality . . . and whether it be in bed, at the table, or even in the high places and the courts of Law. There will remain, as long as people do, some doubters. They will seek out edible bread and good wine and cheese, and they will share it, perhaps lying under the redwood tree, perhaps even on their backsides in a darkened room to the sound of fake bullets from The Box. They may actually eat unfrozen vegetables now and then, in memory of the far-off time when their grandparents cooked in a real kitchen, with wood in the stove and a beautiful fresh smell in the warm air. . . .

Different people have different ideas of pleasure, and that is one of mine.

—AUGUST 1970

# Recollections of 1945

HEINRICH BÖLL

*Translated by Leila Vennewitz*

In March, 1945, I faced the question: if anyone can hold a loaded pistol to anyone's chest and shoot him, where can a deserter hide? In answering the question with, "In the army he is deserting from," I was probably being influenced by Chesterton, whose words I had read as a boy: Where does the wise man hide a leaf? Answer: In the forest. I was not wise, I was not logical, I didn't even go through with it; after only a week I gave up, but before I gave up I had asked myself the question, "What is the best place for a deserter to hide now?" and given myself the answer, "Under a machine gun Model 1942 that he doesn't know how to operate." This camouflage was a good one, but I was still not wise, nor logical, nor able to go through with it. After five miles I found the machine gun too heavy, and I dropped it in a manure pit not far from the village of Drinsahl between Waldbröl and Nümbrecht. That would have been an apt ending to the war. Fortunately it was not my lot to bring the war so aptly, so ingeniously, to an end. As I continued on my way home (my wife was living about eight miles further on), I lost my way, started going east instead of west, and suddenly felt—literally, not figuratively—a pistol against my chest. The muzzle was hard, it was being pressed firmly against my heart; it was the German Army's final (and most impressive) salutation.

The next question is: "How do you organize a commando post?" Answer: "You load a pistol, release the safety catch, take up a position at a street intersection, preferably in a dark doorway, and wait for soldiers who have lost their units or withdrawn from them with peaceful intentions. When a soldier comes in sight, you stride up to him, place the loaded pistol against his chest, and tell him to attach himself forthwith to the newly created commando post. You must be prepared not only actually to shoot but actually to kill. You have the right by virtue of the Führer's orders, so it is not wrong to kill someone who refuses to join the newly created commando post. Later you can justify your action on the basis of emergency orders. When you are dead there is no such thing as emergency-order refusal. Apart from the pistol, the cartridges and the will to kill, all you need is the appropriate historical situation."

The months from March to May, 1945, provided the appropriate historical situation: (1) the Führer's orders; (2) soldiers roaming the countryside in ample numbers.

On April 8, 1945, I became attached to the Brüchermühle commando post in the manner described above, once again I was equipped with a machine gun (which I did not know how to operate), I went through a few hours of acute fear (the wood between Brüchermühle and Eiershagen was situated precisely on the grid which was being systematically shelled by the American artillery), and at noon the following day I put up my hands.

The hamlet of Brüchermühle lies between the villages of Sengelbusch and Löffelsterz, a mile to a mile and a half northwest of Denklingen. Like all the other places mentioned, it is to be found on the map "Sieg-, Sülz-, Agger-, Bröl- und Wahnbachtal," edited by Hans Holtz, Land Surveyor, Coblenz-Pfaffendorf, and published by Schaar and Dathe of Trier (no publication year, unfortunately).

The final stages of my career as a member of the German Army were: the commando post at Brüchermühle, the prisoner-of-war assembly centers at Waldbröl, Rosbach and Sieg, the prisoner-of-war camps at Sinzig-am-Rhein, Nanur-sur-Meuse, Attichy-sur-Aisne, Waterloo near Brussels, and Weeze-am-Niederrhein, and the discharge center at Bonn-am-Rhein, where I was discharged on September 15, 1945.

Discharged from what? I had been taken prisoner by American soldiers, I was the responsibility of the British, and I was guarded by Belgians, who had been allotted the Cologne area in the

British Zone. On September 15, 1945, I was discharged, but from German imprisonment.

Clothing: A Hungarian officer's topcoat, of fine cloth, with red lapels. A flannel shirt, made in England, given me by a kindhearted American Negro who took pity on my nakedness. The shirt was soft, warm, civilian, but on the front, between the patch pocket and the row of buttons, just where the original owner, who had been somewhat taller than I am, must have had his heart, was a bullet hole, neatly darned by a skillful feminine hand. Shoes: American. Trousers: American, of such superior quality that I wore them for the next three years. Socks, cap, handkerchief: German Army. Personal belongings: one tin can, with my name scratched on it, for five months it had been my cup, jug and plate; an empty Belgian beer bottle; four and a half cigarettes, "Belga" brand; two cakes of soap, of Anglo-Saxon origin. Age: not quite twenty-eight. Cash: none. Occupation: student. This description was misleading, it had been but a temporary camouflage preceding the machine gun. This misleading camouflage description turned out to be just as useful during the years to come as it had been in the past. Before distributing ration coupons, government offices demanded proof of "Profession and Occupation," so I quickly established my profession and occupation by registering at the University of Cologne. I made no further use of this misleading description. Soon I possessed a further document bearing the strange description "Work Permit." In this document I was described as an "unskilled laborer"; that was neither camouflage nor misleading. Ever since I was seventeen there had been no doubt as to my profession and occupation: writer. If I had not only practiced but admitted to this occupation, it might quite possibly have led in years gone by to Weimar, to bad company, and in the years ahead to difficulties and delays in documentation.

Under the magnificent trees of the Bonn Hofgarten, on a sunny autumn day, discharged from German imprisonment. The word disguising this illusion is so obvious that I am almost ashamed to reiterate it: discharged.

• • •

In old notebooks, noteworthy housekeeping entries: two pounds of flour, half a pound of butter, 325 marks. A month's salary for a schoolteacher. Bread, cut flowers, 40 marks; two ounces of tea, 75 marks; box of matches, 5 marks; four cigarettes, 32 marks; one ounce of tea, 37.50; ten pounds of potatoes, 75 marks; newspapers, magazines and books, 60 marks. A month's salary for a schoolteacher. Next came three items and two months' salary: briquettes (stolen), 250, 220, 160 marks. A schoolteacher would have had to work for twenty months in a month, but is not a month a month a month?

Electricity was rationed, a black market in kilowatts not yet invented, bribery not possible. Sometimes, however, the profession of writer is also practiced after dark; besides, writers being the shameless creatures they are, they must occasionally warm their hands and feet. Someone showed me how to stop the disk on the meter: you bore a hole underneath in the sealed metal casing, twist some cotton around the tip of a three- or four-inch nail, and push it through the hole against the disk which—rotating white-red, white-red—measures off the units used. When you see that the disk actually stops moving, you wedge the nail firmly into place, watch the disk a few seconds longer to make sure—and the current flows unmetered through the meter into the circuit, spreading light and warmth. Not only was it the wrong trick, I went about it clumsily, the cotton slipped off without my noticing, and the nail left scratches on the disk which convicted me even before I confessed. The proper thing to do is to take off the seal and use a magnet to disable the disk. There were stool pigeons, they were given bonuses when they caught someone not only infringing the "Rationing Regulation" in this way, but also committing theft. The principle which had held for twelve years still held: you can do what you like as long as you don't get caught. First I was annoyed, then relieved, when I was caught.

When the milk was measured out, the pint measure was twice dipped into the milk pail, twice it came out full, twice it was emptied into the milk jug—and yet, how was it that there was always an ounce or two less in the jug than there should have been? Germany's first economic miracle took place long before the date officially marking it. Does economic miracle merely mean economic trick, does economic magic merely mean economic swindle? Is it just a kind of shell game that the gullible ones can't keep away from? O you jugglers of the hunger years, I have seen you practicing your finger exercises for the second economic miracle. How was it that twice two ounces of butter never made a full quarter pound? Don't two-eighths make a quarter a quarter a quarter? Shell game, shell game, which little nutshell hides my time, which your work, which our money? Our time, our work, our money—spirited away. Shell game, where is the next commando post, who is loading his pistol and will hold it against my chest? Your time, money, work—or your life!

Foremost motto of the middle classes: you never get something for nothing. O yes you do: the address was English, the name Irish, and some of the parcels represented thirteen months' salary for a schoolteacher. A gift of time, work, money. Thirteen is a nice number. In Ireland they call it a baker's dozen. When you buy twelve eggs you get—sometimes even today—thirteen. In fact, a gift of a dozen eggs is always thirteen. And a kindhearted Negro who took pity on my nakedness gave me a flannel shirt, and the farmer in Berzbach gave us unskimmed milk every day.

In those days there were more honest black-market dealers than there were honest dealers. Now all we have is a Minister of Finance who is not concerned with prices.

Sometimes people ask me: how can anyone live in Cologne? I shall answer this embarrassing, slyly snobbish question, not for those who ask it but for myself. How can one live in Gelsenkirchen-Rotthausen, in Berlin, Niederdollendorf, Frankfurt, Oberdreisbach or Munich? Presumably by eating one's daily bread, doing one's job, sleeping from time to time, drinking, and so on.

When we saw Cologne again we wept. We walked across from Deutz on the railless temporary bridge, slippery with mud; a British tank coming toward us skidded, and almost pushed us into the Rhine. There it was again: acute fear.

Cologne destroyed possessed something that Cologne undestroyed had never had: grandeur and dignity. Fate had been accurate in its mercilessness. The destruction was complete and, militarily speaking, completely senseless: that was the proper condition for the place we wanted to live in. Tears, and left over from All Saints' Day the wreaths and flowers placed on the rubble sites.

Cologne undestroyed, right up to the wild orgies in the air-raid shelters while the bombs were falling, had not been dignified, or orderly, and in spite of being an important garrison town for nearly a hundred years it had never been militaristic. The toughness concealed beneath the Rhineland sense of humor, a toughness that can turn criminal, was something the orderly and conscientious Prussians had never been able to cope with. Cologne had never really been a big city, it was always a town; its vice lay deeper than the obvious vice of the ordinary big city which is such a favorite movie subject.

Cologne was better, sounder, than any undestroyed rural or small-town idyll where one could have peacefully stolen potatoes, raised tobacco, written soundly, relaxed and gone to sleep.

There came a time—the most German form of the perverted perfection game: "Who's the king of the castle?"—when there was a kind of rivalry among German cities as to which was the most destroyed.

For us, Cologne was sufficiently destroyed. When we went back there to live, there were, I believe, seventy thousand people left out of its three quarters of a million. For years the rubble trolleys remained the only vehicles; for years on every All Saints' Day wreaths and flowers were placed on the rubble sites. (Where could anyone put them now?) Cologne slept longer than other destroyed towns. It had to have "injections," and it got them.

I don't know why I refused to do what was proclaimed with neo-democratic enthusiasm to be the first duty of every returning citizen: to take shovel and rake and help clear away the rubble. It was not just the feeling of having something better to do and of having done enough, it was not just laziness, or indifference toward an inarticulate "will to rebuild." Perhaps the way they stood around in groups, leaning on their shovels and rakes, talking about the war, prisoner-of-war camps, and political errors, reminded me too much of beer-hall cronies and commando posts.

Cologne was a great city, and the only way to have any hope at all was to live in this destroyed city. The question, How can anyone live in

Cologne? has meanwhile become more snobbish and sly than ever. I detect in this question the old (not unwarranted) Prussian distrust toward the Rhineland that fell to Prussia in 1815. If asked at all, the question ought to have been changed long ago to: However can you live in Germany? and from that would follow the second question: Is Cologne German? The answer, surprisingly enough, is Yes. Doubts as to this Yes are always inherent in the first question, no matter who asks it. The last doubts as to this Yes fell away from me as, for the first time since the end of the war, I walked across the railless bridge, slippery with mud, that rainy November day in 1945, across the Rhine from Deutz to Cologne, with my wife, my sister and my brother. In the town were not only seventy thousand people but two madonnas. One was beautiful, later known as the Madonna of the Ruins; the other was not beautiful, but she was tall, very old, earthy, unsymmetrical, with glazed eyes. She stands in St. Mary's chapter house.

—SEPTEMBER 1965

# New York at 6:30 P.M.

DOROTHY PARKER

To write about art now gives me a feeling of deep embarrassment which, in the long ago, I kept hidden under what was known then as "She's having one of her difficult days again, ma'am—screaming and spitting and I don't know what all."

But that, unhappily, was too easy; we outgrow such simple masquerades, and all there is left for the likes of me is a silence not even silver. This occurs when the subject of the adjacent conversation is Art. Oh, I can go as far as "Of course, I don't know anything about painting"—but I cannot even stumble on through the rest of it. Lower you cannot get.

Well, yes, you really can. For here I am burbling on of an American artist and his works, as if—God grant—I knew what I was talking about. The American artist is John Koch; he is just about to crash his middle years, and he is, I should think, as nearly happy as anyone ever gets to be. I know that few of the gifted can accept that as a compliment ("So she says I'm shallow, does she?"), but I mean it to please, and that is why I envy him.

Well, anyway, I know Mr. Koch only through his paintings, and through the almost lyrical tributes to his works. I do not know what school of painting he belongs in; he is not, I believe, avant-garde, and he is, I gather, though I have to strain to take it in, a realist—but not of the ashcan school of the Glackens, Luks, Sloan group. He takes his realism out on the rich. His lovely ladies step out of Edith Wharton, and his graceful gentlemen come from Henry James (whenever you say Edith Wharton, you have to say Henry James right after. If you don't, you'll have bad luck all day).

Mr. Koch, so far as I can pluck from his ungenerous snatches of biography, paints of his times—it seems as if of the times through which he must have been growing up. His pictures are a delight to the eye and a joy to the memories, in case you have such well-bred memories. His favorite time is the autumn of the day—the late afternoon. It was then, in the Old Days, that gracious people gathered together, to speak wittily in soft voices, and laugh gently no matter how funny somebody was. Nobody seemed to be exerting himself and the ladies could take it just as easily, never showing appreciation in a giggle or a screech. They were exquisite people, considerate, one of another, and delicate of tread as cats. One of their sweetest attributes was that they could always be found when you wanted them—they were at home in the late afternoon, and there you could go without a date or an appointment. Theirs were never parties—the cocktail party was not yet alive. I misremember who first was cruel enough to nurture it into life. But perhaps it would be not too much to say, in fact it would be not enough to say, that it was not worth the trouble.

I am jumping a great many of John Koch's paintings when I deal only with the soft spirit of late afternoon in New York, when the sky was Renoir blue and a fire—a real fire—whispered gently under the classic mantelpiece—for he chose many other subjects. He did a succession of still lifes (that looks odd but "still lives" looks even worse). At any rate they somehow never were permanently still. Always the lady, probably the hostess, sat immovable, her back of the straightness achieved by hours of walking about the house with a heavy book on her head; but you had no feeling that she remained motionless. Mr. Koch seemed to have caught her just as she stopped speaking and was about to speak again as soon as she could do so without interrupting.

The regulation still lifes—oh, all right, then, "still lives"—are of furniture, walls, and curtains, but somehow John Koch brought his own gift to them; the rooms empty only for a moment, the curtains had just been drawn by accomplished fingers, the vases of flowers were not "arranged"—simply the blossoms had found the exact place for themselves.

I am always a little sad when I see a John Koch painting. It is nothing more than a bit of nostalgia that makes my heart beat slower—nostalgia for those rooms of lovely lights and lovelier shadows and loveliest people. And I really have no room for the sweet, soft feeling. Nor am I honest, perhaps, in referring to it. For it is the sort of nostalgia that is only a dreamy longing for some places where you never were.

And, I never will be there. There is no such hour on the present clock as 6:30, New York time. Yet, as only New Yorkers know, if you can get through the twilight, you'll live through the night.

—NOVEMBER 1964

# Moving Out

JOHN CHEEVER

The war was over; so was the shortage of building materials and from the windows of our apartment near Sutton Place we could see the horizon beginning to change. Everybody was home who was coming back, the girls still had their dewy furlough looks and, after the smoking and carious ruins of Manila, the City of New York with the sky pouring its light onto the rivers looked like a vision of enlightenment. My children were young and my favorite New York was the one they led me through on Sunday afternoons. A girl in high heels can show you Rome, a drinking companion is the best for Dublin, and I enjoyed the New York my children knew. They liked the Central Park lion house at four o'clock on February afternoons, the highest point of the Queensboro Bridge, and a riverside dock in the East Forties, long gone, where I once saw a couple of tarts playing hopscotch with a hotel room key. Oh, it was a long time ago. You could still hear the *Oklahoma!* score during drinking hours, the Mink Decade was just taking hold and the Third Avenue El still rattled the dishes in Bloomingdale's. The East River views were broader then and there was an imposing puissance to those reaches of light and water. We used to ride and play touch football in Central Park and, in October, with the skiing season in mind, I used to climb the ten flights of stairs to our apartment. I used the back stairs, the only stairs, and I was the only one to use them. Most of the kitchen doors stood open and my climb was a breach of privacy, but what could I do? I used to whistle and sometimes sing to warn the tenants of my approach, but in spite of these precautions I once saw a lady wearing nothing but a girdle while she basted a leg of lamb, a cook drinking whiskey out of a bottle, and a housewife sitting on the lap of the sallow-faced delivery boy from the corner butcher's. On Christmas Eve my children and their friends used to sing carols on Sutton Place—mostly to butlers, everyone else having gone to Nassau, which may have been the beginning of the end.

It was a wonderful life and it didn't seem that it would ever end. In the winter there were those days with a smart polish on the air and the buildings, and then there were the first south winds of spring with their exciting and unclean odors of backyards and all the women shoppers walking east at dusk, carrying bunches of apple blossom and lilac that had been trucked up from the Shenandoah Valley the night before. A French-speaking panhandler used to work Beekman Place (*Je le regrette beaucoup, monsieur . . .* ), and going out to dinner one night we ran into a bagpiper on the Lexington Avenue subway platform who played a Black Watch march between trains. New York was the place where I had met and married my wife, I had dreamed of its streets during the war, my children had been born here and it was here that I had first experienced the feeling of being free from social and parental strictures. We and our friends seemed to improvise our world and to meet society on the most liberal and spontaneous terms. I don't suppose there was a day, an hour, when the middle class got their marching orders, but toward the end of the 1940s the middle class began to move. It was more of a push than a move and the energy behind the push was the changing economic character of the city. It would all be easier to describe if there had been edicts, proclamations and tables of statistics, but this vast population shift was forced by butcher's bills, tips, increased rental and tuition costs and demolitions. Where are the Wilsons? you might ask. Oh, they've bought a place in Putnam County. And the Renshaws? They've moved to New Jersey. And the Oppers? The Oppers are in White Plains. The ranks were thinning and we watched them go with commiseration and some scorn. They sometimes returned for dinner with mud on their shoes, the women's faces red from weeding the vegetable garden. My God, the suburbs! They encircled the city's boundaries like enemy territory and we thought of them as a loss of privacy, a cesspool of conformity and a life of indescribable dreariness in some split-level village where the place name appeared in The New York *Times* only when some bored housewife blew off her head with a shotgun.

That spring, at the closing assembly of my daughter's school, the headmistress took the lectern and announced: "Now school is over and we are *all* going to the country!" We were not going to the country and the exclamation fascinated me because hidden somewhere in her words was a sense, an apprehension of the fact that the rich of the city were getting richer and the friable middle ground where we stood was vanishing. The river views at any rate were vanishing and so were most of the landmarks. Down went a baronial old brewery, up went a deluxe apartment house. Building began on a lot where we used to run the dog and most of the small and pleasant houses in the neighborhood, where people who were less than rich could live, were marked for demolition and would be replaced by the glass towers of a new class. I could see the landscape of my children's youth destroyed before my eyes; and don't we impair the richness of our memories with this velocity of reconstruction? The apartment house where we lived changed hands and the new owners prepared to turn the building into a co-operative, but we were given eight months to find another home. Most people we knew by then lived either in River House or in downtown tenements where you had to put out pots to catch the leaks when it rained. Girls either came out at the Colony Club or came out, so to speak, on the river embankments, and my sons' friends either played football for Buckley or practiced snap-knife shots in the shadows of the bridge.

That was the winter when we never had enough money. I looked for another apartment, but it was impossible to find a place for a family of five that suited my wife and my income. We were not poor enough for subsidized housing and not anything like rich enough for the new buildings that were going up around us. The noise of wrecking crews seemed aimed directly at our residence in the city. In March one of the obligations that I couldn't—or at least neglected to—meet was the electric bill and our lights were turned off. The children took their baths by candlelight and, while they enjoyed this turn of events, the effect of the dark apartment on my own feelings was somber. We simply didn't have the scratch. I paid the light bill in the morning and went out to Westchester a week later and arranged to rent a little frame house with a sickly shade tree on the lawn.

The farewell parties were numerous and sometimes tearful. The sense was that we were being exiled, like so many thousands before us, by invincible economic pressures and sent out to a barren and provincial life where we would get fat, wear ill-fitting clothes and spend our evenings glued to the television set. What else can you do in the suburbs? On the night before we left we went to Riverview Terrace for dinner where I jumped, in an exuberance of regret, out of a first-story window. I don't think you can do that anymore. After the party I walked around the city, beginning my farewells. The customary tinder lights beat up from the streets onto the low clouds overhead. On a sidewalk somewhere in the Eighties I saw a Cuban going through the steps of a rumba, holding a baby in his arms. A dinner party in the Sixties was breaking up and men and women were standing in a lighted doorway calling goodbye and good-night. In the Fifties I saw a scavenger pushing an enormous English perambulator—a carriage for a princess—from ash can to ash can. It was part of the city's imprimatur. It was in the spring and there was a heady, vernal fragrance from Central Park, for in New York the advance of the seasons is not forgotten but intensified. Autumn thunderstorms, leaf fires, the primeval stillness that comes after a heavy snowfall and the randy smells of April all seem magnified by the pavings of the greatest city in the world.

The moving men were due at noon and I took another melancholy walk. I had my shoes shined by a pleasant Italian who always described himself as a dirty-minded man. He blamed it on the smell of shoe polish which he claimed had some venereal persuasions. He had, like many men of his kind, a lively mind and possessed, along with the largest collection of nudist magazines I have ever seen, some exalted memories of Laurence Olivier as Hamlet, or Omletto as he called him. Standing in front of our apartment house was an old lady who not only fed and watered the pigeons that then lived around Queensboro

Bridge, but whose love of the birds was jealous. A workman had put the crusts of his meal onto the sidewalk for the birds and she was kicking the crusts into the gutter. "*You* don't have to feed them," she was telling him. "*You* don't have to worry about them. *I* take care of them. I spend four dollars a week on grain and stale bread and in the summer I change their water twice a day. I don't like strangers to feed them. . . ." The city is raffish and magnificent and she and the shoeshine man would be advocates of its raffishness—those millions of lonely but not discontented men and women who can be overheard speaking with great intimacy to the chimpanzee in the zoo, the squirrels in the park and the pigeons everywhere. That morning the air of New York was full of music. Bessie Smith was singing *Jazzbo Brown* from a radio in the orange-drink stand at the corner. Halfway down Sutton Place a blind man was playing *Make Believe* on a sliding trombone. Beethoven's *Fifth Symphony*, all threats and revelations, was blowing out of an upstairs window. Men and women were sunning themselves on Second Avenue and the vision of urban life seemed to be an amiable one, a bond of imponderables, a shared risk and at least a gesture toward the peaceableness of mankind, for who but a peaceable species could live in such congestion? Fredric March was sitting on a bench in Central Park. Igor Stravinsky was waiting at the corner for the light to change. Myrna Loy was coming out of the Plaza and on lower Sixth Avenue e. e. cummings was buying a bunch of bananas. It was time to go and I got a cab uptown. "I'm not sleeping," the driver said. "I'm not sleeping anymore. I'm not getting my rest. Spring! It don't mean nothing to me. My wife, she's left me. She's shacked up with this fireman, but I told her I'll wait for you, Mildred, I'll wait for you, it's nothing but bestiality you feel for this fireman and I'm waiting for you, I'm keeping the home fires burning. . . ." It was the idiom of the city and one of its many voices, for where else in the world will strangers bare their intimate secrets to one another with such urgency and such speed—and I would miss this.

Like so much else in modern life the pathos of our departure was concealed by a deep cartilage of decorum. When the moving van had closed its doors and departed, we shook hands with the doorman and started for the country ourselves, wondering if we would ever return.

As it happened we returned the next week for dinner and continued to drive back into town regularly to see our friends. They shared our prejudices and our anxieties. "Can you bear it?" we would be asked. "Are you all right out there? When do you think you can get back?"

And we found other evacuees in the country who sat on their suburban lawns, planning to go back when the children had finished college; and when the rain fell into the leaves of the rock maples they asked: "Oh, Charlie, do you think it's raining in New York?"

Now on summer nights the smell of the city sometimes drifts northward on the waters of the Hudson River, up to the wooded, inland banks where we live. The odor is like the stales from some enormous laundry, although I expect that an incurable evacuee could detect in it Arpege, stone-cold gin, and might perhaps even imagine that he heard music on the water; but this is not for me. I sometimes go back to walk through the ghostly remains of Sutton Place where the rude, new buildings stand squarely in one another's river views and where the rents would make your head swim, but now my old friends seem insular in their concern about my exile, their apartments seem magnificent but sooty, like the scenery for the national or traveling company of a Broadway hit, and their doormen only remind me of the fact that I don't have to tip a staff of twenty at Christmas and that in my own house I can shout in anger or joy without having someone pound on the radiator for silence. The truth is that I'm crazy about the suburbs and I don't care who knows it. Sometimes my sons and I go fishing for perch in the Hudson, and when the trains for the city come bowling down along the riverbanks I salute the sometimes embarrassed passengers with my beer can, wishing them Godspeed and prosperity in the greatest city in the world, but I see them pass without a trace of longing or envy.

—JULY 1960

# Why I Live Where I Live

WALKER PERCY

The reason I live in Covington, Louisiana, is not because it was listed recently in *Money* as one of the best places in the United States to retire to. The reason is not that it is a pleasant place but rather that it is a pleasant nonplace. Covington is in the deep South, which is supposed to have a strong sense of place. It does, but Covington occupies a kind of interstice in the South. It falls between places.

Technically speaking, Covington is a nonplace in a certain relation to a place (New Orleans), a relation that allows one to avoid the horrors of total placement or total nonplacement or total misplacement.

Total placement for a writer would be to live in a place like Charleston or Mobile, where one's family has lived for two hundred years. A pleasant enough prospect, you might suppose, but not for a writer—or not for this writer. Such places are haunted. Ancestors perch on your shoulder while you write. Faulkner managed to do it but only by drinking a great deal and by playing little charades, like pretending to be a farmer. It is necessary to escape the place of one's origins and the ghosts of one's ancestors but not too far. You wouldn't want to move to Tucumcari.

Total nonplacement would be to do what Descartes did, live anonymously among the burghers of Amsterdam. Or do what Kierkegaard did, live in the business district of Copenhagen, pop out into the street every half hour, and speak to the shopkeepers so one will be thought an idler. It pleased Kierkegaard to be thought an idler at the very time he was turning out five books a year. On the other hand, a writer in the United States doesn't have to go to such lengths to be taken for an idler. Another type of nonplacement for a southern writer is to live in a nondescript northern place like Waterbury, Connecticut, or become writer in residence at Purdue. This is a matter of taste. It works for some very good writers, like Styron (in Connecticut), for whom the placeness of the South becomes too suffocating. Indeed, more often than not it is only possible to write about the South by leaving it. For me, I miss the South if I am gone too long. I prefer to live in the South but on my own terms. It takes some doing to insert oneself in such a way as not to succumb to the ghosts of the old South or the happy hustlers of the new Sunbelt South.

A popular and often necessary form of nonplacement is to hook up with academe, teaching or visiting in universities. This works for some writers. Indeed it can be a godsend for serious writers who can rarely support themselves by writing. It works if one (a) is a good teacher or (b) is a bad teacher who doesn't care or (c) can both teach and write. For me, teaching is harder work than writing. It is hard enough to deal with words but having to deal with words and students overtaken as they are by their terrible needs, vulnerability, likability, intelligence, and dumbness wears me out. How I respect and envy the gifted teacher!

Total misplacement is to live in another place, usually an exotic place, which is so strongly informed by its exoticness that the writer, who has fled his haunted place or his vacant nonplace and who feels somewhat ghostly himself, somehow expects to become informed by the exotic identity of the new place. A real bummer if you ask me, yet it has worked for some. Hemingway in Paris and Madrid. Sherwood Anderson in New Orleans, Malcolm Lowry in Mexico, Vidal in Italy, Tennessee Williams in Key West, James Jones on the Ile Saint-Louis in Paris. Such a remove is a reasonable alternative to northern ghostliness but unfortunately only a temporary one. Even James Baldwin and Richard Wright had to come home. Northern (by northern, I mean upper North Hemisphere—North America, England, Sweden, Germany) ghostliness tends to evacuate a Latin neighborhood, like a drop of acid on a map of Mexico.

There is a species of consumption at work here. Places are consumed nowadays. The more delectable the place, the quicker it is ingested, digested, and turned to feces. Once I lived in Santa Fe, a lovely placid place, but after a while, the silver-and-turquoise jewelry, the Pueblo Indians, the mesquite, the Sangre de Cristo Mountains, became as commonplace, *used up*, as Dixie beer, good old boys, and Nashville music. After a sojourn in the desert, memories of Louisiana green become irresistible.

Another sort of nonplacement traditionally available to writers, and paradoxically felicitous, is enforced placement in a nonplace—that is, exile or imprisonment. I don't have to tell you how well Cervantes and some other writers have done in jail. My own suspicion is that many American writers secretly envy writers like Solzhenitsyn, who get sent to the Gulag camps for their writings, keep writing on toilet paper, take on the whole bloody state—and win. The total freedom of writers in this country can be distressing. What a burden to bear, that the government not only allows us complete freedom—even freedom for atrocities like *MacBird!*—but, like ninety-five percent of Americans, couldn't care less what we write. Oh, you lucky Dostoyevskys, with your firing squads (imagine shooting an American writer!), exiles, prison camps, nuthouses. True, American writers are often regarded as nuts but as harmless ones. So the exile has to be self-imposed—which has its drawbacks. One goes storming off, holes up in Montmarte or Algiers cursing McCarthyism, racism, TV, shopping centers, consumerism, and no one pays the slightest attention. Months, years, later, one saunters back, hands in pockets, eyes averted—but no one is looking now either. Mailer and Vidal write books reviling the establishment—and make main selection of Book of the Month.

Free people have a serious problem with place, being in a place, using up a place, deciding which new place to rotate to. Americans ricochet around the United States like billiard balls. Swedes, Americans, Germans, the English, play musical chairs with places, usually southern places (all but the French, who think they live in The Place). But for writers, place is a special problem because they never fitted in in the first place. The problem is to choose a place where one's native terror is not completely neutralized (like a writer who disappears into Cuernavaca and coke happily and forever) but rendered barely tolerable.

Here in Covington, one is able to insert oneself into the South, a region celebrated for its strong sense of place and roots, which most southern writers can't stand and have to get away from and so go north, where they can sit in desolate bars and go on about how lovely the South looks—from here. Witness the writers of the agrarian movement in the South, nearly all of whom ended up in northern universities. What makes the insertion possible is that Covington is a nonplace but the right sort of nonplace. Here is one place in the South where a writer can live as happily as a bug in a crack in the sidewalk, where he can mosey out now and then and sniff the air just to make sure this is not just any crack in any sidewalk.

The pleasantest things about Covington are its nearness to New Orleans—which is very much of a place, drenched in its identity, its history, and its rather self-conscious exotica—and its own attractive lack of identity, lack of placeness, even lack of history. Nothing has ever happened here, no great triumphs or tragedies. In fact, people seldom die. The pine trees are supposed to secrete a healthful ozone that has given Covington the reputation of being "the second healthiest place on earth" (I never found out what the first was). I thought this was part of the local moonshine until my friend Steve Ellis, judge and historian, showed me newspaper clippings for a year of a yellow-fever outbreak in New Orleans. Even though Covington received refugees by the hundreds that year, nobody died of yellow fever and only a few people died of any cause.

Covington is a cheerfully anomalous place. Its major streets have New England names—Boston, New Hampshire, Vermont, Rutland—and nobody seems to know why or care. It is the seat of the parish (what counties are called in Louisiana) of St. Tammany. This name, thought up by the first American governor of Louisiana, was probably a joke or a jibe at the French practice of using saints' names, like St. John the Baptist Parish.

When I first saw Covington, having driven over from New Orleans one day, I took one look around, sniffed the ozone, and exclaimed unlike Brigham Young: "This is the nonplace for me!" It had no country clubs, no subdivisions, no Chamber of Commerce, no hospitals, no psychiatrists (now it has all these). I didn't know anybody, had no kin here. A stranger in my own country. A perfect place for a writer! I bought a house the following week.

Another attraction is Covington's rather admirable tradition of orneriness and dissent, its positive genius for choosing the wrong side in the issues of the day, and its abiding indifference to the currents of history. It is a backwater of a backwater. Yet the region was a refuge for Tories in full flight from the crazy American revolutionaries. Shortly thereafter, when several local parishes revolted against Spain to set up their own republic—capital at St. Francisville, flag with one star, which lasted three months—Covington was against it. It liked the Spanish. Then when the United States and Louisiana proposed to annex the Republic of West Florida, we voted against it. We didn't like Louisiana. When Louisiana voted to secede from the Union in 1861, we voted against that too. We liked the Union. Yet when the war was over, slave owners kept their slaves as if the Emancipation Proclamation never occurred. During the years of prohibition, the Little Napoleon bar served drinks.

Things have changed in recent years. We have joined the Sunbelt with a vengeance, are in fact one of the fastest-growing counties in the country. It is worrisome to be written up by *Money* magazine, but more ominous is the plan afoot a build a "theme park" here, like Walt Disney World but bigger.

Covington is now threatened by progress. It has become a little jewel in the Sunbelt and is in serious danger of being written up in *Southern Living*, what with its restored shotgun cottages, live oaks, nifty shops, converted depot. Its politics, no longer strange, have become standard Sunbelt Reagan. There are as many Carter jokes as there used to be Roosevelt and Kennedy jokes in Mississippi. The level of political debate lies somewhere between Genghis Khan and The Incredible Hulk. The center is holding only too well, about ninety degrees to the right of center—which is not necessarily bad. Whenever I get depressed about living in a place where the main political issue is Reagan versus Connally, I have only to imagine what it would be like to live in a McGovernite community. Southern conservatives, in my experience, are more tolerant than northern liberals. That is to say, they put up with "liberal" writers with better grace than Berkeley would put up, say, with Buckley. A southern writer is allowed his eccentricities. The prevailing attitude is a kind of benevolent neglect. As the saying goes in these parts: He may be a son of a bitch, but he's *our* son of a bitch. A minor cultural note: In my opinion, local Yankee racists are worse than southern racists; they don't even like Uncle Toms and Aunt Jemimas. One can only wonder how Abraham Lincoln ever talked these people into fighting a war to free slaves. And the main difference between local country-clubbers (affluent, often midwestern) and the local Klan (poor, southern) is that the former tolerate Jews and Catholics, probably because there are so few Jews and the Catholics are generally as conservative as country-club WASPs.

But these are minor matters. The worst of it is that Covington may be in danger of losing its peculiar distinction of being a pleasant backwater lost, but not too lost, in the interstices of place and time. One of the first things to attract me to Covington was the complaint of a former resident: "My God, you could live back in those pine trees for twenty years and never meet your neighbor—it's as bad as New York." Hmm. Sounds like my kind of place. The best of both worlds: a small southern town, yet one can live as one pleases. There are all manner of folk here—even a writer can make good friends—indeed an unusual and felicitous mix of types, Mississippi WASPs, Creole Catholics, Cajun Catholics, natives, pleasant blacks (who, for reasons that escape me, have remained pleasant), theosophists, every variety of Yankee. Any one group might be hard to take as a majority, but put together the lump gets leavened.

Covington is strategically located on the border between the Bible Belt and the Creole-French-Italian-German South. The two cultures interpenetrate. Good old Mississippi types march in Mardi Gras parades. Cajun types drive Ford Ranger pickups and listen to Loretta Lynn. I FOUND IT! bumper stickers abound (in case you didn't know, IT is Jesus Christ). But there is also the sardonic Catholic rejoinder, I NEVER LOST IT. And then there are stickers in the old eccentric tradition: I LOST MY ANOMIE IN ST. TAMMANY. As well as: GOAT ROPERS NEED LOVE TOO. True.

So it is possible to live in both cultures without being suffocated by the one or seduced by the other. New Orleans may be too seductive for a writer. Known hereabouts as The Big Easy, it may be too easy, too pleasant. Faulkner was charmed to a standstill and didn't really get going until he returned to Mississippi and invented his county. The occupational hazard of the writer in New Orleans is a variety of the French flu, which might also be called the Vieux Carré syndrome. One is apt to turn fey, potter about a patio, and write feuilletons and vignettes or catty romans à clef, a pleasant enough life but for me too seductive.

On the other hand, it is often a good idea to go against demographic trends, reverse the flight to the country, return to the ruined heart of the city. When the French Quarter is completely ruined by the tourists—and deserted by them—it will again be a good place to live. I'm sick of cutting grass. Covington lies at the green heart of green Louisiana, a green jungle of pines, azaleas, camellias, dogwood, grapevines, and billions of blades of grass. I've begun to hear the grass growing at night. It costs twenty-five dollars to get my lawn mower fixed. If my wife would allow it, I would end my days in a French cottage on Rue Dauphine with a small paved patio and not a single blade of grass.

A Chinese curse condemns one to live in interesting and eventful times. The best thing about Covington is that it is in a certain sense out of place and time but not too far out and therefore just the place for a Chinese scholar who asks nothing more than being left alone. One can sniff the ozone from the pine trees, visit the local bars, eat crawfish, and drink Dixie beer and feel as good as it is possible to feel in this awfully interesting century. And now and then, drive across the lake to New Orleans, still an entrancing city, eat trout amandine at Galatoire's, drive home to my pleasant, uninteresting place, try to figure out how the world got into such a fix, shrug, take a drink, and listen to the frogs tune up.

—APRIL 1980

# Staten Island, I Love You!

DAWN POWELL

Staten Island! I fell in love with it the very day I fell in love and the whole affair has the misty charm of a half-forgotten Lehar operetta. The island's history from its earliest patroons, its Walloon and French Huguenot colonists from the Dutch West India Company, its Indians raking the shore's pearl beds for their belts, and its Captain Billop claiming the place for New York Province instead of New Jersey merely by sailing around it in twenty-four hours, makes a stout bed of facts for those who like them. And it is true a ferry will still take you to St. George from Battery Park for a nickel, a miracle even greater than the triumphant completion of the new Verrazano-Narrows Bridge.

But these are basic facts. The real Staten Island buffs have other reasons for their addiction.

What I love about Staten Island is that in the year 1920, fresh sprung from Ohio, conquering New York and knowing everything as I never have since, I was asked by a fair young man in the office next to mine if I would care to go walking Saturday on Staten Island.

"I've always wanted to," I cried, never having heard of the place.

I would have agreed just as eagerly to go mushing over the moon's crust, since I had already decided to marry the man, though I had no yen for walking and had not even caught the young man's name which (we might as well get these happy endings over right at the start) later would be mine.

It was a Prohibition year so naturally part of the hiking equipment was a hip flask of some exquisite blend of lemonade and henbane with a zest of metal rust, but this cannot account altogether for the mysterious haze that enveloped this and all subsequent impressions of the island. First of all I found that the magic ferryboat, churning past chiming bell buoys, mud scows and ocean liners, the Statue of Liberty and little fishing boats, had transported me not to a place but to another time, say fifty years back. Even the St. George terminal, vast and bleak, perfumed with old picnic rejects, peanuts and Bull Durham tobacco, was like the old-time Midwest Junction depot with the music of foghorns and boat whistles instead of engine snorts and blasts. Once on the highway there were the dusty back roads, tangled backyards complete with burdock, lilac, berry bushes, grazing colts, abandoned toys and rusty machinery that belonged to my earliest Ohio memories, though Ohio had already graduated from chicken houses and poison ivy to prize dahlias, rose-trellised pergolas, espaliered fruit trees, swan-shaped hedges and other Garden Club conceits.

In my nostalgic enthusiasm (as a matter of fact, my girlish desire to please) I waxed homesick for sights I'd never seen before, such as a herd of goats ambling along behind a moon-faced farm boy, a trackless trolley line, a Four Corners beer garden with a huge stuffed bear in the yard—was it in Annadale? My companion, who shall be and indeed was called Joe, mistook sheer infatuation for an athletic passion to climb another five miles of hill. From time to time we'd catch a bus or trolley—thank God!—going in any direction, which accounts for us winding up at dusk in the waters of South Beach. We had brought bathing suits—quite a parcel in those overdressed days—and again I feigned rapture over the lovely beach, spangled as it was with melon rinds, broken Moxie bottles, banana peels, wagon wheels, pie tins and l'amour. Somewhere on the fringe we found a peaceful oasis.

"Let's come back to this very spot next Saturday and have a picnic," I suggested craftily.

That was when I learned you never can find the same place again on Staten Island. I never found the stuffed bear again or anyone who ever heard of the inn, or the trackless trolley, or the herd of goats, and by the time I got back to South Beach the melon rinds and broken glass had given way to a stylish boardwalk.

In my years of Staten Island exploration I learned that people as well as places lose themselves here. Except for the old settlers whom you seldom see, nobody can give you any directions because they don't know where they are themselves. All they know is that they're wanted someplace else and they're taking no chances on getting too well acquainted. Hunting for a map-starred beach somewhere in mid-island, we asked the only person we could find on the road where the ocean was.

"I don't know," he said. "I just came out of the house."

Another day we were looking for Meurot's, a local restaurant we had heard praised, and we stopped a man coming out of a movie house in St. George to ask if Meurot's really was the best place in St. George. He looked all around him cautiously as if he had been wrongly accused.

"Listen, folks," he said pleadingly, "I only been to the Black Lagoon," and away he scurried.

Staten Island, it would seem, is the finest hiding place in the country. The solid old burghers, unhappy now over the invasion of their quiet life by the opening of the Verrazano-Narrows Bridge, have never been interested in strangers. They have their lodge, church and school doings, their local politics, and up until recently their spacious old homes; they want no part of the outside world, especially New York City. Like many native islanders elsewhere they hope the necessity of making a living will not oblige them to go further than the nearest town. The old Farmers' Market, a combination Sears Roebuck and county fair, in huge quonsets far out on Richmond Avenue, has long been a weekend supply center for those who dread even the short trip to Jersey. A celebrated writer or front-page criminal may be holed up in the deserted old mansion next door; the burgher's family doesn't care and never heard of him anyway. When Garibaldi took refuge on Staten Island in Rosebank in 1851, his neighbors knew him only as an amiable candlemaker; his past and future plans as a revolutionary were of no interest to them, nor would they have understood the implications. He blazed the trail for a migration of Italians to the island, and the burghers approved their gardening and other crafts and found their anarchism as peaceable as their pizza making, but not as fascinating. Years later, in the Wall Street bomb scare of 1920, Carlo Tresca, the anarchist leader held by the police, managed to slip away on the ferry to vacation quietly with his friends at South Beach while the Manhattan detectives thrashed through less obvious territory. The stolid natives were equally indifferent when Aaron Burr, for reasons not unconnected with difficulties in financial and political skullduggery, took up residence in Port Richmond, where he later died. It is more than possible that in their local absorptions they had never heard of his duel, Madame Jumel, his plots or his lecherous escapades. He was just another customer to the St. James Hotel.

There are other reasons, beyond the reassuring lack of curiosity of the natives, that make Staten Island the perfect hideout.

You wouldn't, for instance, find James Bond heading for a five-cent ferry to track down an international spy holed up in Sailors' Snug Harbor, even if all clues pointed that way. No, he must jet first to Buenos Aires, then to Hong Kong, London, Rio de Janeiro, and possibly the Blue Grotto in Capri, enjoying gourmet meals and luscious sirens all along the way. The lesser James Bonds of the Manhattan squad, even with smaller expense accounts, have no enthusiasm for tracking criminals in the squalid slums of Hoboken or the dreary wastes of Queens or Staten Island. They too enjoy the excuse—rather call it the necessity—for a checkup on Monte Carlo or Las Vegas.

Not so long ago a gentleman Raffles who had been following the society columns assiduously to find out which Westchester socialites were attending balls, leaving their homes open to his tender ministrations, was finally captured with a great deal of front-page éclat. While out on bail, waiting for his trial, the clever fellow slipped off to no-man's-land on the Staten Island ferry. Since the Staten Island press devotes its front pages to the affairs of the Legion Post, with no space for the frivols of Westchester snobs, our man found himself of no interest to Staten Islanders. He had no trouble getting a job as gardener to a country squire and lived in perfect peace, occasionally catching a note in the New York papers about sleuths trailing him through the nightclubs of Paris and even Istanbul. At first their blindness kept him smiling as he trimmed his entries for the local flower show or accepted compliments on his fine mums, but after a year or so he began to feel not only jealous of the pleasures he was affording his enemies, the fuzz, but unwanted. He took to appearing at the St. George ferry terminal whenever he got time out from the gardens, hoping someone on an incoming boat might recognize him as the crackerjack cat burglar they'd read about. Once he even engaged a cop in conversation, containing many a hint of his past, but the cop was in a hurry to put a down payment on a two-family house he'd just brought in Tompkinsville (he showed our man the house plans as freely as he'd have Jack the Ripper). It was almost two years before the cat burglar, now prize gardener, driven mad with ennui, dashed on the ferry for New York and gave himself up to a rather cross group of returned travelers. Is he serving his time in prison now, I wonder, and does he boast of his jewel thefts and hush up his dahlia triumphs? There is no one to tell me.

No one can really tell you about Staten Island. They answer your questions with other questions, or tricky come-ons. You ask how to get to the Lighthouse, and they tell you it's not far from the Buddhist Monastery. Buddhist Monastery here, you shriek? Well, it's really the Jacques Marchais Center of Tibetan Art, they say, around the bend from the Historical Museum at Richmond with its Revolutionary treasures. Naturally, you say, and not too far from that lake that dries up when its sister lake on the mainland overflows, wherever that is.

Does the Verrazano-Narrows Bridge know the wonderland it is opening up or will, alas, the wonders vanish at the first breeze from the real world?

—OCTOBER 1965

# The Golden Age/Time Past

## RALPH ELLISON

*That which we do is what we are. That which we remember is, more often than not, that which we would have liked to have been; or that which we hope to be. Thus our memory and our identity are ever at odds; our history ever a tall tale told by inattentive idealists.*

It has been a long time now, and not many remember how it was in the old days; not really. Not even those who were there to see and hear as it happened, who were pressed in the crowds beneath the dim rosy lights of the bar in the smoke-veiled room, and who shared, night after night, the mysterious spell created by the talk, the laughter, greasepaint, powder, perfume, sweat, alcohol and food—all blended and simmering, like a stew on the restaurant range, and brought to a sustained moment of elusive meaning by the timbres and accents of musical instruments locked in passionate recitative. It has been too long now, some seventeen years.

Above the bandstand there later appeared a mural depicting a group of jazzmen holding a jam session in a narrow Harlem bedroom. While an exhausted girl with shapely legs sleeps on her stomach in a big brass bed, they bend to their music in a quiet concatenation of unheard sound: a trumpeter, a guitarist, a clarinetist, a drummer; their only audience a small, cockeared dog. The clarinetist is white. The guitarist strums with an enigmatic smile. The trumpet is muted. The barefooted drummer, beating a folded newspaper with whisk brooms in lieu of a drum, stirs the eye's ear like a blast of brasses in a midnight street. A bottle of port rests on a dresser, but it, like the girl, is ignored. The artist, Charles Graham, adds mystery to, as well as illumination within, the scene by having them play by the light of a kerosene lamp. The painting, executed in a harsh documentary style reminiscent of W.P.A. art, conveys a feeling of musical effort caught in timeless and unrhetorical suspension, the sad remoteness of a scene observed through a wall of crystal.

Except for the lamp, the room might well have been one in the Hotel Cecil, the building in 118th Street in which Minton's Playhouse is located, and although painted in 1946, sometime after the revolutionary doings there had begun, the mural should help recall the old days vividly. But the décor of the place has been changed and now it is covered, most of the time, by draperies. These require a tricky skill of those who would draw them aside. And even then there will still only be the girl who must sleep forever unhearing, and the men who must forever gesture the same soundless tune. Besides, the time it celebrates is dead and gone and perhaps not even those who came when it was still fresh and new remember those days as they were.

Neither do those remember who knew Henry Minton, who gave the place his name. Nor those who shared in the noisy lostness of New York the rediscovered community of the feasts, evocative of home, of South, of good times, the best and most unself-conscious of times, created by the generous portions of Negro-American cuisine—the hash, grits, fried chicken, the ham-seasoned vegetables, the hot biscuits and rolls and the free whiskey—with which, each Monday night, Teddy Hill honored the entire cast of current Apollo Theatre shows. They were gathered here from all parts of America and they broke bread together and there was a sense of good feeling and promise, but what shape the fulfilled promise would take they did not know, and few except the more restless of the younger musicians even questioned. Yet it was an exceptional moment and the world was swinging with change.

Most of them, black and white alike, were hardly aware of where they were or what time it was; nor did they wish to be. They thought of Minton's as a sanctuary, where in an atmosphere blended of nostalgia and a music-and-drink-lulled suspension of time they could retreat from the wartime tensions of the town. The meaning of time-present was not their concern; thus when they try to tell it now the meaning escapes them.

For they were caught up in events which made that time exceptionally and uniquely *then*, and which brought, among the other changes which have reshaped the world, a momentous modulation into a new key of musical sensibility; in brief, a revolution in culture.

So how *can* they remember? Even in swiftly changing America there are few such moments, and at best Americans give but a limited attention to history. Too much happens too rapidly, and before we can evaluate it, or exhaust its meaning or pleasure, there is something new to concern us. Ours is the tempo of the motion picture, not that of the still camera, and we waste experience as we wasted the forest. During the time it was happening the sociologists were concerned with the riots, unemployment and industrial tensions of the time, the historians with the onsweep of the war; and the critics and most serious students of culture found this area of our national life of little interest. So it was left to those who came to Minton's out of the needs of feeling, and when the moment was past no one retained more than a fragment of its happening. Afterward the very effort to put the fragments together transformed them—so that in place of true memory they now summon to mind pieces of legend. They retell the stories as they have been told and written, glamourized, inflated, made neat and smooth, with all incomprehensible details vanished along with most of the wonder—not how it was as they themselves knew it.

When asked how it was back then, back in the Forties, they will smile, then, frowning with the puzzlement of one attempting to recall the details of a pleasant but elusive dream, they'll say: "Oh, man, it was a hell of a time! A wailing time! Things were jumping, you couldn't get in here for the people. The place was packed with celebrities. Park Avenue, man! Big people in show business, college professors along with the pimps and their women. And college boys and girls. Everybody came. You know how the old words to the *Basin Street Blues* used to go before Sinatra got hold of it? *Basin Street is the street where the dark and the light folks meet*—that's what I'm talking about. That was Minton's, man. It was a place where everybody could come to be entertained because it was a place that was jumping with good times."

Or some will tell you that it was here that Dizzy Gillespie found his own trumpet voice; that here Kenny Clarke worked out the pattern of his drumming style; where Charlie Christian played out the last creative and truly satisfying moments of his brief life, his New York home; where Charlie Parker built the monument of his art; where Thelonius Monk formulated his contribution to the chordal progressions and the hide-and-seek melodic methods of modern jazz. And they'll call such famous names as Lester Young and Ben Webster, Coleman Hawkins, or Fats Waller, who came here in the after-hour stillness of the early morning to compose. They'll tell you that Benny Goodman, Art Tatum, Count Basie, and Lena Horne would drop in to join in the fun; that it was here that George Shearing played on his first night in the U.S.; or Tony Scott's great love of the place; and they'll repeat all the stories of how, when and by whom the word "bebop" was coined here—but, withal, few actually remember, and these leave much unresolved.

Usually, music gives resonance to memory (and Minton's was a hotbed of jazz), but not the music then in the making here. It was itself a texture of fragments, repetitive, nervous, not fully formed; its melodic lines underground, secret and taunting; its riffs jeering—"Salt peanuts! Salt peanuts!" Its timbres flat or shrill, with a minimum of thrilling vibrato. Its rhythms were out of stride and seemingly arbitrary, its drummers frozen-faced introverts dedicated to chaos. And in it the steady flow of memory, desire and defined experience summed up by the traditional jazz beat and blues mood seemed swept like a great river from its old, deep bed. We know better now, and recognize the old moods in the new sounds, but what we know is that which was then becoming. For most of those who gathered here, the enduring meaning of the great moment at Minton's took place off to the side, beyond the range of attention, like a death blow glimpsed from the corner of the eye, the revolutionary rumpus sounding like a series of flubbed notes blasting the talk with discord. So that the events which made Minton's *Minton's* arrived in conflict and ran their course, then the heat was gone and all that is left to mark its passage is the controlled fury of the music itself, sealed pure and irrevocable, banalities and excellencies alike, in the early recordings; or swept along by our restless quest for the new, to be diluted in more recent styles, the best of it absorbed like drops of fully distilled technique, mood and emotion into the great stream of jazz.

Left also to confuse our sense of what happened is the word "bop," hardly more than a nonsense syllable, by which the music synthesized at Minton's came to be known. A most inadequate word which does little, really, to help us remember. A word which throws up its hands in clownish self-depreciation before all the complexity of sound and rhythm and self-assertive passion which it pretends to name; a mask-word for the charged ambiguities of the new sound, hiding the serious face of art.

Nor does it help that so much has come to pass in the meantime. There have been two hot wars and that which continues, called "cold." And the unknown young men who brought a new edge to the sound of jazz and who scrambled the rhythms of those who used the small clear space at Minton's for dancing are no longer so young or unknown; indeed, they are referred to now by nickname in even the remotest of places. And in Paris and Munich and Tokyo they'll tell you the details of how, after years of trying, "Dizzy" (meaning John Birks Gillespie) vanquished "Roy" (meaning Roy Eldridge) during a jam session at Minton's, to become thereby the new king of trumpeters. Or how, later, while jetting over the world in the blasts of his special tilt-belled horn, he jammed with a snake charmer in Pakistan. "Sent the bloody cobra, man," they'll tell you in London's Soho. So their subsequent fame has blurred the sharp, ugly lines of their rebellion even in the memories of those who found them most strange and distasteful.

What's more, our memory of some of the more brilliant young men has been touched by the aura of death, and we feel guilt that the fury of their passing was the price paid for the art they left us to enjoy unscathed: Charlie Christian, burned out by tuberculosis like a guitar consumed in a tenement fire; Fats Navarro, wrecked by the tensions and needling temptations of his orgiastic trade, a big man physically as well as musically, shrunken to nothingness; and, most notably of all, Charlie Parker called "Bird," now deified, worshipped and studied and, like any fertility god, mangled by his admirers and imitators, who coughed up his life and died—as incredibly as the leopard which Hemingway tells us was found "dried and frozen" near the summit of Mount Kilimanjaro—in the hotel suite of a Baroness. (Nor has anyone explained what a "yardbird" was seeking at that social altitude, though we know that ideally anything is possible within a democracy, and we know quite well that upper-class Europeans were seriously interested in jazz long before Newport became hospitable.) All this is too much for memory; the dry facts are too easily lost in legend and glamour. (With jazz we are yet not in the age of history, but linger in that of folklore.) We know for certain only that the strange sound which they and their fellows threw against the hum and buzz of vague signification that seethed in the drinking crowd at Minton's and which, like disgruntled conspirators meeting fatefully to assemble the random parts of a bomb, they joined here and beat and blew into a new jazz style—these sounds we know now to have become the clichés, the technical exercises and the standard of achievement not only for fledgling musicians all over the United States, but for Dutchmen and Swedes, Italians and Frenchmen, Germans and Belgians, and even Japanese. All these, in places which came to mind during the Minton days only as points where the war was in progress and where one might soon be sent to fight and die, are now spotted with young men who study the discs on which the revolution hatched in Minton's is preserved with all the intensity that young American painters bring to the works, say, of Kandinsky, Picasso and Klee. Surely this is an odd swing of the cultural tide. Yet Stravinski, Webern, and Berg notwithstanding, or more recently, Boulez or Stockhausen—such young men (many of them excellent musicians in the highest European tradition) find in the music made articulate at Minton's some key to a fuller freedom of self-realization. Indeed, for many young Europeans the developments which took place here and the careers of those who brought it about have become the latest episodes in the great American epic. They collect the recordings and thrive on the legends as eagerly, perhaps, as young Americans.

Today the bartenders at Minton's will tell you how they come fresh off the ships or planes, bringing their brightly expectant and—in this Harlem atmosphere—startingly innocent European faces, to buy drinks and stand looking about for the source of the mystery. They try to reconcile the quiet reality of the place with the events which fired, at such long range, their imaginations. They come as to a shrine; as we to the Louvre, Notre Dame or St. Peter's; as young Americans hurry to the Café Flore, the Deux Magots, the Rotonde or the Café du Dôme in Paris. For some years now, they have been coming to ask, with all the solemnity of pilgrims inquiring of a sacred relic, to see the nicotine-stained amplifier which Teddy Hill provided for Charlie Christian's guitar. And this is quite proper, for every shrine should have its relic.

Perhaps Minton's has more meaning for European jazz fans than for Americans, even for those who regularly went there. Certainly it has a *different* meaning. For them it is associated with those continental cafés in which great changes, political and artistic, have been plotted; it is to modern jazz what the Café Voltaire in Zurich is to the Dadaist phase of modern literature and painting. Few of those who visited Harlem during the Forties would associate it so, but there *is* a context of meaning in which Minton's and the musical activities which took place there can be meaningfully placed.

Jazz, for all the insistence of the legends, has been far more closely associated with cabarets and dance halls than with brothels, and it was these which provided both the employment for the musicians and an audience initiated and aware of the overtones of the music; which knew the language of riffs, the unstated meanings of the blues idiom, and the dance steps developed from and complementary to its rhythms. And in the beginning it was in the Negro dance hall and nightclub that jazz was most completely a part of a total cultural expression; and in which it was freest and most satisfying, both for the musicians and for those in whose lives it played a major role. As a nightclub in a Negro community then, Minton's was part of a national pattern.

But in the old days Minton's was far more than this; it was also a rendezvous for musicians. As such, and although it was not formally organized, it goes back historically to the first New York center of Negro musicians, the Clef Club. Organized in 1910, during the start of the great migration of Negroes northward, by James Reese Europe, the director whom Irene Castle credits with having invented the fox-trot, the Clef Club was set up on West Fifty-third Street to serve as a meeting place and booking office for Negro musicians and entertainers. Here wage scales were regulated, musical styles and techniques worked out, and entertainment was supplied for such establishments as Rector's and Delmonico's, and for such producers as Florenz Ziegfeld and Oscar Hammerstein. Later, when Harlem evolved into a Negro section, a similar function was served by the Rhythm Club, located then in the old Lafayette Theatre building on 132nd Street and Seventh Avenue. Henry Minton, a former saxophonist and officer of the Rhythm Club, became the first Negro delegate to Local 802 of the American Federation of Musicians and was thus doubly aware of the needs, artistic as well as economic, of jazzmen. He was generous with loans, was fond of food himself and, as an old acquaintance recalled, "loved to put a pot on the range" to share with unemployed friends. Naturally when he opened Minton's Playhouse many musicians made it their own.

Henry Minton also provided, as did the Clef and Rhythm clubs, a necessity more important to jazz musicians than food: a place in which to hold their interminable jam sessions. And it is here that Minton's becomes most important to the development of modern jazz. It is here, too, that it joins up with all the countless rooms, private and public, in which jazzmen have worked out the secrets of their craft. Today jam sessions are offered as entertainment by nightclubs and on radio and television, and some are quite exciting; but what is seen and heard is only one aspect of the true jam session: the "cutting session," or contest of improvisational skill and physical endurance between two or more musicians. But the jam session is far more than this, and when carried out by musicians, in the privacy of small rooms (as in the mural at Minton's) or in such places as Hallie Richardson's shoeshine parlor in Oklahoma City—where I first heard Lester Young jamming in a shine chair, his head thrown back, his horn even then outthrust, his feet working on the foot-rests, as he played with and against Lem Johnson, Ben Webster (this was 1929) and other members of the old Blue Devils orchestra—or during the after hours in Piney Brown's old Sunset Club in Kansas City; in such places as these with only musicians and jazzmen present, then the jam session is revealed as the jazzman's true academy.

It is here that he learns tradition, group techniques and style. For although since the Twenties many jazzmen have had conservatory training and were well-grounded in formal theory and instrumental technique, when we approach jazz we are entering quite a different sphere of training. Here it is more meaningful to speak, not of courses of study, of grades and degrees, but of apprenticeship, ordeals, initiation ceremonies, of rebirth. For after the jazzman has learned the fundamentals of his instrument and the traditional techniques of jazz—the intonations, the mute work, manipulation of timbre, the body of traditional styles—he must then "find himself," must be reborn, must find, as it were, his soul. All this through achieving that subtle identification between his instrument and his deepest drives which will allow him to express his own unique ideas and his own unique voice. He must achieve, in short, his self-determined identity.

In this his instructors are his fellow musicians, especially the acknowledged masters, and his recognition of manhood depends upon their acceptance of his ability as having reached a standard which is all the more difficult for not having been rigidly codified. This does not depend upon his ability to simply hold a job but upon his power to express an individuality in tone. Nor is his status ever unquestioned, for the health of jazz and the unceasing attraction which it holds for the musicians themselves lies in the ceaseless warfare for mastery and recognition—not among the general public, though commercial success is not spurned, but among their artistic peers. And even the greatest can never rest on past accomplishments for, as with the fast guns of the old West, there is always someone waiting in a jam session to blow him literally, not only down, but into shame and discouragement.

By making his club hospitable to jam sessions even to the point that customers who were not musicians were crowded out, Henry Minton provided a retreat, a homogeneous community where a collectivity of common experience could find continuity and meaningful expression. Thus the stage was set for the birth of bop.

In 1941 Mr. Minton handed over his management to Teddy Hill, the saxophonist and former band leader, and Hill turned the Playhouse into a musical dueling ground. Not only did he continue Minton's policies, he expanded them. It was Hill who established the Monday Celebrity Nights, the house band which included such members from his own disbanded orchestra as Kenny Clark, Dizzy Gillespie, along with Thelonius Monk, sometimes with Joe Guy, and later, Charlie Christian and Charlie Parker; and it was Hill who allowed the musicians free rein to play whatever they liked. Perhaps no other club except Clarke Monroe's Uptown House was so permissive, and with the hospitality extended to musicians of all schools the news spread swiftly. Minton's became the focal point for musicians all over the country.

Herman Pritchard, who presided over the bar in the old days, tells us that every time they came "Lester Young and Ben Webster used to tie up in battle like dogs in the road. They'd fight on those saxophones until they were tired out, then they'd put in long distance calls to their mothers both of whom lived in Kansas City, and tell them about it."

And most of the masters of jazz came either to observe or to participate and be influenced and listen to their own discoveries transformed; and the aspiring stars sought to win their approval, as the younger tenor men tried to win the esteem of Coleman Hawkins. Or they tried to vanquish them in jamming contests as Gillespie is said to have outblown his idol, Roy Eldridge. It was during this period that Eddie "Lockjaw" Davis underwent an ordeal of jeering rejection until finally he came through as an admired tenor man.

In the perspective of time we now see that what was happening at Minton's was a continuing symposium of jazz, a summation of all the styles, personal and traditional, of jazz. Here it was possible to hear its resources of technique, ideas, harmonic structure, melodic phrasing and rhythmical possibilities explored more thoroughly than was ever possible before. It was also possible to hear the first attempts toward a conscious statement of the sensibility of the younger generation of musicians as they worked out the techniques, structures and rhythmical patterns with which to express themselves. Part of this was arbitrary, a revolt of the younger against the established stylists; part of it was inevitable. For jazz had reached a crisis and new paths were certain to be searched for and found. An increasing number of the younger men were formally trained and the post-Depression developments in the country had made for quite a break between their experience and that of the older men. Many were even of a different physical build. Often they were quiet and of a reserve which contrasted sharply with the exuberant and outgoing lyricism of the older men, and they were intensely concerned that their identity as Negroes placed no restriction upon the music they played or the manner in which they used their talent. They were concerned, they said, with art, not entertainment. Especially were they resentful of Louis Armstrong whom (confusing the spirit of his music with his clowning) they considered an Uncle Tom.

But they too, some of them, had their own myths and misconceptions: That theirs was the only generation of Negro musicians who listened to or enjoyed the classics; that to be truly free they must act exactly the opposite of what white people might believe, rightly or wrongly, a Negro to be; that the performing artist can be completely and absolutely free of the obligations of the entertainer, and that they could play jazz with dignity only by frowning and treating the audience with aggressive contempt; and that to be in control, artistically and personally, one must be so cool as to quench one's own human fire.

Nor should we overlook the despair which must have swept Minton's before the technical mastery, the tonal authenticity, the authority and the fecundity of imagination of such men as Hawkins,

Young, Goodman, Tatum, Teagarden, Ellington and Waller. Despair, after all, is ever an important force in revolutions.

They were also responding to the nonmusical pressures affecting jazz. It was a time of big bands and the greatest prestige and economic returns were falling outside the Negro community—often to leaders whose popularity grew from the compositions and arrangements of Negroes—to white instrumentalists whose only originality lay in the enterprise with which they rushed to market with some Negro musician's hard-won style. Still there was no policy of racial discrimination at Minton's. Indeed, it was very much like those Negro cabarets of the Twenties and Thirties in which a megaphone was placed on the piano so that anyone with the urge could sing a blues. Nevertheless, the inside-dopesters will tell you that the "changes" or chord progressions and the melodic inversions worked out by the creators of bop sprang partially from their desire to create a jazz which could not be so easily imitated and exploited by white musicians to whom the market was more open simply *because* of their whiteness. They wished to receive credit for what they created, and besides, it was easier to "get rid of the trash" who crowded the bandstand with inept playing and thus make room for the real musicians, whether white or black. Nevertheless, white musicians like Tony Scott, Remo Palmieri and Al Haig who were part of the development at Minton's became so by passing a test of musicianship, sincerity and temperament. Later, it is said, the boppers became engrossed in solving the musical problems which they set themselves. Except for a few sympathetic older musicians it was they who best knew the promise of the Minton moment, and it was they, caught like the rest in all the complex forces of American life which come to focus in jazz, who made the most of it. Now the tall tales told as history must feed on the results of their efforts.

—JANUARY 1959

# Brigitte Bardot and the Lolita Syndrome

SIMONE DE BEAUVOIR

*Translated by Bernard Fretchman*

On New Year's Eve, Brigitte Bardot appeared on French television. She was got up as usual—blue jeans, sweater, and shock of tousled hair. Lounging on a sofa, she plucked at a guitar. "That's not hard," said the women. "I could do just as well. She's not even pretty. She has the face of a housemaid." The men couldn't keep from devouring her with their eyes, but they too snickered. Only two or three of us, among thirty or so spectators, thought her charming. Then she did an excellent classical dance number. "She *can* dance," the others admitted grudgingly. Once again I could observe that Brigitte Bardot was disliked in her own country.

When *And God Created Woman* was shown in first-run houses on the Champs-Elysées in 1956, the film, which had cost a hundred and forty million francs, brought in less than sixty. Receipts in the U.S.A. have come to $4,000,000, the equivalent of the sale of 2,500 Dauphines. B.B. now deserves to be considered an export product as important as Renault automobiles.

She is the new idol of American youth. She ranks as a great international star. Nevertheless, her fellow-countrymen continue to shy away from her. Not a week goes by without articles in the press telling all about her recent moods and love affairs or offering a new interpretation of her personality, but half of these articles and gossip items seethe with spite. Brigitte receives three hundred fan letters a day, from boys and girls alike, and every day indignant mothers write to newspaper editors and religious and civil authorities to protest against her existence. When three young ne'er-do-wells of reputable families murdered a sleeping old man in a train at Angers, the Parent-Teachers Association denounced B.B. to M. Chatenay, the deputy-mayor of the city. It was *she*, they said, who was really responsible for the crime. *And God Created Woman* had been shown in Angers; the young people had been immediately perverted. I am not surprised that professional moralists in all countries, even the U.S.A., have tried to have her films banned. It is no new thing for high-minded folk to identify the flesh with sin and to dream of making a bonfire of works of art, books, and films that depict it complacently or frankly.

But this official prudery does not explain the French public's very peculiar hostility to B.B. Martine Carol also undressed rather generously in her hit films, and nobody reproached her, whereas almost everyone is ready to regard B.B. as a very monument of immorality. Why does this character, fabricated by Marc Allegret and particularly by Roger Vadim, arouse such animosity?

If we want to understand what B.B. represents, it is not important to know what the young woman named Brigitte Bardot is really like. Her admirers and detractors are concerned with the imaginary creature they see on the screen through a tremendous cloud of ballyhoo. In so far as she is exposed to the public gaze, her legend has been fed by her private life no less than by her movie roles. This legend conforms to a very old myth that Vadim tried to rejuvenate. He invented a resolutely modern version of "the eternal female" and thereby launched a new type of eroticism. It is this novelty that entices some people and shocks others.

Love can resist familiarity; eroticism cannot. Its role in the movies dwindled considerably when social differences between the two sexes diminished. Between 1930 and 1940 it gave way to romanticism and sentimentality. The vamp was replaced by the girlfriend, of whom Jean Arthur was the most perfect type. However, when in 1947 the cinema was threatened with a serious crisis, filmmakers returned to eroticism in an effort to win back the public's affection. In an age when woman drives a car and speculates on the stock exchange, an age in which she unceremoniously displays her nudity on public beaches, any attempt to revive the vamp and her mystery was out of the question. The movies tried to appeal, in a cruder way, to the male's response to feminine curves. Stars were appreciated for the obviousness of their physical charms rather than for their passionate or languorous gaze. Marilyn Monroe, Sophia Loren, and Gina Lollobrigida are ample proof of the fact that the full-blown woman has not lost her power over men. However, the dream-merchants were also moving in other directions. With Audrey Hepburn, Françoise Arnoul, Marina Vlady, Leslie Caron, and Brigitte Bardot, they invented the erotic hoyden. For a part in his next film, *Dangerous Connections*, Vadim has engaged a fourteen-year-old girl. The child-woman is triumphing not only in the movies. In *A View From the Bridge*, the Arthur Miller play which has been a hit in the United States and a bigger one in England and France, the heroine has just about reached the age of puberty. Nabokov's *Lolita*, which deals with the relations between a forty-year-old male and a "nymphet" of twelve, was at the top of the best-seller list in America for months. The adult woman now inhabits the same world as the man, but the child-woman moves in a universe which he cannot enter. The age difference re-establishes between them the distance that seems necessary to desire. At least that is what those who have created a new Eve by merging the "green fruit" and "*femme fatale*" types have pinned their hopes on. We shall see the reasons why they have not succeeded in France as well as in the United States.

Brigitte Bardot is the most perfect specimen of these ambiguous nymphs. Seen from behind, her slender, muscular, dancer's body is almost androgynous. Femininity triumphs in her delightful bosom. The long voluptuous tresses of Mélisande flow down to her shoulders, but her hair-do is that of a negligent waif. The line of her lips forms a childish pout, and at the same time those lips are very kissable. She goes about barefooted, she turns up her nose at elegant clothes, jewels, girdles, perfumes, make-up, at all artifice. Yet her walk is lascivious and a saint would sell his soul to the devil merely to watch her dance. It has often been said that her face has only one expression. It is true that the outer world is hardly reflected in it at all and that it does not reveal great inner disturbance. But that air of indifference becomes her. B.B. has not been marked by experience. Even if she has lived—as in *Love Is My Profession*—the lessons that life has given her are too confused for her to have gotten anything out of them. She is without memory, without a past, and, thanks to this ignorance, she retains the perfect innocence that is attributed to a mythical childhood.

The legend that has been built up around Brigitte Bardot by publicity has for a long time identified her with this childlike and disturbing character. Vadim presented her as "a phenomenon of nature." "She doesn't act," he said. "She exists." "That's right," confirmed B.B. "The Juliette in *And God Created Woman* is exactly me. When I'm in front of the camera, I'm simply myself." Brigitte was said not to bother using a comb, but to do up her hair with her fingers. She was said to loathe all forms of worldliness. Her interviews presented her as being natural and unpretentious. Vadim even went further. He painted her as naïve to the point of absurdity. According to him, at the age of eighteen she thought that mice laid eggs. She was moody and capricious. At the gala performance of her film, *Please, Mr. Balzac,* the producer waited in vain for her to show up. At the last minute, he informed the audience that she was not coming. She was described as a creature of instinct, as yielding blindly to her impulses. She would suddenly take a dislike to the decoration of her room and then and there would pull down the hangings and start repainting the furniture. She is temperamental, changeable, and unpredictable, and though she retains the limpidity of childhood, she has also preserved its mystery. A strange little creature, all in all; and this image does not depart from the traditional myth of femininity. The roles that her scriptwriters have offered her also have a conventional side. She appears as a force of nature, dangerous so long as she remains untamed, but it is up to the male to domesticate her. She is kind, she is good-hearted. In all her films she loves animals. If she ever makes anyone suffer, it is never deliberately. Her flightiness and slips of behavior are excusable because she is so young and because of circumstances. Juliette had an unhappy childhood; Yvette, in *Love Is My Profession*, is a victim of society. If they go astray, it is because no one has ever shown them the right path, but a man, a real man, can lead them back to it. Juliette's young husband decides to act like a male, gives her a good sharp slap and Juliette is all at once transformed into a happy, contrite, and submissive wife. Yvette joyfully accepts her lover's demand that she be faithful and his imposing upon her a life of virtual seclusion. With a bit of luck, this experienced, middle-aged man would have brought her redemption. B.B. is a lost, pathetic child who needs a guide and protector. This cliché has proved its worth. It flatters masculine vanity; it reassures mature and maturing women. One may regard it as obsolete; it cannot be accused of boldness.

But the spectators do not believe in this victory of the man and of the social order so prudently suggested by the scenario—and that is precisely why Vadim's film and that of another French director, Autant-Lara, do not lapse into triviality. We may assume that the "little rascal" will settle down, but Juliette will certainly never become a model wife and mother. Ignorance and inexperience can be remedied, but B.B. is not only unsophisticated but dangerously sincere. The perversity of a "Baby Doll" can be handled by a psychiatrist; there are ways and means of calming the resentments of a rebellious girl and winning her over to virtue. In *The Barefoot Contessa*, Ava Gardner, despite her licentiousness, does not attack established values—she condemns her own instincts by admitting that she likes "to walk in the mud." B.B. is neither perverse nor rebellious nor immoral, and that is why morality does not have a chance with her. Good and evil are part of conventions to which she would not even think of bowing.

Nothing casts a sharper light on the character she plays than the wedding supper in *And God Created Woman*. Juliette immediately goes to bed with her young husband. In the middle of the banquet, she suddenly turns up in a bathrobe and, without bothering to smile or even look at the bewildered guests, she picks out from under their very noses a lobster, a chicken, fruit, and bottles of wine. Disdainfully and tranquilly she goes off with the loaded tray. She cares not a rap for other people's opinion. B.B. does not try to scandalize. She has no demands to make; she is no more conscious of her rights than she is of her duties. She follows her inclinations. She eats when she is hungry and makes love with the same unceremonious simplicity. Desire and pleasure seem to her more convincing than precepts and conventions. She does not criticize others. She does as she pleases, and that is what is disturbing. She does not ask questions, but she brings answers whose frankness may be contagious. Moral lapses can be corrected, but how could B.B. be cured of that dazzling virtue—genuineness? It is her very substance. Neither blows nor fine arguments nor love can take it from her. She rejects not only hypocrisy and reprimands, but also prudence and calculation and premeditation of any kind. For her, the future is still one of those adult inventions in which she has no confidence. "I live as if I were going to die at any moment," says Juliette. And Brigitte confides to us, "Every time I'm in love, I think that it's forever." To dwell in eternity is another way of rejecting time. She professes great admiration for James Dean. We find in her, in a milder form, certain traits that attain, in his case, a tragic intensity—the fever of living, the passion for the absolute, the sense of the imminence of death. She, too, embodies more modestly than he, but quite clearly, the credo that certain young people of our time are opposing to safe values, vain hopes, and irksome constraint.

"That is why a vast and traditional-minded rear guard declares that "B.B. springs from and expresses the immorality of an age." Decent or unwanted women could feel at ease when confronted with classical Circes who owed their power to dark secrets. These were coquettish and calculating creatures, depraved and reprobate, possessed of an evil force. From the height of their virtue, the fiancée, the wife, the greathearted mistress, and the despotic mother briskly damned these witches. But if Evil takes on the colors of innocence, they are in a fury. There is nothing of the "bad woman" about B.B. Frankness and kindness can be read on her face. She is more like a Pekingese than a cat. She is neither depraved nor venal. In *Love Is My Profession* she bunches up her skirt and crudely proposes a deal to Gabin. But there is a kind of disarming candor in her cynicism. She is blooming and healthy, quietly sensual. It is impossible to see in her the touch of Satan, and for that reason she seems all the more diabolical to women who feel humiliated and threatened by her beauty.

All men are drawn by B.B.'s seductiveness, but that does not mean they are kindly disposed toward her. The majority of Frenchmen claim that woman loses her sex appeal if she gives up her artifices. According to them, a woman in trousers chills desire. Brigitte proves to them the contrary, and they are not at all grateful to her, because they are unwilling to give up their role of lord and master. The vamp was no challenge to them in this respect. The attraction she exercised was that of a passive thing. They rushed knowingly into the magic trap; they went to their doom the way one throws oneself overboard. Freedom and full consciousness remained their right and privilege. When Marlene displayed her silk-sheathed thighs as she sang with her hoarse voice and looked about her with sultry eyes, she was staging a ceremony, she was casting a spell. B.B. does not cast spells; she is on the go. Her flesh does not have the abundance that, in others, symbolizes passivity. Her clothes are not fetishes and, when she strips, she is not unveiling a mystery. She is showing her body, neither more nor less, and that body rarely settles into a state of immobility. She walks, she dances, she moves about. Her eroticism is not magical, but aggressive. In the game of love, she is as much a hunter as she is a prey. The male is an object to her, just as she is to him. And that is precisely what wounds masculine pride. In the Latin countries, where men cling to the myth of "the woman as object," B.B.'s naturalness seems to them more perverse than any possible sophistication. To spurn jewels and cosmetics and high heels and girdles is to refuse to transform oneself into a remote idol. It is to assert that one is man's fellow and equal, to recognize that between the woman and him there is mutual desire and pleasure. Brigitte is thereby akin to the heroines of Françoise Sagan, although she says she feels no affinity for them—probably because they seem to her too thoughtful.

But the male feels uncomfortable if, instead of a doll of flesh-and-blood, he holds in his arms a conscious being who is sizing him up. A free woman is the very contrary of a light woman. In her role of confused female, of homeless little slut, B.B. seems to be available to everyone. And yet, paradoxically, she is intimidating. She is not defended by rich apparel or social prestige, but there is something stubborn in her sulky face, in her sturdy body. "You realize," an average Frenchman once said to me, "that when a man finds a woman attractive, he wants to be able to pinch her behind." A ribald gesture reduces a woman to a thing that a man can do with as he pleases without worrying about what goes on in her mind and heart and body. But B.B. has nothing of the "easygoing kid" about her, the quality that would allow a man to treat her with this kind of breeziness. There is nothing coarse about her. She has a kind of spontaneous dignity, something of the gravity of childhood. The difference between Brigitte's reception in the United States and in France is due partly to the fact that the American male does not have the Frenchman's taste for broad humor. He tends to display a certain respect for women. The sexual equality that B.B.'s behavior affirms wordlessly has been recognized in America for a long time. Nevertheless, for a number of reasons that have been frequently analyzed in America, he feels a certain antipathy to the "real woman." He regards her as an antagonist, a praying mantis, a tyrant. He abandons himself eagerly to the charms of the "nymph" in whom the formidable figure of the wife and the "Mom" is not yet apparent. In France, many women are accomplices of this feeling of superiority in which men persist. Their men prefer the servility of these adults to the haughty shamelessness of B.B.

She disturbs them all the more in that, though discouraging their jollity, she nevertheless does not lend herself to idealistic sublimation. Garbo was called "The Divine"; Bardot, on the other hand, is of the earth earthy. Garbo's visage had a kind of emptiness into which anything could be projected; nothing can be read into Bardot's face. It is what it is. It has the forthright presence of reality. It is a stumbling-block to lewd fantasies and ethereal dreams alike. Most Frenchmen like to indulge in mystic flights as a change from ribaldry and vice-versa. With B.B. they get nowhere. She corners them and forces them to be honest with themselves. They are obliged to recognize the crudity of their desire, the object of which is very precise—that body, those thighs, that bottom, those breasts. Most people are not bold enough to limit sexuality to itself and to recognize its power. Anyone who challenges their hypocrisy is accused of being cynical.

In a society with spiritualistic pretensions, B.B. appears as something deplorably materialistic and prosaic. Love has been disguised in such falsely poetic trappings that this prose seems to me healthy and restful. I approve Vadim's trying to bring eroticism down to earth. Nevertheless, there is one thing for which I blame him, and that is for having gone so far as to dehumanize it. The "human factor" has lost some of its importance in many spheres. Technical progress has relegated it to a subordinate and at times insignificant position. The implements that man uses—his dwelling, his clothes, etc.—tend toward functional rationalization. He himself is regarded by politicians, brain-trusters, publicity agents, military men, and even educators, by the entire "organization world," as an object to be manipulated. In France, there is a literary school that reflects this tendency. The "young novel"—as it calls itself—is bent on creating a universe as devoid as possible of human meanings, a universe reduced to shiftings of volumes and surfaces, of light and shade, to the play of space and time; the characters and their relationships are left in the background or even dropped entirely. This quest is of interest only to a small number of initiates. It has certainly not influenced Vadim, but he, too, reduces the world, things, and bodies to their immediate presence. In real life, and usually in good novels and films, individuals are not defined only by their sexuality. Each has a history, and his or her eroticism is involved in a certain situation. It may even be that the situation creates it. In *The African Queen*, neither Humphrey Bogart nor Katharine Hepburn, who are presented as aged and worn, arouses desire beforehand. Yet when Bogart puts his hand on Katharine's shoulder for the first time, his gesture unleashes an intense erotic emotion. The spectators identify themselves with the man, or the woman, and the two characters are transfigured by the feeling that each inspires in the other. But when the hero and heroine are young and handsome, the more the audience is involved in their history, the more it feels their charm. It must therefore take an interest in it. For example, in Ingmar

Bergman's *Sommarlek*, the idyll which is related is not set in the past arbitrarily. As a result of this device, we witness the revels of two particular adolescents. The young woman, who has moved us and aroused our interest, evokes her youthful happiness. She appears before us, at the age of sixteen, already weighed down with her entire future. The landscape about her is not a mere setting, but a medium of communication between her and us. We see it with her eyes. Through the lapping of the waters and the clearness of the nocturnal sky, we merge with her. All her emotions become ours, and emotion sweeps away shame. The "summer trifling"—caresses, embraces, words—that Bergman presents is far more "amoral" than Juliette's adventures in *And God Created Woman*. The two lovers have barely emerged from childhood. The idea of marriage or of sin does not occur to them. They embrace with hesitant eagerness and unchaste naïveté. Their daring and jubilation triumphantly defy what is called virtue. The spectator does not dream of being shocked because he experiences with them their poignant happiness. When I saw *And God Created Woman*, people laughed during scenes. They laughed because Vadim does not appeal to our complicity. He "desituates" sexuality, and the spectators become voyeurs because they are unable to project themselves on the screen. This partially justifies their uneasiness. The ravishing young woman whom they surprise, at the beginning of the film, in the act of exposing her nakedness to the sun, is no one, an anonymous body. As the film goes on, she does not succeed in becoming someone. Nonchalantly combining convention and provocation, Vadim does not deign to lure the audience into the trap of a convincing story. The characters are treated allusively; that of B.B. is loaded with too many intentions for anyone to believe in its reality. And the town of St. Tropez is merely a setting that had no intimate connection with the lives of the main characters. It has no effect on the spectator. In *Sommarlek*, the world exists; it reflects for the young lovers their confusion, their anxious desire, their joy. An innocent outing in a boat is as erotically meaningful as the passionate night preceding it and the one to follow. In Vadim's film, the world is absent. Against a background of fake colors he flashes a number of "high spots" in which all the sensuality of the film is concentrated: a strip-tease, passionate lovemaking, a mambo sequence. This discontinuity heightens the aggressive character of B.B.'s femininity. The audience is not carried away once and for all into an imaginary universe. It witnesses, without much conviction, an adventure which does not excite it and which is broken up by "numbers" in which everything is so contrived as to keep it on tenterhooks. It protects itself by snickering. A critic has written that B.B.'s sexuality was too "cerebral" to move a Latin audience. This amounts to making B.B. responsible for Vadim's style, an analytical and consequently abstract style that, as I have said, puts the spectator in the position of a voyeur. The consenting voyeur who feeds on "blue movies" and "peep shows," seeks gratifications other than the visual. The spectator who is a voyeur in spite of himself reacts with annoyance, for it is no fun to witness a hot performance cold-bloodedly. When B.B. dances her famous mambo, no one believes in Juliette. It is B.B. who is exhibiting herself. She is as alone on the screen as the strip-tease artist is alone on the stage. She offers herself directly to each spectator. But the offer is deceptive, for as the spectators watch her, they are fully aware that this beautiful young woman is famous, rich, adulated and completely inaccessible. It is not surprising that they take her for a slut and that they take revenge on her by running her down.

But reproaches of this kind cannot be leveled against *Love Is My Profession*, the film in which B.B. has displayed the most talent. Autant-Lara's direction, Pierre Bost's and Aurenche's scenario and dialogue and Gabin's performance all combine to grip the spectator. In this context, B.B. gives her most convincing performance. But her moral reputation is none the better for it. The film has aroused furious protests; actually it attacks the social order much more bitingly than any of her early ones. The "amoralism" of Yvette, the heroine, is radical. She prostitutes herself with indifference, organizes a holdup and has no hesitation about striking an old man. She proposes to a great lawyer a deal that threatens to dishonor him. She gives herself to him without love. Then she falls in love with him, deceives him and artlessly keeps him informed of her infidelities. She confesses to him that she has had several abortions. However, although the scenario indicates for a moment the possibility of a conversion, she is not presented as being unconscious of the nature of her behavior and capable of being won over to Good, as defined by respectable folk. Truth is on her side. Never does she fake her feelings. She never compromises with what seems to her to be obviously true. Her genuineness is so contagious that she wins over her lover, the old unethical lawyer. Yvette awakens whatever sincerity and dynamism still remain in him. The authors of this film took over the character created by Vadim, but they charged it with a much more subversive meaning: purity is not possible in our corrupt society except for those who have rejected it or who deliberately cut themselves off from it.

But this character is now in the process of evolving. B.B. has probably been convinced that in France nonconformity is on the way out. Vadim is accused of having distorted her image—which is certainly not untrue. People who know B.B. speak of her amiable disposition, her kindness and her youthful freshness. She is neither silly nor scatterbrained, and her naturalness is not an act. It is nevertheless striking that recent articles which pretend to reveal the "real B.B.," "B.B. seen through the keyhole," "the truth about B.B.," mention only her edifying traits of character. Brigitte, we are told again and again, is just a simple girl. She loves animals and adores her mother. She is devoted to her friends, she suffers from the hostility she arouses, she repents of her caprices, she means to mend her ways. There are excuses for her lapses: fame and fortune came too suddenly, they turned her head, but she is coming to her senses. In short, we are witnessing a veritable rehabilitation, which in recent weeks has gone very far. Definitive redemption, for a star, comes with marriage and motherhood.

Brigitte speaks only faintly about getting married. On the other hand, she often declares enthusiastically that she adores the country and dreams of taking up farming. In France, love of cows is regarded as a token of high morality. Gabin is sure of winning the public's sympathy when he declares that "a cow is more substantial than glory." Stars are photographed as much as possible in the act of feeding their chickens or digging in their gardens. This passion for the soil is appropriate to the reasonable bourgeoise that, as we are assured, Brigitte is bent on becoming. She has always known the price of things and has always gone over her cook's accounts. She follows the stock market closely and gives her broker well-informed instructions. During an official luncheon, she is said to have dazzled the director of the Bank of France with her knowledge. To know how to place one's money is a supreme virtue in the eyes of the French bourgeoisie. A particularly imaginative journalist has gone so far as to inform his readers that Brigitte has such a passion for the absolute that she may enter the path of mysticism. Wife and mother, farmerette, businesswoman, Carmelite nun, B.B. has a choice of any one of these exemplary futures. But one thing is certain: on the screen she is already beginning to convert. In her next movie, *Babette Goes to War*, she will play a heroine of the Resistance. Her charming body will be hidden from us by a uniform and sober attire. "I want everyone under sixteen to be able to come and see me," she has been made to say. The film will end with a military parade in which Babette acclaims General de Gaulle.

Is the metamorphosis definitive? If so, there will still be a number of people who will be sorry. Exactly who? A lot of young people belong to the old guard, and there are older ones who prefer truth to tradition. It would be simple-minded to think that there is a conflict of two generations regarding B.B. The conflict that does exist is between those who want mores to be fixed once and for all and those who demand that they evolve. To say that "B.B. embodies the immorality of an age" means that the character she has created challenges certain taboos accepted by the preceding age, particularly those which denied women sexual autonomy. In France, there is still a great deal of emphasis, officially, on women's dependence upon men. The Americans, who are actually far from having achieved sexual equality in all spheres, but who grant it theoretically, have seen nothing scandalous in the emancipation symbolized by B.B. But it is, more than anything else, her frankness that disturbs most of the public and that delights the Americans. "I want there to be no hypocrisy, no nonsense about love," B.B. once said. The debunking of love and eroticism is an undertaking that has wider implications than one might think. As soon as a single myth is touched, all myths are in danger. A sincere gaze, however limited its range, is a fire that may spread and reduce to ashes all the shoddy disguises that camouflage reality. Children are forever asking why, why not. They are told to be silent. Brigitte's eyes, her smile, her presence, impel one to ask oneself why, why not? Are they going to hush up the questions she raised without a word? Will she, too, agree to talk lying twaddle? Perhaps the hatred she has aroused will calm down, but she will no longer represent anything for anyone. I hope that she will not resign herself to insignificance in order to gain popularity. I hope she will mature, but not change.

—AUGUST 1959

# Mrs. Kennedy at the Moment

GLORIA STEINEM

After a privileged childhood; a reign as Debutante of the Year; an education at Vassar, the Sorbonne, and George Washington University; a brief career as an inquiring photographer; a long courtship with a man twelve years her senior who she feared "couldn't be less interested in me"; marriage to that same ambitious young Senator; his several illnesses and near death; his campaign for the Vice-Presidency; the bearing of four children and the death of two; four years as the wife of a Presidential hopeful; two years and ten months as the Thirty-first First Lady of the United States; the witnessing of her husband's murder, and a full year of the rituals and restrictions of mourning, Jacqueline Kennedy, at thirty-five, must decide what to do with her life.

If Jack Kennedy had lived, the problem of how to spend the post–White House years (a problem he rarely discussed) would have been left to him, but his wife's solution was simple. "I'll just retire to Boston," she said, "and try to convince John Jr. that his father was once the President."

Her own special charisma plus the continuing political ambitions of the Kennedy family might have kept her from disappearing as quickly as a Mamie Eisenhower or Bess Truman (Robert Frost predicted after the inauguration that Kennedy would be one of the few Presidents in history who could never be thought of without also thinking of his wife), but there was nothing to indicate she would follow the Eleanor Roosevelt tradition either. Mrs. Kennedy's influence was that of a great beauty, a hostess, and a woman of taste, but she retained a certain boarding-school air ("She's the very best of that sheltered group," said a friend, "but she's still of the group") that made it difficult to take her seriously. No one was surprised when she confided breathily to a reporter: "Housekeeping is a joy to me, I feel this is what I was made for. When it all runs smoothly . . . when the food is good . . . the flowers look fresh . . . I have such satisfaction." Or when she sat, bored and unhappy, leafing through a copy of *Vogue* while her husband campaigned. Or when, in the White House, pregnancy kept her from attending a breakfast given in her honor by Congressional wives, but not from going to New York that evening to see the ballet. Or when she explained at a press conference, "I really do not think of myself as the First Lady, but of Jack as President."

She seemed to be a lovely, well-bred girl who painted a little and wrote a little; whose early heroes—Diaghilev, Oscar Wilde and Baudelaire—valued style at least as much as content; who, in the first winter she was married, took a course in American history to please her husband, but who much preferred eighteenth-century France ("American history is for men," she said); who, while First Lady, vacationed with some of Europe's less-loved capitalists; whose taste was good enough to bring a rare distinction to the White House, but no more eclectic than polite society would allow; who was, in short, the most worthwhile kind of ornament.

Sometimes, being apolitical was an asset. After a few half-hearted denouncements for her lack of involvement in women's peace groups, even the Soviets left her alone. White House correspondent Marianne Means described the galvanic effect she had on anti-American Venezuelan farmers "by appearing like a vision in a lime sheath and greeting them with a warm, simple speech in Spanish." The President was proud of "her concentration on giving historical meaning to the White House furnishings," and a little surprised that she managed the whole thing so well: "Mrs. Kennedy displayed more executive ability," he told a reporter, "than I imagined she had." (And she was working hard. Her mother, Mrs. Hugh Auchincloss, remembered a younger Jackie who wasn't interested in picking out so much as a chair for her room.) Pope John, who had been coached by his secretary to address her as "Madame," opened his arms and said, "Jacqueline!" when he saw her; and Ludwig Bemelmans christened her "Cleopatra of the Potomac" after General de Gaulle put his glasses on to look at her during a state dinner, "and he is so vain that he doesn't know who is in front of him until his aide tells him." She held about twelve formal receptions a year more than Mrs. Eisenhower, entertained about twice as many state visitors, and got Pablo Casals to play in the White House in spite of our aid to Franco's Spain. "There hasn't been such a born giver of feasts in the White House," wrote Katherine Anne Porter, "since Dolley Madison."

But even when her nonpolitical accomplishments turned to pure political gold, she was still regarded as an ornament, a *salonnière* at heart.

Until the assassination.

From the moment she appeared in the bloodstained clothes she refused to change, she became a symbol of high tragedy and courage. "I'd always thought," said one rather cynical lady of the Washington press corps, "that there was nothing Mrs. Kennedy did that I couldn't have done better. I was wrong. I couldn't have gone through that funeral. For the first time, I find myself writing words like 'heroine' with a straight face."

The ceremonies ended, and she moved out of the White House and into retirement, but even her friends looked at her differently. "She's not," said one, "the brittle flower we all thought she was." ("It's just possible," said a journalist who had always scoffed at the value of good schools and "good" families, "that this country actually bred her. There's hope for us all.") Her house was surrounded by patient crowds who waited hours to catch a glimpse of her and then looked away when she appeared, as if ashamed to be caught intruding. "They just waited and waited," recalled a neighbor. "It was as if they were waiting for her to tell them what to do." More than Robert Kennedy or any other member of the family, the odd thaumaturgy of the Kennedy Administration seemed to have passed to her. "When the Kennedys lived here," said a White House guard, "nobody walked by without looking—they couldn't resist it, like people going by a mirror. It wasn't like that with the Trumans or the Eisenhowers, and it isn't with the Johnsons. Now, it's her house in Georgetown that they look at."

The thought of all that power going to waste was more than politicians could bear. Her year of mourning included wearing black and canceling all public appearances and official functions, but within a month after the assassination Mrs. Kennedy's future was being discussed nearly as much as President Kennedy's past. Dean Rusk suggested that she become a touring Goodwill Ambassador, and a Michigan lady legislator passionately advocated her appointment as Ambassador to France, though the "biggest problem might be that . . . other nations might want someone of the same caliber." Clare Boothe Luce, with the questionable sincerity of a Goldwater Republican advising a Democrat, wrote an article proposing that Mrs. Kennedy rise to the podium at the Democratic Convention, make a dramatic plea, and force the delegates to give Robert Kennedy the Vice-Presidency. A politician from Boston suggested that Mrs. Kennedy be Vice-President herself. Civil-rights leaders spoke of her becoming a kind of good-looking Eleanor Roosevelt who would lead Negro children into school, and give fireside, mother-to-mother talks on integration; and a few liberals daydreamed aloud, without much hope, that her marriage to Adlai Stevenson might make him a candidate again. Politicians who feared the power of her endorsement advised that she retire, as widows of other Presidents have done, or stick to culture, or, at the most, run an international salon. Even those who thought her power was more moral than political had ambitious plans: an international newspaper column, a weekly show on Telstar, a campaign to beautify America, a foundation to aid young artists, an appointment as head of UNESCO.

In a pre-assassination article comparing the role of Mrs. Kennedy, then in the White House, to that of Mrs. Roosevelt, sociologist Margaret Mead wrote: "American society accords far greater leeway to widows than to wives—even permitting them to carry on activities initiated by their husbands, in whose shadows they were supposed to live quietly as long as their menfolk were on stage." The same Mrs. Kennedy who had been dismissed as an ornament was being urged to be a leader.

"This November twenty-second, when her retirement is over," said a State Department official, "Jackie could become, if she wanted to, the most powerful woman in the world."

In contrast to the attention lavished on her, the life Mrs. Kennedy was living in retirement seemed to be very simple, or at least very private. Newspapers, desperate for news of her, ran front-page photographs of her walking the dog, taking her daughter to school, or her son to his play group. Books and one-shot magazines on her life sold by the millions—*Jacqueline Kennedy: From Inauguration to Arlington*, and *Jacqueline Kennedy—Woman of Valor (Her Dreams As A Girl, Her Prayers As A Woman, Her Fears As A Mother)*—and a nationwide poll showed that she was the most admired woman in the world. On the suspicion that she might have been pregnant when the President died, at least one magazine delayed a special issue for months, and gave up only after she was photographed in ski clothes in late March. *Time*, *Life*, and *Newsweek* wrote all they could find out about her daily routine which, minus the adjectives and padding, boiled down to the fact that she saw the children in the morning, answered correspondence or worked on plans for the Kennedy Library, played with the children in the afternoon, and sometimes had dinner with friends. The cover of a television semiannual promised "Jacqueline Kennedy: Her Future in TV" (the article said she didn't want one), and a movie magazine headlined "The Men Who Love Jackie Kennedy" (they turned out to be Lyndon Johnson, Dean Rusk, and others who had paid her sympathy calls). When she took John Jr. to a horse show where he was to ride his pony in the lead-line class, well-bred society ladies crowded around in an effort to hear what she was saying to her son. One finally managed it and reported back. What Mrs. Kennedy said was, "Keep your heels down."

Reporters were notified of what her press secretary, Pamela Turnure, called "milestone occasions"—visits to the President's grave with foreign dignitaries, an occasional appearance for the Kennedy Library, her appointment by President Johnson to the White House Preservation Committee—but the rest of her life was, as Miss Turnure said, "pretty insulated." She was surrounded by her protectors: all the members of the Kennedy family plus such old friends as artist William Walton, British Ambassador Sir David Ormsby-Gore and his wife, Mr. and Mrs. Ben Bradlee, Secretary of the Treasury Douglas Dillon and his wife, Franklin Roosevelt, Jr., Mr. and Mrs. Charles Bartlett, Secretary of Defense and Mrs. Robert McNamara, Michael Forrestal, and others.

"We all invited her to small dinners," explained one of that group, "but no matter which one of us gave it, the guest list was always pretty much the same—all friends from the old days—and the conversation always ended in reminiscing."

In the beginning, visitors noticed that her only photograph of the President was one taken while he watched a ceremony on the White House lawn shortly before he died. It showed him from the back. But, by midwinter, she was able to go through her husband's mementos to select "things I hope will show how he really was" for a touring exhibit, and to watch *The Making of a President*, a private screening of a television documentary of the 1960 campaign. (A witness said she looked teary, but "When the film showed Kennedy making wisecracks, she laughed. When he made serious points, she nodded in agreement.")

Still the small dinners continued. ("I never liked them too much before," she said frankly, "and I like them even less now.") Those close to her who felt she should be distracted as well as protected—especially her sister and almost full-time companion, Lee Radziwill—invited outsiders to entertain her, but the new guests were often so fearful of saying the wrong thing that they hung back and said nothing at all. A man described as a "young embassy type" spent an evening as her partner, and found himself reduced to asking politely if she had ever seen a bullfight. ("You just can't go through all that again," observed a guest. "It was like being right back at college.") A New York journalist who sat next to her at dinner found her starved for information. "She wanted to know if Richard Burton's *Hamlet* was good," he said, "and what Shepheard's was like, and which of several current books were worth reading and wouldn't make her sad."

By way of distraction, Mrs. Radziwill invited movie producer George Englund to stop in for a drink and some discussion of a Kennedy Foundation Dinner, on which he was an adviser. For further distraction, Mr. Englund brought along one of his actors, Marlon Brando. The three decided to go out for dinner, and asked Mrs. Kennedy to come along. ("It was very simple and spur-of-the-moment," explained Pamela Turnure. "They just didn't want to leave her there alone.") They chose what was later described by the press as "an Embassy Row Restaurant," The Jockey Club, because it was the only one in which Mrs. Kennedy, during her three years in the White House, had been able to have a private, reporterless meal. (She had lunched there with John Kenneth Galbraith, then Ambassador to India, at the President's suggestion.) But this time it was not so private. Newspaper reporters were everywhere, Brando inquired about backstairs escape routes, and the restaurant manager offered to loan them his car, but it was too late. The story—down to the fact that Brando "smiled slightly as he lit cigarettes"—was carried by newspapers here and abroad.

The fact that she had chosen to make her first social appearance since the assassination with Mr. Brando (which was pretty much the way the no-explanation newspaper report made it appear) lifted the lid on other criticisms. And among those who believed that John F. Kennedy had not yet proven himself as a President, or that the Kennedy family was using the country's grief to continue its power, or that its power was not being used to advance the right causes, or that Mrs. Kennedy should have invited them to one of those small dinners, there had been a kind of underground current of criticism for some time.

That both Kennedy and Lincoln had been assassinated, for instance, was regarded as too small a basis for their identification; and some critics felt there was a clear and faintly sinister effort to identify them. (On her return from Dallas with her husband's body, Mrs. Kennedy had asked Chief-of-Protocol Angier Biddle Duke to find out how Lincoln had been buried, and the precedents he discovered during an all-night investigation were used as guideposts for the Kennedy funeral. Later, she arranged to have a Kennedy inscription added to that in the Lincoln Bedroom of the White House.) There was some resentment of the Eternal Flame she requested for his grave. When schools, bridges, airports, Cape Canaveral, a fifty-cent piece, and the National Cultural Center took on the Kennedy name, resentment grew. Fund raising for the Kennedy Library, the Telstar program celebrating what would have been Kennedy's forty-seventh birthday, the touring exhibit of Kennedy memorabilia, and the designation of his Brookline birthplace as a National Historical Landmark were all greeted as new proofs of excess.

One Washington newspaperman insisted that Kennedy himself—like the Roman Emperor who said on his deathbed, "I fear they will make a god of me"—would not have approved.

Not all the criticism was directed at Mrs. Kennedy. Some felt that the political ambitions of the Kennedy clan made them more her exploiters than her protectors; and others were apprehensive that the family's continuing devotion, however well-meaning, would bolster the group that Washington columnist Mary McGrory had dubbed "the Kennedy irreconcilables," and make the new Administration's work more difficult. Robert Kennedy had tried to slow down the epidemic of renaming, and his sister-in-law had said in her first public statement that it was time people paid attention to the new President and the new First Lady, but, to some, those efforts seemed insincere or not enough.

Some complaints were more picayune. When, on January fourteenth, Mrs. Kennedy made her first television appearance to thank the thousands who had sent messages of sympathy, it coincided with Mrs. Johnson's first White House dinner. As a result, newspapers were full of Mrs. Kennedy and printed little about the dinner. Ladies of the Washington press corps grumbled about Mrs. Kennedy's thoughtlessness, but no one could determine who had planned what first.

President Kennedy was thin-skinned to political criticism but not to personal barbs. (A writer for a national magazine recalled his reaction to a rumor, printed by Dorothy Kilgallen, that Jackie was not really pregnant during the 1960 campaign but was being kept under wraps for political reasons. "He just laughed about it," said the writer, "and added a few amusing comments of his own about what one could expect from that quarter.") For Mrs. Kennedy, the areas of sensitivity seemed to be reversed. She was disturbed by the incident of the Brando dinner and took time to explain to friends how it happened, but she seemed perfectly confident of the ways in which the President's memory would be served best. ("She's less upset by those criticisms than her staff is," said Pamela Turnure. "Once she decides something is right, she just does it.") For a woman whose combativeness, while First Lady, was usually limited to writing letters to *Women's Wear Daily* protesting the hard time given her by that trade paper about where and how she bought her clothes, Mrs. Kennedy was remarkably tough-minded in the face of charges that she was overestimating her husband's historical influence. "He changed our world," she said firmly, "and I hope people will remember him and miss him all their lives."

"She's not political," explained a former Kennedy adviser, "but she is immensely loyal. She didn't like campaigning or being a political wife, but she did it because it mattered to Jack. If he hadn't become President, it would have taken him a while to recover; the whole force of his tremendous energy was concentrated on that goal. If Jackie hadn't become First Lady, she would have smiled gently and said, 'All right. What do we do now?'"

Her loyalty was transferred to her protectors, especially Robert Kennedy. (He is, as she explained in a now-famous quote, "the one I would put my hand in the fire for.") As a nondriver can relax with someone else at the wheel, Mrs. Kennedy seemed able to act on the political counsel of her protectors and not worry about it.

Her controversial "endorsement" of former Press Secretary Pierre Salinger, then running in California's Democratic State primary, was given at Salinger's request, but only with Robert Kennedy's permission. There had been a suggestion that she do more than make a statement: under the guise of spending a few days at Elizabeth Arden's "Maine Chance" beauty farm in Arizona, she was to make a personal appearance in the campaign. ("There was a point there," said one of his supporters, "when Pierre was really worried that he wouldn't make it.") The trip was turned down on the grounds that the public appearance would be inappropriate. ("Can you see Jackie," said an amused friend, "at Maine Chance?") Instead, a telephone interview was granted to California newspaperman Robert Thompson, and the result for Salinger was a helpful statement that "President Kennedy valued his advice and counsel on all major matters." Reportedly, Robert Kennedy approved her giving that support only after it was apparent that Salinger was, in effect, running as a Kennedy. (His slogan was, "Let the man who spoke for two Presidents speak for you," and his staff sent out 4,000,000 postcards bearing a photograph of President Kennedy, the words, "In His Tradition," and a sample ballot with an "X" after Salinger's name.) But getting her to do it seemed to take very little persuading. "She feels it's natural," explained a writer friend of the Kennedys, "to serve her husband's memory by helping his men, the men who will carry on his work. I'm sure she'll keep right on doing it, but of course only if Bobby says so."

Shortly before moving to New York, Mrs. Kennedy apologized for not allowing a picture magazine to do a story on her children. She was sorry to be difficult, she said, but she really hoped her children could grow into their teens without publicity. The editor pointed out that a photograph of Caroline and John Jr. with Robert Kennedy and his children had recently appeared on the cover of *Life*. "Oh," she said, and smiled, "but that was for Bobby." In their temperament and background, Mrs. Kennedy and her brother-in-law have very little in common. (A recent guest at a Kennedy family dinner noted that they had nothing to talk about. "They share a common loss and a basic kind of guts," he said, "and that's about it.") But Robert Kennedy is head of the family now, and Mrs. Kennedy—who instructs her children that "Kennedys don't cry"—seems determined to be loyal.

Her sister, Lee Radziwill, three and a half years younger, often serves as a lightening rod for social criticism of Mrs. Kennedy in much the same way that Robert Kennedy, on political issues, often did for his brother. Any association with so-called frivolous social types (i.e., The Best-Dressed List, The Jet Set, Marlon Brando or Europeans who don't work) as opposed to worthwhile friends who befit a First Lady (i.e., André Malraux, John Steinbeck, Members of the Cabinet, and Americans who work) has been blamed, traditionally, on Mrs. Radziwill. As a doyenne of Paris fashion, a sometime expatriate, and the once-divorced wife of a Polish prince, she is generally regarded as the representative of café society in the woodpile.

"Lee is what Jackie would have been if she hadn't married a Kennedy," explained one intimate, "a charming, witty, intelligent woman who, as the daughter of a rich stockbroker, never acquired much experience of real life or much social conscience." Another theory is that the existing difference between the sisters was only dramatized by their choice of husbands, that Mrs. Kennedy always had been more frank and serious-minded. But they are loyal to each other. (After their joint trip to India in 1963, Mrs. Kennedy said her sister had been "marvelous. . . . I was so proud of her—and we would always have such fun laughing about little things when the day was over. Nothing could ever come between us.") "They've been through a lot together; their parents' divorce, their mother's remarriage and all that," said an old friend. "When the chips are down, it's still the Bouvier girls against the world."

It was partly due to her sister's urging that Mrs. Kennedy decided to leave the Georgetown house with the perpetual crowds outside. She spent more and more weekends in New York, and the press tried vainly to trace her movements. ("When something is published about one of them," explained an anonymous friend, "it's a game with the Kennedys to figure out who told.") She was seen inspecting a cooperative apartment on Fifth Avenue, having lunch with novelist Irwin Shaw, talking to cartoonist Charles Addams at a dinner party, walking on Madison Avenue, and going to church at Bedford Hills, New York. A local newspaper reporter spent much of that Sunday phoning around to the country homes of well-to-do Manhattan families, including that of Mr. and Mrs. James Fosburgh (whom President Johnson had appointed to the White House Preservation Committee), where Mrs. Kennedy was spending the weekend. He also phoned Broadway producer Leland Hayward and his wife—with whom Mrs. Kennedy, Mr. and Mrs. Bennett Cerf, Truman Capote and others had just had lunch—but no one told. It was difficult for her to be anonymous anywhere, but clearly it might be a little less difficult for her and her children in New York.

In July, Mrs. Kennedy announced that her Georgetown house,

whose redecoration she had halted a few months before, and Wexford, her Virginia estate, were being put up for sale. The *Washington Post* regretted "losing a longtime resident and foremost tourist attraction." "She came among us like some wildly unexpected fairy queen," wrote the *Washington Star*, "and with her goes the heart of everyone who had lived in this place when she did." She was breaking her initial resolve to "live in the places I lived with Jack . . . Georgetown, and with the Kennedys at the Cape," and New York rejoiced.

"Of course, the social echelons are excited," said the society press agent Mrs. Stephen Van Rensselaer Strong. "Her presence is a signal honor and will have primary salient impact; she would make any party." "She'll dress up New York," said a fashion writer. "People will go more formally to the good restaurants and theatres because she might be there. It will be chic to be cultural." A spokesman for the Gray Line New York Tours promised that buses would not go off their routes to pass her apartment, "but I see no reason why, if it's on the route, our guides—we call them lecturers—shouldn't point it out." A rumor that east-side bookmakers were taking bets on Mrs. Kennedy's choice for a school for her daughter was squelched by the news that it was a sure thing: "She's enrolled in the second grade at the Convent of The Sacred Heart on Ninety-first Street," said an alumna; "just think how many tickets we can sell for our benefit next year!" With the exception of a few dissenters (a querulous writer in the "Voice of the People" column of the *Daily News* wanted to know "what part of . . . Harlem she will live in as a symbol of her husband's civil-rights bill"), New Yorkers were pleased to receive her, if for rather selfish reasons. But Mayor Wagner was optimistic. "We will give her every opportunity," he said stoutly, "to have as much privacy as she wants."

In anticipation of her emergence into public life in November, some large charity events have already been postponed. (The December benefit performance, in Washington, of *My Fair Lady* was rescheduled in the hope that she could come. It is for the Kennedy Center for the Performing Arts: Mrs. Kennedy is one of the patrons.) Her social secretary, Nancy Tuckerman, has so many requests for Mrs. Kennedy to be sponsor or honorary chairman of charity-social events that she can't list them all. New York hostesses who are not optimistic enough to think that she will come to their parties ("The competition," said one, "is going to be absolutely cutthroat") are trying to spot in advance the functions she might attend. (Any Lincoln Center benefit, any premiere sponsored by the Kennedy Foundation for Retarded Children, the Polish Ball, the National Horse Show, and the Convent of The Sacred Heart's alumnae benefit are the current favorites.)

"I hope," remarked *Glamour* editor Kathleen Casey, "that she has some good advisers and serious friends, because she's going to be set upon by café society and social climbers who will try to attach themselves to her just as they did to the Windsors."

In fact, Mrs. Kennedy has been surrounded by friends, serious and otherwise—by exploiters, distractors who vie to amuse her, and protectors who insulate her from the world—for much of her life, but she is, as William Walton said, "a strong dame." She has survived. "Jackie has always kept her own identity," said Robert Kennedy admiringly, "and been different."

Married to a strong-willed man twelve years her senior, plunged into the Kennedy clan and the role of Senator's wife at twenty-four and the White House at thirty-one, Mrs. Kennedy was often in danger of being submerged. ("I feel," she said after her husband's election, "as though I have just become a piece of public property.") She was so uncertain of being able to remain "a private person" that she rarely cooperated with a press who, for the most part, adored her (she signed a photograph to Pierre Salinger, "from the greatest cross he has to bear"), and once disguised herself in a nurse's uniform and a wig in order to take her daughter out unnoticed. Some of the journalists who went along on her Indian trip had also accompanied Ethel Kennedy and Queen Elizabeth, and they complained that they had got to know "not only Ethel, but the Queen much better than Mrs. Kennedy." A writer who was a personal friend managed to get a few words with her only on the plane going home, and a photographer commented that "She barely said hello to any of us; it was hot as hell and she didn't sweat or let a hair get out of place; she didn't feel well through much of the trip but she never showed it; she was playing the great lady and total stoic."

Yet, at the end of the trip, she saw each newspaperwoman individually and presented her with a note of appreciation and a hand-painted box she had picked out herself. And on the last days NBC reporter Barbara Walters remembered that she relaxed for the first time, as if she had been let out of school: "We met the camel driver whom Lyndon Johnson had invited for a visit, and someone asked if Mrs. Kennedy would like to ride the camel. She was hesitant about it and said, 'No, but Lee would.' Her sister said something like 'Thanks a lot.' It was the first time we had seen that kind of banter between them, and it was obvious that they really liked each other's company. When Lee got off, Mrs. Kennedy got on, riding sidesaddle with her skirt up over her knees. She looked kiddish and charming and as if, finally, she was relaxed and enjoying herself."

Much of the demure, soft-voiced image she presented as she sat, hands folded and immobile through countless public functions, was evidence of the seriousness with which she took her role as First Lady. ("I'm getting good at it," she said. "I just drop this curtain in my mind. . . .") The pose concealed shyness, but it also hid a sharp wit—"It's the unexpectedness of it," said John Kenneth Galbraith, "that makes her so fascinating"—and a strong will—"I wouldn't dream of telling Jacqueline what to do," said her mother; "I never have." At her first press conference after the election, Mrs. Kennedy apologized, with a touch of whimsy, for being unable to speak "Churchillian prose," but when a reporter asked a little condescendingly if she thought she could do "a good job as First Lady," her reply was firm. "I assume," she said, "that I won't fail [him] in any way." Referring of course to her husband.

An interesting case might almost be made for the transference of some of the President's qualities. Robert Kennedy—who was always "the active one while Jack was the sick kid who read the books"—has taken to reading political theory and quoting Thoreau and Emerson. Ted Kennedy—the gay, slightly pampered one—is convalescing with a painful back injury and is said to be using the time to research a book. For Mrs. Kennedy, the change seems to be in attitude: she has acquired a new sense of history and a sense of her own place in it. ("Once, the more I read of history, the more bitter I got," she told writer Theodore H. White. "For a while I thought history was something that bitter old men wrote. But then I realized history made Jack what he was. . . .")

The change is not so great that she plans to accept any formal political responsibility: she has limited herself to work having directly to do with her husband's memory. Her children are still her first concern. ("I was reading Carlyle," she once told a reporter, "and he said you should do the duty that lies nearest you. And the thing that lies nearest me is the children.") She is no longer the dilettantish Bouvier girl, and New Yorkers who hope she will become the center of a glittering social scene are likely to be disappointed. She still has no real interest in politics or activism, but if she or her advisers feel that her role calls for her to act politically, indications are she will do it.

"Her public and private images of herself," explained a former classmate, "are not as different as they used to be. After a few years on her own—if she can survive all the problems and pressures—she just might emerge as the person who, up to now, only her friends have known."

—OCTOBER 1964

# A Clean, Well-Lighted Gym

PETE DEXTER

The first time the fighter came into the gym he went two rounds with a sweet, dumb weight lifter from New Jersey who was just learning to keep his hands up. The worst kind of mismatch.

I didn't know if it was something between them or if the fighter just had a mean streak. A few of them do. Whatever it was, the fighter went after him, turning his weight into his punches, missing some, but dropping enough right hands in so that at the end of the two rounds the whole left side of the weight lifter—without ever having been hit perfect—was blotted pink. It's an honest gym, and if what happened wasn't especially violent, it was still out of place.

I was sitting by the windows with my friend Mickey Rosati at the time, and his son, little Mickey.

The two of them are with each other all day. They work together in their garage downstairs, they run together, they box each other two or three times a week. The kid is a world-class amateur. They know each other inside out—moves and moods—and I've never heard a hard word between them. You get the feeling sometimes that they're the same person, spaced thirty years apart.

Up in the ring, the weight lifter was getting packed into the corner like one shirt too many in a hamper. "What's that about?" I said.

Mickey shook his head. "They're both from Jersey," he said. "Maybe they got on each other's nerves."

The next round was more of the same. When it was over, the weight lifter put an arm around the fighter's shoulders and patted him on the back. "Thanks," he said. You may need to have been in a corner yourself, getting hit with punches you couldn't see, to understand the gratitude you feel when it's over.

The fighter nodded, climbed out of the ring without a word, and sat down on a bench. He'd wanted to hurt him.

The weight lifter had a brother named Dennis. He was fourteen years older—closing in on forty—and two or three times a week the two of them came over the bridge from New Jersey to work out.

The gym sits on a narrow street in South Philadelphia where people park on the sidewalks and kids take sneakers away from each other, tie the laces together, and hang them from the telephone wires. Inside, it's honest and clean; at least, for a gym it's clean. We are not speaking here of Nautilus-center clean, but people have been known to hit the bucket when they spit, and when Mickey's hawk—which is another story—used the ring for a bathroom one afternoon, the spot was scoured with Lysol before anybody fought again. That might not sound like much, but in most gyms, hawk shit will petrify before anybody cleans it up.

The weight lifter liked to box when he could; Dennis didn't. He slapped at the heavy bags and shadowboxed and told stories, and once in a while he mentioned that he ought to be getting paid for his entertainment value. From the beginning Dennis was under the impression that he was entertaining.

During the month or two Dennis and his brother had been coming up, Mickey had spent some time in the ring with the brother, getting him used to the feel of soft punches, showing him how to relax.

At the start, the brother had gone home depressed. Dennis reported this while Mickey was doing sit-ups on an elevated board, his teeth biting a cold cigar. "My brother's got guys terrified of him in Jersey," Dennis said. "He can't believe somebody as old as you could do that to him. All weekend long he's messed up."

Mickey lay back on the board and closed his eyes. "Suddenly," he said, the cigar moving in his teeth, "I don't feel like doing sit-ups no more."

As a step in the mending, Dennis and his brother decided Mickey probably wasn't human, that he couldn't be hurt or tired out. They called him the Machine.

You could see how they might think that. Mickey Rosati is fifty-one years old and left-handed, and he can still fight his ass off. But he is fifty-one years old. His shoulders hurt him after he works out, he gets poison ivy just looking at the woods, and the speed he had when he won twenty-two straight fights back in the Fifties isn't there like it was. On brains and shape, he would still beat most of the four- and six-round fighters at his weight in the world, but he pays more to stay that way than anybody who isn't around him could know.

The fighter was back two weeks later. He came in with Dennis. Mickey was sitting in a chair, holding a cold cigar in his teeth, trying not to scratch his arms. He was just back from the Pocono Mountains, poison-ivyed half to death. He'd gone there for squirrels. Mickey has been hunting since he was seven years old—ever since he went after stray cats in the alleys of South Philadelphia with a baseball bat. As he gets older, though, he gets gentler, and cares less about the shooting and more about just being outside. This weekend, as a mater of fact, he'd left his gun in the cabin.

"This same path, I must've walked it a hundred times," he said. "But this time, I was just walking along, and, you know, there's apples in all those trees. Millions of them. I been through there a hundred times, and I never saw the apples."

Dennis bent over him then. "Hey, Mick, I told this guy you'd give him two or three rounds," he said.

Mickey looked at Dennis, then at the fighter, putting together what was doing. "All right," he said. Mickey will always give you the benefit of the doubt; he will always give you his time.

The fighter dressed and wrapped his hands and then got laced into a pair of black gloves. He loosened up five or ten minutes, then fit his mouthpiece over his teeth and climbed into the ring.

Mickey slipped his unwrapped hands into an old pair of pull-on gloves and got in with him. He doesn't use a mouthpiece or headgear. He seemed about as tall as the fighter, but he was giving away twenty-five pounds and twenty-five years. "Three rounds?" he said.

The fighter said, "I don't know if I'm even in shape to finish one." Mickey has been around gyms all his life and knew better than that.

The bell rang and the fighter came straight at him, throwing right hands and hooks, trying to hurt him. Little Mickey sat down a yard from the ropes and watched.

Mickey took the punches on his arms and gloves and shoulders, moving in and out, relaxed. A minute into the round, he threw a long, slow right hook at the fighter's head, which the fighter blocked, and a short left under his ribs. Which he never saw.

The punch stopped the fighter cold. For two or three seconds he couldn't breathe, he couldn't move his hands. In those seconds, Mickey could have ended it and gone back to his chair and his poison ivy, but he backed off and let him go. And when the fighter could breathe again, he began to find Mickey with some of the right hands.

The gym was quiet, except for the sounds in the ring itself. Mickey and the fighter seemed even for a round and a half, but somewhere in it the fighter got stronger. He used his elbows and shoulders; Mickey gave ground and landed some hooks to the side, but his punches didn't have much on them.

Between rounds Mickey walked in circles, breathing through his teeth, looking at the floor. I thought about being fifty-one years old, working all day pulling transmissions and engines, and then coming upstairs with bad shoulders and poison ivy and having to fight life and death with some kid who didn't even know who you were.

The third round started and the fighter, if anything, was throwing harder now. Mickey let the punches hit his arms and sides and glance off his head, moving in the direction they pushed him. One of them scraped some skin off his eyebrow.

The fighter followed him, forgetting what had happened to him in the first round, forgetting that Mickey hadn't hurt him when he was helpless. And then I heard little Mickey say, "He's got him now." I looked down at him to see how he knew that, and by the time I looked back up, Mickey was hitting the fighter with maybe a dozen clean punches in a row.

For the last minute and a half of the fight, Mickey hit him with everything he threw. When the fighter tried to come back at him, it opened him up for something else.

At the end, he had stopped fighting and was leaning against the ropes covering up. Mickey patted the fighter on the head, climbed out of the ring and worked two hard rounds on the heavy bag, jumped rope, and then put a cigar between his teeth and did sit-ups. Looking happier all the time.

I said to his son, "He shouldn't have to do that."

Little Mickey said, "Yeah, but you know my father. He likes having to do it. . . ."

I looked around the gym—a big clean room with enough windows so you could feel the street—and as nice as it was, that's what it was for. Having to do it. Not every day or every week, but if you're going to box, then once in a while it's going to happen.

And Mickey doesn't own the place by accident. Now and then you've got to let the dog out of the house to run.

Driving home from the gym that night, I told him I wouldn't have patted the fighter on the head, no matter how grateful I was that he tried to kill me.

Mickey said, "Yeah, I should have bit him." His mood was getting better and better. He looked down at his arms, though, touched his neck where the poison ivy was. "Five days," he said, "before it goes away. I lie in bed at night, thinking about scratching it or not."

"That long?"

"The doctor said they got some kind of shot, it gives you the worse case you ever got, and then you don't get it anymore. You can't take the shot when you already got poison ivy, though. You got to be cured, and then they can give it to you, and then they can cure you. Probably."

He shook his head. "Probably," he said, "there's nothing you can do about poison ivy, but stay out of the woods. What good is that?"

—MARCH 1984

# The $20 Theory of the Universe

TOM CHIARELLA

When it comes to the language of money, credit cards are nouns. Dull, concrete, limitless rules and restrictions and creepy fine print, credit cards have all the élan of aluminum foil. Personal checks—the coward's stand-in for cash—are ugly and static pronouns. But a twenty-dollar bill, now, that's a thing of beauty. Nothing static about a twenty. Used correctly, a twenty is all about movement, access, cachet. Forget the other bills. The single won't get you much more than a stiff nod and, these days, the fin is de rigueur. A tenner is a nice thought, but it's also a message that you're a Wal-Mart shopper, too cheap for the real deal. A twenty, placed in the right hand at the right moment, makes things happen. It gets you past the rope, beyond the door, into the secret files. The twenty hastens and chastens, beckons and tugs. The twenty, you see, is a verb. It's all about action.

And me, well, I'm all about action, too, because I am the original twenty-dollar millionaire. Give me a stack of twenties and I'll pass them off as well as any mogul. Maybe better. My fortune rises and falls with the double sawbuck. And because of that, I've always wanted to test myself, to establish the weight and worth of a twenty in the world. So last month I took two grand in twenties, rolled them up, and left for New York. I was going to spend three days greasing palms from gate to gate and see what it got me.

I'm not talking about *buying* here, by the way. When it comes to things with a price tag, a twenty doesn't get you much. You could open one of those stores called EVERYTHING FOR $20, and who the fuck would go in there? Who needs a bunch of art calendars and T-shirts? No one wants to *spend* a twenty. It's a fair amount of money, for one thing. And it won't get you much, for another. Not in the way of merchandise, anyway. No, you have to *give* the twenty. Pass it, release it. This is about as much Zen as I can muster: Stuff your pockets full of twenties and doors will open by themselves.

I started right away. At the airport parking lot in Indianapolis, they offered a car-interior cleaning service for thirty-five dollars. As I was waiting for the shuttle, I started bitching to one of the drivers. "I'd rather pay someone twenty bucks straight cash to get in there and spruce it up for me," I said. The driver stood up on his toes. I asked if he was interested. He'd take twenty now, he said, then talk to the guys in the shop, and they'd put my car in line for detailing so long as I'd slip them another twenty when I got back. So I passed the note and shook hands. Detailing normally costs $120. Fuckin' A. I was *making* money at this point.

When the gate agent wouldn't help me out with my request for the bulkhead seat on my little commuter plane, I set a twenty on the counter. She iced me. An airport is apparently no longer the best place to use a twenty, not since they started x-raying Chuck Taylors. "What's the issue?" she said. I wanted legroom, I told her. She shrugged and shifted me to an exit row. I told her I wanted the *front* seat, pushed the twenty forward, and she started to look pissed. "I don't want your money," she said. "But I want the seat," I said. "The front one." She said it was assigned and all I could do was ask to trade.

On the plane, I approached the woman in seat 1A and held out a twenty. She asked if I was serious. I said yes. She took it and ran to 9B like her pants were on fire.

On the next leg—Cleveland to New York—I skipped the ticket counter altogether, walked straight into first class, and announced that I'd give anyone twenty dollars for his seat. There was some laughter, some nervous ass shifting, and just when I figured no one would bite, a big guy with a beltful of pagers and cell phones took the deal. The flight attendant jumped me when I sat down, asked if money had changed hands. The guy next to me nodded, and she jabbed me with her finger. "I could have you removed from the plane for that," she said, but the flight was crowded and soon she moved on. The guy sitting next to me said he'd never seen that trick before, and he was going to try it next time he didn't get an upgrade. "The FAA would shit their pants if everyone could do that," he said. "You could auction first class away if you had enough time."

I told him that for a forty-seven-minute flight from Cleveland, twenty dollars was about market price. "If I can't get it for twenty dollars," I said, "I don't want it."

He wriggled into his seat and turned away. "Man, there's no price tag on comfort," he said.

I decided right there that this could be a kind of rule for passing the twenty: nothing with a price tag.

The flight attendant, still a little pissed, wouldn't get me my free drink once we took off. So I slipped the guy across the aisle from me twenty dollars to get me three little bottles of single malt. I drank one to flaunt it to the stewardess and pocketed the other two for later.

A twenty should not be a ticket so much as a solution. You have a problem, you need something from the back room, you don't want to wait, you whip out the twenty.

I could have stood in line at the airport cabstand for fifteen minutes like every other mook in the world, freezing my balls off, but such is not the way of the twenty-dollar millionaire. I walked straight to the front of the line and offered a woman twenty bucks for her spot. She took it with a shrug. Behind her, people crackled. "*Hey! Ho!*" they shouted. I knew exactly what that meant. It wasn't good. I needed to get in a cab soon. One of the guys flagging cabs pointed me to the back of the line. That's when I grabbed him by the elbow, pulled him close, and shook his hand, passing the next twenty. I was now down forty dollars for a twenty-dollar cab ride. He tilted his head and nodded to his partner. I peeled another twenty and they let me climb in. As we pulled away, someone in the line threw a half-empty cup of coffee against my window.

That whole event had been too public, too visible. Another lesson learned: The bigger the favor—which is to say, the more *visible* the favor—the more discreet the pass should be. A security guy elbows his way through the crowd to get you up against the stage at a concert and you slip him the twenty quietly, at belt level. Conversely, the smaller the favor, the bigger the flourish. The bellman brings you a bottle of seltzer on a rainy afternoon, you pass that twenty as if the world were watching.

I always grease Bobby H., the bellman at my hotel, and on my first night, within minutes of the pass, he suggested that I might request a room upgrade. He even gave me a room number to ask for. Another twenty at the desk and I was out of two queens, snug in my one king. The next day, we ran the same drill, and *wham*, I was in the minisuite. The twenty after that, I was in a full suite with a view of Times Square. We used a different desk guy each day. When you're passing twenties, Bobby H. told me, you have to spread the wealth. "It's a one-time trick," he said. "You don't want anyone to catch on." Somehow he managed to take a twenty each time, having caught on fully some time ago.

In my favorite midtown coffee shop, the Cafe Edison, they maintain VIP seating for a-holes like Neil Simon and August Wilson who supposedly come here to write. They keep the area roped off and generally empty, even at noon while a line stretches out the door. This has always pissed me off. So when I entered at noon one day, I folded a twenty, slipped it to the old lady at the counter, and she waved me into the VIP like she was whacking me with the back of her hand. I paid way over market for that, since the shop was only half full at the time and it was too far away for the waiter to remember to refill my coffee. Still, people left the restaurant peering at me, working hard to figure who in the world I might be.

I wanted to tell them I was the twenty-dollar millionaire. I wanted to tell them how well my twenties were serving me, even in the last few hours. With a bunch of well-placed bills and some fairly precise requests, a maid had left me forty towels neatly stacked in a single tower on my bed, a bellman had carried my laptop on his shoulder for an hour, the janitor had let me into the subbasement where I could see the subway through a large crack in the foundation, and the bartender hooked up the microphone and let me sing in the hotel bar, without accompaniment, all before lunch hour.

At 3:00 that very morning, I had called an Eighth Avenue bodega and told them I'd give them twenty dollars for a pint of milk and a *Hustler* magazine. The guy who answered the phone had a thick Arabic accent. "You are crazy," he said.

"I'm thirsty."

"Come on, mister," he said. "Come on with that."

"Seriously," I said.

"Mister fucking crazy man, we have no *Hustler*!" he continued. "What is your room number?"

Twenty minutes later, the guy was at my door with a quart of two percent and a shrink-wrapped valu-pack of three *Hustlers*. He sighed and smiled when I gave him the twenty. "It's snowing," he said, as if to explain his relief. But I understood. The twenty is an important contract and no one, on either end, wants it broken.

A twenty can't buy everything. I failed often enough with my twenties that there were times when I doubted whether they could do anything at all. I tried to get into the Guggenheim when it was closed. I pushed the docent to let me roll one ball in the Frick museum's secret bowling alley. I asked a stripper for a big wet kiss. I tried to get an ABC security guard to show me Peter Jennings's car. I attempted to jump to the head of the rotation at a karaoke place. I tried to get into the premier of *Analyze That* by passing a twenty folded in the shape of a ticket. The doorman looked at me like I was a mime.

Then I realized something else: Most people aren't willing to lose their job for twenty bucks, but if they have something they already take for granted—a place in line, a seat, a ticket to a show they've already seen—they'll jump on a twenty like a possum on a wet bag of groceries. It's a matter of opportunity. You have to find your moments.

I never developed any tag lines. I generally presented the bill and asked, "How does this help me?" Though at one point I walked into a one-hour photo place, held out a twenty, and said, "Can I now call this a twelve-minute photo shop?" I needed something better than an hour, having just finished a roll featuring photos of me at the wheel of a street cleaner (requiring one twenty and a promise not to take it out of first gear), but I couldn't get the guy to budge off of sixty minutes. As I was waiting, I asked him if he ever developed dirty pictures.

"Sometimes," he said.

"Do you keep a file?"

He shrugged.

"Does this help me?" I said, whipping out the bill, shooting for as much flourish as I could muster.

"What do you wanna see?"

"You know," I said. "I want to see the file."

He picked up the twenty with two fingers and tucked it in his pocket. "I'll show you what I've got." He pulled a manila envelope from beneath the counter and took out four snapshots. The first three were simple bare asses—in a shower, at a kitchen sink, faceup on a couch. Beneath that was an enlargement of a cat licking a woman's nipple. Pretty cool, but hardly what I expected.

"That's it?" I said.

The guy pursed his lips. "That's all I've got this week. That stuff doesn't stay around here long. The master file would cost a lot more than twenty dollars."

Master file! Damn. Clearly, I had priced myself out of the good stuff by coming forward with the twenty too fast. There is a trick to meeting the market: You can pass out twenties endlessly while people reel you in, inch by inch.

It is the sort of thing that often happens at the better restaurants and clubs, where the twenty is the common currency of exchange. That night, I went straight to the sold-out dinner show at the Carlyle Hotel, where Woody Allen was playing, and slipped the guy at the door twenty dollars for a seat at the bar. He took it, guided me to my chair, and, with the twenty long gone, informed me that there was a three-drink minimum. Worse, I was behind a pole. I told him I wanted a table. He said he'd see what he could do. (This was the line

I most often heard at good restaurants, like Balthazar, where the woman said, "I don't sell seats, but I'll see what I can do," before giving me a three-top next to Fran Tarkenton.)

As the show began, the floor guy at the Carlyle offered me a seat six feet from the bar. Another twenty. He took the money, then told me that the seat had a seventy-five-dollar cover charge. Fuck me. Then, since the rest of the table was open, he seated a beautiful twenty-two-year-old woman in a hard-on quality red dress across from me. Good twenty, I thought, good, good twenty. Then her Italian boyfriend joined us. "We were right next to the drums," she told me. "It was very uncomfortable. I had to give him twenty dollars just to get this crappy seat." The only other thing I heard her say in English that night was to her boyfriend, during a lull: "You don't know how bad I want you right now." And me with my little whiskey sour.

Finally, with about thirty minutes left in the show, I figured out that the people who really want the twenty would be the people sitting at the other tables. People getting dunned just like me. As there was an open seat at the stage-front table, I offered a woman sitting there twenty bucks. She said sure. So there I was, three feet from the stage, having dropped twenties all the way from the door, with Woody Allen launching spit all over me through his clarinet. Worst of all, when the check came, there was a space to tip the captain.

One afternoon, Bobby the bellman alerted me to a corporate meeting at the dinner club next door. "It's all day," he said. "They have very nice buffets."

I decided to scam a lunch. I walked boldly to the door, leaned toward the doorman—you come face-to-face with a lot of young, large black men when you are passing twenties in New York City—and said, "Is this the lunch?" He raised his eyebrows. "I forgot my letter," I said, holding the twenty pressed flat against the palm of my hand and reaching for the shake. He looked confused; I tried to look equally puzzled and said, "Just give me five minutes." He took my hand and nodded me in. I went in and some wag was talking from a dais to a crowd of about two hundred guys in blue shirts. About six or eight people craned their necks to look at me. I went to the buffet, fixed myself a large plate of tiger prawns. I got a beer out of a bucket of ice and sat, balancing it all in my lap. *Good* shrimp. I got another plate before I left. Every once in a while some hungry young exec would turn for a look at me, me with the shrimp legs sticking out of my mouth, me with the huge can of Foster's, and I would nod. It took me fifteen minutes to realize I was listening to a symposium on corporate ethics.

I pressed on. I bought my way into a good table at a Les Paul show with a twenty. I got an usher at NBC to hold a front-row seat for Busta Rhymes on the Carson Daly show. I got a seat at Dos Caminos, Manhattan's jumpingest Mexican restaurant, in five minutes despite the two-hour wait. I cut to the head of the line at the half-price Broadway ticket booth in Times Square. I got my shoes resoled in twenty minutes instead of two weeks. I got a little love by shoving a twenty into a homeless guy's coffee cup.

Finally, I found myself headed back to the hotel, exhausted and down to my last twenty. At the corner of Forty-seventh and Seventh, a guy handed me a flyer. "Mistress Sandra will give you your future," it read. Ten minutes later, I was sitting in Mistress Sandra's overheated apartment with her kids watching *SpongeBob* behind a little fake wall. I felt like dozing, and when I opened my eyes, Mistress Sandra was sitting in front of me. She was a short Mexican woman, mid-forties, wearing a bathrobe. "What are you interested in asking?" she said.

"What can I get for twenty bucks?" I said.

She leaned forward. "What is your real question?"

I repeated myself.

"I do palms for twenty-five dollars," she said.

"Yeah, but I only want to spend twenty dollars," I said, laying the bill on her coffee table.

She shook her head. "Palms must be read together. One palm is no good without the other. Palms cost twenty-five dollars."

The one-palm thing made sense somehow, but I was out of money.

"I can tell you many things," she said. "For instance, you will live to be ninety-seven, God bless you very much."

I was interested now. I fished around in my pocket, looking for one more bill. When I took my hand out, it was grasping two little airplane bottles of single malt. Mistress Sandra raised an eyebrow. I set them on top of my twenty.

"How does this help me?" I asked, having found my real question one more time.

—MARCH 2003

# Repeat After Me

DAVID SEDARIS

Although we'd discussed my upcoming visit to Winston-Salem, my sister and I didn't make exact arrangements until the eve of my arrival, when I phoned from a hotel in Salt Lake City.

"I'll be at work when you arrive," she said, "so I'm thinking I'll just leave the key under the hour ott near the ack toor."

"The what?"

"Hour ott."

I thought she had something in her mouth until I realized she was speaking in code.

"What are you, on a speakerphone at a methadone clinic? Why can't you just tell me where you'll put the goddamned house key?"

Her voice dropped to a whisper. "I just don't know that I trust these things."

"Are you on a cell phone?"

"Of course not," she said. "This is just a regular cordless, but still, you have to be careful."

When I suggested that, actually, she *didn't* have to be careful, Lisa resumed her normal tone of voice, saying, "Really? But I heard . . ."

My sister's the type that religiously watches the fear segments of her local Eyewitness News broadcasts, retaining nothing but the headlines. She remembers that applesauce can kill you but forgets that in order to die, you have to inject it directly into your bloodstream. Announcements that cell-phone conversations may be picked up by strangers mix with the reported rise of both home burglaries and brain tumors, meaning that as far as she's concerned, all telecommunication is potentially life threatening. If she didn't watch it on the news, she read it in *Consumer Reports* or heard it thirdhand from a friend of a friend of a friend whose ear caught fire while dialing her answering machine. Everything is dangerous all of the time, and if it's not yet been pulled off the shelves, then it's certainly under investigation—so there.

"Okay," I said. "But can you tell me *which* hour ott? The last time I was there, you had quite a few of them."

"It's ed," she told me. "Well . . . eddish."

I arrived at Lisa's house late the following afternoon, found the key under the flowerpot, and let myself in through the back door. A lengthy note on the coffee table explained how I might go about operating everything from the television to the waffle iron, each carefully detailed procedure ending with the line, "Remember to turn off and unplug after use." At the bottom of page three, a postscript informed me that if the appliance in question had no plug—the dishwasher, for instance—I should make sure it had completed its cycle and was cool to the touch before leaving the room. The note reflected a growing hysteria, its subtext shrieking, *Oh, my God, he's going to be alone in my house for close to an hour!* She left her work number, her husband's work number, and the number of the next-door neighbor, adding that she didn't know the woman very well so I probably shouldn't bother her unless it was an emergency. "P.P.S. She's a Baptist, so don't tell her you're gay."

The last time I was alone at my sister's place, she was living in a white-brick apartment complex occupied by widows and single, middle-aged working women. This was in the late seventies, when we were supposed to be living in dorms. College hadn't quite worked out the way she'd expected, and after two years in Virginia she'd returned to Raleigh and taken a job at a wineshop. It was a normal enough life for a twenty-one-year-old, but being a dropout was not what she had planned for herself. Worse than that, it had not been planned *for* her. As children, we'd been assigned certain roles—leader, bum, troublemaker, slut—titles that effectively told us who we were. Since Lisa was the oldest, smartest, and bossiest, it was assumed that she would shoot to the top of her field, earning a master's degree in manipulation and eventually taking over a medium-sized country. We'd always known her as an authority figure, and while we took a certain joy in watching her fall, it was disorienting to see her with so little confidence. Suddenly she was relying on other people's opinions, following their advice and withering at the slightest criticism.

"Do you really think so? Really?" She was putty.

My sister needed patience and understanding, but more often than not I found myself wanting to shake her. If the oldest wasn't who she was supposed to be, then what did it mean for the rest of us?

Lisa had been marked Most Likely to Succeed, so it confused her to be ringing up gallon jugs of hearty burgundy. I had been branded Lazy and Irresponsible, so it felt right when I, too, dropped out of college and wound up back in Raleigh. After being thrown out of my parents' house, I went to live with Lisa in her white-brick complex. It was a small studio apartment—the adult version of her childhood bedroom—and when I eventually left her with a broken stereo and an unpaid eighty-dollar phone bill, the general consensus was, "Well, what did you expect?"

I might reinvent myself to strangers, but to this day, as far as my family is concerned, I'm still the one most likely to set your house on fire. While I accepted my lowered expectations, Lisa fought hard to regain her former title. The wineshop was just a temporary setback, and she left shortly after becoming manager. Photography interested her, so she taught herself to use a camera, ultimately landing a job in the photo department of a large international drug company, where she took pictures of germs, viruses, and people reacting to germs and viruses. On weekends, for extra money, she photographed weddings, which really wasn't that much of a stretch. Then she got married herself and quit the drug company in order to earn an English degree. When told there was very little call for thirty-page essays on Jane Austen, she got a real estate license. When told the housing market was down, she returned to school to study plants. Her husband, Bob, got a job in Winston-Salem, so they moved, buying a new three-story house in a quiet suburban neighborhood.

My sister's home didn't really lend itself to snooping, so I spent my hour in the kitchen, making small talk with Henry. It was the same conversation we'd had the last time I saw him, yet still I found it fascinating. He asked how I was doing. I said I was all right, and then, as if something might have drastically changed within the last few seconds, he asked again.

Of all the elements of my sister's adult life—the house, the husband, the sudden interest in plants—the most unsettling is Henry. Technically he's a blue-fronted Amazon, but to the layman, he's just a big parrot, the type you might see on the shoulder of a pirate.

"How you doing?"

The third time he asked, it sounded as if he really cared. I approached his cage with a detailed answer, and when he lunged for the bars, I screamed like a girl and ran out of the room.

"Henry likes you," my sister said a short while later. She'd just returned from her job at the plant nursery and was sitting at the table, unlacing her sneakers. "See the way he's fanning his tail? He'd *never* do that for Bob. Would you, Henry?"

Bob had returned from work a few minutes earlier and immediately headed upstairs to spend time with his own bird, a balding green-cheeked conure named José. I'd thought the two of them might enjoy an occasional conversation, but it turns out they can't stand each other. "Don't even *mention* José in front of Henry," Lisa whispered. Bob's bird squawked from the upstairs study, and the parrot responded with a series of high, piercing barks. It was a trick he'd picked up from Lisa's border collie, Chessie, and what was disturbing was that he sounded exactly like a dog. Just as, when speaking English, he sounded exactly like Lisa. It was creepy to hear my sister's voice coming from a beak, but I couldn't say it didn't please me.

"Who's hungry?" she asked.

"Who's hungry?" the voice repeated.

I raised my hand, and she offered Henry a peanut. As he took it in his claw, his belly sagging to the perch, I understood what someone might see in a parrot. Here was this strange little fatso living in my sister's kitchen, a sympathetic listener turning again and again to ask, "So, really, how are you?"

I'd asked her the same question, and she'd said, "Oh, fine, you know." She's afraid to tell me anything important, knowing I'll only turn around and write about it. In my mind, I'm like a friendly junkman, building things from the little pieces of scrap I find here and there, but my family's started to see things differently. Their personal lives are the so-called pieces of scrap I so casually pick up, and they're sick of it. Our conversations now start with the words, "You have to swear you will never repeat this." I always promise, but it's generally understood that my word is no better than Henry's.

I'd come to Winston-Salem to address the students at a local college, and also to break some news. Sometimes when you're stoned, it's fun to sit around and think of who might play you in the movie version of your life. What makes it fun is that no one is actually going to make a movie of your life. Lisa and I no longer get stoned, so it was all the harder to announce that my book had been optioned, meaning that, in fact, someone was going to make a movie of our lives—not a student, but a real director people had heard of.

"A *what?*"

I explained that he was Chinese, and she asked if the movie would be in Chinese.

"No," I said. "He lives in America. In California. He's been here since he was a baby."

"Then what does it matter if he's Chinese?"

"Well," I said, "he's got . . . you know, a *sensibility.*"

"Oh, brother," she said.

I looked to Henry for support and he growled at me.

"So now we have to be in a movie?" She picked her sneakers off the floor and tossed them into the laundry room. "Well," she said, "I can tell you right now that you're not dragging my bird into this."

The movie was to be based on our preparrot years, but the moment she put her foot down, I started wondering who we might get to play the role of Henry. "I know what you're thinking," she said, "and the answer is no."

Once, at a dinner party, I met a woman whose parrot had learned to imitate the automatic ice maker on her new refrigerator. "That's what happens when they're left alone," she'd said. This was the most disturbing bit of information I'd heard in quite a while. Here was this creature, born to mock its jungle neighbors, and it wound up doing impressions of man-made kitchen appliances. I repeated the story to Lisa, who told me that neglect had nothing to do with it. She then prepared a cappuccino, setting the stage for Henry's pitch-perfect imitation of the milk steamer. "He can do the blender, too," she said.

She opened the cage door, and as we sat down to our coffees, Henry glided down onto the table. "Who wants a kiss?" She stuck out her tongue, and he accepted the tip gingerly between his upper and lower beak. I'd never dream of doing such a thing, not because it's across-the-board disgusting, but because he would have bitten the shit out of me. While Henry might occasionally have fanned his tail in my direction, it was understood that he was loyal to only one person, which, I think, is another reason my sister is so fond of him.

"Was that a good kiss?" she asked. "Did you like that?"

I expected a yes or no answer and was disappointed when he responded with the exact same question: "Did you like that?" Yes, parrots can talk, but unfortunately they have no idea what they're actually saying. When she first got him, Henry spoke the Spanish he'd learned from his captors. Asked if he'd had a good night's sleep, he'd simply say *hola*, much like the Salvadoran women I used to clean with in New York. He goes through phases, favoring an often repeated noise or sentence, and then he moves on to something else. When our mother died, Henry learned how to cry. He and Lisa would set each other off, and the two of them would go on for hours. A few years later, in the midst of a brief academic setback, she trained him to act as her emotional cheerleader. I'd call and hear him in the background screaming, "We love you Lisa!" and "You can do it!" This was replaced, in time, with the far more practical "Where are my keys?"

• • •

After we finished our coffees, Lisa drove me to Greensboro, where I delivered my scheduled lecture. This is to say that I read stories about my family. After the reading, I answered questions about them, thinking all the while how odd it was that these strangers seemed to know so much about my brother and sisters. In order to sleep at night, I have to remove myself from the equation, pretending that the people I love voluntarily choose to expose themselves. It's a delusion much harder to maintain when a family member is actually *in* the audience.

The day after the reading, Lisa called in sick, and we spent the afternoon running errands. Winston-Salem is a city of plazas, mid-size shopping centers each built around an enormous grocery store. I was looking for cheap cartons of cigarettes, so we drove from plaza to plaza, comparing prices and talking about our sister Gretchen. A year earlier, she'd bought a pair of flesh-eating Chinese box turtles with pointed noses and spooky translucent skin. The two of them lived in an outdoor pen and were relatively happy until raccoons dug beneath the wire and chewed the front legs off the female and the rear legs off her husband. "I may have the order wrong," Lisa said, "but you get the picture."

The couple survived the attack and continued to track the live mice that constituted their diet, propelling themselves forward like a pair of half-stripped Volkswagens.

"The sad part is that it took her two weeks to notice it," Lisa said. "Two weeks!" She shook her head and drove past our exit. "I'm sorry, but I don't know how a responsible pet owner could go that long without noticing a thing like that. It's just not right."

According to Gretchen, the turtles had no memories of their former limbs, but Lisa wasn't buying it. "Oh, come on," she said. "They must at least have phantom pains. I mean, how can a living creature not mind losing its legs?" Her eyes misted, and she wiped them with the back of her hand. "My little collie gets a tick and I go crazy." Lisa's a person who once witnessed a car accident saying, "I just hope there isn't a dog in the backseat." Human suffering doesn't faze her much, but she'll cry for days over a sick-pet story.

"Did you see that movie about the Cuban guy?" she asked. "It played here for a while, but I wouldn't go. Someone told me a dog gets killed in the first fifteen minutes, so I said forget it."

I reminded her that the main character died as well, horribly, of AIDS, and she pulled into the parking lot, saying, "Well, I just hope it wasn't a real dog."

I wound up buying cigarettes at Tobacco USA, a discount store with the name of a theme park. Lisa had officially quit smoking ten years earlier and might have taken it up again were it not for Chessie, who, according to the vet, was predisposed to lung ailments. "I don't want to give her secondhand emphysema, but I sure wouldn't mind taking some of this weight off. Tell me the truth: Do I look fat to you?"

"Not at all."

She turned sideways and examined herself in the window of Tobacco USA. "You're lying."

"Well, isn't that what you want me to say?"

"Yes. But I want you to really mean it."

But I *had* meant it. It wasn't the weight I noticed so much as the clothing she wore to cover it up. The loose, baggy pants and oversized shirts falling halfway to her knees: This was the look she'd adopted a few months earlier, after she and her husband had gone to the mountains to visit Bob's parents. Lisa had been sitting beside the fire, and when she scooted her chair toward the center of the room, her father-in-law said, "What's the matter, Lisa? Getting too fat—I mean hot. Getting too hot?"

He had tried to cover his mistake, but it was too late. The word had already been seared into my sister's brain.

"Will I have to be fat in the movie?" she asked me.

"Of course not. You'll be just . . . like you are."

"Like I am according to who?" she asked. "The Chinese?"

"Well, not all of them," I said. "Just one."

Normally, if at home during a weekday, Lisa likes to read eighteenth-century novels, breaking at 1:00 to eat lunch and watch a television program called *Matlock*. By the time we finished with my errands, the day's broadcast had already ended, so we decided to go to the movies—whatever she wanted. She chose the story of a young Englishwoman struggling to remain happy while trying to lose a few extra pounds, but in the end she got her plazas confused and we arrived at the wrong theater just in time to watch *You Can Count on Me*, the Kenneth Lonergan movie in which an errant brother visits his older sister. Normally Lisa's the type who talks from one end of the show to the other. A character will spread mayonnaise onto a chicken sandwich and she'll lean over, whispering, "One time, I was doing that? And the knife fell into the toilet." Then she'll settle back in her seat and I'll spend the next ten minutes wondering why on earth someone would make a chicken sandwich in the bathroom. This movie reflected our lives so eerily that for the first time in recent memory, she was stunned into silence. There was no resemblance between us and the main characters—the brother and sister were younger and orphaned—but like us they'd stumbled to adulthood playing the worn, confining roles assigned to them as children. Every now and then one of them would break free, but for the most part they behaved not as they wanted to but as they were expected to. In brief, a guy shows up at his sister's house and stays for a few weeks until she kicks him out. She's not evil about it, but having him around forces her to think about things she'd rather not, which is essentially what family members do, at least the family members my sister and I know.

On leaving the theater we shared a long, uncomfortable silence. Between the movie we'd just seen and the movie about to be made, we both felt awkward and self-conscious, as if we were auditioning for the roles of ourselves. I started in with some benign bit of gossip I'd heard concerning the man who'd played the part of the brother but stopped after the first few sentences, saying that, on second thought, it wasn't very interesting. She couldn't think of anything, either, so we said nothing, each of us imagining a bored audience shifting in its seats.

We stopped for gas on the way home and were parking in front of her house when she turned to relate what I've come to think of as the quintessential Lisa story. "One time," she said, "one time I was out driving . . ." The incident began with a quick trip to the grocery store and ended, unexpectedly, with a wounded animal stuffed into a pillowcase and held to the tailpipe of her car. Like most of my sister's stories, it provoked a startling mental picture, capturing a moment in time when one's actions seem both unimaginably cruel and completely natural. Details were carefully chosen and the pace built gradually, punctuated by a series of well-timed pauses. "And then . . . and then . . ." She reached the inevitable tailpipe, and just as I started to laugh, she put her head against the steering wheel and fell apart. It wasn't the gentle flow of tears you might release when recalling an isolated action or event, but the violent explosion that comes when you realize that all such events are connected, forming an endless chain of guilt and suffering.

I instinctively reached for the notebook I keep in my pocket, and she grabbed my hand to stop me. "If you ever," she said, "*ever* repeat that story, I'll never talk to you again."

In the movie version of our lives, I would have turned to offer her comfort, reminding her, convincing her, that the action she'd described had been kind and just. Because it was. She's incapable of acting otherwise.

In the real version of our lives, my immediate goal was simply to change her mind. "Oh, come on," I said. "The story's really funny, and, I mean, it's not like *you're* going to do anything with it."

*Your life, your privacy, your bottomless sorrow—it's not like you're going to do anything with it.* Is this the brother I always was or the brother I have become?

I'd worried that, in making the movie, the director might get me and my family wrong, but now a worse thought occurred to me: What if he gets us right?

Dusk. The camera pans an unremarkable suburban street, moving in on a parked four-door automobile where a small, evil man turns to his sobbing sister, saying, "What if I use the story but say that it happened to a friend?"

But maybe that's not the end. Maybe before the credits roll, we see this same man getting out of bed in the middle of the night, walking past his sister's bedroom and downstairs into the kitchen. A switch is thrown, and we notice, in the far corner of the room, a large standing birdcage covered with a tablecloth. He approaches it carefully and removes the cover, waking a blue-fronted Amazon parrot, its eyes glowing red in the sudden light. Through everything that's come before this moment, we understand that the man has something important to say. From his own mouth the words are meaningless, so he pulls up a chair. The clock reads 3:00 A.M., then 4:00, then 5:00, as he sits before the brilliant bird repeating slowly and clearly the words, "Forgive me. Forgive me. Forgive me."

—MAY 2002

# A Few Words About Breasts

NORA EPHRON

I have to begin with a few words about androgyny. In grammar school, in the fifth and sixth grades, we were all tyrannized by a rigid set of rules that supposedly determined whether we were boys or girls. The episode in *Huckleberry Finn* where Huck is disguised as a girl and gives himself away by the way he threads a needle and catches a ball—that kind of thing. We learned that the way you sat, crossed your legs, held a cigarette and looked at your nails, your wristwatch, the way you did these things instinctively was absolute proof of your sex. Now obviously most children did not take this literally, but I did. I thought that just one slip, just one incorrect cross of my legs or flick of an imaginary cigarette ash would turn me from whatever I was into the other thing; that would be all it took, really. Even though I was outwardly a girl and had many of the trappings generally associated with the field of girldom—a girl's name, for example, and dresses, my own telephone, an autograph book—I spent the early years of my adolescence absolutely certain that I might at any point gum it up. I did not feel at all like a girl. I was boyish. I was athletic, ambitious, outspoken, competitive, noisy, rambunctious. I had scabs on my knees and my socks slid into my loafers and I could throw a football. I wanted desperately not to be that way, not to be a mixture of both things but instead just one, a girl, a definite indisputable girl. As soft and as pink as a nursery. And nothing would do that for me, I felt, but breasts.

• • •

I was about six months younger than everyone in my class, and so for about six months after it began, for six months after my friends had begun to develop—that was the word we used, develop—I was not particularly worried. I would sit in the bathtub and look down at my breasts and know that any day now, any second now, they would start growing like everyone else's. They didn't. "I want to buy a bra," I said to my mother one night. "What for?" she said. My mother was really hateful about bras, and by the time my third sister had gotten to the point where she was ready to want one, my mother had worked the whole business into a comedy routine. "Why not use a Band-Aid instead?" she would say. It was a source of great pride to my mother that she had never even had to wear a brassiere until she had her fourth child, and then only because her gynecologist made her. It was incomprehensible to me that anyone could ever be proud of something like that. It was the 1950's, for God's sake. Jane Russell. Cashmere sweaters. Couldn't my mother see that? "*I am too old to wear an undershirt.*" Screaming. Weeping. Shouting. "Then don't wear an undershirt," said my mother. "But I want to buy a bra." "What for?"

I suppose that for most girls, breasts, brassieres, that entire thing, has more trauma, more to do with the coming of adolescence, of becoming a woman, than anything else. Certainly more than getting your period, although that too was traumatic, symbolic. But you could see breasts; they were there; they were visible. Whereas a girl could claim to have her period for months before she actually got it and nobody would ever know the difference. Which is exactly what I did. All you had to do was make a great fuss over having enough nickels for the Kotex machine and walk around clutching your stomach and moaning for three to five days a month about The Curse and you could convince anybody. There is a school of thought somewhere in the women's lib/women's mag/gynecology establishment that claims that menstrual cramps are purely psychological, and I lean toward it. Not that I didn't have them finally. Agonizing cramps, heating-pad cramps, go-down-to-the-school-nurse-and-lie-on-the-cot cramps. But unlike any pain I had ever suffered, I adored the pain of cramps, welcomed it, wallowed in it, bragged about it. "I can't go. I have cramps." "I can't do that. I have cramps." And most of all, gigglingly, blushingly: "I can't swim. I have cramps." Nobody ever used the hard-core word. Menstruation. God, what an awful word. Never that. "I have cramps."

The morning I first got my period, I went into my mother's bedroom to tell her. And my mother, my utterly-hateful-about-bras mother, burst into tears. It was really a lovely moment, and I remember it so clearly not just because it was one of the two times I ever saw my mother cry on my account (the other was when I was caught being a six-year-old kleptomaniac), but also because the incident did not mean to me what it meant to her. Her little girl, her first-born, had finally become a woman. That was what she was crying about. My reaction to the event, however, was that I might well be a woman in some scientific, textbook sense (and could at least stop faking every month and stop wasting all those nickels). But in another sense—in a visible sense—I was as androgynous and as liable to tip over into boyhood as ever.

I started with a 28AA bra. I don't think they made them any smaller in those days, although I gather that now you can buy bras for five-year-olds that don't have any cups whatsoever in them; trainer bras they are called. My first brassiere came from Robinson's Department Store in Beverly Hills. I went there alone, shaking, positive they would look me over and smile and tell me to come back next year. An actual fitter took me into the dressing room and stood over me while I took off my blouse and tried the first one on. The little puffs stood out on my chest. "Lean over," said the fitter (to this day I am not sure what fitters in bra departments do except to tell you to lean over). I leaned over, with the fleeting hope that my breasts would miraculously fall out of my body and into the puffs. Nothing.

"Don't worry about it," said my friend Libby some months later, when things had not improved. "You'll get them after you're married."

"What are you talking about?" I said.

"When you get married," Libby explained, "your husband will touch your breasts and rub them and kiss them and they'll grow."

That was the killer. Necking I could deal with. Intercourse I could deal with. But it had never crossed my mind that a man was going to touch my breasts, that breasts had something to do with all that, petting, my God they never mentioned petting in my little sex manual about the fertilization of the ovum. I became dizzy. For I knew instantly—as naïve as I had been only a moment before—that only part of what she was saying was true: the touching, rubbing, kissing part, not the growing part. And I knew that no one would ever want to marry me. I had no breasts. I would never have breasts.

My best friend in school was Diana Raskob. She lived a block from me in a house full of wonders. English muffins, for instance. The Raskobs were the first people in Beverly Hills to have English muffins for breakfast. They also had an apricot tree in the back, and a badminton court, and a subscription to *Seventeen* magazine, and hundreds of games like Sorry and Parcheesi and Treasure Hunt and Anagrams. Diana and I spent three or four afternoons a week in their den reading and playing and eating. Diana's mother's kitchen was full of the most colossal assortment of junk food I have ever been exposed to. My house was full of apples and peaches and milk and homemade chocolate-chip cookies—which were nice, and good for you, but-not-right-before-dinner-or-you'll-spoil-your-appetite. Diana's house had nothing in it that was good for you, and what's more, you could stuff it in right up until dinner and nobody cared. Bar-B-Q potato chips (they were the first in them, too), giant bottles of ginger ale, fresh popcorn with melted butter, hot fudge sauce on Baskin-Robbins jamoca ice cream, powdered-sugar doughnuts from Van de Kamps. Diana and I had been best friends since we were seven; we were about equally popular in school (which is to say, not particularly), we had about the same success with boys (extremely intermittent) and we looked much the same. Dark. Tall. Gangly.

It is September, just before school begins. I am eleven years old, about to enter the seventh grade, and Diana and I have not seen each other all summer. I have been to camp and she has been somewhere like Banff with her parents. We are meeting, as we often do, on the street midway between our two houses and we will walk back to Diana's and eat junk and talk about what has happened to each of us that summer. I am walking down Walden Drive in my jeans and my father's shirt hanging out and my old red loafers with the socks falling into them and coming toward me is . . . I take a deep breath . . . a young woman. Diana. Her hair is curled and she has a waist and hips and a bust and she is wearing a straight skirt, an article of clothing I have been repeatedly told I will be unable to wear until I have the hips to hold it up. My jaw drops, and suddenly I am crying, crying hysterically, can't catch my breath sobbing. My best friend has betrayed me. She has gone ahead without me and done it. She has shaped up.

Here are some things I did to help:

Bought a Mark Eden Bust Developer.

Slept on my back for four years.

Splashed cold water on them every night because some French actress said in *Life* magazine that that was what *she* did for her perfect bustline.

Ultimately, I resigned myself to a bad toss and began to wear padded bras. I think about them now, think about all those years in high school I went around in them, my three padded bras, every single one of them with different sized breasts. Each time I changed bras I changed sizes: one week nice perky but not too obtrusive breasts, the next medium-sized slightly pointy ones, the next week knockers, true knockers; all the time, whatever size I was, carrying around this rubberized appendage on my chest that occasionally crashed into a wall and was poked inward and had to be poked outward—I think about all that and wonder how anyone kept a straight face through it. My parents, who normally had no restraints about needling me—why did they say nothing as they watched my chest go up and down? My friends, who would periodically inspect my breasts for signs for growth and reassure me—why didn't they at least counsel consistency?

And the bathing suits. I die when I think about the bathing suits. That was the era when you could lay an uninhabited bathing suit on the beach and someone would make a pass at it. I would put one on, an absurd swimsuit with its enormous bust built into it, the bones from the suit stabbing me in the rib cage and leaving little red welts on my body, and there I would be, my chest plunging straight downward absolutely vertically from my collarbone to the top of my suit and then suddenly, wham, out came all that padding and material and wiring absolutely horizontally.

Buster Klepper was the first boy who ever touched them. He was my boyfriend my senior year of high school. There is a picture of him in my high-school yearbook that makes him look quite attractive in a Jewish, horn-rimmed glasses sort of way, but the picture does not show the pimples, which were airbrushed out, or the dumbness. Well, that isn't really fair. He wasn't dumb. He just wasn't terribly bright. His mother refused to accept it, refused to accept the relentlessly average report cards, refused to deal with her son's inevitable destiny in some junior college or other. "He was tested," she would say to me, apropos of nothing, "and it came out 145. That's near-genius." Had the word underachiever been coined, she probably would have lobbed that one at me, too. Anyway, Buster was really very sweet—which is, I know, damning with faint praise, but there it is. I was the editor of the front page of the high-school newspaper and he was editor of the back page; we had to work together, side by side, in the print shop, and that was how it started. On our first date, we went to see *April Love* starring Pat Boone. Then we started going together. Buster had a green coupe, a 1950 Ford with an engine he had hand-chromed until it shone, dazzled, reflected the image of anyone who looked into it, anyone usually being Buster polishing it or the gas-station attendants he constantly asked to check the oil in order for them to be overwhelmed by the sparkle on the valves. The car also had a boot stretched over the back seat for reasons I never understood; hanging from the rearview mirror, as was the custom, was a pair of angora dice. A previous girl friend named Solange who was famous throughout Beverly Hills High School for having no pigment in her right eyebrow had knitted them for him. Buster and I would ride around town, the two of us seated to the left of the steering wheel. I would shift gears. It was nice.

There was necking. Terrific necking. First in the car, overlooking

Los Angeles from what is now the Trousdale Estates. Then on the bed of his parents' cabana at Ocean House. Incredibly wonderful, frustrating necking, I loved it, really, but no further than necking, please don't, please, because there I was absolutely terrified of the general implications of going-a-step-further with a near-dummy and also terrified of his finding out there was next to nothing there (which he knew, of course; he wasn't that dumb).

I broke up with him at one point. I think we were apart for about two weeks. At the end of that time I drove down to see a friend at a boarding school in Palos Verdes Estates and a disc jockey played *April Love* on the radio four times during the trip. I took it as a sign. I drove straight back to Griffith Park to a golf tournament Buster was playing in (he was the sixth-seeded teen-age golf player in Southern California) and presented myself back to him on the green of the 18th hole. It was all very dramatic. That night we went to a drive-in and I let him get his hand under my protuberances and onto my breasts. He really didn't seem to mind at all.

*"Do you want to marry my son?" the woman asked me.*

*"Yes," I said.*

*I was nineteen years old, a virgin, going with this woman's son, this big strange woman who was married to a Lutheran minister in New Hampshire and pretended she was Gentile and had this son, by her first husband, this total fool of a son who ran the hero-sandwich concession at Harvard Business School and whom for one moment one December in New Hampshire I said—as much out of politeness as anything else—that I wanted to marry.*

*"Fine," she said. "Now, here's what you do. Always make sure you're on top of him so you won't seem so small. My bust is very large, you see, so I always lie on my back to make it look smaller, but you'll have to be on top most of the time."*

*I nodded. "Thank you," I said.*

*"I have a book for you to read," she went on. "Take it with you when you leave. Keep it." She went to the bookshelf, found it, and gave it to me. It was a book on frigidity.*

*"Thank you," I said.*

That is a true story. Everything in this article is a true story, but I feel I have to point out that that story in particular is true. It happened on December 30, 1960. I think about it often. When it first happened, I naturally assumed that the woman's son, my boyfriend, was responsible. I invented a scenario where he had had a little heart-to-heart with his mother and had confessed that his only objection to me was that my breasts were small; his mother then took it upon herself to help out. Now I think I was wrong about the incident. The mother was acting on her own, I think: that was her way of being cruel and competitive under the guise of being helpful and maternal. You have small breasts, she was saying; therefore you will never make him as happy as I have. Or you have small breasts; therefore you will doubtless have sexual problems. Or you have small breasts; therefore you are less woman than I am. She was, as it happens, only the first of what seems to me to be a never-ending string of women who have made competitive remarks to me about breast size. "I would love to wear a dress like that," my friend Emily says to me, "but my bust is too big." Like that. Why do women say these things to me? Do I attract these remarks the way other women attract married men or alcoholics or homosexuals? This summer, for example. I am at a party in East Hampton and I am introduced to a woman from Washington. She is a minor celebrity, very pretty and Southern and blonde and outspoken and I am flattered because she has read something I have written. We are talking animatedly, we have been talking no more than five minutes, when a man comes up to join us. "Look at the two of us," the woman says to the man, indicating me and her. "The two of us together couldn't fill an A cup." Why does she say that? It isn't even true, dammit, so why? Is she even more addled than I am on this subject? Does she honestly believe there is something wrong with her size breasts, which, it seems to me, now that I look hard at them, are just right. Do I unconsciously bring out competitiveness in women? In that form? What did I do to deserve it?

As for men.

There were men who minded and let me know they minded. There were men who did not mind. In any case, I always minded.

And even now, now that I have been countlessly reassured that my figure is a good one, now that I am grown up enough to understand that most of my feelings have very little to do with the reality of my shape, I am nonetheless obsessed by breasts. I cannot help it. I grew up in the terrible Fifties—with rigid stereotypical sex roles, the insistence that men be men and dress like men and women be women and dress like women, the intolerance of androgyny—and I cannot shake it, cannot shake my feelings of inadequacy. Well, that time is gone, right? All those exaggerated examples of breast worship are gone, right? Those women were freaks, right? I know all that. And yet, here I am, stuck with the psychological remains of it all, stuck with my own peculiar version of breast worship. You probably think I am crazy to go on like this: here I have set out to write a confession that is meant to hit you with the shock of recognition and instead you are sitting there thinking I am thoroughly warped. Well, what can I tell you? If I had had them, I would have been a completely different person. I honestly believe that.

After I went into therapy, a process that made it possible for me to tell total strangers at cocktail parties that breasts were the hang-up of my life, I was often told that I was insane to have been bothered by my condition. I was also frequently told, by close friends, that I was extremely boring on the subject. And my girl friends, the ones with nice big breasts, would go on endlessly about how their lives had been far more miserable than mine. Their bra straps were snapped in class. They couldn't sleep on their stomachs. They were stared at whenever the word "mountain" cropped up in geography. And *Evangeline*, good God what they went through every time someone had to stand up and recite the Prologue to Longfellow's *Evangeline*: "*. . . stand like druids of eld . . . / With beards that rest on their bosoms.*" It was much worse for them, they tell me. They had a terrible time of it, they assure me. I don't know how lucky I was, they say.

I have thought about their remarks, tried to put myself in their place, considered their point of view. I think they are full of shit.

—MAY 1972

# The Typewriter

An anti-visual theatre piece, 1969
(Originally published as *My Very Last Happening*)

CLAES OLDENBURG

### Site

A large square room with a high ceiling—an Accounting office. An office of maximum desolation austerely functional and penny-pinching. Minimal, grey metal desks, on a hard floor covered with black-and-white-marbled linoleum.

The walls painted a moribund green. A soundproofed ceiling with rows of fluorescent lights.

The desks are placed close to one another in the center of the room. The desks are cleared, except of telephones. Office chairs and smaller tables with office machinery—typewriters, accounting machines, etc., which are under covers, clutter the aisles. Around the room—several wall fans, rotating and turning.

The office selected must be without windows or it must be possible to mask the windows completely. Proper execution of the piece requires absolute darkness.

The size of the audience will depend on the number of desks: one member of the audience to each desk.

**Preparations**

Twelve identical hat trees are placed at regular intervals near the walls around the room. On each tree is hung a small, portable tape recorder fitted with a belt so that it can be fastened to a body around the waist. Each apparatus is provided with a previously recorded tape, ready to play, of a mixture of the following sounds:

(1) Sounds of office machinery, typing, adding, dialing, etc.

(2) Sounds of the body in the office, sneezing, scratching, yawning, etc.

(3) Sounds of object activity in the office, stamping, crumbling, clicking, etc.

Tape recorders with the same material are also fastened under each desk top, or placed in a drawer of each desk. These are turned on just before the audience enters the office. Ten minutes are needed to tie the members of the audience to the tops of the desks. Therefore the first ten minutes of these tapes are blank.

An amplifier capable of very loud sound is placed in the office space at whatever spot is determined to be the most effective. When the audience enters the office, taped musical arrangements such as those heard in lobbies and elevators of office buildings are playing through the amplifier. After ten minutes, the tape changes to a recording of the typewriting of *this scenario*.

The sound of this scenario being typed continues for twenty minutes and should end simultaneously with the sounds of the portable tape recorders and those concealed in the desks. But, unlike the other recorded sounds, the sound of the typing increases gradually in volume. After fifteen minutes, the sound of typing is *extremely loud*, and this volume is maintained for five minutes, which will seem a very long time.

The office space will resound like a battlefield. The contact of a character with paper will sound like the bursting of a shell. The little pauses for thought while writing the scenario become huge spaces charged with tense anticipation of the next crash.

When sound becomes too loud, the body tends to fall asleep.

Each member of the audience is given two large objects to hold—

a giant pencil and a giant typewriter eraser. As many as are needed are reproduced from originals made by the author. A set is placed on the top of each desk, along with (1) a brown Army blanket and (2) a length of thick rope or a giant version of a rubber band, before the audience enters the office.

### Cast and Costume

The following assistants will be needed to perform the piece:

(1) Twelve "Secretaries," six male and six female.
(2) Two pairs of "Floorwashers," male.
(3) Several uncostumed assistants, to handle lighting and sound production through the amplifier.

All the Secretaries, regardless of size and sex, wear the same costume—a pair of black men's pants with black suspenders, a white shirt, and a black-and-white polka-dot tie. They wear nothing underneath. The garments are all of the same size. The pants are 30 inches long in the leg and 36 inches around at the waist. The shirts are 35 inches long in the sleeve and 16 inches around at the neck.

These are the author's sizes.

The pockets of the pants are to be filled with small change.

The Floorwashers wear grey coveralls. They carry big mops and huge buckets of hot smoking water containing a large dose of strong-smelling disinfectant.

All the assistants wear gym shoes.

### Action

The audience is kept in a waiting room or a corridor outside the office until preparations are complete. When the first member of the audience enters the office, timing of the piece begins. The office is brightly lit. Soft music is playing. The needed objects are in place on the desks. Each Secretary has chosen a hat tree, and stands by his (her) tree, giving the audience a courteous smile.

The Floorwashers are aggressively wetting the linoleum. Their action with the mops and water should be directed at the fine shoes of the entering audience members, with the objective of encouraging them to protect themselves by climbing on the desks. Their doing so will be suggested by the twelve Secretaries, who begin first to demonstrate and then to situate the members of the audience on the desk tops. Each audience member is covered with the Army blanket and tied with rope, or giant rubber band, around the whole desk. Once tied, they are given the giant pencil and typewriter eraser to hold in their hands.

The audience is told (not by announcement but quite intimately, by each Secretary) that the giant objects are very fragile and are not to be released. Releasing them would cause them to fall to the floor, to become wet, to be trampled or to be shattered. The audience members can determine with their fingers that the giant objects are indeed very fragile.

There is no alternative for a decent person and, in the total darkness of the performance, the holding on to the objects may reduce anxiety. The details of the objects may be explored by the fingers as a pastime.

The office door is shut. The wall fans spread the stench of heated disinfectant.

When all the members of the audience are tied in place, the Floorwashers depart with their equipment, not bothering to wipe up any pools of water they have made.

The Secretaries return to their posts by the trees.

The fluorescent lamps flicker off, one row after another, leaving the office invisible.

The soft music played during the positioning of the audience continues for a brief while, then stops abruptly.

At this moment, the sounds taped on recorders hidden in the desks should begin, and also the sound of typing carried by the amplifier. At this moment, too, the Secretaries switch on the tape recorders hanging on the hat trees. The Secretaries remove the office costumes, hang them on the trees and strap the operative recorders around their naked waists. They then begin a blind journey through the maze of desks and office equipment, using their hands and feet and other parts of the body to find their way to a hat tree on the opposite side of the office. The trip should take fifteen minutes.

At the end of the period of large scale typing sound (fifteen minutes after the lights go out), each Secretary should have found another tree and another costume hanging on the tree. During the five-minute period of silence that follows, the Secretaries unstrap the recorders, hang them up, and dress again.

The absolute darkness continues, but without recorded sound. Members of the audience, adjusting their ears to the new condition, begin to hear the small real sounds in the space. They hear the breathing, coughing and sounds of the others turning and twisting in their uncomfortable positions. They hear the sound of small change in the pockets of the Secretaries' pants as they dress. If suffering from aural over-stimulation, they may imagine hearing normally unhearable, miniature sounds, such as the dipping of a tea bag into hot water or the sliding of a metal clip on paper.

The five-minute period of silence ends suddenly with the relighting of the fluorescent lamps. They quiver on; the members of the audience rub their eyes.

The music resumes where it ended, recalling the moment when a landing plane recontacts the soothing, sentimental sound that covers the surface of the continent like a natural element. The Secretaries release the audience. The piece is over.

—MAY 1969

# Twilight in the Smog

ORSON WELLES

It used to be easy to hate Hollywood. For me it was no trouble at all. I don't think either of us have mellowed very much since then; but we are getting on a bit and our feelings for each other are scarcely as passionate as they were. For one thing, I no longer live there; I'm not just saying this—I really don't. Formerly this claim was the purest affectation; now it's a fact. It was my melancholy pretense that I was a transient, temporarily employed. There was nothing original about this self-deception. In the film colony a good half of the working population, including many of the oldest inhabitants, keep up their spirits by means of the same ruse. People buy houses and spend half their lives in them without unpacking their bags. By now, however, I think it's safe to announce that I am one of those who got away. I chose freedom—and that was quite a while ago. Nowadays, if I do venture back behind the chromium curtain, it's never without a return ticket to the outside world. Also, I'm very careful about sitting down. This is important. In that peculiar climate one is haunted with the possibility that standing up again might suddenly exceed one's aspirations. Hollywood is a place where a youngish man is ill-advised to indulge in a siesta. Leaving a call for four-thirty won't do him any good. The likelihood remains that when he wakes up he'll be sixty-five years old.

Anyway, as the citrus people are the first to admit, the smog has taken the fun out of life even for the oranges.

When we speak of Hollywood we take in, of course, more than the community of that name: we mean the movie and TV studios in

San Fernando Valley; we include the beach houses, villas and *palazzi* in Santa Monica and Malibu. We mean the film colony that is spread so wide and thin, and the "industry" itself, which no longer dominates the scene as it once did. In the stately homes of Bel Air and Beverly Hills, oil millionaires are at least as numerous as movie stars, and nowadays the luckier studios bristle with oil pumps.

According to the map, Hollywood is a district attached but not belonging to the City of Los Angeles. But this is not strictly accurate: Los Angeles—though huge, populous and rich—has never quite made it as a city. It remains a loose and sprawling confederation of suburbs and shopping centers. As for downtown Los Angeles, it's about as metropolitan as Des Moines or Schenectady.

The metropolitan air is what one misses. Neither the theatre nor its artists are at their best in a suburb. Or a gigantic trailer camp. Whether we work before a camera or behind the footlights, actors are, by nature, city people. Hollywood is most precisely described as a colony. (Colonies are notoriously somewhat cut off from reality, insular, bitchy, and cliquish, snobbish—a bit loose as to morals but very strict as to appearances.) One expects a colony to be an outpost of empire. Hollywood might be called an outpost of civilization (a word which means, after all, "city culture"), but it's also the heart of its own empire of the movies: a capital without a city, yet among its colonies are numbered the great cities of the world. It's as though the colony of Trinidad was the center of the British Commonwealth.

There has never been a real metropolis that did not begin with a market place. Hollywood is a way station on a highway. Drive as far as you like in any direction: wherever you find yourself, it looks exactly like the road to an airport. Any road to any airport.

What is best in any branch of the theatre must always have a certain flavor of tradition. Dear, shabby old Times Square, for instance, has its roots in Rome and the Middle Ages. It was, after all, a kind of market place, and in the old tradition. The saloons and bars of the Broadway area are still the sort of places where show folk have always gathered in Athens and Madrid, in London and Paris and Peking. But Hollywood, which boasts the largest population of actors ever concentrated in a single community, is also the first show-town in history without a pub or a bistro in the traditional sense. In California the tradition of the Mermaid Tavern has given way to the country club. A rigidly standardized middle-class suburbia is replacing the raucous and circusy traditions of the recent past.

Is Hollywood's famous sun really setting? There is certainly a hint of twilight in the smog and, lately, over the old movie capital there has fallen a gray-flannel shadow. Television is moving inexorably westward. Emptying the movie theatres across the land, it fills the movie studios. Another industry is building quite another town; and already, rising out of the gaudy ruins of screenland, we behold a new, drab, curiously solemn brand of the old foolishness.

There must always be a strong element of the absurd in the operation of a dream factory, but now there's less to laugh at and even less to like. The feverish gaiety has gone, a certain brassy vitality drained away. TV, after all, is a branch of the advertising business, and Hollywood behaves increasingly like an annex of Madison Avenue.

Television—live, taped or on film—is still limited by the language barrier, while by nature and economics moving pictures are multilingual. Making them has always been an international affair. Directors, writers, producers and, above all, the stars come to Hollywood from all over the world and their pictures are addressed to a world public. The town's new industry threatens its traditional cosmopolitanism and substitutes a strong national flavor. This could not be otherwise since our television exists for the sole purpose of selling American products to American consumers.

And there's the question of money.

Millions of dollars are being made in television, but a million dollars has never been spent on any television show. Some few of the most lavish "spectaculars" are budgeted at the cost of a B-picture. All the rest of the TV product is made for "quickie" prices, the big money being spread thin to cover the whole season. If there's any conspicuous waste in this new industry it's only in the area of talent. A half-hour television Western multiplied by three equals the playing time of a "program picture." But add the total price of all three and you have less than half the minimum budget for a negotiable second feature. Some TV stars are paid about as much for a week's solo appearance in

Las Vegas as the complete production cost of one of their TV programs—and this includes full cast and crew, script, sets, photography, raw-stock, wardrobe, music, scoring, mixing, processing, insurance—even their own star salaries. This penny-pinching grind runs counter to the town's most venerable instincts, but now, with the biggest of the big film studios limping along on economy programs administered by skeleton staffs, the gold-rush atmosphere which once was Hollywood's own dizzy brand of charm is just a memory.

In its golden age—in the first years of the movie boom—the mood and manner were indeed much like that of the gold rush. There was the frenzy and buccaneering hurly-burly of an earlier California: the vast fortunes found in a day and squandered in a night; the same cheerful violence and cutthroat anarchy. All of that Western turbulence has been silenced now; the wild and woolly charm is just a memory.

Architectural fantasy is in decline, the cheerful gaudiness is mostly gone, the more high-spirited of the old outrages have been razed or stand in ruins. In the "better" residential and business districts a kind of official "good taste" has taken charge. The result is a standardized impeccability, sterile and joyless, but it correctly expresses the community's ardent yearnings toward respectability. There's nothing new about this urge. At my first Hollywood dinner party, twenty years ago, I remember that when the ladies had left us to our port, the host, a studio satrap, admonished me never again to speak of the local product as "the movies"; at least not in good society—the only acceptable usage being "motion pictures."

Right down to this last moment in a long, long history, show folk have been kept quite firmly segregated from respectability. Significantly, the theatre profession had no contact with the middle class. Indeed, it's just recently that we began to employ that very middle-class word, "profession." This was when the mention of art began to embarrass us, and this was the beginning of our fall from grace: when we suddenly aspired to the mediocre rank of ladies and gentlemen. Before that, and in common with all other artists, we had no rank at all, and stood in our own dignity outside of protocol.

Something of what's ailing the new Hollywood, its movies, and us who make them can be traced, I think, back to that first fatal descent into polite society. It really started on that disastrous morning in the last century when the last great English tragedian Henry Irving knelt before Queen Victoria to accept the theatre's first accolade. For Irving, knighthood seemed a giant step out of the old gypsydom, a deliverance from vagabondage; he thought of it as dignifying his "profession"—as sanctifying it with respectability. We can't rebuke him from this distance for imagining that the receipt of royal honors immeasurably elevated the social status of the theatre. Too many of his compatriots agree with him. For my part, I'm convinced that this famous elevation was, in its consequences, nothing less than an abdication from royalty. I don't think that the great leaders of the stage in any country deserve to be ranked with the minor nobility. I think they deserve more. Sir Henry, rising from his knee a dubbed knight, dragged us all, not upward, but sideways—into another dimension, imbedding us squarely and forevermore in the middle class.

What had been invulnerable in our position was the fact that we really had no position whatsoever. For just as long as there was no proper place for us—neither above nor below the salt—an actor was at liberty to sit wherever he was welcome, and this was very often next to the king. (It may be noted that our most distinguished cousins in the British theatre are not today the easy intimates of royalty.) I hold that we had more to give our art and to our audiences when we ourselves were royal bums, draped in our own brand of imperial purple. Our crown was tin, but it was a crown, and we wore it, with a difference, among such other diadems as happened to be gold.

For decades after Irving, the new stage gentry on both sides of the Atlantic made private imitation and public representation of the bourgeois their paramount concern. Then came the movies.

This was an institution "legitimate" actors could look down on with all the priggish contempt formerly lavished by middle-class respectability on the playhouse itself. Hollywood became a word in the language, and in this unlikely outpost—unfettered, unbracketed and largely unconsidered—a motley crew of show folk, in spirit far closer to the circus, to burlesque and *commedia dell'arte* than to the starchy stage world of that epoch, was gaily producing a new art form, and celebrating in the process a brief but exciting renaissance of the old royal nonsense and glory.

That glory had all but died out as the theatre reduced itself into a mere profession. Now—as the making of motion pictures began to be spoken of and to be organized as a mere industry—the glory started dimming in Hollywood.

What's valid on the stage or screen is never a mere professional effort and certainly not an industrial producer. Whatever is valuable must, in the final analysis, be a work of art.

There should be no need to repeat that originality is one of the essential definitions of any work of art, and that every artist is an individual. Just as obviously, the industrial system, by its nature, cannot accommodate originality. A genuine individual is an outright nuisance in a factory.

There used to be something spoken of as "the Hollywood influence." What is more noticeable today is that the rest of America is influencing Hollywood.

As always, much fun is provided by the current sex symbols, but Jayne and Elvis are too patently creatures of the publicity experts—fuzzy carbon copies of the old freewheeling originals, the vamps and sheiks who invented themselves and lived up so gorgeously to their own legends. The recent crop of "Method actors" and the official representatives of the beatnik constituency are rather too sullen in their personal style to add much color to the pallid scene. The biggest noise they make is on their bongo drums and their gestures of protest are no less standardized than the conformist patterns they pretend to reject. They have their own conformism, these eagle scouts of The Actor's Studio—there is no madness in their method.

Of the authentic mavericks the youngest, men like Mitchum and Sinatra, are in their forties. Rock 'n' roll throws up an occasional oddball of a minor sort, but such types are "cool" in the dictionary sense of the word and do nothing to the tepid temperature of the new Hollywood one way or another. Their kind of egotism rages in a sort of monotone and with no exuberance. They hold the mirror up to their own generation. So do their pseudo-suburbanite elders in the film colony. These two groups, the T-shirts and the sports jackets, are more accurate reflections of today's America than were those dazzling pioneers who blazed screenland's frontiers.

One of our producers, by way of explaining the school of neorealism in the Italian cinema, told me that over there, instead of actors, they use people. For good or evil it's certain that the town is overrun with characters who are quite reasonable facsimiles of today's people. It's a solemn thought, but maybe that's what's wrong with Hollywood.

—MARCH 1959

# Holy Water

## JOAN DIDION

Some of us who live in arid parts of the world think about water with a reverence others might find excessive. The water I will draw tomorrow from my tap in Malibu is today crossing the Mojave Desert from the Colorado River, and I like to think about exactly where that water is. The water I will drink tonight in a restaurant in Hollywood is by now well down the Los Angeles Aqueduct from the Owens River, and I also think about exactly where that water is: I particularly like to imagine it as it cascades down the 45-degree stone steps that aerate Owens water after its airless passage through the mountain pipes and siphons. As it happens my own reverence for water has always taken the form of this constant meditation upon where the water is, of an obsessive interest not in the politics of water but in the waterworks themselves, in the movement of water through aqueducts and siphons and pumps and forebays and afterbays and weirs and drains, in plumbing on the grand scale. I know the data on water projects I will never see. I know the difficulty Kaiser had closing the last two sluiceway gates on the Guri Dam in Venezuela. I keep watch on evaporation behind the Aswan in Egypt. I can put myself to sleep imagining the water dropping a thousand feet into the turbines at Churchill Falls in Labrador. If the Churchill Falls Project fails to materialize, I fall back on waterworks closer at hand—the tailrace at Hoover on the Colorado, the surge tank in the Tehachapi Mountains that receives California Aqueduct water pumped higher than water has ever been pumped before—and finally I replay a morning when I was seventeen years old and caught, in a military-surplus life raft, in the construction of the Nimbus Afterbay Dam on the American River near Sacramento. I remember that at the moment it happened I was trying to open a tin of anchovies with capers. I recall the raft spinning into the narrow chute through which the river had been temporarily diverted. I recall being deliriously happy.

I suppose it was partly the memory of that delirium that led me to visit, one summer morning in Sacramento, the Operations Control Center for the California State Water Project. Actually so much water is moved around California by so many different agencies that maybe only the movers themselves know on any given day whose water is where, but to get a general picture it is necessary only to remember that Los Angeles moves some of it, San Francisco moves some of it, the Bureau of Reclamation's Central Valley Project moves some of it and the California State Water Project moves most of the rest of it, moves a vast amount of it, moves more water farther than has ever been moved anywhere. They collect this water up in the granite keeps of the Sierra Nevada and they store roughly a trillion gallons of it behind the Oroville Dam and every morning, down at the Project's headquarters in Sacramento, they decide how much of their water they want to move the next day. They make this morning decision according to supply and demand, which is simple in theory but rather more complicated in practice. In theory each of the Project's five field divisions—the Oroville, the Delta, the San Luis, the San Joaquin and the Southern divisions—places a call to headquarters before nine A.M. and tells the dispatchers how much water is needed by its local water contractors, who have in turn based their morning estimates on orders from growers and other big users. A schedule is made. The gates open and close according to schedule. The water flows south and the deliveries are made.

In practice this requires prodigious coordination, precision, and the best efforts of several human minds and that of a Univac 418. In practice it might be necessary to hold large flows of water for power production, or to flush out encroaching salinity in the Sacramento–San Joaquin Delta, the most ecologically sensitive point on the system. In practice a sudden rain might obviate the need for a delivery when that delivery is already on its way. In practice what is being delivered here is an enormous volume of water, not quarts of milk or spools of thread, and it takes two days to move such a delivery down through Oroville into the Delta, which is the great pooling place for California water and has been for some years alive with electronic sensors and telemetering equipment and men blocking channels and diverting flows and shoveling fish away from the pumps. It takes perhaps another six days to move this same water down the California Aqueduct from the Delta to the Tehachapi and put it over the hill to Southern California. "Putting some over the hill" is what they say around the Project Operations Control Center when they want to indicate that they are pumping Aqueduct water from the floor of the San Joaquin Valley up and over the Tehachapi Mountains. "Pulling it down" is what they say when they want to indicate that they are lowering a water level somewhere in the system. They can put some over the hill by remote control from this room in Sacramento with its Univac and its big board and its flashing lights. They can pull down a pool in the San Joaquin by remote control from this room in Sacramento with its locked doors and its ringing alarms and its constant print-outs of data from sensors out there in the water itself. From this room in Sacramento the whole system takes on the aspect of a perfect three-billion-dollar hydraulic toy, and in certain ways it is. "LET'S START DRAINING QUAIL AT 12:00" was the 10:51 A.M. entry on the electronically recorded communications log the day I visited the Operations Control Center. "Quail" is a reservoir in Los Angeles County with a gross capacity of 1,636,018,000 gallons. "OK" was the response recorded in the log. I knew at that moment that I had missed the only vocation for which I had any instinctive affinity: I wanted to drain Quail myself.

Not many people I know carry their end of the conversation when I want to talk about water deliveries, even when I stress that these deliveries affect their lives, indirectly, every day. "Indirectly" is not quite enough for most people I know. This morning, however, several people I know were affected not "indirectly" but "directly" by the way the water moves. They had been in New Mexico shooting a picture, one sequence of which required a river deep enough to sink a truck, the kind with a cab and a trailer and fifty or sixty wheels. It so happened that no river near the New Mexico location was running that deep this year. The production was therefore moved today to Needles, California, where the Colorado River normally runs, depending upon releases from Davis Dam, eighteen to twenty-five feet deep. Now. Follow this closely: yesterday we had a freak tropical storm in Southern California, two inches of rain in a normally dry month, and because this rain flooded the fields and provided more irrigation than any grower could possibly want for several days, no water was ordered from Davis Dam.

No orders, no releases.

Supply and demand.

As a result the Colorado was running only seven feet deep past Needles today, Sam Peckinpah's desire for eighteen feet of water in which to sink a truck not being the kind of demand anyone at Davis Dam is geared to meet. The production closed down for the weekend. Shooting will resume Tuesday, providing some grower orders water and the agencies controlling the Colorado release it. Meanwhile many gaffers, best boys, cameramen, assistant directors, script supervisors, stunt drivers and maybe even Sam Peckinpah are waiting out the weekend in Needles, where it is often 110 degrees at five P.M. and hard to get dinner after eight. This is a California parable, but a true one.

I have always wanted a swimming pool, and never had one. When it became generally known a year or so ago that California was suffering severe drought, many people in water-rich parts of the country seemed obscurely gratified, and made frequent reference to Californians having to brick up their swimming pools. In fact a swimming pool requires, once it has been filled and the filter has begun its process of cleaning and recirculating the water, virtually no water, but the symbolic content of swimming pools has always been interesting: a pool is misapprehended as a trapping of affluence, real or pretended, and of a kind of hedonistic attention to the body. Actually a pool is, for many of us in the West, a symbol not of affluence but of order, of control over the uncontrollable. A pool is water, made available and useful, and is, as such, infinitely soothing to the western eye.

It is easy to forget that the only natural force over which we have any control out here is water, and that only recently. In my memory California summers were characterized by the coughing in the pipes that meant the well was dry, and California winters by all-night watches on rivers about to crest, by sandbagging, by dynamite on the levees and flooding on the first floor. Even now the place is not all that hospitable to extensive settlement. As I write a fire has been burning out of control for two weeks in the ranges behind the Big Sur coast. Flash floods last night wiped out all major roads into Imperial County. I noticed this morning a hairline crack in a living-room tile from last week's earthquake, a 4.4 I never felt. In the part of California where I now live aridity is the single most prominent feature of the climate, and I am not pleased to see, this year, cactus spreading wild to the sea. There will be days this winter when the humidity will drop to ten, seven, four. Tumbleweed will blow against my house and the sound of the rattlesnake will be duplicated a hundred times a day by dried bougainvillea drifting in my driveway. The apparent ease of California life is an illusion, and those who believe the illusion real live here in only the most temporary way. I know as well as the next person that there is considerable transcendent value in a river running wild and undammed, a river running free over granite, but I have also lived beneath such a river when it was running in flood, and gone without showers when it was running dry.

"The West begins," Bernard DeVoto wrote, "where the average annual rainfall drops below twenty inches." This is maybe the best definition of the West I have ever read, and it goes a long way toward explaining my own passion for seeing the water under control, but many people I know persist in looking for psychoanalytical implications in this passion. As a matter of fact I have explored, in an amateur way, the more obvious of these implications, and come up with nothing interesting. A certain external reality remains, and resists interpretation. The West begins where the average annual rainfall drops below twenty inches. Water is important to people who do not have it, and the same is true of control. Some fifteen years ago I tore a poem by Karl Shapiro from a magazine and pinned it on my kitchen wall. This fragment of paper is now on the wall of a sixth kitchen, and crumbles a little whenever I touch it, but I keep it there for the last stanza, which has for me the power of a prayer:

*It is raining in California, a straight rain*
*Cleaning the heavy oranges on the bough,*
*Filling the gardens till the gardens flow,*
*Shining the olives, tiling the gleaming tile,*
*Waxing the dark camellia leaves more green,*
*Flooding the daylong valleys like the Nile.*

I thought of those lines almost constantly on the morning in Sacramento when I went to visit the California State Water Project Operations Control Center. If I had wanted to drain Quail at 10:51 that morning, I wanted, by early afternoon, to do a great deal more. I wanted to open and close the Clifton Court Forebay intake gate. I wanted to produce some power down at the San Luis Dam. I wanted to pick a pool at random on the Aqueduct and pull it down and then refill it, watching for the hydraulic jump. I wanted to put some water over the hill and I wanted to shut down all flow from the Aqueduct into the Bureau of Reclamation's Cross Valley Canal, just to see how long it would take somebody over at Reclamation to call up and complain. I stayed as long as I could and watched the system work on the big board with the lighted checkpoints. The Delta salinity report was coming in on one of the teletypes behind me. The Delta tidal report was coming in on another. The earthquake board, which has been desensitized to sound its alarm (a beeping tone for Southern California, a high-pitched tone for the north) only for those earthquakes which register at least 3.0 on the Richter Scale, was silent. I had no further business in this room and yet I wanted to stay the day. I wanted to be the one, that day, who was shining the olives, filling the gardens, and flooding the daylong valleys like the Nile. I want it still.

—DECEMBER 1977

# Is Truffaut the Happiest Man on Earth?

FRANÇOIS TRUFFAUT

I am the happiest man in the world and here's why: I walk down a street and I see a woman, not tall but well-proportioned, very dark-haired, very neat in her dress, wearing a dark skirt with deep pleats that swing with the rhythm of her rather quick steps; her stockings, of a dark color, are carefully, impeccably smooth; her face is not smiling, this woman walks down the street without trying to please, as if she were unconscious of what she represented: a good carnal image of woman, a physical image, more than a sexy image, a sexual image. A man walking past her on the sidewalk sees this at once: he looks back, makes a half-turn and falls into step behind her. I watch the scene. Now the man has caught up with the woman, he walks beside her and murmurs something, surely the usual banalities: have a drink, etc. . . . In any event, she turns her head away, walks faster, crosses the street and disappears around the next corner while the man goes off to try his luck farther on.

Now I get into a cab and daydream about the scene a little, such a daily scene in all big cities and not just in Paris. Instinctively I side with the woman against the man and I revise the scene according to my whim of the moment; I tell myself that it would be wonderful if, for once, at the end of a scene of this kind the humiliation had changed hands. I make a note on a page of my memo book and four months later I find myself back on a street behind the Trocadéro, with a camera, a technical crew of twenty-five, and two actors whom

I've chosen, a blond, rather tall man, fairly handsome and well-built, and a woman who, as you may have guessed, is dark-haired, well-proportioned, wearing a skirt with wide pleats. And there I am, in the exercise of my profession which I will allow no one to call useless or uninteresting, and I'm directing the scene. I ask the blond actor to walk, pass the dark-haired woman, look back at her, make a half-turn, catch up with her and say something into her ear. I have not written lines for the man for they will not be heard in the scene, one will guess their implication. Now, the two actors approach the camera which precedes them traveling backward and the dark-haired actress suddenly grabs her pursuer by the coat collar as if to keep him from getting away and, indifferent to what the passersby may think, hurls lines at him that I've been formulating in my head for the last four months before writing them down and giving them to the actress the night before:

"Who are you? Who do you think you are? What do you expect? What are you hoping for? What do women usually say to you? Do they all lie down? Where do you take them? You must think you're some kind of Don Juan, an irresistible man, eh? Is lovemaking especially good with you? Have you ever once looked at yourself in a mirror, just once? Well come and see, look at yourself, take a gook look!"

Then the woman forces her pursuer to look at himself in a store window; terrified by the woman's enraged tone, the man thinks only of running away, he succeeds in pulling free and elbowing his way through the curious crowd that is starting to form. The woman, in turn, begins to walk away, more slowly. "Cut." The scene is "in the can."

That is why I am the happiest of men: I make my daydreams come true and I get paid for it; I am a director.

To make a film is to improve on life, arrange it to suit oneself, it is to prolong the games of childhood, construct something that is at once a new toy and a vase in which one can arrange, as if they were a bouquet of flowers, the ideas one feels at the moment or in a permanent way. Our best film is perhaps the one in which we succeed in expressing, voluntarily or not, our ideas about life and about the cinema.

What do we hope for when we make a film? I agree completely with Jean Renoir when he states: "It all adds up to making your own little contribution to the art of your times." Directing is making decisions from morning to night, *before* the filming, *during* the filming, and *after* the filming. The more the decisions taken fan out through the creative process (which is to say, from the writing of the script to the work on the cutting table), the more the film will present a controlled and personal aspect.

There have been many discussions about what the content of a film should be, should it limit itself to entertainment or inform the public about the great social problems of the day, and I flee such discussions like the plague. I think that every individual should express himself and that all films are useful, be they formalistic or realistic, baroque or engaged, tragic or light, modern or old-fashioned, in color or in black and white, in 35mm or in Super 8, with stars or with unknowns, ambitious or modest. Only the result matters, which is the good the director does himself and the good he does others.

Fifty years ago a dramatist said: "All kinds are allowed except the boring kinds." I would gladly accept this definition on the condition that we could agree on what is boring, which is impossible.

The danger lying in wait for us whenever we give an interview during the course of which we define our work is of indulging in peremptory and definitive statements which are even worse than justifications. In declaring: "The cinema is this and that and only this and that," one slyly implies that one is a terrific guy while all the others are a bunch of bums. We are threatened by our own intolerance, our jealousy, our refusal to accept others, and I believe that we must struggle against this tendency in us. If the critics have maligned us, we declare war on them by saying that they don't know what they are talking about. If the critics have praised us, we blame them anyway because we think they have been too indulgent with the others!

When I started in films in 1954 by becoming Roberto Rossellini's assistant, he was thought of as a "finished" director. The films he made with his wife Ingrid Bergman were dragged through the mud by critics the world over. Rossellini was obviously sad about this state of affairs, but I clearly remember his saying to me one day: "At least I have one consolation in all this, which is that for the last three years I haven't once seen on the faces of the other Italian directors that frightening smirk of jealousy they wore after the success of *Open City, Paisan*, and even more when Ingrid came to share my life."

I have not forgotten these words, but at the time I did not appreciate their truth. When you are a nut about the movies, you love all the members of that family you would so much like to be a part of as a whole, not suspecting for a moment that you are dealing with the family of Orestes and Agamemnon!

Professional jealousy seems despicable to me. In order not to be loathsome, jealousy should go all the way to murder. If you are an embittered director, and Mike Nichols' success, his talents, his youth and his fortune bother you, then you should take a gun and kill Mike Nichols, eliminate him physically. If you do not have this courage, then your jealousy is pitiful, sordid, it makes a wretch of you and you have only one alternative: to accept the existence of Mike Nichols, your fellow.

I like women to be jealous, in all departments: jealous in love and jealous in beauty, for being a woman is a profession as it is, whose only patron is God. When it comes to artists, if we have the good fortune to practice an art and make a living from it, let us not look at ourselves as competitors or rivals but quite simply as other artists. Let us accept the differences between us. Each of us only realizes a part of his dream, but that dream was more or less beautiful, more or less attainable. Let us learn to detect and admire the strong points; we must not say, with a shrug of the shoulders: "Orson Welles? Bah, his films don't make any money," but "Orson Welles is the only filmmaker whose succession of images on the screen gives the impression of music." Directors have quirks, gimmicks or habits which belong to them alone and which help them work. We can call them their style or the tricks of their trade but we must respect and not question them.

Robert Bresson in his films refuses to use professional actors, he is right, *for him*. Alfred Hitchcock refuses to make Westerns or period films, he is right, *for him*. Jean-Luc Godard no longer wants to make films produced and consumed in a society whose destruction he hopes for, he is right, *for him*. Ingmar Bergman does not want to make films outside his country, Sweden, he is right, *for him*. Luis Buñuel no longer wants to use music in his films, he is right, *for him*. Roberto Rossellini only wants to make non-fiction films, he is right, *for him*. Howard Hawks means to almost always place his camera "at the level of the human eye," he is right, *for him*.

These producers are among the greatest in the world, they are orphans because their fathers are dead: Griffith, Lubitsch, Murnau, Dreyer, Mizoguchi, Eisenstein, Sternberg, Stroheim; but they still have brothers, lucky or unlucky, on the active list or out of work, but brothers who are at the same time their fellows: Renoir, Ford, Lang, Kurosawa, Walsh, Vidor, Chaplin and others, fewer and farther between, who were privileged to begin their careers with silent films and become masters of the talkies.

They are all great directors because the films they make resemble them, expressing both their ideas about life and their idea about the cinema, and because these ideas are strong and strongly presented.

You ask me at Esquire: "What advice would you give to future filmmakers?" I don't believe that one can give advice to anyone preparing to practice an artistic profession but I can try to define a few rules which have value for me and for me alone.

*The Public?* Let's not ask for its opinion, only for its money, in order to keep on working. Let's not make a declaration of love to the public; the director of a film, during its shooting, is its first spectator, if the scene works for him it must work for the public. However, when we fail, let's avoid saying: "My film will be understood in ten years," or, about an old failure, let's not say: "Today my film will find its public." This is an illusion, a lack of clarity, and it is preferable to move ahead, to try and make some progress.

*Progress?* It is a joke! We must try to make progress but it is well to know that it will be trifling compared to the wealth that is inside us and is expressed in our first roll of exposed film: all of Buñuel is in *The Andalusian Dog*, all of Welles in *Citizen Kane*, all of Godard in *Breathless*, all of Hitchcock in *The Lodger*.

*Doubts?* We must doubt our talent, we must not doubt our inspiration. We must not say to ourselves: "My God, this is dreadful, while children are dying of hunger in Biafra, I am filming a musical comedy about adultery," but remember that at the moment when we decided to film this musical comedy about adultery, we were in such a state of exaltation that we would have preferred to die rather than give up the project.

*Whose fault is it?* In case of difficulty, never blame others. If the scene is badly written we must not blame the scriptwriter, for the director must be capable of taking a piece of paper and writing what he feels. If the scene is badly acted it is not the actors' fault, we should have directed the scene differently or chosen better actors. If the editing is defective it's the same story, the chief editor carries out orders, he expects imaginative solutions.

Next—useless to give more examples—the same thing goes for the critics and the public. The director can neither expect nor demand from anyone other than himself the same passion, the same interest in the film. For us, it is the distillation of a year of preoccupations and thoughts but for the crew of workers which surrounds us, and is part of the film industry, it is one of the three thousand films produced in the world this year.

*The critics?* We must let them do their jobs. Blaming the critics when they pan us is childish for we should also then contest them when they applaud us. There does exist, for the too severely criticized artist, a psychological consolation that should not be ignored, and that is the "reputation" that grows a little later, mysteriously, not *against* the critics but *outside* them, and it seems to me validly. For example, if we consider Orson Welles' films one by one we notice that they have all been panned; yet, if we ask any film buff at all in the world, he will say that Orson Welles is a great director. Our films are not scientific, the reception the public gives them is not scientific, the portions of talent and luck are not scientific, why should we ask the critics to be scientific? Obviously, I have a good reason for defending the critics: I practiced that profession myself from 1953 to 1957!

The last piece of advice I would give is surely the most important: ignore all advice.

• • •

I have no ideas about what the future evolution of the cinema will be. When reporters come to interview me they often think they give me pleasure by saying: "You and your friends have changed the cinema; today the public no longer goes to the movies to see such and such a star but to see a film by Bergman, by Fellini, by Buñuel, by Godard, or by Truffaut." In reality, that remark causes me more anxiety than pride. I loved the movies when I was twelve, at the time of France's liberation when all the American films appeared on the screens of Paris. I would choose which of these films to go to by looking at the pictures outside the theatre. And then I began, I don't know why, to jot down the director's name in a notebook after I left the theatre each time I had liked the film; but those films were popular, everyone in the audience used the same means to follow the action and understand it. When, on July 6, 1946, I first saw *Citizen Kane*, I immediately felt that it would become my favorite film and knew that I would never forget the name of Orson Welles. But for the past ten years, each time I make a film it is with the hope of arousing the curiosity of strollers who choose their films by looking at the pictures outside the theatre, not bothering about the name of the director.

Today—I'm speaking about the situation in France—the strollers do not go readily into the movie theatres, they get drunk with the images at home. Whenever I go to the movies all I see in the theatre are almost empty rows; the few seats taken hold familiar faces, habitués of the film library, students of the cinema, a few fellow directors, a few impassioned script girls and above all lots of assistant directors, actors and would-be actors.

I realize that Hollywood has been described as a city of bakers where all they make is bread, but what will happen when the bread itself will no longer be eaten except by those who bake it?

When pessimistic thoughts of this sort cross my mind, I reassure myself by remembering the last sequence of a film of Ingmar Bergman's called The *Communicants* in Europe (*Winter Light* in the United States). At the end of *The Communicants*, one sees a priest who has practically lost his faith and finds himself celebrating mass in his church, which is completely empty. The film ends there, with the priest saying mass anyhow. I interpret this scene differently, thinking to myself: "*Yes, Bergman is trying to tell us that spectators all over the world are turning away from the movies but that he thinks we must continue to make films* JUST THE SAME, *even if there is no one in the theatres.*" I interpreted the scene this way and I have no idea whether this was Bergman's thought. In any case, it interested me to see in this ending a parable about the crisis of the cinema in the world.

—AUGUST 1970

# What Makes the Newest Nixon Run?

GARRY WILLS

8:30 A.M., APPLETON, WISCONSIN: This is the place where Joe McCarthy lived and was buried—a place, once, for Nixon to seek out on campaign; then, for a longer time, a place to steer carefully shy of. He has outlived both times, partially. And it is too late to care in any event: the entire American topography is either graveyard, for him, or minefield—ground he must walk delicately, revenant amid the tombstones, whistling in histrionic unconcern.

Not that Appleton wishes to remind him; the townspeople are busy pressing wood into paper, and all they want from Nixon, this time around, is a boost for the local product. Fair enough. Romney, after all, is milking cows in the cheese towns of Wisconsin. The least Nixon can do is fiddle with some pulp.

Appleton's Conway Hotel is offering coffee on one side of its banquet room, but the crowd has already curdled to a standstill half an hour before Nixon's scheduled "remarks." Those standing on the floor cannot see Nixon when he edges through the crowd onto a low platform and says, "Good morning." I am off to one side, where I see nothing but shadow bent distortedly onto the wall by insistent television lights—shadows, rather, since the angled lights give him one dark silhouette and a lighter "ghost" askew of it. Doubled hands rise and dip beside the haloed body, or flail in ghost gestures through it—six dim grades of shadow weaving elusive canons, visual echoes like the sound of "Tricky Dicky," fiction pictures. Six crises endured—six Nixons, which never quite add up or solidify. The hands move in jerky quick apparitions, dark ones unable to escape the haunting light ones, nimble pianist fingers, prestidigitating shadow.

His speech is the standard one of this campaign, but with a bit more partisan bite in it than those delivered in frosty New Hampshire. "Give 'em hell," someone shouts from the floor. "I don't need to," Nixon snaps back. His right hand shadows out, shaking nemesis: "They have given themselves hell." His pitch is to party loyalty: "I have been campaigning twenty years" (it is twenty-two). "I have campaigned in seven national elections" (three times for himself). "I have never campaigned against another Republican, and I'm not going to start it now. The way for a Republican to win is not to show how he can take on other Republicans, but to show how he can take on Lyndon Johnson." (Translation: "I will not accept yesterday's challenge to debate George Romney.")

He goes briskly toward the morning's business. "I'm glad to join the papermakers; but"—his right forefinger waggles its double plumes of shadow—"I want it understood that when we get to Washington we'll cut *down* on the paper work!" He moves to the papermaking gadget, presses a plunger, couches the excess water out of his paper disc, then dries it in a curved toaster. The master of ceremonies, meanwhile, tells him he will be the second President of the United States to have made paper (George Washington was the first). Appleton applauds. On to Stevens Point.

Each of Nixon's stops today will be in different congressional districts— Appleton, eighth; Stevens Point, seventh, largely Democrat, Polish, Catholic. I make my way, up the press bus, to Charlie McWhorter, the walking encyclopedia of Republican politics, and ask why this district was put so high on Nixon's list of places to visit. "Well, it's Mel Laird's district." (In fact, Laird got a federal water-pollution laboratory for the university—Wisconsin State—where Nixon will be speaking.) McWhorter, a veteran of two earlier Nixon campaigns, is riding the press bus, dazzling reporters with his expertise, because there is still no press secretary at this stage of Nixon's campaign. Pat Buchanan, acting press secretary, has other duties which make him fly with Nixon in his rented DC-3 while the press bus pants behind on the ground. "I'm here on pretty short notice myself," Charlie says. "I got the call last Wednesday"—two days before the campaign began. McWhorter, Chairman of the Young Republicans in 1955–58, became Nixon's protegé in the mid-Fifties, and has made a number of other Republicans his protegés. He is a good mixer—one of the mainstays of the Newport Jazz Festival, a bachelor who lives in the Village. On a first-name basis with hundreds of Republicans everywhere, he is supposed to be Nixon's guide to the local situation at each stop.

I used to have a friend in Wisconsin politics; I ask Charlie if he remembers the man. "No. But I'll bet Dick would." (I asked him later; he did.) "There's not much I can tell that man about Republican politics." McWhorter, who has an elfin pinched nose and chin, pushes his glasses up onto his bald head, perches them behind a tongue-of-flame wisp of remaining hair, and lifts his left eyebrow in a tight *circonflexe:* it is his trademark expression—the wise old kewpie doll: "Dick knows almost everything there is to know about the party's inner workings and geography."

12:00 NOON, STEVENS POINT: An hour before the talk, the school's gymnasium is almost full. It has the fresh-staleness of lacquer, basketball, young bodies. About half of the university's six thousand students will eventually squeeze into the gym or be clotted at its entries. I ask a dozen students, here and there, if they ever heard of the Hiss case. "Hess?" One thinks she heard *something* about it. What? "I don't know; just something." The sophomores were born in 1948. Here, at least, Nixon should be able to shed his past. But he isn't. I ask the students what they know about the man. The most frequent answer: "He was the Vice-President, once." (Way back, their voices say.) The second most common answer: "He is called Tricky Dick." Do you know why? "No." But the ghost is there. The third answer: "He was spit on in South America." Do you know why? "No."

It is typical of Nixon that the *indignity* inflicted at his most courageous moment should be remembered. He has called his life a series of crises. He might better have said a series of disasters. Even the victories hurt. He made his one real charge stick—Hiss was convicted, before McCarthy ever made an accusation. But this charge was mingled with all the wild ones that followed, and his role in the Hiss case gave him the reputation of a proto-McCarthy. He vindicated himself in the "Checkers speech." But to do so he had to violate his own privacy; and the experience left him with a permanent air of violation, not of vindication. No one remembers what he *said* to Khrushchev, only that he said it in a kitchen. He walked a fine line of reserve and calm during Eisenhower's illnesses; yet that only contributed to the impression of him as Ike's errand boy. Kennedy's election in 1960 is attributed to his eloquence and "style," Nixon's loss is put down to bad makeup. There is a genius of deflation that follows Nixon about, robbing him, at each crucial moment, of any air of heroism. He has been strong many times; but fate gets photographers to him when he collapses on Bill Knowland's shoulders in tears, or when he snarls at journalists. It is said that he cannot win; that this reputation is a self-fulfilling prophecy. But his real trouble is that he cannot lose—cannot look great in defeat (like Stevenson), bow out gracefully, leave well enough alone, disappear.

But that gaucheness of a man lingering on when he is no longer wanted becomes, at a certain ridiculous extreme, the crazy proof of his importance. He survives. He is always a leftover, and he always finds some job to perform in that capacity. He represents the marginally salvageable past. A part of the McCarthy mood, he could contribute to Ike's kind lobotomy of the electorate: Nixon would do the cutting, Eisenhower the curing—gall and honey. He mobilized the party while the General stood above partisanship. And when he was not mere spear carrier in the regime, he could be the hatchet carrier. The symbolism of McCarthy's exorcism was appropriate: Ike had Nixon repudiate him. Above party himself, barely aware of storms in the lower atmosphere, the General could still have "his" party, in the person of Nixon, disown McCarthy. Then, when reelection time came around, Ike tried to rise to new peaks on Olympus by disowning the disowner. He told his unhappy running mate to "chart his own course" when everyone knew Nixon had no other course to steer by but Ike's elusive coattail, swept up daintily, now, like a skirt not to be soiled with Nixon's touch. But Eisenhower had made too much use of the identification "Nixon-Party" to get rid of him. That would be not only rising above the party, but attacking it. Again, Nixon's past made him marginally useful—by just the margin that kept him from being jettisoned.

Nixon's present followers are trying once again to turn his left-over state to advantage. He is not only left over from the Eisenhower Administration (which came into office during an Asian war, and ended it). The Nixon staff actually calls his defeat at the hands of Kennedy a virtue: there is something glamorous about being a survivor of "the Kennedy era," even if one played the role, in it, of Mordred. Nixon's people like to tell the story of the little girl whose memory of the 1960 debate is that Nixon was "President Kennedy's friend." If one must be a ghost, he might as well be the ghost of Camelot past.

But the pitch at Stevens Point cannot be ghostly. It is all about the future: he comes down hard on a major theme of his new campaign, the "last third of the century" theme. "You can *change* the world. By 2000 A.D., we can wage a successful war against poverty, hunger, misery, and most disease. It is a challenging world, yes! But what an exciting time to be alive!" There is a Camelot in your future.

That is the substance. But much of the speech is mere games that politicians play. "Mel Laird told me . . ." and "As I told Mel Laird. . . ." Stroke. Stroke. The President of the University, Lee Sherman Dreyfus, is a swinger, proud of the fact that his initials are L.S.D. "We're going on a trip together," he told students last fall, when he took office. When he rises to introduce Nixon, he warns the students that what they do will be picked up by the cameras of national TV. "We will be judged by the community of scholars." The meeting is of global concern. (Here he casually puts his hands in his pockets and reveals his own large globe covered with red sweater, a key chain dangling almost to his knees—he must have become a swinger in the Forties.) He introduces those on the platform, including his wife: "Cool it," he growls over the applause, "I've got to live with her." The remark is much appreciated by the students—if not by the community of scholars. L.S.D. is as popular with his students as L.B.J. is unpopular.

So Nixon, skilled at this sort of thing, maneuvers deftly onto the

President's coattail with his opening words. "I asked your President, who I know is a professor of communications, if that included television. He said it does. Maybe if I'd known him in '60, I'd be in the White House now." Yesterday in Green Bay he said that if Vince Lombardi had been coaching him in '60, he might be in the White House. At TV appearances he tells everyone, from the makeup man and the camera crew to the producer and interviewer, that "If only. . . ." Much of the population will soon think Richard Nixon needs *them*, and if only he had known them in 1960. . . . When he is not flattering the President, during his speech, he works on the students: "In the last third of the century, great advances will be made in fields like automation and cybernetics (on which you know far more than I do). . . . You, as students of history, know better than I. . . ." Stroke. Stroke.

The question period goes well. "Mr. Vice-President," begins the first student. "No, Hubert's coming next week." "I mean Mr. former Vice-President." "That's all right; I've been called everything" (a line he used regularly in the '62 campaign—even his jokes are durable). A Eugene McCarthy group has passed out hard questions to be asked; when the first of these is brought up, Nixon unfolds a petition the McCarthy group brought for him to sign, and answers its three requests point by point, disposing of most of the hard questions all at once. A voice shaky with anger says Nixon is a liar unless he is willing to support revolution in Latin America. Nixon, after deploring Castroite violence, calmly ticks off four ways to "revolutionize" the Latin-American economy, agriculture, education, and aid programs. When he finishes, to applause rivaling that of L.S.D., President Dreyfus rises, puts his red globe against the microphone stand, and confirms the success: "Just in case, in November, you're looking for a job—you're a pretty good lecturer; just give me a call."

The students mob him in the corridor, fluttering papers at him for his autograph. The curly black hair, washed far back now on both sides of eroded blunt headland that had been his widow's peak, ducks down as he leaves that little bit of him that politicians play out in ink and energy to every passerby—his name scrawled across I.D. cards, agriculture textbooks, Gene McCarthy questionnaires. When two girls push irritably at the spongy ball of people rolling and breathing all around him, one stops, in mid-struggle, to say, "Boy, he's getting *manhandled.*" The other shrugs superiorly, "Let's face it, he likes it," and huffs her way in. The odd thing about this athletic ceremony is that there is so little respect for it on either side—with the hounds or with the hare.

3:15 P.M., OSHKOSH: The bus rolls into an improbably luxurious motel. In the press room, typewriters cautiously, oh-so-tentatively meditate student response at Stevens Point. *Is* there, then, a *new* new-Nixon—Nixon$^{10}$, already one life beyond the cat's allotment? Those who have to file stories are on the phone; most of those who don't are at the makeshift bar. McWhorter is there, brooding, under raised left triangle of eyebrow, on districts and registrations and voter margins. Then the "real" (well, *pro tem*) press secretary comes in, Pat Buchanan. As usual, he has a black overcoat on, with the collar wrapped up around his lumpy raw face—forty-year-old torpedo, hands on the iron in his pockets? No, he is twenty-nine, a writer, one of Nixon's fresh batch of intellectuals. Pat was, indeed, the very first. He climbed aboard in time to make the '66 campaign swing with Nixon and to accompany him on his '67 tour of the Middle East. Earlier, he caddied for the Vice-President at Burning Tree Club when Nixon had to trudge around the links, a glorified caddy for Ike. Pat was nine at the time of the Hiss case. After a turn as editorial writer on the conservative St. Louis *Globe-Democrat* and some dabbling in the conservative activism of Young Americans for Freedom, he made overtures to Nixon, was invited to New York for a three-hour interview, and became the first of the '68 crop of bright young men. He has proved himself in the interval; he keeps the briefing file on all current affairs, called "the Q and A" (Nixon likes to use lawyer jargon, his talks are full of phrases like "self-serving evidence" and "adversary procedure"). With Ray Price's help, Pat drew up the first version of Nixon's *Pueblo* statement. But, old-timer that he is on this new staff, he was not with "the Boss" (as all the staff call him) in 1960, the Presidential year Pat became old enough to vote—so, while performing a thousand duties by day, he reads up on the '60 campaign at night, using Theodore White's book as his basic text.

Pat has come to the press room to tell me I can ride the plane with Nixon to Chicago tonight; I should get my luggage out of the bus and into one of the staff cars. He also wants to know what the press is making of the Stevens Point performance. Several reporters ask him if the four points Nixon rattled off are part of a position paper on Latin America. "No. He surprised me. I had heard some of that dam-stuff from him in private, but not all put together just this way. That's what's so dam-amazing about this dam-guy: he's got all the dam-information stored up there, and if you touch any dam-subject out it comes." (Pat uses his idiosyncratically turned prefix much as the ancient Greeks scattered particles throughout a sentence, to distribute emphases.) Before the campaign began, Buchanan described for me his Middle East trip, during which the Israeli war broke out: "The Boss was talking to all these dam-officials in Israel, and he knew as much of the dam-position of the Arabs and Russians as they did. He sat there sketching all the dam-possibilities, and amazed the officials. That's the way he is. Take any political situation in the dam-world, and he has war-gamed it this way and that, considering every which way it might go."

7:00 P.M., FOND DU LAC: Ill-omened name for a town that manufactures outboard motors. But another solid Republican district (the sixth, Congressman Steiger's district)—good spot for a Lincoln Day dinner, perhaps the twentieth at which Nixon has had a speech to give (his first was delivered in 1948, at Bill Scranton's invitation, in Pennsylvania). Charlie McWhorter is at the press table, but he keeps bouncing up to greet old friends as they mount the dais or drift by it—young Bill Steiger, plump Ody Fish, Joe this and Jim that. While "Los Banditos" tootle their imitation Tijuana, the Nixons arrive, she ducking her tight nods of acknowledgement, he with his fixed smile behind which the eyes burrow and surface, war-gaming the situation; flash up and move back down—down somewhere, to chambers that *must* exist but have not been plumbed. He has the effrontery, for which he may never be forgiven, of carrying out before the public an embarrassingly private set of eyes, eyes unable to rest vacuously on the pomp of Fond du Lac's Lincoln Day bunting. It would be more decent to leave those eyes at home—at least the intelligent part of them.

I am sitting, now, just below the dais; I see him and not his shadow. There are no multiple images crossing, complicating, in some measure canceling each other. Yet in the very motions of the man there seems some unintended syncopation—not mere duplicity (Tricky Dick), but multiplicity (new Nixons to the nth degree, yet each old one jerking still at one part of his frame or face, giving a lack of focus to him even when he stands, in his customary dark suit, before the lights and cameras).

It is easy to fall down the bottomless pit of Herblockism—the reverse of being star struck. Kennedy was prettier than Nixon—which should not matter to anyone but adolescent girls. Nixon has a pear face, advancing at you about the mouth and jowls, receding from you about the brow and eyes; yet it is worse than phrenology, it is some weird prosopology, to blame ideology on genes, or try to read character from facial contour. Nixon's physical reflexes are not very good; he was a clumsy second-string player on the Whittier College football team. Some of his poor focus is probably nothing more than poor reflexes.

The introduction of the honored guest is standard fare, like our slices of meat glued soggily together: Lincoln "bound up the nation's wounds after the war" (he didn't, he didn't live to). "Even his foes said he was a man of unquestioned integrity" (on the contrary, some of his friends wondered at times if he was a crook). Then something about "illusions of grandeur," and "attributes of computence," and—moving on to Nixon—"simularities between he and the Great Emancipator." It is a speech that could not be given without notes—all *studied* clusters of cliché.

Nixon, on the contrary, rarely speaks from notes, and he likes for everyone to know this: after the introduction, men move the bulky wooden podium away, and Nixon stands there gesturing stiffly, shielded by nothing but the bar of the microphone stand. There is no obvious simularity between he and the Great Emancipator. Nixon is (relatively) short and glib, not the kind to swap pungent stories in the back room. But there are some resemblances. Two big posters with Lincoln's features flank Nixon. The Emancipator, too, was a caricaturist's dream, an ugly fellow easily Herblockized. Both men, despite a natural reticence, were successful courtroom pleaders. Both learned the electoral process inside and out, clean side and dirty, and were proud of the fact that they could play this dangerous game with the best and with the worst—though it was not easy for either of them. Tricky Abe.

But Lincoln, though unimpressive as an orator, knew how to convey some of his private vision in words. He was a classical rhetorician, familiar with all the schoolboy tropes. Yet, like all poets, he used the standard techniques to speak what was original in him. "Bind up the nation's wounds"—the bleeding body politic is an old worn image; but Lincoln made it, irrevocably, his. Nixon, up there, pivots and rattles words impressively; but they have no core. It is not because he has not "made them his" at a certain level. The newsmen have heard them all before. It is easy to take notes (few of the reporters know shorthand): "Let the time . . ." stands for, "Let the time never come when the forces that desire victory have a military superiority over the forces that desire peace." "Some courts . . ." stands for, "Some of the courts have gone too far to weaken the peace forces as against the criminal forces." "Ground . . ." stands for, "There is no ground more important than the ground we stand on. . . ." The words are well-organized, well-rehearsed, carefully weighed. Nixon thinks any basic speech through for almost as many weeks as he spends reciting it. He has infuriated many speech writers by tearing all the threads out and restitching a talk in his own idiom, a resolutely non-heroic idiom. Even his own final draft of "the campaign speech" was too formal for him. As I followed the text the first time he gave it, in New Hampshire, I noticed an impatience with periodicity, an unwillingness to build toward a climax. He kept breaking his own written sentences down into smaller units, piecing them out with "Ands" and "Buts." He shies—as Lincoln did not—from the portentous statement. Yet this personal characteristic does not express personality. It gives his words a stiff matter-of-factness, a disjointedness despite the speech's careful structure. One feels it could break off at any moment, there is no long climb up to a concluding height. The speech does not "swing." It has no rhythm. Its reflexes are faulty.

At this point, I was in danger, once again, of thinking in terms of a beauty contest. The disjointedness of the talk seemed expressed in his face as he scowled (his only expression of thoughtfulness) or grinned (his only expression of pleasure). The features do not quite work together. The famous nose looks detachable. In pictures, its most striking aspect is the ski-jump silhouette ("Bob Hope and I would make a great ad for Sun Valley"), but the aspect that awes one when he meets Nixon is its distressing *width*, and the depth of the ravine running down its center, and its general fuzziness (Nixon's "five-o'clock shadow" extends all the way up to his heavy eyebrows, though—like many hairy men—he is balding above the brows' "timberline"). The nose swings far out; then, underneath, it does not rejoin his face in a straight line, but curves far up again, leaving a large but partially screened space between nose and lip. The whole face's lack of *jointure* is emphasized by the fact that he has no very defined upper lip (I mean the lip itself, the thing makeup men put lipstick on, not the mustache area). The mouth works *down* solely, like Charlie McCarthy's—a rapid but restricted motion, not disturbing the heavy luggage of jowl on either side. When he smiles, the space under his nose rolls up (and in) like the old sunshades hung on front porches. The parts all seem to be worked by wires, a doomed attempt to contrive "illusions of grandeur."

One feels guilty noticing such things. It is embarrassing to feel oneself sinking to the level of Mitch Miller at a Miss America contest. And yet that very sensation increases the difficulty of listening to Nixon's words: one does not like to feel embarrassed by a candidate. That must explain a good deal of the popular antipathy to Nixon. One is *embarrassed* to keep meeting the dog one kicked yesterday.

Dwight Chapin increases the illusion of a Miss America contest: he looks like a young Bert Parks, with regular, lifeless features and patent-leather hair. He was seven at the time of the Hiss case, and still a student during Nixon's last campaign (in '62). After some time spent in an advertising agency, he became Nixon's personal aide, in charge of extracting him from affairs like this and sorting his staff out into cars. Now he tells me where those cars are, and I go to the one behind Nixon's, accompanied by Ray Price.

If Buchanan, with his Y.A.F. background, is the right wing of Nixon's brain trust, Price—who was in charge of the late *Herald Tribune* editorial page—is the left wing. While Buchanan keeps up the Q and A file, Price works on longer-term projects. Like Buchanan, he went with the Boss on one of his study trips, this one to the Orient. Price drew up the Nixon article on Asian policy that appeared in *Foreign Affairs* last fall—a compound of specifics (S.E.A.T.O. is obsolete, we should strengthen A.S.P.A.C.) and slogans (China should be treated with "creative counterpressure," "dynamic detoxification"—and so, evasively, through the alphabet).

Price, a handsome young man, is almost a senior citizen on the new staff. He was seventeen during the Hiss case. He is working, now, on the problems of the cities. What, I ask him, does Nixon mean when he says *some* of the courts have weakened the forces of law? "Well, he doesn't want to place all the blame on the Supreme Court." What other courts does he have in mind? "I don't know for sure. Have the courts convicted many rioters?" No. (Riots are not the best time or place in which to collect the hard evidence that leads to convictions.) But is that what Nixon meant? "You'll have to ask him." That is: since the Birchers have preempted criticism of the Supreme Court, Nixon must try vaguely to attack the court without sounding as if he planned to impeach Earl Warren. Tricky, eh?

I ask Price who Nixon's advisers are—on, say, Asian affairs. "Well, he still has many contacts in the government. I can't name names, of course, since they are still employees of the United States Government, and their position can't be used for partisan purposes by a candidate. Most of his contacts are in the foreign service." How about the academy? "Fewer there; I am trying to get him together with some people. But, primarily he is his own expert."

Nixon, despite his vast knowledge, makes few overtures to intellectuals. Those around him are younger than he is; and most of them either came to him on their own (like Buchanan) or were recruited by Len Garment, a silky-smooth lawyer in Nixon's firm. Garment's great recruiting drive took place last September when he arranged interviews with Nixon for Martin Anderson and Richard Whalen. Anderson (eleven years old when Hiss was investigated) is the author of *The Federal Bulldozer*; he has drawn up Nixon's plan for abolishing the draft (after a Vietnamese settlement) and establishing a computer job-bank for handling unemployment. Whalen—about the same age as Anderson—is the biographer of Joseph Kennedy, the writer-in-residence at Georgetown University's Center for Strategic Studies, and he has a more than recent interest in the Middle East (which plays a big role in Nixon's view of foreign policy, and in his standard speech). Whalen is also interested in the problem of big-city riots (he drew up Nixon's law-and-order speech to the National Association of Manufacturers). Other men were closer at hand during Garment's talent hunt—e.g., John Sears (seven years old in 1948), a young member of the Nixon firm, and Thomas Evans (Ray Price's age), a partner.

10:00 P.M., OSHKOSH: A blowy airport, and the weathered DC-3 that has been tilted up and down in short hops from district to district all day. Mrs. Nixon goes up into the private section with her husband; the rest of the staff fills the twenty seats left in the rear. Rose Mary Woods is in the first seat—the redheaded secretary who joined Nixon's staff when he came to the Senate in 1951 (she had been secretary to a congressman). Rose is the channel through which everyone communicates with the Boss, heroine of the thousand crises that flare up and are extinguished around a public man, who cannot be distracted by them; and villainous to many disgruntled veterans of these crises. She is protective, devoted, inclined to hold a grudge (as newsmen find out when they say bad things about the Boss). Len Hall calls her "the mother hen" who guards an embattled switchboard—though others add that she has no power Nixon does not want to give her. Hall's criticism of the 1960 campaign, which he was supposed to be managing, is that the Boss made all decisions, kept everything in the palm of his hand, wanted to know everything, do everything, "war-game" everything. The instrument for such total control is the indefatigable Rose.

"Nixon's trouble," a campaign manager of one of his rivals said recently, "is that he doesn't understand the way a campaign affects a candidate's judgment. A campaign is like a delicate operation—you have to choose your surgeon carefully, then put yourself in his hands. Nixon not only refuses to take the anesthetic, he keeps popping his head up and telling the doctor to cut a little to the right." There is reason for Nixon to treat campaign mangers with skepticism. As a novice to politics, he put himself in the hands of an old pro, Murray Chotiner, the California kingmaker who had managed Earl Warren and Bill Knowland. But things were done in those early campaigns which Nixon knew nothing of and which have haunted him ever since: the author of the famous "pink paper" used against Helen Douglas told me recently how he and Chotiner whipped it up, one night in a hotel room, and released it without Nixon's ever seeing it. Chotiner kept other things from Nixon, too—the breaking of the Fund scandal, for instance. He also tore up Nixon's telegram of resignation to Ike during that emotional time. Nixon does not trust himself in other's hands now. He began this campaign without a manager (and without a press secretary, issuing the call to McWhorter a mere two days before the campaign's start).

The DC-3's motors pop and backfire in the moist Wisconsin winter—"Where did you dig this one up, Dwight?" The banter of people traveling together, never more than half-relaxed, pops and backfires as the plane rocks over runways, settles down to serious roaring, gets itself determinedly into the air. After we have been airborne for several minutes, Pat Buchanan, muttering about the dam-winds, leans and does stiff-legged involuntary curtsies down the aisle: the Boss will see me now.

Up in the forward cabin, only two lights are on—those picking out the seats on either side of a card table (Quaker Nixon hasn't played poker since his Navy days—he always won). Mrs. Nixon's sedately moderated red hair, in a cottony-puff hairdo, glitters dully under one light. The other picks out her husband's great declivity of nose. Murmuring politely, she puts out a hand to brace herself (it is a redhead's hand, full of freckles) and goes back to talk with Rose. I slide in under the little forward spotlight, as Nixon clicks his own light off, sinks his head back into shadow, and pulls his overcoat around him (the plane is cold as well as noisy, I have to lean forward out of my little pool of light toward his darkness, straining to hear him).

I had been told that Nixon's technique, in these midair interviews, is to filibuster on the first question, so I should ask what I really want to know at the outset—"Give him your high hard one right off"—or I might never get him around to it. Unfortunately, I had no high hard one. Besides, how does one outtrick Tricky? I knew that for the most intricate Q, he would have a well-prepared A. So I didn't fool with Vietnam and stuff. What I would like was some insight into the man muffled in the dark across from me. I remembered that Nixon has referred quite often to Teddy Roosevelt. Sometimes men's heroes reveal their aspirations. I asked if he felt any special affinity to the Republican Roosevelt. "Not so much in ideas." Pause. His answer was quiet, and there was none of that nervous speed of reply that characterizes him in public. "I guess I'm like him in one way only: I like to be in the arena. I have seen those who have nothing to do—I could be one of them if I wanted—the people just lying around Palm Beach. Nothing could be more pitiful." His voice had contempt in it, not pity.

Two things surprised me—the nature of the emotion that showed through, and the fact that it *did* show. His voice had a different timbre to it—a resonance of selfhood, a little unguardedness (very little, he is a politician twenty-four hours a day). Out in the light, he had splintered into shadows. Here in shadow he solidified, drew himself together, stopped gesturing. The first time I saw him was at a reception, where he sailed determinedly through sticky clusters of people, using his hands, out front, for prow; clasping them, sweeping them to make a point (and make a path), making the rounds. On the platform, he keeps his hands in a ball over his stomach—there is no podium to rest them on, and he would have to lift them too far to get a gesture launched if they hung at his sides. His motions are standardized—using one hand to count off points on the other; hammering balled hand into cupped hand; "on the one hand" (left arm woodenly out from the elbow), "on the other" (right arm ditto). But he mixes one special gesture in—a fluttering of the fingers that suggests confetti falling (he used it for comic denial, along with a grimace that turns his eyes up in his head—both are comic in ways not intended).

I had wondered if he keeps his hands so protectively before him in private. I heard conflicting reports: Pat Buchanan said no; but a political figure who had a friendly recent conference with Nixon told me he put his hands together in a prayer-clasp, then flipped them back and forth all through the conversation, saying, "But the *other* side of the coin. . . ." War games.

Now though, in the plane, he wrapped his arms around him in the cold and did not gesture at all. There was no fence out in front of him. And no face. Perhaps they come to much the same thing. It is unfair to judge Nixon as the least pretty of the candidates. But, as he talked without the gesticulating accents in his voice, with no movement of his hands or (so far as I could see into the shadow) of his caricature features, it occurred to me that the face *does* matter, because it affects the man behind it. Perhaps a Rockefeller, or Romney, or Reagan, or Percy, or Lindsay does not live entirely on the surface; still, each one could do so if he wanted—it is a very pleasant surface. And if none of them lives *entirely* there, it pays each to do a good deal of commuting to that pleasant locale. It wouldn't pay Nixon at all. He must be aware that people vote for him despite his appearance; he speaks, always, across a barrier. To carry that barrier about with one, to *be* that barrier, must introduce a painful complexity to one's approach toward fickle things like television and reporters and New Hampshire voters. One gets the impression, watching Nixon's brain turn rapidly in public behind the slowly working mask, that he is challenging one, saying, "Which are you going to advert to? What is important to you?" While he is being tested as a candidate, he feels he is a test of others' seriousness.

*Seriousness.* Responsibility. He has no respect for those "lying around at Palm Beach." All the Republicans who ever had an eye on '68 are extravagantly serious, bad at small talk, not known for their ability to relax. Nixon *had* to play golf, for Ike; or poker, to pass time in the Pacific. Romney hits three balls and runs from shot to shot on the golf course, so he won't waste any time playing *golf*. Rockefeller indulges in art-collecting as a form of philanthropy. Percy exercises feverishly in his private swimming pool. Only Reagan seems to be able to play—but then, he *is* a player, that's his job. If all of them were locked in a room and forbidden to talk about politics, they would bore each other to death within a week.

Part of this comes from the fact that they are all children of the Depression. Nixon, Percy and Reagan worked their way through college in the Thirties, when a college degree was still hard to get, and still worth getting. (Romney tried several times and couldn't make it through.) The Depression even affected Rockefeller, up in his financial stratosphere: he wanted to be a "regular fellow" (the very language he used) at Dartmouth, and asked for a campus job; but he was gently convinced that he would be depriving some poor student of a job he needed to get through college. All of the future candidates were ambitious: they dutifully participated in one sport (the minimum required of campus leaders in the Thirties): football for Nixon and Reagan, soccer for Rockefeller, water polo for Percy. Nixon, Reagan, and Percy were made Class or Student Body presidents. But only Nixon, in this dreary club, got high grades. In a serious field, he outseriouses them all. Locked in that room, under the drone of boredom, he would probably die last. (Romney, appropriately, would go first, singing Mormon hymns of horror at men's shallowness.) Nixon would survive by studying the signs of disintegration in the others. He was known, in law school, for his "iron butt." He "studies" everything—even the procedure for ordering properly sliced tomatoes in a restaurant (a process he described at great length to Mark Harris, to avoid the ordeal of small talk).

Our conversation in the plane moved from the Palm Beach Nixon despises into "the arena." I asked if he thought he could handle the challenges of the Presidency in this almost apocalyptic year, 1968. "Yes. It is a time when a man who knows the world will be able to forge a whole new set of alliances, with America taking the lead in solving the big problems. We are now in a position to give the world all the good things that Britain offered in her Empire without any of the disadvantages of nineteenth-century colonialism." You think we have a kind of manifest destiny? "No, not in Beveridge's sense—though Bowers' book on Beveridge is one of the most instructive I have read." (Score one for Nixon, the grind. I wonder if any of the other candidates ever heard of Claude Bowers? We'll charitably give them Albert Beveridge.) "You asked me if Teddy Roosevelt were my hero. Not in the sense that Wilson is. I think he was our greatest President of this century. You'll notice, too, that he was the best-educated." (Score two for Nixon; he knows he is the only Republican candidate who got high grades in school, and who stayed in school after his four years of college.) "Wilson had the greatest vision of America's world role. But he wasn't practical enough. Take his 'open agreements openly arrived at.' That is not the way diplomacy is conducted. The Vietnamese war, for instance, will be settled at secret high-level negotiations. The Johnson Administration has boxed itself in where it can't undertake these. But a new Administration could and would."

What about the home front? Do you think you could talk to the militant black leaders, to bring civil peace to our cities? "Well, you have to be conceited to be in this business; and this will sound conceited. But I think I could do it as well as any man. I'm very good at one-to-one relationships. You'll notice that I don't have any witness here; I never have Pat take notes on my private interviews. I think that when a third person is present, one is distracted, wondering what *his* reaction is. Or people sometimes show off to the third man. But if there are just two of you, you can concentrate totally on each other." Not on "image." Not on "face." Nixon would like to carry on all his dealings away from the public—he *does* like darkness; he can only be personal where "personality" is not an issue. Revelations like the Fund speech were violations; and he has all the scars of a violated man. A friend close to him in his Vice-Presidential days says he came back from his humiliating encounters with Eisenhower almost in tears, wanting no one to see him. It is easy to make something sinister of his desire to avoid public encounters and broad daylight.

This led to my next question: "Don't you feel it demeaning that you have to get out and shake hands and grin; that you have to worry about makeup and lighting?" "Well, on the television thing, yes. Isn't that a hell of a thing—that the fate of a great country can depend on camera angles? I get so impatient with the whole process that I refuse to take coaching. But as to shaking hands, I like to do that—it brightens people's lives to meet a celebrity; and, as you may have noticed, I'm rather good at it." He is not. I watched him, close up, shaking hands for three hours as an endless line passed by him in New Hampshire. Behind the polite ducking nods, empty jokes, forced amiability, Nixon's mind was almost visibly fidgeting, worrying about the multiple "third person" photographing him, studying him over the line's crawl, criticizing every move. Beside him his wife stood the three hours in high heels, her faced chilled with smiles, her mouth puckering as the ninetieth child went by and had to be admired with a long-distance kiss. Her eyes are not like her husband's, here, there and everywhere; they follow each person who moves by her, some coming close to whisper, some straying wide to size her up—right to left, she keeps them each in focus; but, for the split second when she turns back, left to right, to greet a new face, the eyes blur momentarily, blanking out all unnecessary sensation connected with this ordeal. She is saving herself, in split seconds, all the long afternoon that she spends herself. On her way to the school where these crowds waited for her, newsmen caught Mrs. Nixon and asked how she felt at the outset of another long campaign. She bravely answered, "I love it; one meets so many old friends again." But I watched her hands as she said it; the freckled hands were picking at each other, playing with gloves, trying to still each other's trembling. There is one thing worse than being a violated man—and that's being a violated man's wife.

It intrigued me that Nixon, who is obviously aware of his public handicaps, should think he is good at handshaking. I asked what he meant: "I am able to treat each person as an individual. I have more sympathy with the so-called unimportant people than many intellectuals have. I guess that's why you guys in the press say I do better in the small towns than in the big cities. I admit it. That's true. But some liberals who claim to have so much 'concern' don't give a damn about the individual." That is the answer: it is part of his "one-to-one" philosophy. "The last person who should be arrogant is the intellectual, who *should* know better, but. . . ." He broke off; the contempt had come back into his voice. Palm Beach idlers, arrogant intellectuals. No wonder he thinks he can talk to the common man. He feels—whether happily or not—that he is common. I recalled a memorandum he composed just after the Hiss case (Earl Mazo was allowed to consult it): Hiss, Nixon wrote, "was rather insolent toward me from the time that I insisted on bringing Frankfurter's name in, and from that time my suspicion concerning him continued to grow." Hiss was not only a perjurer; he was "rather insolent toward me." The arrogant intellectual. It was Harvard Law against Whittier College. That helps explain early Nixon outbursts like: "If the American people understood the real character of Alger Hiss, they would boil him in oil."

Romney and Percy and Reagan are Midwesterners. But all three made a great deal of money comparatively early in life, and moved in wide circles. Percy picked out the mansion he lives in now when he was still an impoverished teenager. Romney was an "operator" in Washington lobbyist circles (aluminum, automobiles) long before he went to American Motors. And destiny's tot was sipping his soda in the right drugstore before he was out of his twenties. Nixon, who worked even harder than single-minded men like Percy and Romney, never had any real money until 1960; of all those who made a play for the nomination, he still has "small town" marked all over him, despite his success as a corporation lawyer in New York.

Whittier was a Quaker town of citrus groves when Nixon was growing up in it. Whittier College was a Quaker school. And Nixon's family was so archetypically Quaker that Jessamyn West wrote *The Friendly Persuasion* about his (and her) great-grandfather. After Nixon's successful career in the little Quaker college, his faculty adviser could still recommend him to the Duke Law School in these terms: "If he has any handicap, it is his lack of sophistication." The lack was a militant one. Even little Whittier had its (comparatively) high society—the Franklins, the college social club, affected formal dress among the citrus trees. Nixon founded an underdog group, symmetrically non-Franklinian, called the Orthogonians (squares), with a foursquare slogan of "Beans, Brawn, Brains and Bowels." One has difficulty imagining Alger Hiss's initiation into the Orthogonians. Nixon's first great successes were in debate, at which he excelled—

by the triumph of content over style. The square would outsmart the smart guys, with the help of his "iron butt."

The desire to win was there early—to meet the smart guys, to get out of Whittier. He has described several times the way he yearned after the Santa Fe trains that tore through Whittier. He listened for those trains at night. His attempts to get out of the town began early: in his final year at Duke's law school, he went to New York and applied first to two major firms for a job (one of them was John Foster Dulles's firm); but neither wanted him. Then he lowered his sights considerably and, with his fresh law degree, applied to the F.B.I. to become an agent. The Bureau had just undergone a budget cut, and *they* didn't want him. So he went back to Whittier, joined a small practice and then set up his own—till Pearl Harbor, when he went to Washington to apply for war work (he eased over slowly, slowly, to the Navy, an uneasy transition for a Quaker). Back to Whittier for a political base, and the campaign of a veteran returned from war. Back again to California, after his defeat in 1960. As soon as he thought he was washed up in politics (and so did not need "a base"), he went to New York and a large law firm—the fulfillment of his trip that last year at Duke. Yet he tells people he likes New York because it gives him privacy and not for the city's society or high life or culture. Nixon is the small-town boy in the city—alien there, but not wanting to go home. His footloose habits are not merely part of his determined study of world affairs; he has no real home. In 1960, on Election Day, he drove into Mexico while returns were coming in. On the day of his Senate election, he held a disconsolate picnic by the sea—moving; trying to distract himself, unsuccessfully. He escapes, not to his home but into anonymity and distance—down the Santa Fe track.

Still marked with Whittier, he always feels challenged to win the victory of content over style. And he does his homework still. The great example was the Hiss case. In 1946, "the Communist issue" was just being born. (Nixon now says it had *not* arisen.) The Dies Committee—or Rankin Committee as it was then being called—was already controversial. Eleanor Roosevelt was saying that Communists should not be allowed to teach in American schools—but that she would fear for the health of a campus that had no communist students. A schizophrenia was developing toward our World War II allies. In this period, under Chotiner's guidance, Nixon made an issue of Congressman Jerry Voorhis's support by the C.I.O.'s leftist Political Action Committee; and he won. He did not know much about communism, but he soon put his "iron butt" to work on the subject. In that 1947 class, he sat on the Labor Committee with two other freshmen who were interested in the issue of communism, two conservative Roman Catholics (Catholics had already been guided toward a militant anticommunism party by Pius XI and Pius XII)—Jack Kennedy of heavily Catholic Massachusetts, and Charles Kersten of heavily Catholic (and Polish) Wisconsin. Kersten came from Milwaukee, where the Communist infiltration of unions was a burning issue; he and Kennedy held some Labor Committee hearings in Milwaukee.

Nixon, sizing up his colleagues, decided Kersten knew a great deal about Communism (more, clearly, than young Jack Kennedy); so he formed an alliance with him to study the problem. I asked Nixon about those days when he was new in Washington, when (without knowing it) he was about to be involved in the Hiss case: "Charlie Kersten is a deeply religious man, whose anti-communism is of a philosophical sort. It's too bad he came from that terrible district [the old fifth] where he couldn't get reelected after his third term. He taught me most of what I know about communism." Later, I asked Kersten if this were true: "Not really. I led him to the people who really taught him—especially Father Cronin. But Dick was very curious about communism even before I met him. After some hearing in which he noticed the line of my questioning, he came over and asked me where I had obtained my information. So we tackled the problem together."

Their investigation was simultaneously naïve and sophisticated. The two young congressmen trudged from embassy to embassy of the Iron Curtain lands, asking whether there was a free press, or free speech, in each country. Kersten told me: "I remember the Czechoslovak ambassador was very nervous while we were questioning him, and we didn't know why. The next day we heard about the coup that had put Gottwald in power—what the ambassador, clearly, had been hearing the day before, at the very time when we were asking all those questions about freedom and communism in his country. That was February of '48."

Kersten, a courtly Milwaukee lawyer, had been doing his own homework, and he took Nixon to see his teachers. "I introduced Dick to the then Monsignor Fulton Sheen, who had just finished a book on communism. We spent a long evening discussing it, and he gave us autographed copies. The book had not yet appeared. Then I took him to see Father Cronin." That meeting, in 1947, is the one that determined the outcome of the Hiss case. By seeking out teachers, Nixon stumbled on information that made the encounter of Whittier College with Harvard Law a kind of rigged bout between David and Goliath.

Father John Cronin was a student of John A. Ryan, the pioneer of Catholic social thought. He followed Ryan into the union movement during the Forties, and he has remained true to this heritage by working with civil-rights groups in the Sixties. In the interval—through most of the Fifties, while he was formally employed by the National Catholic Welfare Conference in Washington—he devoted himself to Richard Nixon, as a kind of one-man brain trust. The relationship grew out of their work on the Hiss investigation.

I went to see Father Cronin, who is now a teacher behind the heavily scrolled Renaissance facade of St. Mary's Seminary in Baltimore. He is a white-haired, pink-faced, very gentle man who is known as the most sympathetic listener to seminarians with problems. "Most of the walking wounded make it as far as my door." I asked him how he got involved with Nixon and Hiss. "Early in the Forties, when I was working with the dockside unions in Baltimore, some of my friends came to me with complaints that they were being voted out of union offices by suspiciously packed meetings. I did a little investigating and found these were Communist cadres at work. About that time the F.B.I. approached me to find out what I knew about this. Soon I was in touch with Bill Sullivan [now an Assistant Director of the F.B.I.]. I kept track of what was going on for them. And I got to know many agents intimately. Cardinal—then Archbishop Mooney—heard of my knowledge in this area; so he asked me to prepare a secret report on communism for the American bishops, and I was able to use a great deal of classified material that had come my way." Did the bishops take any action on your report? "About the only immediate recommendation I made was that the bishop take steps to save China by countering our shift of sympathy from the Nationalists. Oddly enough, that was blocked by the inaction of Cardinal Spellman. But by this time I was known, in Catholic circles, as something of an expert on communism. Charlie Kersten heard this, and came to see me. Later, he brought Nixon, and I told him about certain Communists in atomic espionage rings and in the State Department." Did you name names? "Yes." Was one of the names Alger Hiss? "Yes." This was a year and a half before Whittaker Chambers was called by the House committee to confirm testimony given by Elizabeth Bentley—when Hiss was first named publicly as Communist.

There were three things about this episode that interested me in my conversation with Father Cronin: that Nixon did not name Hiss himself (or any of the other people mentioned by Father Cronin); that, when Hiss was brought into the public investigation by Chambers, Nixon did not betray his prior knowledge, or its source; and that, nonetheless, acting on that knowledge, he pursued Hiss with great determination. Just how good his homework had been is revealed by an incident Nixon alluded to during my interview with him on the plane. "Charlie Kersten was the one who told me to go put the evidence before John Foster Dulles." He was referring to a threat that arose at the very outset of the Hiss case. It was a Presidential election year, and Dewey's foreign-policy expert was Dulles. Dulles was also the Chairman of the Carnegie Endowment for International Peace. He had supported Alger Hiss's appointment to the presidency of that organization. And Dulles was convinced that Hiss was innocent of the charges just then coming to the surface. Nixon heard a report that Dulles was going to come to Hiss's defense—thus planting the Republican Party firm in the ranks opposed to Nixon's investigation. He told Kersten about this one afternoon: "I suggested that we go up to New York that very night," Kersten recalls, "and present the evidence to Dulles. We went, and over a period of several hours Dick persuaded not only John Foster Dulles but Allen Dulles too, who was with him." Foster Dulles would later be the most loyal Nixonite in the Eisenhower Administration.

Nixon made another important convert early on—Bert Andrews, chief of the *Herald Tribune*'s Washington Bureau. Andrews had just won a Pulitzer Prize for a story on the inequities of security-clearance procedure; yet Nixon, using his long homework, convinced him, too, that Hiss was lying, and had his help all through the investigation. The "iron butt" was paying off. When Nixon—a first-term congressman, as lowly a creature as exists in Washington—pushed the Hiss case, he seemed to be taking a great risk. It was less than it looked. He had cards all up and down his sleeves, and inside his vest.

Father Cronin told me the story: "Ed Hummer was one of the F.B.I. agents I had worked with. He could have got in serious trouble for what he did, since the Justice Department was sitting on the results of the Bureau's investigation into Hiss—the car, the typewriter, etc. But Ed would call me every day, and tell me what they had turned up; and I told Dick. He knew just where to look for things, and what he would find." Has this been revealed before? "No, but Ed is dead now; they can't do anything to him."

Nixon, the hardworking lawyer, was a hot political property after Hiss's conviction. In 1952 Ike wanted him. Nixon had McCarthy's issue; but, as Father Cronin puts it, he used a rifle instead of a shotgun. Besides, he was young (thirty-nine) and partisan—to balance elderly Ike's ambiguous party background. Then the lawyer was hit with the Fund crisis; and again he did his homework, made his plea—this time a bit ridiculously, since he was both defendant and defending counsel. The impassioned plea to a jury looks strange when delivered through the television set.

"After the Hiss case," Father Cronin says, "I didn't see much of Dick. As a Senator, he concentrated more on his state's problems. But then, when he became Vice-President, I began writing speeches for him. In fact, from 1953 to 1960, I was his only speech writer." How much of your time did you spend on this? "Most of it. I take credit for what was called the new Nixon *that* time around. I was able to give a little background to his treatment of social questions, which I had been studying all my life. Naturally, he tore my speeches apart and remade them in his style; but occasionally he was too busy, and had to deliver the text as I had written it, and that's when he would get the full text printed in The New York *Times*. There is something in Nixon that will not let well enough alone."

Nixon began his '68 campaign with a big political dinner in Concord, New Hampshire. After he had come in, but before his speech, the M.C. was having microphone trouble. Nixon leaped up and tossed one of his standbys over the lectern: "I don't mind his turning the lights off in the White House, but you'd think he'd leave us alone up here in New Hampshire." Then as the M.C. introduced Nixon's two daughters with a feeble joke, the candidate popped up again, but got to the microphone too late for his topper—the M.C. had moved on to another subject. Once more he made a lunge, aborted. It is the story of his life.

As a member of the second string at Whittier, Nixon rarely got into the game: he cost the team too much by his eagerness, which regularly made him leap off side. In interviews he answers rapidly, yet corrects himself just as rapidly: when an interviewer is beginning his second question, Nixon cuts him off with, "To put it in a nutshell . . ." or, "Let me answer it this way. . . ." He boils his answer down, refines it, reworks it three times. Father Cronin says that his speeches get worse from one draft to another: "He keeps simplifying, simplifying. He can't leave well enough alone."

Nixon is not indecisive: it is just that he makes five decisions as he sees fifty new possibilities. He always hears an objector over his shoulder, and shifts his weight to allow attack from that quarter. Len Hall claims Nixon had decided not to debate Kennedy; then he decided he should; then he regretted the decision—"I could win the debate and lose the election"—so that, having accepted the challenge, he did not debate. "He leaned over backwards being obsequious to Kennedy." He tries too hard. He runs so fast after the train that he falls on his face.

And he takes his falls hard. People forget that he is Irish as far back as his family can be traced, both sides—a black Irishman, melancholy, prone to despondency. "He went into a deep depression early in 1960," Father Cronin recalls, "as soon as it was clear that Rockefeller would not be a rival. Instead of organizing his campaign, putting together position papers and all that, he brooded on the responsibility. I think he was overcome by the thought of it." Father Cronin struggles with his pipe, and with an unwillingness to say anything critical of a friend: "Dick has great physical and moral courage, but there is an element of self-doubt very deep in him." Again the uneasiness: "I don't think that Pat helps him." Why not? "Well in the 1956 campaign, Dick prepared the last draft of a speech on a tape recorder; but some aide had not fixed the recorder properly, so nothing was on the tape. After all that work, he had to deliver an earlier draft—mine. His heart was not in it, so he gave it a poor delivery. And Pat chewed the hell out of him in front of the staff." At one point, she made Nixon put his agreement to give up politics in writing. Then, when he told her at a dinner party he meant to run for Governor of California, she "chewed him out" again in public.

Yet, even alone, he goes on. I asked him about his reasons for running as our plane neared Chicago: "There is an awful mood abroad—a desire to just blow everything up. There must be a new vision of America's role if we are to shake ourselves out of this nihilism." He hugs himself almost as if he felt the chill of the world's mood. He has an extraordinary empathy with despondent people—which helps justify his surprising claim that he is "good with people." Pat Buchanan first learned of this after the 1966 tour of duty, when Nixon helped elect many Republicans to office. "I woke up the day after the election; we had won a big victory, but I felt let down, I couldn't understand why, I guess it was just not having the next day's deadline to work at. The Boss called me and must have noticed something in my voice, because he said: 'Are you feeling blue? I know what it's like. Don't stop working altogether, or you'll feel miserable and useless. Taper off gradually, over a week or so, and *then* take a vacation.'"

Another example of this empathy occurred right after the invasion of the Bay of Pigs. Earl Mazo had an appointment with Nixon, who had just returned from seeing Kennedy. "You remember," Mazo told me in Washington, "that was when Kennedy was reaching out for help from everybody—Eisenhower, Nixon, Republicans on the

Hill." Mazo went into Nixon's office and found him on the phone. "He kept making call after call, while I waited for nearly an hour. He was calling Republican officials. Some he asked, others he begged, some he even threatened. He was telling them not to attack Kennedy on this thing. When he finally got to me I said, 'What is this? Here's the perfect issue for your party. Why aren't you using it?' He told me, 'I just saw a crushed man today. He needs our help. I told him to go upstairs and have a drink with his wife, and avoid making any decision until things brighten up a bit.' "

It is advice he has not always followed himself. He has done things in his black moods—sent his resignation to Ike in '52, yielded precipitately in '60 (hurting others on the ticket in areas where votes were still being counted), nagged at the press in '62. He pushes himself very hard, on principle. He thinks, erroneously, that he performs best out on the border line of fatigue, when he has worried a thing to its bitter end. There is a kind of Celtic asceticism about this: "One has to be uncomfortable to do one's best thinking. I don't sleep before a big decision; yet I am at my best then." He has to *punish* himself to earn anything. An Irish Quaker can be quite a puritan.

All those who were considered for the Republican nomination have fundamentalist backgrounds—strict Baptist for Rockefeller, Mormon for Romney, Christian Scientist for Percy, Quaker for Nixon, Goldwaterism for Reagan. In fact, most of them have been lay preachers. Romney did his missionary work. Rockefeller and Nixon both taught Sunday school. Reagan gave the major revivalist speech of 1964. This background shows in the fact that none of those who aspired to candidacy is a smoker, and, though Percy and Romney are the only strict teetotalers, Rockefeller and Nixon rarely take a drink (wine for Rockefeller, beer for Nixon). One might rashly conclude from this that politics is a godly occupation. Or, nearer the truth, that it is a fanatic one. Or that it is a *substitute* for religion. (Or that the candidates' backgrounds are mere coincidence.) But there *is* a similarity in all the Republicans but Nixon—a straightforwardness and lack of mystery that goes with fundamentalist simplicities. Romney and Percy are theological true believers; Reagan is a political one. It gives a certain uncomplicatedness to their efforts and impact. Rockefeller is an example of a more subtle, but still common type—the puritanical self-made man's philanthropic descendant. First-generation millionaires tend to give us libraries. The second and third generations think they should give us themselves. (Naturally, some people want to look this gift horse in the mouth—which may be the reason Rockefeller always has his teeth on display.)

Only in Nixon does the fundamentalism lead to complexity. I asked him—in a plane getting more and more buffeted; it was uncomfortable enough for him to think clearly—what effect his Quaker training had on him. "Oh, I suppose it is the stress on privacy. The Quakers believe in doing their own thing, in not making a display of religion. That's why I never use God's name in speeches, or quote the Bible." But some Quaker prayer meetings have the open prayer. "Yes, but that's not our branch. We have silent prayer—even the silent grace. I have a great respect for other people's privacy. That's why I can't go out and grab people and hug them and carry on. I suppose the Quakerism just strengthened my own temperament here. I'm an introvert in an extrovert profession."

I asked if he thought he could convey his private vision of America's future to public crowds—and I remarked on his lack of rhetorical "grandness," his whittling away at ambitious effects. "Well, there will be some lift in later speeches; but these primaries are not the place for it. I'll have some later. Sure, some is needed. But, you know, people have known me too long for me to come on all of a sudden talking like Adlai Stevenson. If I am to convince people, it will be in simple declarative sentences, by the force of the facts." Content over style. He does not convince *himself* when he is not owning up to Whittier by his manner.

11:30 P.M., CHICAGO: We are on the ground, after nudging slowly through fog onto the Midway field (the original plan, to go to O'Hare, was changed). Nixon keeps talking while the plane empties; walks abstractedly down the aisle trying to remember a book on Wilson he wants to recommend to me; turns at the door—"I'll send you the title. Does Pat have your address?" Rose Woods's brother is the sheriff of Cook County, and he has cars waiting to take us to the Blackstone. I ride with Bob Ellsworth, the interim equivalent of a campaign manager; then, at the hotel, rush to my room and spend two hours copying down everything I can remember of the conversation with Nixon.

I took no notes. I watched him all the time, trying to let him lead the talk, to see where he would take it. He returned most often to Wilson, to the student as President. "But Wilson was not practical enough." Nixon takes great pride in knowing the nuts and bolts of the electoral game; *he* can be as tough and smart as the next guy. He even hurts his small reputation for candor by boasting to newsmen of the pitch he will give to particular audiences. But he is not really "the old pro." He does not delegate authority; his campaign organization is poor; he does not work well with equals; he drives himself to the edge of fatigue; he seems no more successful than Wilson in conveying his private vision of the nation's role. He is not the technician he pretends to be, but a brooding Irish puritan. And a lonely man. These qualities might be handicaps for a President (Lincoln was far more melancholy—was downright neurotic), but they make Nixon the most interesting candidate in either party. One could never be sure what he would do. He still hears the trains in the night. He will probably never catch them. But he hears them.

—MAY 1968

# By Midnight

CHARLES P. PIERCE

*By Midnight* appeared as one piece in "My Day: The Story of April 20, 1999, An Essay in Seven Parts," a series of reactions to the Columbine High School Murders.

By midnight, I was back in a schoolyard, and I was thirteen years old, and three guys had thrown my shoes into a tree.

By midnight, the president had already spoken, and somebody asked him what "concrete" thing could be done about the murderous children, fishing for some sort of political program to cut the unbending unthinkable down to size, and the president paused, just a second, a little touch of Dick Morris in the night, and we were healing again.

By midnight, I was back in another schoolyard, and I was forty-five years old. At the edges of the schoolyard, there were rough and tangled woodlands, where a sniper lay one morning. He was thirteen years old. His accomplice was eleven. The accomplice pulled the fire alarm, and the thirteen-year-old opened up on the children as they streamed out of the school. Four children and a teacher died, and everybody in the country suddenly knew about Jonesboro in Arkansas. And they talked about kids and guns, and they talked about kids and records, and we were healed.

I was there about a year after that shooting, and I spoke to the mother of one of the victims, and she didn't trust what had happened.

People were always telling her to move on, to get beyond what had happened, and she felt cold amnesia creeping into the town around her. Evil, sourceless and sudden, had erupted, and this woman didn't trust the healing because the healing meant forgetting and forgetting meant that what could never happen here could always happen again. And we were healing again, soon to forget, by midnight.

By midnight, I was back in the schoolyard, and I was thirteen years old, and three guys had thrown my shoes into a tree. I do not know what I would have done if I'd had a gun.

—JULY 1999

# My Father, the Spy

JOHN H. RICHARDSON

Mom calls. Dad is in the hospital, on oxygen. It's his heart. I fly down. They live in Mexico in a big adobe house with cool tile floors and high ceilings. Servants move quietly through the rooms. Mom greets me at the door, telling me through tears that she found him last night flopped across the bed with his legs hanging off the edge. He couldn't lift his feet onto the bed, so he just lay there like flotsam for an hour before he started calling for help. When she finally woke up, he apologized for bothering her. Then I laugh, and she smiles through her tears, because it's just so Dad. He's always so polite, so maddeningly self-denying. Sometimes my mom cries out: "Don't ask me what I want! Just tell me what you want!"

I go into his room, and his face is puffy and red, and he looks so very weak. With his dentures out and his head back, he looks like a cartoon of an old codger, lips sucked back over his gums and grizzled chin jutting out. One yellowed tooth stands out in the black hole of his mouth. He's like an apple that's been sitting on a shelf for months, all dried out and sucked down into itself. But when he sees me standing there, his face brightens. He's so grateful to see me, so relieved—and he immediately starts worrying that I've abandoned my important professional responsibilities to come.

A few minutes later, he gets up to go to the bathroom. I've seen him hobbling around the house for years now, and I'm used to frail—he's been juggling congestive heart failure, osteoporosis, cirrhosis, and about a half dozen other major illnesses for almost a decade. But now, the nurse takes one arm, and I take the other, and he leans over so far he's actually hanging by his arms, chest nearly parallel to the floor. He goes three steps and pauses, rests against the bureau, then takes five more steps and rests again. Glancing sideways, I see gray in his cheeks, a whitish gray like dirty marble.

He makes us wait outside the bathroom. He won't be helped in there. So we stand right outside the door, and when the toilet flushes I peek in and see him shuffle to the sink. He's wearing blue pajamas with a tissue folded into the breast pocket like a pocket square. He leans down with his elbows hard against the yellow tiles and washes his hands. On his way out, he stops to put the toilet seat down.

My father was a spy, a high-ranking member of the CIA, one of those idealistic men who came out of World War II determined to save the world from tyranny. Like so many of his colleagues, he ended up bitter at a world that mocked and frustrated and finally vilified him. His bitterness was the mystery of my childhood, turning me stubborn and defiant. Like most sons of unhappy fathers, I had a hole inside me cut to the shape of his sadness, a hole I tried to fill in all the usual ways and never did, because happiness would be too much of a betrayal. My miseries were a tribute to his own—a fucked-up gesture of fucked-up solidarity. So I was always leaving home and coming back and leaving again and coming back again, and often on these visits I would interview him, trying to bridge the gulf between us in the only way I knew. But whenever I pulled out my tape recorder, he would remind me that he had taken an oath of silence. That was always the first thing he said: "You know, son, I took an oath of silence."

In bed at night, he's wheezing and gasping so hard I think he's going to die with each breath. But he goes on as always, worrying about Mom and whether she's adequately covered by insurance and his pension, ground we've been over a million times before. He gives me advice on renting the house out after he dies. He philosophizes for my benefit, as he has all his long life.

"Accidents play such a large part in our lives," he says. "I don't mean accident like car accidents. If it hadn't been for the war, I would have had a very different life."

I've heard this a million times before.

Then he asks me if the doctor thinks this "slump" will get better. In my family we tell the truth, always have, sometimes more than we should, so I say I don't think it will. "There's always a chance, but I don't think so."

He seems relieved at that, seems to relax. Behind his breath, there's a rattle deep in his throat or deeper.

This life began eighty-four years ago in Burma. His father was a wildcat oil engineer from Louisiana (a proud man's way of saying he learned his trade on the job), and his mother was a tough Texas farm girl named Annie Strelsky—Dad never knew if she was Jewish or Polish or Russian and always told me it didn't matter because we were Americans. After the Burma oil boom ended, they moved to Whittier, California, a Quaker town surrounded by orange and lemon groves. Richard Nixon was one class ahead of my dad all through high school and college. Although Dad's parents seem to have been freethinkers—his father was a Freemason and fumed around the house about the night riders who attacked blacks moving into the area—Dad became pious at a young age, teaching Sunday school at a Baptist church. He studied Greek and Latin and by high school graduation could read Cicero in the original. At fourteen, he saw his father die, and he would remember until the day of his own death the sound of his father's last cry and the sight of his body giving one last jerk on the bed. Around that time, he discovered Will Durant's books on philosophy and plunged into study so deeply that within a few years, he suffered some kind of library-induced nervous breakdown and lost his faith in God.

So he transferred from Whittier to Berkeley and the Romantic poets—his letters home mention Pater, Shelley, Keats, Byron, Wordsworth, and Swinburne. He began wearing a "flowing, multicolored tie." He tried to join the Communist party, but they wouldn't have him. He swore to live the life of the mind at whatever cost. "Most of us are satisfied with too little," he wrote a friend, "and we never live even though we think that we do. We're pygmies, we're all the hateful, disgusting things that Swift said that we were, and the damnable thing about it all is that we seem complacently, oily content about the whole matter. By the Lord I'll escape this pygmy state if I have to spend the rest of my life doing it!"

After finishing his degree, he went to Paris, where he studied at the Sorbonne and earned pocket money by cataloging the pornography library of a wealthy French homosexual. After a year of that, he bicycled around Ireland and moved to Germany to study at the University of Heidelberg, where he lived in a *kameradschaft* house with a group of athletic young men who tried to pump him with the glories of national socialism. From his letters home, I get the impression that he was attracted by their health and vigor, but then he saw Hitler speak and was so disturbed, he went back home to study sociology. As he told me years later, he felt that literature hadn't given him "the vocabulary" to argue with those vigorous young Germans. But then his younger brother died of a self-inflicted gunshot wound that was or was not suicide—Dad always believed it was—and Dad drifted through a teaching certificate and a year as an English teacher before moving to the University of Chicago to work on a Ph.D. in anthropology. When the Japanese attacked Pearl Harbor, he tried to sign up right away, but his glasses got him listed 4F. In 1943, his mother died of cancer in his arms and the Army noticed he spoke French and German and asked if he'd mind "wandering the battlefields at night taking papers off of corpses"—which is when he began the long transformation from that romantic young boy in the flowing tie to the complicated and difficult and decent and cruel and tender man I knew as my father.

This afternoon, Dad's pulse goes down to 50 (from 80), and he gasps down lungfuls of air with his head back and lips wide apart, like someone getting mouth-to-mouth. He starts complaining about pain in his chest and pain in his right arm, and then his face seems to slacken into a death mask, his lower lip retracting over his gums almost to the back of his tongue. The nurse shows me the pulse on the chart and goes to call the doctor. Then my sister and the nurse and I all sit around him, stroking him—something we learned from the nurse, a squat young woman whose inward calm is very soothing to us all. At first, I felt awkward about it, stroking his arm for a long time before I got up the nerve to take his hand. I can tell my sister, Jennifer, feels awkward about touching him, too. We are the kind of family that never touched until we said goodbye and then gave each other a hard and awkward hug.

Later, when Jennifer leaves and we are alone in the room, he apologizes. "I'm sorry this is taking so long."

We did not get along when I was a kid. He was distant and preoccupied, and I was (I am told) a natural-born smart-ass. By the time I turned fourteen, I was sneaking out to take drugs, shoplift, and commit acts of petty vandalism, which on at least one occasion prompted the intervention of the local constabulary. That was also the summer he told me he worked for the CIA, but I can't claim high political motives for my rebellion. The only possible connection is that in 1968 he was the kind of guy who would work for the CIA and I was the kind of guy who wanted to drop acid and listen to the White Album over and over. That summer, we moved to Korea, where he brooded on the world's most rigid totalitarian state (just twenty-six miles north of our house!) and I dated Korean bar girls and smoked bushels of dope. Military intelligence officers wrote reports on my activities and sent them to my father, who gave me lectures on being a "representative of my country." Which seemed rather comical to me, since all my fellow representatives were just as whacked as I was; my friend Adrienne had a habit of carving her arm with a razor, Karen was dabbling in heroin, and Peter dropped out of high school and into a reefer haze. So I would bait my father at dinner by defending communism—all your better hippies live on communes, don't they? He would get insanely angry, sputtering his way into a lecture on totalitarianism before leaving the table in disgust. Once I called him paranoid and he exploded into the most gratifyingly paranoid rage I have ever seen. It all came to a boil the day I got beat up by an MP—he called me a girl; I gave him the finger—who charged me with the crime he had committed, assault. When Dad came to get me with his chauffeur and his big black car, he took me to the office of the army general in charge of all Korea and made me apologize for forcing that poor MP to beat me with his club. Not long after that, those helpful men at military intelligence sent Dad a note saying I was a "known user of LSD," and then the army psychiatrists had a crack at me, and before long I was on a plane back to the States—sixteen years old and on my own. If I couldn't get into a college early, I was going to have to support myself. Thanks a lot, Dad. And fuck you very much.

The nurse keeps examining Dad's fingertips, which are turning blue. This is a bad sign. She takes his pulse and goes to call the doctor. Meanwhile, Dad keeps asking the time, which seems ominously significant. Then he keeps trying to tell us something, and Jennifer and I sit close on the edge of the bed, convinced that these are his last words. "*Gee fi ohf*," he says. "*Gee fof*."

Finally, I figure it out. He's trying to say G505—the satellite setting for the *Evans and Novak* show.

"We're here with you," I say.

He smiles sweetly.

In Italy, Dad spent his time rounding up spies with his two best friends, Gordon Messing ("the sloppiest soldier in the U. S. armed forces") and Gordon Mason ("handsome, debonair, witty, sardonic, a great lover"). He also fell in love for the first time, with an Italian baroness whose husband was a fascist officer. And managed to stop an antifascist riot in a small mountain town by climbing onto the hood of his jeep and lecturing the mob on "Aristotle's iron law of politics, to the effect that the anarchy and lawlessness of violence leads to tyranny." But by the end of the war, his romanticism had burned off completely. A letter he wrote to a high school friend shows him changed right down to the rhythms of his prose: "I feel older than the three years would have normally caused, sadder and very tired. I drank hard, played poker and shot craps, made love indiscriminately like all soldiers do. In three years I have hardly read a book, and feel now almost too restless to spend a single evening at home."

Transferred to Salzburg, Dad began arresting Nazis at the rate of fifty a month. (Later, the Austrian Ministry of the Interior officially declared his county "the best and most thoroughly de-Nazified county in all of Austria.") After each conviction, he sat his prisoner down in his office and handed him a scrapbook he had compiled of magazine photos of the camps at Auschwitz and Buchenwald. "I had come to hate the Nazi system," he wrote me years later, "and I mean hate it emotionally as well as intellectually. You will remember that when you were a boy I took you to the Jefferson Memorial in Washington and asked you to remember the words he wrote, carved out above his statue: 'I have sworn upon the altar of God eternal hostility against every form of tyranny over the mind of man.' No better sentence has been written in the English language."

One day, a Soviet official came to Dad's office to bluster against America's recent refusal to repatriate White Russians to Soviet camps, shouting at Dad in "a bullying, overbearing manner, typical of the Soviet style." When Dad lost his patience and threatened to have the MPs drag him away, the official's attitude immediately changed to wheedling conciliation. That made a big impression. "All subsequent experience has convinced me that you can deal with the Communists and the Nazis of this world—and all bullyboy types—only from a position of strength. Their basic human philosophy, if you can call it human, is that of the bully—despise and abuse weakness, defer to strength."

Dad never stops giving me instructions. The doctor told him that fruit is good for you and he wants me to know, too. "Remember that, son—fruit is good for you." He gets obsessed with a lost pill; it was in his bedclothes, he keeps saying. Did he drop it? Did he forget to take it? Should he take another one? A minute later, he worries if the nurse has taken a lunch break. I send her off and help him to the bathroom, and when I hear the flush, I open the door a crack and see him leaning over to wipe off the edge of the toilet bowl. He apologizes for taking so long.

From Salzburg, Dad went to Vienna. Those were the *Third Man* years, when Vienna was a free-for-all of spies, smugglers, and escaping Russian royalists. The Soviets were rushing into the vacuum left by the

Nazis, and their tactics were so brutal that despite the size of Dad's operation—two hundred agents covering half of Eastern Europe—spying on them proved bitterly difficult. Austrian agents often disappeared to firing squads or prison camps. One was stabbed and thrown off a train. Ever the scholar, Dad began reading anticommunist writers like George Orwell and Arthur Koestler. He bought complete sets of the works of Lenin and Marx (still in our library to this day). Years later, one of his colleagues told me that some CIA agents just wanted adventure, travel, notches on the belt. Not Dad. "Your father *believed*," he said, with a lot of respect and maybe a bit of sadness.

As the forties came to a close, the revolution in China and the rumblings of war in Korea seemed to threaten fresh conflict, possibly even another world war. In 1950, a Soviet-inspired coup attempt in Austria sparked riots in several cities. In Vienna, the police almost lost control, and my mother and father—they had met and quickly married that year—were nearly trapped behind the Soviet lines. The atmosphere became so dangerous that Dad's bodyguard stayed at their home every night, sleeping at the foot of the stairs.

Dad wants to hear about the news. I tell him that yesterday they made peace in Ireland.

He's puzzled. "You're in denial?"

"No, Dad, peace in Ireland."

He still loves talking foreign policy, and when I read him the news summary from *Slate* magazine, he says he likes Netanyahu and feels the Israelis can't ever tolerate a Palestinian state.

"Do you think you could eat some Jell-O?" I ask.

He frowns again. "Time to go?"

Then to Athens, in those years one of the biggest CIA posts in the world. Dad and his agents ran operations against the Soviets from Kazakhstan to Hungary, including difficult targets like Bulgaria and Romania. They broadcast free-world news in fourteen languages, dropped leaflets all over Eastern Europe, maintained their own airport and air force of a half dozen planes and a few boats, too. Agent after agent disappeared into Albania, never to return. But Dad never told me about all this. It was Gordon Mason, Dad's old friend and chief of external operations of the Athens station, who finally filled me in. My complaints about the old man's stubborn reticence brought only a smile. "The chief of station in many ways outranks the ambassador in power—the number of people, the prestige, the money, the assets, the contacts," he told me. "Your father was involved in a lot of powerful dealings with a lot of powerful people in the world. But he never flaunted it. He was very modest. You look at him now, and you wonder at the power this man held in his lifetime."

He's too weak to wash his hands. I can tell it upsets him, so I wipe them with a wet washcloth and dry them with a towel. When we get back to the bed, I try to get him to sit up, which is better for his lungs, but he shakes his head. "Why do the so-called right things, when they'll just prolong this condition?"

He lies back, eyes closed, talking intermittently. Some of it is hard to follow. At one point, he says in a tone of surprise, "It's Jimmy Hoffa!"

I tease him. "So you're finally giving up the secrets!"

His eyes open, and he asks what I said. I repeat the whole exchange a couple of times until he understands. Then he gets somber. "It has always been off-limits for the agency to conduct domestic operations," he says.

Dad was ordered to Vietnam early in 1962. When he arrived, the war seemed to be going pretty well, and he plunged into work on the "strategic hamlet" program, a controversial series of armed settlements intended to slow the Vietcong infiltration. Four years in the Philippines had made him one of the CIA's most seasoned counterinsurgency specialists. He met weekly with Ngo Dinh Nhu, President Ngo Dinh Diem's intensely controversial brother. (Nhu later orchestrated the attacks on the rebellious Buddhists.) But toward the end of the year, the Vietcong began to win significant battles, and the Buddhist uprising began, at which point the American reporters on the scene began painting Diem as a paranoid autocrat who didn't have enough popular support to win the war—just another American puppet gone bad. The portrait was a gross simplification but had a pivotal effect on American policy: President Kennedy reacted by sending in a new ambassador, who treated Diem with undisguised contempt. That was Henry Cabot Lodge, still a controversial figure in my house—my mother loathes him. By the summer of 1963, Dad was a lonely figure in the Saigon embassy, the only ranking official who still supported Diem. As he often told me later, he admired Diem's courage and honesty and saw no "credible alternative" among the squabbling generals who would be king. By the time of Nhu's raids on the Buddhist pagodas, Dad was so linked to the Diem regime that he was suspected of complicity in the attacks. "That morning Richardson was a tired and shaken man," David Halberstam wrote in his first Vietnam book, *The Making of a Quagmire*. "He refuted the rumor immediately. 'It's not true,' he said. 'We just didn't know. We just didn't *know*, I can assure you.' "

Then Dad received a fateful cable from his superiors at the CIA. On orders from "the highest authority"—which Dad took to mean President Kennedy—he was instructed that unless he had "overwhelming objections," he was to support Ambassador Lodge and take the actions necessary to mount a coup. Reluctantly, Dad obeyed, sending the legendary CIA agent Lucien Conein (always "Lou" at my house) to encourage General Duong Van "Big" Minh, the primary coup plotter. On August 28, Dad sent a cable to CIA headquarters that later appeared in the Pentagon Papers, a cable he would come to regret: SITUATION HERE HAS REACHED POINT OF NO RETURN . . . WE ALL UNDERSTAND THAT THE EFFORT MUST SUCCEED AND THAT WHATEVER NEEDS TO BE DONE ON OUR PART MUST BE DONE.

The coup fizzled, and *The Times of Vietnam* ran a front-page story accusing Dad of trying to overthrow the government, which got him a place on the hotly rumored assassination lists. Meanwhile, someone began a behind-the-scenes campaign to get Dad fired. On October 2, *The Washington Daily News* ran a story by a Scripps Howard correspondent named Richard Starnes that accused Dad twice by name of disobeying direct orders from Lodge. The headline was "ARROGANT" CIA DISOBEYING ORDERS IN SO. VIETNAM. Citing a "very high United States source," Starnes called Dad's career in Vietnam "a dismal chronicle of bureaucratic arrogance, obstinate disregard of orders, and unrestrained thirst for power." Two days later, Halberstam corrected Starnes on the front page of *The New York Times*, writing that there was "no evidence that the CIA chief has directly countermanded any orders by the ambassador," but he also used Dad's name. "Outed" as a CIA agent, Dad was finished. A day later, he flew back to Washington, where the CIA hid him away for two weeks while newspapers all over the world ran stories about his ouster. *The Washington Evening Star* ran one of the few sympathetic takes: "The crime Mr. Richardson is said to have committed is truly fascinating. He is being charged in the bars of Saigon with declining to overthrow the government of South Viet Nam—incredibobble, as Pogo would say."

One month later, Diem and Nhu were deposed and shot to death, leaving my father with plenty of time to brood on the caveat the CIA chiefs had slipped into that fatal cable: "unless you have overwhelming objections." In retrospect, it seems to have been put there just to give him something to torture himself with for the rest of his life.

Tonight I'm testing Dad's new painkillers. There's mariachi music next door, the jacarandas are in bloom, and Dad's blood pressure just plunged from 100 over 60 to 80 over 50. He sees Jennifer in the hall and doesn't seem to recognize her. "There's the lady who is going to give me my Metamucil," he says. But he still puts on his slippers every time he goes to the bathroom, and he still insists on having a napkin folded into the pocket of his pajamas.

Lying back on the bed with his eyes closed, he asks me: "When did this happen and how? This condition?"

I don't know what to say.

He turns to my mother: "I'm sorry to be such a problem."

"You're not a problem to me," she answers.

"That's important," he says.

I was nine and ten in Vietnam. I remember a French school with chickens in the yard, and Buddhist monks exorcising our house, and the morning I sneaked past the guards at the gate of our house to go to the marketplace. I remember chasing a girl around a schoolyard, trying to untie the ribbon of her dress. I don't remember the day my sister was watching a Disney movie in a local theater and bombs exploded in the lobby, or the day our nanny foiled a kidnapping attempt by hitting a cabdriver with her umbrella and hustling my sister and me out of the cab, or the day one of the kids at my school tried to imitate the Buddhist suicides by pouring gasoline on himself and lighting a match. But I do remember the day my dad didn't come home and my mom sat around without turning on the lights and I got shushed by the servants. Years later, I learned that his helicopter had been shot down in the jungle and she thought he was dead.

Dad tells me that he's been hearing music—emotional music, orchestral, like a movie score. But there is no music playing. A day later, he says he's figured out where the music is coming from. "This music—it's produced by us," he says. "It's a subsidiary of ours."

Later, he murmurs: "Yeah, this is the tail end." He looks at me. "I hope this never happens to you—to be partly killed."

Later still, he frowns, puzzled: "This seems to be just a fragment of me," he says.

Most of Dad's stories are self-deprecating. Talking about Vienna, he tells me not about how powerful he was but about mistakes he made. One time, he was crossing through the Soviet zone and absentmindedly left maps on the backseat detailing the location of military forces in Yugoslavia. Along the way, he gave a young Pole a ride, and when they got to the checkpoint, the Russians became very suspicious and arrested the Pole. "They didn't touch the maps, which would have shown me to be a goddamned spy," Dad told me once, giving me his look of mock alarm. "If they had looked at the maps, I might not be here talking to you."

Years later, an officer of Dad's named Bill Hood centered a spy novel called *Mole* on the Vienna station. Dad appears as the savvy, tough spymaster Joel Roberts. "After six years in Austria," Hood wrote, "Roberts knew every alley in Vienna's *Innere Stadt*." The book tells the true story of the first Soviet counterspy ever recruited by the U.S., but Dad's version of the story is pretty undramatic. "As I recall, he approached some American at his car, got in, and defected," Dad told me. "Later, he was uncovered by the Soviet service and I think executed."

But what about convincing him to go back? Wasn't that a big feather in your cloak?

"I suppose it was, but it was very accidental," he said. "I don't think we deserved any particular merit."

The next day, my sister comes running into the kitchen. Dad's in a lot of pain, wants a shot of something, wants us to take him to the hospital. "I think this is it," she says. But when I get the doctor on the phone, he tells me that once we go to a hospital they'll hook Dad up to machines and keep him alive as long as they can, no matter how vegetative he might get. None of us want that. We stall, and the crisis passes. Dad lies back with his eyes closed, talking out of dreams: "The CIA contact . . ."

I can't catch the rest.

After Vietnam, Dad got kicked upstairs to a desk job as director of training. He brooded and drank, had a heart attack, argued with his superiors about training methods. His friend Frank Wisner (a legendary CIA agent who played an unfortunate role in the Bay of Pigs fiasco) had a mental breakdown and committed suicide. And the war started going to hell, and the hippies started protesting, and, looking back on it now, I can see how it must have seemed bizarre to them, these idealistic men who were just trying to save the world. Suddenly, the very people they had sworn to protect despised them! Nobody cared that most of those CIA excesses were done under orders from American presidents, that it was really the sainted John F. Kennedy who spilled the blood that splashed on Dad. It didn't fit into the sixties script: The hard old men were the bad guys, and, by repudiating them, America would somehow become innocent again.

One day, Dad got a letter from a Vietnamese colonel named Le Quang Tung, who had been the head of Nhu's notorious Special Forces troops, the ones that raided the Buddhist temples. Tung said he was facing a firing squad and wanted to apologize; he was sorry for believing the rumors about Dad and now knew that Dad had never wanted to support the coup.

Dad threw away the letter. A few years ago, I harassed him about it. Didn't he care about history?

He gave me a pitying smile. "I have a feeling history is a pretty vain thing," he said.

We watch sitcoms in the study, then talk. Dad's voice has become a whispery tissue. "I remember the old days in Vienna," he says. "Dean was the youngest major in the Army."

Dean is my uncle, another spy. He's an ocean away, also dying of cancer.

Then we watch *Spin City*, and Dad smiles all the way through it. When it's over, the nurse helps him to bed. "It was a good night," he says.

A few years ago, I had lunch in Georgetown with a couple of Dad's old CIA cronies, Bronson Tweedy and Dave Whipple. Both were age-spotted and bald, with a kind of merry irony. They remembered Dad as a compulsive coffee drinker who had "a slightly ponderous way of expressing himself," as a "tough guy" who took controversial stands. They said he was one of the best, a "pillar" of the clandestine services. They even remembered certain improbable nights in Vienna when he danced to gypsy music till dawn. Then I asked them if they knew why he was so depressed and bitter after Vietnam. At first, they talked about his clashes with the CIA hierarchy and his impolitic but apparently unyielding conviction that the best field agents should be rotated into teaching jobs (first I'd heard of that). Then Tweedy sighed. "One of the reasons was he knew he was serving in a losing war."

Whipple nodded slowly. "An awful lot of people were depressed then."

At ten this morning, Dad wakes out of a nap and calls for me. As I help him into the study, my sister goes to get herself breakfast, but Dad waves his hand. "I think she should be in on this," he says. Dad sits on his little Greek chair waiting. He's hooked up to an oxygen tank, breathing through thin plastic tubes. Every few minutes, he spits blood into a kidney-shaped dish, dabbing at his lips with a napkin.

Finally we're all ready, and he begins. "I feel we're not making any progress," he says. "I feel . . . *I* feel"—he jabs a finger at his chest—"that this could just go on and on. So I want you to call Mike and talk to him."

Mike is his doctor. What Dad means is that he wants me to talk to Mike about giving him some kind of suicide shot. Dad pauses to spit into the dish, and I carry it to the bathroom and wash it out, trying not to look at the bloody phlegm.

"I suppose I could go off the machine," he says, meaning the oxygen. I look over at my mother. As it happens, this very morning a friend of hers sent over some morphine left over from the death of her own husband. I tell Dad about this and say we could always put a batch of it by his bedside if he wants. When he frowns, I try to reassure him, because I know exactly what he's thinking. "It's not like your brother," I say.

"I've always felt bad about my brother's suicide," he says. "I wouldn't want the grandchildren to think their grandfather did that."

"You put up a great fight for eighty-four years, Dad," I say. "It's not like you're taking the easy way out."

My mother and my sister are weeping. The maid vacuums in the hallway.

"I know you feel like it's dragging on," I continue, "but the doctors say it'll just be a week or two more. You're not in pain, your brain is still sharp—and Clinton still hasn't been booted out of office. Why not let nature take its course?"

He seems pleased by that. "Just a week or two?" he says.

I nod.

"And if you start to suffer or just feel you have reached the end of your rope, then know that we do have this alternative," I say. "Talk to me. You don't have to tell Jennifer or Mom. Just come to me."

"Okay, then, we'll wait one more week."

Then we talk about dosage and doctors and make a few terrible jokes about Christianity while my mother and my sister weep nonstop.

"Well that's it, then," Dad finally says. "I think we've covered it all."

But I want to add something. "Dad, I just want to say, I admire you for looking at this straight in the eyes."

He seems very pleased by that. "All right then," he says, with a bit of the old authority. "Go on to what you were doing."

The early years of retirement were the bad years, when Dad earned his cirrhosis bruises. When the dark mood took him, he'd fasten on his completely imaginary money problems or some social error—he was obsessed with politeness to strangers—and pick at it until we were all bloody.

On one binge, he started talking about the Diem coup. He told me that obeying Kennedy's order was the biggest regret of his life. So drunk by then that he may have even cried a little, he said that he wished he had resigned instead of obeying that order. But it came from the president of the United States of America, dammit, with that terrible caveat.

Digging around in my mother's desk a few years ago, I found a series of cryptic notes in my father's handwriting. "Framework of guerrilla war," they began. "Operational involvement vs. analytic detachment. Colby & light at the end of the tunnel. Abandonment of Meos—80,000—one of keenest pangs of defeat—fate of those allied with us. Nat'l interest—cold blooded. Cut our losses but written in human blood."

At the end of these notes, under the heading "Worst episode of my CIA service," I found this:

> WHY DIDN'T I PROTEST MORE?
> MACHINE GUNNER IMAGE—CARRYING OUT ORDERS MENTALITY
> HIGHEST AUTHORITY AND CENTRALIZED INFORMATION AND JUDGEMENT
> EXCESSIVE MODESTY
> PENSION?
> CONCLUSION—LACK OF SUFFICIENT CONVICTION IN THESIS THAT DIEM WAS INDISPENSABLE.

After finding these notes, I asked my father what they meant. "I was probably thinking about that cable that said, Unless you have *overriding objections* to the decision of the president, you should carry out the coup plans," he told me.

And the line about excessive modesty?

"I don't have any comment on that."

Pension?

"That was probably a crude self-interest consideration," he said. "I suppose self-interest plays a role in most people's decisions."

I told him I doubted it played a role in his.

"Have it your way," he said.

Late that night, about two, Dad wanders into the study where I am sleeping and asks, "What do you call those pills?"

"Morphine," I say.

Once, about a year ago, I reminded him that President Kennedy praised him on his fiftieth birthday.

"Kennedy praised me on my birthday?"

I had the quote right there and read it to him. "I know that the transfer of Mr. John Richardson, who is a very dedicated public servant, has led to surmises, but I can just assure you flatly that the CIA has not carried out independent activities but has operated under close control of the Director of Central Intelligence, operating with the cooperation of the National Security Council and under my instructions."

Dad frowned. "I don't remember Kennedy praising me," he said.

"It was on the front page of *The New York Times*," I told him.

He shook his head and shrugged. "I don't remember."

Dad hasn't eaten for three days. The guy who runs the nursing service suggests a synthetic-morphine drip (Mexico forbids real morphine out of deference to the U.S. drug obsession), so I get Dad's doctor on the phone, and he agrees to write the prescription for this packet that Dad can carry around with him like a cassette recorder.

They stick a needle into his belly to start the drip. An hour later, Dad goes into the bathroom and tries to rip it out. I try to convince him to leave it in, and he stands there, his pants around his ankles, saying he just doesn't like it and doesn't want to be hooked up to anything and just doesn't like it, dammit. My mother reminds him how he hated the oxygen mask at first and how he fought the catheter when he needed that last year, and finally he gives in and sits watching *Crossfire*. But as the day goes on, he gets more befuddled and scared. I hate what this is doing to his dignity.

I get angry at the bullshit media cartoons of cold-blooded CIA agents. I'm still annoyed with Don DeLillo because he told an interviewer that the real CIA wasn't as interesting to him as the idea of the CIA as one of the "churches that hold the final secrets," like it's all just a metaphor for the amusement of pretentious novelists. Other countries don't do this. We don't do it with Army Intelligence or the NSA or the FBI. But onto the CIA, we project all our anxieties about being grownups in an ugly world. And it's so easy to point the finger. So easy to sit in an office and write critiques. What's not easy is to choose between the possibility of a global gulag and the lives of thousands of innocent Vietnamese or Guatemalans or Nicaraguans and then to live with that choice—alone, as my father did. And on pile the critics with political motives of their own, which makes them just as dirty as the people who actually take action without the accompanying tragic knowledge, so they gas on and on about poor Salvador Allende because they like those Chilean folksingers, dammit, but Diem—well, hell, wasn't he a bad guy? Didn't he deserve to die? And if I seem a little intemperate about it right now, it's because *The New York Times* fought this gutless paper war right down to my father's obituary, finding some asshole journalist who would say that Dad was sort of a good guy after all because he changed his mind about Vietnam—changed it to agree with *The New York Times!*—even though I told the fucking obit writer over and over that I didn't think he ever really changed his mind, except briefly in a moment of great pressure that he spent the rest of his life regretting. Fucking assholes.

• • •

He sits in the study with the oxygen tube wrapped from nose to tonsure like Salvador Dalí's mustache, and he raises three fingers. "What is that?" he asks.

"It's the morphine, Dad," I say.

This is our new secret code.

Then he starts joking around about turning his back on our cat, which has a vicious streak, giving us that goofy old look of mock alarm—a face I now make to my own kids. "You've still got your sense of humor," I say.

He smiles. "Two things, son," he says. "The first is humor, and the second is courage. I'd like you to tell the grandchildren."

He smiles at the nurse, his face in profile so thin and noble. I want to draw him, to take a photo, to keep this moment somehow. Then Mom comes in and leans down for a kiss. "Long voyage," he says, smiling at her with those bright beady death eyes.

When I was reading up on the old man, I came across a cable written by David Halberstam to his editors at *The New York Times*, dismissing the work of a reporter who'd written articles defending the Diem government. SHE SPENT MOST OF HER TIME INTERVIEWING HEAD OF CIA BRACKET NOW THOROUGHLY DISCREDITED UNBRACKET . . .

In bed a few hours later, I couldn't sleep. Thoroughly discredited? What an arrogant jerk Halberstam was! The fucking guy was sneering at my dad two days after he landed in Saigon! I'm not making this up. It's in his book—two days off the plane, and he thought he knew more about Vietnam than the head of the fucking CIA!

Until that moment, I didn't realize how much I wanted Dad to be right—about Diem, about communism, about everything. It's odd, given how hard I rebelled against him myself. Not to speak of my left-of-center liberal-Democrat politics. What do I care about Ngo Dinh Diem?

At 3:30, we finish watching a movie called *Fly Away Home*. It's about a kid who learns to fly a plane so she can lead a flock of lost geese to Florida. My sister and mother and I all weep through the last half hour, and Dad smiles in perfect Buddhist happiness. When the credits roll, I smile at him. "You liked it," I say.

"*Loved it,*" he says.

Then he sits across from me in his slippers and blue plaid pajamas, reading the paper. He doesn't want to take a nap. "At this point, I take nothing for granted," he whispers.

Halberstam, that asshole, trashed my old man again in 1971. This time, it was in an article for *Playboy,* and without the restraints imposed by the *Times:* "I did not think of J. R. as being a representative of a democracy. He was a private man, responsible to no constituency. Later, I was to think of him as being more representative of America than I wanted, in that he held power, manipulated it, had great money to spend—all virtually unchecked by the public eye. J. R., of course, bristled over the problems of working for a democracy. He disliked the press intensely. It was all too open. How could one counter communism, which was J. R.'s mission—little black tricks that never worked, lots of intelligence (mostly lies) coming in from his agents—with a free press?"

Aside from the line about countering communism, not one word of this pompous shit is true.

Dad can't take a dump. He goes to the bathroom and sits and sits, and it's really hurting him. My sister suggests that this is because he hasn't eaten for four days, so Dad weighs death against constipation and finally decides to drink a protein shake and some prune juice.

The next day, he's still constipated. He wants to go to the hospital, but then decides he doesn't want to go to the hospital even more, so he drinks another shake and more prune juice and starts vomiting almost constantly, spitting up a foul mixture of shake and prune juice and phlegm. Carrying the kidney-shaped dish to the bathroom, I gag and almost vomit myself. I'm starting to hate that infernal little Frankenstein pacemaker that keeps ticking his heart over and over, no matter what the rest of him wants and needs. I can see it under the mottled skin on his chest, hard and round like a hockey puck. Sometimes we joke about passing a magnet over it and putting him out of our misery. Dad nods out, forgets what he's saying, vomits again. Meanwhile, the TV news prattles on and on in the background like an evil guest who won't go away.

Once, I called the CIA public-information office and asked if I could see the old man's personnel records. CIA kids do stuff like this—one (who became a producer for *Unsolved Mysteries*) actually sued the agency under the Freedom of Information Act. A pleasant man named Dennis Klauer called me back with the official response: "Not only no, but hell no—and if you pursue this, we must contact John Richardson Sr. and remind him of his secrecy oath."

At around noon, he says he wants to have another talk, so we gather in the study, and he says pitifully, "My bowels have shut down."

The idiot blathering of CNN continues, distracting him for a moment.

"And something else—what else has shut down? My intestines?"

We turn the sound down and try again.

"Your lungs, you said."

"Yes."

Then the dog starts digging in the trash can, and my mom starts fretting, and my sister says she'll go get the garbage can from the guesthouse, because that one has a lid.

"I wish there was a lid for me," Dad says.

"That's pretty funny, Dad."

"Do you think there's a lid for me?" he asks.

I raise my hands to the heavens, taking the question for whimsy. But he persists.

"Do you think a doctor would do it?"

"What, Dad?"

He dips his head, his eyes going confidential. "Give me a lid for me."

It's odd how very old people get childlike when they tell a secret. For a second, I feel older than he is, and I lean forward and put my hand on his knee. "I don't think a doctor will," I say.

Then he nods so wearily that we try again to convince him to go to bed. But he won't. Never would, never will. Back in the binge days, I would see him walking to the kitchen at dawn with his tequila glass in hand. Sometimes he dropped it, and we would find the bloody footprints later. Now, when his hand droops, I try to pry loose the prune-juice glass without waking him, and he jerks back like I'm trying to steal it. Finally he drinks it down and I say, "As always, Dad, you drank it to the last drop." And I can't help feeling proud of him.

In the kitchen, my mother and I marvel over how tough he is. "It's a lesson in tenacity for me," I say. And she says, "It's a lesson for me that I won't go through that. I'll have my bottle of pills." And I put my hand on her neck and rub, and she shakes it off. "Don't do that!"

I went to his high school once, looked through his old yearbook. There was Richard Nixon looking like a young Richard Nixon. And there was Dad in a basketball uniform. He played on the varsity, never told me. The caption on the photo seems right to me even now: "Never flashy, but always in the thick of the battle, he proved in satisfactory manner to be a very capable guard."

Mom in bed. I say it's getting to be so hard on him. She says it's hard on us, too. Which is a sentiment worth honoring, I think. Weeping, she says she didn't think he'd wake up this morning, talks about maybe calling the doctor. A doctor put her friend Mary to sleep and would wake her up every few days to see if she was still in agony and finally just stopped feeding her through the tube. Maybe Mike would put a lid on him like he asked, put him in a deep sleep. Jennifer says the vet would be the best, and we laugh. And I think, Maybe it's up to me now. Maybe I should just do it and spare them the choice. So I go on the Internet and search for the Hemlock Society and discover it's all philosophy. "Where's the fucking how-to section!" I say.

Jennifer laughs. She's looking over my shoulder. "It's ridiculous," she says. "If you search for 'terrorist handbook,' they'll tell you how to make a pipe bomb."

"Maybe we can use a pipe bomb?"

"Might not work," she says. "He's pretty tough."

When I was twelve, the headmaster of my prep school wrote my dad a letter outlining my many flaws. I found it in my mother's papers a few years ago, furiously underlined by my old man: "His homework shows superficial, if any, preparation. He gives little thought to neatness or accuracy. He does not appear to possess the willingness to apply himself to the task at hand."

This morning, he finally took a dump. He feels much better. But he's so tired he didn't even watch the news, and when he goes to the bathroom again, he asks me to come in with him. Leaning on the edge of the sink, head hanging, he says very emphatically: "Remember—this—is—lung—cancer." When he's finished, I pull up his pants. I see his withered haunches. The pillow-damp hair is stuck wild to his head. But weak as he is, he still insists on washing his hands, leaning over the sink with his elbows on the tiles.

When I was thirteen, he took me on this trout-fishing trip to Nova Scotia. He was a big trout fisher when he was a young guy. I remember it as awkward and dull. We heard the same songs over and over on the radio: "Crimson and Clover," "I Think We're Alone Now," "Happy Together." He stopped the car a lot to pee—from booze, I assume.

I call home, and my youngest daughter says she's fallen in love with a book called *Ella Enchanted*. She loves it so much she took it to a slumber party and read it while the other girls watched the Spice Girls movie. I tell this to Dad. "That makes me very happy," he says. "I couldn't be happier. Tell her I said that."

He's peaceful tonight. Lies quietly, rises only to drink milk or medicine. Asleep at nine. I think the end is coming soon.

When I was fifteen, he started leaving books on my bed: *Waiting for Godot*, *The Trial*, Albert Camus's *Notebooks*. They changed my life, but we never discussed them. He just left them and never said a word.

• • •

In the bathroom, he sits on the toilet for twenty minutes. I sit in a plastic chair across from him. The bathroom is all yellow. There's a black-ink drawing of a rearing horse on the wall above him. I can tell he's thinking deeply about something, and finally he says it. "If—I—need—something, ask—your—mother—first. Because—we—have—the—past."

I want to be sure I know what he means. "If you need something specific, or anything?"

I have to repeat it a few times before he understands me.

"Anything," he finally says. "Because we have the past."

That night, I hear the nurse pounding on his back. He sits there gasping, head hanging, breathing the oxygen from the tubes. When he recovers, he says, "I can't take this anymore."

The nurse does everything she can to help him. It pisses me off. I point to the oxygen, to the pills. "*No está bien; está malo,*" I say in my mangled Spanish: It's not good; it's bad. "*El necesita morir.*"

He needs to die.

At around four, he hisses out his frustration: "I—can't—die."

Looking at my father on his deathbed, I try to picture the romantic Berkeley boy who wore that "flowing, multicolored tie" and quoted Shelley. I'm so sorry I never met him. I used to be angry about it, but now I'm just sorry. And maybe a little bitter. And I don't know if Dad killed him out of shame or if he just held the knife straight while history pushed it in, but I do know that, as time passed, Dad replaced his doubts with convictions and became so absorbed in his war, he forgot that happiness was part of wisdom and that he owed it to himself and to his children to try and earn it. And that is a sad, sad thing. And a dangerous thing, too, because when you become too sure that life is a tragedy, then little by little you begin to accept tragedy, and finally something perverse in you even begins to invite it.

But life is a tragedy, isn't it?

• • •

One last trip to the bathroom. Even now, he won't use the bedpan. The toilet-paper roll is almost empty, and that's when he says his last words:

"Another roll."

I get one from the closet and hand it to him.

Back in his bedroom, he eases into sleep. As the dawn light rises in the window, his breathing starts to change. The agonizing long pauses when you think he's stopped, and then a gasp sucking the air back in for one more round. Long pause and gasp, long pause and gasp. It's horrible. There's something monstrous in those sucking gulps at air, something so hungry and automatic, like his self and will are just the creature of this tyrannical little spark of survivalist life that forces him to go on and on and on. Outside the birds are twittering and then the church bells ring as they do every morning here in Mexico, rolling out into the still, suspended air. Then Dad calms. His breathing gets softer and shallower breath by breath, with no more gasps or gulps, until he's breathing so peacefully, so gently, just skimming off the thin air at the top of his lungs. I move up and sit on the edge of the bed. The bells are finished, and now the garbage trucks rumble by.

The breaths get shorter and shorter and then he just stops.

—MARCH 1999

# CRITICISM *and* POETRY

# The Last Titan

SVEN BIRKERTS

I don't have too many literary heroes anymore—I could count the living ones on the fingers of one hand—so when an editor friend asked me to do an interview with Saul Bellow three years ago, I did not hesitate. Here was my chance to get right next to one of the masters, to feast on his aura. Driving to our meeting, I remember, I was so keyed up that my teeth hurt.

And suddenly we were together, alone in a gloomy office high up in Boston University's School of Theology building, the author of *The Adventures of Augie March*, *Herzog*, and *Humboldt's Gift*, the winner of every prize ever invented, including the Nobel, and me—and I clearly had the drop on the man. How stark the realization: Time passes. I had my questions and my not-so-humble opinions; I had the entitlement of my relative youth.

As for Bellow—I kept trying to shrug off the feeling that I was talking to an old man. But I was. At least he looked and acted the part: rheumy-eyed, slightly hoarse, distracted. I kept simplifying my questions, enunciating with ever more exaggerated care, being nice. I listened, I nodded, but at some level—and this is unforgivable—I cashiered him out. Saul Bellow, I thought, one of the greats, done now.

The rest of this piece is a mea culpa, an object lesson in the hubris of premature condescension. Bellow's new novel, *Ravelstein* (to be published next month), though it may not possess the mural-wall sweep of some of the big novels, towers over his offerings of recent years—towers, indeed, over works of the last few years by his silver-haired juniors Messrs. Updike and Mailer, to name just two who have been squandering their substantial gifts on quick-turnover products.

But it is not just against these various lapses that this work shines. The whole literary culture has changed, gone rhinestone, in a few quick decades, trading off its old artistic anchoring in big things, last things, for easy sensation on one hand and ready laugh-track ironies on the other. We have become in the process so slight as to make me hope Stendhal was wrong, that the novel is not a mirror held up to the reality of the day. Though of course it is.

*Ravelstein*, by contrast, is full of heart and wisdom, and I want to praise it without a pinch of qualification. If this is overpraising it, so be it. The writer, well into his eighties, has hit his number again. He is Bellow, doing the Bellow thing: He is paying homage to greatness of spirit, to the Blakean energy principle. This alone makes him a throwback, a literary pterodactyl in our paved-over midst.

The man is clearly turned on by figures of outsized intellect and spirit. In *Humboldt's Gift* (1975), in my view his greatest book, Bellow fixed to the page in the character of Von Humboldt Fleisher the manic genius of poet Delmore Schwartz, the great friend of his youth. The novel dipped and soared, rode a volatile adrenaline.

In *Ravelstein*, we find some part of that charge recovered. Only now the source appears to be a comrade from the author's later years, the late controversial teacher and ideologue Allan Bloom, author of the conservative cause célèbre *The Closing of the American Mind*.

Plot? Bellow has never been about plot. Moreover, looseness of structure is a courtesy we freely extend to any writer after his third National Book Award. His setup, in other words, is fairly simple. An older man, Chick—Bellow's stand-in—reports on his dealings with his much younger friend, newly anointed culture star Abe Ravelstein, because, as Ravelstein puts it: "There's something in the way you tell anecdotes that gets to me, Chick, and I'd like you to write me up, after I'm gone. . . ."

Ravelstein won't listen to any of Chick's fussy demurrals, either. "Let's not have any bullshit about it. You know perfectly well that I'm about to die." Chick does know. His friend, who is gay, has AIDS; he is sputtering out in brilliant flashes.

At the center, then, holding our full attention, is the grandly cantankerous, chain-smoking, fire-breathing Abe Ravelstein, a man at odds with the whole American intellectual establishment. Arrogant, brutal, he is an antihero intoxicated not just with the grandeur of his own ideas—his denunciations of a Western culture gone slack—but with the drama of thought itself. "Ravelstein, with his bald powerful head, was at ease with large statements, big issues, and famous men, with decades, eras, centuries."

Chick, hovering around his dying friend, reports his bons mots and the dips and spikes of his spirit like a good Boswell. When Ravelstein begins to fail—more in the hospital than out—he struggles to help keep the thread of conversation intact: Ravelstein will march into oblivion like one of his noble philosopher-heroes.

And Chick? What does he get? Moral drubbings, yes, but also a kick in the pants that gets him out of his miserable marriage to Vela, a high-powered scientist. Later, after divorce, Chick takes up with the much younger Rosamund, one of the master's former students. The two eventually travel together to the Caribbean.

Ravelstein's real gift, like Humboldt's, comes only after his death. When Chick gets seriously ill—his vacation turns abruptly from idyll to death march—two things bring him back. One is his promise that he will write about Ravelstein. The other is his friend's example: his courage, his will, the flame of the faith in meaning in the face of death. "You don't easily give up a creature like Ravelstein," Chick concludes, the words affirming his own hard-won intransigence.

*Ravelstein* is—and I mean nothing pejorative here—an old man's book. It stares down infirmity and death and asks the real questions. What will avail us in our deepest moments of desperation? What will we leave behind that might somehow augment those who love us? Bellow's wisdom lies less in any distilled pronouncement and more in the steady pressure of its experienced intelligence. Think what you will of Allan Bloom—I was primed to find him despicable—Ravelstein embodies a force that is beyond ideologies or the piddling niceties of self-presentation. As Chick served his friend, so Bellow has served his. And us. As for retiring the laureate, news came as I was writing this that our most distinguished man of letters is—again—a father. Dare I sin against sophistication and say what I'm thinking? That the energy, the élan vital, that Bellow has been celebrating in so many forms through his long career—in characters like Henderson, Herzog, Humboldt, and now Ravelstein—has come back as karma; that as the life has fed the writing, so has the writing routed its nutrients back into life? Who knows? I only know that I was way off the mark that cloudy March afternoon, that we should all be so lucky.

—APRIL 2000

# Two Poems

DYLAN THOMAS

## FERN HILL

Now as I was young and easy under the apple boughs
About the lilting house and happy as the grass was green,
The night above the dingle starry,
Time let me hail and climb
Golden in the heydays of his eyes,
And honored among wagons I was prince of the apple towns
And once below a time I lordly had the trees and leaves
Trail with daisies and barley
Down the rivers of the windfall light.

And as I was green and carefree, famous among the barns
About the happy yard and singing as the farm was home,
In the sun that is young once only,
Time let me play and be
Golden in the mercy of his means,
And green and golden I was huntsman and herdsman, the calves
Sang to my horn, the foxes on the hills barked clear and cold,
And the sabbath rang slowly
In the pebbles of the holy streams.

All the sun long it was running, it was lovely, the hay
Fields high as the house, the tunes from the chimneys, it was air
And playing, lovely and watery

And fire green as grass.
And nightly under the simple stars
As I rode to sleep the owls were bearing the farm away,
All the moon long I heard, blessed among stables, the night-jars
Flying with the ricks, and the horses
Flashing into the dark.

And then to awake, and the farm, like a wanderer white
With the dew, come back, the cock on his shoulder: it was all
Shining, it was Adam and maiden,
The sky gathered again
And the sun grew round that very day.
So it must have been after the birth of the simple light
In the first, spinning place, the spellbound horses walking warm
Out of the whinnying green stable
On to the fields of praise.

And honored among foxes and pheasants by the gay house
Under the new made clouds and happy as the heart was long,
In the sun born over and over,
I ran my heedless ways,
My wishes raced through the house high hay
And nothing I cared, at my sky blue trades, that time allows
In all his tuneful turning so few and such morning songs
Before the children green and golden
Follow him out of grace.

Nothing I cared, in the lamb white days, that time would take me
Up to the swallow thronged loft by the shadow of my hand,
In the moon that is always rising,
Nor that riding to sleep
I should hear him fly with the high fields
And wake to the farm forever fled from the childless land.
Oh, as I was young and easy in the mercy of his means,
Time held me green and dying
Though I sang in my chains like the sea.

## LAMENT

When I was a windy boy and a bit
And the black spit of the chapel fold,
(Sighed the old ram rod, dying of women),
I tiptoed shy in the gooseberry wood,
The rude owl cried like a telltale tit,
I skipped in a blush as the big girls rolled
Ninepin down on the donkeys' common,
And on seesaw Sunday nights I wooed
Whoever I would with my wicked eyes,
The whole of the moon I could love and leave
All the green leaved little weddings' wives
In the coal black bush and let them grieve.

When I was a gusty man and a half
And the black beast of the beetles' pews,
(Sighed the old ram rod, dying of bitches),
Not a boy and a bit in the wick-
Dipping moon and drunk as a new dropped calf,
I whistled all night in the twisted flues,
Midwives grew in the midnight ditches,
And the sizzling beds of the town cried, Quick!—
Whenever I dove in a breast high shoal,
Wherever I ramped in the clover quilts,
Whatsoever I did in the coal-
Black night, left my quivering prints.

When I was a man you could call a man
And the black cross of the holy house,
(Sighed the old ram rod, dying of welcome),
Brandy and ripe in my bright, bass prime,
No springtailed tom in the red hot town
With every simmering woman his mouse
But a hillocky bull in the swelter

Of summer come in his great good time
To the sultry, biding herds, I said,
Oh, time enough when the blood creeps cold,
And I lie down but to sleep in bed,
For my sulking, skulking, coal black soul.

When I was a half of the man I was
And serve me right as the preachers warn,
(Sighed the old ram rod, dying of downfall),
No flailing calf or cat in a flame
Or hickory bull in milk grass
But a black sheep with a crumpled horn,
At last the soul from its foul mousehole
Slung pouting out when the limp time came;
And I gave my soul a blind, slashed eye,
Gristle and rind, and a roarers' life,
And I shoved it into the coal black sky
To find a woman's soul for a wife.

Now I am a man no more no more
And a black reward for a roaring life
(Sighed the old ram rod, dying of strangers),
Tidy and cursed in my dove cooed room
I lie down thin and hear the good bells jaw—
For, oh, my soul found a Sunday wife
In the coal black sky and she bore angels!
Harpies around me out of her womb!
Chastity prays for me, piety sings,
Innocence sweetens my last black breath,
Modesty hides my thighs in her wings,
And all the deadly virtues plague my death!

—DECEMBER 1957

# Bill Pullman's Face

GREIL MARCUS

Sometimes you can tell what country you're living in by the face you're looking at. In his movies that count, Bill Pullman's face is pushed down, as if by a weight he's suddenly realized he's carrying. He seems to be squinting, sighting some prize on the horizon. But what you're seeing is pure pressure, the weight coming down, the muscles in the face straining to hold it up. The face begins to close, then it stops, and Pullman pulls back to think it all over, caught up in the joke or the horror of it all, wondering if somehow there might be more to the story, even if he knows there isn't.

At forty-four, Pullman has appeared in a lot of movies but a few of them taken together make up as distinct and disquieting a body of work as can be found today in any field. In each of his best roles, in *Malice, The Last Seduction, Lost Highway,* and *The End of Violence,* there comes a moment when his face and the weight pressing on it—the weight of the collapse of a marriage, the collapse of belief, the weight of a world that looks just as it did yesterday but no longer makes any sense at all—become the whole of the drama. The face concentrates motives and events so suggestively that it becomes its own landscape: a window onto an America defined not by hope but by fear, not by judgment but by paranoia, not by mastery but by sin, crime, and error. At its root, it is a Puritan drama, played out in God's country, a country, the face says, that God long ago left to its own devices.

This isn't the Bill Pullman who gets talked about, when he gets talked about. He remains indistinct, confused with Bill Paxton or even Jeff Daniels. "Oh, that everyman guy, sort of blandly handsome," a friend said. "Wasn't he the president in *Independence Day*?" He was. He was also the sheepish grin in *While You Were Sleeping*, the straight man in *Sleepless in Seattle*. "There was this stupid article by some critic comparing some other actor to Bill Pullman, talking about his bland, easygoing roles, never a threat," said a fan. "I don't know what Bill Pullman movies *he'd* been watching." But Pullman's earnest, bumbling nice guy circling Sandra Bullock in *While You Were Sleeping* is only a few steps removed from his humiliated doctor in *The Last Seduction*, who peddles scripts and pharmaceutical cocaine to keep his wife happy. The roles in which Pullman gets lost in the scenery are like a backdrop for the real action, a foundation for the house that's going to be pulled down.

That may be what David Lynch saw; he cast Pullman as the disintegrating saxophone player Fred Madison in *Lost Highway* because, he says, "I always saw something in his eyes. Playing these mild-mannered, guy-next-door characters who most of the time don't get the girl—but I saw the possibility for rage, for insanity. For a leading man. His eyes—it was his eyes. There was a lot more going on there than he was being asked to play." Next door is still where Pullman finds himself, but there was another country to be discovered, to be felt out in the course of a role: a place that has somehow used itself up, a nation sick of its burden of stronger, better, purer, truer, but lacking any other bluff to run, even on itself.

The bluff is called on Pullman's everymen in *Malice*, *The Last Seduction*, and *The End of Violence*—a college dean, a doctor, and a Hollywood producer. (Pullman can make the biggest big shot seem ordinary.) These men are cuckolds, but they're less surprised by that than they are stunned, amused, or even thrilled to find how intertwined the lives they've led are with evil. With his cards face up and worthless, in each role Pullman traces the footsteps of his previous character, and the effect is a feeling of suspension, as Pullman's face seems to contemplate itself more than the world or his enemies, as he tries to read his own mind. If he's not ready to accept that life is a joke, he's beginning to understand the joke life has played on him. There is nothing so pat as a frown, a grimace, a cry of anguish or pain—nothing so cut-and-dried as David Letterman's cynicism, the sallow self-loathing of the men in Richard Ford's fiction, Tom Hanks's firm-handshake-to-the-last, even Ving Rhames's thousand-mile stare. There is no thousand miles in the country Pullman is looking at. A sly, bitter, self-knowing smile floats across Pullman's eyes in the revelatory moments of these three films, followed by acceptance, satisfaction, or terror. Behind any expression is a rising surge of doubt—Pullman's character's doubt about himself, about justice, about the next decision that will ruin his life and leave him stranded.

In *Lost Highway*, the drama is taken past itself. The first shot begins where Pullman's other work ends. We meet Fred Madison in extreme close-up: He looks wasted from the inside out. He looks half dead, and as if he's waiting for the other half to come knocking on the door, and before the opening shot breaks, it will. Madison embarks on a homicidal odyssey, a queerly austere *Twilight Zone*–style splatterfest, an adventure in displacement where the body is felt as little more than a host for disease. The doubt that the country has anything left to say to the ordinary man or woman, the citizen, the one who wants only to be left alone, is replaced by the certainty that it does not. In Pullman's face the country fades out.

"Before," David Lynch says, speaking of *Malice* and *The Last Seduction*, in which Pullman is overshadowed by Nicole Kidman or Alec Baldwin or Linda Fiorentino, "he needed to hold back, to maintain the balance of the movie. He didn't have the power. He needed a movie that revolved around him, where he had the power." It's an odd thing to say about a character who seems powerless even at his most violent, but that may be the point. As an actor, Pullman seems to use no power. You don't think of him as an actor at all. He seems like a figment of someone else's dream—"a dream," as an ancient saying has it, "that is dreaming us." Throughout *Lost Highway*, Pullman appears not so much to inhabit Fred Madison as to merge his character into the spectral bodies of characters from all across the landscape of American film: Paul Muni pleading for understanding in the last shots of *I Am a Fugitive from a Chain Gang*, Tom Neal staring dumbfounded at a body in his bed in *Detour*, Ralph Meeker's sadistic bravado melting like ice in *Kiss Me Deadly*. Near the end of *Lost Highway*, when Pullman rises naked from the desert as a man who must avenge his own crimes, he looks—he fills the air—like no one so much as Gary Cooper: not Mr. Deeds or John Doe or Lou Gehrig or Sergeant York, but Cooper at the end of *High Noon*, somehow realizing that nothing has been settled.

Cooper played a representative man; strangely, perhaps outside of intent, certainly outside of any system of beliefs to be affirmed, Pullman does the same. A picture comes together: the bland, mild-mannered, unsurprising, all but unnoticeable all-American anybody, on any street, in any town, who can at any moment find himself ambushed by all that he trusts—and capable of horrible crimes. He is a representative man in spite of himself: handsome, soft, weak, bitter, still capable of surprise, an American at the dog end of the American century—a man, his face says so clearly, who believes in nothing but that the worst is yet to come. And that might be the power Lynch is talking about. Present in Pullman's face is an America as a nihilist kingdom, where anything can happen and nothing can be said. In the face of this drama, those moments of humor or resolve that spring up and disappear can be the source of the most intense pleasure. But in the end, it's the very disappearance of those moments, when for an instant you smile in the illusion that the man before you knows himself, that makes the drama. Pullman moves off the screen like a frontiersman driven insane by keeping company with no one but himself.

—OCTOBER 1998

# And the Leni Riefenstahl Award for Rabid Nationalism Goes to . . .

TOM CARSON

Last summer, Steven Spielberg's *Saving Private Ryan* surfed on the sort of hype that transcends its own nature—hype with a halo. *Newsweek*'s cover story led with the haggard recollections of real-life Normandy vets, practically obliging moviegoers to thread their popcorn into a rosary. *The New Yorker* lauded *Ryan*'s lack of ideological agendas, an astonishing claim to make about a movie that begins and ends with a luminous Stars and Stripes filling the screen. *Vanity Fair*'s James Wolcott not only hailed Spielberg for "getting it right"—one of the hoopla's mantras—but preemptively bashed any "media-savvy smart-asses" cynical enough to be unmoved. (Talk about the pot painting itself red, white, and blue, if I may speak for the kettles.) On a PR tour undertaken, so he said, only to warn under-fifteens off his movie's graphic carnage, the director piously deprecated its box-office potential, which in $400-mil-and-counting hindsight makes him look like a man wetting his finger to test the breeze while standing inside a wind machine.

And poor Bob Dole, out of luck as usual. If the damn thing had come out two years earlier, he might be president today. A state-of-the-art Spielberg thrill ride disguised as a patriotic hymnal—and vice versa, which was its double-whammy genius—*Ryan* was the pinnacle of our new idolatry of World War II and the generation that fought it, a cultural tic I'd attribute partly to those fin-de-millennium blues and partly to the boomers' predictably startled recognition that their parents are about to die. In a fallacy that, since *Schindler's List*, Spielberg has all but patented, to dislike his movie was to proclaim your snickering contempt for the hell that Dad (or Granddad) went through.

The choir's silliest sing-along was the chant, led by the director, that every previous war flick had been a jingoistic cheesefest starring John Wayne. But Wayne actually made only a handful of uniformed shoot-'em-ups—westerns were his métier—and the most famous, *Sands of Iwo Jima*, is one of the few movies in which he dies, on a sacrificial note that's not much different from *Ryan*'s blubbery finale (except for being less overwrought). It's also an anomaly, since, after V-J Day, few of Hollywood's plenitude of serious-minded war films in the forties and fifties played up battlefield heroics. Flagrant cartoons like 1967's *The Dirty Dozen* don't feature action any more rabble-rousing than Spielberg's pull-out-the-stops last battle, and even movies made during the war didn't go further in portraying the enemy as subhuman. However puerile they could be, one appeal of yesteryear's World War II films is that they were made by and for people who remembered the real thing, lending a been-there-done-that equanimity to their jauntiness that I far prefer to *Ryan*'s fetishistic hysteria. Spielberg's stunning combat scenes were praised for their greater realism by critics chary of admitting that lustrous technology and filmmaking flair also make them more sensational—a turn-on.

If sentimental oomph is the yardstick, nobody can say Spielberg doesn't deliver the goods. Working your adrenal glands and tear ducts simultaneously, he manages something impressive enough to deserve being called dangerous: He makes nostalgia exciting. But in light of the platoon of Oscars that *Ryan*'s likely to take marching home this month—which its technical wizards and splendid cast deserve—last summer's binge could use a bucket of cold water, and this media-savvy smart-ass had his doubts from the get-go. It's absurd for a movie so romantically, primitively rah-rah to be acclaimed for setting the record straight; *Ryan* would hardly be the ultimate World War II film as ultimate Spielberg lollapalooza if it didn't incorporate every cliché of the genre in a way that looks new mostly because it's out to flatten you.

*Ryan* bets the farm on its opening Omaha Beach sequence—instantly famous as the most harrowing portrait of battle in movie history. No question it's intense—hectic but amazingly detailed; the turmoil and clatter never let up. Yet there's often an appalling disjunction between the chaotic slaughter being re-created and the ostentation of the virtuoso filmmaking on display, bragging up distractingly showy effects (the blood flowering from the men shot underwater) when it isn't indulging in pat ironies (the soldier who catches a bullet in the head while marveling at his narrow escape).

More to the point, the intro fudges the average soldier's experience on Omaha in one crucial aspect, which you could figure a glorifier like Stephen Ambrose wouldn't call Spielberg on even if America's favorite D-day wannabe hadn't been on the *Ryan* payroll the whole time *Newsweek* et al. were trotting him out to vouch for its accuracy. Back in bland old 1962, even a spectacular as bowdlerized as *The Longest Day* affectingly showed what *Ryan* does not—that the miserable men on the beach stayed huddled there, panicked into paralysis as the casualties mounted, for several hours. Depicting the same event on a budget most high school pageants would scoff at, for-real invasion vet Samuel Fuller's *The Big Red One* featured a haunting image: the recurring shot of a dead soldier's wristwatch lapped by surf, the water turning redder—the part Spielberg filches—as the morning crawls by. *Ryan*'s beach attackers face a much costlier (in both senses) inferno, which does look more believable. But they also recover to storm the German pillboxes in twenty-five minutes of what's presented to us as real time, lionizing exactly the sort of dauntless heroics the movie was praised for downplaying. Spielberg has gotten huge credit for showing us combat's terrors, but except for Tom Hanks's brief, mute aria of dazed shock, he doesn't show us any of his good guys acting terrified—which means they're superhuman.

On top of that, the celebrated opening is actually superfluous to the story. But it's a brilliant piece of showmanship, since the big number Spielberg pulls off up front half cows and half wows the audience into accepting that the whole movie has been made in the same somber, gritty spirit. It hasn't, of course; commercially speaking, he's not that big a fool. Once Hanks's Captain Miller and his men set off on their rescue mission, trudging from encounter (the reprise of *Full Metal Jacket*'s sniper sequence) to encounter (Ted Danson as the world's oldest paratroop officer) across what no longer looks much like Normandy, the movie comfortably dilates into the longest, most overblown episode of the old TV series *Combat* ever filmed. Measured against the complexity and tension of comparable parts of *The Wild Bunch*—a movie Spielberg's far more indebted to than his interviews suggest but whose opening massacre, unlike this one's, is integral—*Ryan*'s let's-argue-about-the-mission-when-we're-not-killing-Nazis scenes are psychologically and thematically vapid.

For all their sententious airs of high purpose, Spielberg's shaggy-dogface stories just mark time until the slam-bang finale—which the director, ever the movie buff, mounts as a set-piece imitation of the climax of *Rio Bravo*, right down to the mortar rounds being lobbed by hand, just like the sticks of dynamite hurled in the Howard Hawks film. However impressively staged, the last half hour is comic-book stuff on a grand scale, crammed with visual stunting more reminiscent of the Spielberg who directed *Jaws* and *Raiders of the Lost Ark* than the one who did *Schindler's List*—the panzer bursting into view as menacingly as Bruce the shark, the gag of Miller seeming to have blown it up with a pistol shot until the fighter plane that did the job zooms by. In the guise of apotheosizing the GIs' valor, this *Sgt. Fury* extravaganza insults the opening's jittery verisimilitude. One enthusiastic write-up deemed *Ryan*'s big finish "almost unbearably thrilling," which it is. But given the movie's pretensions, didn't it cross anyone's mind that maybe it shouldn't be?

One reason the onscreen debates about the mission's value go in such circles is that the down-to-earth answer to the movie's big question—is one man's life worth risking eight?—is so screamingly obvious: No. It's a weird reversal of the usual proportions of the selfless-gallantry genre, in which one man dies to save many. As a parable of this nation's World War II sacrifices, the story would be truer to what the GIs deserve being honored for if Ryan were a European. Then again, *Saving Monsieur Renault* might not have gripped the modern Stateside audience: Who cares about some damn snail eater? Instead, in a way that's both solipsistic and tautological, saving the world gets redefined as saving ourselves—which must mean we are the world. It isn't lack of patriotism that makes me despise the simplemindedness of the coda's blessing on America—the wife's affirmative answer when the aged Ryan asks, "Have I led a good life?" which symbolically validates our history in the fifty far-from-irreproachable years since World War II. Since the guileless farm boy that Matt Damon plays so marvelously (especially in his big monologue) is also a Jesus figure, the movie amounts to an extrapolation of what must be the ultimate American fantasy—one in which our guns and courage prevent the crucifixion, letting Jesus move to the suburbs and, in old age, take the kids on sentimental journeys back to Golgotha.

But that's only because the saintly Miller has died for him, with an exalted grandeur—far in excess of any earlier World War II film's—that left me more appalled than inspired. To call this an antiwar movie is lunacy; if I were seventeen, I'd have left the theater with a woody to enlist. *Ryan*'s ending elevates a gallant death into the noblest of romantic destinies while transforming the grim necessity of defeating the Axis from a past test of national resolve—which indeed we did meet—into a mystical summons to future greatness: "Earn it." (Question: Even if Americans had just sat on their duffs and played pinochle after 1945, would that mean the GIs died in vain? Of course not.) Hanks has often recounted how his character evolved from the original script's bellicose Medal of Honor winner into the average guy he plays. But the movie's most treacherously brilliant piece of double-dealing is that Miller's actions weren't revised to match; it's precisely because his martyrdom is presented as a triumph of humdrum, ordinary decency—qualities the herrenvolk myth claimed, too—that the hero's Wagnerian finale should leave us queasy. The actor's wonderful performance has moments of great beauty—Miller's bemused reaction to the German loudspeakers blaring, "The Statue of Liberty is kaput," his long scene with Damon. But it's an incoherent part; there's no reason why someone like Miller would keep his past a mystery, except as a gimmick to set up the big speech about fighting to get home that's more shameless than anything in *Bataan*.

The speeches that Spielberg got congratulated for leaving out are the wheezers about fighting to save democracy. But I'd have welcomed some reminder that the United States is one. *Ryan* is actually more reverential of authority, and less tolerant of dissent, than the average Wayne (or war) film—discomfitingly so, since its *dulce et decorum est* therapy for our soft epoch is explicitly divorced from merely utilitarian justifications. The only lesson that Spielberg's robust, good-hearted GIs learn on their way to Valhalla is that they're better off obeying even orders they can't rationalize. For all its pretenses of regret, the movie depicts Americans as a great warrior race—often in distastefully supremacist terms, with the paratroopers who save Miller's men in one shoot-out looming up like olive-drab Terminators; it's as if the only thing wrong with SS men was which side they were on. In a bygone movie era, Barry Pepper's divinely inspired, Scripture-quoting sharpshooter would have been played as a psycho—for satiric purposes in the sixties, and just for yuks after that. Spielberg turns him back into Sergeant York, and his feats make the real one's look like tiddlywinks. Meanwhile, the enemy is shown as lice to be exterminated—people who don't deserve ordinary decency, because they'll only use it against you—and noncombatants are painted as insignificant, if not unworthy. Honestly, I can't see much that Hitler would have wanted changed in *Saving Private Ryan*, except the color of the uniforms.

The giveaway is the Jeremy Davies character—the lily-livered egghead attached to the squad (note that this weak sister isn't even allowed to belong to it), who's treated pretty much the way a Jew would be in a Nazi film. Naturally, he isn't one; instead, Davies's Corporal Upham is an Anglo-Saxon—suspect because he's educated enough to speak foreign languages—whose ultimate baseness is his failure to rescue the strapping, all-American Jewish GI played by Adam Goldberg. But the stereotyping is no less vicious for being reversed. In symbolic terms, it's also tripe; whatever their sins, liberal U. S. intellectuals were hardly spineless about opposing Nazism. In a movie otherwise in control of its own flamboyance, the delirium of this rabid, baiting caricature of the thinker as traitor and coward is a jaw dropper. As soon as he's introduced, Upham grabs a tattletale German helmet instead of a good American one, then gets hit with a scrawny-dick joke—Hanks holding up the stub of pencil that defines him. At a crucial point, he's also used as Spielberg's indictment of his own kind, peering at action he can't participate in and doesn't understand through a rifle scope that subs for a director's viewfinder. When the other men want to shoot a German prisoner, it's Upham who insists that they play by the rules; then the perfidious kraut turns up at the climax, making Upham metaphorically responsible for Miller's death.

There's an obvious paradox here, because when he isn't behind a camera, Spielberg, like Hanks, is among Hollywood's best-known liberals. Yet he's made one of the most mindlessly adulatory war movies of all time—one that treats combat as horrific, but only on the way to making it sublime, and calls the result the ultimate tribute to our national character while egging us on to live up to it. (How? This movie makes fighting Nazism look like an opportunity younger generations have been cheated of.) While I don't think he's a hypocrite, that's mainly because hypocrisy requires some forethought; for all his gifts, Spielberg is less reflective than almost any movie director of his caliber. Now that he's decided to be mature, he's making the witlessly earnest mistake of equating artistic seriousness with momentous topics—the Holocaust, slavery, and now the "good war." But all he can think of to say about them is to state the obvious smashingly—working us over with his full panoply of techniques for inducing excitement and going for primordial effects while remaining oblivious to their implications.

If anything, *Saving Private Ryan* proves just how unreal World War II has become to Americans. There's no way a movie like this could have been made about an event that still felt like part of our national experience. Maybe every last piece of equipment is accurate, but the meanings and behavior are so magnified they're sci-fi; the director is so intent on having us worship these men that he never lets us identify with them. Just like plenty of people who've gushed about *Ryan*, I had a father, too. Mine spent D-day on a destroyer escort off the sector of Omaha that's depicted in the film. So I'm all for tributes, but the fact that we can think a Steven Spielberg blockbuster is an adequate one doesn't mean we've learned how to honor our past. It just means we're movie-mad.

—MARCH 1999

# For the Death of Vince Lombardi

JAMES DICKEY

I never played for you. You'd have thrown
Me off the team on my best day—
No guts, maybe     not enough speed,
Yet running in my mind
As Paul Hornung, I made it here
With the others, sprinting down railroad tracks,
Hurdling bushes and backyard Cyclone
Fences, through city after city, to stand, at last, around you,
Exhausted, exalted, pale
As though you'd said "Nice going": pale
As a hospital wall. You are holding us
Millions together: those who played for you,
And those who entered the bodies
Of Bart Starr, Donny Anderson, Ray Nitschke, Jerry Kramer
Through the snowing tube on Sunday afternoon,
Warm, playing painlessly
In the snows of Green Bay Stadium, some of us drunk
On much-advertised beer     some old     some in other
Hospitals—most, middle-aged
And at home. Here you summon us, lying under
The surgical snows. Coach, look up: we are here:
We are held in this room
Like cancer.

The Crab has you, and to him
And to us you whisper
Drive, *Drive*. Jerry Kramer's face floats near—real, pale—
We others dream ourselves
Around you, and far away in the mountains, driving hard
Through the drifts, Marshall of the Vikings, plunging, burning
Twenty-dollar bills to stay alive, says, still
Alive, "I wouldn't be here
If it weren't for the lessons of football." Vince, they've told us;
When the surgeons got themselves
Together and cut loose
Two feet of your large intestine,
The Crab whirled up,      whirled out
Of the lost gut and caught you again
Higher up. Everyone's helpless
But cancer. Around your bed
The knocked-out teeth like hail-pebbles
Rattle down miles of adhesive tape from hands and ankles
Writhe in the room like vines      gallons of sweat
Blaze in buckets
In the corners      the blue and yellow of bruises
Make one vast sunset around you. No one understands you.
Coach, don't you know that some of us were ruined
For life? Everybody can't win. What of almost all
Of us, Vince? We lost.
And our greatest loss was that we could not survive
Football. Paul Hornung has withdrawn
From me, and I am middle-aged and grey like these others.
What holds us here?
It is that you are dying by the code you made us
What we are by? Yes, Coach, it is true: love-hate is stronger
Than either love or hate. Into the weekly, inescapable dance
Of speed, deception, and pain
You led us, and brought us here weeping,
But as men. Or, you who created us as George
Patton created armies, did you discover the worst

In us: aggression, meanness, deception, delight in giving
Pain to others, for money? Did you make of us, indeed.
Figments    overspecialized, brutal ghosts
Who could have been real
Men in a better sense? Have you driven us mad
Over nothing? Does your death set us free?

Too late. We stand here among
Discarded TV commercials:
Among beer cans and razor blades and hair-tonic bottles,
Stinking with male deodorants: we stand here
Among teeth and filthy miles
Of unwound tapes, novocaine needles, contracts, champagne
Mixed with shower water,
Unraveling elastic, bloody face guards,
And the Crab, in his new, high position
Works soundlessly. In dying
You give us no choice, Coach,
Either. We've got to believe there's such a thing
As winning. The Sunday spirit-screen
Comes on    the bruise-colors brighten    deepen
On the wall    the last tooth spits itself free
Of a linebacker's aging head    knee cartilage cracks,
A boy wraps his face in a red jersey and crams it into
A rusty locker to sob, and we're with you
We're with you all the way
You're going forever, Vince.

—SEPTEMBER 1971

# Hi, This Is Marcel Proust, Reporting from the Hamptons

JOHN LEONARD

I don't know why *Esquire* asked me to write an article about gossip. Jimmy Carter hasn't asked me to write an article about teeth. What do experts need with amateurs? But if one more article on gossip needs to be written, let me begin with the idea of a balloon. There is a Donald Barthelme short story about a balloon that one night expands to occupy the airspace over Manhattan. People have to think about this balloon, to define their relationship with it. Two such balloons that come immediately to mind are Truman Capote and Moby Woodstein.

Somehow, when Mr. Capote's *La Côte Basque, 1965* hit the stands last fall, and one was supposed to be either indignant or rhapsodic, it didn't seem worth the energy. Mr. Capote isn't Saul Bellow after all; he doesn't have any *ideas*. Why get excited about a bunch of expensive people eating naked lunch in a fancy Manhattan restaurant?

For one thing, fancy Manhattan restaurants are approximately as interesting as stamp collections and for the same reason: You mean *this* costs you *that* much money? For another, literary gourmandizing is even less interesting than stamp collections. That, to borrow from E. M. Forster, man goes on "day after day putting an assortment of objects into a hole in his face without becoming surprised or bored" is problematical enough. Writing and reading about it is either absurd or obscene.

For a third thing, if we must have page after page of people putting objects into the holes in their faces, why these particular people? To be fair, they are probably no more interested in me than I am in them. But in what way are they exemplary? In what way are they not superfluous? Their activity—the musical beds, the revolving-door marriages, the Balearic pit stops, the ennui that swells to pique—reminds one of the activity of the snakes Emerson saw on a visit to Walden Pond: "Not to eat, not for love, but only gliding."

A fragment, of course, is a fragment, and Mr. Capote is nothing if not adroit. Given the breathing space of a whole book, he may yet be able to smelt these lumps down to something precious. The ore, however, is outraged. The outrage runs along two parallel lines: Mr. Capote is accused of malicious gossip, and he is accused of betraying the trust of his friends. It's a bum rap.

Novels *are* gossip. (Or at least they used to be, until the postwar French came down with a bad case of epistemological scurvy and perpetrated the *nouveau roman*: vitaminless fiction, marginalia on the hydraulics of perception, psychic liver spots without manners, morals, character, psychology or plot.) Mary McCarthy, in her essay *The Fact of Fiction*, says of Tolstoi, Flaubert, Stendhal, Proust, George Eliot and Charles Dickens that "the voice we overhear in their narratives, if we stop to listen for a minute, putting aside preconceptions, is the voice of a neighbor relating the latest gossip. 'You will hardly believe what happened next,' the novelists from Jane Austen to Kafka (yes indeed) seem to be exclaiming. 'Wait and I'll tell you.' The whole narrative method of Dostoevski could be summed up in those two sentences."

It is so. And why not? That the novel was born of journalism, fathered by Daniel Defoe, is a commonplace. That both were invented to serve the purposes of the new, literate middle class—news, entertainment, tips on self-improvement, the cautionary tale—is equally clear: You will hardly believe what happened next, and it might happen to you, too, if you don't watch your step. (One of the things the traditional novel seemed to be saying over and over again is that you can't be too careful, which is, of course, a working definition of middle-class morality.)

Novelists, naturally, had more leeway than journalists. (Although not so much more leeway than we might imagine. Eighteenth- and nineteenth-century newspapers were no strangers to fiction.) "In the past," writes Wilfrid Sheed, "it was understood that the author made up the names, because he could say more about his people that way, and made up events, because the truth wasn't always good enough. The thrill the reader gets from knowing that he is getting plain gossip instead of heightened, selected, imagined gossip is a cheap, regressive one." Nevertheless, this trafficking in tittle-tattle, this romance of the fact, has always been the principal business, the jumping beans, of the novelist.

When the novel grew up in the nineteenth century, it had to choose a career. The career it chose was the study of class, or the shifting of classes on account of money ("the great solvent of the solid social fabric of the old society," as Lionel Trilling called it), the uncertainties of status, the anatomy of snobbery, how to climb and decline. For all the splendid long-windedness, the garrulous going on about God and war and the Church and the blacking factory, it was almost as though only one big book were being written: *Everything You Always Wanted To Know About Making It but Were Afraid To Ask*. Stendhal wrote this book. So did Jane Austen. Even Dostoevski: "Every situation in Dostoevski, no matter how spiritual," said Trilling, "starts with a point of social pride and a certain number of rubles." Of course: There is very little else we *gab* about.

For middle-class readers, the novel was a bathysphere into these modalities of class and conduct. Its heavy breathing—whether it smelled of lavender or camphor or garlic—was a comfort, an intimacy, a proof of having been *there*, wherever there was supposed to be.

It is sad that Henry James worked so hard to make novel-writing a safe activity for gentlemen, as though the form were a little beneath him and he had to pull it up by its ears until it was exalted enough to talk theory with him. After James, too many novelists, not to mention critics, began to perceive themselves as priests guarding a holy truth, a secret nuance, a kitten in a Baggie, and rubbing it up in the privacy of their self-regard. Nobody is ever going to wait on the dock for a ship from England to bring in their latest chapter, as we did once for Dickens. The novelist's absorption in his own status made possible, on the one hand, books that smelled of the lab instead of our lives and made necessary, on the other hand, the invention of the soap opera.

Our experience has been that society defines the self, and therefore we'd be wise to know as much as possible about the society we live in. Novelists who drop out of society, of *any* and *all* societies, into their deprived selves, tend not to be read and probably don't deserve to be. Whether we are contemplating the snob who imitates the manners of the class above him, or, as is likelier in this country, the bohemian who is imitating the manners of the class below him, we are taking notes, looking for clues. Money, passion, power, pride, status, sex—what are these but the bedsprings of gossip? Given the energy of envy in our emotional marketplace, to speak of "malicious gossip" is to swot the tautological.

Who cares, then, whether one of Mr. Capote's friends might have murdered her husband and gotten away with it, and all of his friends talk about it at La Côte Basque, and he puts what they say into a book he calls a novel? He betrays a trust? They threaten not to invite him to their parties. He expects, according to an interview in *New York* magazine, to be forgiven. One wonders why he wants to be. Such a desire may be more inhibiting for a novelist than the perception of himself as a priest of art. (At least his most recent fragment, as an advertisement for the May issue of *Esquire* so charmingly puts it, "vivisects the literary set." He won't have to worry about not being invited to the parties of the literary set. Members of the literary set are grateful for having been put into novels; someone else is taking them as seriously as they take themselves. Besides, a regrettable plurality of the literary set wants to be invited to Mr. Capote's parties.)

And yet, novels are as much betrayals as they are gossip. "Artists," Elizabeth Hardwick quietly observes, "have often been cruel to others for what they imagined to be advantages to their work." William Faulkner said it more brutally: "The *Ode on a Grecian Urn* is worth any number of old ladies." Dostoevski might not have agreed with Faulkner—Dostoevski never agreed with anybody—since various Karamazovs argue at length whether the happiness of the whole world, much less an ode, would be worth the murder of a little girl. But that didn't prevent Dostoevski from mercilessly satirizing Turgenev in *The Possessed*, and by most accounts Turgenev was one of the nicest guys in nineteenth-century Russia.

The ever-popular roman à clef is the easiest way for writers to betray the trust of their friends. And what important novelist hasn't committed a roman à clef? What else was Proust up to, besides being a genius? Balzac, George Eliot, Dickens again, Dostoevski again, even Flaubert: And who cares whether Madame Bovary was Delphine Delamare or Gustave himself? Nathaniel Hawthorne put all of Brook Farm into *The Blithedale Romance*. Henry Adams used James Russell Lowell in *Democracy* without asking his permission. D. H. Lawrence was unkind to Bertrand Russell in *Women in Love*, as was Somerset Maugham to Thomas Hardy and Hugh Walpole in *Cakes and Ale*. Aldous Huxley and Evelyn Waugh, who made careers out of writing romans à clef, were unkind to everybody.

Thomas Wolfe never made anything up; he just changed the names. Edmund Wilson, when he stooped to fiction, used both Edna St. Vincent Millay and Mary McCarthy. Mary McCarthy, in *The Company She Keeps*, *The Oasis*, and *The Groves of Academe*, used everybody from John Chamberlain to Sidney Hook to Dwight Macdonald to poor old Harold Taylor, who was then young. Randall Jarrell, in reply to Mary McCarthy, and in the wittiest roman à clef ever written, *Pictures from an Institution*, used Mary McCarthy *and* Harold Taylor. In the unwittiest roman à clef ever written, *The Mandarins*, Simone de Beauvoir ripped off Jean-Paul Sartre, Albert Camus, Arthur Koestler and most of postwar Paris café society; then, not content with that, she went all the way to Chicago to trespass against Nelson Algren, who had made the mistake of a fling with her.

More recently: If you read Clancy Sigal's *Going Away* back to back with Doris Lessing's *The Golden Notebook*, you'll find out in *The Golden Notebook* what Mr. Sigal did after he'd gone away. The ever puckish Vladimir Nabokov went so far as to lampoon Alfred Appel, who annotated *Lolita* for him, as Ronald Oranger in *Ada*. Gore Vidal managed the difficult feat of getting Jacqueline Onassis and Anaïs Nin into the same novel, *Two Sisters*. Wilfrid Sheed denies that John Simon was the inspiration for *Max Jamison*, but Mr. Simon was annoyed with those reviewers of *Max Jamison* who didn't mention his name. Wallace Markfield, in *To an Early Grave*, Alan Lelchuk, in *American Mischief*, and Saul Bellow, in *Humboldt's Gift*, stuffed their novels, as though they were suitcases, with most of the New York Jewish intelligentsia.

In fact, almost all novels about intellectuals, whether or not the intellectuals are Jewish and whether or not they live in New York, are likely to be romans à clef, as are almost all novels about the publishing world, newsmagazines, Hollywood, artists' colonies, college life, Washington, D.C., and radical politics. Writers, obviously, are allergic to their surroundings. Betrayal is more important to their craft than punctuation.

And friends of writers have it easier than families of writers. How many novelists *haven't* begun their careers by invading the privacy, violating the trust, of their mothers and fathers, then their relatives, then their hometowns, then their wives or husbands, finally their friends? If they live long enough, they will betray their children, too. The only interesting question is whether the betrayal is worth it, and neither the writer nor those he betrayed will have very much to say about that. As far as I can see, Mr. Capote is guilty only of wanting to go home again after his betrayals.

"A single balloon," says Mr. Barthelme, "must stand for a lifetime of thinking about balloons." Not really. Not when the second balloon is Moby Woodstein.

It came as a surprise, after the syndicated tantrums of the columnists, to read *The Final Days* as a book, not as a series of headlines, sensationalized tidbits and "non-denial denials." The columnists, to be sure, were reviewing the fragments in *Newsweek:* Nixon's weeping, Pat's drinking, Ziegler's shoes, Kissinger's ego. Many concluded that Woodward and Bernstein were, at best, kicking the ex-President when he was down and out in San Clemente (let him rot in peace), or, at worst, fantasizing the whole business. In between, there were accusations of invasion of privacy, distortion, methodological malfeasance and, of course, smarmy-minded gossip-mongering.

The book itself, however, proved to be rather sympathetic to Mr. Nixon. It does not make him out to be a tragic figure: The Southern California version of the Snopes family is incapable of coughing up a tragic figure. Nor does it excuse him: He knew, intermittently, what he was doing. But *The Final Days* suggests, without promiscuous psychologizing, a human dimension hitherto discerned, it seems, only by Julie Eisenhower and William Safire: He talked alone into his tape recorder of flowers and birds; he was capable of despair. On the evidence, he seems to have been less of a crybaby than Kissinger was. For the first time in *my* life—and I grew up in Southern California with the rest of the Snopeses, and Richard Nixon has been part of my life since the 1950 campaign against Helen Gahagan Douglas—I found it possible to feel sorry for him.

Animadversions on the Woodstein methodology put the feet to sleep. They aren't doing anything in *The Final Days* that they didn't do as *Washington Post* reporters when they broke the Watergate story in the first place, except that this time, presumably, they had only to satisfy themselves, and not Ben Bradlee, as to whether a detail had been sufficiently confirmed. (We have come, in the last couple of years, to think of investigative journalists as private detectives in the Sam Spade, Philip Marlowe, Lew Archer antiestablishmentarian mold. Fine. We should remember, then, that in this scheme the editor of the newspaper or magazine becomes the "client." Not the public, but the managing editor—there are still advantages to writing books.)

The process is unlovely; Woodward and Bernstein admitted as much in *All the President's Men*. It involves hunch-playing, intimidation, rule-bending, blind luck, favor-trading, opportunism and a strong stomach. It always has. A. M. Rosenthal, the managing editor of *The New York Times*, has said of Seymour Hersh, the superb investigative reporter who broke the My Lai and the C.I.A. domestic-surveillance stories, that he, Rosenthal, doesn't know how Hersh works and doesn't want to know: The implication is that he wouldn't approve of the methods but knows the results to be consequential. This is tricky terrain; the reporter moves in a shadowland; only the newsroom is full of white light. At least the reporter, unlike the novelist, doesn't betray his sources. Accountability, for the reporter, is outside the purview of this meditation; it may, in the end, be a question of personal conscience. Reliability is another matter and not, for me, at any rate in this case, a complicated one: Do we believe the guys who told us the truth during the cover-up, or do we believe the guys who lied to us during the cover-up?

That Woodstein should on occasion go in for mind reading and a kind of CBS *You Are There* specious omnipresence is sad, silly and unnecessary. Other good reporters, like Gay Talese and David Halberstam, have made the same mistake when liberated into book form. There may be, after all, advantages to having a managing editor, a critical intelligence to review your story. If the truth isn't good enough, change the names. Or, if you aren't writing fiction, find another source.

Still, most of what we learn from *The Final Days* couldn't have come as an astonishment to the boys at the National Press Club bar in Washington, not to mention the offices of the F.B.I. It is the warm coin of gossip in a company town: Nixon's drinking was no more of a surprise to the cognoscenti than the bibulations of Wilbur Mills or the extracurricular activities of the Kennedy brothers. The public didn't know, but why should the public know? A rule of thumbs down among reporters applies to stories about the private lives of politicians unless those lives are so disorderly as to affect the performance of public duties. The rationalizing goes this way: A reporter is not a doctor, a psychologist, a minister, a marriage counselor, God, Synanon, or a common gossipmonger. Reporters, anyway, have their own, perhaps disorderly, private lives.

Amazingly, Jack Anderson subscribes to this scruple, or did on the TV program *60 Minutes* in February, 1975. Eileen Shanahan, of *The New York Times*, dissented, arguing that if a congressman is a closet drunk or a closet Don Juan, it says something pertinent about his character—more pertinent, certainly, than the thousands of words, mindlessly filed, on what he fixes himself for breakfast or the texts of medical bulletins on the state of his chest cold. I would submit that Eileen Shanahan is right. We need only consult our own standards for what constitutes interesting gossip to arrive at a reasonable definition of newsworthiness. We are interested when a man leaves his children; we are not interested in what he ate for breakfast the morning he did so. Clearly, the former is more significant than the latter in explaining the man. It doesn't explain *all* of the man; that would take more reporting, and maybe even a novelist. But, heavily, it pertains.

Trust the hierarchies of gossip; like clichés, gossip connotes a vulgate wisdom, hard-won and more likely than not to consort with truth. If gossip assigns more weight to one behavior than to another, in the slogging on of the species that behavior has proved more revealing of the descent of man, the survival of the fitful. If gossip favors, even *enjoys*, dirt (the failings of character), it is because we suspect ourselves, and the suspicion is a shrewd one. If reporters choose to elaborate on one kind of gossip for their readers and to reserve another kind for anecdotes at dinner parties, and the other kind happens to be the stuff of novels—signifying character—they aren't doing a proper job. The proper job is to ascertain whether interesting gossip is true. To judge by omission is to implicate oneself in a cover-up, to arrogate to oneself the role of arbitrating what the pulpy grey public needs to know and what dazzling power would prefer it didn't, no matter how much it wants to.

In one sense, reporters are doing to journalism what Henry James did to novel-writing: taking it too seriously. Protecting the source is protecting the self, against whom? In ceasing to be an adversary, one becomes an accomplice. Power is spiderlike; out of its bowels it spins secrecy; and webs are sticky. If novelists are allergic to their surroundings, journalists are allured. To abstain from reporting the stupid-drunk incompetence of one important politician, or to giggle privately at womanizing, is to practice for the larger abstention—not reporting preparations for the Bay of Pigs, not wondering aloud what wiretaps of Martin Luther King Jr. really mean, not checking out the bombing of Cambodia. You stick an assortment of lies into a hole in your face without becoming surprised or bored because you like eating at La Côte Basque or Sans Souci. When leaked upon, you smile.

How lucky for us that a couple of crime reporters were assigned to the Watergate caper before we knew the criminals lived at 1600 Pennsylvania Avenue.

"People began, in a curious way, to locate themselves in relation to aspects of the balloon," says Mr. Barthelme. ". . . Each intersection was crucial, meeting of balloon and building, meeting of balloon and man, meeting of balloon and balloon."

Precisely. "The entire *Washington Post* organization has gone bonkers," said a veteran reporter in April. True. *Newsweek*, wholly owned by the *Post*, devoted over twenty pages to the first excerpt of Woodstein, an editorial recap of the excerpt, a George F. Will column on the excerpt, and a Jack Kroll rave review of the movie version of *All the President's Men*. The Saturday before *Newsweek* went to bed, Haynes Johnson, in the *Post*, reported *The Final Days* as though it were to American politics what the Koran is to Islam. That Sunday, Richard Cohen, one of Carl Bernstein's best friends, told us at length about what it's like being a friend of Carl Bernstein. In the two weeks that followed, the *Post* would publish three more essays in self-congratulation—or "autointoxication," as another worthy Washingtonian described it—while *Newsweek* unleashed its letters column, promulgated the second installment, contemplated gossip and, in its book section, reviewed (with reservations) the complete book: "It is absorbing," said Peter Prescott, "nearly intoxicating in its fascination. We need to know almost everything in it. . . ."

Agreed. How, though, to engorge the balloon, instead of losing oneself in it? Robert Redford (as Woodward) and Dustin Hoffman (as Bernstein) effaced themselves in the movie of *All the President's Men*. They turned down their star-light to vouchsafe the murk. They were trying, in a way, to write anonymously. No chance. The public might buy it, but the principals have to have been sidewhelmed. How, on being portrayed on the screen by Redford or Hoffman or Jason Robards or Jack Warden or Martin Balsam, do you resume being merely normal? Isn't your reality attenuated? Can you wear your celebrityhood as anything other than a space helmet?

Ben Bradlee, for instance, is said to have objected to being portrayed by Jason Robards because Robards wasn't handsome enough. Then, having seen the movie at a special screening arranged by Moby Woodstein, Bradlee was so pleased with Robards that he began behaving in the newsroom more like Robards than like Bradlee. Is this true? The story was confirmed, on the Woodstein principle, by two sources; seven other sources said it was preposterous. So much for principles. But is it true in Ben Bradlee's head, in his dreams: Dr. Zhivago hanging tough?

I submit that gossip has become democratized, that, like the nineteenth-century novel, it is a study of Making It, for the purposes of the middle class. Gossip used to be about one's neighbors and one's rulers: hanky-panky next door or in the royal court. In this country, without a royal court, and saddled with an overly pious attitude toward the Presidency, we had to get along with Hollywood and some baseball players. There isn't any Hollywood anymore. The athletes are locked up with their lawyers and agents. There are damned few neighbors, for that matter: Everybody ran off in mobile homes. Where, then, do we find the celebrities about whom to gossip?

We fabricate them. We fabricate, in fact, ourselves. And, typically, we mass-produce. We're a machine for turning out celebrities, the way an assembly line turns out Fords. We haven't, of course, the power of sanction. That's why it was necessary to invent first Ed Sullivan and then Johnny Carson, those priests of the mobile home. Johnny Carson legitimizes celebrityhood. After Johnny Carson, there is no place for a celebrity to go unless it's to a Dean Martin roast. Johnny Carson is the big leagues.

But there are minor leagues for promising celebrities: *People* magazine, Merv Griffin, *New York* magazine, Mike Douglas, *Esquire* magazine, Dinah Shore, the various foxholes of gossip in the daily papers and the newsweeklies, "media" columns and "media" journals.

Take writers. Writers used to go into their rooms and work on their romans à clef. Now they run for mayor, cover moonshots, prizefights and political conventions, go on TV talk shows, do TV commercials, like George Plimpton for the Dry Dock Savings Bank or Truman Capote for the New York *Daily News*. And if they aren't on talk shows or doing commercials, they are in the Hamptons or

Martha's Vineyard, where *People* magazine or *New York* magazine will find them, summer after summer, playing softball or sitting around under the dying copper beech, consuming gin and gossiping about money and other writers. Do you know what Kurt Vonnegut said to Joe Heller about Norman Mailer? Wait and I'll tell you. One stares at these glossy photographs, usually snapped by Jill Krementz: Writers look like anybody else on vacation—debauched kangaroos. It's as though the drawstrings on their swimming suits were broken, and they were about to find their celebrityhood around their knees. Granted because they can rouse themselves to verbalize, they are more interesting than, say, rock stars—Loto and the Six Decorticates, sodomizing an electric bathtub—but to whom, and why?

Then there are the electronic journalists. Electronic journalists are sexier than print journalists. One reason is that electronic journalists have better tailors; they are accustomed, unlike print journalists, to being looked at. Another reason is that, in reporting the news night after night on our TV screens, their faces have become front pages, mirrors of events. History has thickened, substantiated, them. Accustomed as they are to trafficking with momentous occasions, they themselves become occasions when they traffic with us, when they enter a restaurant or a cocktail party, when they visit a talk show or appear on a situation comedy or write an indifferent book. This is hard on the print journalists, who must first go out and *find* a good story, instead of having it handed to them, and then write it up well enough to win a Polk or a Pulitzer Prize, which will encourage a publishing house to let them write a book which, if it is favorably reviewed and sufficiently controversial, might get them an invitation to talk to Edwin Newman or Harrison Salisbury, after which they will buy a new suit and hope that Johnny Carson cares. Otherwise, print journalists will only be talked about in the Press and Media sections of *Time* and *Newsweek*, the Intelligencer section of *New York* magazine, Nora Ephron's Media column in this magazine, Alexander Cockburn's Press Clips column in *The Village Voice*, or, in *[MORE]* magazine, the Rosebuds section, which is preferable, or The Big Apple section, which hurts. For instance, Miss Ephron had to write two books and Carl Bernstein had to write two before their recent marriage could make the big-time gossip columns of *Time, Newsweek* (with a picture) and *The New York Times*. Mike Wallace wouldn't have to operate under that handicap. Barbara Walters made the front page of the *Times* for nothing more compelling than not having decided whether to switch networks.

Oddly enough, critics have a somewhat easier time than reporters on a beat do in getting out of the minor leagues of celebrityhood. Film critics and drama critics are all on the tube. Perhaps this is because they are quoted all the time in advertisements for movies and plays in such big type and therefore have an ethereal presence, a recognition factor, unavailable to journalists who have to work for a living instead of going to movies and plays and using adjectives. Perhaps, too, since their business is quick opinions, they fit in better between commercial interruptions: Feed them a coin and they open their mouths. Still, it's a mystery why anybody in a supermarket would want to pick up a copy of *People* magazine to look at a photo essay on Andrew Sarris and Molly Haskell. Or, God help us, and He didn't, me and my children.

What this adds up to is a media class, serving itself. It consists of novelists who have been coaxed into writing nonfiction books and magazine articles, journalists electronic and otherwise, critics and reviewers, editors and publishers of newspapers and magazines and books, publicity agents, retainers, stringers, relatives and camp followers, all of whom have either Made It, or are trying to, or are trying to keep what they have Made from being taken away by someone who hasn't yet. What they have Made is, of course, anomalous: It has to do with being someone about whom strangers will talk or read; it is characterized by having achieved the company of those about whom one talks and reads.

And how they have Made It, these children of the balloon, is very nicely, thank you. The system works as perfectly as a Möbius strip, a *Washington Post*, a Truman Capote. They talk and write about themselves and each other on their television programs and in their newspapers and magazines and books. They define themselves as celebrities of the new society, and we believe that they are because we believe that celebrities are people who are talked about on television programs and written about in newspapers and magazines and books.

"I met you under the balloon," concludes Mr. Barthelme, "on the occasion of your return from Norway; you asked if it was mine; I said it was. The balloon, I said, is a spontaneous autobiographical disclosure, having to do with the unease I felt at your absence, and with sexual deprivation. . . . Removal of the balloon was easy; trailer trucks carried away the depleted fabric, which is now stored in West Virginia, awaiting some other time of unhappiness, sometime, perhaps, when we are angry with one another."

—AUGUST 1976

# Tampa Stomp

JOHN BERRYMAN

The first signs of the death of the boom came in the summer,
early, and everything went like snow in the sun.
Out of their office windows. There was miasma,
a weight beyond enduring, the city reeked of failure.

The eerie, faraway scream of a Florida panther,
gu-roomp of a bullfrog. One broker we knew
drunk-driving down from Tarpon Springs flew free
when it spiraled over & was dead without one mark on him.

The Lord fled that forlorn peninsula
of fine sunlight and millions of fishes & moccasins
& Spanish moss & the Cuban bit my father
bedded & would abandon Mother for.

Ah, an antiquity, a chatter of ghosts.
Half the fish now in half the time
since those blue days died. We're running out
of time & fathers, sore, artless about it.

—APRIL 1971

# Do You Have What It Takes to Become a Novelist?

JOHN GARDNER

In order to be a good novelist, what a writer needs most is an almost demonic compulsiveness. No novelist is hurt (at least as an artist) by a natural inclination to go to extremes, driving himself too hard, dissatisfied with himself and the world around him and driven to improve on both if he can.

A psychological wound is helpful, if it can be kept in partial control, to keep the novelist driven. Some fatal childhood accident for which one feels responsible and can never fully forgive oneself; a sense that one never quite earned one's parents' love; shame about one's origins—belligerent, defensive guilt about one's race or country upbringing or the physical handicaps of one's parents—or embarrassment about one's own physical appearance: all these are promising signs. It may or may not be true that happy, well-adjusted children can become great novelists; but insofar as guilt and shame bend the soul inward, they are likely, under the right conditions (neither too little discomfort nor too much), to serve the writer's project. By the nature of his work, it is important that one way or another the novelist learn to depend primarily on himself, that he love without too much need and dependency, and that he look inward (or toward some personal standard) for approval and support. Often one finds that novelists are people who learned in childhood to turn, in times of distress, to their own fantasies or to fiction, the voice of some comforting writer, not to human beings near at hand. This is not to deny that it also helps if a novelist finds himself with one or more loved ones who believe in his gifts and in his work.

The best way a writer can find to keep himself going is to live off his (or her) spouse. The trouble is that, psychologically at least, it's hard. Even if one's spouse is rich, it's hard. Our culture teaches none of its false lessons more carefully than that one should never be dependent. Hence the novice or still unsuccessful writer, who has enough trouble believing in himself, has the added burden of shame. That's one reason writers, like other artists, have so often chosen to live off people whom, at some conscious or unconscious level, they need not respect—generous prostitutes, say. It's hard to be a good writer and a guilty person; a lack of self-respect creeps into one's prose. Yet for all that may be said against it, living off one's spouse or lover is an excellent survival tactic. For some businessmen, nothing gives more satisfaction than the artistic achievement of a wife or lover; and some women, in a way that only a cynic would call morbid, derive pride and satisfaction from enabling a husband or lover to do his work. I do not mean that the writer should seek out someone on whom he can feed like a vampire. But if a writer finds himself living, for honest reasons, with someone glad to support his art, he should make every effort to shake off the conventional morality and accept God's bounty, doing everything in his power to make the lover's generosity worthwhile.

With luck, the writer may eventually make money. A novel may be taken by the movies or by the Book-of-the-Month Club, or may for some reason win the hearts of the young. But one ought not to count on it. Most novelists, including very good ones, never make a living from their art. The average income of professional writers is, I think, something like five thousand dollars a year. A young novelist can hardly help hoping that someday he will be published and will find himself free of guilt and debt, but—statistically, at least—shattered expectations are part of the game. One study showed that about seventy percent of those who published a first novel in a given year never went on to publish another. If one is unwilling to write like a true artist, one might do well to put one's energies somewhere else.

The novelist is in a fundamentally different situation from that of the writer of short stories or the poet. Generally speaking, if he wins, he wins more handsomely than they do: a commercially successful artistic novel—especially a third or fourth one—may bring in upwards of $100,000 (no real win by business people's standards; the book may have taken him ten years to write) and in addition may bring stature, honor, maybe love letters from photogenic strangers. None of that is—or ought to be—the reason the novelist chose the genre he works in. He is the particular kind of writer he is, what William Gass has called a "big-breath writer," and in effect he does what is most natural for him. He has, unlike the poet or the short-story writer, the endurance and rhythm of a marathon runner. As Fitzgerald put it, there is a peasant in every good novelist. And he has, besides, the kind of ambition peculiar to novelists: a taste for the monumental. He may begin as a short-story writer; most novelists do. But he quickly comes to find himself too narrowly caged: he needs more space, more characters, more world. So he writes his large book and, as I began by saying, if he wins, he wins handsomely. The trouble is (and this is the point I've been struggling toward), the novelist does not win nearly as often as do poets and writers of short stories. That is why he needs to be a driven man, or at any rate directed by inner forces, not daily or monthly bursts of applause. A good poem takes a couple of days, maybe a week, to write. A good short story takes about the same. A novel may take years. All writers thrive on praise and publication; the novelist is the writer who makes the huge, long-term investment, one that may or may not pay off.

A writer's successes bring him more than praise, publication, or money: they also help him toward confidence. With each success, writers, like stunt riders and ballet dancers, learn to dare more: they take on riskier projects and become more exacting in their standards. They get better. Here the novelist is at a disadvantage in comparison to writers of shorter forms. Especially in his apprenticeship years, when it matters most, success comes rarely.

Let us look more closely at the process a novelist must depend upon. First of all, the serious novelist can seldom push straight through, write from beginning to end, knock off a quick revision, and sell his book. The idea he's developing is too large for that, contains too many unmanageable elements—too many characters, each of whom the writer must not just create but must figure out (as we figure out peculiar people in real life) and then present convincingly. And the story contains too many scenes, too many moments, each of which the writer must imagine and render with all the intensity and care of his being. He may work for weeks, even months, without losing his focus and falling into confusion; but sooner or later—at least in my experience—the writer comes to the realization that he's lost.

His overfamiliarity with the characters, after endless months of writing and rewriting, may lead to his suddenly feeling bored with them, irritated by everything they say or do; or he may become so close to them that, for lack of objectivity, he's baffled by them. Just as we can often predict how casual acquaintances will behave in a given situation, though we cannot make out what we ourselves or those close to us would do, so writers often have a clearer fix on their characters when the novel is still a fresh idea than they can months later, when the writing is well along and the characters are like family. Once during the writing of *Mickelsson's Ghosts* I found the novel's heroine being offered an hors d'oeuvre, and I couldn't tell whether she would accept it or not. I forced the issue, made her refuse it; but then I found myself stuck. It didn't matter a particle which choice she had made, but damned if I could move to the next sentence. "This is ridiculous," I told myself, and tried a little gin—to no avail. It seemed to me now that I knew nothing about this woman. I put the manuscript away and took out my frustration on woodworking tools, making furniture. A week or so later, in the middle of a bandsaw cut, I saw, as if in a vision, the woman taking the hors d'oeuvre. I still didn't understand her, but I was positive I knew what she would do.

Often a novel bogs down because in terms of overall structure—pace, emphasis, and so on—the writer can no longer see the forest for the trees. I've labored with ferocious concentration on a scene, polishing, revising, and tearing up, rewriting, polishing, and revising again, until finally I realize that I have no idea what I'm doing, can't even recall why it was that I thought the scene necessary. Experience has taught me that, unpleasant as it is to do so, I have no choice but to put the manuscript away for a while—sometimes it is months—and then look at it again. When the proper time has elapsed—in other words, when the manuscript is "cold"—the faults stand plain. One may discover that the scene is much too elaborate in relation to scenes before and after it, or that it does not belong in the novel at all, or—this happened to me just once—that the scene is terrific but the rest of the novel has to go. It is hard even for an experienced writer to throw away two hundred pages of unviable writing, or anyway it's hard if one is still close enough to the writing to remember how much time and work it took. A year or two later, taking a fresh look at those bottom-drawer pages, it is easy—even satisfying—to be merciless.

I think there really is no other way to write a long, serious novel. You work, shelve it for a while, work, shelve it again, work some more, month after month, year after year, and then one day you read the whole piece through and, so far as you can see, there are no mistakes. (The minute it's published and you read the printed book you see a thousand.)

So by the nature of the novelist's artistic process, success comes rarely. The worst result of this is that the novelist has a hard time achieving what I've called authority, by which I do not mean confidence—the habit of believing one can do whatever one's art requires—but, rather, something visible on the page, or audible in the author's voice; an impression we get, and immediately trust, that this is a man who knows what he's doing; the same impression we get from great paintings or musical compositions. Nothing seems wasted, or labored, or tentative. We do not get the slightest sense that the writer is struggling to hold in his mind what he's saying, the rhythm with which he's saying it, and how it related to something later in the book. As if without effort, he does it all at once. He snaps into the trance state as if nothing were easier. Probably only an example can suggest what I mean.

Notice the careful, tentative quality of the opening paragraph of Melville's *Omoo*:

"It was in the middle of a bright tropical afternoon that we made good our escape from the bay. The vessel we sought lay with her main top-sail aback about a league from the land, and was the only object that broke the broad expanse of the ocean."

There is, I think, nothing actively bad about this writing; but we get no sense of the speaker's character, no clear mood from the rhythm (we cannot tell how seriously to take the word *escape*), certainly no sense of prose invading the domain of poetry.

Compare what the same writer can do once he's found his booming, authoritative voice:

"Call me Ishmael. Some years ago—never mind how long precisely—having little or no money in my purse, and nothing particular to interest me on shore, I thought I would sail about a little and see the watery part of the world."

*That* is what I mean by authority. No further comment is necessary, but notice how flowing, tricky, and finely balanced it is.

Unlike a poet or a short-story writer, a novelist cannot hope to reach authority by frequent successes. I first declared myself a serious novelist in 1952, when I began *Nickel Mountain*; that is, I decided then that, come hell or high water, a novelist was what I would be. I published my first novel in 1966—not *Nickel Mountain*. I wrote several novels between 1952 and 1966, none of them successful even by my youthful standards. I worked, as I still work, long hours, seven days a week. As a young man I worked a regular eighteen-hour day; now I work less, but now I know more tricks and get more done in an hour. I do not mean to boast about this. Nearly all good novelists work as I do, and there are many good novelists in the world. (Besides, it can't really be called work. A famous basketball player once remarked, "If basketball were illegal, I'd be in prison for life." It's the same with novelists: they'd do what they do even if it were illegal, which, in comparison to basketball, it is.)

So—to return to the subject—a novelist is not likely to develop authority by success after success. In his apprenticeship years he succeeds, like Jack o' the Green, by eating his own white guts. He cannot help being a little irascible: some of his school friends are now rich, perhaps bemused by the fact that one of their smartest classmates is still struggling, getting nowhere, so far as anyone can see.

Hence, if the young would-be novelist is not in some way driven, he will never develop into a novelist. Most don't. Some give up, some get sidetracked. TV and film devour more brilliance and imagination than a thousand Minotaurs. They need the true novelist's originality, but they cannot deal with it except in crippled form. I once visited a successful Hollywood producer, and he gave me a list of what "the American people don't like." They've done marketing research, and they know. The American people don't like movies with snowy landscapes. The American people don't like movies in which the central characters are foreigners. The list went on, but I stopped listening, because the movie I'd come to talk about concerned a Vietnamese immigrant family's first winter in Iowa. What one notices when one hears about Hollywood marketing research is that the only movie one is allowed to write is a cheap imitation of last year's blockbuster.

The would-be novelist can get sidetracked in many ways. He can do TV movies or "real" movies (this is not to deny that we occasionally get fine movies) or moronic TV episodes; he can become a full-time teacher of creative writing; he can move into advertising or porno or pieces for *National Geographic*; he can become an interesting local bum; with a little popular-novel success, he can become a regular on talk shows; he can become a politician or a contributor to *The New York Times* or *The New York Review of Books*. . . .

Nothing is harder than being a true novelist, unless that is all that one wants to be, in which case, though becoming a true novelist is hard, everything else is harder.

Demonic compulsiveness can kill as easily as it can save. The true novelist must be at once driven and indifferent. Drivenness helps only if it forces the writer not to suicide but to the making of works of art, allowing him indifference to whether or not the novel sells, whether or not it's appreciated. Drivenness is trouble for both the novelist and his friends; but no novelist, I think, can succeed without it. Along with the peasant in the novelist, there must be a man with a whip.

As every writer knows—both the experienced and the inexperienced—there is something mysterious about the writer's ability, on any given day, to write. When the juices start flowing, when the writer is "hot," an invisible wall seems to fall away and the writer moves easily and surely from one kind of "reality" into another. In his noninspired state, the writer feels all the world to be mechanical, made up of numbered separate parts: he sees not wholes but particulars, not spirit but matter; or, to put it another way, in this state the writer keeps looking at the words he's written on the page and seeing only words on a page, not the living dream they're meant to trigger. In the writing state—the state of inspiration—the fictive dream springs up fully alive: the writer forgets the words he has written on the page and sees instead his characters moving around their rooms, hunting through cupboards, glancing irritably through their mail, setting mousetraps, loading pistols. The dream is as alive and compelling as one's dreams at night, and when the writer writes down on paper what he has imagined, the words, however inadequate, do not distract his mind from the fictive dream but provide him with a fix on it, so that when the dream flags, he can reread what he's written and find the dream starting up again. *This and nothing else is the desperately sought and tragically fragile writer's process: in his imagination, he sees made-up people doing thing—sees clearly—and in the act of wondering what they will do next, he sees what they will do next, and all this he writes down in the best, most accurate words he can find, understanding even as he writes that he may have to find better words later, and that a change in the words may mean a sharpening or deepening of the vision, the fictive dream or vision becoming more and more lucid, until reality, by comparison, seems cold, tedious, and dead.* This is the process he must learn to set off at will and to guard against hostile mental forces.

Every writer has experienced at least moments of this strange, magical state. Reading student fiction, one can spot at once where the power turns on and where it turns off, where the writer wrote from "inspiration," or deep, flowing vision, and where he had to struggle along on mere intellect. One can write whole novels without once tapping the mysterious center of things, the secret room where dreams prowl. One can easily make up characters, plot, setting, and then fill in the book like a paint-by-numbers picture. But most stories and novels have at least moments of the real thing, some exactly right gesture or startlingly apt metaphor, some brief passage describing wallpaper or the movement of a cat, a passage that somehow shines or throbs as nothing around it does, some fictional moment that, as we say, *comes alive*. It is this experience of seeing something one has written come alive—literally, not metaphorically, a character or scene demonically entering the world by its own strange power, so that the writer feels not the creator but only the instrument, or conjurer, the priest who stumbled onto the magic spell—it is this experience of tapping some magic source that makes the writer an addict, willing to give up almost anything for his art, and makes him, if he fails, such a miserable human being.

The poison or miraculous ointment—it can be either one or both—comes at first in small doses. The usual experience of young writers is that during the process of writing the first draft they feel that all they write is alive, full of interest, but when they look at the writing the next day they find most of it lifeless. Then comes one small moment qualitatively different from the rest: one small dose of the real thing. The more numerous those moments, the more powerful the resulting addiction. The magic moment, notice, has nothing to do with *theme* or, in the usual sense, *symbolism*. It has nothing to do, in fact, with the normal subject matter of literature courses. It is simply a psychological hot spot, a pulsation on an otherwise dead planet, a "real toad in an imaginary garden." These queer moments, sometimes thrilling, sometimes just strange, moments setting off an altered state, a brief sense of escape from ordinary time and space—moments no doubt similar to those sought by religious mystics, or those experienced by people near death—are the soul of art, the reason people pursue it. And young writers sufficiently worried about achieving this state to know when they've done it and feel dissatisfied when they haven't are already on the way to calling it up at will, though they may never come to understand how they do it. The more often one finds the magic key, whatever it is, the more easily the soul's groping fingers come to land on it. In magic, as in other things, success brings success.

No one can really tell the beginning writer whether or not he has what it takes. Most people the young writer asks aren't qualified to judge. They may have impressive positions, even fame, but it's a law of the universe that eighty-seven percent of all people in all professions are incompetent. The young writer must decide for himself, on the available evidence. Here is the evidence to think about:

Verbal facility is a mark of the promising novelist, but some great novelists don't have it, and some quite stupid novelists have it in abundance.

The accuracy and freshness of the writer's eye is of tremendous importance. But one can learn it if one hasn't got it. Usually. One can recognize that the abstract is seldom as effective as the concrete. "She was distressed" is not as good as, even, "She looked away."

Nothing is sillier than the creative-writing teacher's dictum: Write about what you know. But whether you're writing about people or dragons, your personal observation of how things happen in the world—how character reveals itself—can turn a dead scene into a vital one. All human beings see with astonishing accuracy, not that they can necessarily write it down. When husbands and wives have fights, they work brilliantly, without consciously thinking. They go precisely as far as it's safe to go; they find the spouse's weakness, yet they know without thinking just when to hold back. The unconscious is smart. Writers have this brilliance in them as surely as do trout fishermen and mountain climbers. The trick is to bring it out, get it down. Getting it down precisely is all that I mean by "the accuracy of the writer's eye." Getting down what the writer really cares about—setting down what the writer himself notices, as opposed to what any fool might notice—is all that is meant by the *originality* of the writer's eye. Every human being has original vision. Most can't write it down without cheapening or falsifying. Most human beings haven't developed what Hemingway called the "built-in shock-resistant shit detector." But the writer who sets down exactly what he sees and feels, carefully revising time after time until he fully believes it, noticing when what he's said is mere rhetoric or derivative vision, noticing when what he's said is not noble or impressive but silly—that writer, insofar as the world is just, will outlast Gibraltar.

—APRIL 1983

# The More Loving One

W. H. AUDEN

Looking up at the stars, I know quite well
That, for all they care, I can go to hell;
But, on earth, indifference is the least
We have to dread from man or beast.

How should we like it were stars to burn
With a passion for us we could not return?
If equal affection cannot be,
Let the more loving one be me.

Admirer as I think I am
Of stars that do not give a damn,
I cannot, now I see them, say
I missed one terribly all day.

Were all stars to disappear or die,
I should learn to look at an empty sky
And feel its total dark sublime,
Though this might take me a little time.

—APRIL 1958

# FEATURES

# There goes (VAROOM! VAROOM!) that Kandy-Colored (THPHHHHHH!) tangerine-flake streamline baby (RAHGHHHH!) around the bend (BRUMMMMMMMMMMMMMMMMM . . . . . .

TOM WOLFE

*"This is the decade when the postwar babies come of age. In the automobile business, coming of age means the age at which they enter the automobile market. It adds up to twelve and a half million more young people in these age groups by 1970—an increase of more than one million per year!"*

—L. A. IACOCCA, Vice-President of Ford Motor Company and Ford Division General Manager

The first good look I had at customized cars was at an event called a "Teen Fair," held in Burbank, a suburb of Los Angeles beyond Hollywood. This was a wild place to be taking a look at art objects—eventually, I should say, you have to reach the conclusion that these customized cars *are* art objects, at least if you use the standards applied in a civilized society. But I will get to that in a moment. Anyway, about noon you drive up to a place that looks like an outdoor amusement park, and there are three serious-looking kids, like the cafeteria committee in high school, taking tickets, but the scene inside is quite mad. Inside, two things hit you. The first is a huge platform a good seven feet off the ground with a hully-gully band—everything is electrified, the bass, the guitars, the saxophones—and (two) behind the band, on the platform, about two hundred kids are doing frantic dances called the hully-gully, the bird, and the shampoo. As I said, it's noontime. The dances the kids are doing are very jerky. The boys and girls don't touch, not even with their hands. They just ricochet around. Then you notice that all the girls are dressed exactly alike. They have bouffant hairdos—all of them—and slacks that are, well, skintight does not get the idea across; it's more the conformation than how tight the slacks are. It's as if some lecherous old tailor with a gluteus-maximus fixation designed them, striation by striation. About the time you managed to focus on this, you notice that out in the middle of the park is a huge, perfectly round swimming pool; really rather enormous. And there is a Chris-Craft cabin cruiser in the pool, going around and around, sending up big waves, with more of these bouffant babies bunched in the back of it. In the water, suspended like plankton, are kids in Scuba-diving outfits; others are tooling around underwater, breathing through a snorkel. And all over the place are booths, put up by shoe companies and guitar companies and God knows who else, and there are kids dancing in all of them—dancing the bird, the hully-gully, and the shampoo—with the music of the hully-gully band piped all over the park through loudspeakers.

All this time, Tex Smith, from *Hot Rod Magazine*, who brought me over to the place, is trying to lead me to the customized-car exhibit—"Tom, I want you to see this car that Bill Cushenberry built, The Silhouette"—which is to say, here are two hundred kids ricocheting over a platform at high noon, and a speedy little boat barreling around and around and around in a round swimming pool, and I seem to be the only person who is distracted. The customized-car exhibit turns out to be the Ford Custom Car Caravan, which Ford is sending all over the country. At first, with the noise and peripheral motion and the inchoate leching you are liable to be doing, what with bouffant nymphets rocketing all over the place, these customized cars do not strike you as anything very special. Obviously they *are* very special, but the first thing you think of is the usual—you know, that the kids who own these cars are probably skinny little hoods who wear T-shirts and carry their cigarette packs by winding them around in the T-shirt up near the shoulder.

But after a while, I was glad I had seen the cars in this natural setting, which was, after all, a kind of Plato's Republic for teenagers. Because if you watched anything at this fair very long, you kept noticing the same thing. These kids are absolutely maniacal about form. They are practically religious about it. For example, the dancers: none of them ever smiled. They stared at each other's legs and feet, concentrating. The dances had no grace about them at all, they were more in the nature of a hoedown, but everybody was concentrating to do them exactly *right*. And the bouffant kids all had form, wild form, but form with rigid standards, one gathers. Even the boys. Their dress was prosaic—Levis, Slim Jims, sport shirts, T-shirts, polo shirts—but the form was consistent: a stovepipe silhouette. And they all had the same hairstyle: some wore it long, some short, but none of them had a part; all that hair was brushed back straight from the hairline. I went by one of the guitar booths, and there was a little kid in there, about thirteen, playing the hell out of an electric guitar. The kid was named Cranston something or other. He looked like he ought to be named Kermit or Herschel; all his genes were kind of horribly Okie. Cranston was playing away and a big crowd was watching. But Cranston was slouched back with his spine bent like a sapling up against a table looking gloriously bored. At thirteen, this kid was being fanatically cool. They all were. They were all wonderful slaves to form. They have created their own style of life, and they are much more authoritarian about enforcing it than are adults. Not only that, but today these kids—especially in California—have *money*, which, needless to say, is why all these shoe merchants and guitar sellers and the Ford Motor Company were at a Teen Fair in the first place. I don't mind observing that it is this same combination—money plus slavish devotion to form—that accounts for Versailles or St. Mark's Square. Naturally, most of the artifacts that these kids' money-plus-form produce are of a pretty ghastly order. But so was most of the paraphernalia that developed in England during the Regency. I mean, most of it was on the order of starched cravats. A man could walk into Beau Brummel's house at 11 A.M., and here would come the butler with a tray of wilted linen. "These were some of our failures," he confides. But then Brummel comes downstairs wearing one perfect starched cravat. Like one perfect iris, the flower of Mayfair civilization. But the Regency period did see some tremendous formal architecture. And the kids' formal society has also brought at least one substantial thing to a formal development of a high order—the customized cars. I don't have to dwell on the point that cars mean more to these kids than architecture did in Europe's great formal century, say, 1750 to 1850. They are freedom, style, sex, power, motion, color—everything is right there.

Things have been going on in the development of the kids' formal attitude toward cars since 1945, things of great sophistication that adults have not been even remotely aware of, mainly because the kids are so inarticulate about it, especially the ones most hipped on the subject. They are not from the levels of society that produce children who write sensitive analytical prose at age seventeen, or if they do, they soon fall into the hands of English instructors who put them onto Hemingway or a lot of goddamn-and-hungry-breast writers. If they ever write about a highway again, it's a rain-slicked highway and the sound of the automobiles passing over it is like the sound of tearing silk (not that one household in ten thousand has heard the sound of tearing silk since 1945).

Anyway, we are back at the Teen Fair and I am talking to Tex Smith and to Don Beebe, a portly young guy with a white sport shirt and Cuban sunglasses. As they tell me about the Ford Custom Car Caravan, I can see that Ford has begun to comprehend this teen-age style of life and its potential. The way Ford appears to figure it is this: Thousands of kids are getting hold of cars and either hopping them up for speed or customizing them to some extent, usually a little of both. Before they get married they pour *all* their money into this. If Ford can get them hooked on Fords now, after the kids are married they'll buy new Fords. Even the kids who aren't full-time car nuts themselves will be influenced by which car is considered "boss." They use that word a lot, "boss." The kids used to consider Ford the hot car, but then, from 1955 to 1962, Chevrolet became the favorite. They had big engines and were easy to hop up, the styling was simple, and the kids could customize them easily. In 1959, and more so in 1960, Plymouth became a hot car, too. In 1961 and 1962, it was all Chevrolet and Plymouth. Now Ford is making a big push. A lot of the professional hot-rod and custom-car people, adults, will tell you that now Ford is the hot car, but you have to discount some of it, because Ford is laying money on everybody right and left, in one form or another. In the Custom Car Caravan, all the cars have been fashioned out of Ford bodies except the ones that are completely handmade, like the aforementioned Silhouette.

Anyway, Don Beebe is saying, over a loudspeaker, "I hate to break up that dancing, but let's have a little drag racing." He has a phonograph hooked up to the loudspeaker, and he puts on a record, produced by Riverside Records, of drag-strip sounds, mainly dragsters blasting off and squealing from the starting line. Well, he doesn't really break up the dancing, but a hundred kids come over, when they hear the drag-strip sounds, to where Beebe has a slot-racing stand. Slot-racing is a model-train-type game in which two model drag racers, each about five inches long, powered by electricity, run down a model drag strip. Beebe takes a microphone and announces that Dick Dale, the singer, is here, and anybody who will race Dick at the slot-racing stand will get one of his records. Dick Dale is pretty popular among the kids out here because he sings a lot of "surfing" songs. The surfers—surfboard riders—are a cult much admired by all the kids. They have their own argot, with adjectives like "hang ten," meaning the best there is. They also go in for one particular brand of customizing: they take old wood-bodied station wagons, which they call "woodies" and fix them up for riding, sleeping and hauling surfing equipment for their weekends at the beach. The surfers also get a hell of a bang out of slot-racing for some reason, so with Dick Dale slot-racing at the Teen Fair, you have about three areas of the arcane teen world all rolled into one.

Dick Dale, rigged out in Byronic shirt and blue cashmere V-neck sweater and wraparound sunglasses, singer's mufti U.S.A., has one cord with a starter button, while a bouffant nymphet from Newport named Sherma, Sherma of the Capri pants, has the other one. Don Beebe flashes a starting light and Sherma lets out a cry, not a thrilled cry, just nerves, and a model 1963 Ford and a model dragster go running down the slot board, which is about chest high. The slot board is said to be one-twenty-fifth the actual size of a drag strip, which somehow reminds you of those incredible stamp-size pictures in the dictionary with the notation that this is one-hundredth the size of a real elephant. A hundred kids were packed in around the slot racers and did not find it incredible. That is, they were interested in who would win, Dick Dale or Sherma. I'm sure they had no trouble magnifying the slot racers twenty-five times to the size of the full-blown, esoteric world of hot rods and custom cars.

I met George Barris, one of the celebrities of the custom-car world, at the Teen Fair. Barris is the biggest name in customizing. He is a good example of a kid who grew up completely absorbed in this teen-age world of cars, who pursued the pure flame and its forms with such devotion that he emerged an artist. It was like Tiepolo emerging from the studios of Venice, where the rounded Grecian haunches of the murals on the Palladian domes hung in the atmosphere like clouds. Except that Barris emerged from the autobody shops of Los Angeles.

Barris invited me out to his studio—only he would never think of calling it that, he calls it Kustom City—at 10811 Riverside Drive in North Hollywood. If there is a river within a thousand miles of Riverside Drive, I saw no sign of it. It's like every place else out there: endless scorched boulevards lined with one-story stores, shops, bowling alleys, skating rinks, tacos drive-ins, all of them shaped not like rectangles but like trapezoids, from the way the roofs slant up from the back and the plate-glass fronts slant out as if they're going to pitch forward on the sidewalk and throw up. The signs are great, too. They all stand free on poles outside. They have horribly slick doglegged shapes that I call boomerang modern. As for Kustom City—Barris grew up at the time when it was considered sharp to change all the C's to K's. He also sells Kandy Lac to paint cars Kandy Kolors with, and I know that sibilant C in City must have bothered the hell out of him at some point. It's interesting, I think, that he still calls the place Kustom City, and still sells Kandy Kolors, because he is an intelligent person. What it means is, he is absolutely untouched by the big amoeba god of Anglo-European sophistication that gets you in the East. You know how it is in the East. One day you notice that the boss's button-down shirt has this sweet percale roll to it, while your own was obviously slapped together by some mass-production graph keepers who are saving an eighth of inch of cloth per shirt, twelve inches per bolt or the like, and this starts eating at you.

Barris, whose family is Greek, is a solid little guy, five feet seven, thirty-seven years old, and he looks just like Picasso. When he's working, which is most of the time, he wears a heavy white T-style shirt, faded off-white pants cut full with pleats in the manner of Picasso walking along a Mediterranean bluff in the wind at Rapallo, and crepe-sole slipper-style shoes, also off-white. Picasso, I should add, means nothing to Barris, although he knows who he is. It's just that to Barris and the customizers there is no great universe of form and design called Art. Yet that's the universe he's in. He's not building cars, he's creating forms.

Barris starts taking me through Kustom City, and the place looks like any other body shop at first, but pretty soon you realize you're in a *gallery*. This place is full of cars such as you have never seen before. Half of them will never touch the road. They're put on trucks and trailers and carted all over the country to be exhibited at hot-rod and custom-car shows. They'll run, if it comes to that—they're full of big, powerful, hopped-up chrome-plated motors, because all that speed and power, and all that lovely apparatus, has tremendous emotional meaning to everybody in customizing. But it's like one of these Picasso or Miro rugs. You don't walk on the damn things. You hang them on the wall. It's the same thing with Barris' cars. In effect, they're sculpture.

For example, there is an incredible object he built called the XPAK-400 air car. The customizers love all that X jazz. It runs on a cushion of air, which is beside the point, because it's a pure piece of curvilinear abstract sculpture. If Brancusi is any good, then this thing belongs on a pedestal, too. There is not a straight line in it, and only one true circle, and those countless planes, and tremendous baroque fins, and yet all in all it's a rigid little piece of solid geometrical harmony. As a matter of fact, Brancusi and Barris both developed out of a design concept that we can call Streamlined Modern or Thirties Curvilinear—via utterly different roads, of course—and Barris and most custom artists are carrying this idea of the abstract curve, which is very tough to handle, on and on and on at a time when your conventional designers—from architects to the guys who lay out magazines—are all Mondrian. Even the young Detroit car stylists are all Mondrian. Only the aircraft designers have done anything more with the Streamline, and they have only because they're forced to by physics, and so on. I want to return to that subject in a minute, but first I want to tell you about another car Barris was showing me.

This was stuck back in a storeroom. Barris wasn't interested in it anymore since he did it nine years ago. But this car—this old car, as far as Barris was concerned—was like a dream prefiguration of a very hot sports car, the Quantum, that Saab has come out with this year after a couple of years of consultation with all sorts of aerodynamic experts and advance-guard designers. They're beautiful cars—Saab's and Barris'. They're the same body, practically—with this lovely topology rolling down over the tunneled headlights, with the whole hood curving down very low to the ground in front. I told Barris about the similarity, but he just shrugged; he is quite used to some manufacturer coming up with one of his cars five or six years later.

Anyway, Barris and I were walking around the side of Kustom City, through the parking lot, when I saw an Avanti, the new Studebaker sports model, very expensive. This one had paper mock-ups added to the front and the rear, and so I asked Barris about it. That wasn't much, he said; starting with the paper mock-ups, it brought the hood out a foot with a chic slope to it. He was doing the same sort of thing in the back to eliminate that kind of loaf-of-bread look. It really makes the car. Barris doesn't regard this as a very major project. It may end up in something like a kit you can buy, similar to the old Continental kits, to rig up front and back.

If Barris and the customizers hadn't been buried in the alien and suspect underworld of California youth, I don't think they would seem at all unusual by now. But they've had access to almost nothing but the hot-rod press. They're like Easter Islanders. Suddenly you come upon the astonishing objects, and then you have to figure out how they got there and why they're there.

If you study the work of Barris or Cushenberry (the aforementioned Silhouette) or Ed Roth or Darryl Starbird (can you beat that name?), I think you come up with a fragment of art history. Somewhere back in the Thirties, designers, automobile designers among them, came up with the idea of the streamline. It sounded "functional," and on an airplane it is functional, but on a car it's not, unless you're making a Bonneville speed run. Actually, it's baroque. The streamline is baroque abstract or baroque modern or whatever you want to call it. Well, about the time the streamline got going—in the Thirties, you may recall, we had curved buildings (like the showpieces later, at the World's Fair)—in came the Bauhaus movement, which was blown-up Mondrian, really. Before you knew it, everything was Mondrian—the Kleenex box: Mondrian; the format of the cover of *Life* Magazine: Mondrian; those bled-to-the-edge photograph layouts in *Paris-Match*: Mondrian. Even automobiles: Mondrian. They call Detroit automobiles streamlined, but they're not. If you don't believe it, look down from an airplane at all the cars parked on a shopping-center apron, and except that all the colors are pastel instead of primary, what have you got? A Mondrian painting. The Mondrian principle, those straight edges, is very tight, very Apollonian. The streamline principle, which really has no function, which curves around and swoops and flows just for the thrill of it, is very free Dionysian. For reasons I don't have to labor over, the kids preferred the Dionysian. And since Detroit blew the thing, the Dionysian principle in cars was left to people in the teen-age netherworld, like George Barris.

Barris was living in Sacramento when he started customizing cars in 1940. As the plot develops, you have the old story of the creative child, the break from the mold of the parents, the garret struggle, the bohemian life, the first success, the accolade of the esoteric following, and finally the money starts pouring in. With this difference: We're out on old Easter Island, in the buried netherworld of teen-age Californians, and those objects, those cars, they have to do with the gods and the spirit and a lot of mystic stuff in the community.

Barris told me his folks were Greeks who owned a restaurant, and "they wanted me to be a restaurant man, like every other typical Greek, I guess," he said. But Barris, even at ten, was wild about cars, carving streamlined cars out of balsam wood. After a few years, he got a car of his own, a 1925 Buick, then a 1932 Ford. Barris established many of the formal conventions of customizing himself. Early in the game he had clients, other kids who paid him to customize their cars. In 1943 he moved to Los Angeles and landed in the middle of the tremendous teen-age culture that developed there during the war. Family life was dislocated, as the phrase goes, but the money was pouring in, and the kids began to work up their own style of life—as they've been doing ever since—and to establish those fanatic forms and conventions I was talking about earlier. Right at the heart of it, of course, was the automobile. Cars were hard to come by, what with the war, so the kids were raiding junkyards for parts, which led to custom-built cars, mostly roadsters by the very nature of it, and also to a lot of radical, hopped-up engines. All teen-age car nuts had elements of both in their work—customizing and hot-rodding, form and power—but tended to concentrate on one or the other. Barris—and Ed Roth later told me it was the same with him—naturally gravitated toward customizing. In high school, and later for a brief time at Sacramento College and the Los Angeles Art Center, he was taking what he described to me as mechanical drawing, shop, and free art.

I liked this term "free art." In Barris' world at the time, and now for that matter, there was no such thing as great big old fructuous Art. There was mechanical drawing and then there was free art, which did not mean that it was liberating in any way, but rather that it was footloose and free and not going anywhere in particular. The kind of art that appealed to Barris, and meant something to the people he hung around with, was the automobile.

Barris gets a wonderful reflective grin on his face when he starts talking about the old days—1944 to 1948. He was a hot-rodder when hot-rodders were hot-rodders, that's the kind of look he gets. They all do. The professional hot-rodders—such as the Petersen magazine syndicate (*Hot Rod Magazine* and many others) and the National Hot Rod Association—have gone to great lengths to obliterate the memory of the gamey hot-rod days, and they try to give everybody in the field transfusions of Halazone so that the public will look at the hot-rodders as nice boys with short-sleeved sport shirts just back from the laundry, and a chemistry set, such an interesting hobby.

In point of fact, Barris told me, it was a lurid time. Everybody would meet in drive-ins, the most famous of them being the Piccadilly out near Sepulveda Boulevard. It was a hell of a show, all the weird-looking roadsters and custom cars, with very loud varoom-varoom motors. By this time Barris had a '36 Ford roadster with many exotic features.

"I had just come from Sacramento, and I wasn't supposed to know anything. I was a tourist, but my car was wilder than anything around. I remember one night this kid comes up with a roadster with no door handles. It looked real sharp, but he had to kick the door from the inside to open it. You should have seen the look on his face when he saw mine—I had the same thing, only with electric buttons."

The real action, though, was the drag racing, which was quite, but quite, illegal.

"We'd all be at the Piccadilly or some place, and guys would start challenging each other. You know, a guy goes up to another guy's car and looks it up and down like it has gangrene or something, and he says: 'You wanna *go*?' Or, if it was a real grudge match for some reason, he'd say, 'You wanna go for pink slips?' The registrations on the cars were pink; in other words, the winner got the other guy's car.

"Well, as soon as a few guys had challenged each other, everybody would ride out onto this stretch of Sepulveda Boulevard or the old divided highway, in Compton, and the guys would start dragging, one car on one side of the center line, the other car on the other. Go a quarter of a mile. It was wild. Some nights there'd be a thousand kids lining the road to watch, boys and girls, all sitting on the sides of their cars with the lights shining across the highway."

But George, what happened if some ordinary motorist happened to be coming down the highway at this point?

"Oh, we'd block off the highway at each end, and if some guy wanted to get through anyway, we'd tell him, 'Well, Mister, there are going to be two cars coming down both sides of the road pretty fast in a minute, and you can go through if you want to, but you'll just have to take your best shot.'

"They always turned around, of course, and after awhile the cops would come. Then you *really* saw something. Everybody jumped in their cars and took off, in every direction. Some guys would head right across a field. Of course, all our cars were so hopped up, the cops could never catch anybody.

"Then one night we got raided at the Piccadilly. It was one Friday night. The cops came in and just started loading everybody in the wagons. I was sitting in a car with a cop who was off duty—he was a hot-rodder himself—or they would have picked me up, too. Saturday night everybody came back to the Piccadilly to talk about what happened the night before, and the cops came back again and picked up three hundred fifty that night. That pretty well ended the Piccadilly."

From the very moment he was on his own in Los Angeles, when he was about eighteen, Barris never did anything but customize cars. He never took any other kind of job. At first he worked in a body shop that took him on because so many kids were coming by wanting this and that done to their cars, and the boss really didn't know how to do it, because it was all esoteric teen-age stuff. Barris was making next to nothing at first, but he never remembers feeling hard up, nor does any kid out there today I talked to. They have a magic economy or something. Anyway, in 1945 Barris opened his own shop on Compton Avenue, in Los Angeles, doing nothing but customizing. There was that much demand for it. It was no sweat, he said; pretty soon he was making better than $100 a week.

Most of the work he was doing then was modifying Detroit cars—chopping and channeling. Chopping is lowering the top of the car, bringing it nearer to the hood line. Channeling is lowering the body itself down between the wheels. Also, they'd usually strip off all the chrome and the door handles and cover up the wheel openings in the back. At that time, the look the kids liked was to have the body lowered in the back and slightly jacked up in the front, although today it's just the opposite. The front windshield in those days was divided by a post, and so chopping the top gave the car a very sinister appearance. The front windshield always looked like a couple of narrow, slitty little eyes. And I think this, more than anything else, diverted everybody from what Barris and the others were really doing. Hot-rodders had a terrible reputation at that time, and no line was ever drawn between hot-rodders and custom-car owners, because, in truth, they were speed maniacs, too.

This was Barris' chopped-and-channeled Mercury period. Mercuries were his favorite. All the kids knew the Barris styling and he was getting a lot of business. What he was really doing, in a formal sense, was trying to achieve the kind of streamlining that Detroit, for all intents and purposes, had abandoned. When modified, some of the old Mercuries were more streamlined than any standard model that Detroit has put out to this day. Many of the coupes he modified had a very sleek slope to the back window that has been picked up just this year in the "fastback" look of the Rivieras, Sting Rays, and a few other cars.

At this point Barris and the other customizers didn't really have enough capital to do many completely original cars, but they were getting more and more radical in modifying Detroit cars. They were doing things Detroit didn't do until years later—tailfins, bubble tops, twin headlights, concealed headlights, "Frenched" headlights, the low-slung body itself. They lifted some twenty designs from him alone. One, for example, is the way cars now have the exhaust pipes exit through the rear bumper or fender. Another is the bullet-shaped, or breast-shaped if you'd rather, front bumpers on the Cadillac.

Barris says "lifted," because some are exact down to the most minute details. Three years ago when he was in Detroit, Barris met a lot of car designers and, "I was amazed," he told me. "They could tell me about cars I built in 1945. They knew all about the four-door '48 Studebaker I restyled. I chopped the top and dropped the hood and it ended up a pretty good-looking car. And the bubbletop I built in 1954—they knew all about it. And all this time we thought they frowned on us."

Even today—dealing with movie stars and auto manufacturers

and all sorts of people on the outside—I think Barris, and certainly the others, still feel psychologically a part of the alien teen-age netherworld in which they grew up. All that while they were carrying the torch for the Dionysian Streamline. They were America's modern baroque designers—and, oddly enough, "serious" designers, Anglo-European-steeped designers, are just coming around to it. Take Saarinen, especially in something like his T.W.A. terminal at Idlewild. The man in his last years came around to baroque modern.

It's interesting that the customizers, like sports-car fans, have always wanted cars minus most of the chrome—but for different ideals. The sports-car owner thinks chrome trim interferes with the "classic" look of his car. In other words, he wants to simplify the thing. The customizer thinks chrome interferes with something else—the luxurious baroque Streamline. The sports-car people snigger at tailfins. The customizers love them and, looked at from a baroque standard of beauty, they are really not so trashy at all. They are an inspiration, if you will, a wonderful fantasy extension of the curved line, and since the car in America is half fantasy anyway, a kind of baroque extension of the ego, you can build up a good argument for them.

Getting back to Easter Island, here were Barris and the others with their blowtorches and hard-rubber mallets, creating their baroque sculpture, cut off from the rest of the world and publicized almost solely via the teen-age grapevine. Barris was making a fairly good living, but others were starving at this thing. The pattern was always the same: a guy would open a body shop and take on enough hack collision work to pay the rent so that he could slam the door shut at 2 P.M. and get in there and do his custom jobs, and pretty soon the guy got so he couldn't even face *any* collision work. Dealing with all those crusty old arteriosclerotic bastards takes up all your *time*, man, and so they're trying to make a living doing nothing but custom work, and they are starving.

The situation is a lot like that today, except that customizing is beginning to be rationalized, in the sense Max Weber used that word. This rationalization, or efficient exploitation, began in the late Forties when an $80-a-week movie writer named Robert Petersen noticed all the kids pouring money into cars in a little world they had created for themselves, and he decided to exploit it by starting *Hot Rod Magazine*, which clicked right away and led to a whole chain of hot-rod and custom-car magazines. Petersen, by the way, now has a pot of money and drives Maseratis and other high-status-level sports cars of the Apollonian sort, not the Dionysian custom kind. Which is kind of a shame, because he has the money to commission something really incredible.

Up to that time the only custom-car show in the country was a wild event Barris used to put on bereft of any sort of midwifery by forty-two-year-old promoters with Windsor-knot ties who usually run low-cost productions. This car show was utterly within the teenage netherworld, with no advertising or coverage of any sort. It took place each spring—during the high-school Easter vacations—when all the kids, as they still do, would converge on the beach at Balboa for their beer-drinking-Faschung rites, or whatever the Germans call it. Barris would rent the parking lot of a service station on a corner for a week, and kids from all over California would come with their customized cars. First there would be a parade; the cars, about a hundred fifty of them, would drive all through the streets of Balboa, and the kids would line the sidewalks to watch them; then they'd drive back to the lot and park and be on exhibit for the week.

Barris still goes off to Balboa and places like that. He likes that scene. Last year at Pacific Ocean Park he noticed all these bouffant babies and got the idea of spraying all those great puffed-up dandelion heads with fluorescent water colors, the same Kandy Kolors he uses on the cars. Barris took out an air gun, the girls all lined up and gave him fifty cents per, and he sprayed them with these weird brilliant color combinations all afternoon until he ran out of colors. Each would go skipping and screaming away out onto the sidewalks and the beaches. Barris told me, "It was great that night to take one of the rides, like the Bubble Ride, and look down and see all those fluorescent colors. The kids were bopping [dancing] and running around."

The Bubble is a ride that swings out over the ocean. It is supposed to be like a satellite in orbit.

"But the fellows sky-diving got the best look as they came down by parachute."

In 1948 Petersen put on the first custom-car show in the Los Angeles armory, and this brought customizing out into the open a little. A wild-looking Buick Barris had remodeled was one of the hits of the show, and he was on his way, too.

At some point in the Fifties a lot of Hollywood people discovered Barris and the customizers. It was somewhat as if the literary set had discovered the puppeteer, Tony Sarg, during the Thirties and deified him in a very arty, in-groupy way, only I think in the case of Hollywood and Barris there was something a lot more in-the-grain about it. The people who end up in Hollywood are mostly Dionysian sorts and they feel alien and resentful when confronted with the Anglo-European ethos. They're a little slow to note the difference between topsides and sneakers, but they appreciate Cuban sunglasses.

In his showroom at Kustom City, down past the XPAK-400 air car, Barris has a corner practically papered with photographs of cars he has customized or handmade for Hollywood people: Harry Karl, Jayne Mansfield, Elvis Presley, Liberace, and even celebrities from the outside like Barry Goldwater (a Jaguar with a lot of airplane-style dials on the dashboard) and quite a few others. In fact, he built most of the wild cars that show-business people come up with for publicity purposes. He did the "diamond-dust" paint job on the Bobby Darin Dream Car, which was designed and built by Andy DiDia of Detroit. That car is an example, par excellence, of baroque streamlining, by the way. It was badly panned when pictures of it were first published, mainly because it looked like Darin was again forcing his ego on the world. But as baroque modern sculpture—again, given the fantasy quotient in cars to begin with—it is pretty good stuff.

As the hot-rod and custom-car-show idea began catching on, and there are really quite a few big ones now, including one at the Coliseum up at Columbus Circle last year, it became like the culture boom in the other arts. The big names, particularly Barris and Roth but also Starbird, began to make a lot of money in the same thing Picasso has made a lot of money in: reproductions. Barris' creations are reproduced by AMT Models as model cars. Roth's are reproduced by Revel. The way people have taken to these models makes it clearer still that what we have here is no longer a car but a design object, an *objet*, as they say.

Of course, it's not an unencumbered art form like oil painting or most conventional modern sculpture. It carries a lot of mental baggage with it, plain old mechanical craftsmanship, the connotations of speed and power and the aforementioned mystique that the teenage netherworld brings to cars. What you have is something more like sculpture in the era of Benvenuto Cellini, when sculpture was always more tied up with religion and architecture. In a lot of other ways it's like the Renaissance, too. Young customizers have come to Barris' shop, for example, like apprentices coming to the feet of the master. Barris said there were eleven young guys in Los Angeles right now who had worked for him and then gone out on their own, and he doesn't seem to begrudge them that.

"But they take on too much work," he told me. "They want a name, fast, and they take on a lot of work, which they do for practically nothing, just to get a name. They're usually undercapitalized to begin with, and they take on too much work, and then they can't deliver and they go bankrupt."

There's another side to this, too. You have the kid from the small town in the Midwest who's like the kid from Keokuk who wants to go to New York and live in the Village and be an artist and the like, he means, you know, things around home are but *hopelessly*, totally square, home and all that goes with it. Only the kid from the Midwest who wants to be a custom-car artist goes to Los Angeles to do it. He does pretty much the same thing. He lives a kind of suburban bohemian life and takes odd jobs and spends the rest of his time at the feet of somebody like Barris, working on cars.

I ran into a kid like that at Barris'. We were going through his place, back into his interiors—car interiors—department, and we came upon Ronny Camp. Ronny is twenty-two, but looks about eighteen because he has teen-age posture. Ronny is, in fact, a bright and sensitive kid with an artistic eye, but at first glance he seems always to have his feet propped up on a table or something so you can't walk past, and you have to kind of bat them down, and he then screws up his mouth and withdraws his eyeballs to the optic chiasma and glares at you with his red sulk. That was the misleading first impression.

Ronny was crazy over automobiles and nobody in his hometown, Lafayette, Indiana, knew anything about customizing. So one day Ronny packs up and tells the folks, This is it, I'm striking out for hip territory, Los Angeles, where a customizing artist is an artist. He had no idea where he was going, you understand, all he knew was that he was going to Barris' shop and make it from there. So off he goes in his 1960 Chevrolet.

Ronny got a job at a service station and poured every spare cent into getting the car customized at Barris'. His car was right there while we were talking, a fact I was very aware of, because he never looked at me. He never took his eyes off that car. It's what is called semi-custom. Nothing has been done to it to give it a really sculptural quality, but a lot of streamlining details have been added. The main thing you notice is the color—tangerine flake. The paint—one of Barris' Kandy Kolor concoctions—makes the car look like it has been encrusted with chips of some kind of semi-precious ossified tangerine, all coated with a half-inch of clear lacquer. There used to be very scholarly and abstruse studies of color and color symbolism around the turn of the century, and theorists concluded that preferences for certain colors were closely associated with rebelliousness, and these are the very same colors many of the kids go for—purple, creosote yellow, various violets and lavenders and fuchsias and many of these Kandy Kolors.

After he got his car fixed up, Ronny made a triumphal progress back home. He won the trophy in his class at the national hot-rod and custom-car show in Indianapolis, and he came tooling into Lafayette, Indiana, and down the main street in his tangerine-flake 1960 Chevrolet. It was like Ezra Pound going back to Hamilton, New York, with his Bollingen plaque and saying, Here I am, Hamilton, New York. The way Ronny and Barris tell it, the homecoming was a big success—all the kids thought Ronny was all right, after all, and he made a big hit at home. I can't believe the part about home. I mean, I can't really believe Ronny made a hit with a tangerine-flake Chevrolet. But I like to conjecture about his parents. I don't know anything about them, really. All I know is *I* would have had a hell of a lump in my throat if I had seen Ronny coming up to the front door in his tangerine-flake car, bursting so flush and vertical with triumph that no one would ever think of him as a child of the red sulk—Ronny, all the way back from California with his grail.

Along about 1957, Barris started hearing from the Detroit auto manufacturers.

"One day," he said, "I was working in the shop—we were over in Lynwood then—and Chuck Jordan from Cadillac walked in. He just walked in and said he was from Cadillac. I thought he meant the local agency. We had done this Cadillac for Liberace, the interior had his songs, all the notes, done in black and white Moroccan leather, and I thought he wanted to see something about that. But he said he was from the Cadillac styling center in Detroit and they were interested in our colors. Chuck—he's up there pretty good at Cadillac now, I think—said he had read some articles about our colors, so I mixed up some samples for him. I had developed a translucent paint, using six different ingredients, and it had a lot of brilliance and depth. That was what interested them. In this paint you look through a clear surface into the color, which is very brilliant. Anyway, this was the first time we had any idea they even knew who we were."

Since then Barris has made a lot of trips to Detroit. The auto companies, mainly GM and Ford, pump him for ideas about what the kids are going for. He tells them what's wrong with their cars, mainly that they aren't streamlined and sexy enough.

"But, as they told me, they have to design a car they can sell to the farmer in Kansas as well as the hot dog in Hollywood."

For that reason—the inevitable compromise—the customizers do not dream of working as stylists for the Detroit companies, although they deal with them more and more. It would be like René Magritte or somebody going on the payroll of Continental Can to do great ideas of Western man. This is an old story in art, of course, genius vs. the organization. But the customizers don't think of corporate bureaucracy quite the way your conventional artist does, whether he be William Gropper of Larry Rivers, namely, as a lot of small-minded Babbitts, venal enemies of culture, etc. They just think of the big companies as part of that vast mass of *adult* America, sclerotic from years of just being too old, whose rules and ideas weigh down upon Youth like a vast, bloated sac. Both Barris and Roth have met Detroit's Young Stylists, and seem to look upon them as monks from another country. The Young Stylists are designers Detroit recruits from the art schools and sets up in a room with clay and styluses and tells to go to it—start carving models, dream cars, new ideas. Roth especially cannot conceive of anyone having any valid concepts about cars who hasn't come out of the teen-age netherworld. And maybe he's right. While the Young Stylists sit in a north-lit studio smoothing out little Mondrian solids, Barris and Roth carry on in the Dionysian loop-the-loop of streamlined baroque modern.

I've mentioned Ed Roth several times in the course of this without really telling you about him. And I want to, because he, more than any other of the customizers, has kept alive the spirit of alienation and rebellion that is so important to the teen-age ethos that customizing grew up in. He's also the most colorful, and the most intellectual, and the most capricious. Also the most cynical. He's the Salvador Dali of the movement—a surrealist in his designs, a showman by temperament, a prankster. Roth is really too bright to stay within the ethos, but he stays in it with a spirit of luxurious obstinacy. Any style of life is going to produce its celebrities if it sticks to its rigid standards, but in the East a talented guy would most likely be drawn into the Establishment in one way or another. That's not so inevitable in California.

I had been told that Roth was a surly guy who never bathed and was hard to get along with, but from the moment I first talked to him on the telephone he was an easy guy and very articulate. His studio—and he calls it a studio, by the way—is out in Maywood, on the other side of the city from North Hollywood, in what looked to me like a much older and more run-down section. When I walked up, Roth was out on the apron of his place doing complicated drawings and lettering on somebody's ice-cream truck with an airbrush. I knew right away it was Roth from pictures I had seen of him; he has a beatnik-style beard. "Ed Roth?" I said. He said yeah and we started talking and so forth. A little while later we were sitting in a diner having a couple of sandwiches and Roth, who was wearing a short-sleeved T-shirt pointed to this huge tattoo on his left arm that says "Roth" in the lettering style with big serifs that he uses as his signature. "I had that done a couple of years ago because guys keep coming up to me saying, 'Are you Ed Roth?' "

Roth is a big, powerful guy, about six feet four, two hundred seventy pounds, thirty-one years old. He has a constant sort of court attendant named Dirty Doug, a skinny little guy who blew in from out of nowhere, sort of like Ronny Camp over at Barris'. Dirty Doug has a job sweeping up in a steel mill, but what he obviously lives for is the work he does around Roth's. Roth seems to have a lot of sympathy for the Ronny Camp-Dirty Doug syndrome and keeps him around as a permanent fixture. At Roth's behest, apparently, Dirty Doug has dropped his last name, Kinney, altogether, and refers to himself as Dirty Doug—not Doug. The relationship between Roth and Dirty Doug—which is sort of Quixote and Sancho Panza, Holmes and Watson, Lone Ranger and Tonto, Raffles and his sidekick—is part of the folklore of the hot-rod and custom-car kids. It even crops up in the hot-rod comic books, which are an interesting phenomenon in themselves. Dirty Doug, in this folklore, is every rejected outcast little kid in the alien netherworld, and Roth is the understanding, if rather overly pranksterish, protective giant or Robin Hood—you know, a good-bad giant, not part of the Establishment.

Dirty Doug drove up in one of his two Cadillacs one Saturday afternoon while I was at Roth's, and he had just gone through another experience of rejection. He has two Cadillacs, he said, because one is always in the shop. Dirty Doug's cars, like most customizers', are always in the process of becoming. The streaks of "primer" paint on the Cadillac he was driving at the time had led to his rejection in Newport. He had driven to Newport for the weekend. "All the cops have to do is see paint like that and already you're 'one of those hot-rodders,'" he said. "They practically followed me down the street and gave me a ticket every twenty-five feet. I was going to stay the whole weekend, but I came on back."

At custom-car shows, kids are always asking Roth, "Where's Dirty Doug?", and if Dirty Doug couldn't make it for some reason, Roth will recruit any kid around who knows the pitch and install him as Dirty Doug, just to keep the fans happy.

Thus Roth protects the image of Dirty Doug even when the guy's not around, and I think it becomes a very important piece of mythology. The thing is, Roth is not buying the act of the National Hot Rod Association, which for its own reasons, not necessarily the kid's reasons, is trying to assimilate the hot-rod ethos into conventional America. It wants to make all the kids look like candidates for the Peace Corps or something.

The heart of the contretemps between the NHRA Establishment and Roth can be illustrated in their slightly different approach to drag racing on the streets. The Establishment tries to eliminate the practice altogether and restricts drag racing to certified drag strips and, furthermore, lets the people know about that. They encourage the hot-rod clubs to help out little old ladies whose cars are stuck in the snow and then hand them a card reading something like, "You have just been assisted by a member of the Blue Bolt Hot Rod Club, an organization of car enthusiasts dedicated to promoting safety on our highways."

Roth's motto is: "Hell, if a guy wants to go, let him *go*."

Roth's designs are utterly baroque. His air car—the Rotar—is not nearly as good a piece of design as Barris', but his beatnik Bandit is one of the great *objets* of customizing. It's a very Rabelaisian *tour de force*—a twenty-first century version of a '32 Ford hot-rod roadster. And Roth's new car, the Mysterion, which he was working on when I was out there, is another *tour de force,* this time in the hottest new concept in customizing, asymmetrical design. Asymmetrical design, I gather, has grown out of the fact that the driver sits on one side of the car, not in the middle, thereby giving a car an eccentric motif to begin with. In Roth's Mysterion—a bubbletop coupe powered by two 406-horsepower Thunderbird motors—a thick metal arm sweeps up to the left from the front bumper level, as from the six to the three on a clock, and at the top of it is an elliptical shape housing a bank of three headlights. No headlights on the right side at all; just a small clearance light to orient the oncoming driver. This big arm, by the way, comes up in a spherical geometrical arc, not a flat plane.

Balancing this, as far as the design goes, is an arm that comes up over the back of the bubbletop on the right side, like from the nine to the twelve on a clock, also in a spherical arc, if you can picture all this. Anyway, this car takes the streamline and the abstract curve and baroque curvilinear one step further, and I wouldn't be surprised to see it inspiring Detroit designs in the years to come.

Roth is a brilliant designer, but as I was saying, his conduct and his attitude dilutes the Halazone with which the Establishment is trying to transfuse the whole field. For one thing, Roth, a rather thorough-going bohemian, kept turning up at the car shows in a T-shirt. That was what he wore at the big National Show at the New York Coliseum, for example. Roth also insists on sleeping in a car or station wagon while on the road, even though he is making a lot of money now and could travel first class. Things came to a head early this year when Roth was out in Terre Haute, Indiana, for a show. At night Roth would just drive his car out in a cornfield, lie back on the front seat, stick his feet out the window and go to sleep. One morning some kid came by and saw him and took a picture while Roth was still sleeping and sent it to the model company Roth has a contract with, Revel, with a note saying, "Dear Sirs: Here is a picture of the man you say on your boxes is the King of the Customizers." The way Roth tells it, it must have been an extraordinarily good camera, because he says, with considerable pride, "There were a bunch of flies flying around my feet, and this picture showed all of them."

Revel asked Roth if he wouldn't sort of spruce up a little bit for the image and all that, and so Roth entered into a kind of reverse rebellion. He bought a full set of tails, silk hat, boiled shirt, cuff links, studs, the whole apparatus, for $215, also a monocle, and now he comes to all the shows like that. "I bow and kiss all the girls' hands," he told me. "The guys get pretty teed off about that, but what can they do? I'm being a perfect gentleman."

To keep things going at the shows, where he gets $1000 to $2000 per appearance—he's that much of a drawing card—Roth creates and builds one new car a year. This is the Dali pattern, too. Dali usually turns out one huge and (if that's possible anymore) shocking painting each year or so and ships it on over to New York, where they install it in Carstairs or hire a hall if the thing is too big, and Dali books in at the St. Regis and appears on television wearing a rhinoceros horn on his forehead. The new car each year also keeps Roth's model-car deal going. But most of Roth's income right now is the heavy business he does in Weirdo and Monster shirts. Roth is very handy with the airbrush—has a very sure hand—and one day at a car show he got the idea of drawing a grotesque cartoon on some guy's sweat shirt with the air brush, and that started the Weirdo shirts. The typical Weirdo shirt is in a vein of draftsmanship you might call Mad Magazine Bosch, very slickly done for something so grotesque, and will show a guy who looks like Frankenstein, the big square steam-shovel jaw and all, only he has a wacky leer on his face, at the wheel of a hot-rod roadster, and usually he has a round object up in the air in his right hand that looks like it is attached to the dashboard by a cord. This, it turns out, is the gearshift. It doesn't look like a gearshift to me, but every kid knows immediately what it is.

"Kids *love* dragging a car," Roth told me. "I mean they really love it. And what they love the most is when they shift from low to second. They get so they can practically *feel* the r.p.m.'s. They can shift without hardly hitting the clutch at all."

These shirts always have a big caption, and usually something rebellious or at least alienated, something like "MOTHER IS WRONG" or "BORN TO LOSE."

"A teen-ager always has resentment to adult authority," Roth told me. "These shirts are like a tattoo, only it's a tattoo they can take off if they want to."

I gather Roth doesn't look back on his childhood with any great relish. Apparently his father was pretty strict and never took any abiding interest in Roth's creative flights, which were mostly in the direction of cars, like Barris'.

"You've got to be real careful when you raise a kid," Roth told me several times. "You've got to spend time with him. If he's working on something, building something, you've got to work with him." Roth's early career was almost exactly like Barris', the hot rods, the drive-ins, the drag racing, the college (East Los Angeles Junior College and UCLA), taking mechanical drawing, the chopped and channeled '32 Ford (a big favorite with all the hot-rodders), purple paint, finally the first custom shop, one stall in a ten-stall body shop.

"They threw me out of there," Roth said, "because I painted a can of Lucky Lager beer on the wall with an airbrush. I mean, it was a perfect can of Lucky Lager beer, all the details, the highlights, the seals, the small print, the whole thing. Somehow this can of Lucky Lager beer really bugged the guy who owned the place. Here was this can of Lucky Lager beer on *his* wall."

The Establishment can't take this side of Roth, just as no Establishment could accommodate Dadaists for very long. Beatniks more easily than Dadaists. The trick has always been to absorb them somehow. So far Roth has resisted absorption.

"We were the real gangsters of the hot-rod field," Roth said. "They keep telling us we have a rotten attitude. We have a different attitude, but that doesn't make us rotten."

Several times, though, Roth would chuckle over something, usually some particularly good gesture he had made, like the Lucky Lager, and say, "I am a real rotten guy."

Roth pointed out, with some insight, I think, that the kids have a revealing vocabulary. They use the words "rotten," "bad" and "tough" in a very fey, ironic way. Often a particularly baroque and sleek custom car will be called a "big, bad Merc" (for Mercury) or something like that. In this case "bad" means "good," but it also retains some of the original meaning of "bad." The kids know that to adults, like their own parents, this car is going to look sinister and somehow like an assault on their style of life. Which it is. It's rebellion, which the parents don't go for—"bad," which the kids *do* go for, "bad" meaning "good."

Roth said that Detroit is beginning to understand that there are just a hell of a lot of these bad kids in the United States and that they are growing up. "And they want a better car. They don't want an old man's car."

Roth has had pretty much the same experience as Barris with the motor companies. He has been taken to Detroit and feted and offered a job as a designer and a consultant. But he never took it seriously.

"I met a lot of the young designers," said Roth. "They were nice guys and they know a lot about design, but none of them has actually done a car. They're just up there working away on those clay models."

I think this was more than the craftsman's scorn of the designer who never actually does the work, like some of the conventional sculptors today who have never chiseled a piece of stone or cast anything. I think it was more that the young Detroit stylists came to the automobile strictly from art school and the abstract world of design—rather than via the teen-age mystique of the automobile and the teen-age ethos of rebellion. This status-group feeling is very important to Roth, and to Barris, for that matter, because it was only because of the existence of this status group—and this style of life—that custom-car sculpture developed at all.

With the Custom Car Caravan on the road—it has already reached Freedomland—the manufacturers may be well on the way to routinizing the charisma, as Max Weber used to say, which is to say, bringing the whole field into a nice, safe, vinyl-glamorous marketable ball of polyethylene. It's probably already happening. The customizers will end up like those poor bastards in Haiti, the artists, who got too much, too soon, from Selden Rodman and the other folk-doters on the subject of primitive genius, so they're all down there at this moment carving African masks out of mahogany—what I mean is, they never *had* an African mask in Haiti before Selden Rodman got there.

I think Roth has a premonition that something like that is liable to happen, although it will happen to him last, if at all. I couldn't help but get a kick out of what Roth told me about his new house. We had been talking about how much money he was making, and he told me how his taxable income was only about $6200 in 1959, but might hit $15,000 this year, maybe more, and he mentioned he was building a new house for his wife and five kids down at Newport, near the beach. I immediately asked him for details, hoping to hear about an utterly baroque piece of streamlined architecture.

"No, this is going to be my wife's house, the way she wants it, nothing way out; I mean, she has to do the home scene." He has also given her a huge white Cadillac, by the way, unadorned except for his signature—"Roth"—with those big serifs, on the side. I saw the thing, it's huge, and in the back seat were his children, very sweet-looking kids, all drawing away on drawing pads.

But I think Roth was a little embarrassed that he had disappointed me on the house, because he told me his idea of the perfect house—which turned out to be a kind of ironic parable:

"This house would have this big, round living room with a dome over it, you know? Right in the middle of the living room would be a huge television set on a swivel so you could turn it and see it from wherever you are in the room. And you have this huge easy chair for yourself, you know the kind that you can lean back to about ninety-three different positions and it vibrates and massages your back and all that, and this chair is on tracks, like a railroad yard.

"You can take one track into the kitchen, which just shoots off one side of the living room, and you can ride backward if you want to and watch television all the time, and of course in the meantime you've pressed a lot of buttons so your TV dinner is cooking in the kitchen and all you have to do is go and take it out of the oven.

"Then you can roll right back into the living room, and if somebody rings the doorbell you don't move at all. You just press a button on this big automatic console you have by your chair and the front door opens, and you just yell for the guy to come in, and you can keep watching television.

"At night, if you want to go to bed, you take another track into the bedroom, which shoots off on another side, and you just kind of roll out of the chair into the sack. On the ceiling above your bed you have another TV set, so you can watch all night."

Roth is given, apparently, to spinning out long Jean Shepherd stories like this with a very straight face, and he told me all of this very seriously. I guess I didn't look like I was taking it very seriously, because he said, "I have a TV set over the bed in my house right now—you can ask my wife."

I met his wife, but I didn't ask her. The funny thing is, I did find myself taking the story seriously. To me it was a sort of parable of the Bad Guys, and the Custom Sculpture. The Bad Guys built themselves a little world and got onto something good and then the Establishment, all sorts of Establishments, began closing in, with a lot of cajolery, thievery and hypnosis, and in the end, thrown into a vinyl Petri dish, the only way left to tell the whole bunch of them where to head in was to draw them a huge asinine picture of themselves, which they were sure to like. After all, Roth's dream house is nothing more than his set of boiled shirt and tails expanded into a whole universe. And he is not really very hopeful about that either.

—NOVEMBER 1963

# The Transformation of Johnny Spain

CHIP BROWN

Long before the killings, the trials, the fantasies of revolution, Johnny Spain was a six-year-old boy who lived in a small bungalow on the south side of Jackson, Mississippi. His father, Fred, drove a beer truck; his mother, Ann, manufactured TV cabinets. He had an older brother, Charlie, a younger sister, Lissie, a baby brother, Ray. That summer of 1955 his name was Larry Armstrong and he looked pretty much like anybody else's kid except for his hair—"nigger hair," people called it. The children in Choctaw Village liked to put their hands in it, but no barber in Jackson's white parlors would touch it.

Johnny Spain remembers a little from those days, but not much: the time Charlie, his steadfast defender, called him a nigger; the times he hid under the bed when Fred came home; when he heard his father slap his mother and holler, "Take the nigger baby and get out!" He would have entered the first grade that fall were it not for his hair, and the talk and all. Even the superintendent of Jackson's public schools knew about him. Nearly twenty years would pass before children with hair like his would sit in class with whites.

Of what happened next, he recalls virtually nothing. His mother broke the news that he was going to live with a family in California, where he could attend school out of harm's way. She packed his clothes, and then the three of them, Fred and Ann and the boy, piled in the car and eventually he found himself on a train with an elderly woman. He thought his parents would turn up and take him home at any moment, but the sun went down, and morning broke over new country, and the train was streaking west. It was three days to Los Angeles. He would never forget the trestle bridges that traversed the canyons, nor the woman riding with him, but it would be years before he could understand the impact of that journey. This was the child who grew up to be Johnny Spain, the onetime Black Panther, protégé of George Jackson, and sole member of the San Quentin Six convicted of murder. And this is the central fact of his life: a long time ago he boarded a train to Mississippi as a little white boy; when he got off in California, he was black.

Jackson, Mississippi, was burned so thoroughly during the Civil War it got the name Chimneyville, but in the early 1950s "the crossroads of the South" was doing business in furniture, lumber, and cottonseed oil. The population of almost a hundred thousand was two-thirds white and scrupulously segregated. In the 1950 city directory "colored people" were distinguished by a C with a circle around it, and a disclaimer cautioned, "The publishers are very particular in using this, but are not responsible in case of error."

In that year's edition, an Ann and Fred Armstrong are listed. The two children noted would have been Charlie and Larry, and as far as the very particular publishers were concerned, both were white.

Fred Armstrong still lives in Jackson. On a humid June morning I found him sitting in a white T-shirt on the screened-in porch in front of his trailer, a big keg of a man with enormous ears, and the morning paper spread on his lap.

"Mr. Armstrong, can I talk to you about Larry?"

"Larry?" he said.

"Larry . . . Armstrong?"

The name didn't seem to ring a bell.

"Your son . . ."

Finally it clicked. "The nigger?" he said.

We talked through the screen. Fred Armstrong insisted there

wasn't much to tell. What's more, he said, at seventy-six some of the details had escaped him.

"Last time I heard, he'd shot a man or something in California. I think he's out of jail now, maybe he's gotten married."

In Germany during the war, Fred Armstrong had been an Army cook. He opened Armstrong's Café on Monument Street when he got back. He worked nights, his wife Ann worked days. They met at a dance on an Army base, courted by letter, and married on October 6, 1945. He was thirty-four; she was ten years younger.

"At first she took the marriage seriously," he said. "When Charlie was born we were living on Rose Street, we got along pretty good. I was working all the time, she was working. She wasn't bored. We were sleeping together. Then she started slipping out. She come home at 4:00 A.M. one night, and I seen her get out of the car. I slapped her around.

"She got pregnant when I was running the café," he recalled. "I had it two or three years. I sold out in 1948. Then I spent eighteen years in the beer business."

He couldn't remember the name of the man who fathered Larry. He knew him though.

"He come in my café and ate. That boy worked down on State Street at some garage. When he found out I was after him, he skipped."

"What would you have done to him?"

"Back in those days? I probably would have hung him or killed him. Now I look back, it was as much her fault as his. He was about twenty, twenty-five years old. He'd set up at the counter by the cash register. I seen 'em talking, but I didn't think anything about it. She knew all the niggers, they would come in from the cotton mill.

"It happened up there across from the farmers' market. She'd go up there and the nigger went with her. They'd go up in the evening after she got done washing dishes."

"Were you surprised when the baby was born?"

"I was surprised," he said.

"Ann's grandmother was dark-colored," he continued. "I just passed it off. But the boy's hair was nigger hair. I was in the jukebox business, working for Charlie Warren. When that boy was a year old, Charlie told me, 'Fred, that's a nigger baby and you better do something.'

"I said, 'That ain't no nigger baby,' and he said, 'Yes he is.' I really thought it was my own baby until he was a couple of years old. We raised him six years."

"Was he part of the family?"

"Oh, yeah. He ate at the same table and slept in the same house. But the older he got the more he looked like a nigger. People was talking, friends of mine. They'd make remarks: 'When you gonna get rid of that nigger boy?'

"I told 'em after I found out who the father was. Me and her had a talk about it. He didn't rape her, she did it on her own free will. I went down there, I was gonna tell him to take that baby himself. They said he'd quit and went to Chicago.

"I didn't have much to do with Ann after that. I didn't want the boy around. He was a good, disciplined boy. Him and Ray and Charlie played together. But he couldn't go to the white school. Something had to be done.

"I don't know where he is, if he's dead or what. I asked Trina, Charlie's wife, a while ago, 'What ever happened to Larry?' She said he'd shot a man and did some time in California."

"Are you interested in his life?"

"No, no. You get over something like that."

Ann Armstrong and Arthur Cummings converged over a counter top, talking about poetry and baseball.

Arthur came from D'Lo, Mississippi, twenty-five miles southeast of Jackson. He was working as a mechanic. He was a regular at Armstrong's. There was a wall down the middle, whites on one side, blacks on the other. Ann worked both sides of the partition.

"Do you dare play a game of cards?" Ann asked.

"Why not," Arthur said.

Ann was restless, unhappy at home.

"Fred was very abusive," she recalled. "One night he got really rough and threw me down the stairs. He was jealous, but at that point it was all in his mind."

How did the affair get started?

"One thing led to another," she said.

"I knew the seriousness of it," said Arthur. The consequences would have been extreme. But I just didn't worry about those things."

Today Arthur lives in New Orleans. Ann lives in the Northwest under the name of her second husband. She's a diabetic and is legally blind.

When Larry was born, she put him in a crib in her room, rocked him, and talked to him more than she had to Charlie. "I felt more of a responsibility to him. I had the feeling that when he got past me, he'd have nothing."

Fred Armstrong sold the café, and in 1951 the young family moved to a small one-story, two-bedroom house on Stokes Robertson Road, in a poor white neighborhood on the south side of Jackson. Larry was two.

His skin was growing darker, but he played with neighborhood kids. There were chinaberry fights in the fields and baseball games on Wayne and Senie Fortenberry's spacious lawn. Senie was friendly with Ann.

"She told me she was never so shocked in her life the day he was born and they brought the child in," Senie recalled. "She told me her husband accepted Larry as his child. As far as we were concerned he was welcome to play in the yard. I had no problem. You'll find prejudice in all people, but I go by the Scripture.

"Pastor Wayne Todd told Ann—for the child's sake, not the church's—if they could move to a northern city, where the child would be accepted, it would be better. If she couldn't do that, then maybe they should send him to a colored family, a fine Christian family, out of this antagonistic situation."

Into my hand Senie pressed a copy of the New Testament and two gardenias graciously clipped from a fragrant bush. It had upset her to learn that Larry Armstrong had spent the last two decades in jail. She confessed that she had always been afraid something bad would happen to him.

"Why do you think all this happened?"

"It's because of sin—the sins of society, the sins of the parents," she said.

Without identifying herself, Ann called the Jackson school system. She talked to Sykes Elementary School's principal, Jim Bennett, about enrolling Larry. Sykes had opened in 1951 with about four hundred students. The landmark 1954 Supreme Court desegregation ruling had no immediate effect on the student body because there were no blacks in the area.

"If you said to me 'Larry Armstrong' I never would have known who you were talking about," Jim Bennett recalled. "But when you describe the kid, I know immediately who you are talking about.

"John Batte was chairman of the school board and a member of the downtown Kiwanis Club. He was getting calls. He asked me what was I gonna do. I said I couldn't have said no without seeing his birth certificate. If his birth certificate said white, I'd have no choice."

It never came to that. That summer Emmett Till, a fourteen-year-old Chicago boy, was kidnapped and lynched in Money, Mississippi, apparently because he whistled at a white woman. Ann feared for Larry's safety. She said she had gotten calls from the Ku Klux Klan. As it turned out, Fred had found a family to take the child.

The transfer was made in Utica, a pokey town with one stoplight southwest of Jackson, on Route 18.

The Armstrongs stopped at the Corner Grill, a popular white-owned black night spot housed in a hundred-year-old former egg hatchery. They were met by the manager, Iris "Shorty" Davis, a stout, ebullient woman, part Turkish, part black, part Cherokee.

Now on a hot June day, Shorty opened the door and beckoned her visitors in, insisting on whipping up some eggs.

"Fred Armstrong was my beer man," she recalled.

"One day he told me, 'Iris, I'm worried sick.'

"I said, 'Fred, what's wrong?'

"'I got this child at home, he can't go to school with the rest of the children. You can tell he's a colored child.' He wanted me to take the baby here. 'I'm crazy about him,' he said. 'He's smarter than my kids. I just can't keep him.'

"I said, 'I'll tell you what, I can't keep no child here. I got a cousin in California. She wants a child. I'll see if she can take him.'

"He said he'd be glad. So I got on the phone and called Helen, and she said, 'Yeah, I want me a baby.' She loved my kids."

Ann spoke to Helen Spain on the telephone, and a day was arranged—the exact date, no one remembers. Ann recalls the period between the decision to give up Larry and the actual day.

"I felt like I was waiting to die," she said. "I tried to talk to him a lot, but how do you tell a six-year-old he has to go away? I tried to paint as good a picture as I could. I got him some new clothes, made him some cowboy suits, packed his special toys. There was nothing left in me to kill."

"He thought it was going to be an adventure," said Shorty Davis. "He really wanted to go to school. Ann said he wasn't coming back, he'd have a new grandmother. He said would she ever visit, and she said yes, if she had the money."

"It was like closing a casket," Ann said. "I didn't tell him goodbye, I don't tell anybody goodbye, I say 'I'll see you,' or 'Have a nice day.' I know I told him I loved him. He was playing with some other children, and he didn't pay me too much attention."

In subsequent months Ann and Shorty became good friends.

"After I helped her, she looked like she fell in love with me," Shorty said. "She was pitiful. She came down here and talked. She was heartbroken. She never told anybody. I was the one person she could tell what she had done."

The papers were signed, and a new birth certificate was issued for Johnny Larry Spain. The one on which his race is listed as white remains under court seal in Mississippi. Larry Armstrong had a new home, new parents, a new race.

John and Helen Spain are dead today. John was a hardworking electrician. Helen, the daughter of a mixed marriage, was a caterer and cook who once worked for John Wayne.

It was a rocky family from the start. Larry had his own room in a house full of antiques. The Spains lavished him with toys, gave him train sets, expensive clothes, a bicycle.

"They loved him but they didn't know how to show love," said Katie Grissom, the Spains' next-door neighbor. "They were older people. Helen thought by buying him stuff it would make him satisfied. There was something missing."

Larry never thought of Helen as his mother. He came closer to embracing Johnny Spain as his father. His foster father called him Larry. One day the younger Spain announced, "I don't like those old names anymore." He asked to be called Johnny like his dad.

Helen's mother, Mary Davis, lived behind the house. It was she who had traveled with the boy from Jackson to Los Angeles. She was sweet; she smelled of fresh cooking; she always had time for him.

"Do you miss your other mother?" she'd say.

"I don't have another mother."

One day an ambulance pulled into the driveway, and Mary was taken away.

"That was the turning point," Spain recalled in the visitors' center at the California state prison at Vacaville. "I went to the streets after that." Spain is thirty-eight years old now, with wide-set eyes, high cheekbones, and powerful shoulders. A nightstick to the mouth cracked one of his teeth, and a skirmish with an inmate left his nose skewed to the right.

"My tendency was to take flight; I'd run and hide. There were times at Helen and Johnny's when I would get into an argument, and I'd go out of the house and just start running a mile. I would forget everything about the argument, and I would be in this incredible race. I'd see people walking up ahead, and I'd pick a point that would be the finish line. I would make up a story that I'd fallen or had tripped or something to explain why I was always behind. I'd think, here's this guy who's going to make up the distance, and I'd try to catch up."

The Spains sent their foster son to Catholic schools for five years. He refused to cry when the nuns rapped his hand with a ruler, but he broke down in the hall. He saw four schools before he was expelled for good.

"He was like a bottle with a stopper on it," said Gonzalez Cano, a young counselor who ran El Santo Niño, the Catholic Youth Organization center a few blocks down from Spain's house.

Soon, Spain was running with a gang called the Baby Outlaws. He got into fights. The young teenager fired a gun for the first time at a pile of dirt.

In public school Spain was smart enough to measure the amount of work for an A, and then do half for the C. He preferred basketball to studies. He preferred basketball to almost anything. But he was enough of an athlete to excel in football and baseball; he took up tennis and in nine months went to the city championships. Helen cleared a wall for his trophies and ribbons. Sometimes she and Johnny Sr. went to see him play, but Johnny never glanced at the bleachers.

It would not be until years later, when he was in his twenties and facing the ordeal of the San Quentin trial, that he would seek out Ann, his real mother. It was not that he didn't care about Ann, or ache for her. It was hard to explain it to people. She had tried to stay in contact. She sent Christmas presents for a while, and birthday cards, but Spain stopped answering her letters, and they stopped coming finally, and that was fine with him.

His real father, Johnny knew, was probably somewhere out there, too.

But that summer of 1965, Johnny and Helen Spain were his parents, and they looked on helplessly as their foster son's life began to unravel.

Perhaps the times hastened Spain's undoing. It was the summer of Watts. Spain had been hauled before a juvenile court judge as a runaway. He and Helen were not on good terms: her drinking was getting bad. His foster father had taken him into the electrician's business, but after a job at the Beverly Hills home of Earl C. Broady, a black lawyer and future judge, the elder Spain got a humiliating call. Broady's pearl-handled-gun collection was missing.

"I think little John came back and took the guns," Broady said.

Spain was convicted of burglary in 1965 and dispatched to forestry camp to cut firebreaks. The remedy failed. When he challenged the crew chief to a fight, he was turned over to the California Youth Authority and the custody of Howard E. Lambert, a counselor.

Lambert, a white man who died in 1980, was the last stop on the outside. He removed Spain to a foster home and supervised him until December 1966. A decade later Lambert would testify at the San Quentin trial that of the hundreds of kids he'd counseled, Spain was the one he wished he could have raised in his home. Spain had always kept his mixed heritage a secret from his friends. He paid Lambert the ultimate compliment, telling him one day, "You're not white."

In 1966, the year Bobby Seale founded the Black Panther party in Oakland, Spain dropped out of school. On the streets he was known as Caesar. One hot day in July he sat down beside Pinkey Miller in Roosevelt Park. She thought for such a big sports star he was awfully shy. Luckily a firecracker went off, and she had occasion to scream.

"Did that scare you?" he said.

"Oh, yes," she said.

They played basketball; he teased her with magic tricks. They shared hot dogs and danced the Slauson Shuffle at the Friday canteens. Party Pinkey, she was called. She had snaky moves on the dance floor—would have gone on *Soul Train* if her hip hadn't gone out.

"All the girls would speak to me, but they were looking at him," she recalled, sitting in her apartment not far from Johnny Spain's old house. They especially liked his hair. "It was thick and wavy.

"That Christmas, I went baby-sitting in Compton, and I couldn't get in touch with him, he was staying at his foster mother's house. I called and called, I couldn't reach him. I called home the second week, I called my sister Gloria. She said, 'Did you hear what happened to Caesar, he's in jail, he killed somebody.' "

She would not see him again until she recognized his picture ten years later on the front of the Black Panther newspaper and wrote. They would marry in a prison ceremony not long after that.

Four days before Christmas 1966, Spain and two friends, Jonathan Gray and Edward Normant, were walking south on Hill Street. An older white man and his wife were waiting for the bus. Spain asked the woman how far it was to Washington Boulevard.

"About three or four blocks up the street," said Nancy Long.

"Thank you."

Suddenly Nancy Long saw Spain pointing a gun at her husband, Joe.

"Shut up and don't give me any trouble," she heard him say.

"I don't care about that gun," said Long, who had been at the Ringside Bar all evening. "You're not getting my money."

There was a scuffle. Joe Long shouted at his wife, "Sit down!"

And then four shots flashed from the muzzle of the .22.

Spain ran north up Hill Street.

He was caught that night.

During Johnny Spain's twenty-one years in prison, he has seen many psychiatric counselors, read their textbooks, and learned their language. He now wonders if he had seen the face of his stepfather, Fred, in the person of Joe Long. His voice grows soft when he recalls the killing.

"I didn't need the money," he said. "I don't know why I did it. The more I tried to answer why, the larger the question became.

"My connection with my life had been closed off. I was trying to fit in with my peers. We started running together, and we decided to pull this stupid robbery. The guy was drunk, and I didn't have enough sense to stop it. I could have socked him. I didn't have to shoot him. I didn't know what the hell I was doing."

A steam horn blasted, and prisoners began to get up to report for the afternoon count.

"I didn't have the values in my system to appreciate what I was about to do," said Spain. "In east L.A. they taught survival in the crudest form—you survived at the expense of others."

A few days in juvenile hall and the reality sank in. Spain sobbed in his cell. His brother Charlie was on the West Coast and came to the trial. Charlie sat in the courtroom a few rows behind his younger brother, but Spain never acknowledged him.

"I wished I'd turned around and said, 'Charlie, help me,'" Spain recalled. "He'd always helped me when I was little."

That would be the last time the brothers saw each other. They do not communicate today.

Helen and Johnny Spain visited their foster son in jail. "They were kind of destroyed," Spain said. "My mother didn't even ask me why. What difference does it make? You can't change it."

Convicted of first-degree murder, Spain was sentenced to life in prison, and on May 5, 1967, was remanded to the state department of corrections, in whose custody he remains today.

The state prison at Tracy was known as "the gladiator school." Upon arriving, Spain filled out a prison questionnaire.

Q: Who are you?

A: I am Johnny Larry Spain. I am a person in a lot of trouble. I am a person who needs help.

Q: How do you wish to change?

A: I just want to learn to go by the rules.

Q: What are some of your ambitions or goals in life?

A: To be a famous athlete.

Prison psychologists noted: "This emotionally unstable, generally confused young man displays rather marked ambivalency in regard to his racial and masculine adequacy. While continuously he has sought to identify with the Negro culture, he still emotionally tends to relate himself to his Caucasian heritage."

Two years later, inside the walls of Soledad prison, Johnny Spain met George Jackson for the first time.

Spain had been transferred from Tracy in July 1968, a time when the California prisons were anything but immune to the social passions convulsing society at large. Jackson was the field marshal of the Black Panther party and the heart of the swelling prison movement, a campaign by lawyers and activists to reform conditions in the California prison systems. He had begun to compose the incandescent letters that would be published as *Soledad Brother*, the book that would make him an international figure.

Inside prison Jackson was legendary. It was not simply the extent of his teachings. He was a warrior in an environment where a man's life was worth as little as a carton or two of cigarettes. Jackson kept his body tuned, and his mind off sex, with a thousand fingertip push-ups a day. It was said his hands were so tough he could hold them under prison tap water hot enough at the spigot for instant coffee.

In the summer of 1969, an inmate buttonholed Spain and steered him to a lavatory where Jackson was practicing katas—exercises in a martial arts discipline called the Iron Palm.

"Hey George, this is that youngster I was telling you about. He's pretty agile."

"Throw a couple of punches," Jackson said.

"Naw," said Spain, who thought Jackson looked slow and overweight.

"Take your best shot," Jackson urged.

Well, okay, Spain thought, I'm gonna knock you on your butt. He flew at Jackson with a flurry of lefts and rights. He had been the reigning two-on-two champion from the day he set foot in Tracy, and here was this overweight asshole, and *he couldn't touch him*! Jackson was blocking every shot. Spain quit, short of breath and overawed.

"I got better moves with my feet," Jackson said.

Spain saw Jackson every day. Jackson persuaded him to join an Afro-American study group; he called Spain "Comrade" and he put him up for membership in the Black Panther party. Spain began to study Swahili, though he never took an African name. ("I had enough identification problems already.") He studied the life of Che Guevara and the writings of the black psychiatrist Frantz Fanon; he plowed through histories of Cuba and Indochina.

"George would give me a book and say, 'Why don't you read this.' And then we'd discuss it," Spain recalled. "I could read all these technical books rapidly. I read *Das Kapital* in two days."

If there was an urgency to their discussions, it was heightened by the tense atmosphere inside the prison. In January 1970 an influential black prisoner, W. C. Nolan, was killed along with two other black inmates when guards fired into the yard, ostensibly to break up a racial disturbance. To Jackson and Spain and other black prisoners, the killing seemed a deliberate act of murder. They were outraged when Nolan's death was ruled justifiable homicide.

In retaliation for Nolan's death, it is generally believed that Jackson beat rookie guard John Mills and threw him to his death off the third tier. Jackson and two other inmates were charged, and the case of the Soledad Brothers became known nationwide. Jackson was removed from the main line at Soledad.

Eight months later, Jackson's seventeen-year-old brother Jonathan made a desperate bid to free him. Jonathan Jackson barged into a Marin County courtroom, armed a couple of defendants, and took five hostages, including Judge Harold Haley. The swap that Jonathan evidently envisioned never came off. He and two others, including the judge, died in a shoot-out with police.

In Soledad without Jackson, Spain was only drawn deeper into the movement. A month after joining the Black Panther party, he was accused of "being in possession of revolutionary material."

"They brought out letters I had written to Helen," Spain recalled. "They had underlined in red the parts where I was explaining what communication was. Then they found an article from a Black Panther newspaper in my cell. They said it was revolutionary material."

Spain was removed from the general prison population and locked into the Soledad AC (Adjustment Center). That was the beginning of five-and-a-half years of prison-style segregation. In 1971 he was transferred to the hole at San Quentin. They put him in Cell 5.

George Jackson, awaiting trial in the Soledad Brothers case, was in Cell 6.

For virtually twenty-four hours a day Spain and Jackson sat in six-by-eight-foot cells furnished with a steel bunk and mattress, a toilet, and a 60-watt bulb. When tear gas was used to control a recalcitrant inmate, it drifted through the tier, stinging and choking the men in neighboring cells.

"I remember one instance when I kicked a guard," Spain said. "I used to think of it as counterviolence. I thought, I'm not wrong to stand up for myself, I'm not wrong to object if they drop my letters in a mop bucket."

Jackson and Spain talked for hours through the bars. Other prisoners on the tier joined in. At night it was quiet enough to exchange ideas. If Jackson thought a question was simpleheaded, he might say,

"I'm not going to deal with that, I'm going to let Comrade deal with that," and he would pass the query on to Spain. Sometimes it was just Jackson and Spain talking, and the rest of the tier listening. They often talked until dawn.

If there wasn't a discussion, there might be a chess game. Jackson was a pretty fair player. Players used prescriptions pills for pieces, red pain relievers for pawns, muscle relaxants for rooks. Spain didn't know chess, but he listened in his cell as Jackson played. Envisioning the board, he began to see better moves. When Jackson was gone, and there was no one to talk to, he took up the game.

Sixteen years and more than twenty-five thousand pages of testimony later, it is still not clear what happened on the afternoon George Jackson died.

The official story is this: Spain, who worked as a tier tender, had just been locked in his cell after delivering the afternoon meal. At 1:30 P.M. Jackson was let out to visit Stephen Bingham, a radical lawyer whose grandfather had been a U.S. senator from Connecticut. Fifty minutes later Jackson was escorted back from the visiting rooms across the chapel yard to the AC. Two guards conducted a routine strip search. One noticed a shiny object on Jackson's hair. "Okay, let's have it," he said.

Jackson pulled out a gun.

"This is it, gentleman," he said, and alluding to the prison writings of Ho Chi Minh, he said, "The Dragon has come."

Jackson ordered the guards to release the inmates on the tier. Spain was one of the first to come out. Jackson forced a guard named Ken McCray, along with two others, to lie face down on the floor, pillowcases over their heads, electrical cord binding their hands and legs. McCray's throat was cut. Two inmates dragged McCray into Jackson's cell. Another guard, Paul Krasenes, was also dragged in, cut and choking on his own blood and praying. He died. A third guard, Frank DeLeon, was brought in.

Jackson was in control for approximately thirty minutes. The carnage in which three people were seriously wounded and five murdered occurred in about seventeen minutes.

An inmate said he had seen Spain with Jackson as Jackson forced the guard Urbano Rubiaco to open the cells. Spain was also seen entering the killing field of Cell 6. In testimony (unsubstantiated), Officer William L. Hampton went further; he said he saw Spain point a revolver at him.

Around 3:15, the alarm was sounded.

"It's me they want," Jackson said.

He ran toward the door of the Adjustment Center, fired a shot through the windowpanes. Then, with Spain on his heels, Jackson ran into the yard.

Spain heard the first shots that apparently winged Jackson in the legs. He dived for the cover of some bushes by the chapel wall.

Crouched under the brush, Spain saw Jackson fall. "He stumbled by me," Spain said. "I'm not sure if he was hit. I didn't see when he got shot the second time."

Guards surrounded Spain, ordered him to stand with his hands on his head. He was then tossed to the ground and chained on the plaza as the heavily armed guards retook the AC.

Jackson's body lay on the plaza for hours, handcuffed just in case. Some guards sang, "George Jackson's body is a-mouldering in the grave."

Spain was in shock.

"There was a point when I was no longer in the bushes. I did see him lying there, I didn't know if he was dead," Spain recalled.

"I was numb. I really wasn't in San Quentin then. It was like a large part of me had been lifted away—a part of me that could not be hurt any longer."

In the months that followed, Spain had nothing but time to reflect on Jackson's death and the untoward course of his own life. He was indicted on five counts of murder, conspiracy to escape, and lesser charges. In its trial and pretrial phases, the case of the San Quentin Six was then the longest criminal proceeding in American history. Spain was escorted to visiting rooms and court hearings shackled around the waist, hands, and feet with twenty-five pounds of chain.

Over the next two years he would wall out the world. Jackson had been his only friend, but now in a strange way he was free. Eventually he realized it.

"I looked at my life," Spain said. "I was twenty-two years old. People were talking about killing me in the gas chamber. I'm not a terrible person. I thought I was worth more. I had to face facts. I had gotten wrapped up in a political movement, which had some good points, but I was a street kid who didn't know anything—I wanted to help all these people with this revolution I was talking about and I couldn't even write my own mother, for doing what under her circumstances was the only logical thing she could do."

During the time he waited for his case to come to trial, he thought often about the family he had left in Mississippi. He was encouraged in this by an idealistic, dark-haired activist named Cathy Kornblith, whom he had met at a prison banquet in Soledad shortly after Jonathan Jackson's funeral.

Kornblith, then twenty-three, had devoted much of her life to the prison movement. She compiled a newsletter, ferried families to visit relatives in jail, and corresponded with inmates. (Letters to her often began, "My Beautiful Black Queen, I hold you on a pedestal"—not the best way to cut ice with a white feminist.) She was flattered by Spain's attention—his friendship with Jackson conferred upon him a certain status in radical circles—but she soon perceived a quality that set him apart, a quality that grew more pronounced as their friendship deepened.

"He was afraid of family because he didn't have it," she recalled. "He was searching for something. I was really touched by that—his longing to be whole in the context of others."

By 1973 they had exchanged hundreds of letters. When Spain needed a legal investigator to help prepare his defense, Kornblith was the logical choice. Spain's lawyer, former Panther general counsel Charles Garry, felt it was important to emphasize Spain's personal odyssey, a transformation he felt expressed "the story of racism in America." Ann Armstrong's testimony was therefore vital to Spain's defense. Spain had not heard from his mother for years, and despite his longing he shied away. Mississippi was a box of nightmares.

In the spring of 1973, Kornblith found Ann's correct address. As

Spain felt unable to write the letter, Kornblith stepped up—the first of many occasions when she mediated among relatives who found it easier to communicate with a go-between.

In April 1973 Ann Armstrong wrote back:

*Dear Cathy,*

*For weeks and weeks I have not known how to reply to your letter . . . I do trust that you understand that my son being in California in the first place was an act of love. . . . I also trust that you know there is never even a part of one day that he's not in my heart and my prayers. My way in life has been, and is, hard—very hard times, but I am not complaining . . . . Easter will be coming. What do I need to send him and do I send it to you or to Helen? I do not even have an address for him. Do you think he'd like pictures of his family here?*

*Write again, please. . . .*

*Love and many thanks, Ann*

A year would pass before Spain could compose so much as a Mother's Day card. The card—which has since been lost—was their first communication in nearly fifteen years. A month later Ann replied.

6-3-74

5 A.M.

*Dearest Larry—*

*—and this is what you'll always be to me—No words can tell you how very, very happy I was to get your card and your note. I've turned over a whole dictionary in my head trying to find the right words—none came so you'll just have to accept from my heart a reply. Your card and note are the answer to many prayers over the years. I do hope that since you have accepted the fact that "I am your mother" that we can go on from there. . . . There has never been a feeling of rejection on my part—every act of mine toward you—as any of my children, and you are all the same—has always*

*been out of total love for you and anything I've ever done has been with the feeling in my heart that this was right for whichever one was involved for the moment—This includes letting you go to Helen to live when you were six. I sent all the love in this mother's heart with you and kept the tears and agony for myself.*

*I've made many mistakes, one of my biggest, I suppose, is loving too well and not wisely enough. . . .*

*I finally told Nancy [Johnny's half sister] the whole story. All the others have known for a long time. All of them feel that they'd like to write you and place the love we have for one another with you. . . .*

*Please do not wait years and years to write again—even though I'm slow answering I do care—maybe next time will be easier for the both of us.*

*Love, always, Mama*

At San Quentin Ann was reunited with her son. The sight of him, fetched to the visiting room in chains, left her badly shaken. He had dropped forty pounds, lost some teeth, and was suffering from hemorrhoids and severe headaches. The hair that had betrayed him as a child was coming out in his comb.

Spain's trial lasted eighteen months. He threw a manila file at the jury and rattled the shackles during the recitation of the charges. Outraged by the chains, Spain refused to testify. Despite the testimony of Ann, Howard and Lambert, and Ulis Williams, a youth counselor and Olympic track star, the jury convicted Spain in August 1976 on two counts of murder and one count of conspiracy. While never accused of killing anyone, he was found guilty under the legal theory of "vicarious liability," the youngest and only defendant convicted of murder. Two more life terms were added to his jacket.

If anything, prison taught him forbearance. The years that followed as his appeals crept through state and federal courts were marked by periods of hope and of disappointment. In 1977 Spain was finally returned to the general prison population. In 1982 the San Quentin convictions were thrown out by a federal judge, then reinstated by the U.S. Supreme Court. Three years later, they were again vacated by a federal judge who ruled that the chains had prevented Spain from receiving a fair trial.

During this period, Spain became an exemplary inmate. He married Pinkey Miller and was eventually permitted conjugal visits. Their first son, Michael, was born in 1983.

Spain had continued to correspond with Ann, but soon the question of his father became more critical. Faced with the possibility that the state might retry Spain on the original charges, Kornblith, Spain's new attorney, Dennis Riordan, and Spain himself discussed whether it would be useful, if even possible, to find the man Spain had never met, who had disappeared thirty-seven years ago.

His advocates' legal interest in Arthur jibed with an emotional urgency burgeoning in Spain himself. Over the years curiosity had ripened into obsession. There were a million questions Spain had for this man—the sort of questions of origin and identity for which there are few satisfactory answers but which sons need to ask nonetheless.

In 1983 Kornblith got the go-ahead from Riordan to start looking for Arthur. Ann had told her Arthur's name, and she knew that Arthur had repaired brakes at a tractor-trailer company in Jackson, and that he had been born in D'Lo. Kornblith figured she was looking for a man now in his late sixties. She didn't have much luck until she hired another private eye in Jackson, who managed to locate an Arthur Cummings in New Orleans. The man seemed to match the description.

That summer, Kornblith handed Spain a slip of paper with Arthur's name and address. Spain pleaded with her to write him herself, but she refused. "It was his personal journey," she recalled. "I wasn't going to take it for him."

"I used every excuse I could think of not to write," Spain said. "I had to go to school, I had to go to court, I had to read a motion, I was frightened. All of a sudden here was Arthur, here was my father, here was a part of me—a part of what I might have been, things I secretly dreamed about. I didn't want to face that part in my life where I would have to confront him and the possibility that he might not accept who I was."

*Dear Arthur,*

*Writing this letter has been one of the really difficult tasks in my life. My name is John Spain. My mother's name in 1948 was Ann Armstrong. I was born July 30, 1949 in Jackson, Mississippi. I don't know that any of this means anything to you. What I do know is that writing to you, if you are my father, has taken many long years of painful searching, not only to find you, but searching within myself for the courage to touch a part of my past that proved to be one of the most damaging of my life. If you want to confirm whether or not I'm correct about you being my father, I suggest that you call my mother. She has expressed a desire to talk with you, and for what it might be worth, I think you could bring some comfort in her life with a phone call.*

*I have a 35-year-old need to know who my father is. The knowledge would help calm some of the deep, pounding storms within me. I could finally have a piece of the connection I've longed for my whole life. That is important to me. I also have a 9-month-old son, Michael, who needs to have some roots of his own. I want to be able to tell him who his grandfather is. There is much I still want to say, but I think it is necessary (that it could be necessary) for you to inform me of how my presence might influence your life. I have no wish to bring problems to your life. I will send my mother's phone number if you wish me to. If you are my father but do not want to establish communication on an ongoing basis, please inform me of that fact. I am reaching to you, or rather to my father, because I want to know my father. I will not attempt to press for communication if you wish otherwise.*

*Thank you for listening/reading this.*

*Best regards,*
*John Spain*

The letter, dated July 19, 1984, made no mention that Spain was incarcerated in the California state prison at Vacaville, serving three life sentences for murder.

Arthur Cummings routinely stopped by his post-office box. The mail brought little but bills and the weekly copy of *Time* magazine. He was seventy years old and ill and had retired from the tractor-trailer business in Jackson. One day he found a letter from a man who claimed to be his son.

"It was out of the clear blue," he recalled. "The name didn't ring a bell. I opened it. I went over it. I sat there, I read it again. I thought, 'What the hell's going on?' He had the dates, the times, the names correct.

"I always remembered Ann. I always assumed she was just living her life. There used to be a lady in the diplomatic corps—Kennedy or someone appointed her—her name was Ann Armstrong, too. When I'd read her name in the paper, naturally I'd think of Ann."

Arthur wrote back, coincidentally on his son's birthday, July 30, 1984, "I was greatly surprised and overwhelmed receiving a letter from someone I did not know," he wrote. "Your concern about your roots is understandable. I am very sorry to hear of your painful searching. Evidently you believe I am your father, therefore you believe your information is correct. Correct or incorrect there is no problem. It is very awkward for me to write to you. I hope you understand."

In a subsequent letter Spain told his father the whole story and included a prison psychiatric summary. They corresponded fitfully, venturing cautiously into each other's experience. Spain learned, for instance, that he was part of a big family—he had five half brothers and half sisters. But after thirty-five years he wanted more than Arthur could give—maybe more than a man who discovers a son late in life can give. His frustration and hope had coalesced finally in January 1986 in a letter Spain's whole life had been aiming toward.

*Dear Arthur,*

*. . . Being in prison may well have written off any chance I might have had of really knowing one of my parents. There is Ann, you say? Yes there is Ann. She has enough of a time of things just staying about the surface of her own life. . . . I will never come to know Ann, or for that matter any of my brothers or my sister in Mississippi. Those people I can recognize as my family, love to the bitter end, but they cannot escape the harsh, cruel, southern conditioning that will not allow them to embrace any real measure of the*

*child who was sent away thirty years ago. Hell, I can live well enough with that. Although it hurts like you could not imagine sometimes, I can live with that. . . .*

*You were the only real chance I had. You might not be able to understand what it means to me, what hideous creatures loom about me with the threat of you and I never meeting. What happened to you? What was your life like? What forces brought you to this point? I don't know.*

*. . . All and all, I really may have been the best high school athlete in Los Angeles. Those were my greatest years Arthur. My greatest moments in my youth and you don't even know about them. You don't know that I cracked a bone in my leg and was told that I could not play for six months—but played in three weeks because sports was my only valid world when I was growing up. . . .*

*. . . Anything that amounted to good in the Los Angeles years became a threat of some sort to me. I was a good kid in heart, though perhaps too angry at the many things I did not understand. About life. About myself. I was running away from something—that awesome, fleeting, intangible something. I had no idea what it was or where to escape from "it." All I knew was that I had to keep running, faster, farther, and longer. There was no safety for me, no matter how/where I ran. There was only pain and running. Now having gone through so many changes, having been through such an amazing sort of metamorphosis—namely, having grown up—I find myself squarely facing another terrible pain. I know who I am. I want to know who you are. If we don't meet . . . It's not fair. It's just not fair.*

*Please be well,*
*John*

Now it is the fall of 1987 and freedom tantalizes Johnny Spain. He has served twenty-one years in jail on a single conviction for a murder committed when he was seventeen—nearly twice the average sentence for that crime. He has been denied parole twice, but another parole hearing was scheduled for this December. The prosecution theory that Spain was part of a conspiracy to escape—never very credible among many lawyers and authors of books about the case—was further eroded when Stephen Bingham, the lawyer who had been a fugitive for thirteen years, returned to face trial and was acquitted of charges that he had joined the escape conspiracy by smuggling a gun into Jackson in San Quentin. Spain today is an accomplished electrician. His work has earned parole recommendations and letters of support from ninety-three guards—the very men he had scorned as pigs a decade ago.

Nevertheless, the Marin County district attorney plans to retry him on the original San Quentin charges if those convictions are not reinstated. Parole may well be denied again: there are many who agree with David Ross, of the L.A. County D.A.'s office, when he says, "There's no question he's not the black-hearted ogre that he was when he came here, but he's not Rebecca of Sunnybrook Farm, either."

On East Twenty-Third Street, El Santo Niño is closed. Bus benches on the corner of the Hill and Venice are covered with the cyrillic scrawl of L.A. gangs. Under the interstate, some partisan, now no doubt in business school, stopped long enough to write, LONG LIVE THE GREAT PROLETARIAN REVOLUTION.

After a decade of marriage, Pinkey Spain has consented to a divorce. "Johnny is a humanist, he believes in what man can do for man," she says. "I'm a Christian, I believe in God, life after death, heaven and hell." Ann saw her last spring. She and Arthur sometimes talk on the telephone. Arthur writes to Johnny now and then, but they have not met—airfares are expensive and Arthur is a man who stays on the periphery of his children's lives, not wanting to be a bother. When he was hospitalized with a heart condition some years ago, he left blank the lines of the admittance form that asked for next of kin.

Cathy Kornblith talks to Spain at least once a week by phone. She has traced the outermost branches of his family tree, and her conclusion is, "Lots of relatives, no family." The word *struggle* still pops up in her speech, with an odd and anachronistic ring. But the struggle boils down mostly to one man's freedom.

That man—the product of an interracial union when such affairs were felonies in Mississippi, punishable by ten years in jail—never sought to be a symbol. If Johnny Spain has put aside the grander aspirations of his militant youth, he now yearns as intensely for the consolations of ordinary life. He wants to meet his father before his father dies and play with his children before they grow up. He wants to put his hands on a dog, feel the bark of a tree, make a sentimental journey home.

"I don't want to complain," Spain told me. "I believe I have already participated in the biggest revolution in my life, and that is my life. But it's necessary to go beyond history."

Late in the day at Vacaville, I asked him to draw a map of the childhood house on Stokes Robertson Road in Jackson, but he remembered nothing of it, not even the name of the road, and instead drew a map of the house he did remember, on East Twenty-third Street. After he finished the sketch, he ripped a fresh sheet from his legal pad and began again, this time to get the scale right. He drew meticulously, from the mind's eye: front yard, backyard, kitchen, stairs, his room, the small garage where grandmother lived. Up welled the past. Once he had tied his grandmother's apron strings to her rocking chair as she sat dozing. There had been an orchard of trees in the yard—limes, oranges, avocados. He circled the spots where trees had stood, assigned them numbers, and compiled a legend.

"I don't know if they're still there," he said, gazing at the map.

I saw the yard later. Like so much else in his life, they belonged to memory.

—JANUARY 1988

# Phantom of the Opera

MARTIN AMIS

(Originally published as *Ronnie and the Pacemakers*)

The Republican Convention is history now, and history didn't look too good down in New Orleans, sapped and battered by eight years of Ronald Reagan. Before I develop that thought, though, I feel it's high time I said a few words about my family. I have a wife and two little boys. Over here to cover the Convention, I happened to miss them very much. Why, just before I left, my three-year-old gazed up at me with those big blue eyes of his and said I was the best daddy in the whole world. My wife and I love our boys. And they love us. Okay?

On closing night it looked like a day-care center up there on the podium, with the three junior Quayles and Bush's great troupe of grandchildren. They all romped and cuddled among the balloons and spangled confetti. (And what do balloons remind you of? How tall are the people you know who like balloons?) Candidates can't keep their hands off the little ones when they're in public, perhaps because it's the only time they ever see them. The Quayles' first task the next morning, I heard, was to hire someone to mind the kids for three months. This childish spectacle at the Superdome provided a new twist on a familiar image: here were politicians kissing their own babies.

Earlier that evening I was in the Media Lounge eating complimentary popcorn and watching the TV monitor. One half of the screen was occupied by a white-haired lady wearing four tiers of pearls and an expression of wry indulgence; the other half showed schoolchildren in slow motion, raising their hands to teacher.

A journalist came up behind me and said, "What's this?"

"It's an ad for Barbara Bush."

"Jesus Christ, what's going on around here?"

Where has he been? Reagan's is a style-setting administration, and there has been trickle-down. Nowadays, when Chris Evert gets a regular boyfriend, the first thing she does is make an ad about it. On *The Dating Game* the dude will report that his new friend is "open" and "communicative"—"and I admire those skills." Who is the role model of the nascent media-coaching industry? Forces are working on the American self. Thirty-five-year-olds have spent half their adult lives in the Reagan Era. This has gone on long enough.

"George Bush," Barbara confided to the camera, and to the cameramen and lighting men and sound men and media consultants who were crouched around her at the time, was "as strong, decent, and caring as America herself." She had loved "this extraordinarily special man," she went on, "from the moment I laid eyes on him." Early in the election year the Vice-President had decided that the time was right to tell the public about the death of his first daughter. Now here was Barbara with her side of it, revealing how George's strength ("He held me in his arms") had eventually sustained her. It all seemed to shore up the claim of the Texas delegation, which hailed George Bush as "the best father in America."

Of course, you feel a bit of a brute going on about all this stuff. But journalists *are* brutalized by modern Conventions—by these four-day ads for the Party. "This isn't a very interesting Convention so far. It is so well run that there aren't even any lost kids." That was John Steinbeck in 1956. Dressed in eye-hurting orange blazers, Uncle Sam suits, and baseball outfits, the pink elephants of the GOP talk about shopping and eating and how the Giants did against the Dodgers. At this corporate outing there was no danger of any politics coming your way, though there was always the possibility of scandal. In fact the media was in for a nice surprise: it would soon be propitiated by the blood of J. Danforth Quayle. But until that story broke—and Quayle broke with it—we took our cue from the piety on display and lapsed into a mood of ghoulish cynicism.

First you inspect the concourse leading to the burger-shaped Superdome and all the conventional Convention junk, with its air of commercial passion and improvisational verve. GO Pork Rinds—They're Republickin' Good. A blizzard of T-shirts and badges and bumper stickers. Don't Du-Ca-Ca on the USA. At one table someone is hawking Oliver North videos. Across the way are life-size cutouts of Reagan and Bush, and beyond them, an outsize mannequin of Reagan as Rambo (or "Ronbo," as the British tabloids have it): the seventy-seven-year-old sex object is stripped to the waist, a cartridge belt athwart his slabbed chest, and with a giant weapon in his fists. Ronbo is eight feet tall. The slogans and buzz phrases cruelly harp on the stature gap. Beware of Greeks Wearing Lifts. His Only Platform Is Down in His Shoes. Where oh where is the Democrat with Reagan's inches, his Grecian hair, his Mitchum chest!

Next, one was obliged to traipse around the fringe meetings in a wistful search for repulsive policies. Although I was sad to have missed Phyllis Schlafly's Eagle Forum reception, which featured Robert Bork and Jeane Kirkpatrick ("It was great," said one journalist, "Jeane was nuts"), I reposed considerable hope in Pat Robertson, the onetime TV pastor and tithe mogul. Might Pat talk about Armageddon and Rapture? Might he denounce credit cards for harboring the Mark of the Beast? Might he heal my jet lag?

At the hotel a phalanx of news-parched media was pressing at the doors of the Robertson reception. No entry until 6:00, said one of Pat's people, because "everybody in there has waited a year and a half" to hobnob with the great man. "*Please* don't turn this into a press conference." The media was as good as its word. There was no press conference. Instead, Robertson was instantly engulfed by a squirming centipede of mikes and camera tackle; he emerged fifteen minutes later, with an almost audible pop, and was dragged off through a side door by his bodyguard. Still newsless, the newspeople took a few disgusted sips of French cider and trooped off to the Superdome to cover Ronnie Night.

I lingered among the believers, with their fine hair, their thick skins, and their low blink-rates. Many of the women were still shivering from the post-Pat frisson. Their man hadn't won, but they had the feeling that the GOP was gathering him—and them—into its bosom. Clearly Pat hadn't told them what he must know to be the case: that he's finished. The next night, true, he would get his prime-time speech (largely ignored by the cameras) and would thrill the faithful, and the media, with his talk of "disease carriers" who place the healthy "at great risk." But Pat's had it: his valedictory press conference was an ill-attended freak show. He'll just have to go back to his old job, serving God with his miracle-service TV spot and stiffing the fuddled and elderly out of their rent checks and disability allowances.

Pat Robertson at a national convention, equipped with delegates, certainly remains a terrible sight. He is a charlatan of Chaucerian dimensions. To Bush, if not to Reagan, the evangelicals were probably never much more than a useful joke, to be kept happy with promises that can't possibly get past the Senate (like the guff about recriminalizing abortion). Anyway, the video vicarage is now in tatters. Yet another institution in Reagan's dream city comes crashing to the ground—and the National Security Council, and Wall Street, and the Attorney General's office, and the Pentagon. Is it over?

Ronnie Night. First the motorcade and its enthralling expression of personal power: half a six-lane city boulevard sealed off and lined with blinkers and excited cops. Four motorbikes in formation, sirens idling, then six more, then two police cars, then four limousines, then four staff cars (two containing security men, two containing Nancy's helpers and dressers). As soon as the backwash has settled, the cops unplug the bursting sidestreets, and the normal gridlock resumes. No wonder the President looks so young and cheerful: eight years without any traffic.

The time to study Reagan was before he mounted the stage—when he and Nancy took their preliminary seats in the lower gallery. During the imperial entrance, the Reagan face had been divided laterally, the eyes expressing mock alarm, the mouth unqualified gamesomeness. As he settled, a mound of cameras sticklebricked itself into being a few inches from his nose. Reagan jovially waved a hand at the teetering media, as if to say, "Will you look at all these guys?" Then his smile instantly vanished as he fell into an imitation of a serious man listening to a serious speech. Was it imagination, or did I detect, beneath his mask, the dull throb of astonishment that such modest abilities (plus a few gut instincts) had ushered in, not just a Governorship, not just a Presidency, but an American Era? Apart from that, he looks, he looks . . .

What *does* he look like? He looks like a gorgeous old opera-phantom shot full of novocaine. *Esquire*'s caricaturist Steve Brodner is a longtime student of the Reagan face: "Ten years ago the face told you a lot about the man. Now that's all gone." The furtive overlay above the eyes and the wattled dissolution of the jaw have been replaced by clarity and definition. It used to be said that by a certain age a man had the face that he deserved. Nowadays, he has the face he can afford—or the face his handlers decide to go with. One of Dickens's hypocrites has a facial paralysis that gives him a profile of noble immobility; this is the side he presents to his clients, while the hidden half snickers and gloats. With the modern American politician, we must imagine the face *beneath* the face, smarting and flickering with the impostures, the compromises, and the fathomless boredom of public life. Erected by surgeon and makeup man, the face is now the picture window to the soul.

Maureen was there, but Reagan hasn't got any children, or grandchildren, that he can plausibly wheel out and love up. So he goes another way: he loves up Nancy. Reagan has never made any secret of his thralldom to Nancy's talents. With his hints of turbulent nights behind the clipped hedges of Brookline, Dukakis has evidently taken yet another arrow from Reagan's quiver: husbandly romancing has voter appeal. Bush is obviously in a corner on this one with Barbara, who will make TV ads but draws the line at dyeing her hair. Besides, as Bush says with a kind of shrug, it's been forty-three years.

This Convention project of loving up Nancy had begun at a lunch in her honor, where Reagan asked, "What can you say about someone who gives your life meaning? You can say that you love that person, and treasure her." On Ronnie Night, Tom Selleck was Reagan's surrogate on the stage; he spoke of cancer surgery, the war against drugs, and that day when "an assassin nearly took away what she loved most in this life." After Nancy's little address, we got the ad for Ronnie. You know the one: a fifteen-minute collage of newsclips, Bud and Marlboro commercials, and exquisitely lit home movies. So. An actor, then an actress, then an ad; and then another actor—Reagan, with the Speech.

All morning the hall had rung with the words of ardent glozers and fiery mediocrities, chosen for their sex or their skin color or their extremes of youth and age. Punctuated by the tinny clunk of the gavel, the clichés of the peanut-faced orators labored toward you at the speed of sound, chased by the PA echo. . . . Reagan got up there, and after one blooper ("Facts are stupid things"—the crowd winced so fondly, so protectively!), a few jokes, several boasts, and a lot of statistics, shared with his countrymen the gift of the trust in a dream of a vision whose brilliant light in a shining moment showed a sweet day of extra love for a special person between the great oceans. "Here," he exhaustedly concluded, "it's a sunrise every day."

That last revelation can't have been news even in Middle America, which seems to have been in flames all summer. With the Drought, with 50 percent of all counties declared disaster areas, with the unbreathable city air (not to mention the thirty-foot scum line on the beaches of the Northeast), Americans knew all about "our sunlit new day." No need to tell them "to keep alive the fire." Reagan's speech was an apotheosis of a kind: the rhetoric of arcadian green, polluted by reality. Nobody liked it much, even on the floor. Yet the momentum of expectation was so far entrained that the performance somehow passed off as a triumph. This *had* to be the night of rich catharsis, when Reagan's image began its slow wipe, leaving Bush to hurl his first grapple hook across the stature gap.

At lunchtime on the second day the lead local news story was about Convention-related traffic jams. In uniform desperation the media was turning its gaze on the city itself, and duly noting the inevitable contrast between Republicans and New Orleans.

It's true. There is a big difference. Republicans are rich and sober. New Orleans is poor and drunk—and Democrat. Indeed, the city has an air of almost Caribbean laxity. Over Sunday breakfast on my first morning in the French Quarter ("the Quarter"), I watched a teenage girl lurch out of a bar with a beer bottle swinging from her hand. She walked as if she had just come down from Vermont, on horseback; past Big Daddy's Topless and Bottomless Tabletop Dancing she meandered; then she sat on the sidewalk outside a club unceremoniously called the Orgy. No one stared in forgiving New Orleans. But if I'd had a video camera with me, I could have made a good ad for abortion. In the Quarter, everybody knows about the alternative to *choice*. The alternative to legal abortion is illegal abortion. Just more free enterprise.

There is a little voodoo store a couple of blocks farther up Bourbon Street. In the front room there is a tub full of colored ribbons: "MOJO.S FOR—LOVE (red and black) stop CONFUSSION (yellow and BLACK) FOR a good health (diFFerent colors and stripy BLACK) COURTCASE (BLACK and BLACK)." In the back room there is a rectangular chest covered in masks and pinecones: "Pleas do not touch this COFFIN—DANGER—BE WARE of FReddies COFFIN!! PS shit HAPPENing." The store looked far from prosperous. The potency of voodoo, one fears, is definitely on the wane—except in the realm of economics and, perhaps, in that of prophecy. For George Bush was due in town that day. Soon we would hear the sinister creak of Freddie's coffin lid. And shit would be happening.

Like many of the media I began the day by morbidly attending a brunch thrown by the National Rifle Association, with fingers crossed for a few atrocities from the lips of Charlton Heston and Arnold Schwarzenegger. Resplendently present at the bar, Schwarzenegger no-showed on the podium (as he would later monotonously no-show at the Mississippian, Tennessean, and South Carolinian caucus meetings). In the matinee gloom of the curtainless ballroom, Heston was bland and depressingly centrist; we took what solace we could from the opening blasphemies of a local chaplain ("And now a word to our Sponsor. Heavenly Father . . .") and from Phil Gramm's tribute to capital punishment: "If they hurt other people we want them put in jail, and if they kill other people we want them put to death." Hearing this, a couple of elegant young ladies at my table joined in the fierce applause; the palms of their right hands sought their throats in flustered affirmation. Civilized girls. But this isn't civilized. Still, gas chambers and gunslinging aren't news at the end of the Reagan Era. Furloughs are news. The media bitterly decamped to Spanish Plaza to wait for Bush.

Vintage aircraft buzzed the shopping mall, two deejays jabbered into microphones, a fat tug befouled the Mississippi with dyed fountains of red and white and blue, gay protesters took their positions—and into this scene of contemporary pageantry the candidate stepped from the riverboat *Natchez*. . . . Some minutes later there was this frenzied little blond guy waving his arms around and hollering into the mike, and doing pretty well considering he looked about nine years old. Watching him give his cheek a thorough and astonishing wipe after a kiss from Barbara, you might have thought that here was another tearaway Bush grandson. But no: here were three bad decisions (manner, timing, substance) all rolled into one. Here was Dan Quayle.

The TV crews are the Germans of the media. Here they come (watch out), lugging their bazookas and ack-ack launchers, sweating, swearing, and not smiling. They are all elbow and kneecap and have the gracelessness of undisputed muscle. They stand in ranks on crates and platforms, like firing squads. As they focus, their upper lips drag to the left in dead Presley grins. "They got Channel 56 from Jacksonville, Texas, in here," said one crewman at the first Bush-Quayle press conference. "That's how Mickey Mouse it's getting." I peered through the wires and webbing, the jeans and chinos. When the ticket came onto the stage the cameras phutted like a great flock taking to the air. And there was Quayle, confident, plump-faced, handsome, and stupid, all set to go get 'em.

The process that began in those first few minutes would develop into the detailed recycling of a political being, much of it on prime time. The media chomped him up and pooped him out again. And the contraption that is now being buckled onto a horse and sent out on the campaign trail is no longer the "Dan Quayle" to whom Dan Quayle so often, so robotically, refers. He is a hurried creation of the Bush people: the prepped preppy, wired up for a narrow repertoire of frowns and whoops, wired up for limited damage. Facing his first question about Paula Parkinson, Quayle made a gesture of erasure with his hand, said "No" when he meant "Yes," and looked like the kind of man who would want to beat you up if you swore in front of his wife. You don't come on to the media like that. By the next morning there were rumors that Quayle would be dumped from the ticket. Out of the loop for decades, the media was calling, in effect, for a second ballot. The media wasn't just a crowd, busy dispensing free TV. The media was saying that it was a *player.*

Even before the story broke, one remarkable fact had surfaced: here we had yet another major American politician who was quite at sea in the English language, utterly confounded by the simplest declarative sentence. Minutes after the press conference, Bush was blooding his young warrior at the California caucus meeting. Before long, Bush found himself standing there with a look of respectful concentration on his face as Quayle hammered out: "The question today is whether we are going forward, or past to the back." Even this miserable commonplace was too much for him. Indeed, the only sentence Quayle seemed really comfortable with was "Let's go get 'em!" The following night he managed twenty minutes of monosyllabic jingoism on the podium, but a day later, in Huntington, Indiana, his syntax was crazily unspooling all over the courthouse steps. "The Reserve forces is nothing to say is unpatriotic. . . . By serving in Guard somehow is not patriotic, I really do not subscribe to that. . . . And a goal cannot be really a no-win situation."

Quayle was chosen, supposedly, to help ease Bush's passage to the center, a position he tried to occupy in his "soft" acceptance speech, with its Whitmanesque intonations and nudges of moral suasion. Four days later we got a glimpse of the contortions Bush must now attempt, when he addressed the VFW in Chicago and sounded like Spiro Agnew: "[Dan Quayle] did not burn his draft card and he *damned sure* didn't burn the American flag!" No other Veep candidate, no other politician, can ever have won such savage praise for not burning the American flag. Bush chose Quayle, I think, because he responded to and took pleasure in his youth, unaware of the slowly dawning reality that *all* baby boomers are unelectable, by definition (none of us is clean: we've all smoked joints, had sex, worn bell-bottoms, gone to the toilet, and so on). Perhaps Quayle is the fanatically right-wing son that Bush never had. More probably, the young man answered to the young man in Bush, to the frisky kiddishness that remains his central implausibility. By golly. Zip-a-dee-doo-dah. Deep doo-doo. Who does *that* sound like?

One night in New Orleans I fell in with some representatives of the pollster and media-consultant community, people who had worked with Bush, or with "Poppy," as they call him. ("We think Poppy is a regular guy. Mainly because he says *fuck* a lot.") Here, all values are expedient and professionalized, and politics—fascinatingly—is discussed in strictly apolitical terms. I conflate their voices:

"On Spanish Plaza, Quayle looked like he just did a gram of coke. But they only jerked him off the streets of the Quarter an hour before, and that's what power feels like: you're thinking what you were yesterday, what you might be tomorrow. Their first job then was to calm him down. To calm his ass *down*.

"I think everyone's surprised that he seems so vapid. I mean, we're talking Bob Forehead. There's got to be more there. The Bush people are taking shit now but they're smart guys—they must know that Quayle has moves we ain't seen. Hey. What do you get if you cross a chicken with a hawk?"

"I don't know."

"You get a quayle. If he's going to help the ticket he's got to bond with his generation. That's the whole idea, right? He's *got* to express more ambivalence about the war. Maybe you'd want to do that with paid media later on, where you can control everything. It could all help Bush. It could release a lot of emotion, as opposed to canned emotion, and the challenge then is to steer that energy in your direction.

"Right now America is button-punching. If Bush looks like everybody's first husband, then Dukakis is looking like a great first date. The point is, Bush has better guys. Someone like Bob Teeter really earns his money when you're three days from a race and the tracking says you're seven points down and wondering whether to go with an attack spot or just keep with the positive stuff. Like Bush-Dole in New Hampshire. Anyone can do the numbers. It's the analysis. It's like on the *Vincennes*. Hey. How do you tell the difference between an Airbus and an F-14?"

"I don't know."

"Exactly. You don't know either."

At this point we were joined by a young woman from a news network who had spent the day in fruitless search of a Vietnam veteran willing to denounce Dan Quayle. Later, I heard about one of the more recent techniques in market research. You put sixty or seventy people in front of a videotaped stump speech and hand out dials (marked 1–100) on which the audience plots its undulating level of approval. This information goes into a computer. And out comes a tracking graph that gives you an emotional commentary on the speech. Further equipment is available to measure physical responses.

I left with an image of the American electorate, fitted with heartbeat monitor, peter meter, and armpit humidor dial, and pegged out in the political-science lab of the future.

Not that it appears to matter, but in a sense George Bush is everything that Ronald Reagan only seems to be: war hero, sports star, self-reliant achiever, family man. If George is the best father in America, then Ronnie is the worst (he is also, for instance, a war wimp who lied about his record—to Yitzhak Shamir). Yet Reagan has made it all new: the frictionless illusion of a distinguished life is now far catchier than the effortful reality. The only serious omission in Bush's résumé is thirty years in acting school.

Here are three well-placed comments on the Republican nominee. "[Bush's negatives] are not venal negatives, they're warts negatives." "We have a perception problem on some compassion issues." "The guy's got no biceps, no tattoos—he's not up to it." It is evident from his career, and from his autobiography, that Bush has always been prepared to do anything, or anything legal, to get the next job. What the "anything" is in 1988, apart from the usual low blows of a tight race, is a lot of vulgar bull about family (which is ironic, since Barbara Bush must be one of the few remaining housewives in America). After Reagan, though, the messenger is the message, and this messenger tends to pratfall on the steps to the throne. Poor George, with his warts negatives, his compassion-issues perception problem, and his lack of biceps—and of anchors and songbirds and the bruised names of love . . .

Do we get the feeling that the language has taken a beating over the past eight years? It has been an era of euphemism, during which taxes have become revenue enhancements and the lie has turned into the blooper. Reagan bequeaths an economy so unrecognizably deformed that nobody can get a stethoscope close to its chest. He bequeaths the Debt: just as crucially, he bequeaths an atmosphere in which no politician dares discuss it.

Deep, autonomous, imperishable, Reagan's popularity remains the key to everything, including the election. What *is* this woozy affinity between the American people and a *Bonanza* fan who turns in at 10:00 P.M.? Either it is all very simple or it is all very complicated. To adapt the writer Clive James on the singer Barry Manilow: everybody you know despises Reagan, but everyone you don't know thinks he's great. When they see Reagan frowning at his cue cards—instead of wanting less, they want more.

For a decade Reagan has impersonated, with an unguessable degree of sincerity, the kind of American we hear a lot about at election time, if at no other: pious, wise, caring, industrious, independent, and above all *average*. The clear truth that this average American is a vain and shifty prodigal is not something that average Americans are raring to face up to. But then it goes still deeper.

In New Orleans the amplifiers sweltered with that special theme: American exceptionalism. Reagan understands that Americans are "special" (my candidate for the worst word in the current lexicon). They are special—because they really think they're special. Never content just to be, America is also obliged to *mean*; America signifies, hence its constant and riveting vulnerability to illusion. In elevating Reagan—the average American who was special enough to land the best job in the free world—Americans elevate themselves. So perhaps the Era can be viewed as a narcissistic episode: a time when every American was President. Or not every American. Just every American that we don't know.

—NOVEMBER 1988

# Grooving in Chi

TERRY SOUTHERN

Chicago. On the way to the hotel this afternoon, coming from the airport, I saw something right out of a Buñuel movie; in a desolate section that resembles the Jersey flats, four boys each about ten years old and armed with small sticks were flailing wildly at a huge crippled black man who reeled and staggered drunkenly among piles of debris in a deserted lot. The taxi passed within fifty feet of the scene, slowing down as the driver looked directly at it, with no other apparent reaction.

"Wait a minute," I said as we continued past, "they're beating the hell out of that guy back there. We'd better help him."

The driver shrugged and brought the cab to a gradual stop. "The coon's loaded," he muttered, craning his head out the window to look behind us.

"Just back up a little," I suggested, "they'll probably take off."

"Uh-huh," he started slowly backing up, "what if they don't?"

"They're only kids for chrissake," saying this with an almost total lack of conviction as we drew nearer—but as it happened my analysis was correct; after one last flurry, and amidst mucho high-pitched prepuberty screeching of obscenities, the children abandoned their prey and scurried pell-mell across the lot.

"Are you okay?" I asked the Negro, much closer to the curb now, still staggering, but seemingly unscathed. Instead of a direct, or indeed a verbal reply, his response was to seize a large empty and battered ashcan, to raise it over his head, ready to slam it into the side of the taxi.

"Wait," I started to explain, "me friend . . ." but the driver had by now definitely lost interest in the case, and he lurched the car up and away.

"Boy, was that coon ever loaded," he said matter-of-factly about five minutes later.

A curious tableau—did it augur well or mal, conventionwise?

Six P.M. Rendezvous of our hard-hitting little press team—Jean Jack Genet, Willy Bill Burroughs, and yours truly as anchor man, trying to lend a modicum of stability to the group. Also on hand, Esky editor young John Berendt—his job: straighten these weirdos, and K.F.S. ("Keep Flying Speed!"). We met in the queer little Downstairs Lounge, one of several bars in our hotel, the Chicago-Sheraton—and John Berendt was quick to charge us with our respective assignments: "You, Jean Jack Genet, on the alert for all manner of criminality and perversion in high places! You, Big Bill Burroughs, let your keen and experienced eye discern any sign of sense derangement through the use of drugs by these delegates, the nominees, and officials of every station! Now then, you, T. Southern, on double alert for all manner of *absurdity* at this convention!"*

Thus charged, we drank steadily for the next two hours before going to visit grand guy Dave Dellinger, head of National Mobilization to End the War in Vietnam and one of the chief coordinators for the planned demonstrations. Before our meeting, I thought this so-called Dellinger must necessarily be some kind of old-fool-person—a kind of leftover leftist from another era who didn't know where it was at right now, just a compulsive organizer . . . maybe even a monstro-commie-spade-fag. But no, a groove and gas he proved to be.

"Our demonstrations shall be entirely peaceful," he explained (with a certain lack of prophecy) and then went on to describe the coalition and its program. The other two principal groups were the S.D.S. (of Morningside Heights fame) and the fun and ever-loving Yippies. A wise and gentle man, it was this same Dave Dell, editor of

*A typical Southern *jeu d'esprit*, needless to say without basis in fact.—J.B.

*Liberation*, who led the Pentagon March last fall, and so we sat talking in a bare and harshly lit room, the windows of which had been blown out the previous day in some ironic industrial explosion, the glass replaced with a flimsy plastic cloth which flapped absurdly now in the Chicago (Windy City) night breeze, lending a surreal quality to the scene. "We are not seeking a confrontation," said Dave—a term incidentally which proved the most meaningful, both in theory and in fact, of any concept put forward during the convention—"we simply wish to protest the foregone conclusion that it is a closed convention, that there is no possible alternate to Humphrey, as a candidate, and more importantly, of course, to express our continued opposition to the war in Vietnam."

"What's happening with Lincoln Park?"

Early in the afternoon an announcement had been issued by the Office of the Mayor—Richard Daley—to the effect that everyone would have to be out of the park by eleven that night. This edict was fairly inopportune, because about two thousand young yip-yip Yippies had just arrived from various U.S.A.; and with absolutely no other place to go, all hotels full for proverbial months on end, they had ensconced at the Link.

"We're hoping the Mayor will reconsider his decision," said Dellinger, ever boss-reasonable, "that perhaps he will understand the best way to deal with a situation like this might be to accommodate it . . . not to defy it."

This truth was obvious and it immediately brought to mind my own John Jack Lindsay, and how *he* would have handled it, to good advantage, god bless him, strolling down there in shirt sleeves, with some hot dogs to roast, a nice little Panasonic transistorized cassette unit blasting a fine sound, and maybe even a taste of, hrrumph, heehee, *Chicago* Light Green! It was all so apparent how Dumbbell Dick could have cooled it—and not merely have cooled it, but turned it to gross P.R. advan. I began to think of myself as some sort of lean and hungry Pierre Sal, as I grooved there with Dave Dellinger—just grooving on Big Dave and his son, Ray, both too beautiful to be believed—son boss-physical-spiritual, wearing a blue beret, circling catlike bodyguard-style around his father . . . knowing Dad Dave was something else, and that certain lewdies and sick weirdos might venture harm against him.

Suddenly Mister John Jack Genet, knowing no English at all, demanded of our ace trans (Richard Dick Seaver—of Evergreen-Grove fame) if Hugh Hefner was a fag.

Well, really. I mean I'm no prude myself, but when some weird frog starts blasting the Hef, that's when I begin to get a bit uptight. Unfortunately I had nothing at the moment to get up on, much less tight, so I simply lay back, and sort of dropped out, so to speak. Dellinger, of course, knew nothing about Hef sex, nor could (I warrant) care less. In any case the subject was soon dropped in favor of more serious matters—namely where we could find Allen Ginsberg. Allen, it developed, was staying at the Lincoln Hotel, just opposite the park itself; so with Dick Seaver at the wheel, we zoomed across town—toward the very heart of the action, for it was now ten minutes till curfewville, eleven P.M. And quite apparent it was, too, when we reached the scene—the baby-blue police already massed in rows of three . . . nightsticks and Mace at the ready, also gas masks, smoke grenades, and riot guns, a weird sight I can tell you. They lined the sidewalk bordering the park, which was completely dark, except for two or three bonfires glowing in the distance. In the midst of the police formation was a huge armored van, on top of which were several banks of large searchlights; in front of the still dark lights stood three men—the ones on either side holding riot guns, the kind used to fire tear-gas shells, while the man between them made announcements over a gigantic bullhorn:

"This is a final warning. Clear the park. Disperse. You have five minutes to disperse. You have five minutes to get out of this park!"

About then we spotted big Ed Sanders, of Fug and E.V.O. fame, threading his way along the periphery of monstro-fuzz before knifing into the darkness.

"Where's that loony fruit Al Ginsberg?!?" I shouted, rushing to overtake him. Fortunately, just before lowering the boom on me, Ed recognized the remark for the clever and good-natured jibe it was.

"He's doing his thing," he said, pointing, "over by that fire."

We all started walking in that direction. As our eyes became accustomed to the dark, and in the eerie light of the approaching fires, we could now make out figures and faces where before it had been an empty blackness. It is difficult to estimate the number of persons there, but they were everywhere—probably more than two thousand, milling around, seemingly about half of them moving toward the street to get out of the park, the other half just wandering uncertainly in the half-light.

We found Allen, seated in the center of a group of fifty or so, doing his thing, which in this case was the "Om"—leading the others in chanting the word "Om" with varying intonation, pitch, and volume. Sanders explained that at eleven o'clock a rumor that the police were moving in had caused panic and started a general and chaotic flight. Ginsberg however had restored calm by gathering these people around him and doing his Om thing. Now they appeared to be serenity itself, while behind us the bullhorn droned on:

> "FINAL WARNING. THE OFFICERS ARE MOVING IN IN FIVE MINUTES. ANYONE IN THE PARK WILL BE ARRESTED."

We sat down with the others, and joined the Oming, which especially delighted Genet; we stayed there for maybe half an hour, while the circle grew steadily larger, and the "final warnings" were repeated. It was now nearing midnight. Burroughs looked at his watch, and with that unerring awareness of which he is capable, muttered, "They're coming." At that instant, the banks of searchlights blazed up on the armored van which was already moving toward us. Fanned out on each side of the van were about a thousand police.

"Well, Bill, I think we'd better pursue another tactic," I suggested, getting to my feet. What the hell, we were supposed to be here as *observers*, not as participants in any of Allen's crackpot schemes. That the entire reportage team should be busted the first time out was unthinkable. Genet was the most difficult to persuade, but finally, on Ginsberg's insistence, we all went up to his hotel room. By this time the police had made their first contact with the crowd—persons who were actually trying to leave the park, but had been driven back in the opposite direction, so that now people were fleeing all around us. Advancing in the distance, silhouetted against the wall of light, moved this incredible phalanx of strangely helmeted men, swinging their nightsticks as they came. Once it was decided that we should leave, we moved with unfaltering gait—odd how infectious panic can be. Near the street, I glanced back in time to see them reach the place where we had been, and where a dozen or more were still sitting. They didn't arrest them—at least not right away; they beat the hell out of them—with nightsticks, and in one case at least, the butt of a shotgun. They clubbed them until they got up and ran, or until they started crawling away (the ones who were able) and then they continued to hit them as long as they could. The ones who actually did get arrested seemed to have gotten caught up among the police, like a kind of human medicine ball, being shoved and knocked back and forth from one cop to the next, with what was obviously *mounting* fury. And this was a phenomenon somewhat unexpected, which we were to observe consistently throughout the days of violence—that rage seemed to engender rage; the bloodier and the more brutal the cops were, the more their fury increased.

Witnessed an amusing, and perhaps historic, confrontation this P.M. when in the lobby of the Hotel Drake, we chanced across a dramatic encounter between Louis ("I have nothing to hide") Abolafia, the nudist-ticket candidate, and testy Babe Bushnell who's running on the S.C.U.M. (Society for Cutting Up Men) ticket, whose founder, it might be recalled, tried to assassinate Andy Warhol. It was a curious meeting, a sort of "battle of the sexes," you might say. While the Babe shouted her diatribe about the "cutting up" of men, and where exactly the process should begin, Abolafia attempted to detract from her remarks by executing what appeared to be a nude dervish or tarantella. Both candidates had to be dragged from the lobby.

Right after lunch we very dutifully piled into the car and headed for the Convention Hall. It is exactly like approaching a military installation—barbed-wire, checkpoints, the whole bit; Genet was absolutely appalled, I was afraid he was going to be physically sick; Burroughs, of course, was ecstatic; it was all so grotesque that at one point he actually did a little dance of glee. He has a tape recorder, and he applies his cut-up and fragmentation theory to its use—recording speeches by delegates and committee-men, then putting blank spaces in them, and filling the blanks with pieces of other speeches, and finally playing back this composite of clichés and inanities in such a way as to sound like live radio coverage—a possibility which was enhanced by the fact that this particular recorder looks exactly like a portable radio. It was Burroughs' belief that if these tapes were played constantly in the Convention Hall, the subliminal effect—of the repetitions, the non sequiturs, and the general idiocies—would so confound any chance listener as to possibly snap his mind, and thus become a profoundly disruptive factor in the overall "Convention profile."

We had one hell of a time actually getting admitted to the hall, despite all the proper credentials. Burroughs and I, of course, are veritable paragons of fashion and decorum—but Ginsberg and Genet, it must be admitted, are pretty weird-looking guys. In any case the cluster of door cops took one look at our group—which now also included Michael Cooper, an English photographer with shoulder-length hair, a purple suit, and sandals—and then simply turned away, as though we had never arrived. The lieutenant in charge looked at us, though, and just sort of shook his head, a tight little "Who-are-you-kidding?" smile on his lips.

"Our accreditation is all in order, officer," snapped Esky's John Berendt, indicating the door passes around our necks.

"It is, huh?" said the lieutenant, not even bothering to look.

"How about *his* creditation?" he said, pointing to Ginsberg "is it in order too?" And he gave a derisive snort.

"It certainly is," said Berendt, "show him your pass, Allen."

The lieutenant ignored Allen's attempt to show his pass, and fixed on Cooper. "And *he's* got creditation? Hell, he ain't even got any *shoes!*"

This drew some appreciative snickers from the cops in the doorway. Just then another lieutenant arrived and wanted to know what the trouble was, whereupon the first lieutenant simply indicated us with a nod, as though it was that obvious.

"They got passes?" asked the other, and reached out to examine the nearest one.

"You wantta handle this?" said the first lieutenant in a highly annoyed tone, "you handle it. I don't want no part of it." And he turned away, arms crossed, a sullen little-boy expression on his fifty-year-old face.

The other one watched him for a minute, then looked at us again, with perhaps only one iota less suspicion than his colleague.

"Okay, let's go," he said, "I'll take you up to Security."

The Security chiefs were typically F.B.I., C.I.A.—cop-types but a shade less stupid; at least they made a slight effort to disguise their arrogance. In any case, after a thorough checking they let us go on our way, and into the hall. Not that it was necessarily worth it—because, aside from Burrough's tapes, and an occasional hoodlum act on the floor, the events were without interest. It was so flagrantly obvious that the fix was in, and that there was no possibility of altering the outcome. It was in the air; you could see it, you could feel it, you could almost smell it. Worse, like the cheapest sort of wrestling match, where even the *staging* of the deception is inept. The spectacle of grown men behaving like children at a birthday party, cavorting in colored hats and streamers, jumping up and down, standing on chairs, screaming and waving, did not lessen the nausea.

Riding back to the hotel everyone felt depressed, as if the absurdity of it might not be enough after all. We listened to the tapes.

"I wonder what can be in the mind of a politician," someone mused. Seaver translated for Genet, but he was not intrigued. "I wonder," he said, staring at the dashboard of the Ford car we were in, "what can be in the mind of someone who names an automobile 'Galaxie'?"

Near the hotel we passed a procession of about five hundred Yippies, a red flag flying at the fore, and all chanting "Pigs must go! Pigs must go!" We learned that they were parading to the police station to protest the arrest of two of their leaders, Tom Hayden and Wolf Lowenthal. Ginsberg was apprehensive about the growing tension. One of the reasons he had come to Chicago, he explained, was to try and dissuade certain of the more militant leaders from pursuing a program of violence. An hour or so later we went to Grant Park, opposite the Hilton Hotel, where a meeting concerning the Lincoln Park situation was in progress. The parading Yippies had arrived, and one of them had climbed atop a large marble statue commemorating a Civil War Hero. A large number of police, guarding the Hilton, watched the boy with smoldering antagonism—and finally a contingent of them abruptly crossed the street and pulled him down, so forcibly that it broke his arm. A tremendous wave of resentment swept through the crowd and things might have gotten out of hand at that moment, but everyone started leaving for Lincoln Park. They had decided that tonight they would hold it.

We got there around eleven and immediately sensed that there was a different atmosphere from the night before, an air of determination, and about twice as many people—including twenty or thirty priests and ministers. A few helmets were in evidence, and a number of medics, dressed in white with Red Cross armbands, were on hand—but the park was not yet the armed camp it would become. At midnight the police begin to appear; they arrived on the opposite side of the expressway which forms the north boundary of the park—it was a solid line, shoulder to shoulder, five blocks long. Their gas masks were quite conspicuous. About twelve-thirty, one officer crossed the expressway and started issuing "final warnings" on the bullhorn. A few minutes later, a patrol car occupied by four cops with shotguns slowly moved off the expressway and down the sidewalk, through the crowd. Somebody in the crowd threw a brick through the windshield, probably a cop. Incidentally, one of the most insidious aspects of the entire police operation was the use of "confrontation provocateurs." These were cops dressed like hippies whose job it was to incite the crowd to acts of violence which would justify police intervention or, failing that, to commit such acts themselves. It is curiously significant that their artfully dressed undercover men were so flagrantly conspicuous as to be impossible to miss—not due to their appearance, which was indiscernible from the rest of the crowd, even the fact that they were encouraging violence, but due completely to the loud, lewd, tasteless stupidity that characterized their every remark and gesture.

In any case, when the brick hit the windshield, it seemed to me that was our cue to get the hell out of there, so we began a leisurely withdrawal. Behind us now the crowd had surrounded the car, and was rocking it, trying to turn it over. That's when the police charged. They came very fast, clubbing everyone they could catch, and firing tear gas shells ahead of the fleeing crowd—so that it was a question of going through the gas or waiting to get clubbed. Most people chose the gas, and emerged into the street on the south side of the park, groping blindly, face streaming with tears. Our fun party was well ahead of the clubs, but not the gas; no one seemed to escape the gas—the wind was right, and they were using a lot of it. We reached the street adjacent to Allen's hotel, and assumed we were safe—they had wanted us out of the park, and now we were out. But we continued to walk away from it because of the fumes. About three-quarters of the way down the block, we heard yelling ahead and the approach of frantically running footsteps, then the appearance of several dozen people tearing along the sidewalk toward us. "They're coming!" screamed a girl in absolute terror as she passed; running behind her was a boy of sixteen or so, blood covering one side of his face. Now, at the rear of the crowd, we could see the cops, chasing and flailing. We started running with the rest, down the middle of the street, but almost immediately encountered people running in the opposite direction.

"Don't go that way, man," one of them said, "it's a very bad scene back there." We were trapped, and for a moment it was sheer panic, then someone (Berendt or Seaver no doubt) had the inspired thought to try one of the apartment-house doors we were passing, and so the next moment we were all huddled in this small hallway, just as one wave of police swept past, wiping out everyone in its path. Now we had to crouch so as not to be seen through the glass front of the door, because from the other direction they were rushing into the doorways and halls and routing them out. We could hear it happening next door in no uncertain terms. And then it was our turn and, sure enough, in charged four of the finest, with expressions of rage such as I have never seen. In fact, Genet later jestingly insisted that they had not been cops at all but actors who were overplaying their roles.

"You Communist bastards!" one of them snarled, "get the hell outta here! Now move!" And he raised his club at the nearest person, who as it happened was Genet—but the latter, saint that he is, simply looked at the man and shrugged, half lifting his arms in a Gallic gesture of helplessness. And the blow didn't come. Another tribute to Genet's strange power over people. Instead, they pushed and prodded us out onto the street where they talked about taking us to the station; but they were soon distracted by activity farther down the block, and they rushed away. Because it wasn't really us they wanted to get—it was the children.

I talked with Ed Sanders at the park this afternoon. The Yippies have brought a pig, which they are going to try to place in nomination if they can ever get near the hall. The pig is pink, and weighs about a hundred pounds. They keep it in a burlap bag.

Tonight we went to the L.B.J. Un-Birthday Party at the Chicago Coliseum. It was a swinging affair, with a groovy audience who responded enthusiastically when our brutality statements—prepared earlier in the day—were read to them.

Tonight's scene at the park was certainly the strangest yet. About one hundred priests were there, having earlier announced that they would conduct an all-night religious service. A large cross (about ten feet high) had been erected, and several large fires burned nearby. The pattern of events was identical to what had transpired on the previous evenings. Only the presence of the cross, after the smoke and tear gas came rolling in, slowly engulfing it, lent the spectacle an unreal and cinematic quality. As we fled from the park, I witnessed a curious incident, near the lake. A young boy on a bicycle, of apparently no connection whatever with the demonstration, was peddling along the outer path, past six or eight police who were stationed there. They grabbed the bicycle and pushed it and the boy into a lagoon, laughing uproariously the while. By chance a photographer was standing not fifty feet away, and he got a picture of it—published the following day (Wednesday, the 28th) in The Chicago *Daily News.*

• • •

Wednesday, August 28th. This was our biggest, most outlandish day. The plan was to march to Convention Hall, so the crowd began early to form in Grant Park. By four o'clock there must have been seven or eight thousand people. Mayor Daley had refused to issue a parade permit, and the order was that anyone who attempted to march would be arrested forthwith. By now, of course, the National Guard was there in great strength, massed three deep along the Michigan Boulevard side of the park, while on the opposite side, in front of the Hilton, were the police—or "the Pigs" as they were now known by all. Again the order to clear out of the park was given. Under the circumstances (of not being allowed to parade) it was decided that it might be best to regroup elsewhere, so what was intended as a general exodus was begun. And this is where the logic of the Chicago authorities can be proved either insane or sadistic, perhaps both, because the park is joined to Michigan Boulevard by several bridges, and these are the only means of egress; but when the first of the crowd reached the nearest bridge, we found it blocked by soldiers with fixed bayonets. As the crowd continued to accumulate near the bridge, the order to disperse was given again.

"Hey why don't you stick those bayonets up your ass?" someone suggested—a quip which was answered with several quick rounds of tear gas, and the crowd began to scatter wildly across the park. The same thing was experienced at the next two exits—here was a case of *containment* and *dispersal* all in one. "Somebody's wig has snapped," observed Burroughs drily. But it was patently a harassment tactic of the shabbiest order, and one which was to backfire badly. The only way out of the park now was to walk around the lake side by the expressway, a very long route indeed—so that by the time the bulk of the crowd reached Michigan Boulevard, and the Hilton Hotel, they were hopping mad. So were the cops, and you could see the adrenaline rising.

We had all gotten separated during the confusion at the park, so now I found myself alone outside the locked doors of the Hilton, caught up in a seething crowd, and a rapidly growing malaise. I pounded on the glass.

"I'm a guest," I insisted.

"Let's see your key."

"It's at the desk."

"Sorry."

Then by the sheerest chance I spotted a guy I knew, just as he was dangling his key in front of the glass. He was able to get me in, and we immediately went to the hotel bar on Michigan, the windows of which afforded a grandstand view of the melee which followed. By now it had all become like some strange, and sickening, spectator sport.

Bill Styron and John Marquand Jr. were also in the bar and there was a certain undeniable decadence in the way we sat there, drinks in hand, watching the kids in the street getting wiped out. Tear-gas fumes began to permeate even the locked doors, and at the height of the slaughter five or six kids were pushed through a plate-glass window on one side of the bar. The cops rushed in after them.

"Get the hell outta here!" a cop was yelling, which they were trying to do as fast as possible. But something was wrong with one of them, a thin blond boy about seventeen.

"I can't walk," he said.

"You'll walk outta here, you little son of a bitch!" said the cop and clubbed him across the side of the head with his stick. Two of the others seized him by the shirt and started dragging him across the floor of the bar and through the lobby.

Next to me a middle-aged man, wearing a straw hat with a Hubert Humphrey band, watched the incident with distaste.

"Those damn kids," he muttered, "I haven't seen a clean one yet." Then he looked back out into the street where, at that moment, a flying squad of blue helmets and gas masks, clubs swinging, charged straight into a crowd obviously of bystanders.

"Hell," he grunted, "I'd just as soon live in one of those damn police states as put up with that kind of thing."

—NOVEMBER 1968

# Superman Comes to the Supermarket

NORMAN MAILER

For once let us try to think about a political convention without losing ourselves in housing projects of fact and issue. Politics has its virtues, all too many of them—it would not rank with baseball as a topic of conversation if it did not satisfy a great many things—but one can suspect that its secret appeal is close to nicotine. Smoking cigarettes insulates one from one's life, one does not feel as much, often happily so, and politics quarantines one from history; most of the people who nourish themselves in the political life are in the game not to make history but to be diverted from the history which is being made.

If that Democratic Convention which has now receded behind the brow of the Summer of 1960 is only half-remembered in the excitements of moving toward the election, it may be exactly the time to consider it again, because the mountain of facts which concealed its features last July has been blown away in the winds of High Television, and the man-in-the-street (that peculiar political term which refers to the quixotic voter who will pull the lever for some reason so salient as: "I had a brown-nose lieutenant once with Nixon's looks," or "that Kennedy must have false teeth"), the not so easily estimated man-in-the-street has forgotten most of what happened and could no more tell you who Kennedy was fighting against than you or I could place a bet on who was leading the American League in batting during the month of June.

So to try to talk about what happened is easier now than in the days of the convention, one does not have to put everything in—an act of writing which calls for a bulldozer rather than a pen—one can try to make one's little point and dress it with a ribbon or two of metaphor. All to the good. Because mysteries are irritated by facts, and the 1960 Democratic Convention began as one mystery and ended as another.

Since mystery is an emotion which is repugnant to a political animal (why else lead a life of bad banquet dinners, cigar smoke, camp chairs, foul breath, and excruciatingly dull jargon if not to avoid the echoes of what is not known), the psychic separation between what was happening on the floor, in the caucus rooms, in the headquarters, and what was happening in parallel to the history of the nation was mystery enough to drown the proceedings in gloom. It was on the one hand a dull convention, one of the less interesting by general agreement, relieved by local bits of color, given two half hours of excitement by two demonstrations for Stevenson, buoyed up by the class of the Kennedy machine, turned by the surprise of Johnson's nomination as vice-president, but, all the same, dull, depressed in its over-all tone, the big fiestas subdued, the gossip flat, no real air of excitement, just moments—or as they say in bullfighting—details. Yet it was also, one could argue—and one may argue this yet—it was also one of the most important conventions in America's history, it could prove conceivably to be the most important. The man it nominated was unlike any politician who had ever run for President in the history of the land, and if elected he would come to power in a year when America was in danger of drifting into a profound decline.

Depression obviously has its several roots: it is the doubtful protection which comes from not recognizing failure, it is the psychic burden of exhaustion, and it is also, and very often, that discipline of the will or the ego which enables one to continue working when one's unadmitted emotion is panic. And panic it was I think which sat as the largest single sentiment in the breast of the collective delegates as they came to convene in Los Angeles. Delegates are not the noblest sons and daughters of the Republic; a man of taste, arrived from Mars, would take one look at a convention floor and leave forever, convinced he had seen one of the drearier squats of Hell. If one still smells the faint living echo of a carnival wine, the pepper of a bullfight, the rag, drag, and panoply of a jousting tourney, it is all swallowed and regurgitated by the senses into the fouler cud of a death gas one must rid oneself of—a cigar-smoking, stale-aired, slack-jawed, butt-littered, foul, bleak, hard-working, bureaucratic death gas of language and faces ("Yes, those *faces*," says the man from Mars: lawyers, judges, ward heelers, *mafiosos*, Southern goons and grandees, grand old ladies, trade unionists and finks), of pompous words and long pauses which lay like a leaden pain over fever, the fever that one is in, over, or is it that one is just behind history? A legitimate panic for a delegate. America is a nation of experts without roots; we are always creating tacticians who are blind to strategy and strategists who cannot take a step, and when the culture has finished its work the institutions handcuff the infirmity. A delegate is a man who picks a candidate for the largest office in the land, a President who must live with problems whose borders are in ethics, metaphysics, and now ontology; the delegate is prepared for this office of selection by emptying wastebaskets, toting garbage, and saying yes at the right time for twenty years in the small political machine of some small or large town; his reward, one of them anyway, is that he arrives at an invitation to the convention. An expert on local catch-as-catch-can, a small-time, often mediocre practitioner of small-town political judo, he comes to the big city with nine-tenths of his mind made up, he will follow the orders of the boss who brought him. Yet of course it is not altogether so mean as that: his opinion is listened to—the boss will consider what he has to say as one interesting factor among five hundred, and what is most important to the delegate, he has the illusion of partial freedom. He can, unless he is severely honest with himself—and if he is, why sweat out the low levels of a political machine?—he can have the illusion that he has helped to choose the candidate, he can even worry most sincerely about his choice, flirt with defection from the boss, work out his own small political gains by the road of loyalty or the way of hard bargain. But even if he is there for more than the ride, his vote a certainty in the mind of the political boss, able to be thrown here or switched there as the boss decides, still in some peculiar sense he is reality to the boss, the delegate is the great American public, the bar he owns or the law practice, the piece of the union he represents, or the real-estate office, is a part of the political landscape which the boss uses as his own image of how the votes will go, and if the people will like the candidate. And if the boss is depressed by what he sees, if the candidate does not feel right to him, if he has a dull intimation that the candidate is not his sort (as, let us say, Harry Truman was his sort, or Symington might be his sort, or Lyndon Johnson), then vote for him the boss will if he must; he cannot be caught on the wrong side, but he does not feel the pleasure of a personal choice. Which is the center of the panic. Because if the boss is depressed, the delegate is doubly depressed, and the emotional fact is that Kennedy is not in focus, not in the old political focus, he is not comfortable; in fact it is a mystery to the boss how Kennedy got to where he is, not a mystery in its structures; Kennedy is rolling in money, Kennedy got the votes in primaries, and, most of all, Kennedy has a jewel of a political machine. It is as good as a crack Notre Dame team, all discipline and savvy and go-go-go, sound, drilled, never dull, quick as a knife, full of the salt of hipper-dipper, a beautiful machine; the boss could adore it if only a sensible candidate were driving it, a Truman, even a Stevenson, please God a Northern Lyndon Johnson, but it is run by a man who looks young enough to be coach of the Freshman team, and that is not comfortable at all. The boss knows political machines, he knows issues, farm parity, Forand health bill, Landrum-Griffin, but this is not all so adequate after all to revolutionaries in Cuba who look like beatniks, competitions in missiles, Negroes looting whites in the Congo, intricacies of nuclear fallout, and NAACP men one does well to call Sir. It is all out of hand, everything important is off the center, foreign affairs is now the lick of the heat, and senators are candidates instead of governors, a disaster to the old family style of political measure where a political boss knows his governor and knows who his governor knows. So the boss is depressed, profoundly depressed. He comes to this convention resigned to nominating a man he does not understand, or let us say that, so far as he understands the candidate who is to be nominated, he is not happy about the secrets of his appeal, not so far as he divines these secrets; they seem to have too little to do with politics and all too much to do with the private madnesses of the nation which had thousands—or was it hundreds of thousands—of people demonstrating in the long night before Chessman was killed, and a movie star, the greatest, Marlon the Brando out in the night with them. Yes, this candidate for all his record; his good, sound, conventional liberal record has a patina of that other life, the second American life, the long electric night with the fires of neon leading down the highway to the murmur of jazz.

> *"I was seeing Pershing Square, Los Angeles, now for the first time . . . the nervous fugitives from Times Square, Market Street SF, the French Quarter—masculine hustlers looking for lonely fruits to score from, anything from the legendary $20 to a pad at night and breakfast in the morning and whatever you can clinch or clip; and the heat in their holy cop uniforms, holy because of the Almighty Stick and the Almightier Vagrancy Law; the scattered junkies, the small-time pushers, the queens, the sad panhandlers, the lonely, exiled nymphs haunting the entrance to the men's head, the fruits with the hungry eyes and jingling coins; the tough teen-age chicks—'dittybops'—making it with the lost hustlers . . . all amid the incongruous piped music and the flowers—twin fountains gushing rainbow colored: the world of Lonely America squeezed into Pershing Square, of the Cities of Terrible Night, downtown now trapped in the City of lost Angels . . . and the trees hang over it all the like some type of apathetic fate."*
>
> —John Rechy: *Big Table 3*

Seeing Los Angeles after ten years away, one realizes all over again that America is an unhappy contract between the East (that Faustian thrust of a most determined human will which reaches up and out above the eye into the skyscrapers of New York) and those flat lands of compromise and mediocre self-expression, those endless half-pretty repetitive small towns of the Middle and the West whose spirit is forever horizontal and whose marrow comes to rendezvous in the pastel monotonies of Los Angeles architecture.

So far as America has a history, one can see it in the severe heights of New York City, in the glare from the Pittsburgh mills, by the color in the brick of Louisburg Square, along the knotted greedy facades of the small mansions on Chicago's North Side, in Natchez' antebellum homes, the wrought-iron balconies off Bourbon Street, a captain's house in Nantucket, by the curve of Commercial Street in Provincetown. One can make a list; it is probably finite. What culture we have made and what history has collected to it can be found in those few hard examples of an architecture which came to its artistic term, was born, lived and so collected some history about it. Not all the roots of American life are uprooted, but almost all, and the spirit of the supermarket, that homogeneous extension of stainless surfaces and psychoanalyzed people, packaged commodities and ranch homes, interchangeable, geographically unrecognizable, that essence of the new postwar SuperAmerica is found nowhere so perfectly as in Los Angeles' ubiquitous acres. One gets the impression that people come to Los Angeles in order to divorce themselves from the past, here to live or try to live in the rootless pleasure world of an adult child. One knows that if the cities of the world were destroyed by a new war, the architecture of the rebuilding would create a landscape which looked, subject to specifications of climate, exactly and entirely like the San Fernando Valley.

It is not that Los Angeles is altogether hideous, it is even by degrees pleasant, but for an Easterner there is never any salt in the wind; it is like Mexican cooking without chile, or Chinese egg rolls missing their mustard; as one travels through the endless repetitions of that city which is the capital of suburbia with its milky pinks, its washed-out oranges, its tainted lime-yellows of pastel on one pretty little architectural monstrosity after another, the colors not intense enough, the styles never pure, and never sufficiently impure to collide on the eye, one conceives the people who live here—they have come out to express themselves, Los Angeles is the home of self-expression, but the artists are middle-class and middling-minded; no passions will calcify here for years in the gloom to be revealed a decade later as the tesselations of hard and fertile work, no, it is all open, promiscuous, borrowed, half bought, a city without iron, eschewing wood, a kingdom of stucco, the playground for mass men—one has the feeling it was built by television sets giving orders to men. And in this land of the pretty-pretty, the virility is in the barbarisms, the vulgarities, it is in the huge billboards, the screamers of the neon lighting, the shouting farm-utensil colors of the gas stations and monster drugstores, it is in the swing of the sports cars, hot rods, convertibles, Los Angeles is a city to drive in, the boulevards are wide, the traffic is nervous and fast, the radio stations play bouncing, blooping, rippling tunes, one digs the pop in a pop tune, no one of character would make love by it but the sound is good for swinging a car, electronic guitars and Hawaiian harps.

So this is the town the Democrats came to, and with their unerring instinct (after being with them a week, one thinks of this party as a crazy, half-rich family, loaded with poor cousins, traveling always in caravans with Cadillacs and Okie Fords, Lincolns and quarter-horse mules, putting up every night in tents to hear the chamber quartet of Great Cousin Eleanor invaded by the Texas-twanging steel-stringing geetarists of Bubber Lyndon, carrying its own mean high-school principal, Doc Symington, chided for its manners by good Uncle Adlai, told the route of march by Navigator Jack, cut off every six months from the rich will of Uncle Jim Farley, never listening to the mechanic of the caravan, Bald Sam Rayburn, who assures them they'll all break down unless Cousin Bubber gets the concession on the garage; it's the Snopes family married to Henry James, with the labor unions thrown in like a Yankee dollar, and yet it's true, in tranquility one recollects them with affection, their instinct is good, crazy family good) and this instinct now led the caravan to pick the Biltmore Hotel in downtown Los Angeles for their family get-together and reunion.

The Biltmore is one of the ugliest hotels in the world. Patterned after the flat roofs of an Italian Renaissance palace, it is eighty-eight times as large, and one-millionth as valuable to the continuation of man, and it would be intolerable if it were not for the presence of Pershing Square, that square block of park with cactus and palm trees, the three-hundred-and-sixty-five-day-a-year convention of every junkie, pot-head, pusher, queen (but you have read that good writing already). For years Pershing Square has been one of the three or four places in America famous to homosexuals, famous not for its posh, the chic is round-heeled here, but because it is one of the avatars of good old masturbatory sex, dirty with the crusted sugars of smut, dirty rooming houses around the corner where the score is made, dirty book and photograph stores down the street, old-fashioned out-of-the-Thirties burlesque houses, cruising bars, jukeboxes, movie houses; Pershing Square is the town plaza for all those lonely, respectable, small-town homosexuals who lead a family life, make children, and have the Philbrick psychology (How I Joined the Communist Party and Led Three Lives). Yes, it is the open-air convention hall for the small-town inverts who live like spies, and it sits in the center of Los Angeles, facing the Biltmore, that hotel which is a mausoleum, that Pentagon of traveling salesmen the Party chose to house the headquarters of the Convention.

So here came that family, cursed before it began by the thundering absence of Great-Uncle Truman, the delegates dispersed over a run of thirty miles and twenty-seven hotels: the Olympian Motor Hotel, the Ambassador, the Beverly Wilshire, the Santa Ynez Inn (where rumor has it the delegates from Louisiana had some midnight swim), the Mayan, the Commodore, the Mayfair, the Sheraton-West, the Huntington-Sheraton, the Green, the Hayward, the Gates, the Figueroa, the Statler Hilton, the Hollywood Knickerbocker—does one have to be a collector to list such names?—beauties all, with that up-from-the-farm Los Angeles décor, plate-glass windows, patio and terrace, foam-rubber mattress, pastel paints, all of them pretty as an ad in full-page color, all but the Biltmore where everybody gathered every day—the newsmen, the TV, radio, magazine, and foreign newspaperman, the delegates, the politicos, the tourists, the campaign managers, the runners, the flunkies, the cousins and aunts, the wives, the grandfathers, the eight-year-old girls, and the twenty-eight-year-old girls in the Kennedy costumes, red and white and blue, the Symingteeners, the Johnson Ladies, the Stevenson Ladies, everybody—and for three days before the convention and four days into it, everybody collected at the Biltmore, in the lobby, in the grill, in the Biltmore Bowl, in the elevators, along the corridors, three hundred deep always outside the Kennedy suite, milling everywhere, every dark-carpeted grey-brown hall of the hotel, but it was in the Gallery of the Biltmore where one first felt the mood which pervaded all proceedings until the convention was almost over, that heavy, thick, witless depression which was to dominate every move as the delegates wandered and gawked and paraded and set for a spell, there in the Gallery of the Biltmore, that huge depressing alley with its inimitable hotel color, that faded depth of chiaroscuro which unhappily has no depth, that brown which is not a brown, that grey which has no pearl in it, that color which can be described only as hotel-color because the beiges, the tans, the walnuts, the mahoganies, the dull blood rugs, the moaning yellows, the sick greens, the greys and all those dumb browns merge into that lack of color which is an over-large hotel at convention time, with all the small-towners wearing their set, starched faces, that look they get at carnival, all fever and suspicion, and proud to be there, eddying slowly back and forth in that high block-long tunnel of a room with its arched ceiling and square recesses filling every rib of the arch with art work, escutcheons and blazons and other art, pictures I think, I cannot even remember, there was such a hill of cigar smoke the eye had to travel on its way to the ceiling, and at one end there was galvanized-pipe scaffolding and workmen repairing some part of the ceiling, one of them touching up one of the endless squares of painted plaster in the arch, and another worker, passing by, yelled up to the one who was working on the ceiling: "Hey, Michelangelo!"

Later, of course, it began to emerge and there were portraits one could keep, Symington, dogged at a press conference, declaring with no conviction that he knew he had a good chance to win, the disappointment eating at his good looks so that he came off hard-faced, mean, and yet slack—a desperate dullness came off the best of his intentions. There was Johnson who had compromised too many contradictions and now the contradictions were in his face: when he smiled the corners of his mouth squeezed gloom; when he was pious, his eyes twinkled irony; when he spoke in a righteous tone, he looked corrupt; when he jested, the ham in his jowls looked to quiver. He was not convincing. He was a Southern politician, a Texas Democrat, a liberal Eisenhower; he would do no harm, he would do no good, he would react to the machine, good fellow, nice friend—the Russians would understand him better than his own.

Stevenson had the patina. He came into the room and the room was different, not stronger perhaps (which is why ultimately he did not win), but warmer. One knew why some adored him; he did not look like other people, not with press lights on his flesh; he looked like a lover, the simple truth, he had the sweet happiness of an adolescent who has just been given his first major kiss. And so he glowed, and one was reminded of Chaplin, not because they were the least alike in features, but because Charlie Chaplin was luminous when one met him and Stevenson had something of that light.

There was Eleanor Roosevelt, fine, precise, hand-worked like ivory. Her voice was almost attractive as she explained in the firm, sad tones of the first lady in this small town why she could not admit Mr. Kennedy, who was no doubt a gentleman, into her political house. One had the impression of a lady who was finally becoming a woman, which is to say that she was just a little bitchy about it all; nice bitchy, charming, it had a touch of art to it, but it made one wonder if she were not now satisfying the last passion of them all, which was to become physically attractive, for she was better-looking than she had ever been as she spurned the possibilities of a young suitor.

Jim Farley. Huge. Cold as a bishop. The hell he would consign you to was cold as ice.

Bobby Kennedy, the archetype Bobby Kennedy, looked like a West Point cadet, or, better, one of those reconstructed Irishmen from Kirkland House one always used to have to face in the line in Harvard house football games. "Hello," you would say to the ones who looked like him as you lined up for the scrimmage after the kickoff, and his type would nod and look away, one rock glint of recognition your due for living across the hall from one another all through Freshman year, and then bang, as the ball was passed back, you'd get a bony king-hell knee in the crotch. He was the kind of man never to put on the gloves with if you wanted to do some social boxing, because after two minutes it would be a war, and ego-bastards last long in a war.

Carmine DeSapio and Kenneth Galbraith on the same part of the convention floor. DeSapio is bigger than one expects, keen and florid, great big smoked glasses, a suntan like Man-tan—he is the kind of heavyweight Italian who could get by with a name like Romeo—and Galbraith is tall-tall, as actors say, six foot six it could be, terribly thin, enormously attentive, exquisitely polite, birdlike, he is sensitive to the stirring of reeds in a wind over the next hill. "Our grey eminence," whispered the intelligent observer next to me.

Bob Wagner, the mayor of New York, a little man, plump, groomed, blank. He had the blank, pomaded, slightly worried look of the first barber in a good barbershop, the kind who would go to the track on his day off and wear a green transparent stone in a gold ring.

And then there was Kennedy, the edge of the mystery. But a sketch will no longer suffice.

> *". . . it can be said with a fair amount of certainty that the essence of his political attractiveness is his extraordinary political intelligence. He has a mind quite unlike that of any other Democrat of this century. It is not literary, metaphysical and moral, as Adlai Stevenson's is. Kennedy is articulate and often witty, but he does not seek verbal polish. No one can doubt the seriousness of his concern with the most serious political matters, but one feels that whereas Mr. Stevenson's political views derive from a view of life that holds politics to be a mere fraction of existence, Senator Kennedy's primary interest is in politics. The easy way in which he disposes of the question of Church and State—as if he felt that any reasonable man could quite easily resolve any possible conflict of loyalties—suggests that the organization of society is the one thing that really engages his interest."*
>
> —RICHARD ROVERE: *The New Yorker*, July 23, 1960

The afternoon he arrived at the convention from the airport, there was of course a large crowd on the street outside the Biltmore, and the best way to get a view was to get up on an outdoor balcony of the Biltmore, two flights above the street, and look down on the event.

One waited thirty minutes, and then a honking of horns as wild as the getaway after an Italian wedding sounded around the corner, and the Kennedy cortege came into sight, circled Pershing Square, the men in the open and leading convertibles sitting backwards to look at their leader, and finally came to a halt in a space cleared for them by the police in the crowd. The television cameras were out, and a Kennedy band was playing some circus music. One saw him immediately. He had the deep orange-brown suntan of a ski instructor, and when he smiled at the crowd his teeth were amazingly white and clearly visible at a distance of fifty yards. For one moment he saluted Pershing Square, and Pershing Square saluted him back, the prince and the beggars of glamour staring at one another across a city street, one of those very special moments in the underground history of the world, and then with a quick move he was out of his car and by choice headed into the crowd instead of the lane cleared for him into the hotel by the police, so that he made his way inside surrounded by a mob, and one expected at any moment to see him lifted to its shoulders like a matador being carried back to the city after a triumph in the plaza. All the while the band kept playing the campaign tunes, sashaying circus music, and one had a moment of clarity, intense as a *déjà vu*, for the scene which had taken place had been glimpsed before in a dozen musical comedies; it was the scene where the hero, the matinee idol, the movie star comes to the palace to claim the princess, or what is the same, and more to our soil, the football hero, the campus king, arrives at the dean's home surrounded by a court of open-singing students to plead with the dean for his daughter's kiss and permission to put on the big musical that night. And suddenly I saw the convention, it came into focus for me, and I understood the mood of depression which had lain over the convention, because finally it was simple: the Democrats were going to nominate a man who, no matter how serious his political dedication might be, was indisputably and willy-nilly going to be seen as a great box-office actor, and the consequences of that were staggering and not at all easy to calculate.

Since the First World War Americans have been leading a double life, and our history has moved on two rivers, one visible, the other underground; there has been the history of politics which is concrete, factual, practical and unbelievably dull if not for the consequences of the actions of some of these men; and there is a subterranean river of untapped, ferocious, lonely and romantic desires, that concentration of ecstasy and violence which is the dream life of the nation.

The twentieth century may yet be seen as that era when civilized man and underprivileged man were melted together into mass man, the iron and steel of the nineteenth century giving way to electronic circuits which communicated their messages into men, the unmistakable tendency of the new century seeming to be the creation of men as interchangeable as commodities, their extremes of personality singed out of existence by the psychic fields of force the communicators would impose. This loss of personality was a catastrophe to the future of the imagination, but billions of people might first benefit from it by having enough to eat—one did not know—and there remained citadels of resistance in Europe where the culture was deep and roots were visible in the architecture of the past.

Nowhere, as in America, however, was this fall from individual man to mass man felt so acutely, for America was at once the first and most prolific creator of mass communications, and the most rootless of countries, since almost no American could lay claim to the line of a family which had not once at least severed its roots by migrating here. But, if rootless, it was then the most vulnerable of countries to its own homogenization. Yet America was also the country in which the dynamic myth of the Renaissance—that every man was potentially extraordinary—knew its most passionate persistence. Simply, America was the land where people still believed in heroes: George Washington; Billy the Kid; Lincoln, Jefferson; Mark Twain, Jack London, Hemingway; Joe Louis, Dempsey, Gentleman Jim; America believed in athletes, rum-runners, aviators; even lovers, by the time Valentino died. It was a country which had grown by the leap of one hero past another—is there a county in all of our ground which does not have its legendary figure? And when the West was filled, the expansion turned inward, became part of an agitated, overexcited, superheated dream life. The film studios threw up their searchlights as the frontier was finally sealed, and the romantic possibilities of the old conquest of land turned into a vertical myth, trapped within the skull, of a new kind of heroic life, each choosing his own archetype of a neo-renaissance man, be it Barrymore, Cagney, Flynn, Bogart, Brando or Sinatra, but it was almost as if there were no peace unless one could fight well, kill well (if always with honor), love well and love many, be cool, be daring, be dashing, be wild, be wily, be resourceful, be a brave gun. And this myth, that each of us was born to be free, to wander, to have adventure and to grow on the waves of the violent, the perfumed, and the unexpected, had a force which could not be tamed no matter how the nation's regulators—politicians, medicos, policemen, professors, priests, rabbis, ministers, *idéologues*, psychoanalysts, builders, executives and endless communicators—would brick-in the modern life with hygiene upon sanity, and middle-brow homily over platitude; the myth would not die. Indeed a quarter of the nation's business must have depended upon its existence. But it stayed alive for more than that—it was as if the message in the labyrinth of the genes would insist that violence was locked with creativity, and adventure was the secret of love.

Once, in the Second World War and in the year or two which followed, the underground river returned to earth, and the life of the nation was intense, of the present, electric; as a lady said, "That was the time when we gave parties which changed people's lives." The Forties was a decade when the speed with which one's own events occurred seemed as rapid as the history of the battlefields, and for the mass of people in America a forced march into a new jungle of emotion was the result. The surprises, the failures, and the dangers of that life must have terrified some nerve of awareness in the power and the mass, for, as if stricken by the orgiastic vistas the myth had carried up from underground, the retreat to a more conservative existence was disorderly, the fear of communism spread like an irrational hail of boils. To anyone who could see, the excessive hysteria of the Red wave was no preparation to face an enemy, but rather a terror of the national self: free-loving, lust-looting, atheistic, implacable—absurdity beyond absurdity to label communism so, for the moral products of Stalinism had been Victorian sex and a ponderous machine of material theology.

Forced underground again, deep beneath all *Reader's Digest* hospital dressings of Mental Health in Your Community, the myth continued to flow, fed by television and the film. The fissure in the national psyche widened to the danger point. The last large appearance of the myth was the vote which tricked the polls and gave Harry Truman his victory in '48. That was the last. Came the Korean War, the shadow of the H-bomb, and we were ready for the General. Uncle Harry gave way to Father, and security, regularity, order, and the life of no imagination were the command of the day. If one had any doubt of this, there was Joe McCarthy with his built-in treason detector, furnished by God, and the damage was done. In the totalitarian wind of those days, anyone who worked in Government formed the habit of being not too original, and many a mind atrophied from disuse and private shame. At the summit there was benevolence with leadership, regularity without vision, security without safety, rhetoric without life. The ship drifted on, that enormous warship of the United States, led by a Secretary of State whose cells were seceding to cancer, and as the world became more fantastic—Africa turning itself upside down, while some new kind of machine man was being made in China—two events occurred which stunned the confidence of America into a new night: the Russians put up their Sputnik, and Civil Rights—that reluctant gift to the American Negro, granted for its effect on foreign affairs—spewed into real life at Little Rock. The national Ego was in shock: the Russians were now in some ways our technological superiors, and we had an internal problem of subject populations equal conceivably in its difficulty to the Soviet and its satellites. The fatherly calm of the General began to seem like the uxorious mellifluences of the undertaker.

Underneath it all was a larger problem. The life of politics and the life of myth had diverged too far, and the energies of the people one knew everywhere had slowed down. Twenty years ago a post-Depression generation had gone to war and formed a lively, grousing, by times inefficient, carousing, pleasure-seeking, not altogether inadequate army. It did part of what it was supposed to do, and many, out of combat, picked up a kind of private life on the fly, and had their good time despite the yaws of the military system. But today in America the generation which respected the code of the myth was Beat, a horde of half-begotten Christs with scraggly beards, heroes none, saints all, weak before the strong, empty conformisms of the authority. The sanction for finding one's growth was no longer one's flag, one's career, one's sex, one's adventure, not even one's booze. Among the best in the newest of the generations, the myth had found its voice in marijuana, and the joke of the underground was that when the Russians came over they could never dare to occupy us for long because America was too Hip. Gallows humor. The poorer truth might be that America was too Beat, the instinct of the nation so separated from its public mind that apathy, schizophrenia, and private beatitudes might be the pride of the welcoming committee any underground could offer.

Yes, the life of politics and the life of the myth had diverged too far. There was nothing to return them to one another, no common danger, no cause, no desire, and, most essentially, no hero. It was a hero America needed, a hero central to his time, a man whose personality might suggest contradiction and mysteries which could reach into the alienated circuits of the underground, because only a hero can capture the secret imagination of a people, and so be good for the vitality of his nation; a hero embodies the fantasy and so allows each private mind the liberty to consider its fantasy and find a way to grow. Each mind can become more conscious of its desire and waste less strength in hiding from itself. Roosevelt was such a hero, and Churchill, Lenin and DeGaulle; even Hitler, to take the most odious example of this thesis, was a hero, the hero-as-monster, embodying what had become the monstrous fantasy of a people, but the horror upon which the radical mind and liberal temperament foundered was that he gave outlet to the energies of the Germans and so presented the twentieth century with an index of how horrible had become the secret heart of its desire. Roosevelt is of course a happier example of the hero; from his paralytic leg to the royal elegance of his geniality he seemed to contain the country within himself; everyone from the meanest starving cripple to an ambitious young man could expand to the optimism of an improving future because the man offered an unspoken promise of a future which would be rich. The sexual and the sex-starved, the poor, the hard-working and the imaginative well-to-do could see themselves in the President, could believe him to be like themselves. So a large part of the country was able to discover its energies because not as much was wasted in feeling that the country was a poisonous nutrient which stifled the day.

Too simple? No doubt. One tries to construct a simple model. The thesis is after all not so mysterious; it would merely nudge the notion that a hero embodies his time and is not so very much better than his time, but he is larger than life and so is capable of giving direction to the time, able to encourage a nation to discover the deepest colors of its character. At bottom the concept of the hero is antagonistic to impersonal social progress, to the belief that social ills can be solved by social legislating, for it sees a country as all-but-trapped in its character until it has a hero who reveals the character of the country to itself. The implication is that without such a hero the nation turns sluggish. Truman for example was not such a hero, he was not sufficiently larger than life, he inspired familiarity without excitement, he was a character but his proportions came from soap opera: Uncle Harry, full of salty common-sense and small-minded certainty, a storekeeping uncle.

Whereas Eisenhower has been the anti-Hero, the regulator. Nations do not necessarily and inevitably seek for heroes. In periods of dull anxiety, one is more likely to look for security than a dramatic confrontation, and Eisenhower could stand as a hero only for that large number of Americans who were most proud of their lack of imagination. In American life, the unspoken war of the century has taken place between the city and the small town; the city which is dynamic, orgiastic, unsettling, explosive and accelerating to the psyche; the small town which is rooted, narrow, cautious and planted in the life-logic of the family. The need of the city is to accelerate growth; the pride of the small town is to retard it. But since America has been passing through a period of enormous expansion since the war, the double-four years of Dwight Eisenhower could not retard the expansion, it could only denude it of color, character, and the development of novelty. The small town mind is rooted—it is rooted in the small town—and when it attempts to direct history the results are disastrously colorless because the instrument of world power which is used by the small-town mind is the committee. Committees do not create, they merely proliferate, and the incredible dullness wreaked upon the American landscape in Eisenhower's eight years has been the triumph of the corporation. A tasteless, sexless, odorless sanctity in architecture, manners, modes, styles has been the result. Eisenhower embodied half the needs of the nation, the needs of the timid, the petrified, the sanctimonious, and the sluggish. What was even worse, he did not divide the nation as a hero might (with a dramatic dialogue as the result); he merely excluded one part of the nation from the other. The result was an alienation of the best minds and bravest impulses from the faltering history which was made. America's need in those years was to take an existential turn, to walk into the nightmare, to face into that terrible logic of history which demanded that the country and its people must become more extraordinary and more adventurous, or else perish, since the only alternative was to offer a false security in the power and the panacea of organized religion, family, and the F.B.I., a totalitarianization of the psyche by the stultifying techniques of the mass media which would seep into everyone's most private associations and so leave the country powerless against the Russians even if the denouement were to take fifty years, for in a competition between totalitarianisms the first maxim of the prizefight manager would doubtless apply: "Hungry fighters win fights."

Some part of these thoughts must have been in one's mind at the moment there was the first glimpse of Kennedy entering the Biltmore Hotel; and in the days which followed, the first mystery—the profound air of depression which hung over the convention—gave way to a second mystery which can be answered only by history. The depression of the delegates was understandable: no one had too much doubt that Kennedy would be nominated, but if elected he would be not only the youngest President ever to be chosen by voters, he would be the most conventionally attractive young man ever to sit in the White House, and his wife—some would claim it—might be the most beautiful First Lady in our history. Of necessity the myth would emerge once more, because America's politics would now be also America's favorite movie, America's first soap opera, America's best-seller. One thinks of the talents of writers like Taylor Caldwell or Frank Yerby, or is it rather *The Fountainhead* which would contain such a fleshing of the romantic prescription? Or is it indeed one's own work which is called into question? "Well, there's your first hipster," says a writer one knows at the convention, "Sergius O'Shaugnessy born rich," and the temptation is to nod, for it could be true, a war hero, and the heroism is bona fide, even exceptional, a man who has lived with death, who, crippled in the back, took on an operation which would kill him or restore him to power, who chose to marry a lady whose face might be too imaginative for the taste of a democracy which likes its first ladies to be executives of home-management, a man who courts political suicide by choosing to go all out for a nomination four, eight, or twelve years before his political elders think he is ready, a man who announces a week prior to the convention that the young are better fitted to direct history than the old. Yes, it captures the attention. This is no routine candidate calling every shot by safety's routine book ("Yes," Nixon said, naturally but terribly tired an hour after his nomination, the TV cameras and lights and microphones bringing out a sweat of fatigue on his face, the words coming very slowly from the tired brain, somber, modest, sober, slow, slow enough so that one could touch emphatically the cautions behind each word, "Yes, I want to say," said Nixon, "that whatever abilities I have, I got from my mother." A tired pause . . . dull moment of warning, ". . . and my father." The connection now made, the rest comes easy, ". . . and my school and my church." Such men are capable of anything.)

One had the opportunity to study Kennedy a bit in the days that followed. His style in the press conferences was interesting. Not terribly popular with the reporters (too much a contemporary, and yet too difficult to understand, he received nothing like the rounds of applause given to Eleanor Roosevelt, Stevenson, Humphrey, or even Johnson), he carried himself nonetheless with a cool grace which seemed indifferent to applause, his manner somehow similar to the poise of a fine boxer, quick with his hands, neat in his timing, and two feet away from his corner when the bell ended the round. There was a good lithe wit to his responses, a dry Harvard wit, a keen sense of proportion in disposing of difficult questions—invariably he gave enough of an answer to be formally satisfactory without ever opening himself to a new question which might go further than the first. Asked by a reporter, "Are you for Adlai as vice-president?" the grin came forth and the voice turned very dry, "No, I cannot say we have considered *Adlai* as a vice-president." Yet there was an elusive detachment to everything he did. One did not have the feeling of a man present in the room with all his weight and all his mind. Johnson gave you all of himself, he was a political animal, he breathed like an animal, sweated like one, you knew his mind was entirely absorbed with the compendium of political fact and maneuver; Kennedy seemed at times like a young professor whose manner was adequate for the classroom, but whose mind was off in some intricacy of the Ph.D. thesis he was writing. Perhaps one can give a sense of the discrepancy by saying that he was like an actor who had been cast as the candidate, a good actor, but not a great one—you were aware all the time that the role was one thing and the man another—they did not coincide, the actor seemed a touch too aloof (as, let us say, Gregory Peck is usually too aloof) to become the part. Yet one had little sense of whether to value this elusiveness, or to beware of it. One could be witnessing the fortitude of a superior sensitivity or the detachment of a man who was not quite real to himself. And his voice gave no clue. When Johnson spoke, one could separate what was fraudulent from what was felt, he would have been satisfying as an actor the way Broderick Crawford or Paul Douglas is satisfying; one saw into his emotions, or at least had the illusion that one did. Kennedy's voice, however, was only a fair voice, too reedy, near to strident, it had the metallic snap of a cricket in it somewhere, it was more impersonal than the man, and so became the least-impressive quality in a face, a body, a selection of language, and a style of movement which made up a better-than-decent presentation, better than one had expected.

With all of that, it would not do to pass over the quality in Kennedy which is most difficult to describe. And in fact some touches should be added to this hint of a portrait, for later (after the convention), one had a short session alone with him, and the next day, another. As one had suspected in advance the interviews were not altogether satisfactory, they hardly could have been. A man running for President is altogether different from a man elected President: the hazards of the campaign make it impossible for a candidate to be as interesting as he might like to be (assuming he has such a desire). One kept advancing the argument that this campaign would be a contest of personalities, and Kennedy kept returning the discussion to politics. After a while one recognized this was an inevitable caution for him. So there would be not too much point to reconstructing the dialogue since Kennedy is hardly inarticulate about his political attitudes and there will be a library vault of text devoted to it in the newspapers. What struck me most about the interview was a passing remark whose importance was invisible on the scale of politics, but was altogether meaningful to my particular competence. As we sat down for the first time, Kennedy smiled nicely and said that he had read my books. One muttered one's pleasure. "Yes," he said, "I've read . . ." and then there was a short pause which did not last long enough to be embarrassing in which it was yet obvious no title came instantly to his mind, an omission one was not ready to mind altogether since a man in such a position must be obliged to carry a hundred thousand facts and names in his head, but the hesitation lasted no longer than three seconds or four, and then he said, "I've read *The Deer Park* and . . . the others," which startled me for it was the first time in a hundred similar situations, talking to someone whose knowledge of my work was casual, that the sentence did not come out, "I've read *The Naked and the Dead* . . . and the others." If one is to take the worst and assume that Kennedy was briefed for this interview (which is most doubtful), it still speaks well for the striking instincts of his advisers.

What was retained later is an impression of Kennedy's manners which were excellent, even artful, better than the formal good manners of Choate and Harvard, almost as if what was creative in the man had been given to the manners. In a room with one or two people, his voice improved, became low-pitched, even pleasant—it seemed obvious that in all these years he had never become a natural public speaker and so his voice was constricted in public, the symptom of all orators who are ambitious, throttled, and determined.

His personal quality had a subtle, not quite describable intensity, a suggestion of dry pent heat perhaps, his eyes large, the pupils grey, the whites prominent, almost shocking, his most forceful feature: he had the eyes of a mountaineer. His appearance changed with his mood, strikingly so, and this made him always more interesting than what he was saying. He would seem at one moment older than his age, forty-eight or fifty, a tall, slim, sunburned professor with a pleasant weathered face, not even particularly handsome; five minutes later, talking to a press conference on his lawn, three microphones before him, a television camera turning, his appearance would have gone through a metamorphosis, he would look again like a movie star, his coloring vivid, his manner rich, his gestures strong and quick, alive with that concentration of vitality a successful actor always seems to radiate. Kennedy had a dozen faces. Although they were not at all similar as people, the quality was reminiscent of someone like Brando whose expression rarely changes, but whose appearances seems to shift from one person into another as the minutes go by, and one bothers with this comparison because, like Brando, Kennedy's most characteristic quality is the remote and private air of a man who has traversed some lonely terrain of experience, of loss and gain, of nearness to death, which leaves him isolated from the mass of others.

> *"The next day while they waited in vain for rescuers, the wrecked half of the boat turned over in the water and they saw that it would soon sink. The group decided to swim to a small island three miles away. There were other islands bigger and nearer, but the Navy officers knew that they were occupied by the Japanese. On one island, only one mile to the south, they could see a Japanese camp. McMahon, the engineer whose legs were disabled by burns, was unable to swim. Despite his own painfully crippled back, Kennedy swam the three miles with a breast stroke, towing behind him by a life-belt strap that he held between his teeth the helpless McMahon . . . it took Kennedy and the suffering engineer five hours to reach the island."*

The quotation is from a book which has for its dedicated unilateral title, *The Remarkable Kennedys*, but the prose is by one of the best of the war reporters, the former *Yank* editor, Joe McCarthy, and so presumably may be trusted in such details as this. Physical bravery does not of course guarantee a man's abilities in the White House—all too often men with physical courage are disappointing in their moral imagination—but the heroism here is remarkable for its tenacity. The above is merely one episode in a continuing saga which went on for five days in and out of the water, and left Kennedy at one point "miraculously saved from drowning (in a storm) by a group of Solomon Island natives who suddenly came up beside him in a large dugout canoe." Afterward, his back still injured (that precise back injury which was to put him on crutches eleven years later, and have him search for "spinal-fusion surgery" despite a warning that his chances of living through the operation were "extremely limited"), he asked to go back on duty and became so bold in the attacks he made with his PT boat "that the crew didn't like to go out with him because he took so many chances."

It is the wisdom of a man who senses death within him and gambles that he can cure it by risking his life. It is the therapy of the instinct, and who is so wise as to call it irrational? Before he went into the Navy, Kennedy had been ailing. Washed out of Freshman year at Princeton by a prolonged trough of yellow jaundice, sick for a year at Harvard, weak already in the back from an injury at football, his trials suggest the self-hatred of a man whose resentment and ambition are too large for his body. Not everyone can discharge their furies on an analyst's couch, for some angers can be relaxed only by winning power, some rages are sufficiently monumental to demand that one try to become a hero or else fall back into that death which is already within the cells. But if one succeeds, the energy aroused can be exceptional. Talking to a man who had been with Kennedy in Hyannis Port the week before the convention, I heard that he was in a state of deep fatigue.

"Well, he didn't look tired at the convention," one commented.

"Oh, he had three days of rest. Three days of rest for him is like six months to us."

One thinks of that three-mile swim with the belt in his mouth and McMahon holding it behind him. There are pestilences which sit in the mouth and rot the teeth—in those five hours how much of the psyche must have been remade, for to give vent to the bite in one's jaws and yet use that rage to save a life: it is not so very many men who have the apocalyptic sense that heroism is the First Doctor.

If one had a profound criticism of Kennedy it was that his public mind was too conventional, but that seemed to matter less than the fact of such a man in office because the law of political life had become so dreary that only a conventional mind could win an election. Indeed there could be no politics which gave warmth to one's body until the country had recovered its imagination, its pioneer lust for the unexpected and incalculable. It was the changes that might come afterward on which one could put one's hope. With such a man in office the myth of the nation would again be engaged, and the fact that he was Catholic would shiver a first existential vibration of consciousness into the mind of the White Protestant. For the first time in our history, the Protestant would have the pain and creative luxury of feeling himself in some tiny degree part of a minority, and that was an experience which might be incommensurable in its value to the best of them.

As yet we have said hardly a word about Stevenson. And his actions must remain a puzzle unless one dares a speculation about his motive, or was it his need?

So far as the people at the convention had affection for anyone, it was Stevenson, so far as they were able to generate any spontaneous enthusiasm, their cheers were again for Stevenson. Yet it was obvious he never had much chance because so soon as a chance would present itself he seemed quick to dissipate the opportunity. The day before the nominations, he entered the Sports Arena to take his seat as a delegate—the demonstration was spontaneous, noisy and prolonged; it was quieted only by Governor Collins' invitation for Stevenson to speak to the delegates. In obedience perhaps to the scruple that a candidate must not appear before the convention until nominations are done, Stevenson said no more than: "I am grateful for this tumultuous and moving welcome. After getting in and out of the Biltmore Hotel and this hall, I have decided I know whom you are going to nominate. It will be the last survivor." This dry reminder of the ruthlessness of politics broke the roar of excitement for his presence. The applause as he left the platform was like the dying fall-and-moan of a baseball crowd when a home run curves foul. The next day, a New York columnist talking about it said bitterly, "If he'd only gone through the motions, if he had just said that now he wanted to run, that he would work hard, and he hoped the delegates would vote for him. Instead he made that lame joke." One wonders. It seems almost as if he did not wish to win unless victory came despite himself, and then was overwhelming. There are men who are not heroes because they are too good for their time, and it is natural that defeats leave them bitter, tired, and doubtful of their right to make new history. If Stevenson had campaigned for a year before the convention, it is possible that he could have stopped Kennedy. At the least, the convention would have been enormously more exciting, and the nominations might have gone through half-a-dozen ballots before a winner was hammered into shape. But then Stevenson might also have shortened his life. One had the impression of a tired man who (for a politician) was sickened unduly by compromise. A year of maneuvering, broken promises, and detestable partners might have gutted him for the election campaign. If elected, it might have ruined him as a President. There is the possibility that he sensed his situation exactly this way, and knew that if he were to run for President, win and make a good one, he would first have to be restored, as one can indeed be restored, by an exceptional demonstration of love—love, in this case, meaning that the Party had a profound desire to keep him as their leader. The emotional truth of a last-minute victory for Stevenson over the Kennedy machine might have given him new energy; it would certainly have given him new faith in a country and a party whose good motives he was possibly beginning to doubt. Perhaps the fault he saw with his candidacy was that he attracted only the nicest people to himself and there were not enough of them. (One of the private amusements of the convention was to divine some of the qualities of the candidates by the style of the young women who put on hats and clothing and politicked in the colors of one presidential gent or another. Of course, half of them must have been hired models, but someone did the hiring and so it was fair to look for a common denominator. The Johnson girls tended to be plump, pie-faced, dumb sexy Southern; the Symingteeners seemed a touch mulish, stubborn, good-looking pluggers; the Kennedy ladies were the handsomest; healthy, attractive, tough, a little spoiled—they looked like the kind of girls who had gotten all the dances in high school and/or worked for a year as an airline hostess before marrying well. But the Stevenson girls looked to be doing it for no money; they were good sorts, slightly horsy-faced, one had the impression they had played field hockey in college.) It was indeed the pure, the saintly, the clean-living, the pacifistic, the vegetarian who seemed most for Stevenson, and the less humorous in the Kennedy camp were heard to remark bitterly that Stevenson had nothing going for him but a bunch of Goddamn Beatnicks. This might even have had its sour truth. The demonstrations outside the Sports Arena for Stevenson seemed to have more than a fair proportion of tall, emaciated young men with thin, wry beards and three-string guitars accompanied (again in undue proportion) by a contingent of ascetic, face-washed young Beat ladies in sweaters and dungarees. Not to mention all the Holden Caulfields one could see from here to the horizon. But of course it is unfair to limit it so, for the Democratic gentry were also committed half en masse for Stevenson, as well as a considerable number of movie stars, Shelley Winters for one: after the convention she remarked sweetly, "Tell me something nice about Kennedy so I can get excited about him."

What was properly astonishing was the way this horde of political half-breeds and amateurs came within distance of turning the convention from its preconceived purpose, and managed at least to bring the only hour of thoroughgoing excitement the convention could offer.

But then nominating day was the best day of the week and enough happened to suggest that a convention out of control would be a spectacle as extraordinary in the American scale of spectator values as a close seventh game in the World Series or a tied fourth quarter in a professional-football championship. A political convention is after all not a meeting of a corporation's board of directors; it is a fiesta, a carnival, a pig-rooting, horse-snorting, band-playing, voice-screaming medieval get-together of greed, practical lust, compromised idealism, career-advancement, meeting, feud, vendetta, conciliation, of rabble-rousers, fist fights (as it used to be), embraces, drunks (again as it used to be) and collective rivers of animal sweat. It is a reminder that no matter how the country might pretend it has grown up and become tidy in its manners, bodiless in its legislative language, hygienic in its separation of high politics from private life, that the roots still come grubby from the soil, and that politics in America is still different from politics anywhere else because the politics has arisen out of the immediate needs, ambitions, and cupidities of the people, that our politics still smell of the bedroom and the kitchen, rather than having descended to us from the chill punctilio of aristocratic negotiation.

So. The Sports Arena was new, too pretty of course, tasteless in its design—it was somehow pleasing that the acoustics were so bad for one did not wish the architects well; there had been so little imagination in their design, and this arena would have none of the harsh grandeur of Madison Square Garden when it was aged by spectators' phlegm and feet over the next twenty years. Still it had some atmosphere; seen from the streets, with the spectators moving to the ticket gates, the bands playing, the green hot-shot special editions of the Los Angeles newspapers being hawked by the newsboys, there was a touch of the air of promise that precedes a bullfight, not something so good as the approach to the Plaza Mexico, but good, let us say, like the entrance into El Toreo of Mexico City, another architectural monstrosity, also with seats painted, as I remember, in rose-pink, and dark, milky sky-blue.

Inside, it was also different this nominating day. On Monday and Tuesday the air had been desultory, no one listened to the speakers, and everybody milled from one easy chatting conversation to another—it had been like a tepid Kaffeklatsch for fifteen thousand people. But today there was a whip of anticipation in the air, the seats on the floor were filled, the press section was working, and in the gallery people were sitting in the aisles.

Sam Rayburn had just finished nominating Johnson as one came in, and the rebel yells went up, delegates started filing out of their seats and climbing over seats, and a pullulating dance of bodies and bands began to snake through the aisles, the posters jogging and whirling in time to the music. The dun color of the floor (faces, suits, seats and floor boards), so monotonous the first two days, now lit up with life as if an iridescent caterpillar had emerged from a fold of wet leaves. It was more vivid than one had expected, it was right, it felt finally like a convention, and from up close when one got down to the floor (where your presence was illegal and so consummated by sneaking in one time as demonstrators were going out, and again by slipping a five-dollar bill to a guard) the nearness to the demonstrators took on high color, that electric vividness one feels on the side lines of a football game when it is necessary to duck back as the ball-carrier goes by, his face tortured in the concentration of the moment, the thwomp of his tackle as acute as if one had been hit oneself.

That was the way the demonstrators looked on the floor. Nearly all had the rapt, private look of a passion or a tension which would finally be worked off by one's limbs, three hundred football players, everything from seedy delegates with jowl-sweating shivers to livid models, paid for their work that day, but stomping out their beat on the floor with the hypnotic adulatory grimaces of ladies who had lived for Lyndon these last ten years.

Then from the funereal rostrum, whose color was not so rich as mahogany nor so dead as a cigar, came the last of the requests for the delegates to take their seats. The seconding speeches began, one minute each; they ran for three and four, the minor-league speakers running on the longest as if the electric antennae of television was the lure of the Sirens, leading them out. Bored cheers applauded their concluding Götterdämmerungen and the nominations were open again. A favorite son, a modest demonstration, five seconding speeches, tedium.

Next was Kennedy's occasion. Governor Freeman of Minnesota made the speech. On the second or third sentence his television prompter jammed, an accident. Few could be aware of it at the moment; the speech seemed merely flat and surprisingly void of bravura. He was obviously no giant of extempore. Then the demonstration. Well-run, bigger than Johnson's, jazzier, the caliber of the costumes and decoration better chosen: the placards were broad enough, "Let's Back Jack," the floats were garish, particularly a papier-mâché or plastic balloon of Kennedy's head, six feet in diameter, which had nonetheless the slightly shrunken, over-red, rubbery look of a toy for practical jokers in one of those sleazy off–Times Square magic-and-gimmick stores; the band was suitably corny; and yet one had the impression this demonstration had been designed by some hands-to-hip interior decorator who said, "Oh, joy, let's have fun, let's make this *true* beer hall."

Besides, the personnel had something of the Kennedy *élan*, those paper hats designed to look like straw boaters with Kennedy's face on the crown, and small photographs of him on the ribbon, those hats which had come to symbolize the crack speed of the Kennedy team, that Madison Avenue cachet which one finds in the bars like P. J. Clarke's, the elegance always giving its subtle echo of the Twenties so that the raccoon coats seem more numerous than their real count, and the colored waistcoats are measured by the charm they would have drawn from Scott Fitzgerald's eye. But there, it occurred to one for the first time that Kennedy's middle name was just that, Fitzgerald, and the tone of his crack lieutenants, the unstated style, was true to Scott. The legend of Fitzgerald had an army at last, formed around the self-image in the mind of every superior Madison Avenue opportunist that he was hard, he was young, he was In, his conversation was lean as wit, and if the work was not always scrupulous, well the style could aspire. If there came a good day . . . he could meet the occasion.

The Kennedy snake dance ran its thirty lively minutes, cheered its seconding speeches, and sat back. They were so sure of winning, there had been so many victories before this one, and this one had been scouted and managed so well, that hysteria could hardly be the mood. Besides, everyone was waiting for the Stevenson barrage which should be at least diverting. But now came a long tedium. Favorite sons were nominated, fat mayors shook their hips, seconders told the word to constituents back in Ponderwaygot County, treacly demonstrations tried to hold the floor, and the afternoon went by;

Symington's hour came and went, a good demonstration, good as Johnson's (for good cause—they had pooled their demonstrators). More favorite sons, Governor Docking of Kansas declared "a genius" by one of his lady speakers in a tense go-back-to-religion voice. The hours went by, two, three, four hours, it seemed forever before they would get to Stevenson. It was evening when Senator Eugene McCarthy of Minnesota got up to nominate him.

The gallery was ready, the floor was responsive, the demonstrators were milling like bulls in their pen waiting for the *toril* to fly open—it would have been hard not to wake the crowd up, not to make a good speech. McCarthy made a great one. Great it was by the measure of convention oratory, and he held the crowd like a matador, timing their *oles!*, building them up, easing them back, correcting any sag in attention, gathering their emotion, discharging it, creating new emotion on the wave of the last, driving his passes tighter and tighter as he readied for the kill. "Do not reject this man who made us all proud to be called Democrats, do not leave the prophet without honor in his own party." One had not heard a speech like this since 1948 when Vito Marcantonio's voice, his harsh, shrill, bitter, street urchin's voice screeched through the loud-speakers at Yankee Stadium and lashed seventy thousand people into an uproar.

"There was only one man who said let's talk sense to the American people," McCarthy went on, his muleta furled for the *naturales*. "There was only one man who said let's talk sense to the American people," he repeated. "He said the promise of America is the promise of greatness. This was his call to greatness. . . . Do not forget this man. . . . Ladies and Gentlemen, I present to you not the favorite son of one state, but the favorite son of the fifty states, the favorite son of every country he has visited, the favorite son of every country which has not seen him but is secretly thrilled by his name." Bedlam. The kill. "Ladies and Gentleman, I present to you Adlai Stevenson of Illinois." Ears and tail. Hooves and bull. A roar went up like the roar one heard the day Bobby Thomson hit his home run at the Polo Grounds and the Giants won the pennant from the Dodgers in the third playoff game of the 1951 season. The demonstration cascaded onto the floor, the gallery came to its feet, the Sports Arena sounded like the inside of a marching drum. A tidal pulse of hysteria, exaltation, defiance, exhilaration, anger and roaring desire flooded over the floor. The cry which had gone up on McCarthy's last sentence had not paused for breath in five minutes, and troop after troop of demonstrators jammed the floor (the Stevenson people to be scolded the next day for having collected floor passes and sent them out to bring in new demonstrators) and still the sound mounted. One felt the convention coming apart. There was a Kennedy girl in the seat in front of me, the Kennedy hat on her head, a dimpled healthy brunette; she had sat silently through McCarthy's speech, but now, like a woman paying her respects to the power of natural thrust, she took off her hat and began to clap herself. I saw a writer I knew in the next aisle; he had spent a year studying the Kennedy machine in order to write a book on how a nomination is won. If Stevenson stampeded the convention, his work was lost. Like a reporter at a mine cave-in I inquired the present view of the widow. "Who can think," was the answer, half frantic, half elated, "just watch it, that's all." I found a cool one, a New York reporter, who smiled in rueful respect. "It's the biggest demonstration I've seen since Wendell Willkie's in 1940," he said, and added, "God, if Stevenson takes it, I can wire my wife and move the family on to Hawaii."

"I don't get it."

"Well, every story I wrote said it was locked up for Kennedy."

Still it went on, twenty minutes, thirty minutes, the chairman could hardly be heard, the demonstrators refused to leave. The lights were turned out, giving a sudden theatrical shift to the sense of a crowded church at midnight, and a new roar went up, louder, more passionate than anything heard before. It was the voice, it was the passion, if one insisted to call it that, of everything in America which was defeated, idealistic, innocent, alienated, outside and Beat, it was the potential voice of a new third of the nation whose psyche was ill from cultural malnutrition, it was powerful, it was extraordinary, it was larger than the decent, humorous, finicky, half-noble man who had called it forth, it was a cry from the Thirties when Time was simple, it was a resentment of the slick technique, the oiled gears, and the superior generals of Fitzgerald's

Army; but it was also—and for this reason one could not admire it altogether, except with one's excitement—it was also the plea of the bewildered who hunger for simplicity again, it was the adolescent counterpart of the boss's depression before the unpredictable dynamic of Kennedy as President, it was the return to the sentimental dream of Roosevelt rather than the approaching nightmare of history's oncoming night, and it was inspired by a terror of the future as much as a revulsion of the present.

Fitz's Army held; after the demonstration was finally down, the convention languished for ninety minutes while Meyner and others were nominated, a fatal lapse of time because Stevenson had perhaps a chance to stop Kennedy if the voting had begun on the echo of the last cry for him, but in an hour and a half depression crept in again and emotions spent, the delegates who had wavered were rounded into line. When the vote was taken, Stevenson had made no gains. The brunette who had taken off her hat was wearing it again, and she clapped and squealed when Wyoming delivered the duke and Kennedy was in. The air was sheepish, like the mood of a suburban couple who forgive each other for cutting in and out of somebody else's automobile while the country club dance is on. Again, tonight, no miracle would occur. In the morning the papers would be moderate in their description of Stevenson's last charge.

One did not go to the other convention. It was seen on television, and so too much cannot be said of that. It did however confirm one's earlier bias that the Republican Party was still a party of church ushers, undertakers, choirboys, prison wardens, bank presidents, small-town police chiefs, state troopers, psychiatrists, beauty-parlor operators, corporation executives, Boy-Scout leaders, fraternity presidents, tax-board assessors, community leaders, surgeons, Pullman porters, head nurses and the fat sons of rich fathers. Its candidate would be given the manufactured image of an ordinary man, and his campaign, so far as it was a psychological campaign (and this would be far indeed), would present him as a simple, honest, dependable, hard-working, ready-to-learn, modest, humble, decent, sober young man whose greatest qualification for President was his profound abasement before the glories of the Republic, the stability of the mediocre, and his own unworthiness. The apocalyptic hour of Uriah Heep.

It would then be a campaign unlike the ones which had preceded it. Counting by the full spectrum of complete Right to absolute Left, the political differences would be minor, but what would be not at all minor was the power of each man to radiate his appeal into some fundamental depths of the American character. One would have an inkling at last if the desire of America was for drama or stability, for adventure or monotomy. And this, this appeal to the psychic direction America would now choose for itself was the element most promising about this election, for it gave the possibility that the country might be able finally to rise above the deadening verbiage of its issues, its politics, its jargon, and live again by an image of itself. For in some part of themselves the people might know (since these candidates were not old enough to be revered) that they had chosen one young man for his mystery, for his promise that the country would grow or disintegrate by the unwilling charge he gave to the intensity of the myth, or had chosen another young man for his unstated oath that he would do all in his power to keep the myth buried and so convert the remains of Renaissance man as rapidly as possible into mass man. One might expect them to choose the enigma in preference to the deadening certainty. Yet one must doubt America's bravery. This lurching, unhappy, pompous and most corrupt nation—could it have the courage finally to take on a new image for itself, was it brave enough to put into office not only one of its ablest men, its most efficient, its most conquistadorial (for Kennedy's capture of the Democratic Party deserves the word), but also one of its more mysterious men (the national psyche must shiver in its sleep at the image of Mickey Mantle-cum-Lindbergh in office, and a First Lady with an eighteenth-century face). Yes, America was at last engaging the fate of its myth, its consciousness about to be accelerated or cruelly depressed in its choice between two young men in their forties who, no matter how close, dull, or indifferent their stated politics might be, were radical poles apart, for one was sober, the apotheosis of opportunistic lead, all radium spent, the other handsome as a prince in the unstated aristocracy of the American dream. So, finally, would come a choice which history had never presented to a nation before—one could vote for glamour or for ugliness, a staggering and most stunning choice—would the nation be brave enough to enlist the romantic dream of itself, would it vote for the image in the mirror of its unconscious, were the people indeed brave enough to hope for an acceleration of Time, for that new life of drama which would come from choosing a son to lead them who was heir apparent to the psychic loins? One could pause: it might be more difficult to be a President than it ever had before. Nothing less than greatness would do.

Yet if the nation voted to improve its face, what an impetus might come to the arts, to the practices, to the lives and to the imagination of the American. If the nation so voted. But one knew the unadmitted specter in the minds of the Democratic delegates: that America would go to sleep on election eve with the polls promising Kennedy a victory on the day to come, yet in its sleep some millions of Democrats and Independents would suffer a nightmare before the mystery of uncharted possibilities their man would suggest, and in a terror of all the creativities (and some violences) that mass man might now have to dare again, the undetermined would go out in the morning to vote for the psychic security of Nixon the way a middle-aged man past adventure holds to the stale bread of his marriage. Yes, this election might be fearful enough to betray the polls and no one in America could plan the new direction until the last vote was counted by the last heeler in the last ambivalent ward, no one indeed could know until then what had happened the night before, what had happened at three o'clock in the morning on that long dark night of America's search for a security cheaper than her soul.

—NOVEMBER 1960

# Falling

ADRIAN NICOLE LEBLANC

On Thursday, October 13, 1994, Armond Rankins, ten, and Tyrone Johnson, eleven, pushed open the metal doors of Doolittle East Elementary School on the South Side of Chicago and headed home to the Ida B. Wells projects. It had been more than a year since the season of raining children. So many kids had either fallen, jumped, or been thrown from the windows of high-rise projects that the city's authorities felt compelled—perhaps by the accumulating lawsuits—to take action, and window guards were now being installed. On that autumn afternoon, then, when Armond and Tyrone were walking home, families in the projects had reason to believe that if their children were going to die—and their children often did—they wouldn't die by falling from high windows.

Armond and Tyrone (not their real names) had become friends years earlier, around the time Tyrone's daddy, Tommy Jenkins, got locked up, when they were both living at 527 East Browning Street, right behind the school. Last year, with Armond's father, Wade Rankins, also in prison, the boys spent more time together than ever. Both fathers knew that this was the age when boys started doing "dumb shit"—things that could get you into trouble. Already, their sons had been arrested many times, and just a week before that October Thursday, a judge ordered Armond to spend ninety days in home confinement for gun possession. Tyrone's father did not care for the time his son spent with Armond. When Tommy and Tyrone had visited with each other in prison, father had chastised son. "I punched him in the chest—*boom, boom, boom*—and said, '*You better leave that boy Armond alone.*' When a child gets that age," Tommy said, "they father will not only cipher out the wrongs of society, but he gonna give his input to the child." Of course, he had to give his input that day in the restroom of the Stateville Correction Center.

Armond—small, sleepy-eyed, in a too-big T-shirt and dirty jeans—didn't always make it to school. Last year when his dad had been locked up, he'd missed 50 out of 180 school days. His friend Tyrone, a dark, wide-eyed boy, wore the navy pants and white shirt of Catholic school not because he went to one but because his mother liked to dress him proper. If Tyrone's father hadn't been in jail, he would have picked his son up that afternoon.

There was supposed to be safe passage home for schoolkids, a human corridor of feisty tenants willing to stand up to the gangs, but its local ranks had shrunk to three women from the Ida B. Wells project. The women were known by some in the neighborhood as the "snitch bitches." So the children managed the mile home among children—children navigating shorter sisters and brothers to TVs, to community programs, eight-year-old boys and girls heading to their fatherless homes to clean and baby-sit and cook.

That October 13, the two friends shadowed the edge of Madden Park, returning to their homes on the sixty-nine-acre tract of Ida B. Wells, the city's oldest public-housing development, a few blocks from Lake Michigan. First built in 1939 as a series of row houses, the complex grew to include the seven-story "extensions" and the fourteen-story high-rises. The boys cut through the dismal cement lots of the original row-house Ida B.'s, maneuvering around rusted Dumpsters that gangbangers position along the crumbling interior roadway to block rival gangs from drive-by attacks.

As they straggled along, the two tried to figure out how to make their neighbors, eight-year-old Derrick Lemon, a peanut of a boy with a shaved head, and his brother, five-year-old Eric Morse, a little scamp, pay for getting them into trouble. Days earlier, Derrick and Eric had been detained for shoplifting. They told their mother, Toni Morse, thirty-six, that Armond and Tyrone had put them up to it.

Toni and her sister, Arlethea Morse, thirty-nine, had passed the word on to Tyrone's mom.

Around 7:00 that Thursday night, Armond and Tyrone spotted Eric playing outside with Derrick and joined them. It may have been then that they invited the brothers to their clubhouse in a nearby high-rise, 3833 South Langley. The building stands among three similar structures—one now abandoned—in an area known, because of the killing that has occurred there, as the K-zone. The four entered the building peacefully, according to the guard. The brothers rode the sluggish elevator; Armond and Tyrone took the stairs. To the brothers, this may have seemed a race; to Armond and Tyrone, the climb upstairs may have offered one last chance to confer on how they would frighten the younger boys. When the filthy elevator doors slid open on the thirteenth floor—that bank of elevators stopped only on odd-numbered floors—the older boys were waiting. The four proceeded up one more flight, to the top floor, to apartment 1405, the club. The brothers walked in, holding hands.

Like most clubhouses in the projects, this one required special entry—pushing through the plywood door that had been erected just a few hours before. Apartment 1405 had had its share of traffic since its last resident had vacated in July 1993. Ten of the eighteen units on the top two floors remain unoccupied. Danger dwells in empty space, and the higher you go, the more empty space there is. Donald Stubenfield, who lives in the apartment immediately below 1405, often climbed the stairs to clear out the teenagers and children. The night before, he'd gone up to find boys knocking a hole in the wall connecting it to the next apartment, in case they had to escape from the police. His wife, Annie, heard only shuffling this night, however—what sounded like a chair—and she said to herself, "They're being quiet tonight."

The order of the following events is unclear. One account has it that Armond ran to an open window. He called Eric over to watch a fight, but it was a trick. The other story is that Armond and Tyrone began beating Derrick, and Eric jumped to his brother's defense. Either way, within moments, Armond and Tyrone had seized Eric, one grasping him by the shoulders, the other by the legs, and tried to hang him out the window. They failed, according to the police, at least in part because of a window guard. Derrick fought the two boys off, grabbed Eric's arm, and pulled his brother to safety.

But the battle wasn't over. Apparently, Armond continued to struggle with Derrick, trying to hit him with a piece of rubble from the punched-out hole. Meanwhile, Armond removed from another window a plywood square stamped with the standard-issue MUHAMMAD ALI FOUNDATION. This window lacked a guard. Shortly after that, Eric was again in jeopardy, now dangling from the ledge, clinging to Derrick. Eric was an agile child, but he couldn't hang on forever. Nor was Derrick able to maintain his grip, especially after Tyrone bit his fingers. Eric fell. Tyrone later told his father that when he looked out the window, the "baby" was falling backward, flying. Eric Morse, five years old, forty pounds, fourteen stories down, sixty miles per hour at the moment of impact.

As soon as he lost hold of Eric, Derrick flew into the hallway, speeding around corners to the dark stairwell, stumbling, falling. He thought that if he ran fast enough, he might catch his baby brother before he hit the ground.

The rumors quickly floated into the fall air: how the ambulance showed up forty minutes late; how Eric's life could have been saved; how Eric was conscious after he fell and told bystanders what had happened, then died right there on the ground; how Derrick had told a lady on the fourth floor, but she didn't believe him and returned to finish her dinner; how it was drug related, a warning to Eric's mom to pay a debt; how it was, like many kids' deaths in Ida B. Wells, somehow related to a gang.

At the foot of 3833, the crowd that had gathered after the fall was breaking up, and the remaining homicide detectives pooled around their cruisers, talking. Someone pushed out a plywood window board from the high-rise down on them, but it missed.

Within days, a candlelight vigil for Eric took place, described by one girl as everybody marching with their "killing lights." Jesse Madison, director of a nearby boys-and-girls club, said, "For weeks afterward, everybody was running out here to stand at the foot of the window, where he hit, as if it were holy ground."

The police reports cite the motive as revenge for the brothers' having "gotten them [Armond and Tyrone] in trouble." The case is still pending, but as a homicide, it appears open-and-shut. If they are found responsible for first-degree murder, the worst that can happen to the boys is that they'll be sent to an out-of-state locked facility until they turn nineteen, since Illinois has no such facility for children their age. In fact, because of this case, the Illinois legislature passed a bill mandating the construction within the state of locked facilities for juvenile offenders under thirteen.

Taya Sun, who then headed Victim Assistance for the Chicago Housing Authority, worked late the night of October 13. The Victim Assistance office—the first in any housing project in the nation—is located on the first floor of 3833. As Toni rushed to the hospital, Taya took care of Derrick. "He wanted to talk. He wanted to tell someone," Taya remembers. " 'Their mothers really gonna get them,' he said over and over. 'Their mothers'—not the police—'their mothers really gonna get them.' "

Derrick told the police what happened, who did it, and where they lived. "I really liked that kid," says Detective James Riley, an investigator on the case. "He was a great little witness, not totally hysterical." Within forty-five minutes of the killing, at 8:15 P.M., the detectives had picked up Tyrone and Armond. They were hanging out in a crowd, one block away from the high-rise where it happened. A friend of Arlethea Morse's told her that the boys had bragged about throwing someone out a window, but no one had believed them.

According to the police, Tyrone and Armond—interviewed in separate rooms—at first denied their involvement, blaming other boys, then blamed each other. When told that Derrick had explained what happened, they confessed. Press reports claim that Tyrone came up with the plot.

"It was the lack of concern that bothered me," says Riley. "Either they didn't realize or they didn't care—I can't get inside their heads. So young. But you expect a sorry. A tear or at least a crocodile tear. Nothing. That's what sticks to me."

Armond's mother, Shirley Rankins, thirty-eight, recalls managing to ask her son, "What made you do something like that?" and she remembers he gave her a nasty look. "He looked at me like I was crazy, as if I have some nerve asking him like that."

The next morning, Tyrone's father, Tommy, thirty-one, woke up with an odd conviction of trouble. He lay on the mattress in his cell, listening to the radio. His hands began to sweat, his heart started getting tight. On the radio, John Davis of Channel Two News reported that the previous evening, a five-year-old had been pushed to his death from a fourteenth-story window at the Ida B. Wells projects, right across the street from where Tommy's boys now lived with their mother, Sandra. "My son have something to do with that," Tommy thought. Since his cellblock was on lockdown, he couldn't even make a call to find out.

By dying, Eric Morse became a symbol to the world that never knew him. He was compared to Dr. Martin Luther King Jr.—"He gave his life for something moral" (a "debriefer" from social services), a "flower in the desert" (Bill Clinton), and a "saved hero and a saint" (the seventeen-year-old preacher who gave the funeral sermon). To his family, though—his grandmother, mother, eight aunts and uncles, sixteen cousins, and five siblings, including Derrick—Eric remains a boy, dearly loved and sorely missed.

He was a boy who could tell a story right, clear from the beginning to a satisfying end. "He could *tell* it," his aunt Arlethea says with pride. She's a very pretty woman, a housekeeper at the Westin Hotel, who for years lived in 527 East Browning, one of the extensions, the building where Armond and Tyrone had met. "Without a single *uh, uh, uh* or a *you know,*" she says. "It was like you could picture his stories like a movie. When Derrick tries to tell you about a movie, he says, *uh* and *then,* and Eric would say, 'Man, be quiet! Let me tell Auntie!' He remembered details. I gave him one of those Jason movies. Oh, I miss him!"

Eric, just three and a half feet tall, flipped and tumbled his way through the projects. He liked the gymnastic mode of traveling. If he stood more than five feet away from you and you called him over, he flipped and tumbled. If he made a mistake in his routine, he'd get right back up and flip his way toward you again.

With so many aunts and uncles, the children always had spare change. They spent it on candy. "Eric would share," says Arlethea. "Not a lot, but if you asked, he'd give you something. He didn't like it if you begged."

Derrick and Eric looked out for each other. Whenever something happened, says Arlethea, they came together "like quickness." But if Derrick did something wrong, soon enough he'd hear his mother yelling for Eric, because Eric wasn't one for covering things up. "Man, you shoulda told the truth," Eric would tell his big brother. "You shoulda told the truth, 'cuz you shouldn'ta did it!" And he'd fess up to his mom.

Certainly, one thing Derrick and Eric were both reluctant to fess up to was that in late September, they had beaten a few cats to death. They told their aunt Arlethea that Armond and Tyrone had put them up to it. Two weeks later, on a Saturday, a store clerk at Jewel's, the only supermarket in the neighborhood, caught Derrick and Eric shoplifting. The management called their mother, Toni, to pick them up. Again, the boys blamed their actions on Armond and Tyrone and said they were afraid.

That Sunday, Derrick and Eric each received a dollar from their grandmother, Lela Morse, who visited them after attending church. Toni told Lela, "Mama, don't give them any money, you're going to spoil them," but Lela didn't pay her daughter any mind. "They are my grandchildren," Lela says adamantly. "And I give them money if I want." The boys bought nachos with hamburger, and fake tattoos of cartoon characters such as Bugs Bunny and Daffy Duck. In Lela's view, Toni had already spoiled Eric, carrying him all over the place far past the age when he could walk, right up until he was two.

On Monday and Tuesday, Toni kept her sons at home. Tuesday night, she decided to confront Tyrone's mother. Reprimanding someone else's children could be a dangerous thing, so Arlethea went along.

Tyrone's mother, Sandra Johnson, was living in a row house across from 3833. She had moved there from the 527 East Browning extension, where she and Arlethea had met. When Sandra answered the door, Arlethea was relieved. "Girl, I can't do nothing with him," Sandra said, exasperated. "He just come home from jail." But Arlethea thought that the boys had been raised up right. She had seen Tyrone's father, Tommy, taking them to school, picking them up. He cooked while Sandra worked. And they didn't let their children play with just any kids.

Arlethea didn't bother to speak to Shirley, Armond's mother. During that family's growing years at the extensions, she'd seen Shirley overwhelmed. When Shirley had yelled at her sons for starting fires in the courtyards at the East Browning building, they'd screamed back at her, "Fuck you, bitch!" The few times Arletha had wanted to upbraid the boys on anything, she'd made sure she'd spoken to their father, Wade. "I always had a long arm with the kids," she said. "I was the mean lady, but I was a good lady."

On the night Eric fell, Arlethea was walking past the gathering crowd at 3833, on her way home. She saw ambulances and cruisers and kept right on her way. Practical wisdom dictated that in such a situation, you head the other way from trouble. "No bullet is going to say, Oops! I didn't mean to get you," she says.

Around this time, Toni was calling Lela from Wyler Children's Hospital. "Mama, Eric is hurt, I need you," she'd said. Lela said she'd be there as soon as she found a ride—she couldn't walk, it was dark.

When Lela arrived, Toni was hysterical, screaming, lifting her hands to the trauma center's fluorescent lights. The doctor pronounced Eric dead on arrival at 7:56 P.M. of massive internal injuries, and Toni was heading toward a trance. "Get my child's clothes," she told the nurses. "Get my child's clothes. Let's go home. It's late. We got to get home. Please get my baby's clothes."

Lela faced the awful task of identifying Eric's body. When her own son had been shot years before, at Toni's birthday party around the corner from 3833, she couldn't do it. But this time, she had to because she knew what her daughter was going through. Eric's face was bruised. A dried stream of blood ran out of his ear. A blue tube, like a straw, stuck straight up from his little mouth, for breathing. Lela quickly returned to Toni, who had slumped to the floor. "I wish I was dead," Toni was hollering. "I'm going to kill myself and my family. What's it matter now that my baby's gone?" The press had arrived, so the nurses ushered the Morses out a back door. Toni disappeared.

Lela and the police didn't find her until fifteen minutes later, blocks from the hospital, walking without a coat. They had a hard time keeping her in the car. That night, Toni lay in her mother's bed. "She didn't really sleep," Lela says, her eyes welling with tears. "She cried, you know, and she was screaming. She would sit up, '*Oooooohh*, my baby, I love you, Eric!' It was so terrible."

Three caseworkers from the Department of Children and Family Services arrived at Lela's at midnight. The department already knew the Morse family. In fact, it had an open file on them. A DCFS source reported that Eric had been born with heroin in his bloodstream and that an older sister had been removed from the home. This night, Derrick had just returned from the precinct and had bathed and been tucked into bed. The hospital had been required to report that Toni had threatened to kill herself and possibly her children. It was the job of the DCFS to make sure that the city's children were all right.

For three nights, Toni did not sleep.

Even now, she can hardly speak of Eric or his death. And sometimes, when she drinks, she makes a spectacle of her grief.

In the hectic weeks after Eric's death, the press misspelled his name. Friends didn't realize who had died until they saw the Morse family on TV, leaving the Holy Angels Catholic Church funeral service.

Lots of people and organizations called, offering charity. They offered Derrick counseling, horseback riding, clothes for school. They paid the overdue balance on Lela's gas bill, restoring her heat. One organization offered to pay for Eric's burial. Another group said it would take care of the grave, all the way out in suburban Homewood, and spoke of flowers, a tombstone, and how the grave would be kept up right.

When I go to visit the cemetery with Arlethea four months later, an employee directs us to Eric's resting place and quickly drives away. Eric lies near marked plots that are as yet unoccupied, the ground frozen too hard to open up. There's nothing on his grave—no plate, no name, no wooden cross. It's situated on an incline, just a few feet away from where construction workers are drilling. The grave is sinking weirdly into the ground. Across its tiny spread of dirt is the track of a tire tread.

The Morses are religious people. "You just don't know what happened to those children," Lela says of Armond and Tyrone. "They don't just grow up to be violent. There's two sides to every story." She pauses, a gracious, forthright woman who still feels herself blessed.

"'Vengeance is mine, says the Lord,'" she quotes quietly. "Whatever is to be done is his."

Place is an identity. The courtyard where Eric fell sits in the shadow of the high-rise where Armond's life began. His parents met in the building that stands just behind 3833. Wade lived on the ninth floor. Shirley on the eighth. His people were from Mississippi, hers from Tennessee.

Armond was born seven pounds four ounces, with his mother's light skin color and his father's attitude. He loved dogs. He'd find them on the street—pit bulls, mongrels—and they would follow him home. He liked Tyrone's dog, General Grant. Eric's Aunt Arlethea used to give Armond food to feed the dogs. He would lock them up in the basement or in abandoned apartments and try to get the dogs to learn. "He used to train them, and nobody would mess with them," says Shirley. Doris Merrity, his social worker at the school in the Audy Home, the detention center where Armond is now being held, says. "He likes training dogs to be tough. He knows the different types of dogs." He named them Queenie, Blackie, Quincy, Cujo, Spot. Queenie's puppies were stillborn and Wade flushed them down the toilet. Another dog died in a bedroom, and Armond placed it in the incinerator. Armond would like to be a dogcatcher when he grows up.

Since Eric's death, what people remember about Armond are the bad things. In kindergarten, according to teachers at Doolittle, Armond brought crack in for show-and-tell. When the teacher phoned the principal's office, Armond swallowed it. They also remember that Armond once attacked someone with a dog chain.

His father, Wade, forty-five, got locked up for drug possession in 1993. He'd been working as a freelance plumber, he says, and "then I messed up." He'd been messing up for a while. Wade's rap sheet, spanning 1966 through 1993, with the seriousness of the charges decreasing over time, includes five robberies, seven drug possessions, six disorderly conducts, three domestic batteries, two thefts, one gambling charge, and one delinquent-child charge.

Armond's teachers link his increasing troubles to his father's departure. Loss accumulates. Armond's fourteen-year-old brother, Junior, who'd cared for him like a parent, had to move to an aunt's house because he didn't get along with Shirley's new man, whom she had taken up with when Wade went to prison. Armond cut school and went downtown to hustle. Each month added a new charge to his rap sheet. March: solicitation. April: gun possession. May: aggravated battery. July: theft over $300. August: battery and aggravated assault. He and Tyrone would shoplift at Jewel's and at Goldblatt's, another nearby store. Armond broke into the Doolittle school with Tyrone and Tyrone's younger brother, Casanova. Around this time, Armond formed a crew. According to one youth worker, they would shake down younger kids.

Twice, Arnold went to the prison with his grandmother to visit Wade. He didn't say much during the visits. He would get a package of popcorn from the vending machine and pop it in the visiting-room microwave. Then he'd lounge in the chair, his scrawny legs dangling, watch his father, and eat.

Now Armond is eleven years old and still small for his age. He was so tiny as a baby that his parents tucked him into a small dresser drawer with a pillow. Wade and Shirley had a bureau then.

At the Henry C. Hill Correctional Center, where Tyrone's father, Tommy, was recently transferred and is finishing his fourth and final year for aggravated stalking and home invasion, family values are tangible, at least in memo form. In pursuit of a "favorable family atmosphere" in the visiting room, unlike in the wider world, someone—the warden—has figured out what fathers can and cannot do: "Unacceptable behavior incidents" will no longer be tolerated. "Manly behavior is being respectful," the memo reads. In promotion of "positive family interaction . . . it will not be permissible for heads to lay in laps. . . . Legs must be in a normal sitting position [and] there will be no more sitting in the legs of each other." Kids under twelve are exempt.

"Ma'am," a guard says to me as I wait on the vinyl couch, my legs in normal sitting position, "here's your ID. There will be a lady up to shake you down in a second."

Seven percent of the families in Chicago's public-housing projects have two parents. In better times, Tommy and Sandra were one of these, and on top of that, they had the advantage of a car. Tommy had met Sandra when she was a student at Malcolm X College on Chicago's South Side. His friends thought he was dating a square, but the couple stayed together and had two sons and moved into an Ida B. Wells row house. Tommy landed a job at Gateway Concrete Systems, waking up at 3:00 A.M. to be at work by 5:00. Sandra worked afternoons at a clothing store. When Tommy came home in the afternoon, he watched the kids and cooked.

Casanova, their younger son, was the one who gave them trouble. When Tommy would get up for work, he'd find Casanova slumped on the chair downstairs. "He'd put my work boots on and fall back asleep," Tommy remembers. "I'm looking for the boots, and he'd sit over there by the TV, asleep."

"Casanova!" Tommy would say.

"Aww, Daddy," Casanova would say, springing up, "I'm gonna go witcha!"

"No, you ain't," Tommy would reply. "Go get in bed with your mama."

"No, I ain't. I'm goin' witcha."

"Boy, you better get your ass in that bed!"

Every few weeks, after Tommy cashed his check on Wednesdays, he'd take his children to Foot Locker and let them have their pick. The Foot Locker salesgirl would bend down and say, "Whatchu gonna do this week, li'l boyfriend?" to Casanova, who thought he was a ladies' man. Casanova would state definitively: "I want these!" Tyrone was more moderate. He wouldn't run the aisles. He took time to look. It made Tommy feel good, the way the customers would say to his sons, "Oh, how your daddy loves you."

"I would just sit there," Tommy says, "modifying the energy, and let the peoples know that I love my kids."

Tyrone's occasions of acting up usually involved his homework.

He would do the first page of the assignment and dutifully bring it into the kitchen to show Tommy. Then he'd trot back to the TV chair, prop himself up as if he were working, the pen positioned earnestly, and sink back from adult view. "He would peek out," Tommy says; "trying to be slick. Okay, then he go quiet. He got the cover over his head, with the pen in his hand, but he was asleep. 'No, buddy, come on,' I'd say. 'Sit at the table.'" Discipline might mean the belt, but when his sons thought they were due for a spanking, Tommy would reverse it and make them do a lot of work. Sometimes, he just wouldn't let them go to sleep. "Casanova was the bad one, and Ty was the good one," says Tommy, rueful at the unpredictable twist of things.

Tommy sees an analogy between training his Doberman-rottweiler, General Grant, and missteps in raising his son. "I would keep General in the closet, around no one. As soon as he would get out, he was like a mad dog, just like saying you keep a person from what he really want to get out there, once he gets out there, he's gonna go mad. That's what I did. So when Ty knew, My daddy's locked up, *shewwwww!* He went straight to bad company, 'cuz I kept him away from that."

Right now, Tommy has the time to reflect on the random nature of the universe. I call him a philosopher. He disagrees. "This is more sociological," he says. "Philosophy is too vague.

"Seem like the nightmare became a reality," Tommy continues, now crying. "We came out of lockup, I called. I dreaded to hear the truth of the premonitions so deep down inside, laid at the bottom of my stomach. Ty's mama was on the phone, crying. But she didn't have to tell me nothin'. I already knew. When you have a feeling like that—when your love is consolidated with somebody like mine is for Tyrone, a love so strong, so powerful, that no matter what, whatever way the wind blows, no matter whatever storm come through, we always stood it. Me, him, and Casanova. Lotta my brothers, lotta my buddies, is gone now, but I always say, 'Well, I wanna family,' and Tyrone was born in 1983. He's rare." He pauses, looking down.

"Let me reintegrate something. A life has been lost, of course. Eric Morse. Who was he? Why did his life affect mine? And my son?

To cause our futures to be so interrelated I think about that. I think about that baby all the time."

And other inmates remind me. Sometimes, they ask Tommy in the hallway, "How's your shorty?" and "How's your shorty gonna do?"

"I say, 'He's all right, he'll be fine'—what I'm supposed to say?" So Tommy goes about his prison business, waking, reading, doing seventy-five sit-ups a day. A good day is when Tommy's counselor lets him put a phone call through to Tyrone's jail.

The last time they spoke, out of a blue sky Tyrone asked him, "Dada, you getting married?" Tyrone's uncle Mac told the boy that, because Mac doesn't like Tyrone's mom. Tommy told Tyrone, "No matter what, I'll always love you. No matter what happens, I have an obligation to you." The conversation made Tyrone feel better, Tommy knows, because Tyrone laughed.

Before their time was up, Tyrone asked Tommy to explain what obligation meant.

A winter Friday in the projects, the night sky darkening. In the stairwells, as the disappointment and the boredom combine with booze and drugs, the danger amplifies.

Carrying a McDonald's bag, Yvonne, twenty-one—Shirley's oldest child, Wade's stepdaughter—refuses to return to her apartment by the stairs. "The kids be begging for the food," she says, so we step into the elevator, an even more unnerving route back. We're returning from a fairly terrifying trip in search of an open pharmacy that would honor her Medicaid card. She attributes the bad cramps she's having to a missing fallopian tube.

Right now, she's snapping like elastic—rambling, raging, frightening me—and as the elevator doors close, four large boys without smiles slip in. Yvonne's glazed eyes land on one boy's chest. She mumbles about the softness of her pubic hair, how another girl's sorry ass isn't good for shit, then she's back to the subject of her fallopian tube, all the while compulsively twisting her hair and rubbing with her fist a self-inflicted bruise on her temple. It's a scary moment—her words, their desperation, their insane, mocking challenge. It's as if she were saying, "Fuck me" and "Fuck you" at the same time. I keep my gaze down. The boys reject her call. Disgusted, they don't move when we reach her floor, and we squeeze past them.

Is she crazy? High? Yvonne sure has a busted heart. She seeks solace in commotion—jumpy visitors with hollowed eyes, cash transactions at her door, too many trips to the bathroom, bouts of devouring sleep.

Armond's crime, she says, hit her the hardest of the family. She learned about it from a cop who, she says, told her, "We just arrested your brother for murder."

Yvonne's apartment ordinarily gives little refuge. Now that Wade and Shirley have moved in, having been run out of their old apartment in the wake of Armond's arrest, the tension has only gotten worse. While we're out, Emmanual, Yvonne's six-year-old son; Junior, Wade's first son and Armond's older brother; and a succession of neighbor boys are playing, and Wade, who's finished his first bottle of Wild Irish Rose, wants to play, too. The second bottle is open.

A woman from an apartment downstairs arrives to complain about Junior bouncing a basketball against her door. As she's leaving, still within earshot, Junior tells his daddy, "Oh, she's a bitch." Wade responds, "You shouldn't do that," and punches Junior joyfully in the chest. The punch makes a thudding sound. Shirley is disgusted.

The chaos is increasing by increments. "Come over here, boy," Wade sings to his grandson, Emmanual. "Come over here, boy," Wade sings to his grandson, Emmanual. "Come over here and give me a kiss." He grabs the boy and kisses him on the cheek, then bites into his lip, pulling it out with his teeth. Emmanual yelps from the pain; Wade releases his lip and pulls him onto his lap. Emmanual cries for just a moment, then slips away.

The boys love to tease Wade, and the teasing gets him going. They circle him while he sits at the kitchen table and try to snatch his hat, which is embroidered with an S, for *Shirley.* Wade jumps up and chases them down the hallway, but only Emmanual gains the sanctuary of the bathroom. It is the only room in the apartment with a lock. "I'm gonna kick your ass when you get out," Wade says, returning to his chair.

The boys don't want the fun to stop. Junior and a neighbor join voices in a sadistic chorus, pitching, 'C'mon, c'mon, come out!" After some hesitation, Emmanual, hearing the pleas of his allies, opens the door and peeks out. Wade rushes down the hall to the bathroom and kneels down to pound Emmanual in the arms and stomach. The boy wails, scrunched up between the toilet and the wall.

The neighbor boy dives on Wade's back—it is pure glee—until Wade flips him over his shoulder onto the linoleum with a whack. The boy covers his head, shocked, while Junior laughs from the hallway. Now Wade turns his full attention to the neighbor. He punches him, then bends the boy's fingers back until they touch his wrist. Junior stops laughing. Emmanual escapes again.

Violence, tonight, is a way of speaking. Each time, what has started out as horseplay slips into a meaner brand of mayhem. Each episode has its own internal rhythms, and over the course of the evening, they escalate in their brutality. If it were music, it would be getting louder and louder. But here, it's oddly silent, except for the occasional punctuation of a child's cry.

Round six in the living room. Wade's back at the table, and Emmanual is circling, but he's not playing this time, so it's an even more dangerous game. Wade can't resist it. He throws Emmanual to the floor, holds him down, and begins to choke his grandson. He squeezes his throat, oblivious to the boy's crying. The timing now is solely Wade's. "Don't you know I'm taking pictures?" the photographer asks. Twice, he calls out, "Stop." The camera flashes. Wade is in a world of his own. He squeezes, squeezes Emmanual's throat until the boy's tongue pops out. Only when the photographer puts his hand on Wade's back does Wade finally stop.

On this particular night, in this stark apartment, chaos has revealed itself. What seem to be episodes of calm are indistinguishable from hurt's aftermath. Shirley has been heating up ravioli out of a can and sipping wine out of a baby-food jar. She puts the food on the table. Seconds after being choked, Emmanual gets up from the floor and sits down at the table and eats—a lot. Then he heads to the hallway closet and sits inside it, beside a bag of clothes.

If violence is a conversation, its harsh motions another form of speech, what, four months earlier, the wind whipping into the open window of their clubhouse, were Armond and Tyrone trying to say?

Wade's in the doghouse. The chaos of last night is replaced with an angry stillness. It's four in the afternoon the following day; for the family, it's morning. Yvonne's asleep, Emmanual's asleep, and Junior sits quietly with a friend, playing a video game on the fuzzy TV screen. Shirley, in a housedress, her hair in rollers for tomorrow's visit to her son, sweeps the linoleum abruptly. She flings dirt and glass and wrappers past the mounting pile. Sluggishly, Wade dodges pokes of the broom. No wine today, and not much room for lip.

There's the smack of the rag—now she's bleaching—tabletop, dishes, counter. An old dance—her cleaning, him brooding, the children playing low.

Wade twirls the drawstring of his prison-issue sweatpants, his head down. He wanders over to Junior, who's leaning back on his hands. Wade steps on Junior's fingers, as casually as an afterthought. Without looking back, Junior pulls his hand away.

Sunday morning. I arrive with Dunkin' Donuts. Wade sees me coming from the window, and as I sign in downstairs, Shirley's there to meet me. A speedy little girl in the hallway asks, "Can-I-have-a-doughnut? Can-I-have-a-doughnut? Can-I-have-a-doughnut?"

Upstairs, Emmanual is shirtless, a nervous wreck. He approaches the doughnut box, touching it quickly as if it were on fire. Shirley says, "Don't open it!" Wade says, "Leave that box alone, boy!" Emmanual starts to reply, but his protective instincts stifle all but an inarticulate sound. He gets up and stomps down the hall, returning on a pair of plastic roller skates. "Take those off, boy!" Wade yells. Emmanual doesn't and then he does. I open the box. He asks me, "Can I have a doughnut?"

"Can he have a doughnut?" I ask Shirley. She gives him an exasperated look. When he gets a doughnut in one hand, he cries for coffee—which we're sharing—and with enough hopping about, he gets a little in a baby-food jar. He takes a spoonful, then bites into the lemon doughnut as he sprawls on the floor. Powdered sugar and cream cover his face, and Junior says, "It looks like you know what!" At his age, Junior is mostly hormones.

"Stop that!" says Shirley. "Don't be talking like that!"

When Emmanual tosses his unfinished doughnut into the bathroom wastebasket instead of the one in the kitchen, Wade nabs him, holding him by the neck, and socks him in the belly. Shirley commands Emmanual to the bedroom. She dresses him with the help of Wade's sister, who is visiting. They plant Emmanual on the bed, the aunt taking his feet—washing the little toes with a washcloth—Shirley putting on his pants, pulling up the puddled socks. He escapes to flex his biceps at those of us in the kitchen, then zips back into the bedroom between his grandma and his aunt. Emmanual relishes it—a sandwich of better love.

Shirley gruffly wraps him in his coat and dispatches him down to the second floor, where Yvonne spent the night. Shirley tells him to go straight to his mother and she tells him twice.

About an hour later, Shirley and I head out to the store for snacks for Armond to eat—Hot Flames, an orange, coconut chocolate-chip cookies, two packs for a dollar. We cross the street, Wade following our progress from the window. Shirley calls the photographer "a nosy butt." She complains that "he got them pictures of Wade beating them boys," though she concedes that that night was not much different from most others. I ask her how she feels when he beats the kids. "I try to slow him down," she says, "so he don't start beating me." Mostly, she blames what she calls "the wrestling" on the wine. Yet even Wade's stone-cold-sober Sunday voice just telling Emmanual he's going to get it sends the child reeling. When we get back to the apartment, Shirley makes a point of telling me that she's going to get dressed. There's a lot of commotion in the bathroom. Wade's sister comes into the kitchen, sweating. Wade looks stoned and sits by the oven, his back to us.

We head the mile to the Audy Home, past deserted factories, past the Sparkle Car Wash, past abandoned lots. As we arrive, Shirley walks about ten feet behind Wade. We are processed quickly; today, there's not much of a line.

After we're cleared for the fifth floor, we walk toward Armond, past the unit windows. Criminal kids are housed according to aggressiveness, size, and age. Armond is one of the home's tiniest boys. In one cell, a man-boy stretches out the full length of his bed, which he's dragged right up to the glass door. He watches the boys with visitors, sucking his thumb. At Unit 5H, we sign in. I pause at the word *relationship* and register as Armond's out-of-town aunt.

As Armond picks up an extra chair for the assigned table, I survey the room. At the far end, by the TV, the unvisited boys slump on a couch. Almost all have their hands inside their shirts, a few have hands down their pants. In the main section with the tables, there is a Hispanic kid, his hair cropped close with a rat tail and his mother's pink lips perfectly imprinted on his forehead, playing cards. Armond has on an enormous T-shirt and baggy institutional pants tied up by a string. They can't wear belts, he says, "so we don't strangle nobody." He bites his lips a lot at the beginning of the visit and frequently shrugs. Shirley fixes her eyes on him, her chin in her hand, a big smile half covered by her palm. It is a mother's smile. She is pleased to see her son. Wade, though he's descending into depression, also seems lifted by the sight of him.

Armond poses the standard first question to his parents—what did they bring? He pulls snacks from the paper bag noisily, popping the small package of Hot Flames, then opening it. "That boy over there is in for raping his sister," he says after a long pause.

"Which boy?" asks Wade.

"See that boy against the wall?" Armond says.

"That honky?" Wade asks.

"No," says Armond, "that white boy against the wall."

Wade regards Armond with wry amusement. "I said 'that honky,' and he say 'that white boy.' Don't he know what a honky is?"

"She was two," says Armond.

Wade asks, "For real?"

Armond flags the guard to unlock his room so he can show his parents his certificates from the program called BUILD, at the school downstairs. The school social worker says some of his fellow students call him a "baby killer." Armond chronicles the charges of some of the other boys—attempted murder, which he calls "attempt," and manslaughter. "But you ain't in for attempt, are you, Armond? You in for murder," says Wade, with what sounds like pride.

Armond opens the envelope and tosses the certificates on the table. One is for Student of the Week. Shirley and Wade glance at them but don't say a thing. Shirley mutters something about Emmanual.

"Where he is?" asks Armond.

"I dunno. Home playing, I guess," says Shirley.

"What you say Emmanual if you don't know where he is?" Armond says. His face mocks her, as if she's stupid. "You said Emmanual was somewhere, now you sayin' he playin'." It is a reprimand. Armond seems to despise her for her feebleness and her resignation.

"He ain't in kindergarten," Wade says of Emmanual. "He flunked, he got all F's." Wade, in his barely covert contempt for Yvonne, takes it out on her little boy. He competes with his grandson for attention.

"What's your name, Javon?" Wade asks Armond, teasing.

"Armond," Armond says. "Only my *friends* call me Javon."

The social worker told me Armond didn't know his birthday. I ask him about it.

"November 1, 1983," he tries.

"November 21," says Wade.

Armond says sweetly, "1983!"

Then we speak of violence. It's the only time Armond sits up and shows animation. He begins to narrate a gun scene from a movie. This man took a gauge (Wade instructs: "What's a gauge?" and Armond pantomimes holding a gun), and then the guy sliced a potato (Armond holds the imagined knife and slices), and then they stuck the gun right through it. (Wade: "Like a silencer?" and Armond says, "No! Not a silencer!") Armond reacts to the shot—throws his hands up—then bends over to dodge it from his chair, his eyes bright, the story pouring out of him. Two people end up dead.

"Where'd you see that?" Wade asks. "They show a picture like that in here?"

"BUILD," says Armond, naming the program that gave him the certificates.

"They put you in prison and show you motherfucking pictures like that?" says Wade, incredulous. "That is some fucked-up shit." Shirley agrees that it's crazy, and as soon as her reaction is noticed, she wipes the expression away with her hand.

Shirley's area of expertise is silence. When she speaks at all, it is usually to tell Emmanual or Junior or Wade to shut up. During the visit, the only full sentence she says is this: "That guard over there looks like he playing chess, but he's really watching everything them boys do."

Armond tells his parents about a real-life fight, how these boys were kicking it to some guy. He was in his room, and he didn't know what was going on until he heard the chairs flying. He laughs. Shirley and Wade do, too. Wade and Armond turn to the television screen. "They shoulda put the TV in here," Wade says.

All this time, the boy at the table nearest us has been enduring a lecture from his mother. "This embarrasses me to come and see you," she is saying. "I am trying to reach out and touch you, but you don't want to be touched. I can go down on that street and do whatever I want to do, and you stay here." The boy flips through the Polaroids she brought and kicks the table.

Armond watches the boy and giggles. Armond, unlike Wade, owns all the mannerisms of street life—he winks, whistles through his teeth, curls his lip, shakes his head knowingly. He is two months into eleven.

I ask him if he misses home. He shrugs. I ask him if he missed his dad in prison, and he says yes, softly.

"Your dad misses you," I say.

"You visited me in prison," Wade adds. "Now I'm visiting you in prison."

Armond returns to talk of the movies. This one is the film the Audy Home shows to new arrivals. "They is birds and they singing at the beginning, and they show a guy who is in for life, and he behind bars. You was behind bars," Armond says.

"I was behind bars," Wade says sadly.

"I wish we had bars," Armond says.

"You may as well. You can't go nowhere for shit."

Armond looks up at the clock on the wall, which he calls a watch. Wade asks him how long he's been locked up, and Armond can't remember. "I know," says Wade. "When I was in prison, you start to forget what time it is." When we leave, Armond will have dinner. If it's fish or swine, he says, none of the Audy boys will eat it. I ask why, and he smirks. Then he says, "BDs." He means the Black Disciples, a gang. I ask Armond if he is one. He says no.

"When I was in prison, you wasn't supposed to eat pork, and I said, 'I like pork, I'm gonna eat it,'" says Wade.

Wade never ran with a gang, and it's a subject that makes him defensive. He once announced to me, "I am a gang of myself." Another time he told me, "I ain't in a gang, but I am somebody."

Armond is allowed to make a phone call tomorrow. He's had phone privileges before, and Wade would like his son to call him.

Armond recites the number incorrectly.

"You know the number. You said you can call from the school. Why don't you call?" Wade ventures.

Armond shrugs.

"But you gonna do what you gonna do," Wade says, giving up.

The awkwardness increases as the visiting hour shrinks. Wade handles it by renewing his teasing.

"You want to leave with me?" Wade asks, leaning close to Armond's face.

"I can't," Armond says.

"You want to leave with me?" the father says again.

Armond says, "I can't."

"What you mean, you can't?" Wade taunts him.

"I can't," says Armond, his eyes lowered. "You ain't supposed to leave."

"How come you don't come just walking out of here with me?"

Shirley grabs a handful of Armond's hair to get close enough to say goodbye. "Your grandmother gonna get you a pick," she says, and then she gives him a kiss. Wade moves away from Armond slowly, walking backward, being careful not to bang into the empty chairs.

"Goodbye, Armond." Wade says solemnly. As they leave, Shirley and Wade walk slowly down the hall, holding hands.

Wade is in the back of my rental car with a bottle of Wild Irish Rose, and Shirley, with some in a Starbucks cup, is in the front, with me driving. When I ask them if they want to get a drink or something to eat, they agree to but don't feel comfortable going inside anywhere. "People be so nosy." Shirley says, "they all into your business. Everybody look at me like I'm crazy." It exhausts Shirley, the staring, what she imagines them saying.

The court hearings and the public defender make her head hurt; at the last hearing, they found Armond unfit to face charges because of his IQ of 53. They talk about assigning him to a residential placement home, which Shirley calls a "replacement." She doesn't understand what that is, nor does she have enough of a protective shell to experience Armond's predicament as much more than an offense to her, her own failure.

We drive, heading north up Western Avenue, then back, then we turn down toward the Loop. The city's brightness feels like some kind of future.

Chicago is something to behold. "Look at that," says Wade as we drive into the skyline. "With that sight, you can generate some feelings—and some people don't have no feelings at all. How lovely! I learned in prison to appreciate things when you are in there you can't do nothing about." Shirley sighs.

Wade knows all the buildings—the Prudential, the Tribune, the Sun-Times, a hotel where he worked as a bellboy. We head down Michigan Avenue, past the furs, the furniture, the stores. "It's real pretty," Shirley whispers. We pass by jazz clubs—they've never been to one, but Wade knows where they are—go down by the riverfront, back to the lions guarding the Art Institute, by the library. We drive—westward, eastward—and listen to the music, Wade crooning softly to songs of love.

"You remember this?" Wade asks. "Shirley, you remember this? Do you?"

"*Mmmm.*"

"The aid building? You remember, Shirley?"

"*Ahhmmmm.*"

"Do you remember, Shirley? Do you remember?"

"Yeahhh, Mercy Hospital," Shirley says.

We pass the building where they got their marriage blood test twenty-one years ago, for twenty dollars, and the boarded-up Times Cafe, where they danced the "scunch." "The scunch, Shirley!" says Wade with delight. "Oh, Shirley, you remember dancing the scunch!"

We pass a hamburger grill where, in 1980, Wade bought himself a meal. He bought pancakes and sausage and bacon—he remembers exactly, he'd just gotten his paycheck that day—and he couldn't eat it all, there was so much. It was not long after that that Wade lost his job at a body shop. He then filled his days scavenging scraps of brass to sell.

"I wish I could find my sister," says Shirley all of a sudden. Of this youngest sister Shirley is proud. She raised her up from when she was a baby, and her sister has no kids or man, and she reads books.

"She real smart, she ain't got no kids," Shirley says several times. "She wrote me a letter, it was like a whole book. You shoulda seen it—how much she wrote. She wrote about how she wanted me to get my life together and all, how to be ready for you when you came out," she says, turning back to Wade, "how me and you was gonna put our life together the way it was."

"Our life haven't been great, but there's been times it was good," says Wade. "We can have it back just like that."

"We're going to have it back real soon. You'll see, we'll go back to the way it was." In the time I've known her, this is the only hopeful thing Shirley has said.

"That's all I want," says Wade, his voice gurgly with alcohol, emotion. "Our life with me and you and our kids and a place to live of our own."

The moment peaks, and then there is a silence. We pass by the

Audy Home on our way back to Yvonne's. We thought we had escaped it, but the sight takes us back to earlier that evening when Armond had asked his parents to look up and wave to him as we left the detention-center grounds. He told them his window was by a blue sign—we suspect he meant the blue background of a snow-emergency-route sign.

We pulled up under the sign in the car and attempted to spot Armond. There were so many tiny heads pressed up against the large modern windows, ears and arms framed by a dull yellowish light. Some boys, standing on their beds, banged on the glass, others gestured wildly, but to us their attempts at communication were silent, inscrutable.

Wade sat in the backseat of the car, looking up, as Shirley scrunched up to look from the passenger side of the front seat. I suggested to Wade that he get out, since Arnold expected them to be on foot, as they usually walk the mile from the projects to the Audy Home.

"Naw, I can't see him," Wade said, more in defeat than indifference.

"I can't tell which one is him."

Shirley told Wade to get out of the car. As he loped along the sidewalk, Shirley said, "Thass him."

"That ain't him," said Wade, climbing back in.

"Go on back out," she told Wade.

"That ain't him," he said.

"That him?" Shirley asked no one, referring to a small boy leaning his head against the glass.

"Naw, that ain't him," Wade wheezed, the wheezing becoming a cough.

"Well, I don't know," Shirley said, beaten.

"They all look alike," offered Wade.

"Up there," said Shirley, her eyes on the road, "they all look alike when they in there."

We reach Yvonne's neighborhood. From the street, the projects look wrecked. The towers appear substantial, but the way the broken shades and sheets hang and droop from the poorly installed window strips gives the buildings a mismatched, dreary feel. The future, here, is falling.

Shirley doesn't look forward to going up, especially not after a relaxing drive. "It's like she's her maid," Wade says of Shirley, "If she's anybody's maid, she should be mine, but that ain't the way it is." Shirley shops for Yvonne. She cleans, she cooks, she baby-sits. Sometimes, Yvonne goes out to the store and doesn't come back all night. When she returns, sometimes Shirley dares to ask her. "Ain't you bring no cigarettes? Some change?"

"You is the grandmother," Yvonne snaps. "You don't get none of that."

The car idles. Wade climbs out, and Shirley sits with me a moment. She says, "Just because I don't talk don't mean I don't worry about my son."

She opens the door to the cold, bracing herself for the entrance. "Everybody look at me like I'm crazy, but I did the best that I could." She moves into the building, her chin level, Wade walking with his eyes to the ground, a few steps ahead.

—APRIL 1995

# Hell Sucks

MICHAEL HERR

There is a map of Vietnam on the wall of my apartment in Saigon, and some nights, coming back late to the city, I'll lie out on my bed and look at it, too tired to do anything more than just get my boots off. The map is a marvel, especially absorbing because it is not real. For one thing, it is very old. It was left here years ago by a previous tenant, probably a Frenchman since the map was made in Paris. The paper has buckled, and much of the color has gone out of it, laying a kind of veil over the countries it depicts. Vietnam is divided into its older territories of Tonkin, Annam and Cochin China, and to the west, past Laos and Cambodge, sits Siam, a kingdom. That's old, I told the General. That's a really old map.

The General is drawn to it too, and whenever he stops by for a drink he'll regard it silently, undoubtedly noting inaccuracies which the maps available to him have corrected. The waters that wash around my Indochine are a placid, Disney blue, unlike the intense metallic blues of the General's maps. But all of that aside, we both agree to the obsolescence of my map, to the final unreality of it. We know that for years now, there has been no country here but the war. The landscape has been converted to terrain, the geography broken down into its more useful components: corps and zones, tactical areas of responsibility, vicinities of operation, outposts, positions, objectives, fields of fire. The weather of Vietnam has been translated into conditions, and it's gone very much the same way with the people, the population, many of whom can't realize that there is an alternative to war because war is all they have ever known. Bad luck for them, the General says. As well as he knows them (and he knows them well), he seldom talks about them except to praise "their complexity, their sophistication, their survivability." Endearing traits.

Everyone is terribly sorry about what the war is doing to Vietnam and the Vietnamese, especially since the cities have been brought into it, although somehow most of the official expressions of grief have about them that taint of Presidential sorrow, turning a little grinny around the edges. The Tet Offensive changed everything here, made this an entirely different war, made it Something Else. ("Nonsense," a colonel told me. "We're just doing the same things in the cities that we've done in the boonies, why . . . for *years*!" He was not the same man who said, "We had to destroy Bentre in order to save it," but he might have been. He'd be hip to that.) Before Tet, there was some clean touch to jungle encounters, some virtue to their brevity, always the promise of quick release from whatever horror there was. The war went on in bursts, meeting engagements; and covering it—particularly in the Highlands and the Delta, II Corps and IV Corps—you were always a tourist, a tripper who could summon up helicopters like taxis. You would taxi in, the war would break over you suddenly and then go away, and you would taxi out. Enough chances were taken to leave you exhilarated, and, except for the hangovers that any cheap thrill will give you, it was pleasant enough. Now, it is awful, just plain awful, awful without relief. (A friend on the *New York Times* told me that he didn't mind his nightmares so much as his waking impulse to file on them.) It has finally become that kind of conventional war that the Command so longed for, and it is not going well. And for every month that it continues not going well, the scope of its destruction is enlarged. We are not really a particularly brutal people, certainly no more brutal now that we've been in other wars, acquiring it as the war goes on. But our machine is devastating. And versatile. It can do almost everything but stop.

And after all these years, we were caught in midwinter with the blunt truth that our achievement in Vietnam had been less than epic, a fact that touched everyone but the men who run the war. It became finally clear that General Westmoreland did not understand this war ("This is a different war than Americans have ever been asked to fight," he told the Examining Angels. "How is it different?" they asked. "Well, you know, it's just . . . different"), and he was asked to leave it. The immediate official response was manic; after years and years of posing along the rim, the Mission joined hands and leapt through the Looking Glass. It was as though Swift's vault had been plundered to meet the public doubt. They trotted out their kill ratios, their curious estimates of enemy morale (there wasn't any), their poor, salvaged shards of Pacification (that good American idea; it would have worked wonderfully in New Mexico), strange redemption profiles of the countryside's lost security. The same incantations, the heavies, moderates and lights of this statistic-obsessed war, were sung again, and optimism was spent at the same excessive rate which we had previously maintained in the expending of ordnance. This antic Thumbs-Upmanship was best pegged by a British correspondent who compared it all to the captain of the *Titanic* announcing, "There's nothing to be alarmed about, ladies and gentlemen. We're only stopping briefly to take on some ice." And I remembered an Indian lady I once knew who shipped a trunk to her family in Calcutta. She had lost the key but found another, the key to one of her closets, and she mailed that on after the trunk. She knew it wouldn't open the trunk, but she so wanted it to work that she sent it anyway. Strange story, but I expect it might touch our Ambassador, and possibly even our former Commanding General.

When the battle for the Hué was all over, they entered it into the records, gauged its terrible cost and battlegrammed it, so that it took on the dry, tactical stamp of the West Point Atlas of American Wars. When future observers come to it, it will seem that some order had been apparent during the twenty-seven days that it took to get the North Vietnamese and Vietcong forces out of the Imperial City, and that will not be exactly the truth. Hué was not the bloodiest battle of the Vietnam War (unless you enter in the more than four thousand civilian dead and the tens of thousands who were wounded, not likely in any forthcoming revised edition of the W.P.A.O.A.W.), but it was the hardest and the bitterest, and for those of us who were a part of it, even the coldest chronicles will be enough to recall the texture of its dread. If the war was changing, Hué was that turn of the screw which locked the new terms into place for good, taking you beyond that cutoff point where one war becomes just like all other wars. You would get twinges of this feeling any time that you were on the line, with the troops; but still, before Hué, you thought of yourself as a dove or a hawk, felt that our involvement was criminal or proper, obscene or clean. After Hué, all of your lines of reasoning turned into clumsy coils, and all of the talk got on your nerves. Hué finally gave you what you had expected, half yearned for, in the days of the war that ended with the Offensive. It got up memories, vicarious enough, stored from old copies of *Life* magazine, old movie newsreels, Pathé sound tracks whose dirge-disaster music still echoed: the Italian Campaign, the fight for the Reservoir, gruesome camp, evocations of '44 and '50.

Going in, there were sixty of us packed in a deuce-and-a-half, one of eight trucks moving in convoy from Phubai, bringing in over three hundred replacements for the casualties taken in the earliest fighting south of the Perfume River. There had been a harsh, dark storm going on for days, and it turned the convoy route into a mud bed. It was terribly cold in the trucks, and the road was covered with leaves that had either been blown off the trees by the storm or torn away by our heavy artillery. The artillery had done a job here, touched everything. Many of the houses had been completely collapsed, and not one had been left without at least heavy pitting from shell fragments. Hundreds of refugees held to the side of the road as we passed. Many of them had been wounded during the shelling. The kids would laugh and shout the standard, "You you you! Okay?" The old would look on with that quiet tolerance for misery that makes so many Americans uneasy, which is usually misread as indifference. But the younger men and women would often give us looks of unmistakable contempt, pulling their cheering children back from the trucks.

So we sat there, grinning at the bad weather and the discomfort, sharing the first fear, glad that we were not riding point or closing the rear because, man, the middle is good. They had been hitting our convoys regularly, and a lot of trucks had been turned back. The houses that we were passing so slowly made the best kind of cover for snipers, and one B-40 rocket could have made casualties out of a whole truckload of us. All the Grunts were whistling and no two were whistling the same tune, and it sounded like a locker room just before a big game. A friend of mine, Sergeant Dale Dye, a Marine correspondent, sat with a tall yellow flower sticking out of his helmet cover, a really outstanding target, the kind of idiosyncracy the Marines will indulge in. His eyes rollicked, and below his big moustache his wicked, shy smile said, "Oh yes, Charlie's got his shit together here, this will be oh-so-bad, indubitably." It was the same smile I saw later when a sniper's bullet tore up the wall two inches above his head inside the Citadel. Odd cause for merriment in anyone but a Grunt.

There's something you see in the faces of Marines that you'll never see in the Army, some extra character etched in by the training and by more hard times than you'd believe, by constant intimidation, by the widespread conviction that you will get yours if you hang in there long enough. They're each of them like the hardest man on the block (You ain't been cut, you ain't my man) and they all have that wild, haunted, going-West look that says it is perfectly correct to be here where the fighting is worst, where you won't have half of what you'll need, where it is colder than the Nam ever gets. To pass the time, I started reading the stuff they'd written on their helmet covers and flak jackets. There were the names of campaigns and the names of their girls, nicknames (The Entertainer, The Avenger, Short Time Safety Moe), the slogans that touch on their lonely, severe fantasies (Born to Lose, Born to Raise Hell), and general graffiti (Hell Sucks, Time is On My Side, Yossarian Lives, Just You and Me God—Right?). There was nothing on the truck as good as the scrawl on the wall in Khesahn that said, "I Think I'm Falling In Love With Jake," but it passed the time.

And they are all giving you that mock-astonished look. "You mean you don't *have* to be here? And you're *here*?" But they are glad you're here, really very grateful. "Hey, *Esquire*! Hey, you want a story, man? Write this: I'm up there on 881, this was May, I'm up there walkin' the ridgeline an' this Zip jumps up smack into me, lays this AK-47 fuckin' right *into* me, only he's so surprised I got my whole clip off 'fore he knew how to thank me for it. Grease one." After twenty kilometers of this, in spite of the roiling dark sky ahead, we could see the smoke coming up from the far side of the river, from the Citadel of Hué.

The bridge was down that spanned the canal dividing the village of An Cu and the southern sector of Hué, blown the night before by the Vietcong, and the forward area beyond the opposite bank was not thought to be secure, so we bivouacked in the village for the night. It had been completely deserted, and we set ourselves up in empty hootches, laying our poncho liners out over the litter of shattered glass and brick. At dusk, while we were all stretched out along the canal bank eating dinner, two Marine gunships came down on us, strafing us, sending burning tracers up along the canal, and we ran for cover, more astonished than scared. "Way to go, mother-lover, way to pinpoint the motherin' enemy," one of the Grunts screamed, and he set up his M-60 machine gun in case they came back. "I don't guess we gotta take *that* shit." Patrols were sent out, guards posted, and we went to the hootches to sleep. For some reason, we were not even mortared that night.

The next morning we knew that the area must have been secured beyond a reasonable doubt, because the A.R.V.N. were there. Good little fighters, the A.R.V.N.; ask any U.S. adviser in the field. Most of them were not even armed. They needed both hands free for their work that morning, which consisted of thoroughly combing every house and store in the village, turning out drawers, tipping over chests and urns, raiding chicken coops and liquor cabinets, kicking in all the glass cases they could find, and forcibly relieving refugees on the road of radios, wine, ducks, clothing, anything. What they couldn't carry, they wore. One soldier moved up the road in an old felt hat that fell down over his eyes and a blue gabardine overcoat at least eight sizes too large, so that it trailed around him in the mud as he walked. I thought he was going to ask me the way to Floogle

Street, but he only smiled proudly at his good luck and ducked into one of the shops.

It was the same after we'd crossed the canal on a two-by-four and started walking in. We tried to flag down a lift, but the jeeps all seemed to be driven by A.R.V.N. officers out on organized looting parties. We walked along in the open toward the river, talking in an offhanded way about how superb the N.V.A. snipers were supposed to be, until we came across the very first of the hundreds of civilian dead that we were to see in the next weeks: a little girl who had been hit while riding her bicycle and an old man who lay arched over his straw hat. They'd been lying out like that for over a week, and for the first time I was grateful for the cold.

Along the Perfume River's south bank there is a long, graceful park that separates Hué's most pleasant avenue, Le Loi, from the riverfront. People will talk about how they'd sit out there in the sun and watch the sampans moving down the river, or watch the girls bicycling up Le Loi, past the villas of officials and the French-architected university buildings. Many of those villas had been destroyed and much of the university permanently damaged. In the middle of the street a couple of ambulances from the German Mission had been blown up, and the Cercle Sportif was covered with bullet holes and shrapnel. In the park itself, four fat green dead lay sprawled around a tall, ornate cage, inside of which sat a small, shivering monkey. One of the correspondents along stepped over the corpses to feed it some fruit. (Days later, I came back to the spot. The corpses were gone, but so was the monkey. There had been so many refugees and so little food then, and someone must have eaten him.) The Marines of 2/5 had secured almost all of the central south bank and were now fanning out to the west, fighting and clearing one of the major canals. We were waiting for some decision on whether or not U.S. Marines would be going into the Citadel itself, but no one had any doubts about what the decision would be. Didn't it always come to that with the Grunts? Didn't it, every goddam time? We sat there taking in the dread by watching the columns of smoke across the river, receiving occasional sniper rounds, infrequent bursts of .50 caliber, watching the Navy's L.C.U.'s on the river getting shelled from the wall. One Marine next to me was saying that it was just a damned shame, all them poor people, all them nice-looking houses. He was looking at the black napalm blasts and the wreckage along the wall. "Looks like the Imperial City's had the schnitz," he said.

It stayed cold for the next ten days, cold and dark, and that damp gloom was the background for the footage that we all took out of the Citadel. The little sunlight there was caught the heavy motes of dust that blew up from the wreckage of the East Wall, held it until everything you saw was filtered through it. And most of what you saw was taken in from unaccustomed angles, prone positions or quick looks from a crouch; lying flat out, hearing the hard dry rattle of shrapnel scudding against the debris around you, listening to the Marine next to you who didn't moan, "Oh my God, Oh Sweet Jesus, Oh Holy Mother save me," but who sobbed, instead, "Are you *ready* for this? I mean, are you *ready* for this?" Once, when the noise from a six-round mortar attack stopped, I heard some singing in back of me. There were three Grunts huddled together holding onto their helmets, looking more mischievous than scared. "We gotta get out of this place," they sang, "if it's the las' thing we ever do-woo." With all of that dust blowing around, the acrid smell of gunpowder would hang in the air for a long while after the fire fights, and there was also some CS gas that we'd fired at the N.V.A. blowing back in over our positions. It was impossible to get off a clean breath with all of that going on, and of course there was that other smell too, that most special of all smells that came up from shallow graves and from shattered heaps of stone wherever an air strike had passed. It held to the lining of your nostrils and worked itself into the weave of your fatigues, and weeks later, miles away, you would wake up from a dream in the middle of the night and it would be there in the room with you. The N.V.A. had dug themselves so deeply into the wall that air strikes had to destroy it meter by meter, dropping napalm as close as three hundred meters from our positions. Up on the highest point of the wall, on what had once been a tower, I looked across the Citadel's moat and saw the N.V.A. moving quickly among the rubble of the opposing wall. We were close enough to be able to see their faces. A rifle went off a few feet to my right, and one of the figures across the moat started forward and then dropped. A Marine sniper leaned back from his cover and grinned at me.

By the end of that week, the wall had cost the Marines roughly one casualty for every meter taken, a quarter of them K.I.A. 1/5, which came to be known as the Citadel Battalion, had been through every tough battle the Marines had had in the past six months, and now some of its companies were down to below platoon strength. They all knew how bad it was, the novelty of fighting in the streets had become a nasty, spooky joke, and not many of them really believed they'd ever get out alive. Everyone wanted to get wounded.

There was a tough quiet Negro who called himself Philly Dog. He'd been a gang lord in the streets of North Philadelphia, and in Hué he was the best man to be with, the only one who really understood how it was when you had no cover and no rear. He was better here than the hottest jungle fighter, better than those lean, mean Nam veterans with their proficiency badges for coaxing water out of palm roots, filleting snakes and reading moss. Philly Dog was the only scout you could feel right about in Hué.

"Just hold onto it, man," he'd say. "You doan go out there. That's Charlie." He pointed up the road.

We were in among the makings of a former villa, with only the rear wall still standing. I couldn't see anything up the road past one of our tanks, only a few houses, scattered trees and wires and a gigantic portion of collapsed wall.

"How do you know?" I asked.

"'Cause if I was Charlie, that'd be my spot." And he was right, almost every time.

At night, in the battalion C.P., the Major in command would sit reading his maps, staring vacantly at the trapezoid of the Citadel. It could have been a scene in a Norman farmhouse twenty-five years ago, with candles burning on the tables, bottles of red wine arranged along damaged shelves, the cold in the room, the high ceilings, the heavy ornate cross on the wall. The Major had not slept for five nights, and for the fifth night in a row he assured us that tomorrow would get it for sure, the final stretch of the wall would be taken, and he had all the Marines he needed to do it. And one of his aides, a tough mustang of a first lieutenant, would pitch a hard, ironic smile among the Major's stare, a smile that rejected good news and opted for doom, and it was like hearing him say, "The Major here is full of shit, and we both know it."

We found a villa near the C.P. and set ourselves up in it for the night. We never stayed in the same area two nights in a row, since it never took the N.V.A. very long to get us zeroed in. In the living room of the villa there were photographs of a Vietnamese family that had been taken in the States; the father in a dark business suit standing somewhere in New York; Mom, Dad and the kids at Disneyland. The Grunts could never get over the fact that there were wealthy Vietnamese, and these pictures filled them with awe. Dale Dye was there (after the sniper had barely missed him, he had gotten rid of that flower), and some of the guys had found a bottle of Veuve Cliquot. Usually they'd scarf up the 7 Crown or the Calvert's and leave four-star cognacs sitting on the shelves, but the champagne intrigued them. Most of them had never tasted it. One tall kid was saying that where he came from, it only got poured at weddings. Dye popped the cork, and one of them went chasing after it, giggling at how gala this was getting to be. Dye passed the bottle to the tall boy, who put it to his lips as if it might go off before drinking it. "It tickles m' nose," he said, and Dye broke up, shaking his head. "It's a good champagne," he said. "Not a great champagne, but a good champagne."

We slept so soundly that night that a sixty-round mortar barrage a little before dawn failed to wake us.

After the Catholic chaplain was killed, the Protestant had to give communion. His name was Takesian, an Armenian from Boston, one of those hip, blunt clerics who loved to talk, as though talking itself contained ritual powers of redemption. He wasn't one of your grizzled battle chaplains, but he was very brave, and very much affected by the particular ugliness of the Hué fighting. It was not physical fear that put him off, but the mood of bitterness that no one seemed to be able to shake, and he would sit for long stretches by himself, staring at the wounded through his thick steel-rimmed glasses. He was using sliced C-ration white bread and canteen water to deliver the sacraments, and some of the Grunts were skeptical about receiving them from a Protestant. "Listen, you silly bastards," Takesian said. "You could all get your ass shot off any time now out there. Do you think God gives a damn *how* you've been blessed?"

Sometimes one of the companies would find itself completely cut off, and it would take hours for the Marines to get their casualties out. I remember one Marine with a head wound who finally made it up to the Battalion C.P., only to find himself stuck in a stalled jeep. He finally jumped out of the jeep and started to push it, knowing it was the only way out of there. Most of the tanks and trucks which carried casualties had to move up a long, straight road with no cover, and they began calling it Rocket Alley. Every tank the Marines had had been hit at least once there. An epiphany of Hué turned up in John Olson's great photograph in *Life*, the wounded from Delta Company piled hurriedly on the tank. Sometimes, on the way out to the Battalion Aid Station, the more seriously wounded would take on that bad color, the grey-blue fishbelly promise of death that would spread upwards from the chest and cover the face. There was one Marine who had been shot through the neck, and all the way out the corpsmen massaged his chest. By the time they reached the station, though, he was so bad that the doctor triaged him, passed him over to treat the ones that he knew could be saved, and when they put him into the green canvas body bag there was some chance that he was still clinically alive. The doctor had never been in a position before where he had had to choose like that—there were so many wounded—and he never got used to it. During the lulls, he'd step outside for some air, but it was no better out there. The bodies were stacked together, and there was always a crowd of A.R.V.N. standing around staring, death-enthralled like all Vietnamese. Since they did not know what else to do, and not knowing how it would look to the Marines, they would smile vacantly at the bodies there, and a couple of ugly incidents occurred. The Marines who had volunteered for the body details were overworked and became snappish, ripping packs off of corpses angrily, cutting gear away with bayonets, heaving bodies into the green bags. One of the dead Marines had become stiff and they had trouble getting him to fit. "Damn," one of them said, "didn't this mother have big feet on him?" And he finally forced the legs into the canvas. In the station, there was the youngest looking Marine I'd ever seen, so young that his parents must have had to sign for him at enlistment. He'd been caught in the knee by a large piece of shrapnel, and he had no idea at all of what they would do with him now that he'd been wounded. He lay out on the stretcher while the doctor explained how he would be choppered back to the Phubai hospital and then put on a plane to Danang, and then flown back to the States for what would probably be the rest of his hitch. At first the boy was sure that the doctor was kidding him, then he started to believe a little of it, and when he knew that it was true, that he was actually getting out, he couldn't stop smiling, and enormous tears of happiness ran down into his ears.

It was at this point that I began to recognize almost every casualty, remember conversations we'd had days and even hours earlier, and that's when I got out, riding a Medevac chopper with a lieutenant who was covered with blood-soaked bandages. He'd been hit in both legs, both arms, the chest and head, his ears were filled with caked blood, and he asked a photographer named Art Greenspon who was in the chopper if he'd get a picture of him like this so he could mail it to his wife.

But at this point, the battle for Hué was almost over. The Cav was working the northwest corner of the Citadel, and elements of the 101st had come in through what had formerly been an N.V.A. resupply route. Vietnamese Marines and some of the 1st A.R.V.N. Division, who had fought well from the beginning, had been moving the remaining N.V.A down toward the wall. The N.V.A. flag that had flown for so long over the South Wall had been brought down, and in its place an American flag had been put up, a sight which must have thrilled those most xenophobic of all Vietnamese, the people of Hué. Two days later the Hoc Bao, Vietnamese Rangers for whom this privilege had been reserved, stormed through the wall of the Imperial Palace, but there were no enemy troops left inside. Except for a few corpses that bobbed sluggishly in the moat, most of the dead had been buried. Nearly seventy percent of Vietnam's one lovely city was destroyed, and if the landscape seemed desolate, imagine how the figures in that landscape looked.

There were two official ceremonies marking the expulsion of the N.V.A., both flag raisings. On the south bank of the Perfume River, two hundred refugees from one of the camps were recruited to stand in the rain and watch the G.V.N. flag being run up. But the rope snapped, and the crowd, thinking the V.C. had shot it down, broke up in panic. (There was no rain in the stories that the Saigon papers ran, there was no trouble with the rope, and the cheering crowd numbered thousands.) As for the other ceremony, the Citadel was still thought by most people to be insecure, and when the flag finally went up there was no one there to watch it except a handful of Vietnamese troops.

In the first weeks after the Tet Offensive began, the curfew began early in the afternoon, and was strictly enforced. By two-thirty each day Saigon had the look of the final reel of *On the Beach*, a desolate city whose long avenues held nothing but refuse, windblown papers, small, distinct piles of human excrement and the dead flowers and spent firecracker casings of the Lunar New Year. Alive, Saigon had been depressing enough, but once the Offensive began it became so stark that, in an odd way, it was invigorating. The trees along the main streets all looked like they had been struck by lightning, and it became unusually, uncomfortably cold; one more piece of bad luck in a place where nothing was in its season. With so much filth growing in so many streets and alleys, an epidemic of plague was feared, and if there was ever a place that suggested plague, demanded it, it was Saigon in the Emergency. Large numbers of American civilians, the construction workers and engineers who were making it here like they'd never made it at home, began openly carrying weapons, 45's and grease guns and AK's, and no mob of Mississippi sheriff's boys ever promised more bad news. You'd see them at ten in the morning on the terrace of the Continental Hotel, waiting for the bar to open, unable to light their own cigarettes until it did. The crowds on Tu Do Street looked like Ensor processions, and there was a corruption in the air that had nothing to do with government officials on the take.

After seven in the evening, when the curfew became total, nothing but police vehicles and M.P. jeeps moved in the streets, except for a few very young children who raced up and down over the rubbish, running newspaper kites up into the chilling wind. Shortly after dark, I could expect to see the headlights of the General's jeep coming up the street toward my apartment.

The General is a great favorite of the press here. He is commonly thought to be candid, articulate and accessible, which is absolutely the highest compliment the press corps can pay to any member of the American Mission. He is less accessible now that the war has begun to go badly, but he still finds time most nights to drop around for a quick drink, before returning to his headquarters and, I imagine, a late night's work. I have never really understood our growing friendship, since there is not a single point touching the war that we agree on. It is thought by outsiders that the General and I spend our evenings playing chess, but in fact I never learned the game, and its abstractions make the General nervous. My colleagues think that he drinks with me instead of them because I am accredited to a monthly, but of course there's more to it than that. For one thing, the General never condescends to me, while I take a lot of trouble trying not to understand him too quickly. I suppose that we are both, in our own way, aesthetes. The General is an aesthete of insurgency and counterinsurgency, a choreographer of guerilla activity, and he has been at it a long, long time. Some of the older hands here remember seeing him in Vietnam at the time of the Indochina War. He was a captain then, and he would turn up in odd, remote corners of the country dressed in black pajamas. He is supposed to have spoken fluent Vietnamese then, although he now flatly denies any familiarity with that language, which he will actually mimic quite cruelly, breaking into protracted fits of laughter. It's said that he took a break in service during the early Sixties, two years in which he all but completely disappeared. He has no command designation as such, but is connected vaguely with something called Special Operations, about which he refuses to speak.

One is immediately struck by the clean-lined ruggedness of his features, although the longer you observe him the more you notice something delicate there, some softness behind the eyes that is almost feminine. The eyes are ice-blue but not cold, and they suggest his most interesting trait, an originality of mind that one never associates with the Military, and which catches you off balance. It's impossible to guess his age to a certainty (I'd never think of asking him), but he is probably around fifty.

"How's the war going, General?" I'll ask him.

"You're a correspondent, you tell me."

"Seriously."

"Oh, how does it ever go, Mike? Slowly. Damned slowly."

He accepts his drink, lights a Bastos and sinks into a chair.

"We're hurting him," he says. "We know we're hurting him. What we don't know is how much more of it he can take. We're killing him." He raises his glass. "To absent friends."

We talk about many things: Blake, Mexico, the Beethoven Quartets, Oriental women, the Saints, wines, the Elizabethans, classic automobiles and, obviously, Vietnam, which I don't really understand that well. Before the Offensive, we would argue about whether the American position here was morally defensible. I believed it was not, the General believed it was beside the point. In fact (we never said this, but somehow mutually acknowledged it) the subject bored us both. Now, since Tet, I've been more concerned with whether or not our position is even militarily defensible, and the General is optimistic there. Sometimes, he worries about me, about my safety and, even more, about my sanity. I have what he refers to as "this thing about death," an unhealthy fascination with so much of what I've had to see here. He respects it intellectually (one of our other constant topics is suicide) but finally he finds it morbid and unprofitable. Worst of all, he finds that I have a tendency, when discussing the dead, to not only dwell on them, but to personalize them as well. "That way lies you-know-what," he says, tapping his temple; but he lets me get it out, lets me talk about the victims, about the dead and the disposition of the dead.

The first dead I saw in Vietnam was a Cambodian Mercenary serving with the Special Forces in the Seven Mountains Region of the Delta. He had accidentally shot himself in the head while cleaning his .30-caliber rifle. Mercenaries live in a compound with their families, and this one had his parents, his grandparents and his wife with him at the time. The medics bandaged his entire head so that he looked like something you'd see in relief on an old temple wall, some dead prince, very dignified in repose. The women squatted over his body, and their moaning built up into a terrible wail, falling off and beginning again, hour after hour. Some blood and brine from the wound had seeped through the bandages and filled a small dent in the canvas, so that when they carried him from the stretcher some of it spilled over my boots. "Sorry," one of the medics said. "Got some on you." The next dead I saw were in a mass of over one hundred, Vietcong who had tried to overrun the perimeter of an outpost of the 25th Infantry Division near Tayninh. They had been stopped by 105's firing fléchette canisters, thousands of steel shafts that cut them up in the most incredible way, leaving them almost unrecognizable as human beings, although you could see that some of them were very young and some were women. In Cantho, on the morning after the Offensive began, there were around forty V.C. piled up at the end of the airstrip, and one of them was a medic who had died huddled over his aid case. One of the Americans worked him loose with his feet, jammed a cigar into the clenched teeth and photographed it. Another American was screaming at a very young dead, almost sobbing, "There, you silly bastard, there! You got it now? You got it?" Americans often admonish the dead like that, particularly the young ones.

The bodies were all loaded into the back of a truck, where they lay all day, growing stiff in the positions which they had taken in death. When the truck finally started, one of them fell off the back. He was so rigid that he landed exactly on both knees and one elbow (a perfect three-pointer, one of the guys called it) with no other part of him touching the ground, and he had to be lifted up into the truck like a heavy wrought-iron figure.

Later that day, in the provincial hospital at Cantho, the friendly dead began accumulating in the corridors. The Vietcong shelled the hospital for over seven hours from Cantho University, which they had captured and held until it was finally bombed flat, and even if we had wanted to leave we couldn't have. They needed help desperately that day. Over four hundred civilian wounded were brought in, most of them children ("Who shot you, V.C. or U.S.?" the Psywar types kept asking), and we had to cleanse the wounds, cut away dead tissue, or just lean on them, hold them still while the surgeons worked. Outside of the operating rooms there were all of those who were beyond saving, already going grey before death. They just waited there, and you could see they knew. There was an odd piece of graffiti up on the wall of one of the hospital rooms, and I passed it a hundred times that day, always meaning to find out who had written it, and why. It said, "How do you feel about decay, Senator?" In spite of the mortars, a number of Vietnamese came into the hospital carrying wounded children, strangers whom they'd found lying out in the streets, and a number of others came in simply to help. At this point in the fighting the IV Corps Commander, General Manh, was absorbed in constructing a solid five-block perimeter around his house, a strange sort of defense plan considering that the most precious region of the country was at stake, and we were not permitted to drive our jeeps through this perimeter because they drew fire. We had to drive instead through sniper-infested sections of the city, frequently through ambushes along the road, and there were certainly a lot of dead to be seen there.

Of course it is much closer to you when the dead are Americans, and closer still when you've known them. I'm always being told about our comparatively heightened regard for human life, and a lot of us here think that it's exclusively American. I knew a G.I. in Bu Dop who could look at blown-up Vietnamese all day, V.C. or friendly, men, women and children, it didn't much matter. "Hell, they ain't people," he said. "Them're Slopes." But the sight of one quite cleanly killed American made him vomit. The war was a very simple one for him, and you can bet that he had a solution for ending it. But we did agree that it was a bad thing that Americans were getting killed. I'd spent enough hours flying out of combat LZ's in choppers shared with the dead. Often enough, they had no faces left at all, and some died with that wincing sucking-in of breath that shows the full pain of it, some with the dreamy smiles of the drowned, and one that I particularly remember with full staring eyes and a look of mighty outrage, like some Old Testament picture of wrath at the injustice of it. Some just get Blown Away, and sometimes, if they can't reassemble a more or less total corpse from the found parts, they will enter it as Missing. "Shitty way to buy the farm," one kid told me.

For me, though, the very worst dead was a Vietnamese who had been killed near a canal in southern Hué, on the road leading to the Hotel Company C.P. The very top of his head had been shaved off by a piece of debris, so that only the back of his scalp remained connected to the skull. It was like a lidded container whose contents had poured out onto the road to be washed away by the rains. Perhaps something had driven over it, or perhaps it had just collapsed during the ten days or more that it had lain there, but I couldn't get the image out of my mind. I spent that afternoon with the commander of Hotel, checking their defense perimeter. He was a great, decent Marine named Captain Christmas. This was not a wealthy section of Hué. The homes were modest, sometimes nothing more than elaborate hootches, but walking around Hotel's positions you could see that the entire section had been planned and landscaped, its arranged pathways decorated with statues, its gardens formally designed. Christmas was very moved by this, and his men had strict orders to respect the homes, the grounds and the people. But when it came to spending the night there, my nerves gave out. The Grunts probably assumed that I was afraid of a mortar attack, which was ridiculous since one could be and usually was mortared almost anywhere in Hué at any time. It was that dead out there with his hinged scalp. I knew that if I stayed here he would drift in over me that night, grinning and dripping, all rot and green-black bloat. After I'd decided to go, I knew that I'd have to pass him again on the way out, and when the time came I forgot my promise and looked back at him one more time. . . .

The General holds up his hand. He's been leaping forward, listening like a crack therapist, and his eyes have gone narrow. He's been tuned into it, all right.

"Yes. Of course," he says. "It's terrible. I didn't really expect it to happen this way. If they'd listened to me then."

"Who? When?"

He shakes his head and a guarded smile comes over his face. Outside, there is a gecko chittering and screaming and a cluster of magnesium flares are settling down over the perimeter beyond Tan Son Nhut. The General's driver, a giant Khmer called Lurch, is sleeping behind the wheel of the jeep down by the curb.

"Sometimes," the General says, "I think I'm the only man in the world who understands this thing."

"It must be very lonely for you."

"Mike, it comes with the job. But you. If you hate this all so much, why do you stay?"

He has me there. I wait a moment before answering. "Because, General, it's the only war we've got."

And he smiles now. After all that talk, we're speaking the same language again.

—AUGUST 1968

# A Rumor of Resistance

PHILIP CAPUTO

On the Pakistani side of the Khyber Pass, along the road that climbs and twists to Torkam on the Afghan frontier, painted stone tablets add splashes of color to the brown Khyber hills. They stand singly in some places; elsewhere, they cluster like tombstones in a crowded graveyard, odd-looking symbols chiseled on their facades: crossed sabers and crossed rifles, wreaths, crowns, and banners bearing names like DORSETSHIRE and GORDON HIGHLANDERS. The tablets are not tombstones but markers commemorating the exploits of the British regiments that played in the rougher innings of what a nineteenth-century English officer called the Great Game.

There is another kind of memorial on the Afghan side of the border, at a place called Gondabak. It is a stark beige-colored hill, no different from all the other stark beige-colored hills except for the extraordinary number of human bones that have been found under its rocks by the people who look for such things. The bones are all that is left of the 44th Foot, which formed the rear guard of a British and Indian army retreating from Kabul in 1842, the last year of the First Afghan War. At Gondabak, the regiment made one of those last stands that later provided raw material for historical novelists and the Hollywood illusion factory. But it was the real thing for the 44th on that winter's day nearly a century and a half ago: Afghan tribesmen overran the regiment, massacring forty-five hundred troops and twelve thousand camp followers and sparing only a handful. One of them was told to return to India and inform Her Majesty's colonial government that the Khyber Pass could be very hazardous to an Englishman's health.

News of the disaster stunned the British; a punitive expedition was mounted and the defeat avenged; but Afghanistan never became part of the empire upon which the sun never set. That is why the Afghans still sing about the battle, why they talk about it in such detail that you would think it had been fought only yesterday. It was their best inning of the Game, the time when they played the opposition to a shutout.

What was the Great Game? The officer who coined the phrase did not live long enough to explain precisely what he meant by it: an Uzbek emir beheaded him while he was on a diplomatic mission in the area now known as Soviet central Asia. Rudyard Kipling, who died in bed at a respectable age and who popularized the phrase, portrayed the Game in terms of intrigue and high adventure in his novel *Kim* and his short story "The Man Who Would Be King." In these and other tales, Kipling created literature from an idea the British politicians of his day regarded as axiomatic: that an expansionist Russia, pushing south through Turkistan, meant to use Afghanistan as an invasion route to the subcontinent and the warmwater ports of the Arabian Sea and the Persian Gulf. In that sense, the Great Game was understood to mean the rivalry between two imperial powers battling for control of central Asia.

Whatever the Game was—intrigue, adventure, geopolitics, or merely subject matter for celluloid spectacle—its main arena was Afghanistan, a country almost as big as Texas, half of it desert, the other half covered by mountains so high you can look *down* on thunderstorms from the peaks and passes. In response to real or imagined threats, the British invaded the country three times—in 1838, 1878, and 1919—and fought enough skirmishes in between to keep several generations of generals in medals, to make journalistic and political reputations (Winston Churchill was a war correspondent in one Afghan campaign), and to give Kipling plenty of background for his poems and stories about the North-West Frontier.

For the Afghans, the wars against the British were just another chapter in a very long history of resistance to foreign domination. They have fought any number of men who would have been their kings: Greeks under Alexander the Great, Mongols, Scythians, Arabs, Englishmen. The Russians had a go at it in the early eighteenth century and were stopped by the Afghans at a place called Darband in 1725. They made another attempt in Napoleon's time, but their army could not conduct such a long-range campaign and was withdrawn. From then on, the Russians relied on subversion, avoiding direct conflict with the Afghans, whom a Western military analyst described to me as "the most ruthless practitioners of mountain warfare in the world." As any newspaper reader now knows, that long-standing policy ended in December 1979, when a Soviet army of nearly one hundred thousand men began rolling into the mountains of the Hindu Kush to crush a rebellion by Moslem tribesmen against a Marxist government that had taken power in Kabul with considerable help from Moscow.

The invasion revived the Great Game. If Kipling were to return to the North-West Frontier today, he would find enough similarities in the situation to give him a sense of déjà vu and enough dissimilarities to leave him a little bewildered. The old fear of a Russian thrust toward India and the Persian Gulf has been reawakened, but that fear now resides in Washington, not London. Afghan rebels are again sniping from the hills (often with weapons their grandfathers carried in Kipling's day), but they are sniping at an enemy equipped with the lethal technology of the late twentieth century—Mi-24 helicopter gunships, MiG-23 jets, and T-62 tanks. And from what I saw during the two weeks I spent with the guerrillas, the Afghans don't stand a chance of doing to the Soviets what they did to the English at Gondabak; they stand a good chance of losing this time around.

I went to Afghanistan in early May, a few days before the Soviets opened an offensive in Kunar and Nuristan provinces, which lie just over the Pakistani border. I landed in Peshawar, the capital of Pakistan's North-West Frontier and the city where the eight major Afghan rebel factions maintain their headquarters. My object was to cross the frontier clandestinely with one or another of the insurgent groups. "Doing a Dan Rather" is what it's called by the newsmen covering the war, although the CBS newsman was not the first correspondent to slip into Afghanistan, just the most famous and the most photogenic. A reporter's dolling himself up like a Moslem tribesman and sneaking over the border sounds like something out of a bad movie, but with Afghanistan closed to Western journalists it was the only way I could get into the country.

I learned in Peshawar that the Afghans are very liberal when it comes to punctuality. They have elevated the late arrival and the broken appointment to an art form, so I was not just surprised but delighted, stunned, amazed, when Tamim knocked at my door in the Khyber Inter-Continental at 7:20 P.M., only twenty minutes late. He was wearing baggy trousers, sandals, and horn-rimmed glasses that made him look not so much like a guerrilla as like what he'd been before the war began: a student of civil engineering. He looked around the room with a nervousness I thought was caused by the atmosphere of the hotel, a standardized plastic palace that wouldn't have looked out of place if it had been moved to Dayton. Walking in, Tamim began to examine my dresser like a man searching for a hidden microphone.

"Where is the *kibli?*" he asked, referring to the arrowlike symbol that points in the direction a Moslem must face during prayer. "All these rooms have a *kibli*. They're usually attached to this furniture."

*That* was the cause of his anxiety. It was time for the prayer before sunset, and my room lacked a *kibli*. I went to the balcony, saw where the sun was setting, and told Tamim to face the wall against which the couch stood. This he did, spreading a bath towel as a prayer rug.

Turning around, I saw Tamim in the mirror above the dresser, kneeling and bowing, praying with an unselfconsciousness no longer possible in the secular West. Faith is one of the few things the rebels have going for them. At its worst, it is a faith that can quickly degenerate into a mindless, murderous fanaticism; at its best, it is a force that gives the insurgents the spiritual strength to face Soviet planes and tanks.

"We have two choices: to become Russians or to fight," Tamim had told me earlier. "This is our way: to fight and become martyrs for our faith. We'll fight with or without the help of other countries. But if we lose in Afghanistan, eventually you will face the same problem: to fight or become Russians."

He was twenty-six years old, had learned his English while studying in Kabul, and was now a spokesman for his faction, which was called Jamiat-Islami. It was his job to answer questions from that curious, not always honorable fraternity of men who earn their living by covering wars in distant places. I had met Tamim two days before while making my rounds of the various rebel headquarters, trying to find a group willing to smuggle me over the border. A previous attempt with Hisbi-Islami, the largest insurgent group, had turned into a comic misadventure that was less the stuff of Kipling than of *Flashman*, George Fraser's spoof of imperial heroics in Afghanistan.

Dressed in my Moslem-tribesman costume (the disguise was necessary to get me through the numerous checkpoints the Pakistanis had set up in the frontier areas), I had ended up in an Afghan refugee camp at Miran Shah, a town west of Peshawar and about twenty miles inside the Pakistani border. My cover had been blown when I'd started photographing four Russian gunships that, by accident or design, were dropping bombs well inside Pakistani territory. It seemed a good story: the Soviets were attacking a neutral country. The Pakistani security men who'd spotted me didn't think so. They arrested me and, after finding that I didn't have government permission to travel in the frontier provinces, packed me off to Peshawar under guard. I was not returned to my hotel, which is the usual procedure the police follow when they catch a newsman mucking around where he doesn't belong. Instead, I was taken to the headquarters of the North-West Frontier constabulary, where two hard-eyed, no-nonsense young men said they suspected me of being a Russian agent who had slipped into Pakistan to stir up trouble among restive tribesmen. Like many American correspondents, I'd grown accustomed to accusations that I was working for the CIA; but this was the first time I'd been charged with playing for the other team. It was only after hours of interrogation, during which I answered questions of the how-many-home-runs-did-Babe-Ruth-hit variety, that I convinced them I was a patriotic American with no ties to the KGB.

Next day, like a salesman calling on his clients, I paid visits to the seven other guerrilla factions, which are grouped loosely—*very* loosely—under the umbrella of an organization named the Islamic

Alliance for the Liberation of Afghanistan. Most of the rebel headquarters are near the old city, in the shadow of a gloomy fifteenth-century fortress that rises above a chaos of bazaars and narrow streets exotic and sinister enough in appearance to convince you that you are indeed in a dangerous place. I found Jamiat-Islami's offices in a row of storefronts on a street where horse-drawn rickshaws jousted with Hondas and Toyotas. At the entrance, a sentry carrying a Kalashnikov rifle gave me a body search. Another escorted me down a gangway to a courtyard surrounded by rooms where guerrillas recently returned from the front lay on straw mats, their feet dirty and callused, their rifles stacked in a corner. (One look at those Mausers and Lee-Enfields told you that if the CIA is arming rebels, as Tass would have us believe, it is doing so by raiding antique gun shops.) *Mujahedin* is what the guerrillas call themselves; depending on who is translating, it means either "freedom fighters" or "holy warriors."

I was ushered into the political information office, where several men lounged on the floor. Removing my shoes, I walked in and joined them. They served me tea, for the Afghans, like most Moslems, put great store in treating guests hospitably. One of the men asked whom I wished to see. I told him I was looking for Tamim, whose name had been given to me by another correspondent. He said to wait; and while I waited, men drifted in and out of the room or sauntered aimlessly in the courtyard. The place had none of the snap and bustle you expect of a military headquarters. The general atmosphere was the same as that in the other offices I'd visited—casual disorganization.

That is, in fact, one of the weaknesses of the Afghan resistance. To this disorganization, add disunity. The mujahedin are, for the most part, feudal warriors who value personal honor and bravery but who have almost no comprehension of the fact that success in modern warfare requires collective action. The Islamic Alliance for the Liberation of Afghanistan is an alliance in name only; it suffers from the fragmentation that afflicts many revolutionary movements, though not for the usual ideological reasons. As far as their political philosophies go, you can say of the rebel factions what George Wallace said of Democrats and Republicans: there isn't a dime's worth of difference between them. They all espouse some form of fundamentalist Islam. The splits in the resistance have been caused by its leaders, gray-bearded chieftains who have lived long enough to acquire enemies lists longer than Richard Nixon's and who have found in the war a good reason for raising private armies with which they can settle old scores. To put it another way, the Afghans have a penchant for blood feuds, and they often tangle with one another when they aren't fighting the Russians. The day I arrived in Peshawar, a bomb exploded in the building occupied by Jamiat-Islami, killing fourteen people. The guerrillas blamed it on Soviet agents, but Western and Pakistani intelligence sources said a rival Afghan group had set off the bomb.

Tamim entered at last. Folding his legs under him, he sat down. After we'd exchanged courtesies, he made a plea for help: "We are not like the Vietcong. They had assistance from two superpowers, China and Russia. We're alone. Why doesn't America help us?"

I couldn't answer him, beyond saying that America wasn't helping because it had a President who seemed unable to decide what color socks to put on in the morning. Tamim responded with a vow that the Afghans would fight to the last man and the last bullet, regardless.

"Our faith is the strongest barrier against Communism," he said. "The Russians have good weapons. We don't. But we have it in the heart, and we capture weapons from the Russians. And when they get out of their tanks and fight us man to man, we always win."

Tamim neglected to mention that the Russians seldom leave their tanks for that very reason; but he was obviously sincere in his belief that bravery, faith, and the Enfield rifle are a match for the T-62 tank and the Mi-24 gunship.

With all that said, I asked Tamim about the chances of slipping over the border with some of his men. After reflecting a few moments, he suggested a trip to Kunar Province, which would require five to eight days' travel. A party of guerrillas was planning to leave for Kunar the day after tomorrow. He would contact me at seven o'clock on the following evening.

Now, in the hotel room, Tamim finished his prayers and sat on the couch. Lighting a cigarette, he announced rather dramatically: "You will be leaving for Kunar in the morning. A Pakistani security man is always outside our headquarters at seven, so you must be there before then to change clothes. Do you have everything?"

I said I did and showed him my kit: the long shirt, baggy trousers, round Chitrali cap, and capelike blanket worn by Afghan tribesmen; a canteen, hiking boots, a camera and camera bag, and a small, lightweight mountaineer's pack containing a sweater, a change of socks and underwear, notebooks and pens, a Swiss Army knife, and a first-aid kit. Tamim approved of everything, the medical gear especially. "You might need that," he said. "We don't have any doctors."

We were seated beside a dirt path, gazing at the mountain marking the frontier we had just crossed into Afghanistan. Mahmud Hezrat rose, adjusting the pack he had fashioned by wrapping a blanket around his belongings and supplies, then looping and knotting the tag ends into shoulder straps. It weighed thirty or forty pounds, but the thinly built Mahmud carried it with the ease of the old mountain man he was.

"Yusef, stand," he said, meaning that our rest was over. Except for certain military phrases, *stand* and *sit* were the only English words he knew. He did not call me by my first name because he could not pronounce it; I'd told him to address me by my middle name, Joseph, which comes out "Yusef" in Pashto, the primary language of the Afghans.

I stood slowly, as did Steve Bent, a twenty-one-year-old British freelance photographer who had decided to come along. We were both wiped out after climbing over the mountain that stands between Afghanistan and Bedjauer, the Pakistani border town where we'd spent the night. Six thousand feet up, six thousand down.

Ten of us had crossed the frontier that morning: seven teenage mujahedin, all unarmed and carrying sacks of flour, clothing, and rifle ammunition; Bent and I; and the nominal leader, Mahmud Hezrat. He was about fifty, with the large nose and high cheekbones of a Pathan (the dominant ethnic group in Afghanistan and northern Pakistan) and a vague moustache that made him look like a taxi driver who cheats on fares. He wasn't like that at all but utterly trustworthy, the only fighting man in the bunch. The other seven, as far as I could tell, had never seen action.

Below the mountain, our small column moved down a dirt track beside a riverbed that was dry except for a trickle of brown water idling down its middle. Terraced wheat fields rose in alternating bands of green and gold on both sides of the river; mud-walled villages stood atop the hills above the fields, these hills climbing toward still higher hills that rose to meet the Hindu Kush, a great blaze of white far in the distance.

It was beautiful country, but the fields and villages were nearly deserted. You didn't need to be a military expert to figure out why: Kunar Province, this part of it anyway, was a free-fire zone. Mahmud described the destruction in the tone of a park ranger naming species of plants for nature-lovers. Pointing at a huge hole blasted out of a mosque, he said, "Roosie tank." At two craters yawning in the middle of the road: "Roosie bomb." At a house with its roof blown off, its timbers charred: "Roosie rocket." At a row of smashed houses on the far side of the river: "Roosie helicopter." Then, sweeping his arm back in the direction from which we'd come: "*Majer, majer.* Pakistan," meaning that the people had fled to the refugee camps across the border. My immediate impression was that the Russians were playing the Great Game with new weapons but in the same old way. Give the wogs a whiff of grapeshot and make 'em run.

By midafternoon we had been on the move nearly eight hours, and an old bullet wound in my leg, which I'd suffered four years earlier while covering the Lebanese civil war, was hurting like hell. Bent and I were parched, hungry, drenched in sweat, and exasperated by the language barrier, which made it impossible for us to find out why we were sailing off into the wild blue without a rifle among us, where we were going, and how long it would take us to get there. We felt a little like captives being led off to an unknown destination.

Sensing our mood and our exhaustion, Mahmud took us to a mud-brick house owned by a tall, strongly built mujahed named Posli Akhbar. I dubbed him "the gay guerrilla" because, to abbreviate a long story, he showed an extraordinary, indeed an unnatural, affection for Bent and me. Put up in Posli Akhbar's guest room, a dark, dirty hovel abuzz with flies, we were fed a lunch of bread, goat's milk, and tea. Then we collapsed on beds made of woven straw and slept through the afternoon.

In the evening, we made a determined effort to find out from Mahmud where we were headed. The conversation was conducted in pidgin English, pidgin Pashto, and sign language. An hour of this produced some answers. Mahmud showed us an envelope with Pashto script on it: it was a sealed message from Jamiat headquarters to a man named Shair Rahman, whom he described as a *turjoman*, a field commander. Mahmud was a courier. Rahman's position was less than two days' march away, at a place called Kattar. After the message was delivered, we would spend a day or two with Rahman's men, see a bit of the war, and then hike back to Pakistan. I felt reassured; there was a purpose to this expedition, after all. I was also taken with the idea of delivering a message to a guerrilla chieftain. Shair Rahman. It was a grand name, something out of Kipling. We never did find him.

The rain clouds sweeping down the mountains made the Kunar River look like a ribbon of liquid lead. Flecked with the white of the rapids, it swept past us with a low, steady roar. Some distance to the northwest, where the sky was still clear, a squadron of Russian gunships skimmed over a ridgeline, then nosed down out of view. A few minutes later we caught the rumble of bombs and the short, sharp bursts of rockets. Crouched among the boulders on the riverbank, we listened to the bombardment, scanned the skies for helicopters flying in our direction, and waited to board the raft for the river crossing. That, not the Soviet gunships, was my immediate concern. The current boomed along at a good ten or twelve knots, but the raft was the sorriest jury-rigged lash-up I'd ever seen—nothing more than a few logs and lengths of scrap lumber tied to inflated goatskins and steered with two oars made of flat boards tied to poles with old rope. But it was the only way the guerrillas could get to the other side; the ferries downstream at Chigaserai and upstream at Shegul were in Russian hands.

One of the boatmen—actually a boy of no more than fifteen—finished blowing up the goatskins with a bellows and waved us aboard.

"*Bismillah ar-rahman, ar-rahim,*" Mahmud said as we shoved off and spun into the current, the fast water lapping over the skins, the boatmen heaving on the oars. Now the other mujahedin joined in the chant. "*Bismillah ar-rahman, ar-rahim.*" The words mean "In the name of God the all-merciful, the all-loving-kind," and are spoken by Moslems before any important or dangerous undertaking. They are the equivalent to the Christian sign of the cross.

The boatmen got the better of the current and swung the raft at an angle across the river. When it bumped against the opposite bank, the rebels opened their arms wide and cried, "*Allahu akbar*" ("God is great").

We scrambled up a cliff to where a dirt road ran through a mile-wide stretch of flat, open country broken by stone fences. It was the closest thing I'd seen to an actual battlefield since we'd crossed the border. Fresh tank tracks corrugated the road. There were old Russian foxholes ringed by rock parapets, a few burned-out trucks, and scattered bits of spent flares and ammunition. Warning that the fields were sometimes shelled and that armored columns often patrolled the road, Mahmud told us to move quickly. Move quickly we did, Bent loping on his long legs while I hippity-hopped on my gimpy one. Mahmud led us on, running in short sprints, then dropping low to look around, then running again. The other seven, by contrast, sauntered along behind us, filled with the ignorance of death that is one of the privileges of youth.

When we stopped to catch our breath, I told Bent, "I'm sticking close to the old man from now on."

"Why's that?" the Englishman asked in his tough Manchester accent.

"Did you see the way he moved? He's not interested in dying for Islam. He wants to stay alive. That gives us a lot in common."

Getting to our feet, we half-ran, half-walked into a gully, then climbed a trail to the outskirts of a village named Shinqaluq. It was an Edenic spot, with pink wild flowers growing at the trailside, wide-spreading chinar trees for shade and concealment, and a cold spring from which Bent and I could fill our canteens. Three mujahedin armed with collectors' pieces were sitting near a small cave they used as an air-raid shelter. It came in handy a few minutes later, when two gunships appeared over a low ridgeline a quarter mile away. They came on not with the rapid *wap-wap-wap* of American hueys but with a throaty growl, flying straight toward us at low speed and at an altitude of no more than five hundred feet. We scrambled for cover. The cave could hold only two or three men; the rest of us crouched or lay flat under the trees. We could hear the measured throb of the rotor blades as the helicopters flew directly overhead, their slowness suggesting the leisurely confidence of predators with no natural enemies.

It was obvious that these Russian pilots weren't afraid of anything the mujahedin could do to them. And with good reason. The guerrilla beside me was aiming his rifle at the aircraft, and I thought, *Jesus Christ, don't shoot that damn thing and draw their fire,* when I saw that his gun was a breech-loading Martini-Henry. Stamped on the receiver were the initials V.R.—"Victoria Regina"—and the date of manufacture, 1878. Happily, the choppers flew on. The pilots either did not see us or, if they did, decided we weren't worth the waste of ammunition. We waited for several minutes to make sure they had gone for good; then Mahmud shouldered his makeshift pack and spoke the words I was already tired of hearing: "Yusef, stand."

At Kattar, which we reached a day and a half later, a band of guerrillas told us that Shair Rahman had packed his bags. He had been blown out of his position by the Russian bombardment we had heard while crossing the Kunar, and had fled into Nuristan, on the far side of a mountain with the haunting name of Nungalam Tangasaar. It rose some ten or fifteen miles away, all eleven thousand feet of it, its peak white above the timberline. Nuristan is the modern name for Kafiristan, the land where Kipling's Daniel Dravot would have been king; and though a small part of me was curious to see it—its inhabitants are a fair-skinned people who, according to a legend too marvelous to be true, are descendants of a lost legion of Alexander the Great—the larger part of me was not so curious as to want to undergo an eleven-thousand-foot climb.

The march from the Kunar River had been an ordeal for Bent and me. There seemed to be only two directions in eastern Afghanistan:

up and farther up. The Russian troops owned the roads and they owned the river valleys, forcing the mujahedin to stick to the high country.

From Shinqaluq we traveled up a ravine to the foot of a dark mountain called Pandasaar. There we rested in the house of a bearded elder and again ate flat, pie-sized loaves of bread washed down with goat's milk.

It was a killing six-hour trek up the eight-thousand-foot Pandasaar. Through chinar and wild mulberry trees on the lower slopes, through walnut and hazel higher up, we climbed a trail that was steep enough in places to make our thigh muscles quiver. At sunset we reached the summit, too drugged with fatigue to appreciate the view, then slogged down a short distance to a wretched little village of pine-log huts.

Our night camp was the local mosque, a drafty shack with an open doorway and paneless windows. While Bent and I stretched out, our thin blankets not much protection against the wind, Mahmud and the others sat around the fire talking to a few local guerrillas, men whose faces had the color and texture of the leather bandoliers that crisscrossed over their chests. The mujahedin seemed indefatigable. I saw then how smart the Russians were to fight this war with helicopters and tanks. The toughest infantry in the world would be no match for the Afghans in these mountains.

In the morning, peppered with tick bites, we started down the other side of Pandasaar, walking quickly over an upland meadow into the shelter of a pine and cedar forest when two Mi-24 gunships buzzed close by. A few miles off, ten more choppers were clearly visible against the white of the distant mountains. One by one, they dipped down to strafe some valley far below. We could not see the bombardment, but we heard it—a low, rolling rumble.

The trail led us through the pines, then past empty villages where water coursing down chutes made of hollowed logs turned mill wheels that creaked on uselessly because there was no one to put grain into the mills; past fields where goats grazed with no one to herd them; past files of refugees, the children carrying chickens and teakettles, the women burdened with infants slung papoose-style over their backs, the men bent double under enormous bundles of rugs, blankets, and odd bits of furniture. One very old man hopped along like a crippled bird, using two tree branches for crutches. The Russian bombardment kept echoing through the mountains with a sound that made me think of oil drums rolling through a tunnel.

"*Khali*," Mahmud said, using the Arabic word for "empty." Then, "*Majer, majer.* Pakistan."

His reaction to what the Russians were doing—emptying Afghanistan of Afghans—wasn't clear from his flat tone of voice. It was very clear when you looked into his dark, deep-set eyes, in which the tension between fury and sorrow created an intensity that seemed capable of burning holes through a man.

On the trek down Pandasaar, we not only saw the effects of Soviet methods but felt them—in our guts. We had eaten nothing since the previous night. So when we reached Kattar and heard that Shair Rahman had fled to Nuristan, Bent and I hoped Mahmud would give up the chase. He didn't. We went on, into a deep gorge where a river flung itself against the rocks, roaring so loudly that we had to shout to make ourselves heard, then up and up a narrow trail until the sound of the river diminished to a whisper.

Small bands of guerrillas, who seemed to be wandering the countryside aimlessly, passed us along the way. They greeted us with calls of "*Salaam aleikum*" ("Peace be unto you") and fed us a mishmash of contradictory information. Shair Rahman had been killed in the bombing. Shair Rahman lived. Shair Rahman had fled to Kabul, not Nuristan. No, Shair Rahman was still in Kunar, in the village of Gumbier, with an army of four thousand mujahedin.

Off we trekked to Gumbier, where we found not four thousand rebels but four. They were sitting outside the house of a local commander, a proud, dignified-looking man with a thick black moustache, a bullet-studded bandolier, and bad news. Shair Rahman had definitely gone to Nuristan; he had established a new outpost at Amirat, a village in the Waigul River valley on the far side of the mountain called Nungalam Tangasaar. To reach Amirat, we would have to scale the mountain by way of a pass below the peak; we would reach the village late the following afternoon, Allah willing and all that.

The mustachioed chieftain put us up for the night. Bread, goat's milk, tea. Bent and I were hungry to the point that we could hardly eat, tired to the point that we could not sleep. Lying on the wicker cots, we listened to some distant shelling and to the guerrillas talking among themselves. We understood very little, of course, but a few words from the English lexicon of war kept cropping up in their conversation. And it occurred to me that these isolated mountaineers had been talking about other things not long ago—about marriages and tribal disputes and crops and livestock and local scandals. Now it was "helicopter," "bomb," "tank," "rocket."

The pass over Nungalam Tangasaar stood at nine or ten thousand feet, where the air was thin and cold. Even with the sun high, we could see our breath and the steam rising from our bodies. Looking down past a meadow covered with yellow wild flowers and Parnassus grass, down to the dark-green timberline, I felt rather pleased with myself for having made it up the mountain. More than pleased—exhilarated. We had begun the ascent at four in the morning and had finished it around noon, Bent and I sucking the air as greedily as thirsty men drink water.

From atop the pass, where the summit pointed upward like a huge white spike above us, we gazed down on Nuristan, on all the wooded ridges, steep ravines, and glass-clear streams tumbling into the Waigul valley, beyond which more ridges rose toward mountains whose peaks were almost as bright as the sun. It was the kind of country that does the same thing to your heart as the sight of a woman you love passionately; but just to remind us that we weren't on some "Valderee, Valdera" hike in the Bavarian Alps, a formation of Mi-24s appeared, silhouetted against the white mountains. The helicopters swooped down and began to strafe the river Waigul.

This attack did not end after an hour or two; it went on all afternoon. Around four, after we had passed through forests where the pines looked a thousand years old, we started down a steep hillside toward Klaigul, a Nuristani village of flat-roofed houses built in tiers against a cliff. A stream rushed beneath it toward the river, above which helicopters circled and dove. Smoke from their bombs rose in columns over the villages hugging the banks of the Waigul. We could hear tank cannons and the helicopters' miniguns, which fire so rapidly that a single burst sounds like the explosion of a drag racer's engine when the starter's flag goes down. Sometimes a guerrilla's machine gun fired five or ten rounds in reply; this told me that the mujahedin had great fire discipline or, more likely, did not have enough ammunition. Even if they had had enough, it would have been virtually useless against the Mi-24, one of the wonders of late-twentieth-century death engineering. The gunship's armor plating makes it a flying tank, invulnerable to all but the heaviest antiaircraft fire; it is armed with a conventional machine gun in the nose, an under-nose minigun (which shoots six thousand rounds per minute), one hundred twenty-eight rockets, as many as four bombs carried in wing-tip pylons, four air-to-surface missiles, and electronic sensor packs for accurate rocket firing in bad weather or rough terrain.

Watching those helicopters flying at a speed and altitude no American pilot would have dared in Vietnam unless he'd had a death wish, listening to the pitifully brief bursts from the rebel guns, I thought, *This isn't a war, it's a Russian training exercise.*

We did not see them at first; they were below us, lazing along almost at treetop level over the stream, their green fuselages camouflaged against the ridge on the far side. Rising as the stream bed rose, the two gunships appeared suddenly at our eye level and less than half a mile off.

"*Kena!*" ("*Get down!*") Mahmud shouted. The others, Bent among them, ducked under a grove of mulberry trees a hundred feet or so downslope. Mahmud and I were caught on an exposed patch of ground where a few low bushes offered the only concealment. The two of us lay under these, keeping our eyes on the helicopters as they climbed toward the pass. They hung in the air for a moment; then—and I swear this is true, though I know it can't be—the lead chopper seemed to shudder in the excited way a man-o'-war bird shudders just before it swoops down on a school of fish. All right, I was imagining things, hallucinating perhaps—stress and exhaustion do funny things to your brain chemistry—but I can still see that tremor passing through the helicopter the instant before it banked sharply and came down toward us, its rotors flashing in the sun.

Mahmud started to pray. "*Bismillah ar-rahman, ar-rahim.*" He gestured to me to cover my watch with my sleeve so that it wouldn't reflect the sunlight. Both gunships were closing in now low enough for us to see the barrels of both the nose gun and the minigun under the nose. "*Bismillah ar-rahman, ar-rahim.*" Mahmud's praying had become frantic, a desperate appeal, a garble of words in which I could only make out "*Allah.*" Allah, Allah, Allah. The gunships drifted overhead; any slower and they would have been hovering. Miniguns, rocket pods, bomb racks, sensor packs. The whole nine yards. Six thousand rounds a minute. A one-second burst would turn a man into something resembling dog food. And if it had to happen, I hoped it would happen that way—quickly. The only thing I wanted less than to be killed in Afghanistan was to be seriously wounded in Afghanistan. The mujahedin are waging partisan warfare on the thinnest of shoestrings. Not enough modern weapons, not enough ammunition, and, as Tamim had told me, no doctors. No medevacs, either. The injured are evacuated on muleback or camelback. Few survive the trip out. For most, it is slow death.

Mahmud continued to send up his fervent prayers. The choppers were straight overhead, their turbos making a pulsing whine. I don't know if Allah was listening, but the gunships abruptly made a tight turn and headed back toward the Waigul. That river was as far as I cared to go. Mahmud, however, remained faithful to his mission and led us on to Klaigul, which was a mile farther.

We saw our first Nuristanis there. Some were as dark as the Pathans, but others looked as English as the blond, six-foot Bent. Despite the helicopters buzzing nearby and the bombs falling only two miles away, the local mujahedin commander, a twenty-two-year-old ex-teacher who spoke English, took us into his house and treated us with the usual hospitality. We asked our host if he could help by guiding us to Amirat. He shook his head. The Soviet attack was concentrating on Amirat. It was much too dangerous to go there. If Shair Rahman wasn't dead, he was on the run to somewhere.

That was it as far as I was concerned. We had chased this phantom Rahman for four days, often marching fourteen hours a day. We had gone far enough. Using the local commander as an interpreter, I told Mahmud that. Much to my relief, and Bent's as well, he agreed. Gesturing toward the Waigul, he said that the mujahedin there were finished. He had done the best he could; to go on would be foolhardy. In the morning we would start the return trip to Pakistan.

We ended up back on Pandasaar four days later, with plenty of company. Blankets wrapped around our shoulders against the chill, Bent and I sat awaiting our turn to move. In front of us, a file of refugees struggled up a trail toward the crest of the mountain. The men were carrying bundles of mattresses and sheepskins on their backs, bundles that looked big enough to crumple a mule. The women, their silver bracelets and amulets jingling, shambled along, some with infants held to their breasts. Those children old enough to walk walked, as they had been walking since they'd left Nuristan, on bare feet over rocky trails that bit and slashed their skin. They were all going up the mountain: men, women, and kids, the old and the sick, about a thousand people altogether. Bent and I watched, awed by their endurance.

We had left Klaigul and climbed for six hours to another village, where we spent a cold, unhappy night sleeping in a cave. Next morning, with Russian mortar shells thudding in the valley below, the villagers decided they would go with us. They packed whatever could be carried and left everything else behind. One headman ran up to me, pointing at a helicopter with one hand and waving a .303 Enfield cartridge in my face with the other. He shouted in Pashto, but I understood his meaning clearly enough: he and the others were fleeing because those .303s were no defense against the technology and the firepower that the Soviets were throwing at them.

Over the next three days, the original column grew from about a hundred people to a thousand. As far as I could tell, this mass evacuation had not been planned. It seemed as spontaneous as a flash flood, with refugees flowing in from the Waigul and an adjoining river valley, the Pech, which had also come under attack. Perhaps a fifth of the column were mujahedin, men who had been designated to guard their clans and families on the long walk to Pakistan. Their presence made the evacuation look like a retreat, and in some ways it was.

We ran from the Russians, then almost ran into them. All during the three-day march from Nuristan we had heard the sound of the Russian bombing behind us. On the morning of the third day, as the column was beginning to climb Pandasaar, that same sound started coming from somewhere in front of us. We were nearing the pine-log village, the one where Bent and I had slept in the mosque a week before, when we passed a mujahedin patrol coming from the direction of the Kunar River. They gave us the worst possible news: Soviet helicopters were attacking the village of Shinqaluq and the ford over the Kunar River; a column of twenty tanks had also moved in to block the crossing point; the tanks' machine guns had opened up on the rafts and had sunk them, killing three guerrillas and four civilians. There were Russians behind us in the Waigul valley, Russians west of us in the Pech valley, and now Russians in front of us on the Kunar. The door out to Pakistan had been closed. We were cut off, trapped, screwed.

The leaders of the evacuation decided that we could do nothing but wait it out. It was midmorning of the following day when a young mujahed entered the stable where Bent and I were housed and squatted beside the fire we had built to ward off the high-country cold. He and Mahmud fell into a long conversation, after which the old man looked toward heaven and muttered a prayer. It turned out to be a prayer of thanksgiving. The tanks had moved, Mahmud explained in the usual mixture of pidgin and sign language. New rafts—launches, he grandly called them—had been brought up. There was, however, one Russian position upstream from the crossing point and another one downstream. The plan was to move the column through this opening and ferry the whole lot across under cover of darkness. The operation would have to be completed by dawn, to avoid being spotted by Soviet gunships.

Feeling relieved and anxious at the same time, Bent and I went outside to await our turn. The column was organized, more or less, into clan and village groups; along with Mahmud, we had been adopted by the family of a dark-bearded mullah named Gulzada. The four of us idled outside the stable while, inside, Gulzada's youngest daughter baked loaves of flat bread for the trip ahead. His wife and his older daughters huddled nearby, veiling their faces with their shawls. Finally Gulzada shouldered his belongings, and Mahmud turned to me and said, "Yusef, stand."

The flat, upright boulders looked like grave markers in the light of the quarter moon. Led by Mahmud, we stumbled down a gully toward the Kunar. The sound of distant mortar and machine-gun fire punctuated the steady, whispering rush of the river. Moving out of the gully, we started over a stretch of flat ground crisscrossed by tank tracks. Gulzada and his family trailed behind. We clambered down a cliff toward the Kunar, its waters black except where the rapids caught the moonlight. Below, we found hundreds of people crowded onto a narrow, rocky bank.

The ferrying operation was already well under way. Those still waiting their turn raised their hands toward the sky and implored God to grant the others safe passage. It was moving to hear their voices rising in the darkness above the noise of the water, to sense the strength of their hard, simple faith.

The operation went on all night: a thousand people ferried over a wild river on rafts buoyed by inner tubes and inflated goatskins. Our turn came a little after five. It was now fully light, and we would be utterly helpless if any helicopters showed up.

The crossing took only a few minutes. When we got to the other side, I embraced Mahmud and thanked him. He, of course, thanked God. He then took a roll of Afghan currency and paid the boatmen. If courage, honor, and faith are the Pathans' principal virtues, greed is their principal vice. The boatmen were charging twenty *afghanis* per head to take the refugees across.

We saw another, uglier example of Pathan avarice four hours later, on the trail back to Pakistan. The river crossing had split the long column into small bands, and the group Bent, Mahmud, and I were traveling with was waylaid by bandits who lived in the Kunar valley. There were only three of them, led by a vicious young man armed with a Russian machine gun. They were levying a toll on travelers passing through their territory. The mujahedin outnumbered the gang ten to one, and could have shot all three. They didn't because, as Mahmud explained, the bandits' kinsmen—dozens of them—would have come down out of the hills and wiped out the mujahedin in revenge.

Mahmud was the only one to ignore the machine gunner's order to move to the side of the trail. Cool-headedly he walked on, telling Bent and me to do the same. We hugged the embankment to stay out of the machine gun's line of fire. The young man kept yelling and we kept walking, until we rounded a bend to what I hoped was safety. Mahmud flopped down and, in gestures, said that his heart was pounding. From what I could understand of his sign language, he had defied the bandits' orders out of fear that they would have discovered Bent and I were foreigners and held us for ransom. I felt greatly relieved, and grateful, and disgusted. The resistance had enough strikes against it without Afghans' using the war as an opportunity to plunder other Afghans. But then, there are profiteers in every war.

We reached the border two days later, after a hard and happily uneventful march. The combined retreat-evacuation had been successful; no one had been lost or injured. Nevertheless, it was a defeat—a small and perhaps temporary one, but a defeat. Five months of fighting had already created a million refugees and a thousand more had been added, a thousand more people who would not be there to give the mujahedin shelter, food, and intelligence. It was, I thought, the Great Game in reverse. A century and a half ago, the Afghans had driven out one foreign conquerer; now another was driving *them* out.

And many of those primitive mountain people were leaving the terrors of war for those of a new and alien way of life. I recall Gulzada's youngest daughter, a girl of about ten or eleven, letting out a hysterical scream while we were walking down a road toward the refugee camp at Bedjauer. A pickup truck was coming toward us. The truck was what had frightened her. She had never seen one before.

—DECEMBER 1980

# My Favorite Teacher

## ROBERT KURSON

One night twenty years ago, my biology teacher picked up a seventeen-year-old hitchhiker named Jefferson Wesley.

Hitchhikers were rare on Chicago's exclusive North Shore, where kids owned Camaros and carried plenty of taxi cash. Even rarer were high school teachers who picked them up. It was midnight. Mr. Lindwall pulled over his yellow Toyota Land Cruiser and told Wesley to hop in.

Down the road, Mr. Lindwall stopped the Land Cruiser and asked Wesley to wait a second, the spare tire was rattling in back. Wesley said cool.

Mr. Lindwall shut off the headlights, exited the vehicle, and popped open the back hatch. Among a pile of tools, he found his hunting knife, which he unsheathed and poked at Wesley's back. He ordered the boy to bend over and locate the hangman's noose by his feet. Wesley found it and tightened it around his neck in the way Mr. Lindwall instructed.

My teacher climbed back into the driver's seat and explained: The seat belts in this jeep don't unfasten. Put your head between your legs. I'm going to tape your hands behind your back. This noose is attached to a series of pulleys. If you struggle, I can pull tight from here and control you.

Wesley now had good reason to believe he'd be killed. The son of a Chicago cop, he'd heard his share of stories, and in those stories kids wearing nooses didn't live.

2

Recently, I wrote a letter to Mr. Lindwall. It's been twenty years since we've seen each other, I said, but I remember you. I'd like to visit, to catch up and talk about our lives.

What I didn't tell Mr. Lindwall was that I'd never stopped thinking about him. While his name had become a sick punch line to anyone who had known him, I still admired him. And I needed to figure out why.

3

Northbrook, Illinois, happens to a person when life is good. The average home costs $340,000; 97 percent of the kids go to college; and when you buy groceries at Sunset Foods, crimson-vested valets scurry to load your car. Northbrook offers gazebos to its picnickers and electronic scoreboards to its Little Leaguers. Seniors who stroll the downtown's winding lanes enjoy handsome discounts on hand-dipped ice cream.

My family moved to Northbrook when I was fourteen. Fashionable welcome ladies helped me pronounce the name of my new street—Michelline Lane—and instructed me to celebrate my lucky transplant into Glenbrook North High School, the crown jewel in this gilded community and one of the top high schools in the country. My personal high school guidance counselor raved about Glenbrook North's high SAT scores and swimming-pool wing and plans for the multimillion-dollar Center for the Performing Arts. Kids who attend GBN, he said, turn out to be doctors, lawyers, CEOs; in short, adults worthy of living in Northbrook.

You've seen Glenbrook North before. Perhaps not in person but in near-documentary form in *The Breakfast Club*, *Sixteen Candles*, and *Ferris Bueller's Day Off*, the films based on the high school by director and Northbrook favorite son John Hughes (Glenbrook North, '68). Show up at Glenbrook North with the wrong folder, the wrong parents, the wrong nose, and you didn't just amuse students, you sickened them.

Feeling like an alien in high school of course did not make me unique, but it felt so at the time. Looking back, it seems like Glenbrook North decided up front to hate me. My Afro was fucked. My voice was fucked. My clothes were fucked. Even my name—Rob, the most innocuous name on the planet—somehow was fucked. In class, on the bus, in Sunset Foods with my mom on Saturday, just the sight of me offended important students—and at Glenbrook North they were all important. They took to blurting "Rob!" into the air whenever I was around, turning the word into the latest euphemism for *asshole*. "You're such a Rob!" one girl squealed to another in the participation-counts algebra class I was flunking for fear of making a peep. I would have given my life to become invisible at Glenbrook North, but at six three, with my gangly limbs and towering Dr. J. Afro sprawling in all directions, that was impossible.

And soon enough, I came around to Glenbrook North's way of thinking. At home, I'd pound the crap out of my little brother because he still thought my hair looked cool or because he continued to dub himself "the Kurs Jr.," in honor of my nickname from the days in the old neighborhood, where people had liked me. I told my mom to go to hell in front of frail relatives when she remarked at a family wedding that I looked handsome, because who can deal with a parent who's too stupid to see what a hundred rich kids can see so clearly every day in school—that I was as ugly as they came?

Against this backdrop appeared Mr. Lindwall, perhaps the only individual at Glenbrook North more out of place than I was. A giant, bearded bear of a man, Mr. Lindwall lived in a trailer, adored the outdoors, and walked apologetically, with shoulders hunched in, as I did. His potbelly was proof that he didn't belong to any of the many area health clubs, and his baggy pants made him look like a kid whose mom shopped outlet and never knew enough to iron. By all rights, GBN students should have eaten this science teacher alive, sent him and his rusty jeep and corny sweater-vests whimpering back to whatever the hell Yosemite National Redwood Sherwood Forest he crawled out from.

Instead, they embraced him, sensed something safe about him. Mr. Lindwall had an intuition about kids. Before learning names, he divined who required extra attention, who was hurting at home, who needed to call him Rick. He listened for underlying messages, and he understood that sometimes a question about amoebas was really a question about alienation.

Almost immediately, an impressed administration asked him to devote time to the school's "alternatives" program, Northbrook code for the outsider-druggie-loser program. To most teachers, it would have been a baby-sitting sentence. To Mr. Lindwall, it was a calling. In weeks, kids who had been thrown away by mom, by life, by Northbrook, were learning science for "Rick" and calling him the greatest teacher they'd ever had.

My first contact with Mr. Lindwall came in the training room during football season, where he taped athletes' ankles and worked out their aches after school. When I needed treatment, he taught me how to stretch to avoid shinsplints as if I actually fit in at Glenbrook North. And he did this despite my football teammates' obvious and noisy disdain for me—made it seem as if he didn't even hear them blurt out "Rob!" when I climbed onto the training table. Other athletes probably figured Mr. Lindwall's lack of eye contact to be his need to concentrate on their ailments. But I knew that downward stare. This was a man who ached with shame on the inside, who prayed that if he couldn't see you, you couldn't see him. That other people adored Mr. Lindwall made him my favorite teacher in the school, because if Mr. Lindwall could still be liked despite not liking himself, there was hope for me, too.

## 4

Able to manipulate the noose around Jefferson Wesley's neck from the driver's seat, Mr. Lindwall turned on the Land Cruiser's headlights, adjusted the AM radio, and pulled onto Route 120. His trailer home near Northbrook was just twenty miles away, but he zigzagged along side roads for more than an hour in order to disorient the boy.

Perhaps Wesley thought of his mother during this ride. He had hung up on her earlier that evening when she told him to stay where he was, not to walk home, she'd come get him. Or maybe he thought of his girlfriend, Donna, whom he'd seen that night. The couple had planned to attend her turnabout dance next week. They were in love.

The Land Cruiser pulled into the trailer park near Northbrook after 1:00 A.M., and Mr. Lindwall parked it flush against his unit's screen door. He stepped around to Wesley's side, opened the door, removed the noose, and placed a hood over his head. Using a screwdriver, he jimmied the rigged seat-belt buckle until the mechanism clicked. It took only moments to drag the boy backward, heels scraping, into the trailer home.

In the living room, Mr. Lindwall laid Wesley on his back, bound the boy's ankles with athletic tape, removed the hood, and taped his eyes shut. Then he asked Wesley questions. Do you have a girlfriend? Do you poke this girlfriend? Do you masturbate? Does it shoot out? Then Mr. Lindwall went into another room to find a screwdriver and some Vaseline.

## 5

During class one day in my sophomore year, Mr. Popular strutted into my face, preened for his sporto buddies, then announced in front of teachers and students that he'd received an "awesome" blow job from my sister. I punched him in the face and knocked him down. I was 210 pounds, he was no more than 130, and he was clearly beat. But I wasn't done. I kicked him in the face with my boot, not once, not twice, but maybe ten, twelve times while his hysterical friends screamed, "Uncool!" and he was bleeding and begging and microscopes were shattering. In this fog of fury and resentment, I might have killed the kid, but teachers locked on to my arms and pulled me off. Only later, in the dean's office, would I realize that I had been sobbing myself while administering this beating.

Mr. Lindwall, who had been teaching in an adjacent room, rushed over, settled a hand on my shoulder, and used his back to shield me from the jeering students; he couldn't abide them watching me cry.

"You're better than that," he said in a low voice. "You're better than them."

I was stunned. Here was an adult, a man everyone loved, whose instinct was to rush past the kid with the broken face to comfort the kid with the broken feelings. I was right about Mr. Lindwall, I thought as I was led away to the dean's office. He and I come from the same place. We recognize each other.

6

Mr. Lindwall undid Wesley's brown corduroys and pushed them to his ankles, then did the same with his own pants. He ordered Wesley to open his mouth, placed his penis inside, and told Wesley to fellate him. Wesley complied, but Mr. Lindwall could not climax; he withdrew his penis and began masturbating. Near climax, he put his penis back into Wesley's mouth and ejaculated. That done, Wesley pleaded, "That's enough, that's enough, please, no more, that's enough."

An hour passed. Mr. Lindwall tied a knot in a sock, stuffed it into Wesley's mouth, and taped the boy's lips shut. Mr. Lindwall rolled the boy onto his stomach and said, "I'm going to do anal intercourse to you now," but found that he could not maintain an erection, a disaster because Wesley might think him a neuter. Mr. Lindwall scooped out some Vaseline, smoothed it over the screwdriver handle, and dragged the tool over Wesley's buttocks, telling him, "Now I'm going to do it to you." He pushed the tip of the handle inside Wesley's anus and said, "Now I'm doing it to you." A moment later, he removed the tool and told Wesley he had changed his mind.

Mr. Lindwall pulled up the boy's pants and dragged him back into the Land Cruiser, where he fastened the seat belt and reaffixed the noose. All the while, he assured Wesley that he would be dropped off near home. Wesley trembled and shook. Mr. Lindwall put the hood over the boy's head and pulled the noose tight until Wesley's head was down between his knees. Mr. Lindwall started the Land Cruiser and zigzagged back toward Wesley's town.

Near Wesley's home, the boy began to mumble and struggle again. Mr. Lindwall pulled the noose tighter and told him to relax, they were almost there. But the mumbling continued, so Mr. Lindwall turned up the radio because the groans were disturbing him. Near Route 120, he pulled off the road to let the boy out. After removing Wesley's hood, Mr. Lindwall saw that the boy wasn't moving. He loosened the noose and heard the boy gurgle, but he knew the sounds were not words. Wesley was dead.

Mr. Lindwall executed a U-turn and drove back to his home, where he lugged Wesley's corpse to the rear bedroom, undressed and unbound it, then bent it into the fetal position before rigor mortis could set in. He bathed the body, covered it with a blanket, waited until daylight, then drove to the hardware store to buy heavy-duty garbage bags. When he returned, he stuffed the naked body into two of those bags until no skin showed, pushed the heap into the Land Cruiser, and set out for a Wisconsin campground. He dumped the body next to a tree. By Monday morning, he was back at Glenbrook North, teaching sophomores about mitosis.

7

A few weeks after Mr. Lindwall shielded me and told me that I was "better than them," he was charged with the kidnapping, sexual assault, and murder of Jefferson Wesley. He also was being investigated, newspapers said, for the kidnappings and sexual assaults of two other young men nearby. Rumors swirled about more possible victims, ten of them even, about foster children he'd molested and maybe other dead Lindwall bodies out there. "Mr. Lindwall has a toothache," teachers and administrators told students who showed up for his class the morning after his arrest. Then, eventually, they assured the dumbfounded kids that Mr. Lindwall was not anything like what he appeared. He was nothing like us.

8

After a few days, Mr. Lindwall answered my letter:

"I'll be happy to visit with you, Bob. Send me some of your recent writings so I can get a feel for the kind of man you turned out to be. Let's get together in a week. I look forward to it very much."

I shove the letter under a pile of bills in a bottom drawer. What am I looking for from this guy? Do I want him to tell me I'm a good boy? Do I need him to tell me that I wasn't as much of an asshole as all those kids in high school said I was? If so, I need more help than Mr. Lindwall can give me.

The letter stays buried in my drawer for a few days. Then I write back. "Dear Mr. Lindwall, tell me when and where to go. I look forward to seeing you, too."

### 9

To visit an inmate at the Joliet Correctional Center, that inmate must add your name to an approved visitors list. The process takes a few days. I spent those days investigating Mr. Lindwall's case. After all these years, I still didn't really know what had happened, whom he had killed and whom he hadn't, what was rumor and what was fact. I called classmates and teachers, some of whom I still despised, who told me about "Rick" as teacher and colleague. I read newspaper accounts and the lengthy trial transcript, including Mr. Lindwall's detailed confession and speech to the court before sentencing. For the first time since 1979, Mr. Lindwall returned to my life in three dimensions.

### 10

Rick Lindwall loved being a kid. If other ten-year-olds in suburban north Chicago in 1954 tempered their play with a rich-kid demurral, Rick was balls-out rough-and-tumble, a jumping bean with permanent scrapes on his elbows and knees who capped two-hour games of cowboys and Indians with mile-long swims.

Rick Lindwall loved being a kid until he was ten, when he contracted rheumatic fever and his life changed. The disease, which affects the heart, forced the boy to bed for a summer and caused him to miss eight weeks of sixth grade. For a cowboy who had slain thousands of Indians, this wasn't too much to handle. But soon after, other parts of his body betrayed him.

At age twelve, Rick developed breasts. Not just the folds of flesh you find on a fat kid, which he wasn't, but boobs, tits, the real thing. Around the same time, his penis began to shrink and his pubic hair stopped growing, until the horrified child began to wonder if he was still a boy. Rick ached to tell his parents but said nothing; he sensed that these developments had something to do with sex, and sex was taboo in the Lindwall home.

Rick managed to agonize silently for a time, but when his shame turned to despair he had to tell his parents. His father was unapproachable, a Milquetoast of a man too timid even to select a restaurant, so he confided in his mother, a domineering pants-wearer in a June Cleaver era. He begged her for help and told her he hated himself. She declared it a "general" problem and urged as much to the family doctor, who complied by treating the boy with shots and a pat on the back. When the breasts grew larger, Mom and Doc shrugged their shoulders; sure, there were still "bumps" under his sweaters, but listen, kids grow out of things, why ever bring it up again?

Nobody knew in 1956 that Rick Lindwall likely had something called Klinefelter's syndrome. People with this condition have an extra X chromosome and a jumble of sexual characteristics and are sexually sterile. A few injections of testosterone would have made Rick feel like a boy again, might have restored his masculine appearance, at least might have helped him withstand what was to come.

At school, Rick became choice locker-room fodder for boys whose own fresh pubic hair had infused them with newfound bravado. "Where's your bra?" "You're in the wrong class," they singsonged in falsetto, pointing him to the girl's bathroom. It was in the locker room that Rick began to consider himself "God's mistake."

Through junior high and high school, Rick kept no friends and managed just a single date. Consumed by shame, he didn't dare allow anyone to know him, because you don't come across a neuter every day. He kept himself close to sports, which he loved, by becoming the high school's athletic trainer, the guy who tapes the football players. Inside the training room, he found himself captivated by physiques, and, here's the curious thing, not in a sexual way, because Rick still didn't know what sexual feelings were, didn't know they existed. He stared at the jocks to gather information about what he should have been.

At Ripon College in Wisconsin, Mr. Lindwall rushed Delta Upsilon. He hadn't made a friend since he was ten, but these guys liked him, actually wanted him. When he discovered that initiation included a Hell Week during which pledges removed their shirts, he quit. For the remainder of college and into the Air Force, peers ridiculed him mercilessly with the familiar "Where's your bra?" Had he not lucked into a medical discharge, he might have turned suicide in the Air Force. Instead, Mr. Lindwall became a teacher.

Northbrook Junior High was thrilled to get Mr. Lindwall. He was smart, knew his science, and didn't take himself too seriously. The administration believed him ideal for that toughest of junior high classes, sex education. Mr. Lindwall accepted the assignment with equanimity, then dashed to the bookstore to cram the basics. He was twenty-seven years old and had never even masturbated.

Kids at the junior high loved Mr. Lindwall, loved that he dug science the way they dug Led Zeppelin, loved the scientific but silly pictures he drew on their notebooks and arms. They told their parents about him, sometimes so fervently that mom or dad would schedule an appointment just to thank him in person. All the while, he knew little about his subject. If a kid asked a technical question, he'd chuckle and suggest, "Let's check the book for that one!" If a student used sexual slang, he'd approach another teacher after school and ask, "How would you answer a kid who wants to know if you can get VD from eating a girl out?" caring little about the VD part but desperate to know what "eating out" meant.

Mr. Lindwall spent seven years teaching sex ed and science at Northbrook Junior High before getting the call to the big leagues, Glenbrook North High School. There, he impressed the administration as he had at the junior high, and soon he was teaching the bad kids in the "alternatives" program and prompting those freaks to issue their ultimate compliment, *He's cool, but I actually learn shit.* He also settled in as GBN's athletic trainer. Coaches loved the guy because he'd give anything for the team; they called him "Lindoo Can-Do," because what better nickname could you hang on a great guy who always said yes? After victories on the road, the coaches would invite Mr. Lindwall out to Tonelli's for pizza and beer, their treat, but he always took the rain check. In the hallways at Glenbrook North, students, staff, and janitors felt good about themselves when Mr. Lindwall smiled at them. But when they invited him to parties, Mr. Lindwall declined, because who knew if it might require removing your shirt? Or discussing dating. Folks got the message. In the nearly ten years Mr. Lindwall taught in Northbrook, only three people, family included, ever visited him at home.

**11**

A year and three weeks after Mr. Lindwall disposed of Jefferson Wesley, he picked up another late-night hitchhiker. Kelly Smith, eighteen, needed a lift to a tavern.

Mr. Lindwall's method was consistent—rattling tire, hunting knife, noose, tape, hood. His application this time, however, was unthorough. He taped Smith's wrists loosely, allowing the young man to stretch the binds during the circuitous ride back to the trailer.

Once inside, Mr. Lindwall didn't tape Smith's ankles. He forced him down face-first on the carpet, then exited the room, saying he needed to move his Land Cruiser. Smith, believing his execution to be imminent, worked a hand free from behind his back and flung off the hood and noose. He could now make out the figure of his captor outside the front door, so he scrambled for a rear exit. When he could find none, he rushed the front door and came face-to-face with Mr. Lindwall, who ordered him to stop.

Smith hurtled past him and into the trailer park's common area, banging on doors and shrieking, "Help! Help! Police!" Moments later, a squad car arrived and took the teenager to the Glenview police station, just two miles from Glenbrook North High School.

When Smith arrived at the station, he was startled to see Mr. Lindwall parking his Land Cruiser. Officers questioned Smith in the basement and made note of his appearance—white athletic tape around one sleeve of his blue windbreaker, inflamed wrists, three punctures in the back of the jacket. Smith told police his story.

Upstairs, Mr. Lindwall told a different version. He calmly explained that after he had picked up Smith, the two had decided to hit the bars and needed to return to the trailer for money. Inside, he had observed Smith stealing various items and naturally had chased the young man away.

When officers asked if they could search the Land Cruiser and the trailer home, Mr. Lindwall said, Of course—I am a respected member of the community and a teacher at Glenbrook North and I have nothing to hide. At his trailer home, Mr. Lindwall urged the police to look around and said, I want to get to the bottom of this as much as you do and I am a good person and a foster parent who takes in wayward boys.

The two officers worked from front to back. In the bedroom, one found a roll of film marked boys, which Mr. Lindwall said had been taken during a high school camping trip, and hundreds of snapshots of boys, which Mr. Lindwall said showed the same. On a kitchen chair, one officer found a rope inside a hood. The rope is for camping, Mr. Lindwall told them. Outside, with dawn breaking, one officer spotted a noose, a knife, and three rolls of athletic tape and asked Mr. Lindwall if he'd like to tell them what really happened.

## 12

By the time Mr. Lindwall reached trial in the summer of 1980, he was suicidal and had done everything in his power to convince the state to execute him. His confessions were detailed, his memory sharp, and his despair complete as he informed investigators of nine to twelve hitchhikers abducted and molested over the past three years. He advised his lawyers, "Don't work too hard for me; I just want to die."

The state charged Mr. Lindwall with the murder, aggravated kidnapping, and deviate sexual assault of Jefferson Wesley, plus the aggravated kidnappings of Kelly Smith and another young man. Dozens of other charges were put on hold to make the trial manageable.

Reporters shoved for position when opening arguments began Wednesday morning, July 16. Mr. Lindwall's mother and brother had visited with him before the proceedings, visited so loudly in fact that a sheriff's deputy found Judge James M. Bailey in chambers and told him, Sad story, Judge, I just overheard that man's family ask him why he doesn't do everyone a favor and just kill himself.

Mr. Lindwall drooped into court wearing a V-neck sweater-vest, the same style he'd worn countless times to cover his breasts at Glenbrook North, even during sweltering Indian-summer days. During the weeklong trial, witnesses would continue to identify Mr. Lindwall in court by pointing to "the man over there in the tan sweater-vest." For his part, Mr. Lindwall would spend most of the trial with his head in his hands.

The state's case was cinematic and lurid. The other young man told of trick seat belts and nooses and an abduction in which he was masturbated by Mr. Lindwall four times over twelve hours, with respite only when Mr. Lindwall retired to another room to watch the Bears game on TV. Prosecutors dragged the seat from Mr. Lindwall's Land Cruiser into the courtroom, and Kelly Smith climbed in, fastened the inescapable seat belt, slipped the noose around his neck, and allowed lawyers to poke at him with a knife the way Mr. Lindwall had. Smith identified for the jury the athletic tape, the hood, the noose that still bore his gnaw marks. The state's psychiatrist swore Mr. Lindwall was sane.

The public defender called Mr. Lindwall's mother, who testified to her son's boyhood days and his loose-fitting shirts and get-out-of-gym notes. Among the character witnesses from the Glenbrook North faculty was the head of the science department, who averred his teacher's sterling character and reputation. The defense psychiatrist declared Mr. Lindwall insane.

Mr. Lindwall testified, too. He swore that he molested boys not for sexual thrills but to process what they "had," to watch their penises "get real hard and point up toward their heads" while his wouldn't, to watch theirs "spurt out" because his didn't. He claimed to abduct boys only on weekends because he didn't want to upset their weekly routine, they were in school. He insisted that he had never been homosexual and never meant to kill Jefferson Wesley. Such claims were routine and always false inside the Cook County Courthouse, but from the melancholy and self-incriminating Mr. Lindwall, they rang true. Medical witnesses agreed that Wesley's death was most likely accidental.

The jury took two hours to convict Mr. Lindwall on all counts. The next morning, headlines blared from the Chicago daily newspapers, and the city wanted blood. Sensing that the judge had been moved by Mr. Lindwall's story, his lawyer opted to have Bailey decide the sentence rather than the jury. Mr. Lindwall would be allowed to address the court first.

"I have the life of Jefferson Wesley on my conscience, and that's something that will stay there until I die. I would publicly like to apologize to his parents for the terror and grief, the suffering I've put them through. And to the other young men who have had the misfortune of crossing my path, I also apologize and hope that the scars that may remain will soon disappear.

"I am not looking for sympathy, nor am I offering excuses. I believe those of you who knew me deserve an explanation. I also believe there is something to be learned from all that has occurred."

Mr. Lindwall described his boyhood, the cruelty he endured as his body changed, and the impossibility of living as a neuter, as God's mistake. He expressed relief that he had been stopped when he had.

"In closing, if any of you have a problem which hurts you to the point of altering how you feel about yourselves, for God's sake don't keep it to yourself. Don't get trapped into believing that no one can help. If the first person you go to does not ease your concerns, then try someone else. Whatever you do, don't surrender to your problem.

"Nothing I say can bring back Jefferson Wesley, or get rid of all the pain and suffering I've caused. But, God, don't let it happen to somebody else."

While Mr. Lindwall spoke, Judge Bailey scratched these notes into his oversized notebook: "He lived a good life." "No prior criminal record." "Bizarre case." Then he announced to the courtroom, "I must say, the defendant is a very unusual one as far as this court is concerned. In ten years as a judge here and four years as a federal prosecutor, you come across very few defendants like this one. . . . Considering the factors involved here, I have no alternative but to sentence the defendant to the Illinois penitentiary on the murder charge for natural life without parole, and sixty years on the other charges, all to run concurrent. That's it."

Expressionless, Mr. Lindwall gathered his papers just as he had after biology class, waited a moment to make sure no one needed him, then disappeared into the Illinois penal system. He was thirty-six years old.

13

I'm thirty-six years old. Today, I go to see Mr. Lindwall.

The mustard stone walls at the Joliet Correctional Center have stood sentry over 140 years of broken men. The prison, landscaped in pillowy bales of barbed wire, will hold Mr. Lindwall until he dies.

At the sign-in counter, a guard checks a list for my name and informs me that, whoa, the dude I'm here to see never gets any visitors. He points me to a locker for my belongings, then searches me in a no-man's holding zone to make sure I'm not stashing anything in my hair or between my toes—visitors are not allowed to bring anything, not even a pencil, into a visit. I'm moved to a waiting area that sells ice cream sandwiches and Joliet Correctional Center T-shirts, then stamped on the hand with an ultraviolet blotch and led through two sets of iron doors and into the visiting room.

I search for the bushy-bearded, 240-pound teacher, but he's not among the tattooed convicts, their weary-faced women, or yelping kids. Only one man sits alone in this room, but he's got a neatly trimmed gray beard and weighs no more than 160 pounds. He wears his prison-issue blue shirt looser than the other prisoners, and he has kind eyes. Mr. Lindwall and I shake hands.

He apologizes for not remembering me. I'm nervous and can only muster a dopey "Wow, you look great." He says he's in the best shape of his life, jogs every day and lifts weights like this, he says, hoisting two invisible dumbbells and grinning. We sit on bolted-down stools at opposite ends of a pizza-sized table. He fills me in on the incidentals of his everyday life. His day always begins with a hot chocolate, then six hours of laundry folding before working crossword puzzles, the harder the better. He resents Oprah for asking guests, "How did that make you feel?" since he's discovered that nothing "makes" you feel any way—you decide how to feel.

Mr. Lindwall is polite and gracious, but then he turns to me. Why are you interested in me? he asks. For a moment, I strain to recapture the sophisticated explanations I'd rehearsed in the car. Instead, I blurt out, "Was I wrong to like you?"

"You weren't wrong," he says after long consideration. "I was a good teacher and sometimes I was a good person. I did a lot of good things. But I led two separate lives."

"Why did you do it?" I ask.

And then he begins telling me about his crimes.

"I'm not homosexual. These weren't sex crimes. I did them to . . . satisfy my curiosity," he says. "The newspapers said that I never touched any of my foster children. Well, that's not true. And I did other . . . things . . . that didn't, let's say, come out completely. If you think someone like me starts committing crimes when he's thirty-one, you're wrong. These things go back a long, long way.

"Did you know I had already resigned from Glenbrook North before I got caught? I did that because I was going to hurt my own students. The things I was doing weren't satisfying me anymore. I knew I was going to take things to . . . another level. If I hadn't been caught, I would have turned into another Gacy. No. I was going to live as a hermit, and I would have been worse than Gacy."

Mr. Lindwall asks if I remember his trial. I tell him that I'd read the papers and, like everyone else, admired his speech to the court.

"That speech was bullshit," Mr. Lindwall says softly. "I remember believing it at the time—I'm not saying I purposely lied. But I had no feeling for my victims, nothing. It took me years in here before I felt anything for victims, mine or anyone else's.

"Remember Sporto Hall? I remember once, this very sensitive kid walked down Sporto Hall and the jocks were merciless, teasing him, and when this guy came back he was in tears. I embraced him, tried to comfort him. I felt so bad for the kid, I just wanted to ease his pain. But even then, at the very moment I was comforting him, I also wanted to hurt him."

After a while, a guard pokes me and says time's up. Mr. Lindwall apologizes for focusing so much on his crimes and says that he'd like me to come back, so perhaps we can get to know each other better. I am a little disoriented and react by trying to buy him a Mountain Dew for the road. He smiles and says, No thanks, it's not allowed.

Mr. Lindwall shakes my hand as I leave. "I feel like you came here for a reason," he says. "I'm not very religious, so I don't mean this religiously. But I feel like you showed up, I mean right now, at this time, for a purpose. I don't know the purpose, but I appreciate it."

In the parking lot, I scribble out notes:

"Smart. Articulate. Soft voice. Honest."

"Was about to hurt own students."

"Says he was ready to become serial killer, worse than Gacy."

"Other crimes no one knows about."

"Remembers wanting to comfort—but also hurt—'sensitive' kid in GBN hallway."

"Still a good guy."

I'm numb as I pull onto the snowy expressway, back to Northbrook, the place I despised, so of course it's where I now live, and I'm wondering what I have discovered about Mr. Lindwall. Wondering if this is finally over for me. My mind is full and racing, skimming across the surface of the experience like a smooth stone. Is it possible to reconcile fond feelings for someone who had been such a positive influence yet had turned out to be capable of such evil? It happens all the time, I suppose—adults in positions of responsibility betraying impressionable children, sometimes much worse. How is a kid supposed to process that? And I'm driving and thinking about our conversation, about his laundry detail and Oprah and undiscovered crimes and crimes that had been planned and not executed, combing, combing for clues. And then suddenly, halfway between prison and home, I take my foot off the accelerator and the car drifts slowly over to the icy shoulder.

*"Still a good guy."*

Eighteen-wheelers blast by, sending up the snow in a dirty swirl, as I sit there staring straight ahead, engine running. I'm thinking about the sensitive student Mr. Lindwall had comforted yet wanted to hurt.

And I know that Mr. Lindwall was talking about me.

—MARCH 2000

# Everest at the Bottom of the Sea

BUCKY McMAHON

You toss in your seaman's bunk and dream the oldest, oddest beachcomber's dream: Something has siphoned away all the waters of the seas, and you're taking a cold, damp hike down into the world's empty pool. Beer cans, busted pipes, concrete blocks, grocery carts, a Cadillac on its back, all four tires missing—every object casts a long, stark shadow on the puddled sand. With the Manhattan skyline and the Statue of Liberty behind you, you trek due east into the sunrise, following the toxic trough of the Hudson River's outflow—known to divers in these parts as the Mudhole—until you arrive, some miles out, at Wreck Valley.

You see whole fishing fleets asleep on their sides and about a million lobsters crawling around like giant cockroaches, waving confounded antennae in the thin air. Yeah, what a dump of history you see, a real Coney Island of catastrophes. The greatest human migration in the history of the world passed through here, first in a trickle of dauntless hard-asses, and then in that famous flood of huddled masses, Western man's main manifest destiny arcing across the northern ocean. The whole story is written in the ruins: in worm-ridden middens, mere stinking piles of mud; in tall ships chewed to fish-bone skeletons; five-hundred-foot steel-plated cruisers plunked down onto their guns; the battered cigar tubes of German U-boats; and sleek yachts scuttled alongside sunken tubs as humble as old boots.

You can't stop to poke around or fill your pockets with souvenirs. You're on a journey to the continent's edge, where perhaps the missing water still pours into the Atlantic abyss with the tremendous roar of a thousand Niagaras. Something waits there that might explain, and that must justify, your presence in this absence, this scooped-out plain where no living soul belongs. And you know, with a sudden chill, that only your belief in the dream, the focus of your mind and your will on the possibility of the impossible, holds back the annihilating weight of the water.

You wake up in the dark and for a moment don't know where you are, until you hear the thrum of the diesel and feel the beam roll. Then you realize that what awakened you was the abrupt decrease of noise, the engine throttling down, and the boat and the bunk you lie in subsiding into the swell, and you remember that you are on the open sea, drawing near to the wreck of the *Andrea Doria*. You feel the boat lean into a turn, cruise a little ways, and then turn again, and you surmise that up in the pilothouse, Captain Dan Crowell has begun to "mow the lawn," steering the sixty-foot exploration vessel the *Seeker* back and forth, taking her through a series of slow passes, sniffing for the *Doria*.

Crowell, whom you met last night when you hauled your gear aboard, is a big, rugged-looking guy, about six feet two inches in boat shoes, with sandy brown hair and a brush mustache. Only his large, slightly hooded eyes put a different spin on his otherwise gruff appearance; when he blinks into the green light of the sonar screen, he resembles a thoughtful sentinel owl. Another light glows in the wheelhouse: a personal computer, integral to the kind of technical diving Crowell loves.

The *Seeker*'s crew of five divvies up hour-and-a-half watches for the ten-hour trip from Montauk, Long Island, but Crowell will have been up all night in a state of tense vigilance. A veteran of fifty *Doria* trips, Crowell considers the hundred-mile cruise—both coming and going—to be the most dangerous part of the charter, beset by imminent peril of fog and storm and heavy shipping traffic. It's not for nothing that mariners call this patch of ocean where the

*Andrea Doria* collided with another ocean liner the "Times Square of the Atlantic."

You feel the *Seeker*'s engine back down with a growl and can guess what Crowell is seeing now on the forward-looking sonar screen: a spattering of pixels, like the magnetic shavings on one of those draw-the-beard slates, coalescing into partial snapshots of the seven-hundred-foot liner. What the sonar renders is but a pallid gray portrait of the outsized hulk, which, if it stood up on its stern on the bottom, 250 feet below, would tower nearly fifty stories above the *Seeker*, dripping and roaring like Godzilla. Most likely you're directly above her now, a proximity you feel in the pit of your stomach. As much as the physical wreck itself, it's the *Doria* legend you feel leaking upward through the *Seeker*'s hull like some kind of radiation.

"The Mount Everest of scuba diving," people call the wreck, in another useful catchphrase. Its badass rep is unique in the sport. Tell a fellow diver you've done the Great Barrier Reef or the Red Sea, they think you've got money. Tell 'em you've done the *Doria*, they know you've got balls. Remote enough to expose you to maritime horrors—the *Seeker* took a twenty-five-foot wave over its bow on a return trip last summer—the *Doria*'s proximity to the New York and New Jersey coasts has been a constant provocation for two generations. The epitome, in its day, of transatlantic style and a luxurious symbol of Italy's post–World War II recovery, the *Andrea Doria* has remained mostly intact and is still full of treasure: jewelry, art, an experimental automobile, bottles of wine—plus mementos of a bygone age, like brass shuffleboard numbers and silver and china place settings, not so much priceless in themselves but much coveted for the challenge of retrieving them.

But tempting as it is to the average wreck diver, nobody approaches the *Doria* casually. The minimum depth of a *Doria* dive is 180 feet, to the port-side hull, well below the 130-foot limit of recreational diving. Several years of dedicated deep diving is considered a sane apprenticeship for those who make the attempt—that, plus a single-minded focus that subsumes social lives and drains bank accounts. Ten thousand dollars is about the minimum ante for the gear and the training and the dives you need to get under your belt.

And that just gets you to the hull and hopefully back. For those who wish to penetrate the crumbling, mazelike interior, the most important quality is confidence bordering on hubris: trust in a lucid assessment of your own limitations and belief in your decision-making abilities, despite the knowledge that divers of equal if not superior skill have possessed those same beliefs and still perished.

Propped up on your elbows, you look out the salon windows and see the running lights of another boat maneuvering above the *Doria*. It's the *Wahoo*, owned by Steve Bielenda and a legend in its own right for its 1992 salvage of the seven-hundred-pound ceramic Gambone Panels, one of the *Doria*'s lost art masterpieces. Between Bielenda, a sixty-four-year-old native of Brooklyn, and Crowell, a transplanted southern Californian who's twenty years younger and has gradually assumed the lion's share of the *Doria* charter business, you have the old King of the Deep and the heir apparent. And there's no love lost between the generations.

"If these guys spent as much time getting proficient as they do avoiding things, they'd actually be pretty good" is Crowell's backhanded compliment to the whole "Yo, Vinny!" attitude of the New York–New Jersey old school of gorilla divers. Bielenda, for his part, has been more pointed in his comments on the tragedies of the 1998 and 1999 summer charter seasons, in which five divers died on the *Doria*, all from aboard the *Seeker*. "If it takes five deaths to make you the number-one *Doria* boat," Bielenda says, "then I'm happy being number two." He also takes exception to the *Seeker*'s volume of business—ten charters in one eight-week season. "There aren't enough truly qualified divers in the world to fill that many trips," Bielenda says.

To which Crowell's best response might be his piratical growl, "*Arrgh!*" which sums up his exasperation with the fractious politics of diving in the Northeast. He says he's rejected divers who've turned right around and booked a charter on the *Wahoo*. But, hell, that's none of his business. His business is making the *Seeker*'s criteria for screening divers the most coherent in the business, which Crowell believes he has. Everyone diving the *Doria* from the *Seeker* has to be Tri-mix certified, a kind of doctoral degree of dive training that implies you know a good deal about physiology, decompression, and the effects of helium and oxygen and nitrogen on those first two. That, or be enrolled in a Tri-mix course and be accompanied by an instructor, since, logically, where else are you gonna learn to dive a deep wreck except on a deep wreck?

As for the fatalities of the last two summer seasons—"five deaths in thirteen months" is the phrase that has been hammered into his mind—Crowell has been forthcoming with reporters looking for a smoking gun onboard the *Seeker* and with fellow divers concerned about mistakes they might avoid. "If you look at the fatalities individually, you'll see that they were coincidental more than anything else," Crowell has concluded. In a good season, during the fair-weather months from June to late August, the *Seeker* will put about two hundred divers on the *Doria*.

Nobody is more familiar with the cruel Darwinian exercise of hauling a body home from the *Doria* than Crowell himself, who has wept and cursed and finally moved on to the kind of gallows humor you need to cope. He'll tell you about his dismay at finding himself on a first-name basis with the paramedics that met the *Seeker* in Montauk after each of the five fatalities—how they tried to heft one body still in full gear, until Crowell reached down and unhooked the chest harness, lightening the load by a couple hundred pounds. Another they tried to fit into a body bag with the fins still on his feet.

But beyond their sobering effect on those who've made the awful ten-hour trip home with the dead, the accidents have not been spectacularly instructive. Christopher Murley, forty-four, from Cincinnati, had an outright medical accident, a heart attack on the surface. Vince Napoliello, a thirty-one-year-old bond salesman from Baltimore and a friend of Crowell's, "just a good, solid diver," was a physiological tragedy waiting to happen; his autopsy revealed a 90 percent obstructed coronary artery. Charlie McGurr? Another heart attack. And Richard Roost? A mature, skilled diver plain shit-out-of-luck, whose only mistake seems to have been a failure to remain conscious at depth, which is never guaranteed. Only the death of Craig Sicola, a New Jersey house builder, might fit the criticism leveled at the *Seeker* in Internet chat rooms and God knows where else—that a supercompetitive atmosphere, and a sort of taunting elitism projected by the *Seeker*'s captain and his regular crew, fueled the fatalities of the last two seasons.

Did Sicola, soloing on his second trip, overreach his abilities? Maybe so, but exploring the wreck, and yourself in the process, is the point of the trip.

"You might be paying your money and buying your ticket just like at Disney World, but everybody also knows this is a real expedition," says Crowell. "You've got roaring currents, low visibility, often horrible weather, and you're ten hours from help. We're pushing the limits out here."

All this you know because, like most of the guys on the charter, you're sort of a *Doria* buff. . . . Well, maybe a bit of a nut. You wouldn't be out here if you weren't. A lot of the back story you know by heart. How on the night of July 25, 1956, the *Andrea Doria* (after the sixteenth-century Genoese admiral), 29,083 tons of *la dolce vita*, festively inbound for New York Harbor, steamed out of an opaque fogbank at a near top speed of twenty-three knots and beheld the smaller, outbound Swedish liner *Stockholm* making straight for her. The ships had tracked each other on radar but lined up head-on at the last minute. The *Stockholm*'s bow, reinforced for ice-breaking in the North Sea, plunged thirty feet into the *Doria*'s starboard side, ripping open a six-story gash. One *Doria* passenger, Linda Morgan, who became known as the miracle girl, flew from her bed in her nightgown and landed on the forward deck of the *Stockholm*, where she survived. Her sister, asleep in the bunk below, was crushed instantly. In all, fifty-one people died.

Eleven hours after the collision, the *Andrea Doria* went down under a froth of debris, settling onto the bottom on her wounded starboard side in 250 feet of cold, absinthe-green seawater. The very next day, Peter Gimbel, the department-store heir (he hated like hell to be called that) and underwater filmmaker, and his partner, Joseph Fox, made the first scuba dive to the wreck, using primitive double-hosed regulators. The wreck they visited was then considerably shallower (the boat has since collapsed somewhat internally and hunkered down into the pit the current is gouging) and uncannily pristine; curtains billowed through portholes, packed suitcases knocked around in tipped-over staterooms, and shoes floated in ether. That haunted-house view obsessed Gimbel, who returned, most famously, for a monthlong siege in 1981. Employing a diving bell and saturation-diving techniques, Gimbel and crew blowtorched through the first-class loading area doors, creating "Gimbel's Hole," a garage-door-sized aperture amidships, still the preferred entry into the wreck, and eventually raised the Bank of Rome safe. When Gimbel finished editing his film, *The Mystery of the Andrea Doria*, in an event worthy of Geraldo, the safe was opened on live TV. Stacks of waterlogged cash were revealed, though much less than the hoped-for millions.

In retrospect, the "mystery" and the safe seem to have been invented after the fact to justify the diving. Gimbel was seeking something else. He had lost his twin brother to illness some years before, an experience that completely changed his life and made of him an explorer. He got lost in jungles, filmed great white sharks from the water. And it was while tethered by an umbilicus to a decosphere the divers called Mother, hacking through shattered walls and hauling out slimed stanchions in wretchedly constrained space and inches of visibility, always cold, that Gimbel believed he encountered and narrowly escaped a "malevolent spirit," a spirit he came to believe inhabited the *Doria*.

But while Gimbel sought absolute mysteries in a strongbox, salvagers picked up other prizes—the *Andrea Doria*'s complement of fine art, such as the Renaissance-style life-sized bronze statue of Admiral Doria, which divers hacksawed off at the ankles. The wreckage of the first-class gift shop has yielded trinkets of a craftsmanship that no longer exists today—like Steve Bielenda's favorite *Doria* artifact, a silver tea fob in the form of a locomotive with its leather thong still intact. A handful of Northeastern deep divers who knew one another on a first-name basis (when they were on speaking terms, that is) spread the word that it was actually fun to go down in the dark. And by degrees, diving the *Doria* and its two-hundred-foot-plus interior depths segued from a business risk to a risky adventure sport. In the late eighties and early nineties, there was a technical-diving boom, marked by a proliferation of training agencies and a steady refinement of gear. Tanks got bigger, and mixed gases replaced regular compressed air as a "safer" means of diving at extreme depths.

Every winter, the North Atlantic storms give the wreck a rough shake, and new prizes tumble out, just waiting for the summer charters. The *Seeker* has been booked for up to three years in advance, its popularity founded on its reputation for bringing back artifacts. The most sought-after treasure is the seemingly inexhaustible china from the elaborate table settings for 1,706 passengers and crew. First-class china, with its distinctive maroon-and-gold bands, has the most juju, in the thoroughly codified scheme of things. It's a strange fetish, certainly, for guys who wouldn't ordinarily give a shit about the quality of a teacup and saucer. Bielenda and Crowell and their cronies have so much of the stuff that their homes look as if they were decorated by maiden aunts.

Yet you wouldn't mind a plate of your own and all that it would stand for. You can see it in your mind's eye—your plate and the getting of it—just as you saw it last night on the cruise out, when someone popped one of Crowell's underwater videos into the VCR. The thirty-minute film, professionally done from opening theme to credits, ended beautifully with the *Seeker*'s divers fresh from their triumphs, still blushing in their dry suits like lobsters parboiled in adrenaline, holding up *Doria* china while Vivaldi plays. A vicarious victory whose emotions were overshadowed, you're sorry to say, by the scenes inside the *Doria*, and specifically by the shots of *Doria* china, gleaming bone-white in the black mud on the bottom of some busted metal closet who knew how far in or down how many blind passageways. Crowell had tracked it down with his camera and put a beam on it: fine Genoa china, stamped ITALIA, with a little blue crown. The merit badge of big-boy diving, the artifact that says it best: I fuckin' did it—I dove da *Doria*! Your hand reaches out . . .

The cabin door opens and someone comes into the salon, just in time to cool your china fever. It's Crowell's partner Jenn Samulski, who keeps the divers' records and cooks three squares a day. Samulski, an attractive blond from Staten Island who has been down to the *Doria* herself, starts the coffee brewing, and eyes pop open, legs swing out over the sides of the bunks, and the boat wakes up to sunrise on the open sea, light glinting off the steely surface and the metal rows of about sixty scuba tanks weighing down the stern.

On a twelve-diver charter, personalities range from obnoxiously extroverted to fanatically secretive—every type of type A, each man a monster of his own methodology. But talk is easy when you have something humongous in common, and stories are the coin of the lifestyle. You know so-and-so? someone says around a mouthful of muffin. Wasn't he on that dive back in '95? And at once, you're swept away by a narrative, this one taking you to the wreck of the *Lusitania*, where an American, or a Brit maybe—somebody's acquaintance, somebody's friend—is diving with an Irish team. He gets entangled, this diver does, in his own exploration line, on the hull down at 280 feet. His line is just pooling all around him and he's thrashing, panicking, thinking—as everybody always does in a panic—that he has to get to the surface, like *right now*. So he inflates his buoyancy compensator to the max, and now he's like a balloon tied to all that tangled line, which the lift of the b.c. is pulling taut. He's got his knife out, and he's hacking away at the line. One of the Irish divers sees what's happening and swims over and grabs the guy around the legs just as the last line is cut. They both go rocketing for the surface, this diver and his pumped-up b.c. and the Irishman holding on to him by the knees. At 160 feet, the Irishman figures, Sorry, mate, I ain't dying with you, and has to let him go. So the diver flies up to the top and bursts internally from the violent change of depth and the pressurized gas, which makes a ruin of him.

Yeah, he should never have been diving with a line, someone points out, and a Florida cave diver and a guy from Jersey rehash the old debate—using a line for exploration, the cave diver's practice, versus progressive penetration, visual memorization of the wreck and the ways out.

Meanwhile, a couple of the *Seeker*'s crew members have already been down to the wreck to set the hook. The rubber chase boat goes over the bow, emergency oxygen hoses are lowered off the port-side rail, and Crowell tosses out a leftover pancake to check the current.

It slaps the dead-calm surface, spreading ripples, portals widening as it drifts aft. Because the *Doria* lies close to the downfall zone, where dense cold water pours over the continental shelf and down into the Atlantic Trench, the tidal currents can be horrendously strong. Sometimes a boat anchored to the *Doria* will carve a wake as if it were under way, making five knots and getting nowhere. An Olympic swimmer in a Speedo couldn't keep up with that treadmill, much less a diver in heavy gear. And sometimes the current is so strong, it'll snap a three-quarter-inch anchor line like rotten twine. But on this sunny July morning, already bright and heating up fast, Crowell blinks beneath the bill of his cap at the bobbing pancake and calculates the current at just a couple of knots—not too bad at all, if you're ready for it.

Crowell grins at the divers now crowded around him at the stern. "Pool's open," he says.

You can never get used to the weight. When you wrestle your arms into the harness of a set of doubles, two 120-cubic-foot-capacity steel tanks yoked together on metal plates, you feel like an ant, one of those leaf-cutter types compelled to heft a preposterous load. What you've put on is essentially a wearable submarine with its crushed neoprene dry-suit shell and its steel external lungs and glass-enclosed command center. Including a pony-sized emergency bottle bungee-strapped between the steel doubles and two decompression tanks clipped to your waist, you carry five tanks of gas and five regulators. You can barely touch your mittened hands together in front of you around all the survival gear, the lift bags, lights, reels, hoses, and instrument consoles. And yet, for all its awkwardness on deck, a deep-diving rig is an amazing piece of technology, and if you don't love it at least a little you had better never put it on. It's one thing you suppose you all have in common on this charter—stockbrokers, construction workers, high school teachers, cops—you're all Buck Rogers flying a personal ship through inner space.

The immediate downside is that you're slightly nauseated from reading your gauges in a four-foot swell, and inside your dry suit, in expedition-weight socks and polypropylene long johns, you're sweating bullets. The way the mind works, you're thinking, To hell with this bobbing world of sunshine and gravity—you can't wait to get wet and weightless. You strain up from the gearing platform hefting nearly two hundred pounds and duckwalk a couple of steps to the rail, your fins smacking the deck and treading on the fins of your buddies who are still gearing up.

Some of the experienced *Doria* divers from Crowell's crew grasp sawed-off garden rakes with duct-taped handles, tools they'll use to reach through rubble and haul in china from a known cache. Crowell gestures among them, offering directions through the *Doria*'s interior maze. Your goal is just to touch the hull, peer into Gimbel's Hole. An orientation dive. You balance on the rail like old Humpty-Dumpty and crane your neck to see if all's clear on the indigo surface. Scuba lesson number one: Most accidents occur on the surface. There was a diver last summer, a seasoned tech diver, painstaking by reputation, on his way to a wreck off the North Carolina coast. Checked out his gear en route—gas on, take a breath, good, gas off—strapped it on at the site, went over the side, and sank like a dirt dart. His buddies spent all morning looking for him everywhere except right under their boat, where he lay, drowned. He had never turned back on his breathing gas.

And there was a diver on the *Seeker* who went over the side and then lay sprawled on his back in the water, screaming, "Help! Help!" The fuck was the matter with the guy? Turns out he'd never been in a dry suit before and couldn't turn himself over. Crowell wheeled on the guy's instructor. "You brought him out here to make his first dry-suit dive on the *Doria*? Are ya *crazy*?" Then the instructor took an underwater scooter down with him, and he had to be rescued with the chase boat. *Arrgh*! Crowell laments that there are divers going from Open Water, the basic scuba course, to Tri-mix in just fifty dives; they're book-smart and experience-starved. And there are bad instructors and mad instructors, egomaniacal, gurulike instructors.

"You will dive only with me," Crowell says, parodying the Svengalis. "Or else it's a thousand bucks for the cape with the clouds and the stars on it. Five hundred more and I'll throw in the wand."

"Just because you're certified don't make you qualified" is Steve Bielenda's motto, and it's the one thing the two captains can agree on.

You take a couple of breaths from each of your regs. Click your lights on and off. You press the inflator button and puff a little more gas into your buoyancy compensator, the flotation wings that surround your double 120's, and experience a tightening and a swelling up such as the Incredible Hulk must feel just before his buttons burst. Ready as you'll ever be, you plug your primary reg into your mouth and tip the world over . . . and hit the water with a concussive smack. At once, as you pop back up to the surface, before the bubbles cease seething between you and the image of the *Seeker*'s white wooden hull, rocking half in and half out of the water, you're in conflict with the current. You grab the floating granny line and it goes taut and the current dumps buckets of water between your arms and starts to rooster-tail around your tanks. This is two knots? You're breathing hard by the time you haul yourself hand over hand to the anchor line, and that's not good. Breath control is as important to deep divers as it is to yogis. At two hundred feet, just getting really excited could knock you out like a blow from a ball-peen hammer. As in kill you dead. So you float a moment at the surface, sighting down the parabola of the anchor line to the point where it vanishes into a brownish-blue gloom. Then you reach up to your inflator hose and press the other button, the one that splutters out gas from the b.c., and feel the big steel 120's reassert their mass, and calmly, feetfirst, letting the anchor line slide through your mitts, you start to sink.

For the thin air of Everest, which causes exhaustion universally and pulmonary and cerebral events (mountain sickness) seemingly randomly, consider the "thick" air you must breathe at 180 feet, the minimum depth of a dive to the *Doria*. Since water weighs sixty-four pounds per cubic foot (and is eight hundred times as dense as air), every foot of depth adds significantly to the weight of the water column above you. You feel this weight as pressure in your ears and sinuses almost as soon as you submerge. Water pressure doesn't affect the gas locked in your noncompressible tanks, of course, until you breathe it. Then, breath by breath, thanks to the genius of the scuba regulator—Jacques Cousteau's great invention—the gas becomes ambient to the weight of the water pressing on your lungs. That's why breathing out of steel 120's pumped to a pressure of 7,000 psi isn't like drinking out of a fire hose, and also why you can kick around a shallow reef at twenty feet for an hour and a half, while at a hundred feet you'd suck the same tank dry in twenty minutes; you're inhaling many times more molecules per breath.

Unfortunately, it's not all the same to your body how many molecules of this gas or the other you suck into it. On the summit of Everest, too few molecules of oxygen makes you light-headed, stupid, and eventually dead. On the decks of the *Doria*, too many molecules of oxygen can cause a kind of electrical fire in your central nervous system. You lose consciousness, thrash about galvanically, and inevitably spit out your regulator and drown. A depth of 216 feet is generally accepted as the point at which the oxygen in compressed air (which is 21 percent oxygen, 79 percent nitrogen) becomes toxic and will sooner or later (according to factors as infinitely variable as individual bodies) kill you. As for nitrogen, it has two dirty tricks it can play at high doses. It gets you high—just like the nitrous oxide that idiot adolescents huff and the dentist dispenses to distract you from a root canal—starting at about 130 feet for most people. "I am personally quite receptive to nitrogen rapture," Cousteau writes in *The Silent World*. "I like it and fear it like doom."

The fearsome thing is that, like any drunk, you're subject to mood swings, from happy to sad to hysterical and panicky when you confront the dumb thing you've just done, like getting lost inside a sunken ocean liner. The other bad thing nitrogen does is deny you permission to return immediately to the surface, every panicking person's solution to the trouble he's in. It's the excess molecules of nitrogen lurking in your body in the form of tiny bubbles that force you to creep back up to the surface at precise intervals determined by time and depth. On a typical *Doria* dive, you'll spend twenty-five minutes at around two hundred feet and decompress for sixty-five minutes at several stopping points, beginning at 110 feet. While you are hanging on to the anchor line, you're off-gassing nitrogen at a rate the body can tolerate. Violate deco and you are subject to symptoms ranging from a slight rash to severe pain to quadriplegia and death. The body copes poorly with big bubbles of nitrogen trying to fizz out through your capillaries and bulling through your spinal column, traumatizing nerves.

Enter Tri-mix, which simply replaces some of the oxygen and nitrogen in the air with helium, giving you a life-sustaining gas with fewer molecules of those troublesome components of air. With Tri-mix, you can go deeper and stay longer and feel less narced. Still, even breathing Tri-mix at depth can be a high-wire act, owing to a third and final bad agent: carbon dioxide. The natural by-product of respiration also triggers the body's automatic desire to replenish oxygen. When you hyperventilate—take rapid, shallow breaths—you deprive yourself of $CO_2$ and fool the body into believing it doesn't need new oxygen. Breath-hold divers will hyperventilate before going down as a way to gain an extra minute or two of painless $O_2$ deprivation. But at depth (for reasons poorly understood), hypercapnia, the retention of $CO_2$ molecules, has the same "fool the brain" effect. It's a tasteless, odorless, warningless fast track to unconsciousness. One moment you are huffing and puffing against the current, and the next you are swimming in the stream of eternity.

Richard Roost, a forty-six-year-old scuba instructor from Ann Arbor, Michigan, one of the five *Doria* fatalities of the last two seasons, was highly skilled and physically fit. His body was recovered from the *Doria*'s first-class lounge, a large room full of shattered furniture deep in the wreck. It's a scary place, by all accounts, but Roost seemed to be floating in a state of perfect repose. Though he had sucked all the gas from his tanks, there was no sign that he had panicked. Crowell suspects that he simply "took a nap," a likely victim of hypercapnia.

So it is that you strive to sink with utter calm, dumping a bit of gas into your dry suit as you feel it begin to vacuum-seal itself to you, bumping a little gas into the b.c. to slow your rate of descent, seeking neutrality, not just in buoyancy but in spirit as well. Soon you've sunk to that zone where you can see neither surface nor bottom. It's an entrancing, mystical place—pure inner space. Things appear out of nowhere—huge, quick things that aren't there, blocks of blankness, hallucinations of blindness. Drifting, drifting . . . reminds you of something Steve Bielenda told you: "The hard part is making your brain believe this is happening. But, hey, you know what? It really is happening!" You focus on the current-borne minutiae—sea snow, whale food, egg-drop soup—which whizzes by outside the glass of your mask like a sepia-colored silent movie of some poor sod sinking through a blizzard.

Your depth gauge reads 160 feet, and you hit the thermocline, the ocean's deep icebox layer. The water temp plunges to 45 degrees and immediately numbs your cheeks and lips. Your dry suit is compressed paper-thin; you don't know how long you can take the cold, and then something makes you forget about it completely: the *Doria*, the great dome of her hull falling away into obscurity, and the desolate rails vanishing in both directions, and a lifeboat davit waving a shred of trawler net like a hankie, and the toppled towers of her superstructure. And it's all true what they've said: You feel humbled and awed. You feel how thin your own audacity is before the gargantuan works of man. You land fins-first onto the steel plates, kicking up two little clouds of silt. Man on the moon.

You've studied the deck plans of the Grande Dame of the Sea—her intricacy and complexity and order rendered in fine architectural lines. But the *Doria* looks nothing like that now. Her great smokestack has tumbled down into the dark debris field on the seafloor. Her raked-back aluminum forecastle decks have melted like a Dalí clock in the corrosive seawater. Her steel hull has begun to buckle under its own weight and the immense weight of water, pinching in and splintering the teak decking of the promenade, where you kick along, weaving in and out of shattered windows. Everything is moving: bands of water, now cloudy, now clear, through which a blue shark twists in and out of view; sea bass darting out to snatch at globs of matter stirred up by your fins. They swallow and spit and glower. Everywhere you shine your light inside, you see black dead ends and washed-out walls and waving white anemones like giant dandelions bowing in a breeze.

You rise up a few feet to take stock of your location and see that on her outer edges she is Queen of Snags, a harlot tarted up with torn nets, bristling with fishermen's monofilament and the anchor lines of dive boats that have had to cut and run from sudden storms. She's been grappled more times than Moby Dick, two generations of obsessed Ahabs finding in her sheer outrageous bulk the sinews of an inscrutable malice, a dragon to tilt against. In your solitude you sense the bleak bitch of something unspeakably larger still, something that shrinks the *Doria* down to the size of Steve Bielenda's toy-train tea fob: a hurricane of time blowing through the universe, devouring all things whole.

On the aft deck of the *Wahoo*, Steve Bielenda, a fireplug of a man, still sinewy in his early sixties, is kicked back in his metal folding-chair throne. He wears his white hair in a mullet cut and sports a gold earring. He was wild as a kid, by his own account, a wiseguy, wouldn't listen to nobody. The product of vocational schools, he learned auto mechanics and made a success of his own repair shop before he caught the scuba bug. Then he would go out with fishermen for a chance to dive—there weren't any dive boats then—and offered his services as a salvage diver, no job too small or too big. When he sold his shop and bought the *Wahoo*, it was the best and the biggest boat in the business. Now, as the morning heats up, he's watching the bubbles rise and growling out *Doria* stories in his Brooklyn accent.

"When you say Mount Everest to somebody," he says, "you're sayin' something. Same with da *Doria*. It was the pinnacle wreck. It was something just to go there."

And go there he did—more than a hundred times. The first time in '81, with a serious *Doria* fanatic, Bill Campbell, who had commissioned a bronze plaque to commemorate the twenty-fifth anniversary of the sinking; and often with maritime scholar and salvager John Moyer, who won salvage rights to the *Doria* in federal court and hired the *Wahoo* in '92 to put a "tag" on the wreck—a tube of PVC pipe, sealed watertight, holding the legal papers. Tanks were much smaller then, dinky steel 72's and aluminum 80's, compared with the now-state-of-the-art 120-cubic-foot-capacity tanks. "You got air, you got time," is how Bielenda puts it. And time was what they didn't have down at 180 feet on the hull. It was loot and scoot. Guys were just guessing at their decompression times, since the U. S. Navy Dive Tables expected that nobody would be stupid or desperate enough to make repetitive dives below 190 feet with scuba gear. "Extrapolating the tables" was what they called it; it was more like pick a lucky number and hope for the best. But Bielenda's quick to point out that in the first twenty-five years of diving the *Doria*, nobody died. Back then the players were all local amphibians, born and bred to cold-water diving and watermen to the nth degree. Swimming, water polo, skin diving, then scuba, then deep scuba—you learned to crawl before you walked in those days.

A thousand things you had to learn first. "You drive through a tollbooth at five miles an hour—no problem, right? Try it at fifty miles an hour. That hole gets real small! That's divin' da *Doria*. To dive da *Doria* it's gotta be like writin' a song," the captain says, and he hops up from his chair and breaks into an odd little dance, shimmying his 212 pounds in a surprisingly nimble groove, tapping himself here, here, here—places a diver in trouble might find succor in his gear.

"And you oughta wear yer mask strap under yer hood," he tells a diver who's gearing up. "There was this gal one time . . ." and Bielenda launches into the story about how he saved Sally Wahrmann's life with that lesson.

She was down in Gimbel's Hole, just inside it and heading for the gift shop, when this great big guy—John Ornsby was his name, one of the early *Doria* fatalities—comes flying down into the hole after her and just clobbers her. "He rips her mask off and goes roaring away in a panic," Bielenda says. "But see, she has her mask under her hood like I taught her, so she doesn't lose it. It's still right there around her neck."

The blow knocked Wahrmann nearly to the bottom of the wreck, where an obstruction finally stopped her fall seven sideways stories down. But she never panicked, and with her mask back on and cleared, she could find her way out toward the tiny speck of green light that was Gimbel's Hole, the way back to the world. "She climbs up onto the boat and gives me a big kiss. 'Steve,' she says, 'you just saved my life.'"

As for Ornsby, a Florida breath-hold diver of some renown, his banzai descent into Gimbel's Hole was never explained, but he was found dead not far from the entrance, all tangled up in cables as if a giant spider had been at him. It took four divers with cable cutters two dives each to cut the body free. Bielenda has been lost inside of wrecks and has found his way out by a hairbreadth. He and the *Wahoo* have been chased by hurricanes. One time he had divers down on the *Doria* when a blow came up. He was letting out anchor line as fast as he could, and the divers, who were into decompression, they were scrambling up the line hand over hand to hold their depth. The swells rose up to fifteen feet, and Bielenda could see the divers in the swells hanging on to the anchor line, ten feet underwater but looking down into the *Wahoo*! A *Doria* sleigh ride—that's the kind of memories the *Doria*'s given him. Strange sights indeed. He knows he's getting too old for the rigors of depth, but he's not ready to let go of the *Doria* yet, not while they still have their hooks in each other.

Up in the pilothouse of the *Seeker*, Dan Crowell is fitting his video camera into its watertight case, getting ready to go down and shoot some footage inside the wreck. He tries to make at least one dive every charter trip, and he never dives without his camera anymore if he can help it.

The more you learn about Crowell, the more impressed you are. He's a voracious autodidact who sucks up expertise like a sponge. He has worked as a commercial artist, a professional builder, a commercial diver, and a technical scuba instructor, as well as a charter captain. His passion now is shooting underwater video, making images of shipwrecks at extreme depths. His footage of the *Britannic* was shot at a whopping depth of 400 feet. When Crowell made his first *Doria* dive in 1990, a depth of 200 feet was still Mach I, a real psychological and physical barrier. He remembers kneeling in the silt inside Gimbel's Hole at 210 feet and scooping up china plates while he hummed the theme from *Indiana Jones*, "and time was that great big boulder coming at you."

In '91, Crowell didn't even own a computer, but that all changed with the advent of affordable software that allowed divers to enter any combination of gases and get back a theoretically safe deco schedule for any depth. "In a matter of months, we went from rubbing sticks together to flicking a Bic," Crowell says. It was the aggressive use of computers—and the willingness to push the limits—that separated the *Seeker* from the competition. When Bill Nagle, the boat's previous captain, died of his excesses in '93, Crowell came up with the cash to buy the *Seeker*. He'd made the money in the harsh world of hard-hat diving.

Picture Crowell in his impermeable commercial diver's suit, with its hose-fed air supply and screw-down lid, slowly submerging in black, freezing water at some hellish industrial waterfront wasteland. The metaphorical ball cock is stuck and somebody's gotta go down and unstick it. Hacksaw it, blast it, use a lift bag and chains—the fuck cares how he does it? Imagine him slogging through thigh-deep toxic sludge hefting a wrench the size of a dinosaur bone. His eyes are closed—can't see a damned thing down there anyway—and he's humming a tune to himself, working purely by touch, in three-fingered neoprene mitts. Think of him blind as a mole and you'll see why he loves the camera's eye so much, and you'll believe him when he says he's never been scared on the *Andrea Doria*.

"Well, maybe once," Crowell admits. "I was diving on air and I was pretty narced, and I knew it. I started looking around and realized I had no idea where I was." He was deep inside the blacked-out maze of the wreck's interior, where every breath dislodges blinding swirls of glittering rust and silt. "But it just lasted a few seconds. When you're in those places, you're seeing things in postage-stamp-sized pieces. You need to pull back and look at the bigger picture—which is about eight and a half by eleven inches." Crowell found his way out, reconstructing his dive, as it were, page by page.

You've always thought that the way water blurs vision is an apt symbol of a greater blurring, that of the mind in the world. Being matter, we are buried in matter—we are buried alive. This is an idea you first encountered intuitively in the stories of Edgar Allan Poe. Madman! Don't you see? cries Usher, before his eponymous house crashes down on top of him. And the nameless penitent in "The Pit and the Pendulum" first creeps blindly around the abyss, and then confronts the razor's edge of time. He might well be looking into Gimbel's Hole and at the digital readout on his console; he is literature's first extreme deep diver, immersed in existential fear of the impossible present moment. But the diver's mask is also a miraculous extra inch of perspective; it puts you at a certain remove from reality, even as you strike a Mephistophelian bargain with physics and the physical world.

You're twelve minutes into your planned twenty-five-minute bottom time when the current suddenly kicks up. It's as if God has thrown the switch—*ka-chung*!—on a conveyor belt miles wide and fathoms thick. You see loose sheets of metal on the hull sucking in and blowing out, just fluttering, as if the whole wreck were breathing. If you let go, you would be whisked away into open sea, a mote in a maelstrom. The current carries with it a brown band of bad visibility, extra cold, direly menacing. Something has begun to clang against the hull, tolling like a bell. Perhaps, topside, it has begun to blow. Keep your shit together. Control your breath. Don't fuck up. And don't dream that things might be otherwise, or it'll be the last dream you know. Otherwise? Shit . . . this is it. Do something. Act. Now! You're going to have to fight your way back to the anchor line, fight to hold on for the whole sixty-five minutes of your deco. And then fight to get back into the boat, with the steel ladder rising and plunging like a cudgel. What was moments ago a piece of cake has changed in a heartbeat to a life-or-death situation.

Then you see Dan Crowell, arrowing down into Gimbel's Hole with his video camera glued to his eyes. You watch the camera light dwindle down to 200 feet, 210, then he turns right and disappears inside the wreck. Do you follow him, knowing that it is precisely that—foolish emulation—that kills divers here? Consider the case of Craig Sicola, a talented, aggressive diver. On his charter in the summer of '98, he saw the crew of the *Seeker* bring up china, lots of it. He wanted china himself, and if he'd waited, he would've gotten it the easy way. Crowell offered to run a line to a known cache—no problem, china for everybody. But it wouldn't have been the same. Maybe what he wanted had less to do with plates than with status, status within an elite. He must've felt he'd worked his way up to the top of his sport only to see the pinnacle recede again. So he studied the *Doria* plans posted in the *Seeker*'s cabin and deduced where china ought to be—his china—and jumped in alone to get it. He came so close to pulling it off, too.

Dropping down into Gimbel's Hole, he found himself in the first-class foyer, where well-dressed passengers once made small talk and smoked as they waited to be called to dinner. He finessed the narrow passageway that led to the first-class dining room, a huge, curving space that spans the width of the *Doria*. He kicked his way across that room, playing his light off lumber piles of shattered tables. Down another corridor leading farther back toward the stern, he encountered a jumble of busted walls, which may have been a kitchen—and he found his china. He loaded up his goody bag, stirring up storms of silt as the plates came loose from the muck. He checked his time and gas supply—hurry now, hurry—and began his journey back. Only he must have missed the passage as he recrossed the dining room. Easy to do: Gain or lose a few feet in depth and you hit blank wall. He would've sucked in a great gulp of gas then—you do that when you're lost; your heart goes wild. Maybe the exit is inches away at the edge of vision, or maybe you've got yourself all turned around and have killed yourself, with ten minutes to think about it.

Sicola managed to find his way out, but by then he must've been running late on his deco schedule. With no time to return to the anchor line, he unclipped his emergency ascent reel and tied a line off to the wreck. Which was when he made mistake number two. He either became entangled in the line, still too deep to stop, and had to cut himself free, or else the line broke as he ascended. Either way, he rocketed to the surface too fast and died of an embolism. Mercifully, though, right up to the last second, Sicola must have believed he was taking correct and decisive action to save himself. Which, in fact, is exactly what he was doing.

But with a margin of error so slender, you have to wonder: Where the hell does someone like Crowell get the sack to make fifty turns inside that maze? How can he swim through curtains of dangling cables, twisting through blown-out walls, choosing stairways that are now passages, and taking passages that are now like elevator shafts, one after another, as relentlessly as one of the blue sharks that school about the wreck? By progressive penetration, he has gone only as far at a time as his memory has permitted. Only now he holds in his mind a model of the ship—and he can rotate that model in his mind and orient himself toward up, down, out. He's been all the way through the *Doria* and out the other side, through the gash that sank her, and brought back the images. This is what it looks like; this is what you see.

But how does it feel? What's it like to know you are in a story that you will either retell a hundred times or never tell? You decide to drop down into the black hole. No, you don't decide; you just do it. Why? You just do. A little ways, to explore the wreck and your courage, what you came down here to do. What is it like? Nothing under your fins now for eighty feet but the mass and complexity of the machine on all sides—what was once luminous and magical changed to dreary chaos. Drifting down past the cables that killed John Ornsby, rusty steel lianas where a wall has collapsed. Dropping too fast now, you pump air into your b.c., kick up and bash your tanks into a pipe, swing one arm and hit a cable, rust particles raining down. You've never felt your attention so assaulted: It is everything at once, from all directions, and from inside, too. You grab the cable and hang, catching your breath—bubble and hiss, bubble and hiss. Your light, a beam of dancing motes, plays down a battered passageway, where metal steps on the left-hand wall lead to a vertical landing, then disappear behind a low, sponge-encrusted wall that was once a ceiling. That's the way inside the *Doria*.

There is something familiar about that tunnel, something the body knows. All your travels, your daily commutes, the Brownian motion of your comings and goings in the world, straining after desires, reaching for your beloved—they've all just been an approach to this one hard turn. You can feel it, the spine arching to make the corner, a bow that shoots the arrow of time. In the final terror, with your gauges ticking and your gas running low, as dead end leads to dead end and the last corridor stretches out beyond time, does the mind impose its own order, seizing the confusion of busted pipes and jagged edges and forcing them into a logical grid, which you can then follow down to the bottom of the wreck and out—in a gust of light and love—through the wound in her side? Where you find yourself standing up to your waist in water, in the pit the current has gouged to be the grave of the *Andrea Doria*. Seagulls screech in the air as you take off your gear piece by piece and, much lightened, begin to walk back to New York across the sandy plane. And it comes as no surprise at all to look up and behold the *Seeker* flying above you, sailing on clouds. On the stern deck, the divers are celebrating, like rubber-suited angels, breaking out beers and cigars, and holding up plates to be redeemed by the sun.

—JULY 2000

# A Distasteful Encounter with William F. Buckley Jr.

GORE VIDAL

During the evening of May 13, 1944, Christ Episcopal Church at Sharon, Connecticut was vandalized. According to *The Lakeville Journal*: "The damage was discovered by worshipers who entered the church for early communion the following day. The vandalism took on the appearance of similar occurrences in New York, according to witnesses. Honey mixed with feathers was smeared on seats, obscene pictures were placed in prayer books, among other desecrations." According to the local police lieutenant "the crime [was] one of the most abominable ones ever committed in the area."

Twenty-four years later, on Wednesday, August 28, at nine-thirty o'clock, in full view of ten million people, the little door in William F. Buckley Jr.'s forehead suddenly opened and out sprang that wild cuckoo which I had always known was there but had wanted so much for others, preferably millions of others, to get a good look at. I think those few seconds of madness, to use his word, were well worth a great deal of patient effort on my part.

Last month, in a lengthy apologia, Buckley reprinted this exchange which, he proudly tells us, "rocked television." For purpose of reference, I must briefly reprise what happened. On the night of August 28, the Chicago Police riot was at its peak. Predictably, Buckley took the side of the police. This was particularly hard to do since, just before we went on the air, ABC had shown a series of exchanges between police and demonstrators which made it quite clear that the boys in azure blue were on a great lark, beating up everyone in sight. Buckley attacked me for defending the victims. That did it. I was now ready for the *coup de grace*. I began: "The only pro crypto Nazi I can think of is yourself. . . ."* As Buckley knew, there was more to come. He created a diversion: "Now listen, you queer. Stop calling me a pro crypto Nazi or I'll sock you in the goddamn face and you'll stay plastered. . . ." It was a splendid moment. Eyes rolling, mouth twitching, long weak arms waving, he skittered from slander to glorious absurdity. "I was," he honked, "in the Infantry in the last war." Starting as always with the last improvisation first, I said, "You were not in the Infantry, as a matter of fact you didn't fight in the war." I was ready to go into that but by then he was entirely out of control and, as our program faded away on much noise, a few yards from us Hubert Humphrey was being nominated for President. All in all, I was pleased with what had happened: I had enticed the cuckoo to sing its song, and the melody lingers on.

For eleven nights we had "debated" one another on television, first at the Republican Convention in Miami Beach and then at the Democratic Convention in Chicago. The American Broadcasting Company had asked us to discuss politics, and so I had spent a number of weeks doing research on the major candidates as well as on my spar-

*There is some confusion about what was actually said on the telecast. The word "Nazi" was first introduced into the discussion by Howard K. Smith who felt that to raise a Vietcong flag in Grant Park was the equivalent to raising a Nazi flag during the Second War. I said it was not the same thing: officially there is no war between us and Hanoi. More to the point, a sizeable minority in the U.S. disapprove of their government's policy and if flaunting a North Vietnamese flag gives them comfort they have every constitutional right to do so (as it later developed, the "flag" raised was underwear). Buckley once again attacked the dissenters; I defended their right to dissent. Unfortunately, two lines of his preceding my "pro crypto Nazi" remark are not clear on the tape. It is my recollection they had to do with communism and the dissenters' relation to the Great Conspiracy. Whatever they were, my own outburst was not a declarative sentence but the beginning of a response to Buckley which was—so notoriously—cut short. Incidentally, I had not intended to use the phrase "pro crypto Nazi." "Fascist-minded" was more my intended meaning, but the passions of the moment and Smith's use of the word "Nazi" put me off course.

ring partner. From past experience, I knew that as a debater Buckley would have done no research, that what facts he had at his command would be jumbled by the strangest syntax since General Eisenhower faded from the scene, that he would lie ("McCarthy never won a majority in any state he ever ran in . . .") with an exuberance which was almost but not quite contagious; and that within three minutes of our first debate, if the going got tough for him on political grounds, he would mention my "pornographic" novel *Myra Breckinridge* and imply its author was a "*degenerate*." This is of course what happened. This is what always happens when Buckley performs. As columnist or debater, he has made sniggering sexual innuendos about a range of public figures, and there is some evidence that what may have begun as a schoolboy debater's trick to save a losing argument has now become morbid obsession.

Study the technique. Discussing the "left opposition" to President Johnson on the Vietnam war, Buckley writes (June 17, 1966, *Los Angeles Times*): "At the eye of the hurricane, taking advantage of the centrifugal quiet of his station, is Bobby, whose way is swept clean by the ravaging winds of his associates. He must of course occasionally lisp into the act. . . ." Now the late Senator's voice was known to us all and he did not lisp. Why say that he did? Because the word "lisp" suggests softness, weakness, and, above all, effeminacy. The mad cuckoo behind the little door could not resist casting a shadow upon the virility of his enemy, just as the cuckoo astonishingly characterized those who demonstrated against the war in New York, October 1965, as "epicene" and "mincing" slobs, thus slyly assigning to Sodom's banner such unlikely recruits as I. F. Stone, Ossie Davis, and Father Philip Berrigan. Charity forbids me mentioning what he has written or said of many others; it is all, however, in the record, as his great idol Joe McCarthy used to say.

In any event, having indicated that he lost the debates to me by "losing his cool," Buckley now hopes to regain by writing what he lost through performing. From where I sit, it looks as if our old friend Hugh Bris is back in town. Apparently Buckley has spent the better part of a year brooding over his disaster. "I tormented myself," he declares in a tone which, for sheer plangency, has not sounded since

Whittaker Chambers sang among the pumpkins. And so, to relieve his torment, at extraordinary length, he has given us the passion of William Buckley "on experiencing Gore Vidal," a document which deserves at least appendix-status in any study of paranoia American Style. It is obvious that Buckley spent a great deal of effort on this work and though it is about as accurate as those newspaper columns he writes in twenty minutes, it is still a most revealing work—though not, as I hope to demonstrate, in quite the way he thinks.

Buckley begins his tirade with, I should have thought, a most dangerous quotation from *The East Village Other* to the effect that Buckley has been found guilty of exercising "faggot dialectic." The implication is plain. The writer thinks that Buckley is a faggot. He is not alone. Norman Mailer even shouted the word "fag" at Buckley during a Les Crane taping: it was cut from the show . . . how innocent television was before Chicago last summer! Now Buckley's private life should be a matter of no concern to *The East Village Other* or even to that vivacious compendium *The Homosexual Handbook* whose listing of well-known degenerates includes, on page 261, "*William F. Buckley*: Writer, professional candidate, Mr. Buckley hosts a television program and conducts it with a flourish and a zest, with such brilliant gestures and hand movement, that Gore Vidal is reported to have called him 'the Marie Antoinette of American politics.' " Now to include Buckley in a list of homosexuals is doubtless slanderous. In any case, every public figure is vulnerable to this sort of rumor, which is why it seems to me odd that someone like Buckley, himself suspect, should be so quick to smear others as "queers." It is a most unbecoming trait in him, and more than a little mad.

Buckley's reaction to being called a "faggot logician" in *The East Village Other* was very peculiar. Quoting with obvious excitement from a series of personal ads in the paper soliciting homosexual partners, he asks, "why is faggotry okay, but the imputation of it discreditable?" This is sophistical, to say the least. When Buckley imputes faggotry to others, he means no compliment; nor were the liberal editors of the paper paying him a compliment by calling him a "faggot logician." Though Buckley is hardly a logician, he is—at his level—a kind of syllogist, and this is what I think he is trying to say:

If liberals think faggotry okay and I call one of them a faggot, why is that wrong in their eyes since there is nothing wrong in being one? Yet when they call *me* one, they imply there is something very wrong about being a faggot.

I believe I can straighten this out for him. People often use terms which are blunt but not necessarily unkind. Agnew's "fat Jap," let us say, or Aristophanes needling Socrates for being a pederast which Buckley reminded us of in his garble of classical history ("I really loved your novel *Julian*," Bill whispered softly to me in Miami as we waited to go on the air) when Aristophanes was himself an apologist for pederasty (read Plato's *Symposium* for the inside story and don't forget you saw it here first!). People have a tendency to be ambiguous about sex and sexual words. Succumbing to his constant vice of name-dropping, Buckley described how at Chicago Paul Newman ticked him off for having shouted "you queer" at me. Buckley described the conversation accurately except for Newman's last statement, "You," said Newman with that preciseness that made him such a formidable campaigner in the 1968 primaries, "are a male c-asterick-asterick-t." Now this did not mean that the heterosexual movie star and father of six in any way deplored the c-asterick-asterick-t. ("The last fantasy which is of course the first reality." *Myra Breckinridge*, p. 245), it just meant that the word "hysterical" derives from the Greek noun for womb, and by his own admission Buckley was a "madman" that night. In other words, it is possible to designate someone as a faggot in one context while, in another, regard the whole subject with a permissive eye. By Newman's standard, Buckley behaved like a male womb, by mine he was hysterical, and since that anomaly—the male womb—ought to be excised, I hope that this present exercise will prove to be a successful hysterectomy.

Just as I had predicted, no sooner had I begun to discuss the various political positions of Nixon and Reagan, Buckley launched an attack on *Myra Breckinridge*, as a pornographic potboiler, even though he now admits in his *mea culpa* that he had not read the book at the time he attacked it. Would that he were always so candid! But his motive was plain. *Myra Breckinridge* is about a homosexual who becomes a woman, falls in love with a girl and then becomes, more or less, a man again. To connect me with the book would mean, to certain simple souls, that the author was a homosexual who had become a woman who had then become a man, etc.—because books are true, aren't they? This is pretty simpleminded reasoning but Buckley himself has a simple mind; it is only his neurosis that is rich and strange. Needless to say, identifying authors with their works is a feckless game. Simply to go by their books, Agatha Christie is a mass murderess, while William Buckley is a practicing Christian. But we are dealing now with tribal emotions. There was nothing that Buckley was not prepared to invoke in order to keep me from establishing him as anti-black, anti-Semitic, and pro-war. After I had pointed out, pleasantly I hope, how much he resembled Myra Breckinridge, particularly in his use of logic, I was able to get the subject back to politics. I confronted him with a series of statements he had made. He then did something I have never seen anyone do on television before or since. He simply denied having written what I said he had written. It was the obverse of Joe McCarthy's, "I have a paper here in my hand." This time I had the paper with each statement neatly checked and dated, and he denied it all. As Goebbels used to say, in somewhat similar circumstances, the big lie is always more powerful than the small plausible one. Still upset over those quotations, he now tells us that he carefully checked his records and the dates I had given him and so on were wrong.

He makes a great to-do over my statement that he favored the atom-bombing of North Vietnam, on the ground that my quote was from the *National Review*, 23 February 1968. Apparently there is no such issue. The quote, as prepared for me by my researcher, and which, incidentally, appeared in Buckley's *On the Right* column of 22 February 1968, reads, "The use of limited atomic bombs for purely military operations is many times easier to defend on the morality scale than one slit throat of a civilian for terrorism's sake." I thought this most illustrative of the Buckley morality scale. But then, denying he had made the statement, he writes, "Could Vidal have had in mind a column, written about that time, though never published in *National Review*, advocating the use of tactical nuclear weapons in Vietnam? Who knows? Yes, I have advocated (and most ardently continue to do so) their use. . . ." He then appeals to the reader: what is he to do with someone who invents facts on television? There is a solemn lunacy about all this. Incidentally, in the text of his article that I was sent by Esquire, *he crossed out the following exchange from our first performance*:

**Vidal:** According to you, it's [the people] made nothing but errors since 1932 with an eight-year interregnum of a man you didn't much admire. In fact you criticized Richard Nixon for his unctuous love and attention of the great general. Unctuous is a rather good word.

**Buckley:** I can account for these errors other than by using the neurotic terms that you're so fetched by. . . .

Buckley crossed out this exchange. Reading it, I wondered why. Admittedly, his response makes no sense—just which of the terms I had used was "neurotic"? A few lines later I understood the reason for the cut.

"Vidal suddenly switched the topic, electing to allude to my 'intimacy' with Reagan and Nixon."

Buckley does indeed like to give the impression that he is "the tablet keeper of history" for the movers and shakers, and his journalism is filled with little anecdotes as to how Reagan introduced him as a speaker one night in California, or "I have had exclusive interviews with Mr. Rockefeller and Mr. Nixon in recent weeks." (*National Review*, 9 April 1968.) I knew, as shall be later demonstrated, that in the words of *The Wall Street Journal*, his ". . . ideological stance seem[s] to have closed off for him, at least for the present, any close public contact with political figures in the major parties." (31 January 1967.)

"In order to do so, [Vidal] assigned to the word 'neurosis' a meaning I have never heard it given, not even by conventional neurotics."

Aware that I had simply played back the word "neurotic," Buckley thought it wise to suppress that part of the dialogue which showed him as provocateur. He then gave the following exchange:

**Vidal:** Since you're in favor of the invasion of Cuba, in favor of bombing the nuclear potentiality of China, since you're in favor of nuclear bombing of North Vietnam, I'd be very worried about your kind of odd neurosis [I meant "neurotic"] being a friend of anybody who might be a President. . . .

Denying everything, Buckley did admit, righteously, that: "I advocated the liberation of Cuba at the same time that Mr. Kennedy ordered the liberation of Cuba."

**Vidal:** No, no, Bill, keep to the record. You said we should enforce the Monroe Doctrine and invade Cuba the sooner the better in your little magazine whose name will not pass my lips.

I then gave the date when he favored an invasion—20 April 1965, four years after Kennedy's attempt at "liberation." ("What Republican leader had done anything to dramatize the need for the restoration of the Monroe Doctrine and *all that it signifies* in terms of *our axiomatic obligation* to our own hemisphere?" [Italics mine] *N.R.* 20 April 1965.) He continues with my testimony, beginning:

**Vidal:** You favored bombing Red China's nuclear production facilities the 17th of September 1965 in *Life* magazine, and you suggested the atom bombing of North Vietnam in your little magazine which I do not read but I'm told about, the 23rd of February 1968. So you're very hawkish, and if both Nixon and Reagan are listening to you, I'm very worried for the country.

Buckley abandons the transcript to observe, "I told him he was misquoting me." Was I? Here is what I quoted from *Life* magazine September 17, 1965: "I have advocated bombing Red China's nuclear production facilities. . . . How do we justify the bombing in terms of world opinion? On the grounds that the good guys of this earth have got to keep the bad guys from getting nuclear bombs."

On television I called Buckley a warmonger because the preemptive strike which he favors against China would lead to a war with China, because the use of nuclear weapons against the North Vietnamese would undoubtedly bring the Chinese into that already disastrous operation, and because his call for an invasion of Cuba is plainly a call for war. I quoted him accurately. And his response? I had invented everything. I suspect that the thought of a Republican administration in 1969 made him not want to be reminded of more zealous days. Always ambitious to be accepted by the nation's establishment, he wanted desperately to appear to be in the placid mainstream of our political life—yet there I was revealing him as an eccentric war-lover of the right. He was not happy. As we left the studio, after the first debate, he whispered to me, "You'll be sorry."

During the next twelve debates, I did my best to discuss the issues. I came to each session armed with quotations from Nixon, et al. Buckley came with a set of prejudices, uncompromised by fact. He was at a constant disadvantage and he knew it. The best he could do was simply say that whatever source I quoted was false. He makes particularly heavy weather in his epilogue of my quotation from Nixon: "I am opposed to pensions in any form as it [sic] makes loafing more attractive than working." According to Buckley, "no politician in the history of the world ever said that, and most probably no non-politician." The second part of this hyperbole is quite mad: most right-wingers say this sort of thing all the time. As for the first part, Nixon did make the statement, and it can be found in *Labor*, 18 October 1952.

When the evidence was too clearly against Buckley, he would again revert to sexual innuendo, attacks on *Myra*, and, finally, Bobby Kennedy. With unexpected naïveté, Buckley thought I would be embarrassed to have the audience reminded that I had written unkind things about Bobby. The opposite is true. And so, contrary to expectation, I enjoyed Buckley's reading of Bobby's letter to him, suggesting that not blood but Gore be sent to the Vietcong. I also noted that at the end of the letter Bobby had scribbled, "And please, when you put it in—please don't twist it." He knew Buckley. Needless to say, this part was not read aloud on the air.

Apropos of the second Kennedy murder, Buckley quotes from an interview I gave to the German magazine *Stern* in which I said that I thought it significant that Sirhan was brought up in Pasadena, a city rich in anti-Jews, anti-blacks, anti-poor. In fact, Orange County, California, is one of the strongholds of the virulent Right Wing. Now obviously Pasadena is not solely responsible for making Sirhan do what he did, but it was certainly a contributing factor. You cannot live unaffected in a community where so many tote guns and talk loudly about how this Commie and that Jew and that nigger ought to be shot. Needless to say, Buckley defends Pasadena. He then quotes various unflattering things I had written about Bobby, asking rhetorically, "Was that the passage that caught the eye of Sirhan?" This is pure Goebbels. But where Buckley is more than usually bird-brained is that I can quote him at equal length in dispraise of Bobby, and I, too, can cry, "Is this the phrase that caught the madman's eye and drove him to kill?"

Yet there is a demagogic strategy in all this. If one is lying, accuse others of lying. On television this sort of thing is enormously effective in demoralizing the innocent and well-mannered who, acting in good faith, do not lie or make personal insults. Buckley has made many honorable men look dishonest fools by his demagoguery, and by the time they recover from his first assault and are ready to retaliate, the program is over. Fortunately, I had Buckley night after night and was so able to remind him and the audience of those facts he found inconvenient. My favorite exchange occurred when we were discussing Eugene McCarthy. At the end of one debate, in which I had claimed that McCarthy was the popular choice of the party, if not of its leaders, Buckley suddenly exclaimed, "McCarthy never won a clear majority in any state he ever ran in. Name one state. Name *one*!" Honking and hissing, flapping his arms, he made it impossible for me to answer that McCarthy had won the Wisconsin primary by fifty-seven percent, a clear majority. The next night, however, I brought up the subject again. Buckley began to writhe. He tried to deny the figures. Then tried to deny saying what he had said. Finally: "But Wisconsin was an uncontested primary and I meant a *contested* primary." I pointed out that since there were other names on the ballot, that meant a contest and, in any case, that is not what he had said, et cetera. Childish. Typical. Appealing? To whom, I wonder.

As the debates continued their turbulent way, Buckley began to show the strain. His hands shook, eyes grew wild, he sweated constantly. As I doggedly and, probably rather boringly, discussed the positions of the candidates, he would go off on wild tangents of his own. I lived in Europe (I also live in America). I was a pornographer. I was making up my newspaper quotations. Whenever he did this, I would reply in kind. Although careful to avoid discussing his personal life, I set out to establish him not only as a war-lover but as a totalitarian, in the general sense of someone with an authoritarian disposition who wishes to use the state for such ends as placing the "chronic welfare cases" of New York City in "rehabilitation centers" outside the city (a proposal made in the mayoralty campaign of 1965). No matter what I said, he denied it. Yet here are some of the quotations:

"I am convinced that Martin Luther King belongs behind bars along with everyone else who conspires to break the law."

After King's death, he wrote:

> *"The martyrdom [King] seemed sometimes almost to be seeking may commend him to history and to God, but not likely to Scarsdale, New York, which has never credited the charge that the white community of America conspires to ensure the wretchedness of the brothers of Martin Luther King. . . ."*

After Adam Clayton Powell was suspended from Congress, the *National Review* printed a lip-smacking comment wittily subtitled, "The Jig Is Up, Baby."

> *"If the entire Negro population in the South were suddenly given the vote and were to use it as a block and pursuant to directives handed down by some more demagogic Negro leaders, chaos would ensue."*

This statement is a paradigm of the Buckley technique, and should be analyzed. If the Negroes are given the vote, and if they all decided to vote as a block, and the leader of the block was Rap Brown, say, then there would be chaos. Conclusion: don't give them the vote. Yet (a) there is no evidence that they would necessarily vote in any more of a self-serving block than those New York Irish cops who voted for Buckley; (b) it is well known that extremist black leaders like Rap Brown have almost no influence among the Southern blacks; (c) how could there be "chaos" when the only choice offered the blacks in a general election like that of 1968 would be Nixon or Humphrey? Perhaps their block support of Humphrey is Buckley's idea of chaos. In any case, the thought of the blacks exercising their constitutional right to vote is displeasing to one who regards the blacks not only of America but of Africa with distaste, even going so far as to characterize Patrice Lumumba and Joseph Mobutu as "semi-savages in the Congo." (*The New York Times*, 23 August 1961.)

In his epilogue, Buckley had some good fun with my statistics on poverty. I am supposed to have said, sometimes there were forty million poor and at other times twenty million, and so on.

The point to throwing doubt on my statistics (supplied by the Department of Health, Education and Welfare) was to give the impression that poverty is really not much of a problem. But then Buckley's attitude toward the poor is singularly cruel. "It is estimated that in New York one half of the chronically poor are disorganized poor, who cannot be persuaded even to flush their own toilets." (*N.R.*, 4 June 1968.) He also affects not to understand my reference to garbage thrown out of the windows of Harlem. I was not able to complete the sentence on television. But here it is. During a television exchange with Buckley, James Baldwin blamed the white owners of the black slums for their condition. Buckley's response: And I suppose the white landlords go pitty-pat uptown and throw the garbage out the windows.

I first became aware of the Buckleys as a family when I was running for Congress as a Democrat in upstate New York, close to Sharon, Connecticut, where the Buckleys live. Campaigning in Amenia (a town I carried) I heard a good deal about the family, none of it flattering. Until then, I had been vaguely aware of someone called

William F. Buckley Jr. who had written an attack on the faculty of Yale's "intellectual drive toward agnosticism and collectivism," a defense of Joe McCarthy and McCarthyism as "a movement around which men of goodwill and stern morality can close ranks," and who edited an unsuccessful magazine called *National Review* (according to *The Wall Street Journal*, January 31, 1967, between 1955 and 1964, the operating deficit was $2,181,000; it is now more). I had dismissed him as a sort of Right Wing Liberace.

Then, on a January night in 1962, on *The Jack Paar Show*, there was a discussion of the Right Wing. I mentioned Buckley in a half sentence, something to do with his dismissal of Pope John's encyclical *Mater et Magistra* as "a venture in triviality." Buckley was not mentioned again. Then, unfortunately, this was the opportunity he had been waiting for, according to Buckley, "Paar was evidently pressured to invite me to reply." Needless to say, Paar was not seriously "pressured" by anyone except Buckley who rang him up and asked for "equal time." Buckley had now managed to get himself on national television. It was a heady moment. The fact that Paar cut him up badly made no difference. Buckley had finally hit the big time as a TV entertainer, and that was all that mattered. It is a source of some pain to me that, unwittingly, I helped Buckley lose his richly deserved anonymity.

We met for the first time on David Susskind's program of September 23, 1962. For two hours, we debated. I had been reluctant to appear with Buckley on the ground that simply to sit next to him would make me look the same sort of nut of the Left Wing that he was of the Right. But Susskind persuaded me. It is my recollection that the program was dull.

We next met in San Francisco, 1964, during the Goldwater convention. We appeared for an hour on a program moderated by Susskind. Here is Buckley's version of what happened: ". . . .Vidal announced . . . that I had that very afternoon importuned Barry Goldwater to accept a draft of an acceptance speech I had written for him, and that Goldwater had brusquely turned me down, all of this in the presence of 'John Jones,' a Goldwater aide. I told him that I had not laid eyes on Goldwater that afternoon. . . ." I never said

Buckley went to Goldwater . . . in fact, just the opposite. It was, all in all, a fine comic interlude, beginning earlier the day of the telecast, when Douglas Kiker, then of the New York *Herald Tribune*, took Norman Mailer and me to see Goldwater's press secretary "John Jones." What "Jones" said about Goldwater was to be off the record. I could not resist, however, asking what Buckley's role would be in the campaign if Goldwater were the nominee. "Jones" sighed. "That guy! The telephone's been ringing all day, him wanting to talk to the Senator. Then he sent over some stuff for the acceptance speech and I took it in to the Senator, and he said, 'What's all that crap?'" I confess to having prepared a trap for Buckley. Once we were on air, I inquired innocently as to what his role would be in a Goldwater campaign. Buckley looked positively roguish, his *éminence* becoming more *grise* by the moment. I egged him on. He grew more and more expansive about his relations with Goldwater. Hinted at closeness. Then, to my shame, I allowed the trap to shut. I repeated—somewhat paraphrased—what "Jones" had told Mailer, Kiker and me. Buckley raved: it was all lies! The next day "Jones," quite predictably, wrote Buckley a letter denying what he had said and Buckley sent a copy to me with a covering letter to the effect that he never wanted to see me again. I found this sentiment agreeable. In any case, aside from my two witnesses, Mailer and Kiker, events proved me right: Buckley played no part in the campaign of '64, and the G.O.P. national chairman Dean Burch ascribed this to "a matter of personality."

After San Francisco, Buckley tells us he decided not to debate me again and declares that "over the intervening years I had never asked him to appear on *Firing Line* [Buckley's television program]"; according to Buckley, this "exclusion gravelled him." Here we have two misstatements. First, I was hardly "gravelled" at the thought of not appearing on *Firing Line*. Second, I was one of the first people approached to appear on *Firing Line*. As Buckley's luck would have it, the producer of the program rang me while I was giving an interview to Gerald Walker. I turned the producer down flat, hung up, then explained to Walker that one of the regrets of my life was allowing Buckley to use me to get himself attention. Walker recorded all this in his interview, which appeared in *Writer's Yearbook*, 1965.

• • •

Now before we return to Chicago and the crack-up, I think I should answer certain charges Buckley has made about my work. I am, apparently, such a dedicated proselytizer for homosexuality that I have, in the words of *National Review*'s daintiest hack, produced in *Romulus* (a play taken from Dürrenmatt about the last Roman emperor) ". . . the most offensive instance of 'inside theatre' . . . effeminate. . . ." In actual fact, there is nothing "effeminate" about the play. No character is a homosexual, and the subject is never mentioned. Buckley also quotes New Haven's maven for all drama seasons Robert Brustein as objecting to the play as an "effeminate charade." What can they mean? They mean, simply, that the leading actor, Cyril Ritchard (now a widower, but for years a happily married man) is known as a camp actor—and doesn't camp mean effeminate mean homosexual? Since no one listens in the theatre (or to television), the actual drama went unnoticed. Fortunately, the text can be found with Dürrenmatt's original in a Grove Press edition, and the curious will discover that this "effeminate charade" is a thoughtful meditation on power and responsibility, and makes no mention of sex of any kind. The *N.R.* writer also tells us that "[Vidal] once wrote a scenario about Billy the Kid . . . as a misunderstood homosexual." (A) Leslie Stevens wrote the screenplay for *The Left Handed Gun*, based upon a television play by me; (B) in neither version was Billy the Kid shown to be homosexual.

Now for *Myra Breckinridge*. As literary critic, Buckley is—how to put it?—lightly equipped. But that does not deter him. He will take on any subject with insolent pluck, confident that his readers are bound to be even more ignorant than he. He is probably right. To support his case against *Myra*, he quotes most selectively, from some of the more troubled American reviews. Now I am not about to explain or defend my work, but since he has quoted at length from such obscure periodicals as *The Critic* (a house organ for the Knights of Columbus?), I shall quote from two well-known English critics.

First, Michael Ratcliffe in *The Times* (London): "Most British reviews have taken Mr. Vidal with total seriousness, up to a point, but to conclude, as some have, that *Myra Breckinridge* is a novel about sex as the source of all ultimate power is greatly to underrate its subtlety. Gore Vidal remains, after all, a proclaimed classicist, a writing professional and a patrician who suffers fools and shamateurs less gladly than ever . . . and it is impossible when reading *Myra Breckinridge* not to sense his impatience that the headlong flight into apparent sexual libertarianism has produced a nightmare of idiotic thinking and cant and even that, as an anthropological phenomenon, sex has become wildly overrated. . . . Mr. Vidal has drawn the line between absurdity and obscenity, between satire and daft thinking with such a delicate exactness that future sociologists will be hard put to distinguish the fantasy from the real thing."

Second, Brigid Brophy in *The Listener*: "The high baroque comedy of bad taste is a rare genre. *Myra Breckinridge* belongs to it and is a masterpiece: the funniest event since *Some Like It Hot* (and some can't recommend more highly than that). . . . The trans-sex fantasy explodes, I suspect, at a level even deeper than the one from which it liberates the homosexual imprisoned in every heterosexual and also, of course, the heterosexual in every homosexual (for what, after all, was a respectable, presumed-exclusive queer like Myron doing taking such an erotically detailed interest in lady film stars?). . . . Because the baroque is so analytically formal, the baroque mode and his baroque subject matter are a perfect metaphor for Mr. Vidal's satiric purpose.

"He finds intellectual sloppiness destructive. He destroys it by an explosive, centrifugal force far more inherently destructive than its enemy, but which he controls and creatively deploys into an artistic form."

In England literary critics tend to write about books for the newspapers; in the United States journalists like Buckley do most of the reviewing, with the result that one gets a good deal of intellectual sloppiness and much moralizing at the Billy Graham level. Muddling *Myra*'s views with my own, Buckley indicates that I prefer homosexuality to heterosexuality. Now I want to make one thing absolutely clear, as Richard Nixon would say: I do not prefer homosexuality to heterosexuality—or, for that matter, heterosexuality to homosexuality. Unhappily, somewhere along the way, those who write for newspapers decided that since I thought homosexuality as *natural* as heterosexuality, I must then hate heterosexuality and love homosexuality. One of the sad characteristics of popular journalism is that what *ought* to be true is true. Contrary evidence is not admitted, including the two million words which I have published in the last twenty-five years, nowhere stating that homosexuality ought to be the preferred form of sexuality. It is true that at one point *Myra* makes a case for homosexuality on the ground that it might help contain the population explosion. That was a joke. Incidentally, though Buckley quotes at length from the scene in which Rusty is raped, he makes no mention of the many pages devoted to Myra's attempted seduction of Mary-Ann and the long and I think quite beautiful apostrophe to the uterine mystery.

> "*But tonight she was subtly changed. I don't know whether it was the snaps at Scandia or the cold bright charm of the powerful Letitia or the knowledge that Rusty would never be hers again but whatever it was, she allowed my hand to rest a long moment on the entrance to the last fantasy which is of course the first reality. Ecstatically, I fingered the lovely shape whose secret I must know or die, whose maze I must thread as best I can or go mad for if I am to prevail I must soon come face to face with the Minotaur of dreams and confound him in the charneled lair, and in our heroic coupling know the last mystery: total power achieved not over man, not over woman but over the heraldic beast, the devouring monster, the maw of creation itself that spews us forth and sucks us back into the black oblivion where stars are made and energy waits to be born in order to begin once more the cycle of destruction and creation at whose apex now I stand, once man, now woman, and soon to be privy to what lies beyond the uterine door, the mystery of creation that I mean to shatter with the fierce thrust of a will that alone separates me from the nothing of eternity; and as I have conquered the male, absorbed and been absorbed by the female, I am at last outside the human scale, and so may render impotent even familiar banal ubiquitous death whose mouth I see smiling at me with moist coral lips between the legs of my beloved girl who is the unwitting instrument*

*of victory, and the beautiful fact of my life's vision made all too perfect flesh."*

While we are on Buckley's favorite subject, sex, I will try to unmuddle his distortion of what I have said about bisexuality. We are all bisexual to begin with. That is a fact of our condition. And we are all responsive to sexual stimuli from our own as well as from the opposite sex. Certain societies at certain times, usually in the interest of maintaining the baby supply, have discouraged homosexuality. Other societies, particularly militaristic ones, have exalted it. But regardless of tribal taboos, homosexuality is a constant fact of the human condition and it is not a sickness, not a sin, not a crime . . . despite the best efforts of our puritan tribe to make it all three. Homosexuality is as natural as heterosexuality. Notice I use the word "natural," not normal. Buckley likes the word normal. It conjures up vigorous Minute Men with rifles shooting Commies, while their wives and little ones stay home stitching hoods. But what is the sexual norm? By definition it is what most people do most frequently. Therefore, the norm is neither homosexual nor heterosexual. The most frequent (if not most preferred!) sexual outlet of most people most of the time is masturbation, making onanism the statistical norm from which all else is deviation. Yet I don't think even Mrs. Portnoy's son would want to make a case for that particular normality.

As for being an "evangelist of bisexuality," I am not an evangelist of anything in sexual matters except a decent withdrawal of the state from the bedroom. There will, of course, always he morbid twisted men like Buckley sniggering and giggling and speculating on the sexual lives of others, and nothing's to be done about them. But the sex laws must be changed. It was Dr. Kinsey who pointed out that if all the laws were enforced, ninety percent of the men in the United States would be in jail. One final point: Buckley quotes an American reviewer who was horrified at my explicit description of a male body (as usual, no mention of the equally explicit description of a female body). To me this reviewer's objection perfectly reflects the sickness of the society we live in. On the one hand, such critics hold that we are made in the very image of God, a bit of proud, primitive lunacy still obtaining in certain Christian sects, and yet, without any awareness of paradox, they also hold nudity to be obscene, the body disgusting, and certain parts of it horrifying. Yet if we are made in God's image, the body must be divine. Conversely, if the body is vile, then its maker must be vile. Unfortunately, our primitives are beyond mere logic. They have their tribal prejudices and find both comfort and glory in their confusion.

"The only pro crypto Nazi I know is you," I said to Buckley on the night of August 28. He tells us that this so maddened him, he went to pieces with righteous anger. Looking and sounding not unlike Hitler, but without the charm, he began to shriek insults in order to head me off, and succeeded, for by then my mission was accomplished: Buckley had revealed himself. There was no need to discuss his anti-Semitic background. He had demonstrated most vividly what I could only have stated. But now that he has seen fit to relive his failure at Chicago, I am now obliged to write what I chose not to say on the air.

William F. Buckley Sr. was a Texan and an oil speculator who made a small fortune and had ten children. Politically, he was a perfect example of what Professor Richard Hofstader has called the "paranoid style" in American political life. A nouveau riche of limited intelligence but powerful prejudices, Buckley Sr. felt that he should have more influence in the country than indeed he had. In this he follows what Professor Hofstader has shown to be a classic pattern. Whenever a member of one of the immigrant groups to the United States moves from poverty to affluence, his first response is a sense of letdown that he is still no closer to the levers of power than he was before. If he is of a paranoid disposition, he will suspect conspiracy; he will blame *them*. The John Birch Society is a particular haven for this kind of malcontent. It seems likely that Buckley Senior felt insufficiently acknowledged. Despite the legend of his great fortune, he was never listed in *Who's Who in America*, *Current Biography*, *Poor's Register of Corporations, Directors, and Executives*, or even the *Social Register*. Like a cut-rate Joe Kennedy, he then decided to compensate through his children. They were taught total conservatism. They were privately tutored. All were sent to England to acquire patrician accents. William Jr.'s did not quite take. The result was a vigorous, highly articulate brood who, in the words of one (John), "are all good conservatives and, thank heavens, we all married conservatives." The family is as devoted to one another as the Kennedys, and on the important issues, they think alike. When Buckley Junior was attacking the faculty at Yale for "collectivist" tendencies, two sisters opened up separate fronts at Smith and Vassar.

Though Buckley Jr. is usually candid about his love of war and distaste for the blacks, he is extremely wary of appearing anti-Semitic. In this he resembles Robert Welch, though not the late irrepressible George Lincoln Rockwell. Very seldom does he betray his actual feelings as he did on Tex McCrary's radio program 25 September 1964. ". . . they [the Jews] tend to construct an engaging political myth, centered around the Hitlerian experience, which more or less suggests that Hitler was the embodiment of the ultra-Right, and that the true enemies of Hitler, many of them—that the true enemies were, in fact, many of them Communists during the early Thirties. And under the circumstances they, I think, emotionally feel a kind of toleration for Communist excesses in this country. . . ." Arnold Forster of the Anti-Defamation League of B'nai B'rith answered Buckley four days later on the same program. To Buckley's charge that Jews feel a kind of toleration for Communist excesses in this country, Forster replied: "That of course, Tex, is nothing more than insidious slander. . . . And notice how easy he finds it to generalize, Tex, about Jews. Millions of human beings in one group." The question of course is why does Buckley find it so easy insidiously to slander, in Forster's phrases, millions of human beings? I know the answer and Buckley, knowing that I knew it at Chicago, terrified that I would discuss it on the air, saw fit to interrupt me with calculated hysterics.

On March 4, 1944, Mr. and Mrs. Sully Berman bought a house on the green at Sharon. The Bermans were Jews. Now in Sharon, there was a gentleman's agreement to keep out Jews. Needless to say, the arrival of the Bermans was considered by the village gentry to be a betrayal of that agreement, and the town's wrath was directed not so much at the Bermans as at the real-estate agent who had done such an un-Christian thing as to admit Jews to Sharon. The agent was Mrs. Francis James Meadows Cotter. Her husband was the Episcopal minister at Sharon, and Rector of Christ Church. The Cotters were a well-liked family, and their two daughters were contemporaries and friends of the young Buckleys. Buckley Sr., however, was a most unforgiving man. He complained loudly and bitterly about what Mrs. Cotter had done and, like Henry II, vowed revenge. Shortly thereafter, on Saturday, May 13, Christ Episcopal Church was vandalized. Honey and feathers were poured over the velvet cushions of the pews. Prayer books were defaced. Obscene photographs were inserted in the Bible.

There was considerable uproar the next morning when the Reverend Cotter and his flock assembled. Who had done it? The high-spirited Buckleys were immediately suspected. Acting on a tip, detectives went to the Buckley house and there found the magazines from which had been torn the nudes, the oatmeal and syrup containers still set out on the kitchen table. Minimal sleuthing revealed which of the young Buckleys had been in town that night. The detectives then confronted the three vandals and got them to sign confessions. The case came to court June 10, and the three (one was in college and two were in prep school) were found guilty by a Justice of the Peace and each fined $100 for damaging the church. Buckley Sr. did his best to take further revenge on the Cotters, even going so far as to request the Episcopal Bishop of Connecticut to remove Cotter from Christ Church, but by then village sentiment was entirely on the side of the Cotters and Buckley Sr. dropped the matter. But he had made his point as far as his family was concerned and therein lies the key to his son's character. Buckley Jr. has never accepted any view of the world other than his father's. He is forever the little boy trying to impress Daddy by hating what Daddy hates. To be fair, Buckley Sr.'s prejudices were not much different from those of, let us say, Joe Kennedy or Senator Gore, my grandfather, but Joe Kennedy's sons and Senator Gore's grandson changed as they made their way in the world, learned charity or at least good sense, but not Bill—he is still the schoolboy debater echoing what he heard in his father's house, and for this postponed maturity he must suffer the fate of having been irrelevant to his own time, a mere entertainer with a gift for mischief.

"A man like Titus Oates occurs like a slip of the tongue, disclosing the unconscious forces, the nightside of an age. . . ." So wrote Graham Greene and so one might write of Buckley. In examining Eichmann's career Hannah Arendt came to the conclusion that evil could be banal. Buckley's career suggests that evil can be fatuous. But banal or fatuous, the result is the same if to the fool or his friends falls the power of the state. Buckley is not of course a "pro crypto Nazi" in the sense that he is a secret member of the Nazi party (and I respond to Buckley's charming apology to me with mine to him if anyone thought I was trying to link him to Hitler's foreign and domestic ventures). But in a larger sense his views are very much those of the founders of the Third Reich who regarded blacks as inferiors, undeclared war as legitimate foreign policy, and the Jews as sympathetic to international communism.

Since I began this operation with a story from *The Lakeville Journal*, a sense of symmetry impels me to end with another newspaper quotation. During Buckley's campaign for Mayor of New York, *The New York Times* took exception to his "slurs on Negroes," and accused him of pandering to "brutish instincts." Buckley wanted to know to what brutish instincts he was appealing, and *The Times* made answer, "Those instincts are fear, ignorance, racial superiority, religious antagonism, contempt for the weak and afflicted, and hatred for those different from oneself."

—SEPTEMBER 1969

# The Long Fall of One-Eleven Heavy

MICHAEL PATERNITI

It was summer; it was winter. The village disappeared behind skeins of fog. Fishermen came and went in boats named *Reverence, Granite Prince, Souwester.* The ocean, which was green and wild, carried the boats out past Jackrock Bank toward Pearl Island and the open sea. In the village, on the last shelf of rock, stood a lighthouse, whitewashed and octagonal with a red turret. Its green light beamed over the green sea, and sometimes, in the thickest fog or heaviest storm, that was all the fishermen had of land, this green eye dimly flashing in the night, all they had of home and how to get there—that was the question. There were nights when that was the only question.

This northerly village, this place here of sixty people, the houses and fences and clotheslines, was set among solid rocks breaching from the earth. It was as if a pod of whales had surfaced just as the ocean turned to land and then a village was built on their granite backs. By the weathered fishing shacks were anchors rusted like claws and broken traps and hills of coiled line. Come spring, wildflowers appeared by the clapboard church. The priest said mass. A woman drew back a curtain. A man hanged himself by the bridge. Travelers passing through agreed it was the prettiest earthly spot, snapping pictures as if gripped by palsy, nearly slipping off the rocks into the frigid waves.

Late summer, a man and woman were making love in the eaves of a garishly painted house that looked out on the lighthouse—green light revolving, revolving—when a feeling suddenly passed into them, a feeling unrelated to their lovemaking, in direct physical opposition to it: an electrical charge so strong they could taste it, feel it, the hair standing on their arms, just as it does before lightning strikes. And the fishermen felt it, too, as they went to sea and returned, long ago resigned to the fact that you can do nothing to stop the ocean or the sky from what it will do. Now they too felt the shove and lock of some invisible metallic bit in their mouths. The feeling of being surrounded by towering waves.

Yes, something terrible was moving this way. There was a low ceiling of clouds, an intense, creeping darkness, that electrical taste. By the lighthouse, if you had been standing beneath the revolving green light on that early-September night, in that plague of clouds, you would have heard the horrible grinding sound of some wounded winged creature, listened to it trail out to sea as it came screeching down from the heavens, down through molecule and current, until everything went silent.

That is, the waves still crashed up against the granite rock, the green light creaked in its revolutions, a cat yowled somewhere near the church, but beyond, out at sea, there was silence. Seconds passed, disintegrating time . . . and then, suddenly, an explosion of seismic strength rocked the houses of Peggy's Cove. One fisherman thought it was a bomb; another was certain the End had arrived. The lovers clasped tightly—their bodies turning as frigid as the ocean.

That's how it began.

It began before that, too, in other cities of the world, with plans hatched at dinner tables or during long-distance calls, plans for time together and saving the world, for corralling AIDS and feeding the famine-stricken and family reunions. What these people held in common at first—these diplomats and scientists and students, these lovers and parents and children—was an elemental feeling, that buzz of excitement derived from holding a ticket to some foreign place. And what distinguished that ticket from billions of other tickets was the simple designation of a number: SR111. New York to Geneva, following the Atlantic coast up along Nova Scotia, then out over Greenland and Iceland and England, and then down finally into Switzerland, on the best airline in the world. Seven hours if the tailwinds were brisk. There in time for breakfast on the lake.

In one row would be a family with two grown kids, a computer-genius son and an attorney daughter, setting out on their hiking holiday to the Bernese Oberland. In another would be a woman whose boyfriend was planning to propose to her when she arrived in Geneva. Sitting here would be a world-famous scientist, with his world-famous scientist wife. And there would be the boxer's son, a man who had grown to look like his legendary father, the same thick brow and hard chin, the same mournful eyes, on a business trip to promote his father's tomato sauce.

Like lovers who haven't yet met or one-day neighbors living now in different countries, tracing their route to one another, each of them moved toward the others without knowing it, in these cities and towns, grasping airline tickets. Some, like the Swiss tennis pro, would miss the flight, and others, without tickets, would be bumped from other flights onto this one at the last minute, feeling lucky to have made it, feeling chosen.

In the hours before the flight, a young blond woman with blue, almost Persian eyes said goodbye to her boyfriend in the streets of Manhattan and slipped into a cab. A fifty-six-year-old man had just paid a surprise visit to see his brother's boat, a refurbished sloop, on the Sound, just as his two brothers and his elderly mother came in from a glorious day on the water, all that glitter and wind, and now he was headed back to Africa, to the parched veldts and skeletal victims, to the disease and hunger, back to all this worrying for the world.

Somewhere else, a man packed—his passport, his socks—then went to the refrigerator to pour himself a glass of milk. His three kids roughhoused in the other room. His wife complained that she didn't want him to fly, didn't want him to leave on this business trip. On the refrigerator was a postcard, sent randomly by friends, of a faraway fishing village—the houses and fences and clotheslines, the ocean and the lighthouse and the green light revolving, revolving. He had looked at that postcard every day since it had been taped there. A beautiful spot. Something about it. Could a place like that really exist?

All of these people, it was as if they were all turning to gold, all marked with an invisible X on their foreheads, as of course we are, too, the place and time yet to be determined. Yes, we are burning down; time is disintegrating. There were 229 people who owned cars and houses, slept in beds, had bought clothes and gifts for this trip, some with price tags still on them—and then they were gone.

Do you remember the last time you felt the wind? Or touched your lips to the head of your child? Can you remember the words she said as she last went, a ticket in hand?

Every two minutes an airliner moves up the Atlantic coast, tracing ribboned contrails, moving through kingdoms in the air, demarcated by boundaries, what are called corridors and highways by the people who control the sky. In these corridors travel all the planes of the world, jetliners pushing the speed of sound at the highest altitudes, prop planes puttering at the lowest, and a phylum in between of Cessnas and commuters and corporate jets—all of them passing over the crooked-armed peninsulas and jagged coastlines and, somewhere, too, this northern village as it appears and disappears behind skeins of fog.

The pilot—a thin-faced, handsome Swiss man with penetrating brown eyes and a thick mustache—was known among his colleagues as a consummate pilot. He'd recently completed a promotional video for his airline. In it, he—the energetic man named Urs—kisses his perfectly beautiful wife goodbye at their home before driving off, then he is standing on the tarmac, smiling, gazing up at his plane, and then in the cockpit, in full command, flipping toggles, running checks, in command, toggles, lights, check, command.

So now here they were, in their corridor, talking, Urs and his copilot, Stephan. About their kids; both had three. About the evening's onboard dinner. It was an hour into the flight, the plane soaring on autopilot, the engine a quiet drone beneath the noise in the main cabin, the last lights of New England shimmering out the west side of the aircraft, and suddenly there was a tickling smell, rising from somewhere into the cockpit, and really, how could it be?—smoke. Toggles, lights, check, but the smoke kept coming. The pilot ran through his emergency checklists, switching various electrical systems on and off to isolate the problem. But the smoke kept coming. He was breathing rapidly, and the copilot, who wasn't, said, We have a problem.

Back in the cabin, the passengers in 30B and 16D were sipping wine and soda, penning postcards at thirty-three thousand feet. In first class, some donned airline slippers and supped on hors d'oeuvres while gambling on the computer screens in front of them. Slots, blackjack, keno. Others reclined and felt the air move beneath them—a Saudi prince, the world-famous scientist, the UN field director, the boxer's son, the woman with Persian eyes—an awesome feeling of power, here among the stars, plowing for Europe, halfway between the polar cap and the moon, gambling and guzzling and gourmanding. No one knew that even now, the pilot was on the radio, using the secret language of the sky to declare an emergency:

Pan, pan, pan, said Urs. We have smoke in the cockpit, request deviate, immediate return to a convenient place. I guess Boston. (Toggles, lights, check, breathe.)

Would you prefer to go into Halifax? said air-traffic control, a calm voice from a northern place called Moncton, a man watching a green hexagon crawl across a large, round screen, this very flight moving across the screen, a single clean green light.

Affirmative for one-eleven heavy, said the pilot. We have the oxygen mask on. Go ahead with the weather—

Could I have the number of souls on board . . . for emergency services? chimed in Halifax control.

Roger, said the pilot, but then he never answered the question, working frantically down his checklist, circling back over the ocean to release tons of diesel to lighten the craft for an emergency landing, the plane dropping to nineteen thousand feet, then twelve thousand, and ten thousand. An alarm sounded, the autopilot shut down. Lights fritzed on and off in both the cockpit and the cabin, flight attendants rushed through the aisles, one of the three engines quit in what was now becoming a huge electrical meltdown.

Urs radioed something in German, *emergency checklist air conditioning smoke*. Then in English, Sorry . . . Maintaining at ten thousand feet, his voice urgent, the words blurring. The smoke was thick, the heat increasing, the checklists, the bloody checklists . . . leading nowhere, leading—We are declaring emergency now at, ah, time, ah, zero-one-two-four. . . . We have to land immediate—

The instrument panel—bright digital displays—went black. Both pilot and copilot were now breathing frantically.

Then nothing.

Radio contact ceased. Temperatures in the cockpit were rising precipitously; aluminum fixtures began to melt. It's possible that one of the pilots, or both, simply caught fire. At air-traffic control in Moncton, the green hexagon flickered off the screen. There was silence. They knew what was coming: the huge fuck, the something terrible. God save them. One controller began trembling, another wept.

It was falling.

Six minutes later, SRIII plunged into the dark sea.

The medical examiner woke to a ringing phone, the worst way to wake. Ten-something on the clock, or was it eleven? The phone ringing, in the house where he lived alone, or rather with his two retrievers, but alone, too, without wife or woman. He lived near the village with the lighthouse, had moved here less than three years ago from out west, had spent much of his life rolling around, weird things following him, demons and disasters. Had a train wreck once, in Great Britain, early in his career, a Sunday night, university students coming back to London after a weekend at home. Train left the tracks at speed. He'd never seen anything like that in his life—sixty dead, decapitations, severed arms and legs. These kids, hours before whole and happy, now disassembled. Time disintegrating in the small fires of the wreckage. After the second night, while everyone kept their stiff upper lips, he sobbed uncontrollably. He scared himself—not so much because he was sobbing, but because he couldn't stop.

There'd been a tornado in Edmonton—it couldn't possibly have been, but, yes, a tornado, twenty-three dead. And then another train wreck in western Canada, in the hinterlands fifty miles east of Jasper. Twenty-five dead in a ravine. He'd nearly been drummed out of the job for his handling of that one. The media swarmed to photograph mangled bodies, and the medical examiner, heady from all the attention and a bit offended by it, knowing he shouldn't, stuffed some towels and linens on a litter, draped them with a sheet, and rolled the whole thing out for the flashing cameras. Your dead body, gentlemen.

Later, when they found out—oh, they hated him for that. Called for his head.

This had been a frustrating day, though, driving up to New Glasgow, waiting to take the stand to testify in the case of a teenage killer, waiting, waiting, four, five, six hours, time passing, revolving, nothing to do in that town except pitter here and there, waiting. Got off the stand around six, home by nine, deeply annoyed, too late to cook, got into the frozen food, then to bed, reading the paper, drifting, reading, drifting. And now the phone was ringing, a woman from the office: a jet was down. Without thinking, he said, It's a mistake. Call me back if anything comes of it. Set the phone in its cradle, and a minute later it rang again.

There's a problem here, she said.

I'll get on my way, he said, and hung up. He automatically put a suitcase on the bed, an overnight bag, and then it dawned on him: There'd been no talk about numbers yet, the possible dead. There could be hundreds, he knew that, yes, he did know that now, didn't he? He walked back and forth between his cupboard and his bed, flustered, disbelieving, *hundreds*, and then the adrenaline started to move, with hypodermic efficiency. Hundreds of bodies—and each one of them would touch his hands. And he would have to touch them, identify them, confer what remained of them to some resting place. He would have to bear witness to the horrible thing up close, what it did up close, examine it, notate, dissect, and, all the while, feel what it did, feel it in each jagged bone.

Flustered, disbelieving, it took him forty minutes to pack his bag with a couple pairs of khakis, some underwear, shirts, a pair of comfortable shoes, some shaving gear, should have taken five minutes.

He was a sensitive, empathetic man—at least he thought so (did his ex-wife? did his two faraway daughters?)—with a sharp if morbid sense of humor, a kind of loner in this northern place, Nova Scotia, where clans had carved out their lives over centuries and generations, where someone's great-great-grandfather had once fished someone else's great-great-grandfather from a storm at sea. He was an outsider, had always been, which qualified him for what was now coming, lurching toward him at the speed it would take him to drive in that thick night, in the warm rain that now fell like pieces of sky, from his home to his office.

No, he didn't know then, as he left his retrievers, Dan and Deputy, behind, as he closed the door on his house, everything freezing in time as he did, magazines fanned on a table, milk in the refrigerator, didn't know that summer would pass and fall would arrive, that the leaves would vanish from the trees before he returned.

But now all he did was drive, doing the math: There were twelve in the office and six in the morgue. The local hospitals might be able to cough up thirty more, but that didn't even begin to cover it. Where the hell were they going to find enough body bags?

More phones rang, more people woke. The coast guard, the Mounties, ministers, presidents. The navy, the airline, the media, everyone scrambling to figure out what was going on; without realizing it, everyone was now caught in the spreading fire. In the village, boats left for sea. The fishermen rolled from their beds, threw on rain gear, buddied up, and started out, unquestioning, reflexively. (You couldn't keep the sea and sky from what it would do.) Many of the fishermen thought they were going in search of survivors, were convinced of it, owing to the legacy of shipwrecks in these parts, which often meant someone was out there somewhere in all that inky black, in a yellow raft, waiting for help, cold, shivering, alive, waiting, waiting, waiting for *them*.

The television reporter stood on the shore, with a growing cabal of other reporters, fellow parasites. He stood apart, shifting from foot to foot, antsy, squinting out at the ocean. Shit, where? Others worked their cell phones, frantically scrounging for the story, but still nobody knew anything. Someone living in a trailer home nearby claimed to have seen a huge flash on the horizon; another said the plane had come so close to the village that you could see inside, cabin lights flickering on and off, people lit, then black, see those last moments playing out from the ground.

These waters were his, that's what the reporter thought. He'd sailed these coves and inlets all summer long, sailed past the lighthouse so many times it seemed a natural outcropping of the landscape. He was a solid, good-looking man who spoke quickly, moved at a clip, all of forty-two, with just-thinning hair. He'd worked twenty years on the nautical beat, covering the navy and ship sinkings and whatever else came along. He never forgot to register a name, and then never forgot it, kept a card catalog in his head that connected everyone to everyone else. One of his great strengths. And when he saw what looked like falling stars in the distance, parachute flares, he knew that was where the plane was. He turned to the cameraman.

We need to be under those, he said, pointing to the falling stars.

Before he left the office, he'd stashed extra cell-phone batteries in his pocket. You never knew, or maybe you already did. And now, in this night, in the seamless dark (there was no marking land but for the lighthouse, green light revolving), he was on his way in a hired boat with a cameraman. The wind blew, heavy swells, ten-foot waves, on his way, to see what? And why? He was as bad as the others, wasn't he? A fucking parasite. There were a lot of people on that plane, he knew that. At the UN, they called it the diplomatic shuttle: dinner meeting in Manhattan, breakfast meeting in Geneva. And now here they were, lost off the coast of this forgotten place.

It took an hour in those seas. The parachute flares and spotlights were blinding at first, the smell of diesel overwhelming. Sea King helicopters whirred overhead, flashing white beams; boats drifted through the wreckage, aimlessly, the water a bottomless black. They couldn't see anything, just heard it on the VHF radio, fishermen talking to one another: I got something over here. I think she's alive. Then thirty seconds passed. I need a body bag. And then other voices, this morbid call and response:

*We got another one.*
*Over here, too.*
*Need a body bag, now!*
*Jesus, we got a foot in the water.*
*We have an arm.*
*We need a body bag! Who's got body bags?*

Then the reporter saw a half-inflated life raft. Alive—someone was alive! But when they came upon it, it was empty, had inflated on impact. There were shoes fanning everywhere around them, hundreds and hundreds of shoes, in procession, riding the water's windrows—some with the laces still tied up. And underwear and ripped shirts, Bibles and stuffed animals. Money floating on the surface of the ocean now. Dollars and marks, rupees and francs and drachmas. You'd haul up a purse and expect to find a wallet, a driver's license, lipstick, anything, and it would be empty.

The plane had hit the water at more than four hundred miles per hour, nose first, two engines still firing, very unusual, extremely rare; the jet was two hundred feet long, and the tail rammed straight into the nose, everything exploding into more than one million pieces. Later, someone would be in charge of counting pieces at the military base, in a hangar where bits of the plane would fill thousands of crates and cardboard boxes. At impact, the bodies on board had been what the medical examiner would call degloved, simply shorn from the bones. You couldn't pick them up in your hands. You had to scoop them in nets.

No one has survived this crash, the television reporter told the world. From what we are seeing, there are no survivors.

But, said an anchorperson, the coast guard is calling this a search and rescue.

There are no survivors.

Until dawn, he was the only reporter under the parachute flares, a bizarre, surreal time, no believer in God, but you could feel something, 229 of them in this place. There were body parts and shoes—he'd dream about them for a long time. He was beamed into television sets around the world. No survivors. He told the pilot's wife that her husband was dead. He told the famous boxer that his son was dead. He told the father of the woman with Persian eyes that his daughter was dead.

When he finally came to shore the next day, when he stood near the lighthouse, green light revolving, doing more live feeds, carefully choosing his words for the world, running on adrenaline, he noticed a large man glaring at him. The man was a very big man, with a pockmarked face and greased-back hair, scary looking, glaring. And the reporter thought, He's going to kick my ass for being a parasite, for feeding off all these bodies.

When the reporter finished, the oversized man started for him and the reporter could do nothing but ready himself for the blow. But it never came. Something else did.

I want to thank you, he said. You told me my fiancée was dead. I got a phone call last night, in New York, and I was told there might be survivors and I thought, Well, if anybody survived this it was her, because we're gonna get married—and everyone was saying there are survivors, and you told me she was dead. You told me the truth. I needed to hear that.

Needed to hear that? This man needed to hear that? Yesterday the reporter had been covering some minor promotion ceremony at the military base; today he had told the world they could say goodbye to these 229 human beings, the ones with X's on their foreheads, the ones turning to gold, once wearing shoes, ghosts now, goodbye. And then the big man was gone, too, before the reporter could offer thanks back, or rather condolences, before he could think to ask the living man's name.

It was early morning in Geneva, and the father of the woman with the blue Persian eyes—a slight, erudite man with fine hair turning from orange to gray, turning at that very moment even—sat before a television, watching the reporter, in disbelief. He woke his wife and asked, Did she phone last night? And his wife said, She'll be phoning soon to have you fetch her in Zurich. And he said, She won't; the plane has crashed.

His wife roused herself, still half tangled in sleep, and stared at the reporter, listening, trying to grasp words that made no sense. It's all right, she said. There's nothing to worry about. We'll wait for her call.

The phone rang. It was her boyfriend in New York. What plane did she take? he asked. And the father said, But you tell me? No, he said, because we parted company at four in the afternoon, and she didn't know which plane she was on. And can you please tell me that she was on the Zurich flight?

No, the father said. And then he called the airline and insisted they tell him whether his daughter had been on the Zurich flight. We cannot, a voice said. But you must. You must. . . . There was silence, then a rustling of papers. We have to tell you, the voice said, she is not on the list.

Thank you, said the father.

Then he told his wife, and she said, Until they phone us with the news, we have to believe. And the man said, But darling, they're not going to phone with news like that. They'd come to the door—

And before he'd finished his sentence, the doorbell rang.

Grief is schizophrenic. You find yourself of two minds, the one that governs your days up until the moment of grief—the one that opens easily to memories of the girl at six, twelve, eighteen—and the one that seeks to destroy everything afterward. The man was fifty-eight and he'd given his daughter every advantage he could afford; the circumstances of his life—his work for a luxury-car company and then a fine-watch company—had given her the riding lessons and top-notch education and summer home in France. But then she'd given so much of herself, too. She'd been a championship swimmer and show jumper. She had a great knack for simplifying things, for having fun, for enjoying the moment so fully that those around her wanted to live inside those moments with her. She was contagious and beautiful and twenty-four, with those amazing eyes. She was about to come home and take a job.

After she was gone, the husband and wife made a promise to each other: They would stop their imaginations at that place where their daughter had boarded the plane, their minds would not wander past that particular rope. As usual, he broke the promise, unable to divert his mind from picturing his daughter at the end—it's possible she, like all of them, was unconscious at impact from the crushing g-forces inside the aircraft. Or that she suffered horribly, screaming, the flash of an entire life playing before her eyes. Whom did she sit next to in those moments? What was said?

The man couldn't help but imagine the pilots, too, their fate connected to a recurring dream he'd had for many years of himself as a pilot, trying to land a jet on a motor launch and not knowing what the hell he was doing. Though his wife stopped her mind on the gangplank as her daughter stepped into the jet, he followed his girl into the sea.

Nothing made sense, time was disintegrating, everything was a confusion, chaos. Walking through town, he'd see the river and have to keep himself from slipping into it. He'd go to the station and hold back from throwing himself before a train: how good it would feel, a matter of time now, not whether but *when*—today? Tomorrow? What would it feel like?

Since he couldn't sleep, he drank a bottle of Scotch daily, then couldn't remember anything. He followed the news accounts, half-heartedly reading words like *investigation, black box, recovery effort, debris field*. There had been a Picasso on board the plane and millions in rubies and diamonds. One day a postcard arrived from his daughter, detailing her stay in New York. Authorities called, wanting to send some of her effects (others now slept with ripped shirts and favorite sweaters, passports and stuffed animals), but the thought horrified him. What was worse, what the man could never have foreseen after thirty years of marriage, after having done so much to put a life together, was how quickly it became undone. He'd spent his life stitching up a beautiful life—the watch on his wrist a mysterious blue, cost the same as a small house. Now he didn't want to be with anybody, just alone, and his wife, his best friend—his wife had stopped at the gangplank. How could she? How could she not follow their beloved daughter into the ocean? Silly words comforted her while they enraged him; having family nearby was a source of strength for her, torment for him. This response or that response of hers seemed so . . . wrong. And in his mind he was asking: What's the point of this life? And she said, We must forget.

There was one thing that made him feel better. He flew alone to the northern village a few days after the crash, thinking he'd have to identify his daughter, drove down along the coast road to the lighthouse. (The media was now encamped here, among the houses and rocks and clotheslines, long-range lenses trained on anybody shedding a tear, beaming the image to the world.) He came to this village, and he felt something, some part of him rising, too. He knew he was going mad—and yet he could feel these waves churning inside him, his daughter there, too. When he returned to Geneva, he simply went back to devising ways to kill himself.

The full severity of the crash dawned on the medical examiner only the morning after, when he rode a Sea King out to the debris field. The fishermen and others in Zodiacs kept shuttling body parts to a huge command ship, the captain on the radio to these men talking in calm tones. (Many would later say it was that voice, that reassuring voice, that pulled them through that night.) The media had already begun a body count, based on the body bags coming ashore, and yet there were no bodies out here whatsoever, not one intact body in those bags, which were running out fast. But for one, they couldn't identify a single soul visually.

Back at the military base, the medical examiner set up in Hangar B, refrigerated trucks called reefers parked outside to hold the remains. There were huge fans and scented candles to mask the smell, the whole place lit and flickering like a church. Like the strangest church. On one wall hung a huge diagram of the plane, a seating chart, and as the remains of a passenger were identified by dental records or DNA, by a distinctive tattoo or a wedding ring, a blue dot was placed on the passenger's seat. The medical examiner would eventually be in charge of four hundred people here—a cadre of pathologists and DNA experts, morticians, media liaisons, and staff. But when he came back to the hangar after having been at sea that first time, he thought, What if I go now, bugger off right now? But where? Back to his dogs? No, what he realized as the parts began to fill the hangar and the reefers, as the stench became overpowering, was that he was too afraid to leave. With each passing day inside the hangar, there was nowhere to vanish but inside these people, these bodies.

One day he was waiting to go on the stand in dead-end New Glasgow, killing time, and the next this complete Armageddon. There were three hundred family members gathered now at a hotel, and the medical examiner was asked to address them. Others spoke first—officials, the president of the airline, offering their deepest sorrow to these people—and then he stood up nervously, cleared his throat, perhaps recalling that day years before when he'd made a body out of rolled-up towels for the media, how simple and, well, hilarious that had been. But how do you tell grieving family members the average body is now in one hundred pieces, one hundred little stars? (A fisherman saw a human heart on the surface of the water.) You will never see your loved ones again, he said. Those were the first words out of his mouth, and the crowd let out a massive exhalation, as if hit in the stomach. One man began sobbing uncontrollably and was led from the room. Not only are they dead, *you will never see them again.*

He'd said it. However painful, he knew this much: If you look away, if you self-justify or obfuscate, then you're stuck with the lie. You may make it through the moment, but in a day, a week, a year, it will bring you down, like cheetahs on a gazelle. Yes, he told them. If anything, they could see their own fear in his eyes, feel their quaver in his voice, their tears welling in his eyes. No stiff upper lip here. Fuck the macho and whatever it was that made you a man. (There was a heart on the surface of the water.) He vowed he would not betray these people, there'd be no fake body under a sheet. He'd try to talk to each of them, answer their concerns and desires, treat each body as if he himself were the next of kin: the father, the son, the lover, the brother.

Inside the hangar, days and nights of horrific work, checking dental records, X rays, fingerprints. And on several occasions the medical examiner took fingers from which they could not get accurate prints, decomposed fingers, made an incision, and stuck his own finger inside, went inside these bodies, *became* them, so that he could lay an accurate mark of them on paper, return them to their rightful place. He knew each passenger by name and blood type. He found himself intensely identifying with some, one in particular, a newspaper executive, a man named John Mortimer—couldn't shake him and his wife from his mind. He put himself in that seat next to John Mortimer's wife, tried to imagine the dreadful plummet, the smash of atoms. He tried to do the math: A loving couple falls through the sky at four hundred miles per hour, with maybe six minutes until impact: What did they say? What could be done?

Day after day, more blue dots came to fill the seats of the imaginary plane. He was not a believer in God, but a priest had come to the hangar, and the medical examiner said, Do you feel it? And the priest said, The souls are hovering. And the medical examiner looked up and said, Yes. Yes they are.

Then that November day came when they were done. There would be more dredging, hundreds of pounds of remains to come, jagged bones in piles (the plane hitting so hard some were embedded with quarters and nickels), clean as a whistle from the currents of the sea, but they were basically done. There were only a few technicians left in the hangar and they were going to shut it down, and the medical examiner came in early, when no one was there.

He knew it was perverse, but he didn't want it to end. He was convinced that his entire life, one full of mistakes and masterstrokes, had been leading to this moment. He was exhausted, flirting with a breakdown. He knew that, could feel it, but he knew, too, that if he'd run, the cheetahs would have caught him, somewhere out there on the veldt they would have dragged him down. It was fall, the leaves off the trees. A season had passed. How many seasons had passed? Nothing made sense. He was going back to his life (his dogs, the daughter who thought he was grandstanding now, saw his public empathy as something he'd never once offered her), his best self traded back for his flawed self, and he stood for a long while in silence, time disintegrating. When he turned to walk away—even later when he retired and packed up and moved back west—most of him stayed right here.

The passengers were blue dots now, and yet they were still alive. After that first night, even as time passed and the story fell from the news, the television reporter had been driven deeper into it; he learned the names, who connected to whom. He tracked the possible causes of the crash: a spark thrown from the wiring of the elaborate entertainment system, the flammability of the Mylar insulation. He was haunted by the prospect that if the pilot had landed immediately, hadn't gone by the book, dallying with checklists, just put the jet down, everyone might be alive.

But then he met the pilot's wife. He went to Zurich, flew in the cockpit of the same kind of jet that had crashed, with one of the dead pilot's best friends, an awesome feeling of power up in that kingdom of sky, plowing for Europe. He met the pilot's wife at her expensive home in a ritzy neighborhood with a lap pool and lots of sunlight inside. The woman was startlingly attractive, especially when she smiled, which wasn't often these days. In her former life, when she wanted to go to Manhattan or Hong Kong or Tokyo, she didn't go first-class, she went in the cockpit. And when her husband spoke, a dozen people jumped. They'd met when she was a flight attendant, and now here she was describing how she and her three children were trying to carry on without their father, her husband, Urs.

She told a story about going to the crash site, on board a boat that took the families there, about how hard it had been for everyone, how the kids were down, very down, and coming back, over the side, in the water, there were suddenly dolphins running in the ocean, an amazing vision, like electrical currents, these dolphins up from the deep and slipping alongside them. Not too long after, she decided that she was going back to work as a flight attendant, for the same airline. Her first flight was the New York–Geneva route, on the same type of aircraft as the one her husband had ridden into the sea.

There were others, too, people so moved by the graciousness of those in this northern place that they returned or even bought property to be closer. One man sailed his sloop here, in honor of the brother who'd taught him to sail in the first place, the brother trying to save the world. The boxer, now an old man of seventy-eight but once a world champion, came despite himself and said he felt lighter when he left, after looking out from the lighthouse at the spot where his son's life ended. It somehow made him feel lighter. Others came and saw the hangar where the remains had been, the hangar where the million pieces of plane were still boxed and numbered, seats over here, armrests over there. The three jet engines were there, too, big, hulking things with mangled rotors.

How did these people do it? How did they go on? How could they? One woman whom the reporter had interviewed in New York had a box of stuff that had once been her daughter's: a French-English dictionary, a cup, a pair of binoculars, some glasses, a locket that she, the mother, had given her. She spent hours touching these things. And then another woman, who lost her husband, heard that they had found parts of his hand, had tested its DNA, and she asked that the remains be sent directly to her, though usually the remains were sent to funeral homes or hospitals. The reporter knew a counselor who spent four hours on the phone with the wife who had her husband's hand, and she finally sent the police because the woman was trying to put it back together. I can get the thumb, she said, but I can't get the next part.

The reporter didn't have the luxury of a breakdown, what with three kids. He still had the nightmares—shoes and body parts. He saw a therapist a few times, and she told the reporter to put the dream in a box, take the image of that black, bottomless sea and the debris field with its body parts and shoes, the smell of diesel drenching everything, and place it all in a box, take the box and put it high on a shelf. He did that, and he got past it. Yes, in an imaginary closet somewhere in his head, in an imaginary box, was everything that had actually, really, horrifically happened, and now sometimes, on a very good day, after some beers, maybe watching hockey or roughhousing with the kids, he could imagine for a moment that it hadn't.

One day, the man from Geneva boarded a plane and came back to the village, left his wife behind, riffled through his closet of finely tailored suits and ridiculous leather dress shoes and packed some jerseys and books and left, for good, the only remnant of his former life that wristwatch with the stunning blue face, the same color as the sea here on certain windswept days, the color of his daughter's eyes.

The man left his wife, yes, but to save her from him. It sounded odd, but it was true. They'd made a promise and he'd broken it. He kept following his daughter into the ocean.

The last time he came to the village in this northern place, he saw a roadside restaurant and convenience store for sale nearby, and now, knowing nothing about restaurants or convenience stores, he bought it. It was a barnlike building with living quarters on the second floor, in some disrepair, but if grief was schizophrenic, then maybe here he could find a balancing point for his life before he lost his daughter and his life after. He had never conceived of the possibility that anything he did could be undone, let alone that he himself would become undone. But he'd become undone.

So he set to work, seven days a week, up at five-thirty, readying the coffee, cleaning the grill, playing opera on the stereo, checking the weather in the cove that let onto the ocean, a stunning place, and his daughter in this place. He'd open the doors at seven, and at seven-thirty a man named Leroy came to clean. They said he'd been half a man, a backward boy, before he'd been given this job, mopping floors and cleaning toilets at the restaurant. Now he was coming into his own. When the man asked him to do something, he smiled and saluted and said, Okay, copy ya!

The man redid the walls, opened up the dining space, began to build a large deck. He'd once traveled to the Middle East to sell hundreds of thousands of dollars' worth of watches at a time, and now he cooked Surf 'n' Turf burgers ($5.52) and Bacon & Egg Double Deckers ($2.99) just to hear someone, anyone, say, I think I've been sufficiently sufficed. Thank you kindly. He joked and laughed with the fishermen and the construction crews and the older men, too, who came just to sit and drink coffee. He stood in the middle of his restaurant in a rugby jersey, wearing a white apron, near a photograph of his daughter, and told a story about her.

She was sent to convent school when she was six years old, her hair cut incredibly short, not like it was at the end, long and streaked blond. There was an open school day, a parents' day, and they organized games for the kids. In one of the games you could fish for goldfish with a net, and his daughter came to him and said, Oh, can you imagine! All my life, my whole life, I've wanted a goldfish! I can't remember when I haven't wanted a goldfish! And the man looked at his daughter, who was beaming at him, her eyes lit all the blues of the world, and he laughed, her whole life and she was just six years old, sweet and precocious and it really was too funny. Well, a quarter of her life was over by then, doesn't seem—but it was, it was funny.

No, he hadn't left his wife. He talked to her every day, his best friend. But Geneva was her home and this was his now, this village. His beard had gone more gray over the winter here. Who could ever imagine where life would carry you, humbled and hopeful, lost and found and lost again as a storm blew in from sea? There would be a day when he and his wife would be together again. They would reach an understanding, and they would perhaps travel down to Morocco, to Marrakech, a place they'd loved for its colors and light, for its people, together again, released, absolved, together.

It would be a strange, wonderful resolution, thought the man, imagining it. They would make themselves clean. But now, there were hungry men at a table, and so this man with the spectacular wristwatch tied on his apron, went to the grill. This man, though he was hungry, too, he fed the others first.

It was summer; it was winter. The village disappeared behind skeins of fog. Fishermen came and went in their boats, boats that had been at the crash site all those seasons ago, under that dark ceiling of night clouds, in those swells of black, bottomless water. One of the men fished a baby from the sea, kneeling on deck, lit by the parachute tracers, holding fast to what was left of the child, time disintegrating. Those who braved the night said that something happened out there, something horrible, and then—and this is the odd part—something beautiful. In the strange, eerie silence, everything drenched in diesel, you could feel it, almost taste it, something rising up from this spot, up through the ocean, through the men who stood out there in boats, among the shoes, something rose through them, like electricity.

At the edge of the rocks stood the lighthouse, green light revolving, revolving. Sometimes, in the heaviest storm, that was all the fishermen had of land, this green eye dimly flashing in the night, all they had of home, and how to get there, that was the question. And there were other questions that lingered, too, when they dared to consider them. Even at noon on the brightest days of the year, especially on the brightest days of the year, when the wind whipped the laundry on the line, the questions lingered. Yes, what had happened here? And why did the clothes on the line look as if they were filled by bodies, though there were no bodies in sight anymore?

—JULY 2000

# PROFILES

# Frank Sinatra Has a Cold

GAY TALESE

Frank Sinatra, holding a glass of bourbon in one hand and a cigarette in the other, stood in a dark corner of the bar between two attractive but fading blondes who sat waiting for him to say something. But he said nothing; he had been silent during much of the evening, except now in this private club in Beverly Hills he seemed even more distant, staring out through the smoke and semidarkness into a large room beyond the bar where dozens of young couples sat huddled around small tables or twisted in the center of the floor to the clamorous clang of folk-rock music blaring from the stereo. The two blondes knew, as did Sinatra's four male friends who stood nearby, that it was a bad idea to force conversation upon him when he was in this mood of sullen silence, a mood that had hardly been uncommon during this first week of November, a month before his fiftieth birthday.

Sinatra had been working in a film that he now disliked, could not wait to finish; he was tired of all the publicity attached to his dating the twenty-year-old Mia Farrow, who was not in sight tonight; he was angry that a CBS television documentary of his life, to be shown in two weeks, was reportedly prying into his privacy, even speculating on his possible friendship with Mafia leaders; he was worried about his starring role in an hour-long NBC show entitled *Sinatra—A Man And His Music*, which would require that he sing eighteen songs with a voice that at this particular moment, just a few nights before the taping was to begin, was weak and sore and uncertain. Sinatra was ill. He was the victim of an ailment so common that most people would consider it trivial. But when it gets to Sinatra it can plunge him into a state of anguish, deep depression, panic, even rage. Frank Sinatra had a cold.

Sinatra with a cold is Picasso without paint, Ferrari without fuel—only worse. For the common cold robs Sinatra of that uninsurable jewel, his voice, cutting into the core of his confidence, and it affects not only his own psyche but also seems to cause a kind of psychosomatic nasal drip within dozens of people who work for him, drink with him, love him, depend on him for their own welfare and stability. A Sinatra with a cold can, in a small way, send vibrations through the entertainment industry and beyond as surely as a President of the United States, suddenly sick, can shake the national economy.

For Frank Sinatra was now involved with many things involving many people—his own film company, his record company, his private airline, his missile-parts firm, his real-estate holdings across the nation, his personal staff of seventy-five—which are only a portion of the power he is and has come to represent. He seemed now to be also the embodiment of the fully emancipated male, perhaps the only one in America, the man who can do anything he wants, *anything*, can do it because he has money, the energy, and no apparent guilt. In an age when the very young seem to be taking over, protesting and picketing and demanding change, Frank Sinatra survives as a national phenomenon, one of the few prewar products to withstand the test of time. He is the champ who made the big comeback, the man who had everything, lost it, then got it back, letting nothing stand in his way, doing what few men can do: he uprooted his life, left his family, broke with everything that was familiar, learning in the process that one way to hold a woman is not to hold her. Now he has the affection of Nancy and Ava and Mia, the fine female produce of three generations, and still has the adoration of his children, the freedom of a bachelor, he does not feel old, he makes old men feel young, makes them think that if Frank Sinatra can do it, it can be done; not that *they* could do it, but it is still nice for other men to know, at fifty, that it can be done.

But now, standing at this bar in Beverly Hills, Sinatra had a cold, and he continued to drink quietly and he seemed miles away in his private world, not even reacting when suddenly the stereo in the other room switched to a Sinatra song, *In the Wee Small Hours of the Morning*.

It is a lovely ballad that he first recorded ten years ago, and it now inspired many young couples who had been sitting, tired of twisting, to get up and move slowly around the dance floor, holding one another very close. Sinatra's intonation, precisely clipped, yet full and flowing, gave a deeper meaning to the simple lyrics—"In the wee small hours of the morning / while the whole wide world is fast asleep / you lie awake, and think about the girl. . . ."—it was like so many of his classics, a song that evoked loneliness and sensuality, and when blended with the dim light and the alcohol and nicotine and late-night needs, it became a kind of airy aphrodisiac. Undoubtedly the words from this song, and others like it, had put millions in the mood, it was music to make love by, and doubtless much love had been made by it all over America at night in cars, while the batteries burned down, in cottages by the lake, on beaches during balmy summer evenings, in secluded parks and exclusive penthouses and furnished rooms, in cabin cruisers and cabs and cabanas—in all places where Sinatra's songs could be heard were these words that warmed women, wooed and won them, snipped the final thread of inhibition and gratified the male egos of ungrateful lovers; two generations of men had been the beneficiaries of such ballads, for which they were eternally in his debt, for which they may eternally hate him. Nevertheless here he was, the man himself, in the early hours of the morning in Beverly Hills, out of range.

The two blondes, who seemed to be in their middle thirties, were preened and polished, their matured bodies softly molded within tight dark suits. They sat, legs crossed, perched on the high bar stools. They listened to the music. Then one of them pulled out a Kent and Sinatra quickly placed his gold lighter under it and she held his hand, looked at his fingers: they were nubby and raw, and the pinkies protruded, being so stiff from arthritis that he could barely bend them. He was, as usual, immaculately dressed. He wore an oxford-grey suit with a vest, a suit conservatively cut on the outside but trimmed with flamboyant silk within; his shoes, British, seemed to be shined even on the bottom of the soles. He also wore, as everybody seemed to know, a remarkably convincing black hairpiece, one of sixty that he owns, most of them under the care of an inconspicuous little grey-haired lady who, holding his hair in a tiny satchel, follows him around whenever he performs. She earns $400 a week. The most distinguishing thing about Sinatra's face are his eyes, clear blue and alert, eyes that within seconds can go cold with anger, or glow with affection, or, as now, reflect a vague detachment that keeps his friends silent and distant.

Leo Durocher, one of Sinatra's closest friends, was now shooting pool in the small room behind the bar. Standing near the door was Jim Mahoney, Sinatra's press agent, a somewhat chunky young man with a square jaw and narrow eyes who would resemble a tough Irish plainclothesman if it were not for the expensive continental suits he wears and his exquisite shoes often adorned with polished buckles. Also nearby was a big, broad-shouldered two-hundred-pound actor named Brad Dexter who seemed always to be thrusting out his chest so that his gut would not show.

Brad Dexter has appeared in several films and television shows, displaying fine talent as a character actor, but in Beverly Hills he is equally known for the role he played in Hawaii two years ago when he swam a few hundred yards and risked his life to save Sinatra from drowning in a riptide. Since then Dexter has been one of Sinatra's constant companions and has been made a producer in Sinatra's film company. He occupies a plush office near Sinatra's executive suite. He is endlessly searching for literary properties that might be converted into new starring roles for Sinatra. Whenever he is among strangers with Sinatra he worries because he knows that Sinatra brings out the best and worst in people—some men will become aggressive, some women will become seductive, others will stand around skeptically appraising him, the scene will be somehow intoxicated by his mere presence, and maybe Sinatra himself, if feeling as badly as he was tonight, might become intolerant or tense, and then: headlines. So Brad Dexter tries to anticipate danger and warn Sinatra in advance. He confesses to feeling very protective of Sinatra, admitting in a recent moment of self-revelation: "I'd kill for him."

While this statement may seem outlandishly dramatic, particularly when taken out of context, it nonetheless expresses a fierce fidelity that is quite common within Sinatra's special circle. It is a characteristic that Sinatra, without admission, seems to prefer: *All the Way; All or Nothing at All*. This is the Sicilian in Sinatra; he permits his friends, if they wish to remain that, none of the easy Anglo-Saxon outs. But if they remain loyal, then there is nothing Sinatra will not do in turn—fabulous gifts, personal kindnesses, encouragement when they're down, adulation when they're up. They are wise to remember, however, one thing. He is Sinatra. The boss. *Il Padrone*.

I had seen something of this Sicilian side of Sinatra last summer at Jilly's saloon in New York, which was the only other time I'd gotten a close view of him prior to this night in this California club. Jilly's, which is on West Fifty-second Street in Manhattan, is where Sinatra drinks whenever he is in New York, and there is a special chair reserved for him in the back room against the wall that nobody else may use. When he is occupying it, seated behind a long table flanked by his closest New York friends—who include the saloonkeeper, Jilly Rizzo, and Jilly's azure-haired wife, Honey, who is known as the "Blue Jew"—a rather strange ritualistic scene develops. That night dozens of people, some of them casual friends of Sinatra's, some mere acquaintances, some neither, appeared outside of Jilly's saloon. They approached it like a shrine. They had come to pay respect. They were from New York, Brooklyn, Atlantic City, Hoboken. They were old actors, young actors, former prizefighters, tired trumpet players, politicians, a boy with a cane. There was a fat lady who said she remembered Sinatra when he used to throw the *Jersey Observer* onto her front porch in 1933. There were middle-aged couples who said they had heard Sinatra sing at the Rustic Cabin in 1938 and "We knew then that he really had it!" Or they had heard him when he was with Harry James's band in 1939, or with Tommy Dorsey in 1941 ("Yeah, that's the song, *I'll Never Smile Again*—he sang it one night in this dump near Newark and we danced . . ."); or they remembered that time at the Paramount with the swooners, and him with those bow ties, The Voice; and one woman remembered that awful boy she knew then—Alexander Dorogokupetz, an eighteen-year-old heckler who had thrown a tomato at Sinatra and the bobby-soxers in the balcony had tried to flail him to death. Whatever became of Alexander Dorogokupetz? The lady did not know.

And they remembered when Sinatra was a failure and sang trash like *Mairzy Doats*, and they remembered his comeback and on this night they were all standing outside Jilly's saloon, dozens of them, but they could not get in. So some of them left. But most of them stayed, hoping that soon they might be able to push or wedge their way into Jilly's between the elbows and backsides of the men drinking three-deep at the bar, and they might be able to peek through and see him sitting back there. This is all they really wanted; they wanted to see him. And for a few moments they gazed in silence through the smoke and they stared. Then they turned, fought their way out of the bar, went home.

Some of Sinatra's close friends, all of whom are known to the men guarding Jilly's door, do manage to get an escort into the back room. But once they are there they, too, must fend for themselves. On the particular evening, Frank Gifford, the former football player, got only seven yards in three tries. Others who had somehow been close enough to shake Sinatra's hand did *not* shake it; instead they just touched him on the shoulder or sleeve, or they merely stood close enough for him to see them and, after he'd given them a wink of recognition or a wave or a nod or called out their names (he had a fantastic memory for first names), they would then turn and leave. They had checked in. They had paid their respects. And as I watched this ritualistic scene, I got the impression that Frank Sinatra was dwelling simultaneously in two worlds that were not contemporary.

On the one hand he is the swinger—as he is when talking and joking with Sammy Davis, Jr., Richard Conte, Liza Minelli, Bernie Massi, or any of the other show-business people who get to sit at *the* table; on the other, as when he is nodding or waving to his *paisanos* who are close to him (Al Silvani, a boxing manager who works with Sinatra's film company; Dominic Di Bona, his wardrobe man; Ed Pucci, a 300-pound former football lineman who is his aide-de-camp), Frank Sinatra is *Il Padrone*. Or better still, he is what in traditional Sicily have long been called *uomini rispettati*—men of respect:

men who are both majestic and humble, men who are loved by all and are very generous by nature, men whose hands are kissed as they walk from village to village, men who would *personally* go out of their way to redress a wrong.

Frank Sinatra does things *personally.* At Christmas time, he will personally pick dozens of presents for his close friends and family, remembering the type of jewelry they like, their favorite colors, the sizes of their shirts and dresses. When a musician friend's house was destroyed and his wife was killed in a Los Angeles mud slide a little more than a year ago, Sinatra personally came to his aid, finding the musician a new home, paying whatever hospital bills were left unpaid by the insurance, then personally supervising the furnishing of the new home down to the replacing of the silverware, the linen, the purchase of new clothing.

The same Sinatra who did this can, within the same hour, explode in a towering rage of intolerance should a small thing be incorrectly done for him by one of his *paisanos.* For example, when one of his men brought him a frankfurter with catsup on it, which Sinatra apparently abhors, he angrily threw the bottle at the man, splattering catsup all over him. Most of the men who work around Sinatra are big. But this never seems to intimidate Sinatra nor curb his impetuous behavior with them when he is mad. They will never take a swing back at him. He is *Il Padrone.*

At other times, aiming to please, his men will overreact to his desires: when he casually observed that his big orange desert jeep in Palm Springs seemed in need of a new painting, the word was swiftly passed down through the channels, becoming ever more urgent as it went, until finally it was a *command* that the jeep be painted *now,* immediately, yesterday. To accomplish this would require the hiring of a special crew of painters to work all night, at overtime rates; which, in turn, meant that the order had to be bucked back up the line for further approval. When it finally got back to Sinatra's desk, he did not know what it was all about; after he had figured it out he confessed, with a tired look on his face, that he did not care when the hell they painted the jeep.

Yet it would have been unwise for anyone to anticipate his

reaction, for he is a wholly unpredictable man of many moods and great dimension, a man who responds instantaneously to instinct—suddenly, dramatically, wildly he responds, and nobody can predict what will follow. A young lady named Jane Hoag, a reporter at *Life*'s Los Angeles bureau who had attended the same school as Sinatra's daughter, Nancy, had once been invited to a party at Mrs. Sinatra's California home at which Frank Sinatra, who maintains very cordial relations with his former wife, acted as host. Early in the party Miss Hoag, while leaning against a table, accidentally with her elbow knocked over one of a pair of alabaster birds to the floor, smashing it to pieces. Suddenly, Miss Hoag recalled, Sinatra's daughter cried, "Oh, that was one of my mother's favorite . . ."—but before she could complete the sentence, Sinatra glared at her, cutting her off, and while forty other guests in the room all stared in silence, Sinatra walked over, quickly with his finger flicked the *other* alabaster bird off the table, smashing it to pieces, and then put an arm gently around Jane Hoag and said, in a way that put her completely at ease, "That's okay, kid."

Now Sinatra said a few words to the blondes. Then he turned from the bar and began to walk toward the poolroom. One of Sinatra's other men friends moved in to keep the girls company. Brad Dexter, who had been standing in the corner talking to some other people, now followed Sinatra.

The room cracked with the clack of billiard balls. There were about a dozen spectators in the room, most of them young men who were watching Leo Durocher shoot against two other aspiring hustlers who were not very good. This private drinking club has among its membership many actors, directors, writers, models, nearly all of them a good deal younger than Sinatra or Durocher and much more casual in the way they dress for the evening. Many of the young women, their long hair flowing loosely below their shoulders, wore tight, fanny-fitting Jax pants and very expensive sweaters; and a few of the young men wore blue or green velour shirts with high collars and narrow tight pants, and Italian loafers.

It was obvious from the way Sinatra looked at these people in the poolroom that they were not his style, but he leaned back against a high stool that was against the wall, holding his drink in his right hand, and said nothing, just watched Durocher slam the billiard balls back and forth. The younger men in the room, accustomed to seeing Sinatra at this club, treated him without deference, although they said nothing offensive. They were a cool young group, very California-cool and casual, and one of the coolest seemed to be a little guy, very quick of movement, who had a sharp profile, pale blue eyes, blondish hair, and squared eyeglasses. He wore a pair of brown corduroy slacks, a green shaggy-dog Shetland sweater, a tan suede jacket, and Game Warden boots, for which he had recently paid $60.

Frank Sinatra, leaning against the stool, sniffling a bit from his cold, could not take his eyes off the Game Warden boots. Once, after gazing at them for a few moments, he turned away; but now he was focused on them again. The owner of the boots, who was just standing in them watching the pool game, was named Harlan Ellison, a writer who had just completed work on a screenplay, *The Oscar.*

Finally Sinatra could not contain himself.

"Hey," he yelled in his slightly harsh voice that still had a soft, sharp edge. "Those Italian boots?"

"No," Ellison said.

"Spanish?"

"No."

"Are they *English* boots?"

"Look, I donno, man," Ellison shot back, frowning at Sinatra, then turning away again.

Now the poolroom was suddenly silent. Leo Durocher, who had been poised behind his cue stick and was bent low, just froze in that position for a second. Nobody moved. Then Sinatra moved away from the stool and walked with that slow, arrogant swagger of his toward Ellison, the hard tap of Sinatra's shoes the only sound in the room. Then, looking down at Ellison with a slightly raised eyebrow and a tricky little smile, Sinatra asked: "You expecting a *storm?*"

Harlan Ellison moved a step to the side. "Look, is there any reason why you're talking to me?"

"I don't like the way you're dressed," Sinatra said.

"Hate to shake you up," Ellison said, "but I dress to suit myself."

Now there was some rumbling in the room, and somebody said, "Com'on, Harlan, let's get out of here," and Leo Durocher made his pool shot and said, "Yeah, com'on."

But Ellison stood his ground.

Sinatra said, "What do you do?"

"I'm a plumber," Ellison said.

"No, no, he's not," another young man quickly yelled from across the table. "He wrote *The Oscar.*"

"Oh, yeah," Sinatra said, "well I've seen it, and it's a piece of crap."

"That's strange," Ellison said, "because they haven't even released it yet."

"Well, I've seen it," Sinatra repeated, "and it's a piece of crap."

Now Brad Dexter, very anxious, very big opposite the small figure of Ellison, said, "Com'on, kid, I don't want you in this room."

"*Hey,*" Sinatra interrupted Dexter, "can't you see I'm talking to this guy?"

Dexter was confused. Then his whole attitude changed, and his voice went soft and he said to Ellison, almost with a plea, "*Why do you persist in tormenting me?*"

The whole scene was becoming ridiculous, and it seemed that Sinatra was only half-serious, perhaps just reacting out of sheer boredom or inner despair; at any rate, after a few more exchanges Harlan Ellison left the room. By this time the word had gotten out to those on the dance floor about the Sinatra-Ellison exchange, and somebody went to look for the manager of the club. But somebody else said that the manager had already heard about it—and had quickly gone out the door, hopped in his car and drove home. So the assistant manager went into the poolroom.

"I don't want anybody in here without coats and ties," Sinatra snapped.

The assistant manager nodded, and walked back to his office.

It was the morning after. It was the beginning of another nervous day for Sinatra's press agent, Jim Mahoney. Mahoney had a headache, and he was worried but not over the Sinatra-Ellison incident of the night before. At the time Mahoney had been with his wife at a table in the other room, and possibly he had not even been aware of the little drama. The whole thing had lasted only about three minutes. And three minutes after it was over, Frank Sinatra had probably forgotten about it for the rest of his life—as Ellison will probably remember it for the rest of *his* life: he had had, as hundreds of others before him, at an unexpected moment between darkness and dawn, a scene with Sinatra.

It was just as well that Mahoney had not been in the poolroom; he had enough on his mind today. He was worried about Sinatra's cold and worried about the controversial CBS documentary that, despite Sinatra's protests and withdrawal of permission, would be shown on television in less than two weeks. The newspapers this morning were full of hints that Sinatra might sue the network, and Mahoney's phones were ringing without pause, and now he was plugged into New York talking to the *Daily News*'s Kay Gardella, saying: ". . . that's right, Kay . . . they made a gentleman's agreement to not ask certain questions about Frank's private life, and then Cronkite went right ahead: 'Frank, tell me about those associations.' *That* question, Kay—*out!* That question should never have been asked. . . ."

As he spoke, Mahoney leaned back in his leather chair, his head shaking slowly. He is a powerfully built man of thirty-seven; he has a round, ruddy face, a heavy jaw, and narrow pale eyes, and he might appear pugnacious if he did not speak with such clear, soft sincerity and if he were not so meticulous about his clothes. His suits and shoes are superbly tailored, which was one of the first things Sinatra noticed about him, and in his spacious office opposite the bar is a red-muff electrical shoe polisher and a pair of brown wooden shoulders on a stand over which Mahoney can drape his jackets. Near the bar is an autographed photograph of President Kennedy and a few pictures of Frank Sinatra, but there are none of Sinatra in any other rooms in Mahoney's public-relations agency; there once was a large photograph of him hanging in the reception room but this apparently bruised the egos of some of Mahoney's other movie-star clients and, since Sinatra never shows up at the agency anyway, the photograph was removed.

Still, Sinatra seems ever present, and if Mahoney did not have legitimate worries about Sinatra, as he did today, he could invent them—and, as worry aids, he surrounds himself with little mementos of moments in the past when he did worry. In his shaving kit there is a two-year-old box of sleeping tablets dispensed by a Reno druggist—the date on the bottle marks the kidnapping of Frank Sinatra, Jr. There is on a table in Mahoney's office a mounted wood reproduction of Frank Sinatra's ransom note written on the aforementioned occasion. One of Mahoney's mannerisms, when he is sitting at his desk worrying, is to tinker with the tiny toy train he keeps in front of him—the train is a souvenir from the Sinatra film, *Von Ryan's Express*; it is to men who are close to Sinatra what the PT-109 tie clasps are to men who were close to Kennedy—and Mahoney then proceeds to roll the little train back and forth on the six inches of track; back and forth, back and forth, click-*clack*-click-*clack*. It is his Queeg-thing.

Now Mahoney quickly put aside the little train. His secretary told him there was a *very* important call on the line. Mahoney picked it up, and his voice was even softer and more sincere than before. "Yes, Frank," he said. "Right . . . right . . . yes, Frank. . . ."

When Mahoney put down the phone, quietly, he announced that Frank Sinatra had left in his private jet to spend the weekend at his home in Palm Springs, which is a sixteen-minute flight from his home in Los Angeles. Mahoney was now worried again. The Lear jet that Sinatra's pilot would be flying was identical, Mahoney said, to the one that had just crashed in another part of California.

On the following Monday, a cloudy and unseasonably cool California day, more than one hundred people gathered inside a white television studio, an enormous room dominated by a white stage, white walls, and with dozens of lights and lamps dangling: it rather resembled a gigantic operating room. In this room, within an hour or so, NBC was scheduled to begin taping a one-hour show that would be televised in color on the night of November 24 and would highlight, as much as it could in the limited time, the twenty-five-year career of Frank Sinatra as a public entertainer. It would not attempt to probe, as the forthcoming CBS *Sinatra* documentary allegedly would, that area of Sinatra's life that he regards as private. The NBC show would be mainly an hour of Sinatra singing some of the hits that carried him from Hoboken to Hollywood, a show that would be interrupted only now and then by a few film clips and commercials for Budweiser beer. Prior to his cold, Sinatra had been very excited about this show; he saw here an opportunity to appeal not only to those nostalgic, but also to communicate his talent to some rock-and-rollers—in a sense, he was battling The Beatles. The press releases being prepared by Mahoney's agency stressed this, reading: "If you happen to be tired of kid singers wearing mops of hair thick enough to hide a crate of melons . . . it should be refreshing to consider the entertainment value of a video special titled *Sinatra—A Man And His Music. . . .*"

But now in this NBC studio in Los Angeles, there was an atmosphere of anticipation and tension because of the uncertainty of the Sinatra voice. The forty-three musicians in Nelson Riddle's orchestra had already arrived and some were up on the white platform warming up. Dwight Hemion, a youthful sandy-haired director who had won praise for his television special on Barbra Streisand, was seated in the glass-enclosed control booth that overlooked the orchestra and stage. The camera crews, technical teams, security guards, Budweiser ad men were also standing between the floor lamps and cameras, waiting, as were a dozen or so ladies who worked as secretaries in other parts of the building but had sneaked away so they could watch this.

A few minutes before eleven o'clock, word spread quickly through the long corridor into the big studio that Sinatra was spotted walking through the parking lot and was on his way, and was looking fine. There seemed great relief among the group that was gathered; but when the lean, sharply dressed figure of the man got closer, and closer, they saw to their dismay that it was not Frank Sinatra. It was his double. Johnny Delgado.

Delgado walks like Sinatra, has Sinatra's build, and from certain facial angles does resemble Sinatra. But he seems a rather shy individual. Fifteen years ago, early in his acting career, Delgado applied for a role in *From Here To Eternity.* He was hired, finding out later that he was to be Sinatra's double. In Sinatra's latest film, *Assault on a*

*Queen*, a story in which Sinatra and some fellow conspirators attempt to hijack the *Queen Mary*, Johnny Delgado doubles for Sinatra in some water scenes; and now, in this NBC studio, his job was to stand under the hot television lights marking Sinatra's spots on the stage for the camera crews.

Five minutes later, the real Frank Sinatra walked in. His face was pale, his blue eyes seemed a bit watery. He had been unable to rid himself of the cold, but he was going to try to sing anyway because the schedule was tight and thousands of dollars were involved at this moment in the assembling of the orchestra and crews and the rental of the studio. But when Sinatra, on his way to his small rehearsal room to warm up his voice, looked into the studio and saw that the stage and orchestra's platform were not close together, as he had specifically requested, his lips tightened and he was obviously very upset. A few moments later, from his rehearsal room, could be heard the pounding of his fist against the top of the piano and the voice of his accompanist, Bill Miller, saying, softly, "Try not to upset yourself, Frank."

Later Jim Mahoney and another man walked in, and there was talk of Dorothy Kilgallen's death in New York earlier that morning. She had been an ardent foe of Sinatra for years, and he became equally uncomplimentary about her in his nightclub act, and now, though she was dead, he did not compromise his feelings. "Dorothy Kilgallen's dead," he repeated, walking out of the room toward the studio. "Well, guess I got to change my whole act."

When he strolled into the studio the musicians all picked up their instruments and stiffened in their seats. Sinatra cleared his throat a few times and then, after rehearsing a few ballads with the orchestra, he sang *Don't Worry About Me* to his satisfaction and, being uncertain of how long his voice could last, suddenly became impatient.

"Why don't we tape this mother?" he called out, looking up toward the glass booth where the director, Dwight Hemion, and his staff were sitting. Their heads seemed to be down, focusing on the control board.

"Why don't we tape this mother?" Sinatra repeated.

The production stage manager, who stands near the camera

wearing a headset, repeated Sinatra's words exactly into his line to the control room: "Why don't we tape this mother?"

Hemion did not answer. Possibly his switch was off. It was hard to know because of the obscuring reflections the lights made against the glass booth.

"Why don't we put on a coat and tie," said Sinatra, then wearing a high-necked yellow pullover, "and tape this. . . ."

Suddenly Hemion's voice came over the sound amplifier, very calmly: "Okay, Frank, would you mind going back over. . . ."

"Yes I *would* mind going back," Sinatra snapped.

The silence from Hemion's end, which lasted a second or two, was then again interrupted by Sinatra saying, "When we stop doing things around here the way we did them in 1950, maybe we . . ." and Sinatra continued to tear into Hemion, condemning as well the lack of modern techniques in putting such shows together; then, possibly not wanting to use his voice unnecessarily, he stopped. And Dwight Hemion, very patient, so patient and calm that one would assume he had not heard anything that Sinatra had just said, outlined the opening part of the show. And Sinatra a few minutes later was reading his opening remarks, words that would follow *Without a Song*, off the large idiot-cards being held near the camera. Then, this done, he prepared to do the same thing on camera.

"Frank Sinatra Show, Act I, Page 10, Take 1," called a man with a clapboard, jumping in front of the camera—*clap*—then jumping away again.

"Did you ever stop to think," Sinatra began, "what the world would be like without a song? . . . It would be a pretty dreary place. . . . Gives you something to think about, doesn't it? . . ."

Sinatra stopped.

"Excuse me," he said, adding, "*Boy*, I need a drink."

They tried it again.

"Frank Sinatra Show, Act I, Page 10, Take 2," yelled the jumping guy with the clapboard.

"Did you ever stop to think what the world would be like without a song? . . ." Frank Sinatra read it through this time without stopping. Then he rehearsed a few more songs, once or twice interrupting the orchestra when a certain instrumental sound was not quite what he wanted. It was hard to tell how well his voice was going to hold up, for this was early in the show; up to this point, however, everybody in the room seemed pleased, particularly when he sang an old sentimental favorite written more than twenty years ago by Jimmy Van Heusen and Phil Silvers—*Nancy*, inspired by the first of Sinatra's three children when she was just a few years old.

*"If I don't see her each day*
*I miss her. . . .*
*Gee what a thrill*
*Each time I kiss her. . . . "*

As Sinatra sang these words, though he has sung them hundreds and hundreds of times in the past, it was suddenly obvious to everybody in the studio that something quite special must be going on inside the man, because something quite special was coming out. He was singing now, cold or no cold, with power and warmth, he was letting himself go, the public arrogance was gone, the private side was in this song about the girl who, it is said, understands him better than anybody else, and is the only person in front of whom he can be unashamedly himself.

Nancy is twenty-five. She lives alone, her marriage to singer Tommy Sands having ended in divorce. Her home is in a Los Angeles suburb and she is now making her third film and is recording for her father's record company. She sees him every day; or, if not, he telephones, no matter if it be from Europe or Asia. When Sinatra's singing first became popular on radio, stimulating the swooners, Nancy would listen at home and cry. When Sinatra's first marriage broke up in 1951 and he left home, Nancy was the only child old enough to remember him as a father. She also saw him with Ava Gardner, Juliet Prowse, Mia Farrow, many others, has gone on double dates with him. . . .

*"She takes the winter*
*And makes it summer. . . .*
*Summer could take*
*Some lessons from her. . . . "*

Nancy now also sees him visiting at home with his first wife, the former Nancy Barbato, a plasterer's daughter from Jersey City whom he married in 1939 when he was earning $25 a week singing at the Rustic Cabin near Hoboken.

The first Mrs. Sinatra, a striking woman who has never remarried ("When you've been married to Frank Sinatra . . ." she once explained to a friend), lives in a magnificent home in Los Angeles with her younger daughter, Tina, who is seventeen. There is no bitterness, only great respect and affection between Sinatra and his first wife, and he has long been welcome in her home and has even been known to wander in at odd hours, stoke the fire, lie on the sofa and fall asleep. Frank Sinatra can fall asleep anywhere, something he learned when he used to ride bumpy roads with band buses; he also learned at that time, when sitting in a tuxedo, how to pinch the trouser creases in the back and tuck the jacket under and out, and fall asleep perfectly pressed. But he does not ride buses anymore, and his daughter Nancy, who in her younger days felt rejected when he slept on the sofa instead of giving attention to her, later realized that the sofa was one of the few places left in the world where Frank Sinatra could get any privacy, where his famous face would neither be stared at nor cause an abnormal reaction in others. She realized, too, that things normal have always eluded her father: his childhood was one of loneliness and a drive toward attention, and since attaining it he has never again been certain of solitude. Upon looking out the window of a home he once owned in Hasbrouck Heights, New Jersey, he would occasionally see the faces of teen-agers peeking in; and in 1944, after moving to California and buying a home behind a ten-foot fence on Lake Toluca, he discovered that the only way to escape the telephone and other intrusions was to board his paddle boat with a few friends, a card table and a case of beer, and stay afloat all afternoon. But he has tried, insofar as it has been possible, to be like everyone else, Nancy says. He wept on her wedding day, he is very sentimental and sensitive. . . .

What the hell are you doing up there, Dwight?"

Silence from the control booth.

"Got a party or something going on up there, *Dwight?*"

Sinatra stood on the stage, arms folded, glaring up across the cameras toward Hemion. Sinatra had sung *Nancy* with probably all he had in his voice on this day. The next few numbers contained raspy notes, and twice his voice completely cracked. But now Hemion was in the control booth out of communication; then he was down in the studio walking over to where Sinatra stood. A few minutes later they both left the studio and were on the way up to the control booth. The tape was replayed for Sinatra. He watched only about five minutes of it before he started to shake his head. Then he said to Hemion: "Forget it, just forget it. You're wasting your time. What you got there," Sinatra said, nodding to the singing image of himself on the television screen, "is a man with a cold." Then he left the control booth, ordering that the whole day's performance be scrubbed and future taping postponed until he had recovered.

Soon the word spread like an emotional epidemic down through Sinatra's staff, then fanned out through Hollywood, then was heard across the nation in Jilly's saloon, and also on the other side of the Hudson River in the homes of Frank Sinatra's parents and his other relatives and friends in New Jersey.

When Frank Sinatra spoke with his father on the telephone and said he was feeling awful, the elder Sinatra reported that *he* was also feeling awful: that his left arm and fist were so stiff with a circulatory condition he could barely use them, adding that the ailment might be the result of having thrown too many left hooks during his days as a bantamweight almost fifty years ago.

Martin Sinatra, a ruddy and tattooed little blue-eyed Sicilian born in Catania, boxed under the name of "Marty O'Brien." In those days, in those places, with the Irish running the lower reaches of city life, it was not uncommon for Italians to wind up with such names. Most of the Italians and Sicilians who migrated to America just prior to the 1900's were poor and uneducated, were excluded from the building-trades unions dominated by the Irish, and were somewhat intimidated by the Irish police, Irish priests, Irish politicians.

One notable exception was Frank Sinatra's mother, Dolly, a large and very ambitious woman who was brought to this country at two months of age by her mother and father, a lithographer from Genoa. In later years Dolly Sinatra, possessing a round red face and blue eyes, was often mistaken for being Irish, and surprised many at the speed with which she swung her heavy handbag at anyone uttering "Wop."

By playing skillful politics with North Jersey's Democratic machine, Dolly Sinatra was to become, in her heyday, a kind of Catherine de Medici of Hoboken's third ward. She could always be counted upon to deliver six hundred votes at election time from her Italian neighborhood, and this was her base of power. When she told one of the politicians that she wanted her husband to be appointed to the Hoboken Fire Department, and was told, "But, Dolly, we don't have an opening," she snapped, "*Make* an opening."

They did. Years later she requested that her husband be made a captain, and one day she got a call from one of the political bosses that began, "Dolly, congratulations!"

"For what?"

"*Captain* Sinatra."

"Oh, you finally made him one—thank you very much."

Then she called the Hoboken Fire Department.

"Let me speak to *Captain* Sinatra," she said. The fireman called Martin Sinatra to the phone, saying, "Marty, I think your wife has gone nuts." When he got on the line, Dolly greeted him:

"Congratulations, *Captain* Sinatra!"

Dolly's only child, christened Francis Albert Sinatra, was born and nearly died on December 12, 1915. It was a difficult birth, and during his first moment on earth he received marks he will carry till death—the scars on the left side of his neck being the result of a doctor's clumsy forceps, and Sinatra has chosen not to obscure them with surgery.

After he was six months old, he was reared mainly by his grandmother. His mother had a full-time job as a chocolate dipper with a large firm and was so proficient at it that the firm once offered to send her to the Paris office to train others. While some people in Hoboken remember Frank Sinatra as a lonely child, one who spent many hours on the porch gazing into space, Sinatra was never a slum kid, never in jail, always well-dressed. He had so many pants that some people in Hoboken called him "Slacksey O'Brien."

Dolly Sinatra was not the sort of Italian mother who could be appeased merely by a child's obedience and good appetite. She made many demands on her son, was always very strict. She dreamed of his becoming an aviation engineer. When she discovered Bing Crosby pictures hanging on his bedroom walls one evening, and learned that her son wished to become a singer too, she became infuriated and threw a shoe at him. Later, finding she could not talk him out of it—"he takes after me"—she encouraged his singing.

Many Italo-American boys of his generation were then shooting for the same star—they were strong with song, weak with words, not a big novelist among them: no O'Hara, no Bellow, no Cheever, nor Shaw; yet they could communicate *bel canto*. This was more in their tradition, no need for a diploma; they could, with a song, someday see their names in lights . . . *Perry Como* . . . *Frankie Laine* . . . *Tony Bennett* . . . *Vic Damone* . . . but none could see it better than *Frank Sinatra*.

Though he sang through much of the night at the Rustic Cabin, he was up the next day singing without a fee on New York radio to get more attention. Later he got a job singing with Harry James's band, and it was there in August of 1939 that Sinatra had his first recording hit—*All or Nothing at All*. He became very fond of Harry James and the men in the band, but when he received an offer from Tommy Dorsey, who in those days had probably the best band in the country, Sinatra took it; the job paid $125 a week, and Dorsey knew how to feature a vocalist. Yet Sinatra was very depressed at leaving James's band, and the final night with them was so memorable that, twenty years later, Sinatra could recall the details to a friend: ". . . the bus pulled out with the rest of the boys at about half-past midnight. I'd said good-bye to them all, and it was snowing, I remember. There was nobody around and I stood alone with my suitcase in the snow and watched the taillights disappear. Then the tears started and I tried to run after the bus. There was such spirit and enthusiasm in that band, I hated leaving it. . . ."

But he did—as he would leave other warm places, too, in search of something more, never wasting time, trying to do it all in one generation, fighting under his *own* name, defending underdogs, terrorizing top dogs. He threw a punch at a musician who said something anti-Semitic, espoused the Negro cause two decades before it became fashionable. He also threw a tray of glasses at Buddy Rich when he played the drums too loud.

Sinatra gave away $50,000 worth of gold cigarette lighters before he was thirty, was living an immigrant's wildest dream of America. He arrived suddenly on the scene when DiMaggio was silent, when *paisanos* were mournful, were quietly defensive about Hitler in their homeland. Sinatra became, in time, a kind of one-man Anti-Defamation League for Italians in America, the sort of organization that would be unlikely for them because, as the theory goes, they rarely agreed on anything, being extreme individualists: fine as soloists, but not so good in a choir; fine as heroes, but not so good in a parade.

When many Italian names were used in describing gangsters on a television show, *The Untouchables*, Sinatra was loud in his disapproval. Sinatra and many thousands of other Italo-Americans were resentful as well when a small-time hoodlum, Joseph Valachi, was brought by Bobby Kennedy into prominence as a Mafia expert, when indeed, from Valachi's testimony on television, he seemed to know less than most waiters on Mulberry Street. Many Italians in Sinatra's circle also regard Bobby Kennedy as something of an Irish cop, more dignified than those in Dolly's day, but no less intimidating. Together with Peter Lawford, Bobby Kennedy is said to have suddenly gotten "cocky" with Sinatra after John Kennedy's election, forgetting the contribution Sinatra had made in both fundraising and in influencing many anti-Irish Italian votes. Lawford and Bobby Kennedy are both suspected of having influenced the late President's decision to stay as a house guest with Bing Crosby instead of Sinatra, as originally planned, a social setback Sinatra may never forget. Peter Lawford has since been drummed out of Sinatra's "summit" in Las Vegas.

"Yes, my son is like me," Dolly Sinatra says, proudly. "You cross him, he never forgets." And while she concedes his power, she quickly points out, "He can't make his mother do anything she doesn't want to do," adding, "Even today, he wears the same brand of underwear I used to buy him."

Today Dolly Sinatra is seventy-one years old, a year or two younger than Martin, and all day long people are knocking on the back door of her large home asking her advice, seeking her influence. When she is not seeing people and not cooking in the kitchen, she is looking after her husband, a silent but stubborn man, and telling him to keep his sore left arm resting on the sponge she has placed on the armrest of a soft chair. "Oh, he went to some terrific fires, this guy did," Dolly said to a visitor, nodding with admiration toward her husband in the chair.

Though Dolly Sinatra has eighty-seven godchildren in Hoboken, and still goes to that city during political campaigns, she now lives with her husband in a beautiful sixteen-room house in Fort Lee, New Jersey. This home was a gift from their son on their fiftieth wedding anniversary three years ago. The home is tastefully furnished and is filled with a remarkable juxtaposition of the pious and the worldly—photographs of Pope John and Ava Gardner, of Pope Paul and Dean Martin; several statues of saints and holy water, a chair autographed by Sammy Davis, Jr. and bottles of bourbon. In Mrs. Sinatra's jewelry box is a magnificent strand of pearls she had just received from Ava Gardner, whom she liked tremendously as a daughter-in-law and still keeps in touch with and talks about; and hung on the wall is a letter addressed to Dolly and Martin: "The sands of time have turned to gold, yet love continues to unfold like the petals of a rose, in God's garden of life. . . may God love you thru all eternity. I thank Him, I thank you for the being of one. Your loving son, Francis. . . ."

Mrs. Sinatra talks to her son on the telephone about once a week, and recently he suggested that, when visiting Manhattan, she make use of his apartment on East Seventy-second Street on the East River. This is an expensive neighborhood of New York even though there is a small factory on the block, but this latter fact was seized upon by Dolly Sinatra as a means of getting back at her son for some unflattering descriptions of his childhood in Hoboken. "What—you want me to stay in *your* apartment, in *that* dump?" she asked. "You think I'm going to spend the night in *that* awful neighborhood?"

Frank Sinatra got the point, and said, "Excuse *me*, Mrs. Fort Lee."

After spending the week in Palm Springs, his cold much better, Frank Sinatra returned to Los Angeles, a lovely city of sun and sex, a Spanish discovery of Mexican misery, a star land of little men and little women sliding in and out of convertibles in tense tight pants.

Sinatra returned in time to see the long-awaited CBS documentary with his family. At about nine P.M. he drove to the home of his former wife, Nancy, and had dinner with her and their two daughters. Their son, whom they rarely see these days, was out of town.

Frank Jr., who is twenty-two, was touring with a band and moving cross country toward a New York engagement at Basin Street East with The Pied Pipers, with whom Frank Sinatra sang when he was with Dorsey's band in the 1940's. Today Frank Sinatra, Jr., whom his father says he named after Franklin D. Roosevelt, lives mostly in hotels, dines each evening in his nightclub dressing room, and sings until two A.M., accepting graciously, because he has no choice, the inevitable comparisons. His voice is smooth and pleasant, and improving with work, and while he is very respectful of his father, he discusses him with objectivity and in an occasional tone of subdued cockiness.

Concurrent with his father's early fame, Frank, Jr. said, was the creation of a "press-release Sinatra" designed to "set him apart from the common man, separate him from the realities: it was suddenly Sinatra, the electric magnate, Sinatra who is supernormal, not super*human* but super*normal*. And here," Frank, Jr. continued, "is the great fallacy, the great bullshit, for Frank Sinatra *is* normal, *is* the guy whom you'd meet on a street corner. But this other thing, the supernormal guise, has affected Frank Sinatra as much as anybody who watches one of his television shows, or reads a magazine article about him. . . .

"Frank Sinatra's life in the beginning was so normal," he said, "that nobody would have guessed in 1934 that this little Italian kid with the curly hair would become the giant, the monster, the great living legend. . . . He met my mother one summer on the beach. She was Nancy Barbato, daughter of Mike Barbato, a Jersey City plasterer. And she meets the fireman's son, Frank, one summer day on the beach at Long Branch, New Jersey. Both are Italian, both Roman

Catholic, both lower-middle-class summer sweethearts—it is like a million bad movies starring Frankie Avalon. . . .

"They have three children. The first child, Nancy, was the most normal of Frank Sinatra's children. Nancy was a cheerleader, went to summer camp, drove a Chevrolet, had the easiest kind of development centered around the home and family. Next is me. My life with the family is very, very normal up until September of 1958 when, in complete contrast to the rearing of both girls, I am put into a college-preparatory school. I am now away from the inner family circle, and my position within has never been remade to this day. . . . The third child, Tina. And to be dead honest, I really couldn't say what her life is like. . . ."

The CBS show, narrated by Walter Cronkite, began at ten P.M. A minute before that, the Sinatra family, having finished dinner, turned their chairs around and faced the camera, united for whatever disaster might follow. Sinatra's men in other parts of town, in other parts of the nation, were doing the same thing. Sinatra's lawyer, Milton A. Rudin, smoking a cigar, was watching with a keen eye, an alert legal mind. Other sets were watched by Brad Dexter, Jim Mahoney, Ed Pucci; Sinatra's makeup man, "Shotgun" Britton; his New York representative, Henri Giné; his haberdasher, Richard Carroll; his insurance broker, John Lillie; his valet, George Jacobs, a handsome Negro who, when entertaining girls in *his* apartment, plays records by Ray Charles.

And like so much of Hollywood's fear, the apprehension about the CBS show all proved to be without foundation. It was a highly flattering hour that did not deeply probe, as rumors suggested it would, into Sinatra's love life, or the Mafia, or other areas of his private province. While the documentary was not authorized, wrote Jack Gould in the next day's New York *Times*, "it could have been." Immediately after the show, the telephones began to ring throughout the Sinatra system conveying words of joy and relief—and from New York came Jilly's telegram: "WE RULE THE WORLD!"

The next day, standing in the corridor of the NBC building where he was about to resume taping his show, Sinatra was discussing the CBS show with several of his friends, and he said, "Oh, it was a gas."

"Yeah, Frank, a helluva show."

"But I think Jack Gould was right in The *Times* today," Sinatra said. "There should have been more on the *man*, not so much on the music. . . ."

They nodded, nobody mentioning the past hysteria in the Sinatra world when it seemed CBS was zeroing in on the *man*; they just nodded and two of them laughed about Sinatra's apparently having gotten the word "bird" on the show—this being a favorite Sinatra word. He often inquires of his cronies, "How's your bird?"; and when he nearly drowned in Hawaii, he later explained, "Just got a little water on my bird"; and under a large photograph of him holding a whisky bottle, a photo that hangs in the home of an actor friend named Dick Bakalyan, the inscription reads: "Drink, Dickie! It's good for your bird." In the song, *Come Fly With Me*, Sinatra sometimes alters the lyrics—". . . just say the words and we'll take our birds down to Acapulco Bay. . . ."

Ten minutes later Sinatra, following the orchestra, walked into the NBC studio which did not resemble in the slightest the scene here of eight days ago. On this occasion Sinatra was in fine voice, he cracked jokes between numbers, nothing could upset him. Once, while he was singing *How Can I Ignore the Girl Next Door*, standing on the stage next to a tree, a television camera mounted on a vehicle came rolling in too close and plowed against the tree.

"Kee-rist" yelled one of the technical assistants.

But Sinatra seemed hardly to notice it.

"We've had a slight accident," he said, calmly. Then he began the song all over from the beginning.

When the show was over, Sinatra watched the rerun on the monitor in the control room. He was very pleased, shaking hands with Dwight Hemion and his assistants. Then the whisky bottles were opened in Sinatra's dressing room. Pat Lawford was there, and so were Andy Williams and a dozen others. The telegrams and telephone calls continued to be received from all over the country with praise for the CBS show. There was even a call, Mahoney said, from the CBS producer, Don Hewitt, with whom Sinatra had been so angry a few days before. And Sinatra was *still* angry, feeling that CBS had betrayed him, though the show itself was not objectionable.

"Shall I drop a line to Hewitt?" Mahoney asked.

"Can you send a fist through the mail?" Sinatra asked.

*He has everything, he cannot sleep, he gives nice gifts, he is not happy, but he would not trade, even for happiness, what he is. . . .*

*He is a piece of our past—but only we have aged, he hasn't . . . we are dogged by domesticity, he isn't . . . we have compunctions, he doesn't . . . it is our fault, not his. . . .*

*He controls the menus of every Italian restaurant in Los Angeles; if you want North Italian cooking, fly to Milan. . . .*

*Men follow him, imitate him, fight to be near him . . . there is something of the locker room, the barracks about him . . . bird . . . bird. . . .*

*He believes you must play it big, wide, expansively—the more open you are, the more you take in, your dimensions deepen, you grow, you become more what you are—bigger, richer. . . .*

*"He is better than anybody else, or at least they think he is, and he has to live up to it."* —NANCY SINATRA, JR.

*"He is calm on the outside—inwardly a million things are happening to him."* —DICK BAKALYAN

*"He has an insatiable desire to live every moment to its fullest because, I guess, he feels that right around the corner is extinction."*

—BRAD DEXTER

*"All I ever got out of any of my marriages was the two years Artie Shaw financed on an analyst's couch."* —AVA GARDNER

*"We weren't mother and son—we were buddies."*

—DOLLY SINATRA

*"I'm for anything that gets you through the night, be it prayer, tranquilizers or a bottle of Jack Daniel."* —FRANK SINATRA

Frank Sinatra was tired of all the talk, the gossip, the theory—tired of reading quotes about himself, of hearing what people were saying about him all over town. It had been a tedious three weeks, he said, and now he just wanted to get away, go to Las Vegas, let off some steam. So he hopped in his jet, soared over the California hills across the Nevada flats, then over miles and miles of desert to The Sands and the Clay-Patterson fight.

On the eve of the fight he stayed up all night and slept through most of the afternoon, though his recorded voice could be heard singing in the lobby of The Sands, in the gambling casino, even in the toilets, being interrupted every few bars however by the paging public address: ". . . Telephone call for Mr. Ron Fish, Mr. Ron Fish . . . *with a ribbon of gold in her hair. . . .* Telephone call for Mr. Herbert Rothstein, Mr. Herbert Rothstein. . . *memories of a time so bright, keep me sleepless through dark endless nights. . . .*"

Standing around in the lobby of The Sands and other hotels up and down the strip on this afternoon before the fight were the usual prefight prophets: the gamblers, the old champs, the little cigar butts from Eighth Avenue, the sportswriters who knock the big fights all year but would never miss one, the novelists who seem always to be identifying with one boxer or another, the local prostitutes assisted by some talent in from Los Angeles, and also a young brunette in a wrinkled black cocktail dress who was at the bell captain's desk crying, "But I want to speak to Mr. Sinatra."

"He's not here," the bell captain said.

"Won't you put me through to his room?"

"There are *no* messages going through, Miss," he said, and then she turned, unsteadily, seeming close to tears, and walked through the lobby into the big noisy casino crowded with men interested only in money.

Shortly before seven P.M., Jack Entratter, a big grey-haired man who operates The Sands, walked into the gambling room to tell some men around the blackjack table that Sinatra was getting dressed. He also said that he'd been unable to get front-row seats for everybody, and so some of the men—including Leo Durocher, who had a date, and Joey Bishop, who was accompanied by his wife—would not be able to fit in Frank Sinatra's row but would have to take seats in the third row. When Entratter walked over to tell this to Joey Bishop, Bishop's face fell. He did not seem angry; he merely looked at Entratter with an empty silence, seeming somewhat stunned.

"Joey, I'm *sorry*," Entratter said when the silence persisted, "but we couldn't get more than six together in the front row."

Bishop still said nothing. But when they all appeared at the fight, Joey Bishop was in the front row, his wife in the third.

The fight, called a holy war between Muslims and Christians, was preceded by the introduction of three balding ex-champions, Rocky Marciano, Joe Louis, Sonny Liston—and then there was *The Star-Spangled Banner* sung by another man from out of the past, Eddie Fisher. It had been more than fourteen years ago, but Sinatra could still remember every detail: Eddie Fisher was then the new king of the baritones, with Billy Eckstine and Guy Mitchell right with him, and Sinatra had been long counted out. One day he remembered walking into a broadcasting studio past dozens of Eddie Fisher fans waiting outside the hall, and when they saw Sinatra they began to jeer, "Frankie, Frankie, I'm *swooning*, I'm *swooning*." This was also the time when he was selling only about 30,000 records a year, when he was dreadfully miscast as a funny man on his television show, and when he recorded such disasters as *Mama Will Bark*, with Dagmar.

"I growled and barked on the record," Sinatra said, still horrified by the thought. "The only good it did me was with the dogs."

His voice and his artistic judgment were incredibly bad in 1952, but even more responsible for his decline, say his friends, was his pursuit of Ava Gardner. She was the big movie queen then, one of the most beautiful women in the world. Sinatra's daughter Nancy recalls seeing Ava swimming one day in her father's pool, then climbing out of the water with that fabulous body, walking slowly to the fire, leaning over it for a few moments, and then it suddenly seemed that her long dark hair was all dry, miraculously and effortlessly back in place.

With most women Sinatra dates, his friends say, he never knows whether they want him for what he can do for them now—or will do for them later. With Ava Gardner, it was different. He could do nothing for her later. She was on top. If Sinatra learned anything from his experience with her, he possibly learned that when a proud man is down a woman cannot help. Particularly a woman on top.

Nevertheless, despite a tired voice, some deep emotion seeped into his singing during this time. One particular song that is well remembered even now is *I'm A Fool to Want You*, and a friend who was in the studio when Sinatra recorded it recalled: "Frank was really worked up that night. He did the song in one take, then turned around and walked out of the studio and that was that. . . ."

Sinatra's manager at that time, a former song plugger named Hank Sanicola, said, "Ava loved Frank, but not the way he loved her. He needs a great deal of love. He wants it twenty-four hours a day, he must have people around—Frank is that kind of guy." Ava Gardner, Sanicola said, "was very insecure. She feared she could not really hold a man . . . twice he went chasing her to Africa, wasting his own career. . . ."

"Ava didn't want Frank's men hanging around all the time," another friend said, "and this got him mad. With Nancy he used to be able to bring the whole band home with him, and Nancy, the good Italian wife, would never complain—she'd just make everybody a plate of spaghetti."

In 1953, after almost two years of marriage, Sinatra and Ava Gardner were divorced. Sinatra's mother reportedly arranged a reconciliation, but if Ava was willing, Frank Sinatra was not. He was seen with other women. The balance had shifted. Somewhere during this period Sinatra seemed to change from the kid singer, the boy actor in the sailor suit, to a man. Even before he had won the Oscar in 1953 for his role in *From Here to Eternity*, some flashes of his old talent were coming through—in his recording of *The Birth of the Blues*, in his Riviera-nightclub appearance that jazz critics enthusiastically praised; and there was also a trend now toward L.P.'s and away from the quick three-minute deal, and Sinatra's concert style would have capitalized on this with or without out an Oscar.

In 1954, totally committed to his talent once more, Frank Sinatra was selected Metronome's "Singer of the Year," and later he won the U.P.I. disc-jockey poll, unseating Eddie Fisher—who now, in Las Vegas, having sung *The Star-Spangled Banner*, climbed out of the ring, and the fight began.

Floyd Patterson chased Clay around the ring in the first round, but was unable to reach him, and from then on he was Clay's toy, the bout ending in a technical knockout in the twelfth round. A half hour later, nearly everybody had forgotten about the fight and was back at the gambling tables or lining up to buy tickets for the Dean Martin-Sinatra-Bishop nightclub routine on the stage of The Sands. This routine, which includes Sammy Davis, Jr. when he is in town, consists of a few songs and much cutting up, all of it very informal, very special, and rather ethnic—Martin, a drink in hand, asking Bishop: "Did you ever see a Jew jitsu?"; and Bishop, playing a Jewish waiter, warning the two Italians to watch out "because I got my own group—the *Matzia*."

Then after the last show at The Sands, the Sinatra crowd, which now numbered about twenty—and included Jilly, who had flown in from New York; Jimmy Cannon, Sinatra's favorite sports columnist; Harold Gibbons, a Teamster official expected to take over if Hoffa goes to jail—all got into a line of cars and headed for another club. It was three o'clock. The night was young.

They stopped at The Sahara, taking a long table near the back, and listened to a baldheaded little comedian named Don Rickles, who is probably more caustic than any comic in the country. His humor is so rude, in *such* bad taste, that it offends no one—it is *too* offensive to be offensive. Spotting Eddie Fisher among the audience, Rickles proceeded to ridicule him as a lover, saying it was no wonder that he could not not handle Elizabeth Taylor; and when two businessmen in the audience acknowledged that they were Egyptian, Rickles cut into them for their country's policy toward Israel; and he strongly suggested that the woman seated at one table with her husband was actually a hooker.

When the Sinatra crowd walked in, Don Rickles could not be more delighted. Pointing to Jilly, Rickles yelled: "How's it feel to be Frank's tractor? . . . Yeah, Jilly keeps walking in front of Frank clearing the way." Then, nodding to Durocher, Rickles said, "Stand up Leo, show Frank how you slide." Then he focused on Sinatra, not failing to mention Mia Farrow, nor that he was wearing a toupee, nor to say that Sinatra was washed up as a singer, and when Sinatra laughed, everybody laughed, and Rickles pointed toward Bishop: "Joey Bishop keeps checking with Frank to see what's funny."

Then, after Rickles told some Jewish jokes, Dean Martin stood up and yelled, "Hey, you're always talking about the Jews, never about the Italians," and Rickles cut him off with, "What do we need the Italians for—all they do is keep the flies off our fish."

Sinatra laughed, they all laughed, and Rickles went on this way for nearly an hour until Sinatra, standing up, said, "All right, com'on, get this thing over with. I gotta go."

"Shaddup and sit down!" Rickles snapped. "I've had to listen to you sing. . . ."

"Who do you think you're talking to?" Sinatra yelled back.

"Dick Haymes," Rickles replied, and Sinatra laughed again, and then Dean Martin, pouring a bottle of whisky over his head, entirely drenching his tuxedo, pounded the table.

"Who would ever believe that staggering would make a star?" Rickles said, but Martin called out, "Hey, I wanna make a speech."

"Shaddup."

"No, Don, I wanna tell ya," Dean Martin persisted, "that I think you're a great performer."

"Well, thank you, Dean," Rickles said, seeming pleased.

"But don't go by me," Martin said, plopping down into his seat, "I'm drunk."

"I'll buy that," Rickles said.

By four A.M. Frank Sinatra led the group out of The Sahara, some of them carrying their glasses of whisky with them, sipping it along the sidewalk and in the cars; then, returning to The Sands, they walked into the gambling casino. It was still packed with people, the roulette wheels spinning, the crapshooters screaming in the far corner.

Frank Sinatra, holding a shot glass of bourbon in his left hand, walked through the crowd. He, unlike some of his friends, was perfectly pressed, his tuxedo tie precisely pointed, his shoes unsmudged. He never seems to lose his dignity, never lets his guard completely down no matter how much he has drunk, nor how long he has been up. He never sways when he walks, like Dean Martin, nor does he ever dance in the aisles or jump up on tables, like Sammy Davis.

A part of Sinatra, no matter where he is, is never there. There is always a part of him, though sometimes a small part, that remains *Il Padrone*. Even now, resting his shot glass on the blackjack table, facing the dealer, Sinatra stood a bit back from the table, not leaning against it. He reached under his tuxedo jacket into his trouser pocket and came up with a thick but *clean* wad of bills. Gently he peeled off a one-hundred-dollar bill and placed it on the green-felt table. The dealer dealt him two cards. Sinatra called for a third card, overbid, lost the hundred.

Without a change of expression, Sinatra put down a second hundred-dollar bill. He lost that. Then he put down a third, and lost that. Then he placed two one-hundred-dollar bills on the table and lost those. Finally, putting his sixth hundred-dollar bill on the table, and losing it, Sinatra moved away from the table, nodding to the man, and announcing, "Good dealer."

The crowd that had gathered around him now opened up to let him through. But a woman stepped in front of him, handing him a piece of paper to autograph. He signed it and then *he* said, "Thank you."

In the rear of The Sands' large dining room was a long table reserved for Sinatra. The dining room was fairly empty at this hour, with perhaps two dozen other people in the room, including a table of four unescorted young ladies sitting near Sinatra. On the other side of the room, at another long table, sat seven men shoulder-to-shoulder against the wall, two of them wearing dark glasses, all of them eating quietly, speaking hardly a word, just sitting and eating and missing nothing.

The Sinatra party, after getting settled and having a few more drinks, ordered something to eat. The table was about the same size as the one reserved for Sinatra whenever he is at Jilly's in New York; and the people seated around this table in Las Vegas were many of the same people who are often seen with Sinatra at Jilly's or at a restaurant in California, or in Italy, or in New Jersey, or wherever Sinatra happens to be. When Sinatra sits to dine, his trusted friends are close;

and no matter where he is, no matter how elegant the place may be, there is something of the neighborhood showing because Sinatra, no matter how far he has come, is still something of the boy from the neighborhood—only now he can take his neighborhood with him.

In some ways, this quasi-family affair at a reserved table in a public place is the closest thing Sinatra now has to home life. Perhaps, having had a home and left it, this approximation is as close as he cares to come; although this does not seem precisely so because he speaks with such warmth about his family, keeps in close touch with his first wife, and insists that she make no decision without first consulting him. He is always eager to place his furniture or other mementos of himself in her home or his daughter Nancy's, and he also is on amiable terms with Ava Gardner. When he was in Italy making *Von Ryan's Express*, they spent some time together, being pursued wherever they went by the *paparazzi*. It was reported then that the *paparazzi* had made Sinatra a collective offer of $16,000 if he would pose with Ava Gardner; Sinatra was said to have made a counter offer of $32,000 if he could break one *paparazzi* arm and leg.

While Sinatra is often delighted that he can be in his home completely without people, enabling him to read and think without interruption, there are occasions when he finds himself alone at night, and *not* by choice. He may have dialed a half-dozen women, and for one reason or another they are all unavailable. So he will call his valet, George Jacobs.

"I'll be coming home for dinner tonight, George."

"How many will there be?"

"Just myself," Sinatra will say. "I want something light, I'm not very hungry."

George Jacobs is a twice-divorced man of thirty-six who resembles Billy Eckstine. He has traveled all over the world with Sinatra and is devoted to him. Jacobs lives in a comfortable bachelor's apartment off Sunset Boulevard around the corner from Whiskey à Go Go, and he is known around town for the assortment of frisky California girls he has as friends—a few of whom, he concedes, were possibly drawn to him initially because of his closeness to Frank Sinatra.

When Sinatra arrives, Jacobs will serve him dinner in the dining room. Then Sinatra will tell Jacobs that he is free to go home. If Sinatra, on such evenings, should ask Jacobs to stay longer, or to play a few hands of poker, he would be happy to do so. But Sinatra never does.

This was his second night in Las Vegas, and Frank Sinatra sat with friends in The Sands' dining room until nearly eight A.M. He slept through much of the day, then flew back to Los Angeles, and on the following morning he was driving his little golf cart through the Paramount Pictures movie lot. He was scheduled to complete two final scenes with the sultry blonde actress, Virna Lisi, in the film *Assault on a Queen*. As he maneuvered the little vehicle up the road between the big studio buildings, he spotted Steve Rossi who, with his comedy partner Marty Allen, was making a film in an adjoining studio with Nancy Sinatra.

"Hey, Dag," he yelled to Rossi, "stop kissing Nancy."

"It's part of the film, Frank," Rossi said, turning as he walked.

"In the garage?"

"It's my Dago blood, Frank."

"Well, cool it," Sinatra said, winking, then cutting his golf cart around a corner and parking it outside a big drab building within which the scenes for *Assault* would be filmed.

"Where's the fat director?" Sinatra called out, striding into the studio that was crowded with dozens of technical assistants and actors all gathered around cameras. The director, Jack Donohue, a large man who has worked with Sinatra through twenty-two years on one production or other, has had headaches with this film. The script had been chopped, the actors seemed restless, and Sinatra had become bored. But now there were only two scenes left—a short one to be filmed in the pool, and a longer and passionate one featuring Sinatra and Virna Lisi to be shot on a simulated beach.

The pool scene, which dramatizes a situation where Sinatra and his hijackers fail in their attempt to sack the *Queen Mary*, went quickly and well. After Sinatra had been kept in the water shoulder-high for a few minutes, he said, "Let's move it, fellows—it's cold in this water, and I've just gotten over one cold."

So the camera crews moved in closer, Virna Lisi splashed next to

Sinatra in the water, and Jack Donohue yelled to his assistants operating the fans, "Get the waves going," and another man gave the command, "*Agitate!*" and Sinatra broke out in song. "Agitate in rhythm," then quieted down just before the cameras started to roll.

Frank Sinatra was on the beach in the next situation, supposedly gazing up at the stars, and Virna Lisi was to approach him, toss one of her shoes near him to announce her presence, then sit near him and prepare for a passionate session. Just before beginning, Miss Lisi made a practice toss of her shoe toward the prone figure of Sinatra sprawled on the beach. As she tossed her shoe, Sinatra called out, "Hit me in my bird and I'm going home."

Virna Lisi, who understands little English and certainly none of Sinatra's special vocabulary, looked confused, but everybody behind the camera laughed. She threw the shoe toward him. It twirled in the air, landed on his stomach.

"Well, that's about three inches too high," he announced. She again was puzzled by the laughter behind the camera.

Then Jack Donohue had them rehearse their lines, and Sinatra, still very charged from the Las Vegas trip, and anxious to get the cameras rolling, said, "Let's try one." Donohue, not certain that Sinatra and Lisi knew their lines well enough, nevertheless said okay, and an assistant with a clapboard called, "419, Take 1," and Virna Lisi approached with the shoe, tossed it at Frank lying on the beach. It fell short of his thigh, and Sinatra's right eye raised almost imperceptibly, but the crew got the message, smiled.

"What do the stars tell you tonight?" Miss Lisi said, delivering her first line, and sitting next to Sinatra on the beach.

"The stars tell me tonight I'm an idiot," Sinatra said, "a gold-plated idiot to get mixed up in this thing. . . ."

"Cut," Donohue said. There were some microphone shadows on the sand, and Virna Lisi was not sitting in the proper place near Sinatra.

"419, Take 2," the clapboard man called.

Miss Lisi again approached, threw the shoe at him, this time falling short—Sinatra exhaling only slightly—and she said, "What do the stars tell you tonight?"

"The stars tell me I'm an idiot, a gold-plated idiot to get mixed up in this thing. . . ." Then, according to the script, Sinatra was to continue, ". . . do you know what we're getting into? The minute we step on the deck of the *Queen Mary*, we've just tattooed ourselves," but Sinatra, who often improvises on lines, recited them: ". . . do you know what we're getting into? The minute we step on the deck of that mother's-ass ship. . . ."

"*No*, no," Donohue interrupted, shaking his head, "I don't think that's right."

The cameras stopped, some people laughed, and Sinatra looked up from his position in the sand as if he had been unfairly interrupted.

"I don't see why that can't work . . ." he began, but Richard Conte, standing behind the camera, yelled, "It won't play in London."

Donohue pushed his hand through his thinning grey hair and said, but not really in anger, "You know, that scene was pretty good until somebody blew the line. . . ."

"Yeah," agreed the cameraman, Billy Daniels, his head popping out from around the camera, "it was a pretty good piece. . . ."

"Watch your language," Sinatra cut in. Then Sinatra, who has a genius for figuring out ways of not reshooting scenes, suggested a way in which the film could be used and the "mother" line could be recorded later. This met with approval. Then the cameras were rolling again, Virna Lisi was leaning toward Sinatra in the sand, and then he pulled her down close to him. The camera now moved in for a close-up of their faces, ticking away for a few long seconds, but Sinatra and Lisi did not stop kissing, they just lay together in the sand wrapped in one another's arms, and then Virna Lisi's left leg just slightly began to rise a bit, and everybody in the studio now watched in silence, not saying anything until Donohue finally called out:

"If you ever get through, let me know. I'm running out of film."

Then Miss Lisi got up, straightened out her white dress, brushed back her blonde hair and touched her lipstick, which was smeared. Sinatra got up, a little smile on his lips, and headed for his dressing room.

Passing an older man who stood near a camera, Sinatra asked, "How's your Bell & Howell?"

The older man smiled.

"It's fine, Frank."

"Good."

In his dressing room Sinatra was met by an automobile designer who had the plans for Sinatra's new custom-built model to replace the $25,000 Ghia he has been driving for the last few years. He also was awaited by his secretary, Tom Conroy, who had a bag full of fan mail, including a letter from New York's Mayor John Lindsay; and by Bill Miller, Sinatra's pianist, who would rehearse some of the songs that would be recorded later in the evening for Sinatra's newest album, *Moonlight Sinatra*.

While Sinatra does not mind hamming it up a bit on a movie set, he is extremely serious about his recording sessions; as he explained to a British writer, Robin Douglas-Home: "Once you're on that record singing, it's you and you alone. If it's bad and gets you criticized, it's you who's to blame—no one else. If it's good, it's also you. With a film it's never like that; there are producers and scriptwriters, and hundreds of men in offices and the thing is taken right out of your hands. With a record, you're *it*. . . ."

*But now the days are short*
*I'm in the autumn of the year*
*And now I think of my life*
*As vintage wine*
*From fine old kegs. . . .*

It no longer matters what song he is singing, or who wrote the words—they are all his words, his sentiments, they are chapters from the lyrical novel of his life.

*Life is a beautiful thing*
*As long as I hold the string. . . .*

When Frank Sinatra drives to the studio, he seems to dance out of the car across the sidewalk into the front door; then, snapping his fingers, he is standing in front of the orchestra in an intimate, air-tight room, and soon he is dominating every man, every instrument, every sound wave. Some of the musicians have accompanied him for twenty-five years, have gotten old hearing him sing *You Make Me Feel So Young*.

When his voice is on, as it was tonight, Sinatra is in ecstasy, the room becomes electric, there is an excitement that spreads through the orchestra and is felt in the control booth where a dozen men, Sinatra's friends, wave at him from behind the glass. One of the men is the Dodgers' pitcher, Don Drysdale ("Hey, Big D," Sinatra calls out, "*hey*, baby!"); another is the professional golfer Bo Wininger; there are also numbers of pretty women standing in the booth behind the engineers, women who smile at Sinatra and softly move their bodies to the mellow mood of his music:

> "*Will this be moon love*
> *Nothing but moon love*
> *Will you be gone when the dawn*
> *Comes stealing through. . . .*"

After he is finished, the record is played back on tape, and Nancy Sinatra, who has just walked in, joins her father near the front of the orchestra to hear the playback. They listen silently, all eyes on them, the king, the princess; and when the music ends there is applause from the control booth, Nancy smiles, and her father snaps his fingers and says, kicking a foot, "*Ooba-deeba-boobe-do!*"

Then Sinatra calls to one of his men.

"Hey, Sarge, think I can have a half-a-cup of coffee?"

Sarge Weiss, who had been listening to the music, slowly gets up.

"Didn't mean to wake ya, Sarge," Sinatra says, smiling.

Then Weiss brings the coffee, and Sinatra looks at it, smells it, then announces, "I thought he'd be nice to me, but it's *really* coffee. . . ."

There are more smiles, and then the orchestra prepares for the next number. And one hour later, it is over.

The musicians put their instruments into their cases, grab their coats, and begin to file out, saying good-night to Sinatra. He knows them all by name, knows much about them personally, from their bachelor days, through their divorces, through their ups and downs, as they know him. When a French-horn player, a short Italian named Vincent DeRosa, who has played with Sinatra since The Lucky Strike "Hit Parade" days on radio, strolled by, Sinatra reached out to hold him for a second.

"Vicenzo," Sinatra said, "how's your little girl?"

"She's fine, Frank."

"Oh, she's not a *little* girl anymore," Sinatra corrected himself, "she's a big girl now."

"Yes, she goes to college now. U.S.C."

"That's great."

"She's also got a little talent, I think, Frank, as a singer."

Sinatra was silent for a moment, then said, "Yes, but it's very good for her to get her education first, Vicenzo."

Vincent DeRosa nodded.

"Yes Frank," he said, and then he said, "Well, good-night, Frank."

"Good-night, Vicenzo."

After the musicians had all gone, Sinatra left the recording room and joined his friends in the corridor. He was going to go out and do some drinking with Drysdale, Wininger, and a few other friends, but first he walked to the other end of the corridor to say good-night to Nancy, who was getting her coat and was planning to drive home in her own car.

After Sinatra had kissed her on the cheek, he hurried to join his friends at the door. But before Nancy could leave the studio, one of Sinatra's men, Al Silvani, a former prizefight manager, joined her.

"Are you ready to leave yet, Nancy?"

"Oh, thanks, Al," she said, "but I'll be all right."

"Pope's orders," Silvani said, holding his hands up, palms out.

Only after Nancy had pointed to two of her friends who would escort her home, and only after Silvani recognized them as friends, would he leave.

The rest of the month was bright and balmy. The record session had gone magnificently, the film was finished, the television shows were out of the way, and now Sinatra was in his Ghia driving out to his office to begin coordinating his latest projects. He had an engagement at The Sands, a new spy film called *The Naked Runner* to be shot in England, and a couple more albums to do in the immediate months ahead. And within a week he would be fifty years old. . . .

*Life is a beautiful thing*
*As long as I hold the string*
*I'd be a silly so-and-so*
*If I should ever let go. . . .*

Frank Sinatra stopped his car. The light was red. Pedestrians passed quickly across his windshield but, as usual, one did not. It was a girl in her twenties. She remained at the curb staring at him. Through the corner of his left eye he could see her, and he knew, because it happens almost every day, that she was thinking, *It looks like him, but is it?*

Just before the light turned green, Sinatra turned toward her, looked directly into her eyes waiting for the reaction he knew would come. It came and he smiled. She smiled and he was gone.

—APRIL 1966

# Can You Say . . . "Hero"?

TOM JUNOD

Once upon a time, a little boy loved a stuffed animal whose name was Old Rabbit. It was so old, in fact, that it was really an unstuffed animal, so old that even back then, with the little boy's brain still nice and fresh, he had no memory of it as "Young Rabbit" or even "Rabbit"; so old that Old Rabbit was barely a rabbit at all but rather a greasy hunk of skin without eyes and ears, with a single red stitch where its tongue used to be. The little boy didn't know why he loved Old Rabbit; he just did, and the night he threw it out the car window was the night he learned how to pray. He would grow up to become a great prayer, this little boy, but only intermittently, only fitfully, praying only when fear and desperation drove him to it, and the night he threw Old Rabbit into the darkness was the night that set the pattern, the night that taught him how. He prayed for Old Rabbit's safe return, and when, hours later, his mother and father came home with the filthy, precious strip of rabbity roadkill, he learned not only that prayers are sometimes answered but also the kind of severe effort they entail, the kind of endless frantic summoning. And so when he threw Old Rabbit out the car window the *next time*, it was gone for good.

You were a child once, too. That's what Mister Rogers said, that's what he wrote down, once upon a time, for the doctors. The doctors were ophthalmologists. An ophthalmologist is a doctor who takes care of the eyes. Sometimes, ophthalmologists have to take care of the eyes of children, and some children get very scared, because children know that their world disappears when their eyes close, and they can be afraid that the ophthalmologist will make their eyes close forever. The ophthalmologists did not want to scare children, so they asked Mister Rogers for help, and Mister Rogers agreed to write a chapter for a book the ophthalmologists were putting together—a chapter about what other ophthalmologists could do to calm the children who came into their offices. Because Mister Rogers is such a busy man, however, he could not write a chapter himself, and he asked a woman who worked for him to write it instead. She worked hard at writing the chapter, until one day she showed what she had written to Mister Rogers, who read it and crossed it all out and wrote a sentence addressed directly to the doctors who would be reading it: "You were a child once, too."

And that's how the chapter began.

The old navy-blue sport jacket comes off first, then the dress shoes, except that now there is not the famous sweater or the famous sneakers to replace them, and so after the shoes he's on to the dark socks, peeling them off and showing the blanched skin of his narrow feet. The tie is next, and scanty black batwing of a bow tie hand-tied at his slender throat, and then the shirt, always white or light blue, whisked from his body button by button. He wears an undershirt, of course, but no matter—soon that's gone, too, as is the belt, as are the beige trousers, until his undershorts stand as the last impediment to his nakedness. They are boxers, egg-colored, and to rid himself of them he bends at the waist, and stands on one leg, and hops, and lifts one knee toward his chest and then the other and then . . . Mister Rogers has no clothes on.

Nearly every morning of his life, Mister Rogers has gone swimming, and now, here he is, standing in a locker room, seventy years old and as white as the Easter Bunny, rimed with frost wherever he has hair, gnawed pink in the spots where his dry skin has gone to flaking, slightly wattled at the neck, slightly stooped at the shoulder, slightly sunken in the chest, slightly curvy at the hips, slightly pigeoned at the toes, slightly aswing at the fine bobbing nest of himself . . . and yet when he speaks, it is in *that* voice, *his* voice, the famous one, the unmistakable one, the televised one, the voice dressed in sweater and sneakers, the soft voice, the reassuring one, the curious and expository one, the sly voice that sounds adult to the ears of children and childish to the ears of adults, and what he says, in the midst of all his bobbing nudity, is as understated as it is obvious: "Well, Tom, I guess you've already gotten a deeper glimpse into my daily routine than most people have."

Once upon a time, a long time ago, a man took off his jacket and put on a sweater. Then he took off his shoes and put on a pair of sneakers. His name was Fred Rogers. He was starting a television program, aimed at children, called *Mister Rogers' Neighborhood*. He had been on television before, but only as the voices and movements of puppets, on a program called *The Children's Corner.* Now he was stepping in front of the camera as Mister Rogers, and he wanted to do things right, and whatever he did right, he wanted to repeat. And so, once upon a time, Fred Rogers took off his jacket and put on a sweater his mother had made him, a cardigan with a zipper. Then he took off his shoes and put on a pair of navy-blue canvas boating sneakers. He did the same thing the next day, and then the next . . . until he had done the same things, *those* things, 865 times, at the beginning of 865 television programs, over a span of thirty-one years. The first time I met Mister Rogers, he told me a story of how deeply his simple gestures had been felt, and received. He had just come back from visiting Koko, the gorilla who has learned—or who has been taught—American Sign Language. Koko watches television. Koko watches *Mister Rogers' Neighborhood*, and when Mister Rogers, in his sweater and sneakers, entered the place where she lives, Koko immediately folded him in her long, black arms, as though he were a child and then . . . "She took my *shoes* off, Tom," Mister Rogers said.

Koko was much bigger than Mister Rogers. She weighed 280 pounds, and Mister Rogers weighed 143. Koko weighed 280 pounds because she is a gorilla, and Mister Rogers weighed 143 pounds because he has weighed 143 pounds as long as he has been Mister Rogers, because once upon a time, around thirty-one years ago, Mister Rogers stepped on a scale, and the scale told him that Mister Rogers weighs

143 pounds. No, not that he *weighed* 143 pounds, but that he *weighs* 143 pounds. . . . And so, every day, Mister Rogers refuses to do anything that would make his weight change—he neither drinks, nor smokes, nor eats flesh of any kind, nor goes to bed late at night, nor sleeps late in the morning, nor even watches television—and every morning, when he swims, he steps on a scale in his bathing suit and his bathing cap and goggles, and the scale tells him he weighs 143 pounds. This has happened so many times that Mister Rogers has come to see that number as a gift, as a destiny fulfilled, because as he says, "the number 143 means 'I love you.' It takes one letter to say 'I' and four letters to say 'love' and three letters to say 'you.' One hundred and forty-three. 'I love you.' Isn't that wonderful?"

The first time I called Mister Rogers on the telephone, I woke him up from his nap. He takes a nap every day in the late afternoon—just as he wakes up every morning at five-thirty to read and study and write and pray for the legions who have requested his prayers; just as he goes to bed at nine-thirty at night and sleeps eight hours without interruption. On this afternoon, the end of a hot, yellow day in New York City, he was very tired, and when I asked if I could go to his apartment and see him, he paused for a moment and said shyly, "Well, Tom, I'm in my bathrobe, if you don't mind." I told him I didn't mind, and when, five minutes later, I took the elevator to his floor, well, sure enough, there was Mister Rogers, silver-haired, standing in the golden door at the end of the hallway and wearing eye-glasses and suede moccasins with rawhide laces and a flimsy old blue-and-yellow bathrobe that revealed whatever part of his skinny white calves his dark-blue dress socks didn't hide. "Welcome, Tom," he said with a slight bow, and bade me follow him inside, where he lay down—no, *stretched out*, as though he had known me all his life—on a couch upholstered with gold velveteen. He rested his head on a small pillow and kept his eyes closed while he explained that he had bought the apartment thirty years before for $11,000 and kept it for whenever he came to New York on business for the Neighborhood. I sat in an old armchair and looked around. The place was drab and dim, with the smell of stalled air and a stain of daguerreotype sunlight on its closed, slatted blinds, and Mister Rogers looked so at home in its gloomy familiarity that I thought he was going to fall back asleep when suddenly the phone rang, startling him. "Oh, hello, my dear," he said when he picked it up, and then he said that he had a visitor, someone who wanted to learn more about the Neighborhood. "Would you like to speak to him?" he asked, and then handed me the phone. "It's Joanne," he said. I took the phone and spoke to a woman—his wife, the mother of his two sons—whose voice was hearty and almost whooping in its forthrightness and who spoke to me as though she had known me for a long time and was making the effort to keep up the acquaintance. When I handed him back the phone, he said, "Bye, my dear," and hung up and curled on the couch like a cat, with his bare calves swirled underneath him, and one of his hands gripping his ankle, so that he looked as languorous as an odalisque. There was an energy to him, however, a fearlessness, an unashamed insistence on intimacy, and though I tried to ask him questions about himself, he always turned the questions back on me, and when I finally got him to talk about the puppets that were the comfort of his lonely boyhood, he looked at me, his gray-blue eyes at once mild and steady, and asked, "What about you, Tom? Did you have any special friends growing up?"

"Special friends?"

"Yes," he said. "Maybe a puppet, or a special toy, or maybe just a stuffed animal you loved very much. Did you have a special friend like that, Tom?"

"Yes, Mister Rogers."

"Did your special friend have a name, Tom?"

"Yes, Mister Rogers. His name was Old Rabbit."

"Old Rabbit. Oh, and I'll bet the two of you were together since he was a very young rabbit. Would you like to tell me about Old Rabbit, Tom?"

And it was just about then, when I was spilling the beans about my special friend, that Mister Rogers rose from his corner of the couch and stood suddenly in front of me with a small black camera in hand. "Can I take your picture, Tom?" he asked. "I'd like to take your picture.

I like to take pictures of all my new friends, so that I can show them to Joanne. . . ." And then, in the dark room, there was a wallop of white light, and Mister Rogers disappeared behind it.

Once upon a time, there was a boy who didn't like himself very much. It was not his fault. He was born with cerebral palsy. Cerebral palsy is something that happens to the brain. It means that you can think but sometimes can't walk, or even talk. This boy had a very bad case of cerebral palsy, and when he was still a little boy, some of the people entrusted to take care of him took advantage of him instead and did things to him that made him think that he was a very bad little boy, because only a bad little boy would have to live with the things he had to live with. In fact, when the little boy grew up to be a teenager, he would get so mad at himself that he would hit himself, hard, with his own fists and tell his mother, on the computer he used for a mouth, that he didn't want to live anymore, for he was sure that God didn't like what was inside of him any more than he did. He had always loved Mister Rogers, though, and now, even when he was fourteen years old, he watched the Neighborhood whenever it was on, and the boy's mother sometimes thought that Mister Rogers was keeping her son alive. She and the boy lived together in a city in California, and although she wanted very much for her son to meet Mister Rogers, she knew that he was far too disabled to travel all the way to Pittsburgh, so she figured he would never meet his hero, until one day she learned through a special foundation designed to help children like her son that Mister Rogers was coming to California and that after he visited that gorilla named Koko, he was coming to meet her son.

At first, the boy was made very nervous by the thought that Mister Rogers was visiting him. He was so nervous, in fact, that when Mister Rogers did visit, he got mad at himself and began hating himself and hitting himself, and his mother had to take him to another room and talk to him. Mister Rogers didn't leave, though. He wanted something from the boy, and Mister Rogers never leaves when he wants something from somebody. He just waited patiently, and when the boy came back, Mister Rogers talked to him, and then he made his request.

He said, "I would like you to do something for me. Would you do something for me?" On his computer, the boy answered yes, of course, he would do *anything* for Mister Rogers, so then Mister Rogers said, "I would like you to pray for me. Will you pray for me?" And now the boy didn't know how to respond. He was thunderstruck. Thunderstruck means that you can't talk, because something has happened that's as sudden and as miraculous and maybe as scary as a bolt of lightning, and all you can do is listen to the rumble. The boy was thunderstruck because nobody had ever *asked* him for something like that, ever. The boy had always been prayed *for*. The boy had always been the *object* of prayer, and now he was being asked to pray for Mister Rogers, and although at first he didn't know if he could do it, he said he would, he said he'd try, and ever since then he keeps Mister Rogers in his prayers and doesn't talk about wanting to die anymore, because he figures Mister Rogers is close to God, and if Mister Rogers likes him, that must mean God likes him, too.

As for Mister Rogers himself . . . well, he doesn't look at the story in the same way that the boy did or that I did. In fact, when Mister Rogers first told me the story, I complimented him on being so smart—for knowing that asking the boy for his prayers would make the boy feel better about himself—and Mister Rogers responded by looking at me at first with puzzlement and then with surprise. "Oh, heavens no, Tom! I didn't ask him for his prayers for *him*; I asked for *me*. I asked him because I think that anyone who has gone through challenges like that must be very close to God. I asked him because I wanted his *intercession*."

On December 1, 1997—oh, heck, once upon a time—a boy, no longer little, told his friends to watch out, that he was going to do something "really big" the next day at school, and the next day at school he took his gun and his ammo and his earplugs and shot eight classmates who had clustered for a prayer meeting. Three died, and they were still children, almost. The shootings took place in West Paducah, Kentucky, and when Mister Rogers heard about them, he said, "Oh, wouldn't the world be a different place if he had said, 'I'm going to do something really *little* tomorrow,'" and he decided to dedicate a week of the Neighborhood to the theme "Little and Big." He wanted to tell children that what starts out little can sometimes *become* big, and so they could devote themselves to little dreams without feeling bad about them. But how could Mister Rogers *show* little becoming big, and vice versa? That was a challenge. He couldn't just say it, the way he could always just say to the children who watch his program that they are special to him, or even sing it, the way he could always just sing "It's You I Like" and "Everybody's Fancy" and "It's Such a Good Feeling" and "Many Ways to Say I Love You" and "Sometimes People Are Good." No, he had to show it, he had to demonstrate it, and that's how Mister Rogers and the people who work for him eventually got the idea of coming to New York City to visit a woman named Maya Lin.

Maya Lin is a famous architect. Architects are people who create big things from the little designs they draw on pieces of paper. Most famous architects are famous for creating big famous buildings, but Maya Lin is more famous for creating big fancy things for people to look at, and in fact, when Mister Rogers had gone to her studio the day before, he looked at the pictures she had drawn of the clock that is now on the ceiling of a place in New York called Penn Station. A clock is a machine that tells people what time it is, but as Mister Rogers sat in the backseat of an old station wagon hired to take him from his apartment to Penn Station, he worried that Maya Lin's clock might be *too* fancy and that the children who watch the Neighborhood might not understand it. Mister Rogers always worries about things like that, because he always worries about children, and when his station wagon stopped in traffic next to a bus stop, he read aloud the advertisement of an airline trying to push its international service. "Hmmm," Mister Rogers said, "*that's* a strange ad. 'Most people think of us as a great domestic airline. We *hate* that.' Hmmm. *Hate* is such a strong word to use so lightly. If they can hate something like that, you wonder how easy it would be for them to hate something more important." He was with his producer, Margy Whitmer. He had makeup on his face and a dollop of black dye combed into his silver hair. He was wearing beige pants, a blue dress shirt, a tie, dark socks, a pair of dark-blue boating sneakers, and a purple, zippered cardigan. He looked very little in the backseat of the car. Then the car stopped on Thirty-fourth Street, in front of the escalators leading down to the station, and when the doors opened—

"Holy shit! It's Mister Fucking Rogers!"

—he turned into Mister Fucking Rogers. This was not a bad thing, however, because he was in New York, and in New York it's not an insult to be called Mister Fucking Anything. In fact, it's an honorific. An honorific is what people call you when they respect you, and the moment Mister Rogers got out of the car, people wouldn't stay the fuck away from him, they respected him so much. Oh, Margy Whitmer tried to keep people away from him, tried to tell people that if they gave her their names and addresses, Mister Rogers would send them an autographed picture, but every time she turned around, there was Mister Rogers putting his arms around someone, or wiping the tears off someone's cheek, or passing around the picture of someone's child, or getting on his knees to talk to a child. Margy couldn't stop them, and she couldn't stop him. "Oh, Mister Rogers, thank you for my childhood." "Oh, Mister Rogers, you're the father I never had." "Oh, Mister Rogers, would you please just hug me?" After a while, Margy just rolled her eyes and gave up, because it's always like this with Mister Rogers, because the thing that people don't understand about him is that he's *greedy* for this—greedy for the grace that people offer him. What is grace? He doesn't even know. He can't define it. This is a man who loves the simplifying force of definitions, and yet all he knows of grace is how he *gets it*; all he knows is that he gets it from God, through man. And so in Penn Station, where he was surrounded by men and women and children, he had this *power*, like a comic-book superhero who absorbs the energy of others until he bursts out of his shirt.

"If Mister Fucking Rogers can tell me how to read that fucking clock, I'll watch his show every day for a fucking *year*"—that's what someone in the crowd said while watching Mister Rogers and Maya Lin crane their necks at Maya Lin's big fancy clock, but it didn't even matter whether Mister Rogers could read the clock or not, because every time he looked at it, with the television cameras on him, he leaned back from his waist and opened his mouth wide with astonishment, like someone trying to catch a peanut he had tossed into the air, until it became clear that Mister Rogers could show that he was astonished all *day* if he had to, or even forever, because Mister Rogers lives in a *state* of astonishment, and the astonishment he showed when he looked at the clock was the same astonishment he showed when people—absolute strangers—walked up to him and fed his hungry ear with their whispers, and he turned to me, with an open, abashed mouth, and said, "Oh, Tom, if you could only hear the stories I hear!"

Once upon a time, Mister Rogers went to New York City and got caught in the rain. He didn't have an umbrella, and he couldn't find a taxi, either, so he ducked with a friend into the subway and got on one of the trains. It was late in the day, and the train was crowded with children who were going home from school. Though of all races, the schoolchildren were mostly black and Latino, and they didn't even approach Mister Rogers and ask him for his autograph. They just sang. They sang, all at once, all together, the song he sings at the start of his program, "Won't You Be My Neighbor?" and turned the clattering train into a single soft, runaway choir.

He finds me, of course, at Penn Station. He finds me, because that's what Mister Rogers *does*—he looks, and then he finds. I'm standing against a wall, listening to a bunch of mooks from Long Island discuss the strange word—χάρις—he has written down on each of the autographs he gave them. First mook: "He says it's the Greek word for grace." Second mook: "Huh. That's cool. I'm glad I know that. Now, what the fuck is grace?" First mook: "Looks like you're gonna have to break down and buy a dictionary." Second mook: "Fuck that. What I'm buying is a ticket to the fucking *Lotto*. I just met Mister Rogers—this is *definitely* my lucky day." I'm listening to these guys when, from thirty feet away, I notice Mister Rogers looking around for someone and know, immediately, that he is looking for me. He is on one knee in front of a little girl who is hoarding, in her arms, a small stuffed animal, sky-blue, a bunny.

"Remind you of anyone, Tom?" he says when I approach the two of them. He is not speaking of the little girl.

"Yes, Mister Rogers."

"Looks a little bit like . . . *Old Rabbit*, doesn't it, Tom?"

"Yes, Mister Rogers."

"I thought so." Then he turns back to the little girl. "This man's name is Tom. When he was your age, he had a rabbit, too, and he loved it very much. Its name was Old Rabbit. What is yours named?"

The little girl eyes me suspiciously, and then Mister Rogers. She goes a little knock-kneed, directs a thumb toward her mouth. "Bunny Wunny," she says.

"Oh, that's a *nice* name," Mister Rogers says, and then goes to the Thirty-fourth Street escalator to climb it one last time for the cameras. When he reaches the street, he looks right at the lens, as he always does, and says, speaking of the Neighborhood, "Let's go back to my place," and then makes a right turn toward Seventh Avenue, except that this time he just *keeps going*, and suddenly Margy Whitmer is saying, "Where is Fred?" Where is Fred?" and Fred, he's a hundred yards away, in his sneakers and his purple sweater, and the only thing anyone sees of him is his gray head bobbing up and down amid all the other heads, the hundreds of them, the thousands, the millions, disappearing into the city and its swelter.

Once upon a time, a little boy with a big sword went into battle against Mister Rogers. Or maybe, if the truth be told, Mister Rogers went into battle against a little boy with a big sword, for Mister Rogers didn't *like* the big sword. It was one of those swords that really isn't a sword at all; it was a big plastic contraption with lights and sound effects, and it was the kind of sword used in defense of the universe by the heroes of the television shows that the little boy liked to watch. The little boy with the big sword did not watch Mister Rogers. In fact, the little boy with the big sword didn't know who Mister Rogers *was*, and so when Mister Rogers knelt down in front of him, the little boy with the big sword looked past him and through him, and when Mister Rogers said, "Oh, my, that's a big sword you have," the boy didn't answer, and finally his mother got embarrassed and said, "Oh, honey, c'mon, that's *Mister Rogers*," and felt his head for fever. Of course, she knew who Mister Rogers was, because she had grown up with him, and she knew that he was good for her son, and so now, with her little boy zombie-eyed under his blond bangs, she apologized, saying to Mister Rogers that she knew he was in a rush and that she knew he was here in Penn Station taping his program and that her son usually wasn't *like* this, he was probably just tired. . . . Except that Mister Rogers wasn't going anywhere. Yes, sure, he was taping, and right there, in Penn Station in New York City, were rings of other children wiggling in wait for him, but right now his patient gray eyes were fixed on the little boy with the big sword, and so he stayed there, on one knee, until the little boy's eyes finally focused on Mister Rogers, and he said, "It's not a sword; it's a death ray." A death ray! Oh, honey, Mommy *knew* you could do it. . . . And so now, encouraged, Mommy said, "Do you want to give Mister Rogers a hug, honey?" But the boy was shaking his head no, and Mister Rogers was sneaking his face past the big sword and the armor of the little boy's eyes and whispering something in his ear—something that, while not changing his mind about the hug, made the little boy look at Mister Rogers in a new way, with the eyes of a child at last, and nod his head yes.

We were heading back to his apartment in a taxi when I asked him what he had said.

"Oh, I just knew that whenever you see a little boy carrying something like that, it means he wants to show people that he's strong on the outside.

"I just wanted to let him know that he was strong on the inside, too.

"And so that's what I told him.

"I said, 'Do you know that you're strong on the inside, too?'

"Maybe it was something he needed to hear."

He was barely more than a boy himself when he learned what he would be fighting for, and fighting against, for the rest of his life. He was in college. He was a music major at a small school in Florida and planning to go to seminary upon graduation. His name was Fred Rogers. He came home to Latrobe, Pennsylvania, once upon a time, and his parents, because they were wealthy, had bought something new for the corner room of their big redbrick house. It was a television. Fred turned it on, and, as he says now, with plaintive distaste, "there were people throwing *pies* at one another." He was the soft son of overprotective parents, but he believed, right then, that he was strong enough to enter into battle with *that*—that machine, that medium—and to wrestle with it until it yielded to him, until the ground touched by its blue shadow became hallowed and this thing called television came to be used "for the broadcasting of grace through the land." It would not be easy, no—for in order to win such a battle, he would have to forbid himself the privilege of *stopping*, and whatever he did right he would have to repeat, as though he were already living in eternity. And so it was that the puppets he employed on *The Children's Corner* would be the puppets he employed forty-four years later, and so it was that once he took off his jacket and his shoes . . . well, he was Mister Rogers for good. And even now, when he is producing only three weeks' worth of new programs a year, he still winds up agonizing—*agonizing*—about whether to announce his theme as "Little and Big" or "Big and Little" and still makes only two edits per televised minute, because he doesn't want his message to be determined by the cuts and splices in a piece of tape—to become, despite all his fierce coherence, "a message of fragmentation."

He is losing, of course. The revolution he started—a half hour a day, five days a week—it wasn't enough, it didn't *spread*, and so, forced to fight his battles alone, Mister Rogers is losing, as we all are losing. He is losing to *it*, to *our* twenty-four-hour-a-day pie fight, to the dizzying cut and the disorienting edit, to the message of fragmentation, to the flicker and pulse and shudder and strobe, to the constant, hivey drone of the electroculture . . . and yet still he fights, deathly afraid that the medium he chose is consuming the very things he tried to protect: childhood and silence. Yes, at seventy years old and 143 pounds, Mister Rogers still fights, and indeed, early this year, when television handed him its highest honor, he responded by telling television—gently, of course—to just *shut up* for once, and television listened. He had already won his third Daytime Emmy, and now he went onstage to accept Emmy's Lifetime Achievement Award, and there, in front of all the soap-opera stars and talk-show sinceratrons, in front of all the jutting man-tanned jaws and jutting saltwater bosoms, he made his small bow and said into the microphone, "All of us have special ones who have loved us into being. Would you just take, along with me, *ten seconds* to think of the people who have helped *you* become who you are. . . . Ten seconds of silence." And then he lifted his wrist, and looked at the audience, and looked at his watch, and said softly, "I'll watch the time," and there was, at first, a small whoop from the crowd, a giddy, strangled hiccup of laughter, as people realized that *he wasn't kidding*, that Mister Rogers was not some convenient eunuch but rather a *man*, an authority figure who actually expected them to do what he asked . . . and so they did. One second, two seconds, three seconds . . . and now the jaws clenched, and the bosoms heaved, and the mascara ran, and the tears fell upon the beglittered gathering like rain leaking down a crystal chandelier, and Mister Rogers finally looked up from his watch and said, "May God be with you" to all his vanquished children.

Once upon a time, there was a little boy born blind, and so, defenseless in the world, he suffered the abuses of the defenseless, and when he grew up and became a man, he looked back and realized that he'd had no childhood at all, and that if he were ever to have a childhood, he would have to start having it now, in his forties. So the first thing he did was rechristen himself "Joybubbles"; the second thing he did was declare himself five years old forever; and the third thing he did was make a pilgrimage to Pittsburgh, where the University of Pittsburgh's Information Sciences Library keeps a Mister Rogers archive. It has all 865 programs, in both color and black and white, and for two months this past spring, Joybubbles went to the library every day for ten hours and watched the Neighborhood's every episode, plus specials—or, since he is blind, *listened* to every episode, *imagined* every episode. Until one night, Mister Rogers came to him, in what he calls a visitation—"I was dreaming, but I was awake"—and offered to teach him how to pray.

"But Mister Rogers, I *can't* pray," Joybubbles said, "because every time I try to pray, I forget the words."

"I know that," Mister Rogers said, "and that's why the prayer I'm going to teach you has only three words."

"What prayer is that, Mister Rogers? What kind of prayer has only three words?"

"Thank you, God," Mister Rogers said.

The walls of Mister Rogers' Neighborhood are light blue and fleeced with clouds. They are tall—as tall as the cinder-block walls they are designed to hide—and they encompass the Neighborhood's entire stage set, from the flimsy yellow house where Mister Rogers comes to visit, to the closet where he finds his sweaters, to the Neighborhood of Make-Believe, where he goes to dream. The blue walls are the ends of the daylit universe he has made, and yet Mister Rogers can't *see* them—or at least can't know them—because he was born blind to color. He doesn't know the color of his walls, and one day, when I caught him looking toward his painted skies, I asked him to tell me what color they *are*, and he said, "I imagine they're *blue*, Tom." Then he looked at me and smiled. "I imagine they're blue."

He has spent thirty-one years imagining and reimagining those walls—the walls that have both penned him in and set him free. You would think it would be easy by now, being Mister Rogers; you would think that one morning he would wake up and think, Okay, all I have to do is be *nice* for my allotted half hour today, and then I'll just take the rest of the day off. . . . But no, Mister Rogers is a stubborn man, and so on the day I ask about the color of his sky, he has already gotten up at five-thirty, already prayed for those who have asked for his prayers, already read, already written, already swum, already weighed himself, already sent out cards for the birthdays he never forgets, already called any number of people who depend on him for comfort, already cried when he read the letter of a mother whose child was buried with a picture of Mister Rogers in his casket, already played for twenty minutes with an autistic boy who has come, with his father, all the way from Boise, Idaho, to meet him. The boy had never spoken, until one day he said, "X the Owl," which is the name of one of Mister Roger's puppets, and he had never looked his father in the eye until one day his father had said, "Let's go to the Neighborhood of Make-Believe," and now the boy is speaking and reading, and the father has come to thank Mister Rogers for saving his son's life. . . . And by this time, well, it's nine-thirty in the morning, time for Mister Rogers to take off his jacket and his shoes and put on his sweater and his sneakers and start taping another visit to the Neighborhood. He writes all his own scripts, but on this day, when he receives a visit from Mrs. McFeely and a springer spaniel, she says that she has to bring the dog "back to his owner," and Mister Rogers makes a face. The cameras stop, and he says, "I don't like the word *owner* there. It's not a good word. Let's change it to 'bring the dog *home*.'" And so the change is made, and the taping resumes, and this is how it goes all day, a life unfolding within a clasp of unfathomable governance, and once, when I lose sight of him, I ask Margy Whitmer where he is, and she says, "Right over your shoulder, where he always is," and when I turn around, Mister Rogers is facing me, child-stealthy, with a small black camera in his hand, to take another picture for the album that he will give me when I take my leave of him.

Yes, it should be easy being Mister Rogers, but when four o'clock rolls around, well, Mister Rogers is *tired*, and so he sneaks over to the piano and starts playing, with dexterous, pale fingers, the music that used to end a 1940s newsreel and that has now become the music he plays to signal to the cast and crew that a day's taping has wrapped. On this day, however, he is premature by a considerable extent, and so Margy, who has been with Mister Rogers since 1983—because nobody who works for Mister Rogers ever *leaves* the Neighborhood—comes running over, papers in hand, and says, "Not so fast there, buster."

"Oh, please, sister," Mister Rogers says. "I'm done."

And now Margy comes up behind him and massages his shoulders. "No, you're not," she says, "*Roy* Rogers is done. *Mister* Rogers still has a ways to go."

He was a child once, too, and so one day I asked him if I could go with him back to Latrobe. He thought about it for a second, then said, by the way of agreement, "Okay, then—tomorrow, Tom, I'll show you childhood." Not *his* childhood, mind you, or even *a* childhood—no, just "childhood." And so the next morning, we swam together, and then he put back on his boxer shorts and the dark socks, and the T-shirt, and the gray trousers, and the belt, and then the white dress shirt and the black bow tie and the gray suit jacket, and about two hours later we were pulling up to the big brick house on Weldon Street in Latrobe, and Mister Rogers was thinking about going inside.

There was nobody home. The doors were open, unlocked, because the house was undergoing a renovation of some kind, but the owners were away, and Mister Roger's boyhood home was empty of everyone but workmen. "Do you think we can go in?" he asked Bill Isler, president of Family Communications, the company that produces *Mister Rogers' Neighborhood*. Bill had driven us there, and now, sitting behind the wheel of his red Grand Cherokee, he was full of remonstrance. "No!" he said, "Fred, they're *not home*. If we wanted to go into the house, we should have *called* first. Fred . . ." But Mister Rogers was out of the car, with his camera in his hand and his legs moving so fast that the material of his gray suit pants furled and unfurled around both of his skinny legs, like flags exploding in a breeze. And here, as he made his way through thickets of bewildered workmen—this skinny old man dressed in a gray suit and a bow tie, with his hands on his hips and his arms akimbo, like a dance instructor—there was some kind of wiggly jazz in his legs, and he went flying all around the outside of the house, pointing at windows, saying there was the room where he learned to play the piano, and there was the room where he saw the pie fight on a primitive television, and there was the room where his beloved father died . . . until finally we reached the front door. He put his hand on the knob; he cracked it open, but then, with Bill Isler calling caution from the car, he said, "Maybe we *shouldn't* go in. And all the people who made this house special to me are not here, anyway. They're all in heaven."

And so we went to the graveyard. We were heading there all along, because Mister Rogers *loves* graveyards, and so as we took the long, straight road out of sad, fading Latrobe, you could still feel the *speed* in him, the hurry, as he mustered up a sad anticipation, and when we passed through the cemetery gates, he smiled as he said to Bill Isler, "The plot's at the end of the yellow-brick road." And so it was; the asphalt ended, and then we began bouncing over a road of old blond bricks, until even that road ended, and we were parked in front of the place where Mister Rogers is to be buried. He got out of the car, and, moving as quickly as he had moved to the door of his house, he stepped up a small hill to the door of a large gray mausoleum, a huge structure built for six, with a slightly peaked roof, and bronze doors, and angels living in the stained glass. He peeked in the window, and in the same voice he uses on television, *that* voice, at once so patient and so eager, he pointed out each crypt, saying, "There's my father, and there's my mother, and there, on the left, is my place, and right across will be Joanne. . . ." The window was darkened glass, though, and so to see through it, we had to press our faces close against it, and where the glass had warped away from the frame of the door—where there was a finger-wide crack—Mister Rogers's voice leaked into his grave, and came back to us as a soft, hollow echo.

And then he was on the move again, happily, quickly, for he would not leave until he showed me all the places of all those who'd loved him into being. His grandfather, his grandmother, his uncles, his aunts, his father-in-law and mother-in-law, even his family's servants—he went to each grave, and spoke their names, and told their stories, until finally I headed back down to the Jeep and turned back around to see Mister Rogers standing high on a green dell, smiling among the stones. "And now if you don't mind," he said without a hint of shame or embarrassment, "I have to go find a place to relieve myself," and then off he went, this ecstatic ascetic, to take a proud piss in his corner of heaven.

Once upon a time, a man named Fred Rogers decided that he wanted to live in heaven. Heaven is the place where good people go when they die, but this man, Fred Rogers, didn't want to *go* to heaven; he wanted to *live* in heaven, here, now, in this world, and so one day, when he was talking about all the people he had loved in this life, he looked at me and said, "The connections we make in the course of a life—maybe that's what *heaven* is, Tom. We make so *many* connections here on earth. Look at us—I've just met you, but I'm invested in who you are and who you will be, and I can't help it."

The next afternoon, I went to his office in Pittsburgh. He was sitting on a couch, under a framed rendering of the Greek word for grace and a biblical phrase written in Hebrew that means "I am my beloved's, and my beloved is mine." A woman was with him, sitting in a big chair. Her name was Deb. She was very pretty. She had a long face and a dark blush to her skin. She had curls in her hair and stars at the centers of her eyes. She was a minister at Fred Rogers's church. She spent much of her time tending to the sick and the dying. Fred Rogers loved her very much, and so, out of nowhere, he smiled and put his hand over hers. "Will you be with me when I die?" he asked her, and when she said yes, he said, "Oh, thank you, my dear." Then, with his hand still over hers and his eyes looking straight into hers, he said, "Deb, do you know what a great prayer you are? Do you know that about yourself? Your prayers are just wonderful." Then he looked at me. I was sitting in a small chair by the door, and he said, "Tom, would you close the door, please?" I closed the door and sat back down. "Thanks, my dear," he said to me, then turned back to Deb. "Now, Deb, I'd like to ask you a favor," he said. "Would you lead us? Would you lead us in prayer?"

Deb stiffened for a second, and she let out a breath, and her color got deeper. "Oh, I don't know, Fred," she said. "I don't know if I want to put on a *performance*. . . ."

Fred never stopped looking at her or let go of her hand. "It's not a performance. It's just a meeting of friends," he said. He moved his hand from her wrist to her palm and extended his other hand to me. I took it, and then put my hand around her free hand. His hand was warm, hers was cool, and we bowed our heads, and closed our eyes, and I heard Deb's voice calling out for the grace of God. What is grace? I'm not certain; all I know is that my heart felt like a spike, and then, in that room, it opened and felt like an umbrella. I had never prayed like that before, ever. I had always been a great prayer, a powerful one, but only fitfully, only out of guilt, only when fear and desperation drove me to it . . . and it hit me, right then, with my eyes closed, that this was the moment Fred Rogers—Mister Rogers—had been leading me to from the moment he answered the door of his apartment in his bathrobe and asked me about Old Rabbit. Once upon a time, you see, I lost something, and prayed to get it back, but when I lost it the second time, I didn't, and now this was it, the missing word, the unuttered promise, the prayer I'd been waiting to say a very long time.

"Thank you, God," Mister Rogers said.

—NOVEMBER 1998

# Nick Nolte Is Racing the Clock to Repair the Damage

DANIEL VOLL

There's a strip mall in Malibu. The surf crashes right across the highway. At the RadioShack, Eric the audio geek helps me select a new microcassette recorder. He asks what I'm up to. I tell him I'm interviewing a guy.

"Who?" he asks. "I don't want to be pushy."

"It's okay," I shrug. "It's Nick Nolte."

"Cool—why didn't you say so? He comes in here all the time hunting parts for his microscope. Science is his thing. He's got a *big* microscope."

Nolte's rural six-acre compound is a few miles north of RadioShack, back in the hills, away from the ocean. I push a buzzer, the gate opens, and I drive in. Lush grounds, a canopy of trees. A couple houses on the property. Gardeners everywhere. A big yellow Lab with a plastic megaphone around its neck bounds out of the main house. The doors to the house are open. I follow the dog inside.

Nolte is standing in the center of a large room, wearing a black long-sleeved T-shirt and wide-striped Calvin Klein pajama bottoms. He's barefoot. Face tanned and lined, eyes sunk in. Strong neck. Lean as a bull rider. His hair is the same tawny color as the Labrador's and flies back over his ears and floats above his forehead and down into his eyes. He peers through his hair at me, and there is an energy to those eyes, a crazy vitality. He is mixing a little something in a small cup, a brown potion, looks earthy. There's a dropper and a spoon and he's stirring and then he drinks it down. I wait for him to say something. But he just looks at me. Finally, I shake his hand and say, "Congratulations on the Nobel prize. Can we talk about your latest science project?"

"Great!" Nolte says, sort of rubbing his hands together. "I've evolved deep into dark-field blood work. Let's go upstairs."

Up the stairs we tramp, through a construction zone of plastic walls with zippers, sawhorses, and power saws, into a massive, high-ceilinged upper room that looks over a garden. This is his bedroom and laboratory. A schoolboy's dream of a room. A Buddha watches over the large, book-strewn bed. Naked women with trumpets adorn lamps. Another dog comes in and sniffs us out. And then there it is, in an alcove where he does his work: a vintage, professional-grade Ortholux microscope.

Nolte stands in front of the microscope, eyes wide, a sideways look, mouth cocked open. "My blood?" he asks. "Or yours?"

I tell him I'm squeamish about needles.

He looks at me and growls, voice deep as a lion's. "You'll have to get over that if you want to do blood work."

He pricks his finger, squeezes a drop of his blood. "We don't want the first drop. We want to get down a little deeper." He squeezes again, a second perfect drop onto a glass slide, which he slips under the microscope. "Our blood tells us everything. By watching your blood, you become connected to yourself in a way that you have never before been connected." He's flipping switches. Light passes through the iris, illuminating the blood cells. The picture is projected on a nearby monitor.

"Yes, *yes*, that's it!" He's pointing to cells moving on the screen. "Here's a real good cell structure, perfectly round. When you're young, the red cells are plump and shimmering—that's what you want." He points out a dying cell. "I've watched my blood degenerate over twenty-four hours. You'll actually see long strings of bacteria coming out of them as they decay." He lingers on the word *decay*, giving it a couple more syllables.

The blood cells are quite beautiful, but all of a sudden the microscope is smoking. It's like a magnifying glass that has been left in the sun and now there's fire inside. "Whoa," he says, surprised, blowing at the smoke. "*Whoa!* Who's been messing with this?"

He tries to close the iris, but it's too hot. "We're screwed," he says. "Oh, shit!" He might have burned himself a little. "Oh, Aidan, *Aidan*, what have you *done*?" he moans. The smoke starts up again. Small puffs of it, like smoke signals.

"Brawley!" Nolte bellows, calling his twelve-year-old son.

Brawley is in a room across the hall, and I'm sent to hunt him down. I unzip the plastic sheeting and walk into the space that Brawley calls his cave. He and his best friend, Aidan, are hunched over separate computers playing EverQuest. The game takes nine hours to cross a virtual landscape. The room is pitch-black except for the glowing monitors, and it's throbbing, incredibly loud. I have to shout to get their attention.

The microscope is still smoldering as the boys shuffle into the lab, wanting to know what happened. They crowd around Nolte's shoulders, looking at it.

"Somebody's been on this while I was out of the house," Nolte says. "*That* is my paranoid conclusion." He looks at Aidan, a chubby kid with acne, a real whiz kid, who says, "I get blamed for everything around here. I could be fifty miles away and you'd still blame me."

Aidan is the son of Brawley's shrink. They met when Aidan's dad was trying to help Brawley cope with Nick's divorce from Brawley's mom six years ago. Then the shrink himself got divorced, and now the two boys are best friends. Sometimes Aidan sleeps on the floor next to Brawley's bed.

The boys want to check out the iris of the microscope, and Nolte cuts a flashlight on. "Maybe it's an aging problem," Aidan says. They all peer through the smoke at the inner workings. Even though Nolte is fifty-eight, and Brawley and Aidan are twelve and thirteen, the three confer like colleagues, and that is, in truth, the relationship. They hang out here, for weeks sometimes, without visitors, plotting new science projects, along with Nolte's girlfriend, the comedic actress Vicki Lewis. The compound is tricked out with ten computers, each with a large color monitor, and Nolte has his own Internet server. To Brawley and Aidan, he's just Nick. No big deal. He's a grown-up kid with a credit card and the best toys.

But his blood work has been interrupted, and his frustration is beginning to show. He doesn't want to scold, doesn't want to accuse, because Brawley's a good kid, and he's still working out this postdivorce relationship. Anyway, you can't yell at them, because if you yell, they'll just sneak around and do bad-boy things. Aw, hell. "Maybe I shouldn't let the two of you in here for a while," Nolte says. "Let's shut it down for now, let it cool down."

"We should test his blood type!" Brawley suggests.

Yes! Let's test his blood type! Nolte is immediately back in motion. Suddenly, all three of them are looking at me hungrily.

Aidan swabs my fingertip with alcohol. "This will hardly hurt at all," he says. "Wanna hear a joke? Something to get your mind off it? Okay, how many blonds can you fit into a van? I mean—oh, shit, that's not it. I mean, four blonds die in a minivan—what's the tragedy?"

He pricks my finger, and Nick squeezes a drop of blood onto the test strip.

"The van could've held eight!" Aidan cries.

Nolte says, "Brawley, Aidan, read this to me. What's the protocol?"

"Um, protocol," Aidan says. "Step one, okay, mix in for thirty seconds, rub it across the thing for thirty seconds."

Brawley studies how the blood instantly starts breaking up, like red paint left in the rain. "I betcha it's A negative," he says. "Me and Aidan are the same type. A negative."

As he waits for the results, Nolte looks over at the wreckage of the microscope, flipping switches again, and says, "It's absolutely *broken. Now* I'm frustrated." He breathes. *Maintain.* He's not going to yell. He knows it can get fixed, damage can be repaired—that's one of the things he's learned. You just have to go to the expert. He knows a guy who can fix it, but still, he's feeling a little jangled. Meanwhile, Brawley was right. I'm A negative.

Nolte pushes away from the microscope. "Who wants a shot of B-12?" he asks.

No, thank you, I say. My needle problem. Maybe coffee? Or a drink?

"*No, no!*" he says. "This is better."

There is a small, gray medical cabinet on his desk. One drawer labeled SYRINGES. Another drawer TOURNIQUETS. He takes out a narrow-gauge needle.

"Don't worry," Brawley says. "He does this all the time."

Every night, for instance, before he goes to bed, Nolte fills a syringe with .5cc of human growth hormone, which is generally illegal unless you are a dwarf, and shoots it into his stomach. Someday, he figures, we'll all just take a pill, encoded with all the testosterone and hormones our body needs, guided toward specific tissues, to retard aging. Until then, he'll keep buying on the underground market. "All the old hippies are doing it now," he says. A lot of corporate executives. "If Charlie Rose and Larry King aren't on human growth hormones," he says, laughing, "they're thinking about it. I guarantee you, they all want to keep a step ahead of the competition.

"And if I'm feeling a little stressed," Nolte says, "I'll come in and shoot a little B with a little pull of folic acid, which is good for the heart, and a little B-12."

In *North Dallas Forty*, he played an over-the-hill football player who shoots painkillers into his knee. "I like needles," the broken-down ballplayer declared. "Anything to keep me in the game."

"Nothing to it," Nolte says. When he's *really* stressed or feeling depleted, he fills an IV bag with thirteen different vitamins and minerals, puts a tourniquet around his arm, and drips them through a needle into his bloodstream. The procedure takes more than an hour, and he figures he does it several times a week, often while in bed.

Well, I guess a little B-12 never hurt anyone. I offer my right arm, but he waves it off. "Need your right butt cheek, just off the hip." He swabs me with alcohol. The needle doesn't go in readily, and he's got to jab it in a second time. Right into muscle. The boys are watching me, and I try not to wince, but the damn needle stings, and immediately I feel the stuff hit my bloodstream. My forehead warms. My feet tingle. An incredible humming rush for about a minute. I'm feeling a little light-headed, I tell Nolte.

"Man, he doesn't look good," Brawley says.

You sure you only put B-12 in there? I ask.

The room has begun to spin, and the boys ease me down onto the floor, where I rest on a round Feldenkrais mat, which feels like a soft, white buoy. I am quite woozy and sweating, and I hear something strange emanating from somewhere—I'm not sure where—a singsongy, possibly computer-generated voice. A very pleasant, clipped voice. Sad Man, a life-sized papier-mâché figure, is seated near the bed, his head bowed in a posture of sadness. Nolte pats Sad Man on the head as he passes. Books are strewn about—scientific journals, Philip Roth's *American Pastoral*, *Better Sex Through Chemistry*.

From this angle I also see Nolte is filling up another syringe for himself, mixing a vitamin cocktail, holding it above his head, thumping it, squinting. Nolte pulls down his pajamas a bit on one side, exposing a few inches of skin, from his waist to his right cheek, a lean flank for a guy almost sixty.

After shooting up, he's feeling a bit strange himself. He's looking a little worried now, too. You sure you didn't mix the wrong thing? I ask. "No," he says, "I think I'm picking up your vibe. A kind of placebo effect."

When the room stops spinning, the boys help me up, each taking an arm.

"I could give you some ozone," Nolte says. "It will make you feel better."

Ozone? Like the hole?

"This works. I can prove it to you. Bad things can't live in it. Viruses can't live in it, bacteria can't. Cancer can't. Gets more oxygen into your plasma. It's all about getting oxygen into your brain. Everything I do is about getting more oxygen. Need oxygen."

He sits me down. There's a cylinder the size of a standard fire extinguisher bolted to the wall, next to the microscope. He hands me a tube with a nosepiece at the end. "Here, take this." I stick the two soft tubes up my nostrils and breathe deeply, holding this stuff in and, man, is it a buzz. Buzz.

"Have a cigarette," he says, handing me a Marlboro. "The ozone'll scrub the nicotine before it gets into your system."

It's illegal, he tells me, to claim that ozone has medical benefits, but he's convinced it's changed his life, and he's got tanks of it bolted to walls in rooms all over the property. Next to the toilet, in the gym, in his office, in the greenhouse. "If you write 'Nolte uses ozone for medical use,' they may come asking," he says. "They may not. But I'm telling you it works."

He turns to Brawley. "Anybody else need some B-12?"

"Nah, I'll have some raspberries," says Brawley.

"Raspberries! Strawberries! *Great idea!*" Nick yelps. "C! We need vitamin C!" Sometimes he'll just stand out there in his berry patch and eat until he's full, a whole meal. It is late in the afternoon, the golden hour, and this will be Nolte's first meal of the day. And so there he goes, enraptured, the energy of a child, all action, pushing down the hall and out the door and into the garden to pick some plump, juicy organic fruit.

To kill a neuron, Nolte says, you really have to go at it. A night out with amphetamines just won't do it. "You've gotta do amphetamines and maybe some heroin and then a couple of gallons of vodka and then Drāno."

And then you pay a doctor to take a nuclear brain scan so that you can see what you have done. Before us is Nolte's brain. Floating in the glowing yellows and reds are islands of neurons that are dead or misfiring. This is the brain of an actor.

When Nolte's doctor first saw this scan, he wanted to know if he'd ever been knocked out. "Well, doc," Nolte said, "I was an alcoholic; there was drug use." The doctor said, "Well, you've experienced the equivalent of blunt trauma."

There has been quite a lot of damage, he says. Nolte honors the damage, and he considers it a gift, a special knowledge. There's a black binder on the table. It's a three-ring binder labeled CONFIDENTIAL, and it contains the story of Nick Nolte's life. It's a rather clinical story, in black and white and X ray and MRI and brain scan and full-body nuclear PET scan in living color. It is sort of the scrapbook of this whole Nolte reclamation project, which is what his life in the last decade or so has become. This black binder is one of many such binders in Nolte's house. He analyzes and thinks and collects the effects of every character that he plays. To build a real character, it pays to understand his damage. This particular binder, the confidential one, is really just the dossier on another character. Most people don't have such a detailed accounting of their own dysfunctions, their failures, their fuckups, their rate of decay, and their halting human efforts in the face of such. Most people would just rather not know how they stack up against the inevitable. But of course, most people have not had as much of a god's hand in willfully accelerating their own demise as Nick Nolte has, and if a man has the power to find the violence inside to harm himself and bring on the end, then he must surely, Nolte feels, be able to find the grace to reverse the process.

It is, at the very least, an interesting hobby.

"Here's the blunt trauma," he says, pointing to dark areas on the brain scan, which is otherwise a gorgeous swirl of color. His fingers are stained from the strawberries.

To increase Nolte's brain function, his doctor prescribed the same treatment that Edward Teller, the father of the H-bomb, used to jump-start his own brain after he had a stroke: sessions in a hyperbaric chamber, the kind they stick divers into when they have the bends. Nolte spent ten hours in one. The goal was to push oxygen into his plasma so that it would be picked up by the brain and metabolized, and where once had been darkness and stupor and death would be bright colors and vitality and life. A new brain.

Like a schoolboy who's just won the prize, he hands me another brain scan taken after these sessions. "See how these yellow streaks don't shoot clear out to the sides anymore? That means the surface is metabolizing." The dark areas are now blue and yellow. Neurons, he says. Neurons that are *firing*.

"I've had some success." He flips to a chart. "It means my body is almost daily repairing everything that's damaged. And you never can get to zero, because life itself means a certain amount of destruction. You have to use things up in order to live."

Flipping through the black binder, we stop on a recent psychiatric workup, and I read the following aloud:

*Results suggest that the patient possesses traits associated with histrionic, narcissistic, and antisocial qualities, which indicate that the patient may seek reassurance or approval from others or may be uncomfortable in situations where he or she is not the center of attention. He may react to criticism with feelings of humiliation. His personality requires attention from others, and he may have a sense of self-importance. His personality type also tends to be a rule-breaker.*

*The patient's attention as assessed was found to be abnormal. Results indicate anxiety-induced attention deficit, which he committed several times, in the second, third, and fourth quarters of the test. This is also indicative of anxiety or impulsivity.*

*Notable: He has very rapid brain speed. Approximately at age forty, with a voltage of 5.03, which may cause him to be prone to addiction. His memory is in the very superior range—no doubt this aids him as an actor.*

"All true," he says.

Nick Nolte is indeed an actor. And he says that in those years when he was working away at destroying himself with the drugs and the alcohol, he was taking some roles that in their way were destroying him, too.

You see, big movies are toxic. Of course, just because movies are small doesn't make them good. But Nolte is a constant; he is ever present. Whatever role he undertakes, there he'll be, digging, digging, going deep, trying to find something, trying to talk to ghosts. These movies, he says—whether last year's *Affliction*, for which he was nominated for an Oscar, or *Mother Night*, or a pair of new ones, *Simpatico*, from the Sam Shepard play, and *Breakfast of Champions*—they are having the same effect as the ozone. If he chooses them, breathes them in, lives them, they will restore him, cleanse him, clear out the bad stuff, all those movies he shot for $7 million apiece—*I Love Trouble*, *Mulholland Falls*, *Blue Chips*—that led him to a heart murmur in the early nineties. And so he's sucking them in, these little movies, because they are like a drug, and if he had to make *Yet Another 48 Hours*, it just might take him around the bend. Eddie Murphy told him that he wanted to do what Nolte was doing, those artistically satisfying, small, gritty movies. Nolte told him he'd have to cut his salary. "Oh, man, I can't do that," Murphy said. "I have my needs."

Now Nolte beckons me into the bathroom. "You want some tea?" he says, waving me in. "This is the best tea. Made in China." We troop into the bathroom, Brawley and Aidan following. The computers have crashed, the server's down, and the boys are at loose ends. Nolte brews the tea on a bureau across from the shower. A tank of ozone is bolted to the wall next to the toilet. He hands me a framed mug shot of himself. Nabbed by the feds at twenty for selling draft cards. Got a forty-five-year sentence, suspended. A felon, he's never voted.

It's a large bathroom, with a huge tub in one corner, a deep, splendid tub with a Jacuzzi. Laminated script pages from his upcoming film are stacked next to the tub. Every morning, he comes in here, turns on the Jacuzzi, and reads his pages. When he was preparing for *The Thin Red Line*, he'd soak in here and yell, *Move those damn troops! Take that goddamn hill!* Pajamas are scattered on the floor. All over the room—in fact, all over this house—are quotes that serve as affirmations, trying to buck Nolte up. One on the bathroom wall reads: "Why are you frightened of being alone? Because you are faced with yourself as you are, and you find that you are empty, dull, stupid, ugly, guilty, and anxious." Nolte thinks it's from Krishnamurti, but he's not sure. The twelve steps of AA are taped to the wall, at his left elbow when he's in the tub. The page is mottled and water-stained. He used to go to meetings regularly, but it wasn't quite enough. Then he discovered science. Now Scotch-taped floor to ceiling on the shower door are pages and pages of large-type definitions from a book on brain chemistry—*addiction* and *craving brain* and *inescapable stress* and so on.

It's dark outside now. The room is illuminated only by a small penlight that Nolte is holding. There is a window above the tub. A large gray-and-white cat with white-socked feet is on the roof, staring into the window. "Coyotes have been trying to ambush him for years," Brawley says. "So he lives on the roof." Nolte opens the window and calls out, "Kitty, kitty, kitty, come in, man, come in." The cat rubs up against Nolte's hand. It's very big. Nolte steps into the empty bathtub, picks the cat up off the roof, and hands it to me. "He's real affectionate," Nolte says.

Brawley and Aidan vanish into their cave, hoping to get back online. I follow Nick down the wide, wooden stairs, carrying the cat, its claws sinking deep into my arm. I am hearing water trickling. I look to the ceiling. The Labrador, its tail banging the wall, comes around the corner. The cat is holding on to my forearm for dear life. Now the floor is wet all around our feet, and we're slipping our way down the stairs. I feel wetness running down my pants. The cat has been pissing straight out into the air. Nolte now looks down for the first time and sees the puddle he's standing in.

"Oh, *Jesus*, who pissed all over the place?"

"It wasn't me," says Aidan, sticking his head out of the cave. "I need your credit-card number. Brawley and I found plans for an ultralight on the Internet."

"You know where the card is," Nolte says.

The cat leaps from my arms and runs. Nolte crouches down with a towel and is sopping up the mess. He looks up at my pee-stained khakis. "Looks like you're going to need some pajamas," he says.

He bounds up the stairs and tosses some down. They are like his, soft, with white piping. I put them on and wait for him to come back. A few minutes later, he slowly descends the stairs, rubbing his butt and screwing up his face a little.

"Had to give myself another hit of B-12."

Eating slips his mind sometimes. It is midnight and, save for a handful of berries, he hasn't eaten. I am faint from hunger.

"You hungry?" he asks.

He pulls on a flimsy pair of canvas shoes, gets us each a small flashlight, picks up a basket. "To the garden!" he says. "I'll cook you some dinner."

The garden is ringed with garlic plants to keep rabbits and gophers out. Only one gopher has gotten past the garlic, but it's driving Nolte crazy. The holes he and the gardeners have dug on their hunt for the gopher are wide and deep enough to fit a body in, tunneling in one direction and another. "We throw poison in," he says, "and the gopher throws it back out."

Tall corn is in our faces as we hunt for tomatoes, which are flourishing between the cornstalks. Vines all around our feet. And we're looking for squash. And we keep coming upon watermelon. Nolte is on his knees, rooting around in his pajamas. "Oooooo, squash, squash, squash," he mutters to himself. "Oh, these are nice. I'll have some of these. I'll take some of those. These are butternuts. I'm gonna slice 'em and steam 'em a little bit in olive oil with some of the Vidalias."

As he's scooting down the rows, sizing up the butternuts, he's talking about this year's Academy Awards. "Everybody gets devastated," Nolte says, "or everybody gets elated, a little bit. But usually everybody gets devastated. It's horrible, it's rejection. No matter that you're one of only a few actors that have been nominated, or you're one of just a few directors—in the final analysis you're a loser. How can you be happy in that situation?

"Listen, I was glad for Roberto Benigni, you know?" Nick says. "But it's not fun. It's never fun to lose." During the commercial break, after the best-actor award was presented, Nolte saw that Edward Norton and Ian McKellen, his fellow nominees, were no longer in their seats.

"I knew those fuckin' guys were at the bar. So I excuse myself and I find 'em, and I say, 'Motherfuckers!' And Ian says to me right off the bat, deadpan, 'You know, Nick, I don't really see why you expected to get the award. You do nothing but play yourself.' I look at Ian, who played a homosexual artist in *Gods and Monsters*, and I say, 'Look who's calling the kettle fuckin' black,' and then we both turn to Ed, who played a skinhead in *American History X*, and say, 'What'd you think? Bald head and tattoos were gonna win?' And we all just started laughing."

Nolte sat on his hands when they honored Elia Kazan. Sean Penn is Nick's friend. Penn's dad was blacklisted. Kazan, of course, named names. "He was a great director," he says. "No question. So we would have had to do without *On the Waterfront*. So what?"

In another decade of his life, he'd be having this conversation on a barstool. But we're inside now, back in the kitchen, and he's slicing up squash and Kentucky wonder beans and sautéing onions in olive oil, mixing it all with brown rice.

Not that he's an AA purist. He drank on Oscar night. "My soul needed that one," he says. "If I have that occasional drink, I can, you know, end up drinking for a day or so, but I no longer have that illusion that drinking is the only way to deal with life. And invariably, after a coupla days, the body is just aching and hurting, and the soul is in pain 'cause you're destroying it."

The food is all gone and it's 1:00 A.M. and Aidan is worrying about his pimples. "I have the next experiment!" Nolte yells, charging in from another room. He has a jar in his hands. Brawley and Aidan watch him as if he were a magician and a white rabbit might pop out of his hat at any moment. He opens the jar and begins to goop an organic mud mask on Aidan's face. Aidan recoils. "Hey, what's that?" he hollers.

Nick answers, almost tenderly. "Here, you put it on like this." He shows him by applying it to his own face. "It's good for you."

The phone rings. It's Vicki, calling from her office thirty feet away. She's been in there scissoring apart the dresses she wore on her recently canceled TV show, *NewsRadio*—miniskirts, pink taffeta bridesmaid's gowns. Making them into a quilt. "Come on out, baby," Nolte says. "Yeah, he's still here. It's an interview, but it evolved. You gotta come out; it's my big hurrah."

Brawley asks if it's true that there are benefits to playing video games. "Dad, since I play so many video games, I have more of those little roots. . . . What are they?"

"Dendrites," Nolte says. "The more challenged the brain is, the more dendrites it builds. They help make more connections."

Aidan pipes up. "How many do you think I have? 'Cause I do, like, problem solving every day in school. And complicated math." The mask is drying on Aidan's face, pulling his eyes apart. With the paste smeared high into his hairline, Nick looks like the fool from *King Lear*.

Brawley has clear skin, looks very much like his father, and has actually played Nolte as a boy in two films. He was also the kid in

*Ransom*. "After doing *Ransom*," he says, "it was confusing. All of a sudden I understood who all those people were who kept stopping my dad on the street. I thought he had a lot of friends. Now I understood—you get in the movies, you get a lot of friends you don't know." He pulls me aside. "Is it true my dad won the Nobel prize?" he asks quietly.

Nolte is at the computer, a cigarette in his mouth, typing with one finger. It's the middle of the night. Aidan is right next to him at another terminal, his complexion much improved, and a panel of blinking red lights means that Brawley is in the next room, playing EverQuest. Aidan has found a medical-surplus store on-line. He's clicking through the screens, yelling out prices of used electron microscopes.

Nolte says, "We don't want to get too complicated. There are setup protocols that would take us all day."

"The way an electron microscope works," Aidan says, "is they incinerate the stuff you're sampling, and it searches for higher electrons it might give off."

"Wow, would that be fun!" Nolte says, his voice pitched high with excitement.

Nolte is working on his lines for his next movie, *Trixie*, with Emily Watson, in which he plays a senator falsely accused of murder. On the screen, he highlights a speech from the script, then he leans back and waits for the computer to recite it to him.

"I-could-even-have-you-arrested," says the clipped, high-pitched computer voice. "I-am-guilty-of-absolutely-no-wrongdoing-anywhere."

"See how she sounds?" he says. He's rubbing his forehead with a fist, eyes closed, just listening as his right hand, fingers spread wide, tilts outward, dipping and rising in concert with the voice. The voice is amplified throughout the upper room.

He used to ask friends to speak random passages from scripts into tape recorders, just to learn the words in a new way. "I'll have him punched," he repeats along with the computer, which answers,

"May-I-say-I-find-you-attractive? You're-so-fresh-and-unspoiled. Is-it-okay-that-I-say-that? Does-that-scare-you-hon?"

The phone rings. It's Alan Rudolph calling from Canada, where he'll be directing *Trixie*, starting in a few weeks. There's the matter of a little S&M to discuss. Nolte sits and listens, pushing his hair off his forehead. He'll be shorn as the senator, hair white. "Do I literally beat her up?" he asks Rudolph. He listens for a few moments, nodding his head. "Well, that's something she and I can figure out."

The computer murmurs in the background. "I'm-single. Are-you-married? A-woman's-sexual-temperature-is-never-lost-on-me. Even-nice-guys-have-nasty-ideas. What-color-underpants-are-you-wearing-right-now?"

Nolte is pacing in his pajamas, intense on the phone. "I think I'll have prepared well enough to be—like we did with Julie in *AfterGlow* with that restaurant scene—I want to be able to be that free with it so we can go anywhere we want to go. I've got the second scene, the big, long one, pretty much that free . . . and that's the one I've been really concentrating on. The other one, it's me and her, you know. It's tricky." He hangs up the phone.

He finds that as time goes by, the roles stay with him more and more. They become sort of encoded. He figures it's the way he prepares in the first place, but he can't help continuing to sort of live them after they're done. After *Jefferson in Paris*, he had to have his windows redone and a gazebo built to match Monticello's. After *U Turn*, the raven that had perched atop the shoulder of his sadistic, incestuous character stayed on here with Nick. The bird died not long ago and is buried in the yard. In the new adaptation of Kurt Vonnegut's *Breakfast of Champions*, Nolte steals the movie as a cross-dressing car-lot manager.

"I designed my own dress," he says. "I told the costumer, 'It has to feel sensual. It has to be what the men don't get to wear, you know, the silk and this kind of thing.' So I took this one little dress, a sheer red dress, and I had it on and said, 'This would be good, but he'd probably like the silk to flow down here.' And then I took the dress and I spun it around backward, so the top was cut down here and the straps crossed here. Now I was bare-breasted—a Phoenician woman. That was key to the character."

He wants the dress this second. "I loved shaving my chest!" he says. He gets up off his chair to leave the lab. The computer voice croons to him, "A-woman's-sexual-temperature-is-never-lost-on-me." Dark-field photos of his sperm are on the table near the scans of his brain. He is pulling open drawers. One is filled with bottles, another with Scotch tape. He throws open the doors of a large armoire. He's saying he thinks he's found the undergarments, sheer and red. "I know it's here somewhere. I swear it! I'll find the dress!"

—OCTOBER 1999

# Tennis Player Michael Joyce's Professional Artistry as a Paradigm of Certain Stuff about Choice, Freedom, Limitation, Joy, Grotesquerie, and Human Completeness

DAVID FOSTER WALLACE

(originally published as *The String Theory*)

When Michael Joyce of Los Angeles serves, when he tosses the ball and his face rises to track it, it looks like he's smiling, but he's not really smiling—his face's circumoral muscles are straining with the rest of his body to reach the ball at the top of the toss's rise. He wants to hit it fully extended and slightly out in front of him; he wants to be able to hit emphatically down on the ball, to generate enough pace to avoid an ambitious return from his opponent. Right now it's 1:00 Saturday, 22 July 1995, on the Stadium Court of the Stade Jarry tennis complex in Montreal. It's the first of the qualifying rounds for the Canadian Open, one of the major stops on the ATP's "hard-court circuit,"[1] which starts right after Wimbledon and climaxes at NYC's U.S. Open. The tossed ball rises and seems for a second to hang, waiting, cooperating, as balls always seem to do for great players. The opponent, a Canadian college star named Dan Brakus, is a very good tennis player. Michael Joyce, on the other hand, is a world-class tennis player. In 1991 he was the top-ranked junior in the United States and a finalist at Junior Wimbledon,[2] is now in his fourth year on the ATP tour, and is as of this day the 79th best tennis player on planet earth.

A tacit rhetorical assumption here is that you have very probably never heard of Michael Joyce of Brentwood/LA. Nor of Florida's Tommy Ho. Nor of Vince Spadea, nor of Jonathan Stark or Robbie Weiss or Steve Bryan—all American men in their twenties, all ranked in the world's top 100 at one point in 1995. Nor of Jeff Tarango, 68th in the world, unless you remember his unfortunate psychotic break in full public view during last year's Wimbledon.[3]

You are invited to try to imagine what it would be like to be among the hundred best in the world at something. At anything. I have tried to imagine; it's hard.

---

1. Comprising Washington, Montreal, LA, Cincinnati, Indianapolis, New Haven, and Long Island, this is possibly the most grueling part of the Association of Tennis Professionals' yearly tour, with three-digit temperatures and the cement courts shimmering like Moroccan horizons and everyone wearing a hat and even the spectators carrying sweat towels.

2. Joyce lost that final to Thomas Enqvist, now ranked in the ATP's top twenty and a potential superstar and in high-profile attendance here at Montreal.

3. Tarango, 27, who completed three years at Stanford, is regarded as something of a scholar by Joyce and the other young Americans on tour. His little bio in the *1995 ATP Player Guide* lists his interests as including "philosophy, creative writing, and bridge," and his slight build and receding hairline do in fact make him look more like an academic or a tax attorney than a world-class tennis player. Also a native Californian, Tarango's a friend and something of a mentor to Michael Joyce, whom he practices with regularly and addresses as "Grasshopper." Joyce—who seems to like pretty much everybody—likes Jeff Tarango and won't comment on his on-court explosion at Wimbledon except to say that Tarango is "a very intense guy, very intellectual, that gets kind of paranoid sometimes."

Stade Jarry's Stadium Court facility can hold slightly over 10,000 souls. Right now, for Michael Joyce's qualifying match, there are 93 people in the crowd, 91 of whom appear to be friends and relatives of Dan Brakus. Michael Joyce doesn't seem to notice whether there's a crowd or not. He has a way of staring intently at the air in front of his face between points. During points he looks only at the ball.

The acoustics in the near-empty Stadium are amazing—you can hear every breath, every sneaker's squeak, the authoritative *pang* of the ball against very tight strings.

Professional tennis tournaments, like professional sports teams, have distinctive traditional colors. Wimbledon's is green; the Volvo International's is light blue. The Canadian Open's is—emphatically—red. The tournament's "title sponsor," du Maurier cigarettes,[4] has ads and logos all over the place in red and black. The Stadium Court is surrounded by a red tarp festooned with corporate names in black capitals, and the tarp composes the base of a grandstand that is itself decked out in red-and-black bunting, so that from any kind of distance the place looks like either a Kremlin funeral or a really elaborate brothel. The match's umpire and linesmen and ballboys all wear black shorts and red shirts emblazoned with the name of a Quebec clothing company.[5] The big beach umbrella that's spread and

---

4. Title sponsors are as important to ATP tournaments as they are to collegiate bowl games. This year the Canadian Open is officially called the "du Maurier Omnium Ltée." But everybody still refers to it as the Canadian Open. There are all types and levels of sponsors for big tennis tournaments—the levels of giving and of commensurate reward are somewhat similar to PBS fundraising telethons. Names of sponsors are all over the Canadian Open's site (with variations in size and placement corresponding to levels of fiscal importance to the tournament), from the big FedEx signs over the practice courts to the RADO trademark on the serve-speed radar display on the show courts. On the scarlet tarp and the box seats all around the Stadium and Grandstand Courts are the names of other corporate sponsors: TANDEM COMPUTERS/APG INC., BELL SYGMA, BANQUE LAURENTIENNE, IMASCO LIMITÉE, EVANS TECHNOLOGIES INC., MOBILIA, BELL CANADA, ARGO STEEL, etc.

5. Another way to be a sponsor: supply free stuff to the tournament and put your name on it in really big letters. All the courts' tall umpire-chairs have a

held over each seated player at end-change breaks has a lush red head and black stem that looks hot to hold.

Stade Jarry's Stadium Court is adjoined on the north by the Grandstand Court, a slightly smaller venue with seats on only one side and a capacity of 4,800. A five-story scoreboard lies just west of the Grandstand, and by late afternoon both courts are rectangularly shadowed. There are also eight nonstadium courts in canvas-fenced enclosures scattered across the grounds. Professional matches are under way on all ten Stade Jarry courts today, but they are not exactly Canadian Open matches, and for the most part they are unwatched.

The Stade Jarry grounds are all spruced up, and vendors' tents are up, and Security is in place at all designated points. Big TV trailers line the walkway outside the stadium, and burly men keep pulling complicated nests of cable out of ports in the trailers' sides.

There are very few paying customers on the grounds on Saturday, but there are close to a hundred world-class players: big spidery French guys with gelled hair, American kids with peeling noses and Pac-10 sweats, lugubrious Germans, bored-looking Italians. There are blank-eyed Swedes and pockmarked Colombians and cyperpunkish Brits. There are malevolent Slavs with scary haircuts. There are Mexican players who spend their spare time playing two-on-two soccer in the gravel outside the Players' Tent. With few exceptions, all the players have similar builds: big muscular legs, shallow chests, skinny necks, and one normal-sized arm and one monstrously huge and hypertrophic arm. They tend to congregate in the Players' Tent or outside the Transportation Trailer awaiting rides in promotional BMWs back to the Radisson des Gouverneurs, the tournament's designated hotel. Many of these players in the "Qualies," or qualifying rounds, have girlfriends in tow, sloppily beautiful European girls with sandals and patched jeans and leather backpacks, girlfriends

---

sign that says they're supplied by TROPICANA; all the bins for fresh and unfresh towels say WAMSUTTA; the drink coolers at courtside (the size of trash barrels, with clear plastic lids) say TROPICANA and EVIAN. The players who don't individually endorse a certain brand of drink tend as a rule to drink Evian, orange juice being a bit heavy for on-court rehydration.

who set up cloth lawnchairs and sun themselves next to their players' practice courts.[6] At the Radisson des Gouverneurs the players tend to congregate in the lobby, where there's a drawsheet for the Qualies up on a cork bulletin board and a multilingual tournament official behind a long desk, and the players stand around in the air-conditioning in wet hair and sandals and employ about forty languages and wait for results of matches to go up on the board and for their own next matches' schedules to get posted. Some of the players listen to personal stereos; none seem to read. They all have the unhappy self-enclosed look of people who spend huge amounts of time on planes and waiting around in hotel lobbies, the look of people who have to create an envelope of privacy around them with just their expressions. Most of these players seem either extremely young—new guys trying to break onto the Tour—or conspicuously older, like over 30, with tans that look permanent and faces lined from years in the trenches of tennis's minor leagues.

The Canadian Open, one of the ATP Tour's "Super 9" tournaments that weigh most heavily in the calculation of world ranking, officially starts on Monday, 24 July. What's going on for the two days right before it is the Qualies. This is essentially a competition to determine who will occupy the eight slots in the Canadian Open's main draw designated for "qualifiers." It is a pre-tournament tournament. A qualifying tourney precedes just about every big-money ATP event, and money and prestige and lucrative careers are often at stake in Qualie rounds, and often they feature the best matches of the whole tournament, and it's a good bet you haven't heard of Qualies.

The realities of the men's professional tennis tour bear about as much resemblance to the lush finals you see on TV as a slaughterhouse does to a well-presented cut of restaurant sirloin. For every Sampras–Agassi final we watch, there's been a week-long tournament, a pyramidical single-elimination battle between 32, 64, or 128

6. Most of the girlfriends have something indefinable about them that suggests extremely wealthy parents whom the girls are trying to piss off by hooking up with an obscure professional tennis player.

players, of whom the finalists are the last men standing. You probably know that already. But a player has to be eligible to enter that tournament in the first place. Eligibility is determined by ATP computer ranking. Each tournament has a cutoff, a minimum ranking required to get entered in the main draw. Players below that ranking who want to get in have to compete in a kind of pre-tournament. That's the easiest way to explain what Qualies are. In actual practice the whole thing's quite a bit messier, and I'll try to describe the logistics of the Canadian Open's Qualies in just enough detail to suggest their complexity without boring you mindless.

The du Maurier Omnium Ltée has a draw of 64. The sixteen entrants with the highest ATP rankings get "seeded," which means their names are strategically dispersed in the draw so that (barring upsets) they won't have to meet each other until the latter rounds.[7] Of the seeds, the top eight—here Agassi, Sampras, Chang, the Russian Yevgeny Kafelnikov, Croatia's Goran Ivanisevic, South Africa's Wayne Ferreira, Germany's Michael Stich, and Switzerland's Marc Rosset, respectively—get "byes," or automatic passes into the tournament's second round. This means that there is actually room for 56 players in the main draw. The cutoff for the 1995 Canadian Open isn't 56, however, because not all of the top 56 players in the world are here.[8] Here the cutoff is 85. You'd think that this meant anybody with an ATP ranking of 86 or lower would have to play the Qualies,

7. The term "seeding" comes from British horticulture and is pretty straightforward. A player seeded First is expected statistically to win, Second to reach the finals, Third and Fourth the semis, etc. A player who reaches the round his seed designates is said to have "justified his seed," a term that seems far more rich in implications and entendres. Serious tennis is full of these multisemiotic terms—"love," "hold" and "break," "fault," "let" as a noun, "heat," "moon," "spank," "coming in," "playing unconscious," and so on.

8. Except for the four Grand Slams, no tournament draws all the top players, although every tournament would obviously like to, since the more top players are entered, the better the paid attendance and the more media exposure the tournament gets for itself and its sponsors. Players ranked in the world's top twenty or so, though, tend to play a comparatively light schedule of tournaments, taking time off not only for rest and training but to compete in wildly

but here too there are exceptions. The du Maurier Omnium Ltée, like most other big tournaments, has five "wild card" entries into the main draw. These are special places given either to high-ranked players who entered after the required six-week deadline but are desirable to have in the tournament because they're big stars (like Ivanisevic, #6 in the world but a notorious flakeroo who "*forgot*" to enter till a week ago and got a last-minute wild card) or to players ranked lower than 85 whom the tournament wants because they are judged "uniquely deserving" (read "Canadian"—the other four players who get wild cards here are all Canadian, and two are Quebecois).

By the way, if you're interested, the ATP Tour updates and publishes its world rankings weekly, and the rankings constitute a nomological orgy that makes for truly first-rate bathroom reading. As of this writing, Mahesh Bhupathi is 284, Luis Lobo 411. There's Martin Sinner and Guy Forget. There's Adolf Musil and Jonathan Venison and Javier

---

lucrative exhibitions that don't affect ATP ranking. (We're talking *wildly* lucrative, like millions of dollars per annum for the top stars.) Given the sharp divergence of interests between tournaments and players, it's not surprising that there are Kafkanly complex rules for how many ATP tournaments a player must enter each year to avoid financial or ranking-related penalties, and commensurately complex and crafty ways players have for getting around these rules and doing pretty much what they want. These will be passed over. The thing to realize is that players of Michael Joyce's station tend to take way less time off; they try to play just about every tournament they can squeeze in unless they're forced by injury or exhaustion to sit out a couple weeks. They play so much because they need to, not just financially but because the ATP's (very complex) set of algorithms for determining ranking tends to reward players for entering as many tournaments as they can.

And so even though several of the North American hard-court circuit's tournaments are Super 9's, a fair number of top players skip them, especially European clay-court players, who hate DecoTurf and tend to stick to their own summer clay-court circuit, which is European and comprises smaller and less lucrative tournaments (like the Dutch Open, which is concurrent with the Canadian and has four of the world's top twenty entered this year). The claycourters tend to pay the price for this at the U.S. Open, which is played on hard sizzling DecoTurf courts.

Frana and Leander Paes. There's—no kidding—Cyril Suk. Rodolfo Ramos-Paganini is 337, Alex Lopez-Moron 174. Gilad Bloom is 228 and Zoltan Nagy is 414. Names out of some postmodern Dickens: Udo Riglewski and Louis Gloria and Francisco Roig and Alexander Mronz. The 29th-best player in the world is named Slava Dosedel. There's Claude N'Goran and Han Shin (276 but falling fast) and Haracio de la Pensa and Marcus Barbosa and Amos Mansdorf and Mariano Hood. Andres Zingman is currently ranked two places above Sander Groen. Horst Skoff and Kris Goossens and Thomas Hagstedt are all ranked higher than Martin Zumpft. One more reason the tournament industry sort of hates upsets is that the ATP press liaisons have to go around teaching journalists how to spell and pronounce new names.

So, skipping a whole lot more complications, the point is that eight slots in the Canadian Open's main draw are reserved for qualifiers, and the Qualies is the tournament held to determine who'll get those eight slots. The Qualies itself has a draw of 64 world-class players—the cutoff for qualifying for the Qualies is an ATP ranking of 350.[9] The Qualies won't go all the way through to the finals, only to the quarters: the eight quarterfinalists of the Qualies will receive first-round slots in the Canadian Open.[10] This means that a player in the Qualies will need to win three rounds—round of 64, round of 32, round of 16—in two days to get into the first round of the main draw.[11]

---

9. There is no qualifying tournament for the Qualies itself, though some particularly huge tournaments have meta-Qualies. The Qualies also have tons of wildcard berths, most of whom here are given to Canadian players, e.g. the collegian that Michael Joyce is beating up on right now in the first round.

10. These slots are usually placed right near the top seeds, which is the reason why in the televised first rounds of major tournaments you often see Agassi or Sampras smearing some totally obscure guy—that guy's usually a qualifier. It's also part of why it's so hard for somebody low-ranked enough to have to play the Qualies of tournaments to move up in the rankings enough so that he doesn't have to play the Qualies anymore—he usually meets a high-ranked player in the very first round and gets smeared.

11. Which is another reason why qualifiers usually get smeared by the top players they face in the early rounds—the qualifier is playing his fourth or fifth

The eight seeds in the Qualies are the eight players whom the Canadian Open officials expect will make the quarters and thus get into the main draw. The top seed this weekend is Richard Krajicek,[12] a 6'5" Dutchman who wears a tiny white billed hat in the sun and rushes the net like it owes him money and in general plays like a rabid crane. Both his knees are bandaged. He's in the top twenty and hasn't had to play Qualies for years, but for this tournament he missed the entry deadline, found all the wild cards already given to uniquely deserving Canadians, and with phlegmatic Low Country cheer decided to go ahead and play the weekend Qualies for the match practice. The Qualies' second seed is Jamie Morgan, an Australian journeyman, around 100th in the world, whom Michael Joyce beat in straight sets last week in the second round of the main draw at the Legg Mason Tennis Classic in Washington. Michael Joyce is seeded third.

If you're wondering why Joyce, who's ranked above the #85 cutoff, is having to play the Canadian Open Qualies at all, gird yourself for one more bit of complication. The fact is that six weeks ago Joyce's ranking was *not* above the cutoff, and that's when the Canadian entry deadline was, and that's the ranking the tournament committee went on when they made up the main draw. Joyce's ranking jumped from 119 to around 80 after this year's Wimbledon, where he beat Marc Rosset (ranked 11 in the world) and reached the round of sixteen. Despite a bout of mononucleosis that kept him in bed through part of the spring, Joyce is having his best year ever as a pro and has jumped from 140 in the world to 79.[13] But he was not in the world's top 85 as of early June, and so he has to qualify in Montreal. It seems to me that Joyce, like Krajicek, might be excused for brooding darkly on the fact that four wild cards in the Canadian's main

---

match in three days, while the top players usually have had a couple days with their masseur and creative-visualization consultant to get ready for the first round. If asked, Michael Joyce will detail all these asymmetries and stacked odds the same way a farmer will speak of poor weather, with an absence of emotion that seems deep instead of blank.

12. (pronounced KRY-chek)

13. At a certain point this summer his ranking will be as high as 62.

draw have been dispensed to Canadians ranked substantially lower than 85, but Joyce is stoic about it.[14]

The Qualie circuit is to professional tennis sort of what AAA baseball is to the major leagues: somebody playing the Qualies in Montreal is undeniably a world-class tennis player, but he's not quite at the level where the serious TV and money are. In the main draw of the du Maurier Omnium Ltée, a first-round loser will earn $5,400 and a second-round loser $10,300. In the Montreal Qualies, a player will receive $560 for losing in the second round and an even $0.00 for losing in the first. This might not be so bad if a lot of the entrants for the Qualies hadn't flown thousands of miles to get here. Plus there's the matter of supporting themselves in Montreal. The tournament pays the hotel and meal expenses of players in the main draw but not in the Qualies.[15] The eight survivors of the Qualies, however, will get their weekend expenses retroactively picked up by the tournament. So there's rather a lot at stake: some of the players in the Qualies are literally playing for their

---

14. It turns out that a portion of the talent required to survive in the trenches of the ATP Tour is emotional; Joyce is able to keep from getting upset about stuff that struck me as hard not to get upset about. When he points out that there's "no point" getting exercised about unfairnesses you can't control, I think what he's really saying is that you either learn how not to get upset about it or you disappear from the Tour. The temperamental behavior of many of the game's top players—which gives the public the distorted idea that most pro players are oversensitive brats—is on a qualifier's view easily explainable: top players are temperamental because they can afford to be.

15. The really top players not only have their expenses comped but often get paid outright for agreeing to enter a tournament. These fees are called "guarantees" and are technically advances against prize money: in effect, an Agassi/Sampras/Becker will receive a "guarantee" of the champion's prize money (usually a couple hundred thousand) just for competing, whether he wins the tournament or not. This means that if top seed Agassi wins the Canadian Open, he wins $254,000 U.S., but if he loses, he gets the money anyway. (This is another reason why tournaments tend to hate upsets, and, some qualifiers complain, why all sorts of intangibles from match scheduling to close line-calls tend to go the stars' way.) Not all tournaments have guarantees—the Grand Slams don't, because the top players will show up for Wimbledon and the French, Australian,

supper, or for the money to make airfare home or to the site of the next Qualie.

You could think of Michael Joyce's career as now kind of on the cusp between the major leagues and AAA ball. He still has to qualify for some tournaments, but more and more often he gets straight into the main draw. The move up from qualifier to main-draw player is a huge boost, both financially and psychically, but it's still a couple plateaux away from true fame and fortune. The main draw's 64 or 128 players are still mostly the supporting cast for the stars we see in televised finals. But they are also the pool from which superstars are drawn. McEnroe, Sampras, and even Agassi had to play Qualies at the start of their careers, and Sampras spent a couple years losing in the early rounds of main draws before he suddenly erupted in the early '90s and started beating everybody.

Still, most main-draw players are obscure and unknown. An example is Jacob Hlasek[16], a Czech who is working out with Switzerland's Marc Rosset on one of the practice courts this morning when

---

and U.S. Opens on their own incentive—but most have them, and the less established and prestigious a tournament, the more it needs to guarantee money to get the top players to come and attract spectators and media (which is what the tournament's title sponsor wants, very much).

Guarantees used to be against ATP rules and were under the table; they've been legal since the early '90s. There's great debate among tennis pundits about whether legal guarantees have helped the game by making the finances less shady or have hurt the game by widening the psychological gap between the stars and all the other players and by upping the pressure on tournaments to make it as likely as possible that the stars don't get upset by an unknown. It is impossible to get Michael Joyce to give a straight answer on whether he thinks guarantees are good or bad—it's not like Joyce is muddled or Nixonianly evasive about it, but rather that he can't afford to think in good/bad terms, to nurture resentment or bitterness or frustration. My guess is that he avoids these feelings because they make it even harder to play against Agassi and the rest, and he cares less about what's "right" in the grand scheme than he does about maximizing his own psychological chances against other players. This seems totally understandable, though I'm kind of awed by Joyce's evident ability to shut down lines of thinking that aren't to his advantage.

16. (pronounced YAkob hLAsick)

I first arrive at Stade Jarry.[17] I notice them and come over to watch only because Hlasek and Rosset are so beautiful to see; at this point I have no idea who they are. They are practicing groundstrokes down the line—Rosset's forehand and Hlasek's backhand—each ball plumb-line straight and within centimeters of the corner, the players moving with the compact nonchalance I've since come to recognize in pros when they're working out: the suggestion is one of a very powerful engine in low gear. Jacob Hlasek is 6'2" and built like a halfback, his blond hair in a short square East European cut, with icy eyes and cheekbones out to here: he looks like either a Nazi male model or a lifeguard in hell and seems in general just way too scary ever to try to talk to. His backhand's a one-hander, rather like Lendl's, and watching him practice it is like watching a great artist casually sketch something. I keep having to remember to blink. There are a million little ways you can tell that somebody's a great player—details in his posture, in the way he bounces the ball with his racquet-head to pick it up, in the casual way he twirls the racquet while waiting for the ball. Hlasek wears a plain gray T-shirt and some kind of very white European shoes. It's midmorning and already at least 90° and he isn't sweating. Hlasek turned pro in 1982, six years later had one year in the top ten, and for the last decade has been ranked in the 60s and 70s, getting straight into the main draw of all the big tournaments and usually losing in the first couple rounds. Watching Hlasek practice is probably the first time it really strikes me how good these professionals are, because even just fucking around, Hlasek is the most impressive tennis player I've ever seen.[18] I'd be surprised if anybody reading this has ever heard of

17. It took forever to get there from the hotel because I didn't yet know that press can, with some wangling, get rides in the courtesy cars with the players, if there's room. Tennis journalism is apparently its own special world, and it takes a little while to learn the ins and outs of how media can finagle access to some of the services the tournament provides: courtesy cars, VIP treatment in terms of restaurant reservations, even free laundry service at the hotel. Most of this stuff I learned about just as I was getting ready to come home.

18. Joyce is even more impressive, but I hadn't seen Joyce yet. And Enqvist is even more impressive than Joyce, and Agassi live is even more impressive than

Jacob Hlasek. By the distorted standards of TV's obsession with Grand Slam finals and the world's top five, Hlasek is merely an also-ran. But last year he made $300,000 on the tour (that's just in prize money, not counting exhibitions and endorsement contracts), and his career winnings are over $4,000,000 U.S., and it turns out his home base for a long time was Monte Carlo, where lots of European players with tax issues end up living.

Michael Joyce is listed in the ATP Player Guide as 5'11" and 165 pounds, but in person he's more like 5'9". On the Stadium Court he looks compact and stocky. The quickest way to describe him would be to say that he looks like a young and slightly buff David Caruso. He is fair-skinned and has reddish hair and the kind of patchy, vaguely pubic goatee of somebody who isn't quite able yet to grow real facial hair. When he plays in the heat he wears a hat.[19] He wears Fila clothes and uses Yonex racquets and is paid to do so. His face is childishly full, and while it isn't freckled it somehow seems like it *ought* to be freckled. A lot of professional tennis players look like lifeguards—that kind of extreme tan that looks like it's penetrated to the subdermal layer and will be retained to the grave—but Joyce's fair skin doesn't tan or even burn, though he does get red in the face when he plays, from effort.[20] His on-court expression is grim

---

Enqvist. After the week was over, I truly understand why Charlton Heston looks gray and ravaged on his descent from Sinai: past a certain point, impressiveness is corrosive to the psyche.

19. During his two daily one-hour practice sessions he wears the hat backwards, and also wears boxy plaid shorts that look for all the world like swimtrunks. His favorite practice T-shirt has FEAR: THE ENEMY OF DREAMS on the chest. He laughs a lot when he practices. You can tell just by looking at him out there that he's totally likable and cool.

20. If you've played only casually, it is probably hard to understand how physically demanding really serious tennis is. Realizing that these pros can move one another from one end of the 27' baseline to the other pretty much at will, and that they hardly ever end a point early by making an unforced error, might stimulate your imagination. A close best-of-three-set match is probably equivalent in its demands to a couple hours of basketball, but we're talking full-court basketball.

without being unpleasant; it communicates the sense that Joyce's attentions on-court have become very narrow and focused and intense—it's the same pleasantly grim expression you see on, say, working surgeons and jewelers. On the Stadium Court, Joyce seems boyish and extremely adult at the same time. And in contrast to the Canadian opponent, who has the varnished good looks and Pepsodent smile of the stereotypical tennis player, Joyce looks terribly *real* out there playing as he sweats through his shirt,[21] gets flushed, whoops for breath after a long point. He wears little elastic braces on both ankles, but it turns out they're mostly prophylactic.

---

21. Something else you don't get a good sense of on television: tennis is a very sweaty game. On ESPN or whatever, when you see a player walk over to the ballboy after a point and request a towel and quickly wipe off his arm and hand and toss the wet towel back to the (rather luckless) ballboy, most of the time the towel thing isn't a stall or a meditative pause—it's because sweat is running down the inside of the player's arm in such volume that it's getting all over his hand and making the racquet slippery. Especially on the sizzling North American summer junket, players sweat through their shirts early on, and sometimes also their shorts (Sampras always wears light-blue shorts that sweat through everyplace but his jockstrap, which looks funny and kind of endearing, like he's an incontinent child—Sampras is surprisingly childlike and cute on the court, in person, in contrast to Agassi, who's about as cute as a Port Authority whore.)

And they drink enormous amounts of water, staggering amounts. I thought I was seeing things at first, watching matches, as players seemed to go through one of those skinny half-liter Evian bottles every second side-change, but Michael Joyce confirmed it. Pro-grade tennis players seem to have evolved a metabolic system that allows rapid absorption of water and its transformation into sweat. I myself—who am not pro-grade, but do sweat like a pig—drink a lot of water a couple hours before I play but don't drink anything during a match. This is because a couple swallows of water usually just makes me want more, and if I drink as much as I want I end up with a protruding tummy and a sloshing sound when I run.

(Most players I spoke with confirm, by the way, that Gatorade and All-Sport and Boost and all those pricey electrolytic sports drinks are mostly bullshit, that salt and carbs at table and small lakes of daily $H_2O$ are the way to go. The players who didn't confirm this turned out to be players who had endorsement deals with some pricey sports-drink manufacturer, but I personally saw at least one such player dumping out his bottle's pricey electrolytic contents and replacing them with good old water, for his match.)

It's 1:30 P.M. Joyce has broken Brakus's serve once and is up 3–1 in the first set and is receiving. Brakus is in the multibrand clothes of somebody without an endorsement contract. He's well over six feet tall, and like many large male collegians his game is built around his serve.[22] At 0–15, his first serve is flat and 118 mph and way out to Joyce's backhand, which is a two-hander and hard to lunge effectively with, but Joyce lunges plenty effectively and sends the ball back down the line to the Canadian's forehand, deep in the court and with such flat pace that Brakus has to stutter-step a little and backpedal to get set up—clearly he's used to playing guys for whom 118 mumps out wide would be an outright ace or at least produce such a weak return that he could move up easily and put the ball away—and Brakus now sends the ball back up the line high over the net, loopy with topspin, not all that bad a shot considering the fierceness of the return, and a topspin shot that'd back most tennis players up and put them on the defensive, and but Michael Joyce, whose level of tennis is such that he moves *in* on balls hit with topspin and hits them on the rise,[23] moves in and takes the ball on the rise and hits a backhand cross so tightly angled that nobody alive could get to it. This is kind of a typical Joyce–Brakus point. The match is carnage of a particular high-level sort: it's like watching an extremely large and powerful predator get torn to pieces by an even larger and more powerful predator. Brakus looks pissed off after Joyce's winner, makes some berating-himself-type noises, but the anger seems kind of pro forma: it's not like there's

---

22. The taller you are, the harder you can serve (get a protractor and figure it out), but the less able to bend and reverse direction you are. Tall guys tend to be serve-and-volleyers, and they live and die by their serves. Bill Tilden, Stan Smith, Arthur Ashe, Roscoe Tanner, and Goran Ivanisevic were/are all tall guys with serve-dependent games.

23. This is mind-bogglingly hard to do when the ball's hit hard. If we can assume you've played Little League or sandlot ball or something, imagine the hardest-hit grounder of all time coming at you at shortstop, and then you not standing waiting to try to knock it down but actually of your own free will running forward *toward* the grounder, then trying not just to catch it in a big soft glove but to strike it hard and reverse its direction and send it someplace frightfully specific and far away.

anything Brakus could have done much better, not given what he and the 79th-best player in the world have in their respective arsenals.

Michael Joyce—whose realness and approachability and candor are a big reason why he's whom I end up spending the most time watching and talking to—will later say, in response to my dry observation that a rather disproportionate number of unranked Canadians seem to have gotten wild cards into the Montreal Qualies, that Brakus "had a big serve, but the guy didn't belong on a pro court." Joyce didn't mean this in an unkind way. Nor did he mean it in a kind way. It turns out that what Michael Joyce says rarely has any kind of spin or slant on it; he mostly just reports what he sees, rather like a camera. You couldn't even call him sincere, because it's not like it seems ever to occur to him to *try* to be sincere or nonsincere. For a while I thought that Joyce's rather bland candor was a function of his not being very bright. This judgment was partly informed by the fact that Joyce didn't go to college and was only marginally involved in his high school academics (stuff I know because he told me it right away).[24] What I discovered as the tournament wore on was that I can be kind of a snob and an asshole, and

24. Something else that's hotly debated by tennis authorities is the trend of players going pro at younger and younger ages and skipping college and college tennis and plunging into the stress and peripatetic loneliness of the Tour, etc. Michael Joyce skipped college and went directly onto the pro tour because at 18 he'd just won the U.S. National Juniors, and this created a set of overwhelming inducements to turn pro. The winner at the National 18-and-Under Singles automatically gets a wild card into the U.S. Open's main draw for that year. In addition, a year's top junior comes to the powerful but notoriously fickle and temporary attention of major clothing and racquet companies. Joyce's victory over the 128-man National field at Kalamazoo MI in 1991 resulted in endorsement offers from Fila and Yonex worth around $100,000. $100,000 is about what it takes to finance three years on the Tour for a very young player who can't reasonably expect to earn a whole lot of prize-money.

Joyce could have turned down that offer of a three-year subsidy and gone to college, but if he'd gone to college it would have been primarily to play tennis. Coaches at major universities apparently offered Joyce inducements to come play for them so literally outrageous and incredible that I wouldn't repeat them here even if Joyce hadn't asked me not to.

that Michael Joyce's affectless openness is a sign not of stupidity but of something else.

Advances in racquet technology and conditioning methods over the last decade have dramatically altered men's professional tennis. For much of the twentieth century, there were two basic styles of

---

The reason why Michael Joyce would have gone to college primarily to play tennis is that his interest in the academic and social aspects of collegiate life interest him about as much as hitting 2500 crosscourt forehands while a coach yells at you in foreign languages would interest you. Tennis is what Michael Joyce loves and lives for and *is*. He sees little point in telling anybody anything different. It's the only thing he's devoted himself to, and he's given massive amounts of himself to it, and as far as he understands it it's all he wants to do or be. Because he started playing at age two and competing at age seven, however, and had the first half-dozen years of his career directed rather shall we say *forcefully* and *enthusiastically* by his father (who Joyce estimates spent probably around $250,000 on lessons and court-time and equipment and travel during Michael's junior career), it seemed reasonable to ask Joyce to what extent he "*chose*" to devote himself to tennis. Can you "*choose*" something when you are forcefully and enthusiastically immersed in it at an age when the resources and information necessary for choosing are not yet yours?

Joyce's response to this line of inquiry strikes me as both unsatisfactory and marvelous. Because of course the question is unanswerable, at least it's unanswerable by a person who's already—as far as he understands it—"*chosen*." Joyce's answer is that it doesn't really matter much to him whether he originally "*chose*" serious tennis or not; all he knows is that he loves it. He tries to explain his feelings at the Nationals in 1991: "You get there and look at the draw, it's a 128 draw, there's so many guys you have to beat. And then it's all over and you've won, you're the National Champion—there's nothing like it. I get chills even talking about it." Or how it was just the previous week in Washington: "I'm playing Agassi, and it's great tennis, and there's like thousands of fans going nuts. I can't describe the feeling. Where else could I get that?"

What he says aloud is understandable, but it's not the marvelous part. The marvelous part is the way Joyce's face looks when he talks about what tennis means to him. He loves it; you can see this in his face when he talks about it: his eyes normally have a kind of Asiatic cast because of the slight epicanthic fold common to ethnic Irishmen, but when he speaks of tennis and his career the eyes get round and the pupils dilate and the look in them is one of love. The love is not

top-level play. The "offensive"[25] style is based on the serve and the net game and is ideally suited to slick (or "fast") surfaces like grass and cement. The "defensive" or "baseline" style is built around foot-speed, consistency, and groundstrokes accurate enough to hit effective passing shots against a serve-and-volleyer; this style is most effective on "slow" surfaces like clay and Har-Tru composite. John McEnroe and Bjorn Borg are probably the modern era's greatest exponents of the offensive and defensive styles respectively.

There is now a third way to play, and it tends to be called the "power baseline" style. As far as I can determine, Jimmy Connors[26] more or less invented the power-baseline game back in the '70s, and in the '80s, Ivan Lendl raised it to a kind of brutal art. In the '90s, the majority of young players on the ATP Tour now have a P.B.-type game. This game's cornerstone is groundstrokes, but groundstrokes hit with incredible pace, such that winners from the baseline are

---

the love one feels for a job or a lover or any of the loci of intensity that most of us choose to say we love. It's the sort of love you see in the eyes of really old people who've been happily married for an incredibly long time, or in religious people who are so religious they've devoted their lives to religious stuff: it's the sort of love whose measure is what it has cost, what one's given up for it. Whether there's "*choice*" involved is, at a certain point, of no interest . . . since it's the very surrender of choice and self that informs the love in the first place.

25. (aka serve-and-volley; see Note 22)

26. I don't know whether you know this, but Connors had one of the most eccentric games in the history of tennis—he was an aggressive "power" player who rarely came to net, had the serve of an ectomorphic girl, and hit everything totally spinless and flat (which is inadvisable on groundstrokes because the absence of spin makes the ball so hard to control). His game was all the stranger because the racquet he generated all his firepower from the baseline with was a Wilson T2000, a weird steel thing that's one of the single shittiest tennis racquets ever made and is regarded by most serious players as useful only for home defense or prying large rocks out of your backyard or something. Connors was addicted to this racquet and kept using it even after Wilson stopped making it, forfeiting millions in potential endorsement money by doing so. Connors was eccentric (and kind of repulsive) in lots of other ways, too, none of which are germane to this article.

not unusual.[27] A power baseliner's net game tends to be solid but uninspired—a P.B.er is more apt to hit a winner on the approach shot and not need to volley at all. His serve is competent and reasonably forceful, but the really inspired part of a P.B.er's game is usually his return or serve.[28] He usually has incredible reflexes and can hit winners right off the return. The P.B.er's game requires both the power and aggression of an offensive style and the speed and calculated patience of a defensive style. It is adjustable both to slick grass and to slow clay, but its most congenial surface is DecoTurf,[29] the type of slow abrasive hard-court surface now used at the U.S. Open and at all the broiling North American tournaments leading up to it, including the Canadian Open.

Boris Becker and Stefan Edberg are contemporary examples of the classic offensive style. Serve-and-volleyers are often tall,[30] and tall Americans like Pete Sampras and Todd Martin and David Wheaton are also offensive players. Michael Chang is an exponent of the pure defensive style, as are Mats Wilander, Carlos Costa, and a lot

---

27. In the yore days before wide-body ceramic racquets and scientific strength-training, the only two venues for hitting winners used to be the volley—where your decreased distance from the net allowed for greatly increased angle (get that protractor out)—and the defensive passing shot . . . i.e., in the tactical language of boxing, "punch" v. "counterpunch." The new power-baseline game allows a player, in effect, to punch his opponent all the way from his stool in the corner; it changes absolutely everything, and the analytic geometry of these changes would look like the worst calculus final you ever had in your life.

28. This is why the phenomenon of "breaking serve" in a set is so much less important when a match involves power-baseliners. It is one reason why so many older players and fans no longer like to watch pro tennis as much: the structural tactics of the game are now wholly different from when they played.

29. © Wichita KS's Koch Materials Company, "A Leader in Asphalt-Emulsions Technology."

30. John McEnroe wasn't all that tall, and he was arguably the best serve-and-volley man of all time, but then McEnroe was an exception to pretty much every predictive norm there was. At his peak (say 1980 to 1984), he was the greatest tennis player who ever lived—the most talented, the most beautiful, the most tormented: a genius. For me, watching McEnroe don a polyester blazer

of the Tour's Western Europeans and South Americans, many of whom grew up exclusively on clay and now stick primarily to the overseas clay-court circuits. Americans Jim Courier, Jimmy Arias, and Aaron Krickstein all play a power-baseline game. So does just about every young new male player on the Tour. But the style's most famous and effective post-Lendl avatar is Andre Agassi, who on 1995's summer circuit is simply kicking everyone's ass.[31]

Michael Joyce's style is power-baseline in the Agassi mold: Joyce is short and right-handed and has a two-handed backhand, a serve that's just good enough to set up the baseline attack, and a great return of serve that's the linchpin of his game. Like Agassi, Joyce takes the ball early, on the rise, so it always looks like he's moving forward in the court even though he rarely comes to net. Joyce's first serve usually comes in around 95 mph,[32] and his second serve is in the low 80s, but it has so much spin on it that the ball turns weird shapes in the air and bounces high and wide to the first-round Canadian's backhand. Brakus stretches for the ball and floats a slice return, the sort of weak return that a serve-and-volleyer'd be rushing up to the net to put on the fly. Joyce does move up, but only to midcourt, right around his own service line, where he lets the floater land and bounce up all ripe, and he winds up his forehand and hits a winner crosscourt into the deuce corner, very flat and hard, so that the ball makes an emphatic sound as it hits the scarlet tarp behind Brakus's end of the court. Ballboys move for the ball and reconfigure complexly as Joyce walks back to serve another point. The

---

and do stiff lame truistic color commentary for TV is like watching Faulkner do a Gap ad.

31. One answer to why public interest in men's tennis has been on the wane in recent years is an essential and unpretty *thuggishness* about the power-baseline style that's come to dominate the Tour. Watch Agassi closely sometime—for so small a man and so great a player, he's amazingly devoid of finesse, with movements that look more like a Heavy Metal musician's than an athlete's.

The power-baseline game itself has been compared to Metal or Grunge. But what a top P.B.er really resembles is film of the old Soviet Union putting down a rebellion. It's awesome, but brutally so, with a grinding, faceless quality about its power that renders that power curiously dull and empty.

applause of the tiny crowd is so small and sad and shabby-sounding that it'd almost be better if people didn't clap at all.

As with Lendl and Agassi and Courier and many P.B.ers, Joyce's strongest shot is his forehand, a weapon of near-Wagnerian aggression and power. Joyce's forehand is particularly lovely to watch. It's more spare and textbook than Lendl's whip-crack forehand or Borg's great swooping loop; by way of decoration there's only a small loop of flourish[33] on the backswing. The stroke itself is completely horizontal, so Joyce can hit through the ball while it's still well out in front of him. As with all great players, Joyce's side is so emphatically to the net as the ball approaches that his posture is a classic contrapposto.

As Joyce on the forehand makes contact with the tennis ball, his left hand behind him opens up, as if he were releasing something, a decorative gesture that has nothing to do with the mechanics of the stroke. Michael Joyce doesn't know that his left hand opens up at impact on forehands: it is unconscious, some aesthetic tic that started when he was a child and is now inextricably hardwired into a stroke

---

32. (compare Ivanisevic's at 130 mph or Sampras's at 125, or even this Brakus kid's at 118).

33. The loop in a pro's backswing is kind of the trademark flourish of excellence and consciousness of same, not unlike the five-star chef's quick kiss of his own fingertips as he presents a pièce or the magician's hand making a French curl in the air as he directs our attention to his vanished assistant.

34. All serious players have these little extraneous tics, stylistic fingerprints, and the pros even more so because of years of repetition and ingraining. Pros' tics have always been fun to note and chart, even just e.g. on the serve. Watch the way Sampras's lead foot rises from the heel on his toss, as if his left foot's toes got suddenly hot. The odd Tourettic way Gerulaitis used to whip his head from side to side while bouncing the ball before his toss, as if he were having a small seizure. McEnroe's weird splayed stiff-armed service stance, both feet parallel to the baseline and his side so severely to the net that he looked like a figure on an Egyptian frieze. The odd sudden shrug Lendl gives before releasing his toss. The way Agassi shifts his weight several times from foot to foot as he prepares for the toss like he needs desperately to pee. Or, here at the Canadian Open, the way the young star Thomas Enqvist's body bends queerly back as he tosses, limboing back from the toss, as if for a moment the ball smelled very bad—this tic derives from Enqvist's predecessor Edberg's own weird spinal arch

that is itself unconscious for Joyce, now, at 22, after years of hitting more forehands over and over than anyone could ever count.[34]

Agassi, who is 25 (and of whom you have heard and then some), is kind of Michael Joyce's hero. Just last week, at the Legg Mason Tennis Classic in Washington D.C., in wet-mitten heat that had players vomiting on-court and defaulting all over the place, Agassi beat Joyce in the third round of the main draw, 6–2 6–2. Every once in a while now during this Qualie match Joyce will look over at his coach next to me in the player-guest section of the Grandstand and grin and say something like "Agassi'd have killed me on that shot." Joyce's coach will adjust the set of his sunglasses and say nothing—coaches are forbidden to say anything to their players during a match. Joyce's coach, Sam Aparicio,[35] a protégé of Pancho Gonzalez, is based in Las Vegas, which is also Agassi's home town, and Joyce has several times been flown to Las Vegas at Agassi's request to practice with him, and is apparently regarded by Agassi as a friend and peer—these are facts Michael Joyce will mention with as much pride as he evinces in speaking of victories and world ranking.

There are big differences between Agassi's and Joyce's games, though. Though Joyce and Agassi both use the Western forehand

---

and twist on the toss. Edberg also has this strange sudden way of switching his hold on the racquet in mid-toss, changing from an Eastern forehand to an extreme backhand grip, as if the racquet were a skillet.

35. Who looks rather like a Hispanic Dustin Hoffman and is an almost unbelievably nice guy, with the sort of inward self-sufficiency of truly great teachers and coaches everywhere, the Zen-like blend of focus and calm developed by people who have to spend enormous amounts of time sitting in one place watching closely while somebody else does something. Sam gets 10% of Joyce's gross revenues and spends his downtime reading dense tomes on Mayan architecture and is one of the coolest people I've ever met either inside the tennis world or outside it (so cool I'm kind of scared of him and haven't called him once since the assignment ended, if that makes sense). In return for his 10%, Sam travels with Joyce, rooms with him, coaches him, supervises his training, analyzes his matches, and attends him in practice, even to the extent of picking up errant balls so that Joyce doesn't have to spend any of his tightly organized practice time picking up errant balls. The stress and weird loneliness of pro tennis—where everybody's in the same community, sees each other every week, but is

grip and two-handed backhand that are distinctive of topspinners, Joyce's groundstrokes are very "flat"—i.e., spinless, passing low over the net, driven rather than brushed—because the actual motion of his strokes is so levelly horizontal. Joyce's balls actually look more like Jimmy Connor's balls than like Agassi's.[36] Some of Joyce's groundstrokes look like knuckleballs going over the net, and you can actually see the ball's seams just hanging there, not spinning. Joyce also has a hitch in his backhand that makes it look stiff and slightly awkward, though his pace and placement are lethal off that side; Agassi's own backhand is flowing and hitchless.[37] And while Joyce is far from slow, he lacks Agassi's otherworldly footspeed. Agassi is every bit as fast as Michael Chang, and watch A.A. on TV sometimes as he's walking between points: he takes these tiny violently pigeon-toed steps, the stride of a man whose feet weigh basically nothing.

Michael Joyce also—in his own coach's opinion—doesn't "see" the ball in the same magical way that Andre Agassi does, and so

---

constantly on the diasporic move, and is each other's rival, with enormous amounts of money at stake and life essentially a montage of airports and bland hotels and non-home-cooked food and nagging injuries and staggering long-distance bills, and people's families back home tending to be wackos, since only wackos will make the financial and temporal sacrifices necessary to let their offspring become good enough at something to turn pro at it—all this means that most players lean heavily on their coaches for emotional support and friendship as well as technical counsel. Sam's role with Joyce looks to me to approximate what in the latter century was called that of "companion," one of those older ladies who traveled with nubile women when they went abroad, etc.

36. Agassi's balls look more like Borg's balls would have looked if Borg had been on a year-long regimen of both steroids and methamphetamines and was hitting every single fucking ball just as hard as he could—Agassi hits his groundstrokes as hard as anybody who's ever played tennis, so hard you almost can't believe it if you're right there by the court.

37. But Agassi does have this exaggerated follow-through where he keeps both hands on the racquet and follows through almost like a hitter in baseball, which causes his shirtfront to lift and his hairy tummy to be exposed to public view—in Montreal I find this repellent, though the females in the stands around me seem ready to live and die for a glimpse of Agassi's tummy. Agassi's

Joyce can't take the ball as early or generate quite the same amount of pace off his groundstrokes. This business of "seeing" is important enough to explain. Except for the serve, power in tennis is a matter not of strength but of timing. This is one reason why so few top tennis players are muscular.[38] Any normal adult male can hit a tennis ball with pro pace; the trick is being able to hit the ball both hard and accurately. If you can get your body in just the right position and time your stroke so you hit the ball in just the right spot—waist-level, just slightly out in front of you, with your weight moving from your back leg to your front leg as you make contact—you can both cream the ball and direct it. And since ". . . just the right . . ." is a matter of millimeters and microseconds, a certain kind of vision is crucial.[39] Agassi's vision is literally one in a billion, and it allows him to hit his groundstrokes as hard as he can just about every time. Joyce, whose hand-eye coordination is superlative, in the top 1% of all athletes everywhere (he's been exhaustively tested), still has to take some incremental bit of steam off most of his groundstrokes if he wants to direct them.

---

S.O. Brooke Shields is in Montreal, by the way, and will end up highly visible in the player-guest box for all Agassi's matches, wearing big sunglasses and what look to be multiple hats. This may be the place to insert that Brooke Shields is rather a lot taller than Agassi, and considerably less hairy, and that seeing them standing together in person is rather like seeing Sigourney Weaver on the arm of Danny DeVito. The effect is especially surreal when Brooke is wearing one of the plain classy sundresses that make her look like a deb summering in the Hamptons and Agassi's wearing his new Nike on-court ensemble, a blue-black horizontally striped outfit that together with his black sneakers make him look like somebody's idea of a French Resistance fighter.

38. (Though note that very few of them wear eyeglasses, either.)

39. A whole other kind of vision—the kind attributed to Larry Bird in basketball, sometimes, when he made those incredible surgical passes to people who nobody else could even see were open—is required when you're hitting: this involves seeing the other side of the court, i.e. where your opponent is and which direction he's moving in and what possible angles are open to you in consequence of where he's going. The schizoid thing about tennis is that you have to use both kinds of vision—ball and court—at the same time.

I submit that tennis is the most beautiful sport there is,[40] and also the most demanding. It requires body control, hand-eye coordination, quickness, flat-out speed, endurance, and that strange mix of caution and abandon we call courage. It also requires smarts. Just one single shot in one exchange in one point of a high-level match is a nightmare of mechanical variables. Given a net that's three feet high (at the center) and two players in (unrealistically) a fixed position, the efficacy of one single shot is determined by its angle, depth, pace, and spin. And each of these determinants is itself determined by still other variables—for example, a shot's depth is determined by the height at which the ball passes over the net combined with some integrated function of pace and spin, with the ball's height over the net *itself* determined by the player's body position, grip on the racquet, degree of backswing, angle of racquet face, and the 3-D coordinates through which the racquet face moves during that interval in which the ball is actually on the strings. The tree of variables and determinants branches out, on and on, and then on even farther when the opponent's own positions and predilections and the ballistic features of the ball he's sent you to hit are factored in.[41] No CPU yet existent could compute the expansion of variables for even a single exchange—smoke would come out of the mainframe. The sort of thinking involved is the sort that can be done only by a living and highly conscious entity, and then only *un*consciously, i.e. by combining talent with repetition to such an extent that the variables are

40. Basketball comes close, but it's a team sport and lacks tennis's primal mano a mano intensity. Boxing might come close—at least at the lighter weight-divisions—but the actual physical damage the fighters inflict on each other makes it too concretely brutal to be really beautiful: a level of abstraction and formality (i.e. "play") is probably necessary for a sport to possess true metaphysical beauty (in my opinion).

41. For those of you into business stats, the calculus of a shot in tennis would be rather like establishing a running compound-interest expansion in a case where not only is the rate of interest itself variable, and not only are the determinants of that rate variable, and not only is the interval in which the determinants influence the interest rate variable, but the principal *itself* is variable.

combined and controlled without conscious thought. In other words, serious tennis is a kind of art.

If you've played tennis at least a little, you probably think you have some idea of how hard a game it is to play really well. I submit to you that you really have no idea at all. I know I didn't. And television doesn't really allow us to appreciate what real top-level players can do—how hard they're actually hitting the ball, and with what control and tactical imagination and artistry. I got to watch Michael Joyce practice several times, right up close, like six feet and a chain-link fence away. This is a man who, at full run, can hit a fast-moving tennis ball into a one-foot-square area 78 feet away over a yard-high net, hard. He can do this something over 90% of the time. And this is the world's 79th-best player, one who has to play the Montreal Qualies.

It's not just the athletic artistry that compels interest in tennis at the professional level. It's also what this level requires—what it's taken for the 100th-ranked player in the world to get there, what it takes to stay, what it would take to rise even higher against other men who've paid the same price he's paid.

Bismarck's epigram about diplomacy and sausage applies also to the way we Americans seem to feel about professional athletes. We revere athletic excellence, competitive success. And it's more than attention we pay; we vote with our wallets. We'll spend large sums to watch a truly great athlete; we'll reward him with celebrity and adulation and will even go so far as to buy products and services he endorses.

But we prefer not to countenance the kinds of sacrifices the professional-grade athlete has made to get so good at one particular thing. Oh, we'll pay lip service to these sacrifices—we'll invoke lush clichés about the lonely heroism of Olympic athletes, the pain and analgesia of football, the early rising and hours of practice and restricted diets, the privations, the prefight celibacy, etc. But the actual facts of the sacrifices repel us when we see them: basketball geniuses who cannot read, sprinters who dope themselves, defensive tackles who shoot up bovine hormones until they collapse or explode. We prefer not to consider the shockingly vapid and primitive comments uttered by athletes in postcontest interviews, or to imagine what impoverishments in one's mental life would allow people actually to think in the simplistic way great athletes seem to think. Note the way "up-close and personal profiles" of professional athletes strain so hard to find evidence of a rounded human life—outside interests and activities, charities, values beyond the sport. We ignore what's obvious, that most of this straining is farce. It's farce because the realities of top-level athletics today require an early and total commitment to one pursuit. An almost ascetic focus.[42] A subsumption of almost all other features of human life to their one chosen talent and pursuit. A consent to live in a world that, like a child's world, is very serious and very small.

Playing two professional singles matches on the same day is unheard of, except in Qualies.[43] Michael Joyce's second qualifying round is at 7:30 Saturday night. He's playing an Austrian named Julian Knowle, a tall and cadaverous guy with pointy Kafkan ears. Knowle uses two hands off both sides[44] and throws his racquet when he's mad. The match takes place on Stade Jarry's Grandstand Court, which seems more like a theater than an arena because it has seats and bleachers only on the east side. But the Grandstand's also more intimate: the box seats start just a few yards from the court surface, and you're

---

42. Sex- and substance-issues notwithstanding, professional athletes are in many ways our culture's holy men: they give themselves over to a pursuit, endure great privation and pain to actualize themselves at it, and enjoy a relationship to perfection that we admire and reward (the monk's begging bowl, the RBI-guru's eight-figure contract) and love to watch even though we have no inclination to walk that road ourselves. In other words they do it "for" us, sacrifice themselves for our (we imagine) redemption.

43. In the Qualies for Grand Slams like Wimbledon and the U.S. Open, players sometimes have to play two three-out-of-five-set matches in one day; it is little wonder that the surviving qualifiers often look like concentration-camp survivors by the time they get to the main drawn and you see them getting annihilated by a healthy and rested top seed in the televised first round.

44. Meaning a two-handed forehand, whose pioneer was a South African named Frew McMillan and whose most famous practitioner today is Monica Seles.

close enough to see a wen on Joyce's cheek or the abacus of sweat on Herr Knowle's forehead. It's not as hot here at night, but it's humid, and the high-power lights all have those curious rainbow globes of diffraction around them, plus orbiting bugs. The Grandstand can hold maybe 1,500 people, and tonight there are exactly four human beings in the audience as Michael Joyce basically beats the everliving shit out of Julian Knowle, who will be at the Montreal airport tonight at 1:30 to board the red-eye for a kind of minor-league clay tournament in Poznan, Poland.

During this afternoon's match Joyce wore a white Fila shirt with two different-colored sleeves. Onto his sleeve was sewn a patch that says POWERBAR; Joyce is paid $1000 each time he wears this patch in play. Plus, this afternoon, a hat—in the afternoon sun, pretty much all the players in the Qualies wear hats. For tonight's match Joyce wears a pinstripe Jim Courier–model Fila shirt with one red sleeve and one blue sleeve. The patch is on the blue sleeve. He has a red bandanna around his head, and as he begins to perspire in the humidity his face turns the same color as the bandanna. It is hard not to find this endearing. Julian Knowle has an abstract pastel shirt whose brand is unrecognizable. He has very tall hair, Knowle does, that towers over his head at near-Beavis altitude and doesn't diminish or lose its gelled integrity as he perspires.[45] Knowle's shirt, too, has sleeves of different colors. This seems to be the fashion constant this year among the qualifiers: sleeve-color asymmetry.

The Joyce–Knowle match takes slightly more than an hour. This including delays caused when Knowle throws his racquet and has to go retrieve it or when he walks around in aimless circles muttering blackly to himself in some High-German dialect. Knowle's tantrums seem a little contrived and insincere to me, though, because he rarely loses a point as a result of doing anything particularly wrong. Here's

45. The idea of what it would be like to perspire heavily with large amounts of gel in your hair is sufficiently horrific to me that I approach Knowle after the match to ask him about it, only to discover that neither he nor his coach spoke enough English or even French to be able to determine who I was, and the whole sweat-and-gel issue will, I'm afraid, remain a matter for your own imagination.

a typical point in this match: it's 1–4 and 15–30 in the sixth game. Knowle hits a 110 mph slice serve to Joyce's forehand; Joyce hits a very flat and penetrating drive crosscourt, so that Knowle has to stretch and hit his forehand on the run, something that's not particularly easy to do with a two-handed forehand. Knowle gets to the forehand and hits a thoroughly respectable shot, loopy with topspin and landing maybe only a little bit short, a few feet behind the service line, whereupon he reverses direction and starts scrambling back to get in the middle of the baseline to get ready for his next shot. Joyce, as is SOP, has moved in on the slightly short ball and takes the ball on the rise just after it's bounced, driving a backhand even flatter and harder into the exact same place he hit his last shot, the spot Knowle is scrambling away from. Knowle is now forced to reverse direction and get back to where he was.[46] This he does, and he gets his racquet on the ball, but only barely, and sends back a weak little USDA Prime loblet that Joyce, now in the actual vicinity of the net, has little trouble blocking into the open court for a winner. The four people clap, Knowle's racquet goes spinning into the blood-colored tarp, and Joyce walks expressionlessly back to the deuce court to receive again whenever Knowle gets around to serving. Knowle has slightly more firepower than the first round's Brakus: his groundstrokes are formidable, probably even lethal if he has sufficient time to get to the ball and get set up. Joyce simply denies him that time. Joyce will later admit that he wasn't working all that hard in this match, and he doesn't need to. He hits a few spectacular winners, but he also makes very few unforced errors, and his shots are designed to make the somewhat clumsy Knowle move a lot and to deny him the time and the peace ever to set up his game. This strategy is one that Knowle cannot solve or interdict: he hasn't got the tools for it. This may be one reason why Joyce is unaffronted by having to play the Qualies for Montreal: barring some kind of injury or neurological dysfunction, he's not going to lose to somebody like Austria's Julian Knowle—Joyce is simply on a different plateau from the mass of these Qualie players.

---

46. What Joyce has done is known as "wrong-footing" his opponent, though the intransigent Francophone press here keep calling the tactic a "*contre-pied*."

The idea that there can be wholly distinct levels to competitive tennis—levels so distinct that what's being played is in essence a whole different game—might seem to you weird and hyperbolic. I have played probably just enough tennis to understand that it's true. I have played against men who were on a whole different, higher plateau than I, and I have understood on the deepest and most humbling level the impossibility of beating them, of "solving their game." Knowle is technically entitled to be called a professional, but he is playing a fundamentally different grade of tennis from Michael Joyce's, one constrained by limitations Joyce does not have. I feel like I could get on a tennis court with Julian Knowle. He would beat me, perhaps badly, but I don't feel like it would be absurd for me to occupy the same 78 x 27–foot rectangle as he. But the idea of me playing Joyce—or even hitting around with him, which was one of the ideas I was entertaining on the flight to Montreal, to hit around with a hot young U.S. pro—is now revealed to me to be absurd and in a certain way obscene, and during this night match I resolve not even to let Joyce[47] know that I used to play competitive tennis, to play seriously and (I'd presumed) rather well. This makes me sad.

Sunday, the second day of the Qualies, is mostly a rainout. It rains off and on all day. The umpire, courtside in his tall chair, decides when the rain's falling hard enough to suspend play. A second-round match between the world's 219th- and 345th-ranked players gets suspended four different times and takes most of the day to complete. What happens when it rains is reminiscent of baseball. The players are hustled off back to the Players' Tent but can't leave because it could stop raining any minute; they have to just sit there, match-ready. The spectators (there are slightly more on the second day) stay where they are, but little fungal domes of umbrella start appearing all over the stands. The local Quebec reporters up in the Press Box curse in French and bring out newspapers or hand-held

47. Who is clearly such a fundamentally nice guy that he would probably hit around with me for a little while just out of politeness, since for him it would be at worst somewhat dull. For me, though, it would be obscene.

video games or begin telling one another long sexual-adventure stories that my French is just good enough to establish as tiresome.

When it stops raining and stays stopped long enough for the umpire to give the old raised thumb, there's suddenly a flurry of custodial activity down on the Stadium Court, a Chinese fire drill of ballboys and linesmen turned groundskeepers. Strange and expensive-looking machinery appears from nowhere and is brought to bear: huge riding-mowerish forced-air machines go over the court, bludgeoning the pooled rainwater and spreading it out; then a platoon of squeegees goes over every cm of the surface; then portable blowers—rather like leaf-blowers, with an over-the-shoulder strap and a wand attachment—are applied to the persistent individual wet spots that always beset a drying court.

This article is about Michael Joyce and the untelevised realities of the Tour, not me. But since a big part of my experience of the Canadian Open and its players was one of sadness, it might be worthwhile to spend a little time letting you know where I'm coming from w/r/t these players. As a young person I played competitive tennis, traveling to tournaments all over the Midwest. Most of my best friends were also tennis players, and on a regional level we were fairly successful, and we thought of ourselves as extremely good players. Tennis and our proficiency at it were tremendously important to us—a serious junior gives up a lot of his time and freedom to develop his game,[48] and it can very easily come to constitute a big part of his identity and self-worth. The other fourteen-year-old Midwest hotshots and I knew that our

48. The example of Michael Joyce's own childhood, though, shows that my friends and I were comparative sluggards, dilettantes. He describes his daily schedule thusly: "I'd be in school till 2:00. Then, after, I'd go [driven by father] to the [West End Tennis] Club [in Torrance, CA] and have a lesson with [legendary, wildly expensive, and unbelievably hard-ass Robert] Lansdorp [former childhood coach of, among others, Tracy Austin] from 3:00 to 4:00. Then I'd have drills from 4:00 to 6:00, then we'd drive all the way home—it's like half an hour—and I'm like, 'Thank God, I can watch TV or go up and talk with [friends] on the phone or something,' but Dad is like, 'You didn't practice your serve yet.' At twelve or thirteen [years old], you're not going to want to do it. [No lie, since two hours of serious

fishpond was somehow limited; we knew that there was a national level of play and that there existed hotshots and champions at that level. But levels and plateaux beyond our own seemed abstract, somehow unreal—those of us who were the hotshots in our region literally could not imagine players our own age who were substantially better than we.

A child's world turns out to be very small. If I'd been just a little bit better, an actual regional champion, I would have qualified for national-level tournaments, and I would have gotten to see that there were fourteen-year-olds in the United States who were playing tennis on a level I knew nothing about.

My own game as a junior was a particular type of the classic defensive style, a strategy Martin Amis describes as "craven retrieval." I didn't hit the ball all that hard, but I rarely made unforced errors, and I was fast, and my general approach was simply to keep hitting the ball back to the opponent until the kid screwed up and either made an unforced error or hit a ball so short and juicy that even I could hit a winner off it. It doesn't look like a very glamorous or even interesting way to play, now that I see it here in bald retrospective print, but it was interesting to me, and you'd be surprised how effective it was (on the level at which I was competing, at least). At age twelve, a good competitive player will still generally miss after four or five balls (mostly because he'll get impatient or grandiose). At age sixteen, a good player will keep the ball in play for more like maybe seven or eight shots before he misses. At the collegiate level, too (at least in Division III), opponents were stronger than junior players but not markedly more consistent, and if I could keep a rally going to seven or eight shots, I could usually win the point on the other guy's mistake.[49]

---

drills alone were usually enough to put your correspondent in a fetal position for the rest of the day.] You need somebody to make you do it. [This is one way of looking at it.] But then, after like a hundred or so serves, I start to get into [standing by himself out on the Joyces' tennis court in their backyard with a huge bucket of balls and hitting serve after serve to no one in what must by then have been the gathering twilight], I like it, I'm glad I'm doing it."

49. An important variable I'm skipping is that children are (not surprisingly) immature and tend to get angry with themselves when they screw up, and so a

I still play—not competitively, but seriously—and I should confess that deep down somewhere inside I still consider myself an extremely good tennis player, real hard to beat. Before coming to Montreal, I'd seen professional tennis only on television, which as has been noted does not give the viewer a very accurate picture of how good pros are. I thus further confess that I arrived in Montreal with some dim unconscious expectation that these professionals—at least the obscure ones, the nonstars—wouldn't be all *that* much bet-

---

key part of my strategy involved putting the opponent in a position where he made a lot of unforced errors and got madder and madder at himself, which would ruin his game. Feelings of self-disgust at his errors, or (even better for me) bitter grievance at the universe for making him have "bad luck" or an "off day" would mount until usually by sometime in the second set he'd sink into a kind of enraged torpor and *expect* to miss, or occasionally he'd even have a kind of grand Learesque tantrum, complete with racquet-hurling and screamed obscenities and sometimes tears. This happened less and less as I got older and opponents got more mature, and by the time I was in college only genuine head-cases could be counted on to get so mad that they'd basically make themselves lose to an inferior player (viz. me). It's something of a shock, then, to watch Joyce do to his third-round Qualies opponent what I used to do to twelve-year-old rich kids, which is essentially to retrieve and avoid errors and wait for this opponent to have a temper tantrum. Because Sunday was a rainout, Joyce's third round is played Monday at 10:00 A.M., at the same time that some of the main draw's first rounds are beginning. Joyce's opponent is a guy named Mark Knowles, 25, the 1986 U.S. Junior Indoor Champion, a native of the Bahamas, now known primarily as a doubles player but still a serious opponent, ranked in the world's top 200, somebody on Joyce's plateau.

Knowles is tall and thin, muscular in the corded way tall thin people are muscular and has an amazing tan and tight blond curls and from a distance is an impressive-looking guy, though up close he has a kind of squished, buggy face and the slightly bulging eyes of a player who, I can tell, is spring-loaded on a tantrum. There's a chance to see Knowles up close because he and Joyce play their match on one of the minor courts, where spectators stand and lean over a low fence only a few yards from the court. I and Joyce's coach and Knowles's coach and beautiful girlfriend are the only people really seriously standing and watching, though a lot of spectators on their way to more high-proFle matches pass by and stop and watch a few points before moving on. The constant movement of civilians past the court aggrieves Knowles no end and sometimes he shouts caustic things to people who've started walking away while a point is still in progress.

ter than I. I don't mean to imply that I'm insane: I was ready to concede that age, a nasty ankle injury in '91 that I haven't bothered to get surgically fixed yet, and a penchant for nicotine (and worse) meant that I wouldn't be able to compete physically with a young unhurt professional; but on TV (while eating junk and smoking) I'd seen pros whacking balls at each other that didn't look to be moving substantially faster than the balls I hit. In other words, I arrived at my first professional tournament with the pathetic deluded pride that attends ignorance. And I have watched the Qualies—not even the main draw yet, mind you, but the competition between 64 fairly low-ranked world-class players for the eight qualifying slots in the Canadian Open field—with a mixture of awe and sad surprise. I have been brought up sharply. I do not play and never have played the same game as these low-ranked pros.

The craven game I spent so much of my youth perfecting would not work against these guys. For one thing, pros simply do not make unforced errors in seven points necessary for me to win a game. For another thing, they will take any shot that doesn't have simply ferocious depth and pace on it and—given even a fractional moment to

---

"Don't worry about it!" is one thing Knowles shouted at someone who moved. "We're only playing for money! We're only professionals! Don't give it a second thought!" Joyce, preparing to serve, will stare affectlessly straight ahead while he waits for Knowles to finish yelling, his expression sort of like the one Vegas dealers have when a gambler they're cleaning out is rude or abusive, a patient and unjudging look whose expression is informed by the fact that they're extremely well compensated for being patient and unjudging.

Sam Aparicio describes Knowles as "brilliant but kind of erratic," and I think the coach is being kind, because Knowles seems to me to belong on a Locked Ward for people with serious emotional and personality disorders. He rants and throws racquets and screams scatological curses I haven't heard since junior high. If one of his shots hits the top of the net-cord and bounces back, Knowles will scream "I must be the luckiest guy in the world!", his eyes protruding and mouth twisted. For me he's an eerie echo of all the rich and well-instructed Midwest kids I used to play and beat because they'd be unable to eat the frustration when things didn't go their way. He seems not to notice that Joyce gets as many bad breaks and weird bounces as he, or that passing spectators are equally distracting to both players. Knowles seems to be one of these

line up a shot—hit a winner off it. For yet another thing, their own shots have such ferocious depth and pace that there's no way I'd be able to hit more than a couple of them back at any one time. I could not meaningfully *exist* on the same court with these obscure, hungry players. Nor could you. And it's not just a matter of talent or practice. There's something else.

Monday commences the main draw, and the grounds are packed. Most of the Qualies' players are in planes high above some ocean somewhere by now.

Going to a major ATP tournament is like a cross between going to a major-league ball game and going to the fair. You can buy a Grounds Pass and wander from match to match, sampling the fare. You can also buy specific expensive tickets for big-name matches in the Stadium and Grandstand. In the early rounds, these headline matches tend to feature the high seeds and household names—Agassi, Sampras, Chang—against main draw also-rans like Jacob Hlasek.[50]

---

people who view the world's inconveniences as speciFc and personal, and it makes my stomach hurt to watch him. When he hits a ball against the fence so hard it seems to damage the ball, the umpire gives him a warning, but in the sort of gentle compassionate voice of a kindergarten teacher to a kid who's known to have A.D.D. I have a hard time believing that someone this of-the-wall could rise to a serious pro plateau, though it's true that when Knowles isn't letting his attention get scattered he's a gorgeous player, with Guid strokes and marvelous control over spin and pace. His read on Joyce is that Joyce is a slugger (which is true), and his tactic is to try to junk him up—change pace, vary spins, hit drop shots to draw Joyce in, deny Joyce pace or rhythm—and because he's Joyce's equal in Frepower the tactic is sound. Joyce wins the Frst set in a tiebreaker. But three times in the tiebreaker Knowles yells at migratory spectators "Don't worry! It's only a tiebreaker in a professional match!" and is basically a wreck by the time the Frst set is over, and the second set is perfunctory, a formality that Joyce concludes as fast as possible and hurries back to the Players' Tent to pack carbohydrates and Fnd out whether he has to play his Frst round in the main draw later this same day.

50. Hlasek lost in the first round of the main draw Tuesday morning to obscure American Jonathan Stark, who then lost to Sampras in the second round on Wednesday in front of a capacity Stadium crowd.

Being a tennis spectator is different from being at a baseball game, though. Whether crowd-noise or -movement is any more distracting to someone getting ready to serve than it is to someone getting ready to shoot a freethrow, players and tournaments act like it is, and play itself is supposed to be conducted in as close to funereal silence as possible.[51] If you've got a seat for a Stadium match, you can leave and return only during the break that happens after every odd-numbered game, when the players get to sit under red umbrellas for a second. Ushers cordon off the exits during play, and a concession-laden mass of spectators always stretch from just behind these ropes all the way down the slanted ramps into the Stadium's bowels, waiting to get back in.

Stade Jarry has the same sort of crumbling splendor that characterizes a lot of Montreal. The Stadium/Grandstand structure used to house the Expos before Montreal built Olympic Stadium, and it's grimy and old and creaks alarmingly when crowds enter or exit. The "Players' Lounge," which at most tournaments is a temperature-controlled salon with plush chairs and video games and multiple massage rooms, is at Stade Jarry just a big tent with canvas partitions around the locker room, no video games, just one TV, and no AC. The parking lots are inadequate and tufted with crabgrass, and the easements between courts and facilities on the ground are either dirt or some kind of blacktop that's decayed back to the point where it's just about dirt too. The whole thing's due to be torn down after the '95 Open's over, and a new Flushing Meadow–type tennis complex is going to be built by Tennis Canada[52] and a whole bunch of the corporations whose names are on the Stadium's brothelish bunting.

---

51. This is in the Stadium and Grandstand, where the big names play, this ceremonial hush. Lesser players on the outlying courts have to live with spectators talking during points, people moving around so that whole rickety sets of bleachers rumble and clank, food service attendants crashing carts around on the paths just outside the windscreen or giggling and flirting in the food-prep tents just on the other side of several minor courts' fences.

52. This is Canada's version of the U.S.T.A., and its logo—which obtrudes into your visual field as often as is possible here at the du Maurier Omnium—consists

The tournament site's surrounding Parc du Jarry, on the other hand, is exquisite. From the top row of the Stadium's seats you can look out in the sunshine and see rolling grass, a public pool, a pond replete with stately fowl. In the distance to the north is the verdigrised dome of a really big church; to the west is the EKG skyline of downtown Montreal.

But also you can wander between matches, stand around watching the practice courts, join the lines for the restrooms, or elbow-fight with little kids and autograph hunters outside the Players' Tent. Or you can buy concessions. There's a booth outside one entrance to the Stadium Court that sells only Evian water. There's Spanish peanuts and fudge you can buy by the gram and eat or buy by the kilo and take home.[53] The whole Stade Jarry grounds have a standard summer-touristic reek of fried foods—French fires in cups, nachos, and in paper trays small spiraled fried things I decline to examine closely. There are two booths for Richard D's Bars, a kind of Quebecois cognate for Dove Bars (and not quite as good, but pretty good). There are only two men's rooms open to the public,[54] and the lines for both always resemble a run on a midsize branch bank. There's the Rado® Smash Booth, where for $3.00 Canadian you can step inside a large cage with a much-handled racquet and hit a serve into a frayed-looking net and have the speed of your serve appear on a big liquid-crystal display above the cage. Most of the people availing themselves of the Rado® Smash Booth are men, whose girlfriends watch dutifully as the men step inside the cage with the same

---

of the good old Canadian maple leaf with a tennis racquet for a stem. It's stuff like Tennis Canada's logo you want to point to when Canadians protest that they don't understand why Americans make fun of them.

53. (though best of luck getting fudge home in this heat . . .)

54. "Le Média" has its own facilities, though they're up in the Press Box, about five flights of rickety and crowded stairs up through the Stadium's interior and then exterior and then interior, with the last flight being that dense striated iron like a fire escape and very steep and frankly dangerous, so that when one has to "aller au pissoir" it's always a hard decision between the massed horror of the public rest rooms and the Sisyphean horror of the Press bathroom, and I learn by the second day to go very easy on the Evian water and coffee as I'm wandering around.

testosteronic facial expression of men at fairs testing their marksmanship or sledge-swinging prowess—and the American men tend to be very pleased and excited at the displayed speed of their serve until it dawns on them that the readout's in kph instead of mph. There are hot dogs and hamburgers and the ambient sizzle-sound of same over near the Grandstand entrances. Just east of the Grandstand and the second men's room, there's a whole sort of cafeteria in a big tent with patio tables arrayed on Astroturf that's laid over a low deck of extremely flimsy boards so that your table trembles and your Evian bottle falls over every time somebody walks by. Starting on Monday there are a lot of Canadian girls in really short tight shorts and a lot of muscle-shirted Canadian boyfriends who scowl at you if you react to the girlfriends in the way the girlfriends' tight shorts seem designed to make anyone with a healthy endocrine system react.

There are old people who sit on red Stade Jarry park benches all day without moving.

At just about every gate and important door on the Stade Jarry grounds there are attendants, young Quebeckers paid by the tournament—whether their function is security or what remains somewhat unclear—who sit all day with walkie-talkies and red and black du Maurier visors and the catatonically bored expressions of attendants everywhere.

There are four separate booths that sell good old U.S. soft drinks, you'll be glad to know, although the booths' promo-signs for "Soft Drinks" translate literally into "Gaseous Beverages," which might explain why most Canadian Open spectators opt for Evian instead of soft drinks.

Or you can stand in front of the Canadian Open Stringer's Tent and watch the Official ATP Tour Stringer work through a small mountain of racquets, using pliers and shears and what looks like a combination blacksmith's anvil and dentist's chair. Or you can join the battalion of kids outside the Players' Tent all trying to get their Official ATP Player Trading Cards[55] autographed by players entering

55. (a recent and rather ingenious marketing move by the ATP—I buy several just for the names)

or exiting, and you can witness a kind of near-riot when the passing player turns out to be Sampras or Courier or Agassi, and you can even get stiff-armed by a bodyguard in wraparound shades when Brooke Shields passes too close in her own wraparounds and floppy hat.

If the mood for more serious consumption strikes, you can walk due east of the Stadium complex to the Promenade du Sportif, a kind of canvas strip mall selling every product even remotely associated with the Canadian Open: Prince, Wilson, Nike, Head, Boost® Vitamin/Energy Drink (free samples available), Swatch, Nature Valley Granola Bars,[56] Sony, and DecoTurf Inc.

And at this tournament you can (U.S. readers may want to sit down for this part) actually *buy* du Maurier–brand cigarettes—by the carton or broad flat Europack—from a special red and black booth right outside the main entrance to the Stadium Court.[57] People in Quebec smoke—heavily—and this booth does serious business. No part of Stade Jarry is nonsmoking, and at matches so many spectators are chain-smoking du Maurier cigarettes that at times a slight breeze will carry the crowd's exhaled cloud of smoke out over the court, transforming the players into nacreous silhouettes for a moment before the cloud ascends. And, in truth, accredited media don't even have to *buy* the du Mauriers; Press Box employees will give packs out free to journalists, though they don't announce this or make a big big deal of it.

It's the little things like public smoking that remind you that Canada's not home. Or e.g. Francophone ads, and these ads' lack of even a pretense of coy subtlety—someplace between the Radisson des Gouverneurs and Stade Jarry is a huge billboard for some kind of Quebecois ice cream. It's a huge photo of an ice cream cone poised at

---

56. It's not at all clear what N.V.G.B.'s have to do with the Omnium, and no free samples are available.

57. Du Maurier cigarettes are like Australian Sterlings or French Gauloise—full-bodied, pungent, crackly when inhaled, sweet and yeasty when exhaled, and so strong that you can feel your scalp seem to leave your skull for a moment and ride the cloud of smoke. Du Maurier–intoxication may be one reason why the Canadian Open crowds seem so generally cheery and expansive and well-behaved.

a phallic 45°, jutting, the dome of ice cream unabashedly glansular, and underneath is the pitch: "Donnez-moi ta bouche."[58] The brand's own trademark slogan, at the bottom, is that it's "La glace du lait plus lechée." One of the nice things Michael Joyce and his coach do is usually let me ride with them in their courtesy car[59] between the hotel and Jarry, to sort of lurk and soak up atmosphere, etc. We pass this billboard several times a day. Finally one time I point up at the glistening phallic ad and ask Joyce whether the ad strikes him as a little heavy, overt, uncoy. Joyce looks up at the billboard—maybe for the first time, because in the car he's usually staring commuterishly straight ahead, either gathering himself into a prematch focus or exiting gradually from same—and turns to me and says in all earnestness that he's tried this particular brand of Canadian ice cream and it's not all that good.

Plus, of course, once the main draw starts, you get to look up close and live at name tennis players you're used to seeing only as arrays of pixels. One of the highlights of Tuesday's second round of the main draw is getting to watch Agassi play MaliVai Washington. Washington, the most successful black American on the Tour since Ashe, is unseeded at the Canadian Open but has been ranked as high as #11 in the world, and is dangerous, and since I loathe Agassi with a passion it's an exciting match. Agassi looks scrawny and faggy and, with his shaved skull and beretish hat and black shoes and socks and patchy goatee, like somebody just released from reform school (a look you can tell he's carefully decided on with the help of various paid image-consultants,

58. (="Give me your mouth"—not subtle at all)

59. These are usually luxury cars provided by some local distributorship in return for promotional consideration. The Canadian Open's courtesy cars are BMWs, all so new they smell like glove compartments and so expensive and high-tech that their dashboards look like the control panels of nuclear reactors. The people driving the courtesy cars are usually local civilians who take a week off from work and drive a numbingly dull route back and forth between hotel and courts—their compensation consists of free tickets to certain Stadium matches and a chance to rub elbows with professional tennis players, or at least with their luggage.

and now cultivates). Washington, who's in dark-green shorts and a red shirt with dark-green sleeves, was a couple of years ago voted by *People* one of the 50 Prettiest Human Beings or something, and on TV is indeed real pretty but in person is awesome. From twenty yards away he looks less like a human being than like a Michelangelo anatomy sketch: his upper body the V of serious weight lifting, his leg muscles standing out even in repose, his biceps little cannonballs of fierce-looking veins. He's beautiful but doomed, because the slowness of the Stadium Court makes it impractical for anybody except a world-class net man to rush the net against Agassi, and Washington is not a net man but a power-baseliner. He stays back and trades groundstrokes with Agassi, and even though the first set goes to a tiebreaker you can tell it's a mismatch. Agassi has less mass and flat-out speed than Washington, but he has vision and timing that give his groundstrokes way more pace. He can stay back and hit nuclear groundstrokes and force Washington until Washington eventually makes a fatal error. There are two ways to make a fatal error against Agassi: the first is the standard way, hitting it out or into the net or something; the second is to hit anything shorter than a couple feet inside the baseline, because anything that Agassi can move up on he can hit for a winner. Agassi's facial expression is the slightly smug self-aware one of somebody who's used to being looked at and automatically assumes the minute he shows up anywhere that everybody's looking at him. He's incredible to see play in person, but his domination of Washington doesn't make me like him any better; it's more like it chills me, as if I'm watching the devil play.

Television tends to level everybody out and make them seem kind of blandly handsome, but at Montreal it turns out that a lot of the pros and stars are interesting- or even downright funny-looking. Jim Courier, former #1 but now waning and seeded tenth here,[60]

60. He will lose badly to Michael Stich in the round of 16, the same Stich whom Michael Joyce beat at the Lipton Championships in Key Biscayne four months before; and in fact Joyce will himself beat Courier in straight sets next week at the Infiniti Open in Los Angeles, in front of Joyce's family and friends, for one of the biggest wins of his career so far.

looks like Howdy Doody in a hat on TV, but here he turns out to be a very big boy—the "Guide Média" lists him at 175 pounds but he's way more than that, with large smooth muscles and the gait and expression of a Mafia enforcer. Michael Chang, 23 and #5 in the world, sort of looks like two different people stitched crudely together: a normal upper body perched atop hugely muscular and totally hairless legs. He has a mushroom-shaped head, ink-black hair, and an expression of deep and intractable unhappiness, as unhappy a face as I've ever seen outside a Graduate Writing Program.[61] P. Sampras, in person, is mostly teeth and eyebrows, and he's got unbelievably hairy legs and forearms, hair in the sort of abundance that allows me confidently to bet that he has hair on his back and is thus at least not 100% blessed and graced by the universe. Goran Ivanisevic is large and tan and surprisingly good-looking—at least for a Croat; I always imagine Croats looking ravaged and katexic and like somebody out of a Munch lithograph—except for an incongruous and wholly absurd bowl haircut that makes him look like somebody in a Beatles tribute band. It is Ivanisevic who will beat Joyce in three sets in the main draw's second round. Czech former top-ten Petr Korda is another clastic-looking mismatch: at 6'3" and 160, he has the body of an upright greyhound and the face of—eerily, *uncannily*—a fresh-hatched chicken (plus soulless eyes that reflect no light and seem to "see" only in the way that fish's and birds' eyes "see").

And Wilander is here—Mats Wilander, Borg's heir, top-ten at age eighteen, #1 at 24, now 30 and unranked and trying a comeback after

---

61. Chang's mother is here—one of the most infamous of the dreaded Tennis Parents of the men's and women's Tours, a woman who's reliably rumored to have done things like reach down her child's tennis shorts in public to check his underwear—and her attendance (she's seated hierophantically in the player-guest boxes courtside) may have something to do with the staggering woe of Chang's mien and play. Thomas Enqvist ends up beating him soundly in the quarterfinals on Wednesday night. (Enqvist, by the way, looks eerily like a young Richard Chamberlain, the Richard Chamberlain of *The Towering Inferno*, say, with this narrow, sort of rodentially patrician quality. The best thing about Enqvist is his girlfriend, who wears glasses and when she applauds a good point sort of hops up and down in her seat with refreshing uncoolness.)

years off the Tour, here cast in the role of the wily old mariner, winning on smarts. Tuesday's best big-name match is between Wilander and Stefan Edberg,[62] 28 and Wilander's own heir[63] and now married to Annette Olson, Wilander's S.O. during his own glory days, which adds a delicious personal cast to the match, which Wilander wins 6–4 in the third. Wilander ends up getting all the way to the semifinals before Agassi beats him as badly as I have ever seen one professional beat another professional, the score beating 6–0 6–2 and the match not nearly as close as the score would indicate.

Even more illuminating than watching pro tennis live is watching it with Sam Aparicio, Joyce's coach, who knows as much about tennis as anybody I've talked to and isn't obnoxious about it. Sam watches a lot of pro matches, scouting stuff for Michael. Watching tennis with him is like watching a movie with somebody who knows a lot about the technical aspects of film: he helps you see things you can't see alone. It turns out, for example, that there are whole geometric sublevels of strategy in a power-baseline game, all dictated by various P.B.ers' strengths and weaknesses. A P.B.er depends on being able to hit winners from the baseline. But, as Sam teaches me to see, Michael Chang can usually hit winners only at an acute angle, from either corner. An "inside-out" player like Jim Courier, on the other hand, can hit winners only at obtuse angles, from the center out. Hence canny and well-coached players tend to play Chang "down the middle" and Courier "out wide." One of the things that makes Agassi so good is that he's capable of hitting winners from anywhere on the court—he has no geometric restriction. Joyce, too, according to Sam,

62. Who himself has the blond bland good looks of a professional golfer, and is reputed to be the single dullest man on the ATP Tour and possibly in the whole world, a man whose hobby is purported to be "staring at walls" and whose quietness is not the quietness of restraint but of blankness, the verbal equivalent of a dead channel.

63. (Just as Enqvist now appears to be Edberg's heir . . . Swedish tennis tends to be like monarchic succession: they tend to have only one really great player at a time, and this player is always male, and he almost always ends up #1 in the world for a while. This is one reason marketers and endorsement-consultants are circling Enqvist like makos all through the summer.)

can hit a winner at any angle. He just doesn't do it quite as well as Agassi, or as often.

Michael Joyce in close-up person, like eating supper or riding in a courtesy car, looks slighter and younger than he does on-court. From close up he looks his age, which to me is basically a fetus. He's about 5'9" and 160; he's muscular but quietly so, without much definition. He likes to wear old T-shirts and a backwards cap. His hairline is receding in a subtle young-man way that makes his forehead look a little high. I forget whether he wore an earring. Michael Joyce's interests outside tennis consist mostly of big-budget movies and genre novels of the commercial paperback sort that one reads on planes. In other words, he really has no interests outside tennis. He has a tight and long-standing group of friends back home in LA, but one senses that most of his personal connections have been made via tennis. He's dated some. It's impossible to tell whether he's a virgin. It seems staggering and impossible, but my sense is he might be. Then again, I tended to idealize and distort him, I know, because of how I felt about what he could do on the court. His most revealing sexual comment is made in the context of explaining the odd type of confidence that keeps him from freezing up in a match in front of large crowds or choking on a point when there's lots of money at stake.[64] Joyce, who usually needs to pause about five beats to think before he answers a question, thinks the confidence is partly a matter of temperament and partly a function of hard work:

"If I'm in like a bar, and there's a really good-looking girl, I might be kind of nervous. But if there's like a thousand gorgeous girls in the stands when I'm playing, it's a different story. I'm not nervous then, when I play, because I know what I'm doing. I know what to do out there." Maybe it's good to let these be his last quoted words.

Whether or not he ends up in the top ten and a name anybody will know, Michael Joyce will remain a figure of enduring and paradoxical fascination for me. The restrictions on his life have been, in my opin-

64. Nerves and choking are a huge issue in a precision-and-timing sport like tennis, and a "bad head" washes more juniors out of the competitive life than any sort of deficit in talent or drive.

ion, grotesque; and in certain ways Joyce himself is a grotesque. But the radical compression of his attention and self has allowed him to become a transcendent practitioner of an art—something few of us get to be. It's allowed him to visit and test parts of his psyche that most of us do not even know for sure we have, to manifest in concrete form virtues like courage, persistence in the face of pain or exhaustion, performance under wilting scrutiny and pressure.

Michael Joyce is, in other words, a complete man (though in a grotesquely limited way). But he wants more. Not more completeness; he doesn't think in terms of virtues or transcendence. He wants to be the best, to have his name known, to hold professional trophies over his head as he patiently turns in all four directions for the media. He is an American and he wants to win. He wants this, and he will pay to have it—will pay just to pursue it, let it define him—and will pay with the regretless cheer of a man for whom issues of choice became irrelevant long ago. Already, for Joyce, at 22, it's too late for anything else; he's invested too much, is in too deep. I think he's both lucky and un-. He will say he is happy and mean it. Wish him well.

—JULY 1996

# Gorgeous Dan

JOHN IRVING

The University of Iowa field house is a reservoir of people with different purposes. It is a Saturday morning in November. The Hawkeye Marching Band is practicing at the end of the field house near the vending machines. It is Dad's Day on campus, and Iowa's football team will, predictably, lose 31–0 to Michigan several hours from now. Since the field house is close to the stadium, many early arrivals to that game have parked their cars nearby and are killing time. Since it's cold, they're killing time indoors, wandering through the field house as if the building were a kind of random museum. There are the "Dads" of former Iowa football teams wearing little black golf caps with a yellow "I" stitched above the visor. And there are Moms with blankets and cushions for the stadium, and picnic baskets they will open later in the field house, up high in some choice balcony seats no one would mind having for a basketball game. Lani Jo Gill, Iowa's baton twirler, sits in the second row of bleachers, a glitter of gold in her coin-encrusted bathing suit; she flicks her baton; she sits there as languidly as a beached mermaid.

Three regulation-size mats are laid together on the field-house floor, next to the area where the basketball team is practicing; the wrestling team is gathering for a workout. They are loosening up, tumbling, doing their sit-ups and neck bridges and touching their toes. An audience gathers around the wrestlers.

Then the word goes around. Someone among the fans has been following more than football. He knows that the Iowa wrestling coach has a new assistant this year. Out on those mats is the best wrestler in the world. The people killing time don't have more than a couple of genuine wrestling fans among them, but everyone is interested in someone who's the "best"—at *anything*. A murmur starts going around: Dan Gable is helping out at the wrestling workouts this year. The champion of the World Games at Sofia, the gold medalist at the Munich Olympics—the winningest wrestler in the sport today and wrestling's closest approximation to a celebrity. A legend of physical conditioning, he runs more miles, lifts more weights, and puts in more wrestling hours than any other competitor in the sport. Dan Gable has been appointed "supervisor of physical-fitness programs for athletes at the University of Iowa," a title which protects his amateur standing under Olympic rules. Officially, he's not *salaried* for anything connected with the sport of wrestling.

A white-haired man in a "Dad's" black Iowa cap approaches a trainer who's juggling some spools of adhesive tape. "Which one is Gable?" In the half-speed skirmishes in progress on the mat, the football fans look for obvious winners. One of Iowa's co-captains, Jan Sanderson, is mistaken for Gable. Sanderson, a five-foot, six-inch, 168-pounder, is an impressively muscular wrestler. He *looks* like he's tough, and he is. His nose is split from his left nostril to near the corner of his eye. *That* looks impressive. The football fans don't know the split nose is from the rugby season which Sanderson has just finished; someone with cleats stepped on his face.

The trainer with his spools of tape looks bored. He squints at the wrestlers and shakes his head. "Gable's not here yet," he says. Disappointed, the football fans wander away. When Dan Gable comes barefoot out of the locker room, carrying his dirty-white wrestling shoes under his arm, wearing his ear guards askew—like a relaxed disc jockey between numbers—no one notices him at all.

Dan Gable started wrestling when he was seven years old. He won his first championship when he was twelve—a Y.M.C.A. tournament in Waterloo, Iowa, Gable's hometown. Waterloo, the big city of Black Hawk County, is wrestling country. Gable grew up with wrestling the way most American boys grow up with football, basketball, and baseball. His father took him to the matches; his father and his father's friends talked wrestling around the kitchen table. He was the lone son of the family, and his basement was provided with a set of barbells (a present from his parents when he was thirteen) and a wrestling mat (a present when he was fifteen). Gable says he wrestled his way to three consecutive State Championships before he had even entered high school—all alone, in the basement of his house, he would wrestle one pretended opponent after another. He'd work out with the barbells between matches.

His first *real* competition was at the Y.M.C.A., and the sport was swimming. He says the first time he stepped out of the pool—the last one to finish—he wanted to feel as good as the swimmer who stepped out first. He wanted to win.

He did, but not swimming. He won three consecutive State Wrestling Championships at West High of Waterloo. He developed a style of training which other wrestlers have envied, and also thought—candidly—was a bit crazy. As a high-school sophomore, there were wrestlers on the West High team who could beat him. When they'd leave practice, Gable would stay. He says he used to think, as he was working out in overtime, that he was gaining on them—working when they were showering, sipping milk shakes, taking it easy. Through college, he kept that perspective. "When I'd get tired and want to stop," he says, "I'd wonder what my next week's opponent was doing, I'd wonder if he was still working out. When I could *see* him still working, I'd start pushing myself. When I could *see* him in the shower, I'd push myself harder, I knew I was putting in more time. You've got to have a tough *mind*. If you know you haven't cheated, physically, in your preparation, that makes you mentally tough." What made him mentally tough was knowing—when he faced *anybody*—that he could go as hard as he could from start to finish, and the other guy would give out before he would. "You have to get high for every match," he says.

Gable got high enough to compile three State Championships in high school and two National Championships at Iowa State University. He approached the last match of his college career, the finals of his third N.C.A.A. tournament, with a record of one hundred and eighty-one wins, no ties, no losses. If Gable won his third N.C.A.A.

title, he'd become the first wrestler in history to go undefeated and untied through high school and college.

He was not unnoticed. *Sports Illustrated*, anticipating the unprecedented perfect record, photographed Gable as he worked his way toward the finals, interviewing him, setting up what would have been one of the biggest spreads a major sports magazine ever gave to amateur wrestling. In the past year Gable had received two dozen letters a week. In his third National Championships, at Northwestern University, the crowd flocked to whatever mat Gable was wrestling on. He didn't disappoint anybody. He pinned his first five opponents, needing slightly more than four minutes for each. As the three-day tournament was winding up to that last showdown, 31,000 fans and almost 400 wrestlers were convinced Dan Gable was unbeatable. A number of good wrestlers had gone out of their way—gaining weight or losing it—to avoid the 142-pound class, conceding that the weight class *belonged* to Gable.

But there was one wrestler who came to Evanston, Illinois, unimpressed. A sophomore at the University of Washington, Larry Owings had wrestled Gable before—in the 1968 Olympic trials, when Owings was a high-school senior and Gable was already a National Champion. Gable had beaten him. Owings had made up his mind that he'd wrestle Gable again, and take him. He went out of his way to put himself in Gable's weight class. He dropped from 173 pounds. Owings says he "almost had to stop eating completely to make 142."

That took a sense of purpose which Dan Gable could understand. Owings walked out on the mat against Gable about as mentally tough—about as high—as Dan Gable says you have to be.

"I had a letdown," Gable says.

Gable is a crowd pleaser. He comes out shooting and he'll shoot right through to the end. Gable took Owings down in twenty-seven seconds of the opening period (2–0, Gable); Owings escaped twenty-nine seconds later and worked a takedown on Gable with a fireman's carry, just as the first period ended (3–2, Owings). Owings escaped to start the second period, then—*amazingly*—took Gable down again (6–2, Owings). Gable lost another point for intentionally going off the mat (7–2, Owings). Then, *slam-bang*, Gable got a reversal, Owings an escape, and Gable another takedown (8–6, Owings). By the end of the second period, 8500 fans were on their feet and screaming.

Owings started the third and last period on top; Gable reversed him and tied the score (8–8). Then Gable got tough. He rode Owings around, looking for the pin, wearing him down and picking up riding time at a point a minute. Owings finally got free with only a minute and three seconds remaining on the clock (9–8, Owings), but Gable had better than a two-minute riding-time advantage (10–9, Gable). When there were only thirty seconds left, Owings slipped under Gable's arm; they were locked tight, chest to chest, when Owings looked down and saw Gable's feet. "I knew I had to go for them," Owings says. He got *one* of them—enough for the takedown (11–10, Owings); he also picked up two predicament points for driving Gable's shoulders near the mat (13–11, Owings). Gable needed a takedown to tie it; he had seventeen seconds to get one. But Gable didn't seem to know about the predicament points against him. He appeared to think it was all tied up, and in a few seconds they'd be going into an overtime period. He shot a takedown, missed it; Owings shot back—he missed, too—and they both rolled off the mat. The referee stopped the clock. When Gable walked back on the mat, there were only three seconds left and he knew by the din of the crowd that he'd lost his first one. At the buzzer, it was Owings who tried for one more takedown; holding him off, Gable just stood there, dropping down on one knee: 13–11, *Owings*.

In one hundred and eighty-two matches, Dan Gable had finally lost one. *Sports Illustrated* ran a brief article, without photographs, on the Owings-Gable match; mainly, the article was about Larry Owings and his great upset.

Gable says he never felt he was even in the match. He felt tired, listless, "like I was losing all the way. Even though it was a close match, and I could have won it right up to the end, I *felt* like I was getting beat the whole time."

"I always dream a lot," Dan Gable says.

He has reddish-blond hair; a sparse, fair moustache, so close to his skin color that it's almost unnoticeable. He's five-foot-nine; in normal clothes, he looks small. He is thick-shouldered rather than broad-shouldered; he wears tight pants and his legs, relative to the rest of him, appear skinny. He has a bobbing, athletic walk; if you're following him, it's comic. He swings his arms; he *touches* things as he walks past them, tapping a car fender, flicking a parking meter. If there's a small stone on the sidewalk, he'll kick it along in front of him, playing with it. He is no stroller; when he walks, he hurries; the object of walking is to get somewhere. The feeling Gable gives off is restless energy; he has to burn up a lot of it before he can relax.

This is a noncompetitive year for Gable, which is why he's in the Iowa field house this Saturday. He's decided to take a year off from the active wrestling circuit (even the Russian-American matches this spring) and devote himself to coaching and making up his mind about whether he'll compete again. But for a wrestler who's not competing, he's still in better shape than most who are. Less than ten pounds over his Olympic weight (149.5), Gable could weigh in with a week's notice.

Out of normal dress, in wrestling tights, Gable no longer looks small. His wrists resemble ankles, his forearms approach the size of the normal human calf, his upper arms are respectable thighs. He has no hips, no ass, like a ten-year-old boy; his legs are as sinewy as a sprinter's. Like a turtle, he can make his neck disappear. I imagine I've seen young girls with waists that are smaller around than Dan Gable's neck. His shoulders are a big man's knees. It is not a *beautiful* body; it has no Greek design and the muscles lack the definition desired by beach prima donnas. Gable's body is pure function; it looks built to perform. It is no more pretty than an axhead. It is no more elaborate than a hammer.

In sixteen years of wrestling, Gable has had no serious injury to his torso. A knee injury almost caused him to miss the Olympics; an operation was suggested, but he was worried that he'd heal more slowly from the operation than from the injury. He declined the operation and worked at ways to wrestle with one good knee. In learning to defend the weak knee, he says he became a smarter wrestler.

He has the philosophy—"most of the time"—that you wrestle differently in practice than you do in a match. In practice, Gable lets people get in on him; he lets them *almost* take him down. He purposefully exposes himself to vulnerable positions so that no position he might ever find himself in—in a match—will feel unfamiliar. As a consequence, he appears the most knowledgeable and unawkward wrestler in the sport: he never looks surprised. In a match, of course, he'll give no easy openings to anyone. And even in practice, he won't give you a shot at that bad knee.

"He's the smartest guy I ever wrestled," says Fred Penrod, Iowa's 190-pounder. "You get the feeling he always knows what you're going to do before you do it."

"I *do* know," Gable says. He says it like he might say, "I wear a size-nine shoe."

Gable wrestles in constant contact with an opponent; he won't stand back and shoot from the outside. "I've got to have my hands on you," he says. He makes quick contact and keeps it, as if by touching you he can read the signals your body's sending that you wish you could conceal. "Once he gets hold of you," says a frustrated Iowa wrestler, "he can do it to you *blind*." There have been very good blind wrestlers in the sport, actually: some wrestlers are familiar with coaches who hold blindfolded workouts, insisting that a wrestler must learn not to telegraph a move to his opponent—and learn to feel the opponent who telegraphs his moves.

Dan Gable *controls* a wrestling match. His reflexes flow into one another. Most wrestlers have an initial move which, if countered, they can offset with *another* move, a re-counter, which their opponent might counter again, and so on, until someone's chain of reactions comes up shorter. The wrestler who scores extends his chain of reactions the longest.

Fred Penrod, who outweighs Gable by almost forty pounds, says, "You've got to get to him first. If you don't get him on the first move, you're in trouble, because he'll keep moving at you and make you react, and then he'll move again, and you'll react again, and then he'll do something else—until you make the wrong reaction." Penrod is a frequent workout partner with Gable at Iowa because his strength and weight advantage can take a little edge away from Gable's superior ability. Occasionally, Penrod can make his first move work. "Sometimes," he says, "I can just catch him and make something work that probably wouldn't work if he were my size. I can just bull him over, *sometimes*." Eventually, Gable just wears Penrod down.

When he's exhausted one opponent, Gable's wrestling (and coaching) method is to go pick a fresh partner.

"The only way we can give him enough of a workout to satisfy him," says Iowa co-captain Jan Sanderson, "is to line up and take turns. We each get a minute with Dan, then a fresh guy goes in. Gable stays in there, wrestling a minute with all of us. After he's been out there a long while, we begin to get to him."

Jon Marks, a big, cheerful, ardent wrestling fan, and a non-wrestling roommate of Gable's in Iowa City, knew Dan when he wrestled for Iowa State and, after he'd graduated, when he prepared for the World Games in Bulgaria and the Munich Olympics. Marks says that in the last year of workouts before Munich, Gable would go home to Waterloo every weekend to see his parents. Gable would bring along someone to work out with, so he wouldn't miss a day of wrestling. "Eventually," Marks says, "Dan would be bringing home five or six guys every weekend, and his Mom would have to feed them all. The only way he could get enough of a workout was to bring home five or six. He'd wear out any two or three wrestlers before he even started to get tired. He'd even work out with Chris Taylor. And he could give Taylor a real workout too."

Taylor, a bronze medalist in the unlimited class at the Olympics, lost only one freestyle match at Munich—a disputed 3–2 decision to the defending World Champion and Russian gold medalist, Alexander Medved. Chris Taylor weighs 400 pounds. He has a weight advantage over Gable of 250 pounds.

At Munich, Gable suffered a cut over one eye in the first match, but he was never even pushed. He began with a pin over Yugoslavia, followed with a 20–0 decision over West Germany, then pinned Greece and decisioned Kikuo Wada of Japan (the silver medalist), 6–0. In his fifth match Gable pinned Poland, moving into the finals without having had a point scored on him in five matches and winning three by falls. He was, he admits, cautious in the last one; he had not wrestled Ruslan Ashuraliev of the Soviet Union before. After the World Games in Bulgaria, and several dual meets in this country and in the Soviet Union, the Russians promised to find a wrestler who would beat Gable in Munich. Gable decisioned Ashuraliev 3–0; he dominated the match, entirely, working a neat single-leg takedown in each of the first two periods and winning a caution point when Ashuraliev was called for stalling in the third. Russia ended up with a bronze medal. Gable took the gold without losing a point to anyone.

And if the great loss of his career haunted him for long, he dispelled his own and anyone else's doubts about the 1970 match with Larry Owings by soundly beating Owings in the Olympic trials for Munich. Gable controlled the whole match, says he never felt in danger, says he knew he shouldn't have lost to him the first time. He beat Owings 7–1, ". . . just being careful. No mistakes."

Oddly, in two N.C.A.A. championships that Larry Owings wrestled in—after his stunning upset of Gable—he could never win another title.

"Owings never got up again," Gable says. "He was never so high as when he beat me."

It's "getting high" that makes Gable wonder whether he'll wrestle again himself. In a career of more than three hundred matches, he says he got up for every one—before and after Owings. "If you put them all together, that's almost a whole year of psyching yourself up as high as you can go, every day. Maybe that's enough. And," he adds, the favorite son of Waterloo, "my Mom and Dad would like me to stop."

But forget, for a moment, the picture of Midwest regularity. He had an older sister, once; she had graduated from high school and was living at home, working in Waterloo, when Gable and his mother and father took a fishing trip to the Mississippi. That was after he'd won his first State Championship for West High of Waterloo, his sophomore year. The Gables were called home from their fishing when Dan's sister, Diane, was found dead in the Gable home. A neighborhood boy, and a former high-school classmate of Diane's, had raped and murdered her and mutilated her body with a knife.

"It *must* have had some influence on Dan," says Jon Marks, but Gable rarely speaks of it. Only this: that when his mother and father wanted to sell the house and move, Dan insisted that they keep the house and stay. "So we can remember her," he said. The Gables stayed.

Mack Gable, Dan's father, is a former wrestler, ruddy-faced, short, and thickly built. Dan's mother, Kate, is a young-looking, statuesque brunette. They have followed Dan's wrestling everywhere. Diane's death must have made their interest in Dan all the stronger ("He's their whole life," says Marks.)

We are going to Solon, Iowa, where Dan Gable is giving a speech. Gable is dressed in his summer-weight Olympic team blazer and blue-striped bell-bottoms. A red, white, and blue sports shirt is open at his throat. He puts a ski parka over the costume because it's twenty-eight degrees and snowing outside. In his car, he searches for something among piles of jogging suits. "Where's the medal?" he says. "They always want to see the medal," he explains, and shows it to me—the big gold one with his name and "freestyle wrestling at 68 kg" written in German.

He wears glasses to drive, and he drives fast, finding the Cedar Rapids station for twenty-four-hour country-and-western music and singing along.

We are going to Saint Mary's Auditorium for a banquet in honor of Solon's first football championship. Gable is the guest speaker; he could go to such a banquet every night, he says, but he doesn't normally accept such a small-town affair. The Solon coach, Dan Wheater, is a friend.

We get to Solon half an hour early ("I hate to be early, anywhere," Gable says). Gable takes off his glasses when he gets out of the car; we find a bar. Inside, Gable drinks one beer swiftly; he's thirsty; in an average workout, he loses six pounds. "I eat and drink what I want," he explains. Unlike most wrestlers, Gable has never dieted. He works out so hard and so long that he can wrestle in the weight class nearest his natural weight. He thinks the weight-cutting habit of wrestlers is bad for them, mentally, and that "if they simply wrestled as hard as they could, all the time, they wouldn't have to worry about losing enough weight to wrestle the smaller guys."

The Solon Gala Football Banquet is hosted by the town firemen, and you quickly get the feeling that the entire town is being honored for the conference title. Sixty-four football players and four coaches receive awards.

I am sitting next to a priest who's supposed to give the blessing before we eat. A fireman comes up to whisper to him that some people at the end of the banquet hall have already been served—*worse,* have already begun to eat. "Is it too late to say Grace, Father?" he asks.

"I don't think it matters," the priest says. He stands up at the table, *chinks* a heavy milk glass with his spoon, cups his hands to his mouth, and *hollers* for attention.

Dan Gable sits at the guest table up on the stage; he drums his fingers on the tabletop; he jiggles one knee up and down, up and down. When Coach Wheater introduces him as "the best athlete in the world," there is prolonged, stand-up applause. "He's as good a wrestler as that Alcindor or Kareem Abdul-Jabber, or whatever his name is, is a basketball player!" Wheater says.

Gable is not used to much talking, but he is familiar enough with giving this kind of speech so that he isn't self-conscious. "Because of athletics," he says, "I feel I can handle about everything."

His speech is a sincere, personal pep talk. He admits that he wants to "inspire" people. "I want to talk about life overall in general," he begins. He starts out telling how he pretended he was a football player when he was a kid. "I'd move all the furniture around, make a kind of obstacle, pretend I'd have to dodge between a chair and a table without touching them and dive on the couch." The couch was the end zone. "I was always the ball carrier," he says. Like the imaginary wrestling season, undefeated, in his basement.

He honors his parents. "They never pushed me, but they were behind me a hundred percent."

He talks about losing to Larry Owings. "Because I made that mistake, it made me a better wrestler." Set goals. Work harder than anybody else. Believe in yourself.

It is not a long speech. It takes longer to sign the autographs—to let people touch, pick up, weigh in their hands and put around their necks his Olympic gold medal. The adults are as interested as the kids, and even more shy. A woman, one of the Moms who got our applause, is smoothing her dress at the foot of the stairs leading to the stage. She has almost the body and every bit of the bounce of the cheerleaders (also awarded). Her friends tease her.

"Go on, you look *fine*!" they say. "You're just going to shake his hand, not *wrestle* with him!"

Titters at the mere idea!

"If you wrestled him, you know who'd win!"

"Oh, I *know*!" she says, delighted, feigning a swoon.

But more people seem interested in the medal than are actually interested in talking to Gable.

One of the junior-high waitresses asks *me* for my autograph; I don't mistake for a minute that it's because she's read my novels. It's because I came in with *him*. "I'm not even famous," I tell her.

In tone with the optimism of Gable's speech, she tells me, comfortingly, "Well, maybe one day you *will* be!" She is a bubble of belief in herself; I sign her paper napkin, under Dan Gable's name.

*Girls?* When would he have had the time?

"There's nobody special to him right now," says Joe Wells, one of Gable's roommates in Iowa City. "There was a girl at Ames, when Dan was at Iowa State. I know Dan liked her, but they didn't really spend that much time together. And she married someone else." Joe Wells is an ex-wrestler, a former Big Ten middleweight who's kept himself in wrestling shape—though he's a light-heavyweight now. Wells first saw Gable when Dan was a high-school wrestler attending a summer wrestling clinic at the University of Iowa. He remembers being struck by "this little red-haired kid who never talked to anybody and wrestled very tough, and—I couldn't believe it!—actually took *notes*!" Two years later, Wells was on the Iowa team which made a recruiting tour of the Iowa high schools; Wells realized who the little red-haired kid was. "We wanted him at Iowa," Wells says, "but he went to Iowa State."

That little red-haired kid, who, as Wells observed, actually took *notes*, has been a model of all work and no play, and an idol of sportswriters who find Joe Namath's off-the-field image in bad taste. But Gable has not escaped having his own, ironic version of a binge. Gable's one binge that gained the public eye was an evening many of us might have regarded as a night off, but it was still as contradictory to his image as losing.

In the spring before Munich, in Ames, Iowa, Gable returned to his apartment, drained from a workout; he was so tired he came straight home in his wrestling gear, planning to shower at his apartment. He discovered a keg of beer and half the Iowa State wrestling team in his living room; they were throwing a party for a high-school recruit. "I was thirsty," Gable says. "I drank four beers real fast, then took a shower. I was feeling pretty good, you know, but I wasn't drunk."

With a quarter of an inch of beer left in a paper cup, Gable stepped out on the street with two friends. "They were obviously watching the party," Gable says, because a cop arrested him on the spot. The charge? Drinking an intoxicant on a public street—what was left in the paper cup. With complete forgiveness, Gable says, "It was a new cop who got me. He didn't know who I was. When I got to the jail, the other cops—who all knew me—said they wouldn't have bothered me, but since I'd been brought to jail, they had to keep me."

They kept him just four hours, but it was headline material for every newspaper in the Midwest.

On learning that Gable had been arrested, Iowa State's 177-pounder—and a roommate of Gable's that year—was enraged. "I'm going to protest," he announced, with a fair portion of the keg inside him, and left the party wearing nothing but his I.S.U. gym shorts. It was a cold spring night and the 177-pounder rode a bicycle up to the nearest traffic light, where he grabbed the door handle of a stopped car. He let the car tow him the two miles downtown to the police station. Somewhere downtown, a surprised policeman witnessed the near-naked wrestler hurtling alongside the car; when the cop realized that the wrestler was *attached* to the car, he arrested him. "I am protesting the fact that Dan Gable is in jail," the 177-pounder offered in his defense. Obligingly, the cop took the 177-pounder to where Gable was.

"I was glad to have the company," Gable says.

The part of the story which most of the Midwest headlines missed was more revealing of Gable than this accidental night on the town. When the 177-pounder was deposited in jail with Gable, he discovered Gable doing chin-ups from a pipe that ran across the ceiling of his cell.

At heart, the little red-haired kid was still taking notes.

Dan Gable still has much to learn about the bizarre problems of the famous. He announced to the local papers his brainchild for the Iowa wrestling team's publicity: "mat maids," girls who would be scorers and timekeepers for the wrestling matches. The "Chairperson" for the Council of Associated University Women attacked Gable with little regard for his innocence. In a university town, the movement considers nothing to be trivial—and little with a sense of humor.

"Those feminists are crazy," Dan Gable says.

Gable has attracted other "crazies." A visitor to his parents' home in Waterloo came from Miami Beach with vague real-estate "deals" and glowing with praise for Dan Gable as "the kind of man America needs more of." The man worked himself into quite an agitated state in the Gables' kitchen, then peeled off his shirt, kicked off his shoes, stripped down to his boxer underwear ("Right in front of my mother," says Dan) and said he wanted to wrestle the Olympic sensation *there* on the kitchen floor. He'd come all the way from Miami Beach, he said, to wrestle the World Champion.

Gable says the man was in his fifties, "with a pretty fair pot belly." He suggested that the wrestling mat in the famous basement was softer than the kitchen floor, and led the man downstairs. "I asked him if he wanted some sweat clothes, or a jock," Gable says, "and he asked me, 'Are *you* going to wear a jock?' I told him I wasn't and he said he wouldn't wear one either, to be fair." The man, Gable says, had obviously never wrestled before. "He danced all around me, whooping and getting out of breath and batting the back of my head with his hands. Then he grabbed my fingers and tried to bend them back, like he'd seen the pro wrestlers do on TV, probably, and I thought he might bust them. I mean, it *hurt*. So I worked a little foot-kick on him and he just sat down on the mat, looking sort of surprised, and he grabbed the back of his neck like he'd been hurt. 'I just remembered,' he said, 'the doctor told me not to do anything too strenuous. I got a bad neck.'"

So it was over, the man dressed himself, wheezing like a winded hog, clapping Gable on the back, saying how it had all been a real pleasure and what did his family want for Christmas? "I thought maybe he'd come to get me to wrestle him so he could sue me if I hurt him in my own house," Gable says. But the man left quickly, promising to see them all again, "going on about what we all wanted for Christmas."

Gable's mother told him he might expect more of these encounters. I tell him it's like the westerns where the retired gunfighter is always getting picked on by some fool who wants to see if he's faster. Gable thinks it over. He shrugs.

Ten years ago I retired from the 130-pound class, after about eight years of wrestling. I was never *that* good a wrestler, but at the University of Pittsburgh I got to wrestle a number of people who *were* very good. I weigh three pounds less than Dan Gable right now; I'm a former lightweight, ten years out of shape, lapsed into the middleweight class.

Gable is very kind to me. In sympathy with my wretched condition, he consents to wrestle only takedowns. We will just shoot takedowns, then go back up to the neutral position on our feet and shoot takedowns again. After a takedown occurs, he promises not to press any advantage down on the mat (the part of wrestling which is *really* exhausting—when you're fighting off a pin or just carrying the weight of the man who's riding you). These are ideal conditions for me; we work only a two-minute period at a time, letting me recuperate between rounds—encouraging my lungs to re-inflate.

The first unsettling feeling when you're wrestling Gable is that you can't feel where his weight is. He feels completely uncommitted; you can't sense how he's leaning, which way he's getting ready to go. He doesn't seem to be driving you or pulling you, yet he's always *moving*—giving you quick shoves and tugs, keeping you constantly off-balance. You know if you just *stand* there, he'll move on you; so you feel hurried into moving first, and always, when you move, you have no certain sense of what he's set up for. Worse, you never feel quite balanced yourself.

I have a favorite series of first moves and counters—a cross-leg pull which, if you miss it, sets up a duck-under to the other side; if you miss the duck-under there's a leg waiting to be picked up. I could usually work that, at least once—even on wrestlers I lost to. It was down on the mat where I lost most of my matches; on the feet I was what my old coach called, "a halfway-decent wrestler." So I set up for my one score on Dan Gable, trying to get him to step across his body with his left leg—toward me. I spend thirty seconds trying to conceal how I want him to step, and then he steps. He just sticks his left leg in front of me; it's a gift—it's *bait*, I realize, feeling uncannily inept; he *knows* I want his left leg, so he is offering it. Clearly, a trap. I hesitate, and of course you *never* hesitate, so he takes me down while I'm making up my mind.

Next time I fake going for the right leg and come back for the left; it isn't there; I come back for the duck-under to his right side. To my surprise I come up behind him; I pick him up at the right hip. Good penetration, that's called; all I have to do is fall on him, but as we fall he does *something*, somehow, and I lose my balance. Rather than fall on him, I pull him on top of me.

That's the consistent feeling with Gable; you feel you've almost got something and then, stupidly, you lose your balance. After losing your balance a *lot*, you suspect you're not simply losing it all by yourself.

I lie on my back on the warm-up mat, re-discovering breathing, slowly—staring up at the ceiling dome of the field house. A kind of cork insulation—like wood, the color of sand—panels the ceiling between the latticework of girders. Way up there—a four-story ceiling, at least—a butter knife is stuck into the cork paneling. It's too high up to notice if you're not looking for it; Jon Marks pointed it out to me and told me how it got there.

Six years ago, after an inter-squad match, one of the losers—who'd just lost the starting position in his weight class—stomped off the mat and went slamming in a fury toward the training room. Before he got there, something on the floor caught his eye. It was a butter knife. No one knows how it got there. He picked it up, swore, spun around; with the knife held in his hand like a discus, he released the knife upward—heaving it with such velocity, miraculously threading the network of girders, that it stuck forever in the ceiling of the field house dome.

Lying on my back on the warm-up mat, I cannot imagine a losing wrestler with enough strength left for such a throw. I have been counting takedowns. At two points per takedown (college scoring), it is 24–0, Gable.

The wrestlers are down on the mat in the referee's position, one man on his hands and knees, the other man in a position of advantage behind him—one arm around the bottom man's waist, palm on the belly button, the other hand on the bottom man's elbow. They wait for the signal from Gable to go.

Dan Gable paces the mat, setting up the conditions. "Okay!" he hollers. "Bottom man's got ten seconds to get *out* of there. You *got* to get away. Top man's *got* to hold him down. Ready? *Wrestle*!"

Frantic, the bottom wrestlers lunge to get free; desperate, the top men try to ride. Ten seconds is over very quickly. "Who got out?" Gable yells. "Raise your hands." Only a few wrestlers raise their hands. "Okay!" Gable shouts. "*Again!* Ten seconds. . . ."

The wrestlers' breathing grows heavier. I shut my eyes, thinking of my own lungs. The thudding of their bodies carries on a current to the warm-up mat and into my head. My throat has closed like a sphincter muscle. I have the familiar "cotton-mouth," which feels worse than cotton—like some dry, hot, furry animal has gone to sleep, or died, on my tongue. "Move!" Gable grunts. "If you're not tired, you're not working hard enough!" The wrestlers' breathing whistles like a violent storm. I think of the butter knife. The man who did that should have his own special award enshrined in the Big Ten Trophy Gallery at the main entrance to the field house. "Again!" says Dan Gable. "Ten seconds left and you *need* that one point. . . ." The wrestlers groan, but they're not complaining. "*Move!*"

I open my eyes. Dan Gable is peering down at me. He kicks, gently, at my slack calf. "Ready?" he says; he grins. He nods his head toward the mat. Do I want to try some *more* takedowns? Gable is very generous with his time.

I remember Fred Penrod, the 190-pounder, saying, "It's an honor to wrestle him. I mean, you know he's the best in the world—so you want to wrestle *better* against him and you really get up for it."

I get up. My sweat stings a mat burn under one eye; the skin over that cheekbone feels stretched tight. My lying down has stiffened me up. We find a space between the careening bodies, Gable hunching his shoulders, twisting his neck; he touches his toes once and he's loose. He bounces out in front of me, letting me come to him. Warily, I snatch one of his wrists; he seizes the wrist of my free hand. It is chess in the pawn phase. And I feel caught up with his impossible-to-follow rhythm, again—like a dancer unfamiliar with the music, trying to find the secret place. Suddenly, I'm enjoying myself. I don't have to suffer the frustration of a competitor; no longer involved with winning, I can simply marvel at how he's going to trap me next. He's moving me by my arm, my whole right side is vulnerable; I compensate, which with Gable always means that you *overcompensate*. I plant my left leg like a tree, all my weight on it; when he drops down to pick it up, I can't possibly move it away.

Up again, looking for loopholes, I begin to relax. Too tired to think, I've fooled myself into believing that the old instincts have returned to me. "Wrestling is a conditioned reflex," my old coach used to say. Meaning, you have to learn it, it *doesn't* come naturally, but you have to learn it so well that it *becomes* natural—like yawning when you see another person yawn, only quicker.

And there is his leg. I take the bait without hesitation. His counter amazes me; I'm on my back with the suspicion that someone has lifted that mat *up* to meet me. My eyes find the butter knife in the ceiling. I must indeed appear to be a very bad wrestler, but I don't mind. I go after him again. When I make contact, he's like a machine who sets us both in motion; it's *his* motion, even when you think it's yours.

"It's like wrestling a computer," Fred Penrod says.

But the contact is euphoric to me. When Dan Gable lays his hands on you, you are in touch with grace.

—APRIL 1973

# Zimmer

SCOTT RAAB

Like love, Zimmer's all around us. All you need are eyes to see.

I can't explain. All I can tell you is that there's this diner in north Jersey—well, you got a million and one diners in north Jersey, but this is the Nevada Diner in Bloomfield, and it's just before nine on a dead-of-winter Saturday morning, and I'm waiting for a pal, smoking and shivering and pacing the sidewalk between the Nevada and Frankie's Future-Matic Car Wash. My universe has shrunk to this: The kid's got the flu, the wife's got the sheeshing hormonals, and me, I've got a heartburn that may well rule out the corned-beef hash. Goddammit.

Just behind me is a shop that sells baseball cards, autographed balls, vintage pennants—all stuff I wouldn't take for free. But something—some*one*—else is here this morning.

Zim.

Right over my shoulder stands Don Zimmer in pinstripes, a life-sized cardboard Zimmer in the window of the shop with arms crossed and a don't-mess-with-me scowl plastered on his puss, and suddenly I am all smiles. Even the hash seems possible.

Ecce Zimmer: Earthly explanations abound for any thorny manifestation of godhood, but what surpasseth the clarity borne of belief, the peace yielded by surrender to faith? How do the hit-and-run and the run-and-hit differ? What constitutes a balk? And why can't Chuck Knoblauch heave the fucking ball to first?

The icon in the window does not speak. It does not speak, but it holds a message, a beckoning. The curb is packed with blackened snow; the baseball season is a distant dream, gray and hidden as the sun. Zim is here and yet . . . Zim is not here.

I shall make a pilgrimage.

I shall seek, in perfect knowledge, perfect peace.

I shall go to Florida—to Treasure Island, Florida—and see Zim.

It shall be warm. We shall eat pancakes. We shall fish and play the ponies and warm our bones beneath the Florida sun.

I shall sit at the calcified knobs that once were his knees and summon the courage to ask of Zim the question burning in my soul:

Why does Joe Torre wear a wristwatch in the dugout?

"It's funny ya would ask that. Tell ya the truth, I never even noticed it. Why he wears a watch? I never even thought of it till now, but as it comes to my mind, he does. I really don't know the reason. There's one thing baseball does that no other sport does—it doesn't go by time. No clock. That's right."

His voice is old gravel and fresh wonder. There is more to his reply, much more: about cigars, which Zim puffs once in a while—he gave up chew a few years back, though his cheeks still bulge like an autumn squirrel's—but never in uniform, because that would not be right; about how the film version of Joe Torre's autobiography took liberties with this sort of thing, which left Zim feeling wronged; and about watches, which Zim himself, now that he thinks of it, can't recall ever wearing during his life in spikes.

To score a run, you must take three left turns. That, too, is how Don Zimmer answers—or doesn't—any question.

He is neither roly nor poly. He is seventy, an aging, battered shortstop, a born jock who is wearing the flannels of a pro baseball team for the fifty-third consecutive year, with a black belt hemming his boiler, a stubbled noggin the size of an Easter ham planted atop an obscured neck, slitted eyes, and a second chin like a wheel of Camembert. Stout, sure, but his arms—those pipes that inspired Roy Campanella to nickname him Popeye—are still thick and iron-strong.

The living-room walls are greenish blue, some hue between aqua and turquoise. The house is simple, neat, and calm, with a sliding glass back door leading to a small, lush yard and, just beyond, a warm cove of the Gulf. Soot, Zim's high school honey—he wed her at home plate in class-A Elmira in 1951, with his teammates in two rows holding a canopy of bats—has gone to ski in Colorado for the week.

The last time Soot took a trip while Zim stayed home, the smoke detector started chirping. Zim thought it was the television, but when he turned the TV off, the noise wouldn't stop. When Soot called and he described it, she told him what the noise was and which drawer she kept the fresh batteries in and Zim, to whom all this was news, managed to bust the plastic clamp inside the smoke detector and slice up the back of his thumb pretty good. And that's it as far as housekeeping goes when Soot is away.

"How d'ya make the bed?" Zim growls. "Close the door. She's gone all week—the door's closed for a week."

It may be the only saddish thing about Zimmer—no doubt the happiest guy I've ever met—that after devoting his life to the game, he has come to be seen as a mascot. Jeter rubs his grizzled dome for luck before the game. Knoblauch lines a foul ball into the dugout and it finds Zimmer's skull—God surely must love that old mushmelon to have fixed upon it so indelible a bull's-eye—and the next night Zim's back on the bench with an army helmet and a jack-o'-lantern grin. He is Popeye, Zip, Yoda, Buffalo Head, and Gerbil, but he is also one of the last Brooklyn Dodgers, one of the original New York Mets, and still one of the most recognized faces in the sport thirty-five years after he finished playing it.

"There's Pee Wee and I," says Zim, pointing to one of many framed black-and-whites on the wall. "Pee Wee Reese, captain, the only one in the world. He was like a father to me, God rest his soul. Hey, here's one for ya—who's in that picture?"

I see Zim and Yogi and Tommy Lasorda and some old duffer named Gerald Ford.

"That's it—playin' in a golf tournament. See this picture here? That's my son, my daughter-in-law, my wife, and I. That was up in Mr. Yawkey's office one night. We had a party."

Zimmer managed Tom Yawkey's Red Sox from 1976 to 1980. Between parties, the Boston media and fans roasted him without mercy.

"Every day," Zim says. "I left the ballpark one night, and sittin' right by the dugout is my wife and my daughter—she lives up in New Hampshire, but it's only, like, forty-five minutes north, and I'm drivin' her up to her house. My wife's sittin' in the front, and my daughter's in the back and she's cryin'. I turned around and said, 'What's wrong with you?' She said, 'Daddy, I'm so tired of people booin' you in this town, and I'm worried that yer gonna get fired.'

"I said, 'Don't go to the game no more. Stay home. If it's gonna bother ya, stay home.'

"Don't tell me it didn't hurt—day after day, hour after hour, the same shit. It's gotta bother ya. But it's baseball. If you don't like it, get out. Get a job. That's the way I looked at it. And that's the way it was."

There is old school as a slogan of self-advertisement and then there is old school as the baseball way of life Zimmer still loves too much to leave behind.

"Yeah. Yeah, or I wouldn't go back. When last season was over, I got the goddamn flu, last day of the World Series. I was on my back for three weeks. I was sick, and my knee still wasn't right, and I was ready to give it up. I got over the flu. My knee I can manipulate—" and I'll be damned if Zim doesn't roll up one pant leg to display a bony spur jutting just south of the ruined joint. It's a tame phrase, "knee replacement," but this looks ghastly. And painful.

"I can get by. I get by," he says. "Hey, this is the first trophy—this was my first trophy in the Pony League, class D. Oh, what a year I had there. I hit twenty-four home runs, I was rookie of the year, most valuable player. That's the year I stole sixty-three bases. See, it's all tarnished now, ya know, it's so old. That was my first trophy."

That was 1950. The inscription on the plaque says PLAYER MOST LIKELY TO SUCCEED. "They weren't wrong," I say.

"No," Zim mumbles. "No."

Two generations before Jeter and Nomar and the nonpareil A-Rod, there came a shortstop who could mash and glide and fire cannonballs and run like a deer: Don Zimmer, who didn't just steal sixty-three bases in the Pony League in 1950—ten times he stole *home.*

Having survived a half century of professional baseball, two near-fatal beanings, three Subway Series spanning four decades, four managerial firings, and, as Boston's skipper, Bucky Dent's wind-kissed pop fly over the Green Monster, you'd think maybe Zim would've gained a mythic heft, a modicum of gravitas.

Nah. But hand him a fungo bat or a shot at the exacta in the fifth at Tampa Bay Downs and he gets by. He's flying to Vegas in a couple of days to shoot craps, then he'll hook up with Soot in Palm Springs for a buddy's wedding and come home to hit the golf course for the first time in a long while—and on the second day of spring training, he'll shoot the first hole in one of his life and walk into the clubhouse the following morning to a standing ovation. He'll tell the boys, Yeah, but I still managed to shoot 140. For nine. Not only that: He teed up the same ball on the next hole and drove it smack into the water.

There is no explanation other than this: He is Zim.

Not that he's any piece of cake. Soot had warned me on the phone that his driving directions can be iffy, and when I call him from my hotel, he names every exit off I-275 South and then tells me to pull into a roadside lot just after crossing onto, no shit, Treasure Island, and call again for the directions to his house—which I miss on my first pass, but on the second, there he is in his driveway, laughing and waving, and it would be hard to miss Don Zimmer, standing in a Yankees sweatshirt and khaki pants, waving at you.

We head over to the pancake house in the Zimmobile, a Grand Marquis, two-tone, cream and gold, spoked wheels, vinyl top—the Florida Edition, it brags above the rear bumper. The front license plate reads POPPY, which is what his grandkids call him. Everybody knows Zimmer at the pancake house because he eats there nearly every day of the off-season, usually with Soot. This morning it's Zim and me and Zim's pal Gene Kirby, whose first baseball job was turning the stiles at old Dunn Field in Cleveland, before it was renamed League Park. Kirby doesn't hear so well anymore, but he can still run down the roster of the 1926 Indians, which he proceeds to do while Zimmer taunts the waitress.

"When we gonna eat?" he barks. "Tomorrow?"

She comes over with three menus and a kindly smile, having danced this dance with him a few thousand times already.

"I don't need no menu. I just didn't know if you was ever gonna wait on us. I'm gonna have a western omelette."

"You don't want the ham?" she asks.

"I'm gonna have a western omelette."

"You want the hamburger in it instead?"

"Please," Zimmer grunts.

"Egg Beaters?"

"I don't care. And a glass of milk. White toast. *White* toast."

"I know. White toast."

"*White.*"

"I know."

He tilts his great round head and locks his tiny eyes with hers.

"Yer capable of makin' a mistake, y'know."

At the dock behind the pancake house, our chartered boat awaits. We are heading out into the Gulf of Mexico, beyond the horizon's edge, three doughty men—plus Skipper Dave—girded for battle with the fearsome grouper fish.

Skipper Dave has a special spot an hour away upon the smiling sea, a roaring, skimming, sun-sprayed, perfect ply, past the casino boats and loggerhead turtles, past all sight of land and weight of care. No cell-phone call can reach me here; here is only blue sky and salt water—and Zimmer, grinning past our wake, the vast, speckled bulb of his cranium naked, glinting. And Kirby, who once upon a time broadcast the Game of the Week with marble-mouthed Dizzy Dean. How sweet is this? So sweet that when we reach Skipper Dave's spot, where the grouper frolic on the ledges eighty feet below us, and he cuts the engines and turns on the lite rock, even Seals & Crofts simpering "Summer Breeze" sounds fine. *That* sweet.

And then the grouper strike. They strike and strike—my line. A couple of grunts hit first, followed by a big boy.

"You gotta reel now," says Skipper Dave. "You gotta reel."

Yes. Of course. This spooly thing down by my hand.

"Keep it tight," Zim barks. "You're right-handed. That's right. Keep it up. Look at this. He's got a good one."

"Gawd," says Kirby. "Oh, fer chrissakes—"

The grouper is not huge—a couple of feet long, all of maybe eight pounds. But sinewy, you know. Desperate-strong. I mean, he was fighting for his life and shit. Okay, look: The truth is that I needed Skipper Dave's help to boat the goddamn thing.

"You get two, three more," says Zim, "and we'll throw *you* in. This sumbitch come outta the snow, zero degrees, wind—he's got three fish. Your fuckin' boss is walkin' down the street, it's 18 degrees."

Don Zimmer, giving *me* shit: This must be heaven. The waves are lapping, sucking at the boat. There is no clock. Motes in eternity's vast eye, we live and die alone in a blank cosmos, and yet . . . we're all connected. I'm out on the ocean with a small-case baseball god, our hooks sunk deep into the brine of life. O the oneness of it all—and suddenly Kirby nearly flies off the boat and into the Gulf.

"I got something," he croaks, but it looks as if something's got him. "Oh, Jesus," he moans.

"All right," Zim says. "Just keep it up. *Up*. Keep winding."

"I can't," says Kirby, squeezing out the words like a man laboring at stool. "I . . . can't . . . wind . . . it."

"You're all right," says Zimmer, laughing. "Keep goin'. C'mon. Don't stop now. Don't you let this fish get away, you sonuvabuck."

"Oh, Jeez."

"Keep goin'," Zimmer cries. "Just keep goin'."

"Would *some*body help me, fer chrissakes?" Kirby wheezes.

The skipper reels it in; Kirby sees it and starts cackling.

"You sonuvabitch," Zimmer barks. "Your face was all red, and the veins on your neck—you looked just like Gil Hodges in a meeting, pissed off. That was worth the trip out, no matter what happens."

Zim hooks nothing but a wee porgy, round and shimmering blue-gold in the sun. He admires it a minute before Dave unhooks it and tosses it back.

"Look at that," says Zimmer. "Is that a beautiful thing? I don't care how big they are—I just wanna catch the pretty ones."

Beams burst off him like a Buddha at the glimmer of satori.

"I love this," Zimmer says with a child's glee. "I'll tell you that—I *love* this. I do. I love this. I really do."

• • •

It was July 7, 1953, the first time. Old-school style: no batting helmet, shitty lighting, dirty balls. He was twenty-two years old, had played his way up to one of Brooklyn's triple-A teams, and was sitting on .300 with twenty-three homers and sixty-three RBIs when a curveball that didn't curve caught him square above the left ear, fracturing his skull.

For six days afterward, he slept while the blood in his brain boiled and pooled. To relieve the clotting, the medicos drilled three holes in the left side of his head, one in the right. (Despite what legend says, they never stuck a plate in there; they filled the holes with tantalum, a rare metal.) He had to learn to talk and see and feel again; his weight dropped from 170 to 124 during his month in the hospital. The Dodgers' front-office men came and told him not to worry about playing ball again: They'd always have a job for him in the organization.

The only work he wanted was at shortstop, though, and he came to spring training in '54 to claim it. The major leagues had sixteen teams back then, and Zimmer had already spent five years in the minors proving that he was good enough to start at short for nearly all of them. But Brooklyn was a mini dynasty and Pee Wee was still the man, so Zim began the season back in triple-A. He made it to the Show when Pee Wee hurt his back that year, saw action in twenty-four games, and in 1955, when the Boys of Summer beat the Yanks in the World Series—for the first and last time in eight tries—Zimmer was the backup at both short and second base. In eighty-eight games that season, he hit fifteen home runs and drove in fifty.

The second time was June 23, 1956—and this time it was worse. Hal Jeffcoat, pitching for the Reds, came up and in with a fourth-inning fastball—two Dodgers already had taken Jeffcoat deep, and somebody was going to pay—crushing Zimmer's cheek and nearly taking out his eye. The docs blindfolded him for two weeks, then put a pair of pinhole glasses on him for another six weeks so he wouldn't move the eye.

Zim was never the same player after that, never what he could have, *should* have, been. He spent nine more seasons wandering the bigs—he even tried converting to catcher for the Washington Senators in 1964–65—but rarely as a regular. He wound up a career .235 hitter, then played in Japan in '66 for thirty grand ($9,000 more per year than he ever made playing in the majors), then hooked on with Cincinnati in '67 as the manager of their double-A club in Knoxville.

Zimmer's anything but bitter about his playing days, and he will wave you off if you dare accuse him of courage. Still, despite—or because of—the head-hunting he survived, Zim has no pity for new-school batters who get concussed and then kvetch.

Particularly Mike Piazza of the Mets, who caught a Roger Clemens heater with his head last summer. We're at dinner at a little Italian place near the dog track when I ask Zimmer about it.

"When Piazza said that in his mind, 'No doubt he threw at me,' that stinks. Is Piazza the only sumbitch in America ever got hit in the head with a ball? That's what burned my ass. There's only one man in the world that knows—the guy who threw it. This guy"—Zim's talking about Clemens—"he's mean. He'll pitch inside like you're supposed ta pitch. The other guys are pussyfoot—they don't wanna pitch inside. Piazza made a little man out of himself. Fuckin' cry. I don't care who knows it, I lost a little respect for Piazza. I got hit in the head, and I know the cocksucker threw at me—fuckin' buried me. The Dodgers wanted me to say that, and so did the press. But even though in my heart I knew, I'd never say that. The prick never called me, never sent a get-well card, nothin'. I was in the hospital twenty fuckin' days, I never heard from him. But I'd still never say that he threw at me purposely. Even though everybody knew this was a nasty cocksucker—there's always the one chance that he didn't, that the ball got away."

You fancy old school? That's *old* old school, brother. So's this: When I grab the dinner check, Zim's ready to rumble.

"I get the check," he growls.

"I am getting the check," he snarls when I insist.

"Don't tell me I'm not getting the check"—he's almost shouting now—"*I'm buyin' yer dinner.*"

Yo, Popeye—it's all yours.

The racetrack ain't like fishing, not to Zimmer. He gets to the clubhouse early, an hour before post time, and joins his crew in the lounge. There's Big John, a retired mailman from Boston; Otto, Big John's brother; George, a developer and builder in St. Pete; and Zim. Friendly guys—"We are horse degenerates," Big John tells me—but they're here to gamble, not kibitz. Every day.

The table is piled high with programs, racing forms, and scratch paper. From where we sit, I can see twenty-one TV screens, soundless. They're racing live in Philadelphia and Maryland, and later in California, Hong Kong, Australia. Dogs, too, and jai alai.

When I ask Zim if I can bet along with him, he says no.

"I don't want nobody bettin' wit' me. If I knew I was pickin' a winner, I'd say climb aboard. I'm gonna try to pick winners. Sometimes I do. Sometimes I don't. Yer just as well off to look in there"—he points to my program—"and pick what ya like."

When the waitress comes, I get the Trifecta Salad—tuna, chicken, egg.

"That's a winner," Zim grunts. He had it for lunch the other day.

"Scott," he says a little later. "The only thing I can tell ya, I am betting on the 1-horse at Tampa. That's all I can tell ya. That's who I'm bettin' on. I love the 1-horse in this race. I don't know what he's gonna do, but I love him."

Pirate's Wager is the 1-horse. I put a deuce on 1 and ten clams on the 2-horse, Air Lisa, to win, because my wife's name is Lisa and she breathes air. Pirate's Wager never threatens. Air Lisa goes off at five-to-one and wins. "The 1 run like a stiff, my man," says Zim, shaking his head. "The 1 run terrible."

After a while, Zim and I take a break and wander out to sit in the grandstand, just past the finish line. He's wearing black slacks and loafers and a tomato-red Banlon shirt. His face and head are pinkish from yesterday's Gulf sun. The air today is warm, full of gulls and the smell of manure. Spring training's as near as the turf inside the oval track, but Zim seems a little sour. I ask him if he's picked any winners yet today. "When yer busted, ya go home," he grumbles. "If ya got money, ya stay."

Jacques Barzun once wrote that "whoever wants to know the heart and mind of America had better learn baseball." I'm not sure that was ever true—today, ten minutes of *Survivor* probably says more about us than a month at any ballpark—but if you want to know baseball's heart, mind, *and* soul, you had better learn Don Zimmer.

"I'm a bench coach," Zim says. "Thirty years ago, there was no such thing—you were a coach. Now they got a title for a bench coach, which is a joke. People say, What is the job of a bench coach? I say, Very simple—I sit next to Torre on the bench. When he plays hit-and-run that works, I say, 'Nice goin', Skipper,' and if it doesn't work, I go down to the other end of the bench, get a drink, and get out of his way. We only got one manager. I don't want no credit for doin' anything. I sit next to Joe like a bump on a log—that's the way I leave it."

The truth is this: Joe Torre doesn't make a move without asking Zimmer what he thinks. Not that Torre *has* to ask; Zimmer managed nearly two thousand major league games himself and isn't shy with the suggestions, which is why Torre hired him in the first place.

Zim won't talk retirement, won't look past this season. He left baseball once, in 1995. He was coaching third base for the Colorado Rockies and he wasn't having fun, so he decided to hang it up. He left in the fifth inning of a game in early June so nobody would make a fuss about honoring him.

"I didn't wanna make no big thing of it," he explains. "I came in very quiet, and that's the way I'd like ta go out."

So he wished Don Baylor, then the Rockies' manager, good luck, drove home, and watched the last three innings on TV with Soot. A few months later—Zim had just cashed his first social security check, the only money he's ever pocketed outside of baseball—Joe Torre got the Yankees job and asked him to climb aboard.

What about now, I ask—the Yankees, four World Series wins in five years, a new memoir, *Zim*, on the shelves. Surely now he'd have some sort of Don Zimmer Day in the Bronx.

"I don't want no day," Zim says. "Hey, it's been a great ride for me, a great life. Everything I have I owe to baseball. Baseball owes me nothin'. Ain't nobody has to give me nothin'. I would be embarrassed if I had a day somewhere. I don't want no day. I want friends, to live my life the way I wanna live it."

He falls silent. Then he hears the pounding of hooves and sees he's missed a bet.

"What the hell's these horses comin'? Oh, they're outta the chute. I liked 1 and 8, top and bottom." Zimmer checks the tote board.

"Naw," he says, relieved. "This ain't even the race. I wasn't even payin' attention."

—JULY 2001

# Old

MIKE SAGER

Morning filters through the bedroom window in delicate, slanted rays, dust motes and sounds and memories drifting in the air. Doves coo, a horseshoe clangs, quails skitter across the rain gutter. The clock radio on the night table whirs and vibrates; the number card flops: 6:33.

The old man sleeps on his left shoulder on the right side of the bed. His name is Glenn Brown Sanberg. He is ninety-two. He is peaceful in repose in plaid pajamas, a colorful floral spread pulled snugly to his neck. He has white, flyaway hair and bushy eyebrows, a flaky irritation at the point on his forehead from which his pompadour once issued. His cheeks are soft and deeply furrowed, speckled here and there with brown spots. His mouth is open, top lip buckled a bit over the gum line, chin stubbled with fine white whiskers. His left hand rests upon the pillow on the unmussed side of the bed, a queen.

Starlings chatter. Water gurgles in an ornamental pond. A draft horse pulls a wagon full of housewares down a cobblestone street. Glenn stirs, sighs, floats toward wakefulness. He thinks of the lake cabin he once built. Laying the foundation, he used a pancake turner for a trowel. He thinks of woodpeckers, of ducks, of fresh blueberries. A Studebaker with a rumble seat. A player piano in a speakeasy. Stealing apples from an orchard, buckshot whistling overhead, the double row of brass buttons on the blue serge uniform of the town constable. Smoking corn silk under the porch. Joan leaning against the radiator in his office in the collection department at the Mayo Clinic, drying her stockings on a cold, rainy day.

The paper thuds against the front door. Glenn's eyelids flutter. An electric golf cart hums past, tires swishing through sprinkler runoff. He thinks of an address book left behind at a riverside telephone booth, a thermos left behind at a seaside hotel. Mount Rushmore. Old Faithful. Shaking hands with Lawrence Welk. Napping on his favorite divan. The odd, modest undershirt and boxers worn by his Mormon son-in-law.

He opens his eyes, blinking against the light. Through the cracks in the partially opened vertical blinds, he can see the sky, a wan blue, vectored with contrails, overhung with wispy clouds. He thinks of the cold, clear sky of a northern Minnesota winter. He thinks of Joan digging in the garden, a smudge of mud on her nose. Dad sitting in President Eisenhower's chair in the White House, a proud and grave expression on his face. Tom bagging his first buck with the Savage .303. Mickey reeling in a fat pike on a sparkling mountain lake. Little Eleanor, limp in her bed, scarlet fever. Joan falling against a door. Lucy falling against the curb. Ann Black, front row center at the Greek Week songfest, legs crossed, dark eyes beaming. Jeffy's warm, tiny hand inside of his.

A lawn mower sputters and coughs, catches, begins to drone. Glenn slides his left hand beneath the covers, places it palm down beside his hip. He reaches behind himself with his right arm, grabs a handful of bedspread. Pushing with one hand, pulling with the other, he rolls himself over onto his back with a grunt. There is little pain to speak of—a twinge of nagging soreness, perhaps, in the knuckles, the left shoulder, the right hip, the neck—but there is a certain acute stiffness in his muscles and ligaments and joints that enfeebles his every action, renders his every movement a task. Think of the first few turns on a rusty lug after it has finally come unstuck—such is the effort. Winded, Glenn lets his head settle into the pillow. He thinks of hoeing weeds in a five-acre bean patch on a hot summer day. Walking across a golf course in the early morning, meeting Lucy at the fountain for a sip of water and a little hug. Martin Luther King Jr. at the Lincoln Memorial. Eleanor in the car on the way to her freshman year of college: "Don't drive so fast, Daddy."

Stretching both arms above his head, he yawns deeply, luxuriantly, then brings his right hand forward, uses his thumb and forefinger to wipe away the cakey dryness that has accumulated at the corners of his mouth. His hand trembles. He's not sure when it began, this shaking. His son pointed it out not long ago when he came to visit. Glenn was taken aback by the revelation; he simply hadn't noticed. You live in your body every day of your life. Things change slowly, inexorably, in increments too small to measure. You gain weight, you lose weight, your hair falls out. Your skin slackens, your voice thins, your bones become brittle, your ankles swell. Your prostate and a piece of your colon are removed. Your back bends with the weight of gravity and passing time. You wake up twice during the night to pee; once in a while, you wet your pants. Crossing your legs has become a project that requires your hands; getting out of a chair has become a gymnastic routine; eating a bowl of soup has become a logistical feat. Whenever you go to the store, you can't remember if you have coffee at home. There are two blue cans of Maxwell House in your refrigerator, six more in your cupboard. You buy another can just to be sure. There is a tiny droplet of moisture suspended from the bottom of your nose. There is food crusted on the front of your shirt, the crotch of your pants, the tips of your shoes. You ask people questions several times over. Sometimes, just as you're asking, you realize that you've already asked this same question, that you've already heard the answer. You go ahead and ask again anyway. It's too embarrassing to do anything else. Your parents and your five siblings and your spouse have all died. Your late-life companion has moved on to constant care. You visit her three times a day. She lights up when you're around. Your children have entered their own retirement years in distant states. People talk to you as if you were a four-year-old; they are always trying to give you hard candies. You are old, diminished, alone. You can't even cut your own toenails. The podiatrist does it for fifty-five dollars. His nurse calls to remind you about your appointment. It was thirty minutes ago.

All of this happens; everything changes. But the odd part is, you don't really notice. You're aware of it, sure, but somehow it doesn't integrate. Deep down, to yourself, you are always just you, the same pair of eyes in the mirror, the same familiar voice inside your head still wondering, "When will I feel grown up?"

Glenn runs his pink tongue around the inside of his mouth, tries to swallow. He is thirsty, but he can wait, the thought of the effort needed to get himself a glass of water displaced for the moment by the pure, sensual pleasure of lingering beneath the covers with no place special to go. It isn't all bad, this diminishment, this narrowing of the circle of friends and activity and influence and competence. You can see it as a long, slow march toward death. Or you can see it as a distillation, a paring down—as the last leg of a journey, the jump-off point, perhaps, for a great new adventure in the next world, a chance to reunite with your loved ones. It is truly a second childhood, only this time you're the one in charge, as long as you still live on your own, as long as you can still dress yourself and feed yourself and get to the store. As long as you still have your driver's license. You can wear the same clothes two days in a row. You can stay up half the night watching *National Geographic* videos. You can nap. You can eat dessert for dinner, pour mocha crème on your cornflakes, stay in bed until you feel like getting up.

At the moment, Glenn feels like staying in bed. He places his hands behind his head, interlaces his fingers. He pans the room, eyes blue and elfin, the eyes of his grandfather, a blacksmith from Sweden, and of his father, a school superintendent from Minnesota. There is Lucy's wig hanging from a hook on the towel rack in the bathroom. Joan's desk, Mother's lamp. A copy of the *Physicians' Desk Reference*. A Snoopy doll holding a tiny box of Whitman's chocolates. Portraits of Lucy's kids and grandkids and great-grandkids. A small, silver frame on a dresser with a picture of Joan on their wedding day. Joan: She was quite a gal. She wasn't a superwoman, but he never knew anybody who was more honest. The first time he saw her, she was leaning against the radiator in his office in the collection department at the Mayo Clinic, drying her stockings on a cold, rainy day. She could read him like a book. One night in bed, in the dark, she slapped him. He doesn't remember what the argument was about. Boy oh boy oh boy. Right on the cheek: *Slap*! That was a wake-up call. Yes sirree. A female voice, digitized, robotic, calls out from the living room: "6:30 A.M."

Glenn's brow furrows. He sighs. *Where am I?* he wonders.

He closes his eyes. The lids tremble with concentration. You can be ninety-two years old and have your eyesight, as Glenn does, need glasses only for reading. You can have hearing good enough to pick out whispers in a crowded room, reflexes good enough to drive on busy streets. You can have a medicine chest with nary a prescription pill or bottle of ibuprofen in evidence. But when you get to be Glenn's age, things are different; things like this happen all the time: A situation comes up and suddenly you are stymied, baffled, lost, confused; the information needed proves elusive. *Why did I come into this room? When did they board up this bank? What's Tom's daughter's name? Wasn't the meeting supposed to be here? When did I order these pictures of myself from Olan Mills? Where am I?*

Glenn knows that he knows the answer. He knows that he knows where he lives. He just can't put his finger on it right now—this little scrap of knowledge stored, along with so many other disparate pieces of information gathered over a lifetime, somewhere in the crammed and dusty attic of random rooms that is his memory, an archive chockablock with electrobiochemical renderings of pictures and dates and facts and ideas, words of wisdom, personal milestones, nouns and verbs and adjectives particular to his life. Like the facts that he was born in Bird Island, Minnesota, in 1905, graduated from the University of North Dakota in 1927, married Joan in 1929, just before the Depression. He was an air-raid warden in Minneapolis during World War II, stepped down as executive vice-president of the American Society of Association Executives in 1964, lost Joan in 1987. Twenty-nine years he's been retired. He knows that fact, too, can do the math in his head right now if he chooses. He knows that Tom lives in Chicago, that Jeffy lives in Oregon and deals in lumber, that Saturday is the most dangerous day of the week to drive your car. That in order to live happily in retirement, you must find something to be important to. That the best excuse is the one you never make.

That you should back up your files on a floppy disk. That the knocking noise in the hot-water heater is probably due to sediment buildup. That you need to separate the laundry before you wash. That it is best to eat the biggest strawberry last. That the first income-tax law was enacted by the U. S. Congress in 1862. That if you are big enough, your troubles will always be smaller than you.

Lying there with his fingers interlaced behind his head, his lids trembling with concentration, Glenn searches the borders of his awareness for the information he seeks. *Come on, Sanberg, you old coot. Boy oh boy oh boy. You're in a fine state, Sanberg. You don't even know where you are!*

The voice that is speaking, the old familiar one inside his head, the one he grew up with, seems oddly amused at the turn of events. A little embarrassed, a bit nonplussed, just the slightest bit self-pitying, the words punctuated with a phlegmy, nervous laugh, *Ah ha ha!* You learn to go with the flow in these matters, to let nature take its course. Patience: That is what you learn with age. You can rage against the dying of the light, or you can feel fortunate that it's not yet totally dark, that there's still time left and things to see, things to remember, even things to forget. Glenn thinks of the other places where he has woken up, the other places he has called home. The cabin they named Spikehorn—the best idea he ever had, enlisting the whole family to build from scratch a one-room cabin in the woods. The three-bedroom house in Minneapolis—he hated to leave the place, but the nation's capital was calling, and he was a man of some ambition. The trailer in McAllen, Texas, their third abortive attempt at finding a place of retirement—too many old farmers with creased necks, nothing to do, too much bingo, and too much square dancing, no way to spend the rest of your life. You don't think about it when you're young, even when you're middle-aged, even when you first retire, but if you're lucky, if you're blessed with hardy genes, as Glenn has been—and that is the only reason he can give for his longevity and good health, the fact that his father died at eighty-nine of the colon cancer they caught in Glenn a few years back, and that his mother died at ninety-three of natural causes—then your retirement years can last for a period of time that is longer than your youth, almost as long as your working adulthood. It's been almost thirty years since Glenn had to set an alarm clock.

Now, as he lies in bed with his eyes closed, it comes to him at last: the answer he's been seeking, materializing out of the shadows, floating toward him like an autumn leaf. Of course, of course. Of course! *Ah ha ha!* He is in Sun City, Arizona, fifteen miles northwest of downtown Phoenix. Nine thousand acres, forty thousand residents, almost all of them over fifty-five. City of Volunteers, home of the Active Retirement Lifestyle, the nation's first large-scale experiment in retirement living. Glenn's home since 1972.

He studies the sky through the cracks in the blinds, a bit amused, a bit relieved. *Sanberg, you old coot! You ain't dead yet!* Doves coo, a lawn mower drones, quails skitter across the rain gutter. Another fine day in Sun City. Another fine day of retirement. Another fine day to—

His brow furrows. He sighs. *What day is this?* he wonders.

The waitress unlocks the door, and Glenn steps lightly across the threshold. He is a handsome man, five feet ten, 190 pounds, with a prominent nose and a broad, friendly chin, another trait passed down from his father. He is wearing a crisp, pale-blue guayabera shirt that he washed and ironed himself and navy-blue flared trousers, polyester, with western stitching. He tips two fingers to his forehead in a modified salute. His eyes twinkle. "Thank ya kindly, ma'am."

"No problem, dear," says the woman, thin and sixtyish, with a cigarette rasp. "How you doin' this morning?"

"Pretty good for an old coot," he says cheerfully.

She smiles wide, lays a hand on his shoulder. "You're just the cutest thing!"

Glenn arches his bushy white eyebrows, makes his mouth an O of surprise. He attempts a step or two of soft shoe, then takes his leave, stage left, heading at his usual good clip toward the banquet room at the rear of Nancy's Country Cupboard. He has an odd, stiff, jaunty gait, torso rigid and bent slightly forward, arms pumping from the elbows, feet working from the knees, weight shifting quickly from side to side, the sole of his left shoe scuffing the floor. Seeing him walk, you detect pride and good nature in the face of adversity; you sense that here is a man who understands the value of progress made one step at a time. A man undeterred by what he cannot do, focused instead on what he can, determined to do it well. He holds his head high.

Had this been a Monday morning, Glenn would have driven his '91 Buick Park Avenue the three hundred yards from his garage to what he likes to call the Chamber of Commerce, the snack bar in the main building of Royal Oaks, his fifth residence since retirement. Had this been a Wednesday, he would have tidied up a bit in anticipation of a visit from Maria the cleaning lady, a pretty young Mexican woman who tells him stories about her little boy. On other days, he might have had a meeting of the Lakes Club board of directors, or the Sun City Community Fund grants committee, or the New Horizons club, wherein outsiders are invited to dinner to discuss topics of general interest, from health care to the state of today's teens.

Thursdays are his busiest, with a Lions Club meeting at noon and his weekly column due at four o'clock. For almost thirty years, in various venues, Glenn has been writing a newspaper column called "Retired in Style." It began in 1952, long before he retired, as an extracurricular attempt to satisfy his lifelong desire to be a writer. A self-published weekly broadsheet containing words of wisdom, encouragement, and solidarity for busy executives like himself, it was called LIFT, as in, "Have you given someone a lift today?" A sort of support group in the form of a newsletter, with subscribers all over the country, LIFT was a bit ahead of its time in sentiment and sensibility, rather touchy-feely in an era of Sputnik and Joe McCarthy. Later, when he retired, Glenn remembered how lost his father had been without something important to do in his golden years. Never much for hobbies, he decided to make the column a late-life career. For five years, "Retired in Style" was carried by *The Arizona Republic*, the major daily in Phoenix. When the long drive downtown to drop off his offerings became problematic, he switched to the *Daily News-Sun*, the chronicle of Sun City and environs, a snappy little afternoon paper conveniently located two blocks from his house. True to his late-found profession, he waits until the last possible moment to flip on his Gateway computer, which features Windows 95, WordPerfect, and America

Online. He writes about what he knows, what he thinks, what he sees, what he remembers, what he reads. Increasingly, he writes about what he's already written, borrowing material from the reams of old clippings he keeps filed in the den he uses for an office. He usually finishes thirty minutes before deadline, then drives it over. The column runs Saturdays on the front page of the second section, along with his picture.

Had this been a Sunday, Glenn would have driven a hundred yards to the constant-care center and picked up Lucy for church. Though he spent most of his life with the Methodists, he now attends Faith Presbyterian, Lucy's church. He sometimes finds comfort in prayer, in the calm, meditative state it brings, in the fellowship of worship with others. He doesn't subscribe to the whole hellfire-and-brimstone story. His beliefs are centered more on the kind of living you do than on what happens when you die. He's not hung up on denomination, either. The way he figures it, God is God is God no matter what house you're in, and Lucy cared more than he did about which church they attended. Faith Presbyterian was also the sponsor of the Royal Oaks Life Care Community, where Glenn and Lucy moved three years ago when they decided to set up house together. A sort of retirement development within a retirement community, Royal Oaks offers laundry, housecleaning, repair services, a cafeteria, social workers, and shuttle vans to shopping and doctors. Within Royal Oaks are three grades of living arrangements—ranch-style duplex garden homes, assisted-living apartments, and full-care nursing facilities. For $40,000 down, $800 a month, Glenn will have food, housing, and care for the rest of his life.

As it is, today turns out to be Tuesday—a fact he finally confirmed by consulting the newspaper tossed every morning from his driveway to his front door by a friendly neighbor on his daily walk—and Glenn has come to Nancy's. For twenty years, Tuesday mornings have been reserved for the Walk-Jog Club. Once upon a time, all the members would jog or walk for an hour and then convene in Nancy's banquet room for the $1.99 breakfast special. Nobody jogs anymore. The big joke these days is how they lose a half pound walking, then gain a pound and a half at breakfast. Glenn contents himself with driving the mile or so to the restaurant and walking one circuit around the parking lot. At his age, you need to get your circulation going, relieve some of the stiffness, but there's no sense getting all worked up. Actuarial tables say that Glenn will likely be dead in 3.4 years. He knows this. He's all right with it. As he often says: "It's been a good life."

Glenn enters the banquet room, the first to arrive. He takes a seat at one of the two large, round tables that have been set up to accommodate the group. He looks around. He sighs. He pats the tabletop like a set of bongos, pat-a-pat-pat.

A man enters, takes a seat across from Glenn. He is in his early eighties. Glenn can't remember his name. "Good to see you," says Glenn.

"How do?" says the man.

"Pretty good for an old coot."

"I'll say," says the man. It occurs to Glenn that he was once a banker. Possibly from Chicago. He is wearing his official Walk-Jog Club T-shirt.

Glenn points to his own chest with a crooked finger. "Looks like I forgot to wear my T-shirt."

"Yeah, well," says the banker, pinching his T-shirt between a crooked thumb and forefinger. "I came to find out if there's anybody still alive down here."

"Alive and kickin'!" says Glenn. He pushes a fist into the air before him, rah-rah.

Soon the others begin to arrive. The younger crowd, sixties and seventies, goes to one table; the others go to Glenn's. Big John is a retired attorney. Edith, in a wide-brimmed straw hat, was one of the founding members of the club. Harold is a retired Westclox executive from somewhere back east; Pearl is his wife. The banker, it turns out, is named Frank. The only other person at the table in his nineties is Reggie. He carries a wireless contraption that he places on the table; it helps him hear. His speech is nearly unintelligible, his glasses are thick, and he walks with a slow shuffle. Though the median age in Sun City is about seventy-four and 25 percent of the residents are over eighty, ninety-two-year-old men who are up and around and healthy like Glenn are a rare commodity. The life expectancy of an American male today is seventy-three years. According to the Census Bureau, there are about fifty-three thousand ninety-two-year-old men in the country, but that number is increasing. All told, people over ninety are the fastest-growing demographic group in America. Edith pours him a cup of decaf coffee from the carafe on the table. They wait to order. No one needs a menu.

"It was a nice breezy walk, wasn't it?" says Frank. "We were bucking the breeze going, but we got a nice rear-end push on the way back."

"Is that what it was?" asks Edith, raising her eyebrows.

"Oh!" exclaims Frank. "You mean you thought that rear-end push was me?"

Edith swats the air in his direction. Everyone laughs. Glenn is sitting with his arms crossed casually, like an executive at a meeting. "You can't beat a little good, clean fun, now can you?" says Glenn.

"No sirree, you can't," says John.

"Nope," says Edith.

"Did I tell you about my Northern Tissue stock?" asks Frank.

"Go ahead if you must," says John, rolling his eyes.

"I guess you're going to anyway," says Edith.

"I bought a hundred shares, but I got wiped out on it," says Frank. He crosses his arms, proud of himself.

"Groan!" says Glenn.

And so it goes. The food comes: oatmeal and eggs and French toast, lots of warm syrup. They chat about summering in Utah, motor homes, cruises up the Colorado, bus trips to Laughlin, Nevada, to play the one-armed bandits. About the traffic on Bell Road, the exploits of sons and daughters, the times they played golf in the 115-degree heat. They swap stories about the legendary Del Webb, the six-foot-four-inch former minor-league pitcher who built Bugsy Siegel's casino, who once owned the Yankees, who, almost forty years ago now, saw acres and acres of sun-bleached cotton fields in the Arizona desert and envisioned a new kind of lifestyle for people in the winter of their lives, the next logical post-Levittown step for the citizens who peopled the American century.

Sitting back with his arms crossed, tossing out a reminiscence here, a comment or a bon mot there, asking a question when the conversation hits a lull, Glenn has the relaxed air of a man at a cocktail party in the 1950s. You can imagine him in a dark suit and skinny tie, puffing on a pipe, passing pleasant time with pleasant associates over a manhattan, two cherries. Since he came here, in fact, Sun City has impressed Glenn as being just like that, like one big floating cocktail party without the booze, a gathering of familiar, friendly acquaintances, all of them of similar type and class and background, with shared values and customs. People from a genteel era, a time when men wore sport coats to baseball games, held doors open for ladies, paid their bills on time, gave backyard cookouts for neighbors, had a friendly word for all, whether they meant it or not.

Glenn pats the tabletop like a set of bongos, pat-a-pat-pat. It is a pleasant feeling, this comradeship, this diversion, this activity that takes him outside his ranch-style duplex garden home, outside his own head. But it is also somewhat hollow and boring. Glenn may be old, but he still knows the difference between acquaintances and true friends, between quality time and killing time. Though he's been living among these same people for many years, he doesn't really know them, and they don't know him, his little offerings in the newspaper every week notwithstanding. They have no idea that he married into the Mayo family, helped set up the world-famous clinic's first collection department. That he started his own successful business, went on to be executive secretary of the American Collectors Association. That by the time his career was at its peak, he could claim good friends among top people in the White House. Like the trophies and plaques and framed citations stored in dusty boxes in his garage, none of that matters much anymore; it happened so long ago now, he can hardly remember the details. You spend thirty or forty or fifty years bulking up your résumé, throwing your weight around, polishing your reputation, playing the game, planting your legacy. It matters what you do in life, it really does—the impressions you leave, the contributions you make, the money you earn, the people you touch, the children you send off into the world. But as the end draws near, as the scope of your life narrows, none of that seems very important anymore, none of that *is* very important anymore. What becomes important are things like your health and the state of the weather, things like putting one foot in front of the other, making sure the chair doesn't roll out from under you when you go to stand, getting a phone call now and then from your sons or daughter, tasting a warm, sweet Entenmann's bear claw. Being able to sit with yourself at the end of another day and feel that you have no regrets about the time you've spent on earth, that you've done your best to live a good life, to give others a lift.

A woman named Barbara comes over from the younger table. She is carrying a newspaper clipping, two inches square: an obituary. She is in her early sixties, the only one in the room wearing shorts.

"There she is, Miss America," sings Frank.

Barbara throws him a dismissive look, walks over to John, shows him the clipping. "Is this the Bob Thompson from Sun City West that used to walk with us?"

John tilts his head up, reads down through the bottom of his trifocals. "Sure," he says, "that was him."

"How old was he?" asks Edith.

"Says here he was eighty-four," says John.

"Bob Thompson?" asks Harold. "Which one was he?"

"Remember?" reminds Pearl, his wife. "Little Bob Thompson. He used to . . . what do you call that? Race walk."

"He used to jog with the boys, then his legs gave out and he got to walkin'," John confirms.

"So that was Bob Thompson," says Harold.

"Guess so," says Frank.

"Yep," says John.

"Hmmm," says Edith.

"Hey, Miss America," says Frank. "Did I tell you the one about my Northern Tissue stock?"

"Say yes!" exclaims Edith.

"Say yes!" exclaims John.

"No matter what, say yes!" exclaims Glenn.

Everybody laughs.

• • •

Glenn struts into Lucy's place, full of vigor and good cheer, a fresh pink rose in his hand. The room is a standard nursing-home double painted in pastels. "How you doing, old gal?"

"I never know," says Lucy. She is a small woman with large, brown glasses and short, gray hair, sitting on the edge of the narrow bed. She giggles a nervous laugh, *Ha ha ha.*

"I like that black-and-white outfit."

"Do you?" She looks down to see what she's wearing, adjusts the drape of her blouse. "I have to stop and think. Where am I? Who am I?" She giggles again, *Ha ha ha.*

"That's all right, dear," says Glenn. "I have to do that, too." He reaches out with a trembling hand and cups her cheek.

Lucy sighs, leans her face into his palm. "Oh, well," she says. She has been in the constant-care center for almost two years. Her Alzheimer's is still at an early enough stage that in her good moments she seems to be aware of what is happening to her, this process that is slowly taking her away from the world. It seems to embarrass and frustrate her, yet at the same time she seems resigned and good-humored, willing to accept what comes. She no longer complains about the food, no longer asks about going home. Rarely is she sad or angry anymore. During her active lifetime, she was smart, pleasant, witty, a little feisty, willing to see the silver lining. Now it is as if the disease is slowly distilling her to her essence, rendering her a fond memory of herself. "It's really a very nice day," she says. She is a bit difficult to understand without her dentures.

"A little breezy out there right now."

"It's a little tricky."

"It's always a little tricky," says Glenn. He laughs nervously, *Ah ha ha!* He is embarrassed and frustrated, too. He visits three times a day. He makes it a policy to stay upbeat, though he secretly wonders sometimes why he bothers to come at all. He always hopes, whenever he walks through the door to her room, that this time things will be different, that this time Lucy will show signs of getting well. He knows she won't get well. More often than not, a few moments after he arrives, he feels ready to leave. He sticks it out anyway. It's a rough deal, this thing. Having her here is very tough. A real push/pull, if you know what he means. If he didn't show up, she probably wouldn't know. Yet something deep compels him to return time after time, day after day, with a cheery expression on his face: a deep gratitude for the years they spent together, for what they meant to each other. A deep solace in knowing that he is not alone here in Sun City. He steps to the bed, turns, slowly lowers himself down next to her.

Glenn and Lucy met many years ago in Minneapolis. She and her husband, they called him Bake, lived near the Sanbergs. He was an accountant for the railroad. The two couples were quite friendly, members of the same social club. Glenn and Bake hunted together. Lucy worked for a time as Glenn's secretary. Years later, her daughter had a summer job with him. When Glenn and Joan came to Sun City for the first time to check it out, the Bakers and another couple were their hosts.

When Joan died in 1987, just before Thanksgiving, Glenn got a call late at night from the hospital, saying she was gone. It all happened so fast. That summer, vacationing in Logan, Utah, she had fallen and hit her head. Four months later, she was dead. Fifty-eight years of married life were over. He never thought he'd be the one who was left behind. He listened to the words, delivered by a stranger, a nurse, over the telephone. Then he replaced the receiver on its cradle. "I'm all alone," he said, speaking out loud into the darkness. He will forget a lot of things before his time is up, but he will never forget that.

It was rough for a while, real rough, boy oh boy oh boy, though he came to enjoy the parade of widows with their casseroles who started showing up at his door. He learned how to sort the laundry and make coffee, how to fend for himself after so many years as a husband. He was doing okay; it wasn't great, but he was getting along. Then one day he ran into Lucy. Bake had died a few years before; Joan and Glenn had helped her through her grief. Now, coincidentally, both Glenn and Lucy were on a walking kick. He began phoning her in the mornings to say he was leaving for his walk, and she'd leave, too, and they'd meet at the water fountain on the golf course, a point equidistant from their houses. At first, they'd just hang around and talk. Soon, they were giving each other a little hug. That's the thing you come to miss the most: a little hug, the warmth of someone next to you, her body against yours, her breath on your neck. They began eating meals together, some days at his place, some at hers. Lucy took Joan's place in a way that was very positive, Glenn believes, and he thinks he took Bake's place in the same way. After a few years, they decided to cut out the foolishness and move in together.

Before they finalized their plans, however, they went to see the pastor of Lucy's church. They told him their intention, to live together in the open, out of wedlock. He regarded them gravely. Then he cracked a smile. "Go for it!" he said. Three other words that Glenn will never forget.

Glenn and Lucy had similar likes and dislikes. They both played golf and bridge, enjoyed dancing. They both cared about who was president, who was senator, what was going on in the world. She was easy to be with, very accessible, had a sense of humor, was a very sharp gal, a college graduate, very involved throughout her life with the American Field Service. You couldn't put anything over on her. She was that kind, like Joan in many respects. They went on trips to see each other's children, drove all the way to Florida, took a cruise once through the Panama Canal. In the years they lived and traveled together, they slept in the same bed—he on the right, she on the left—but never had sexual intercourse. Thinking about it, Glenn wonders if it was kind of unusual to be so close and yet never be intimate in that way. Their spouses had been their lifelong lovers, their only lovers. And so it remained, though it wasn't like he couldn't have, physically—he still feels the call now and then. No matter. They were at an age in life when that wasn't very important anymore.

Then one day Lucy fell against the curb in the parking lot. It didn't seem like that big of a deal—a few cuts and scratches, a badly bruised hip. But tests at the hospital revealed Alzheimer's. She never returned home. He still keeps her things in their proper places in the house, the way they were the day she left with him to go out for a simple lunch at the Lakes Club—the wig hanging from a hook on the towel rack, the pictures of her family on the walls. To do otherwise would be unthinkable.

Lucy leans her head against Glenn's shoulder. Glenn looks distractedly around the room. Through the doorway, he can see the slow procession of Royal Oaks residents up and down the central corridor, aged figures caterpillar-walking in their wheelchairs, pushing with their hands and padding with their feet, eyes fixed on the distance. A woman is slumped in her wheelchair just outside Lucy's door. She is holding a teddy bear. "Help me," she calls again and again. "I have to make a BM."

Glenn notices the rose in his hand, holds it out in front of Lucy. "I brought you this rose. It's from our yard."

"No kidding?"

"Yeah, right from our yard."

"Our yard?"

"The one at the house."

"It's lovely this time of year."

"Yes it is, dear, yes it is." He puts the rose on the dresser. "I had breakfast this morning with Harold and Pearl. Frank was there, too."

"How are their families doing? Or are you only interested in whether or not the little boy can jump the fence?"

"I guess so," says Glenn. He laughs, *Ah ha ha!* Lucy looks at him questioningly. She seems to realize that she is not making sense. She laughs. *Ha ha ha.*

"My whole back is bad," says Lucy.

"Itchy?"

"It's just wonderful when they come by and scratch."

"Here, allow me, madam," Glenn says with mock formality. He shifts his weight, moves his arm slowly behind her back, begins to scratch.

A look of pure bliss crosses Lucy's face. "*Oooooooh, ahhhhhhh, ooooooo*," she purrs. She closes her eyes, shrugs her shoulders, wriggles her back. "It's almost worth paying extra," she says. "*Ahhhhhh.*"

"You can leave me a tip."

"Absolutely!"

"Boy oh boy oh boy," says Glenn. He laughs, *Ah ha ha!* He continues scratching.

• • •

Glenn slips beneath the floral spread, rolls effortfully onto his left side, one hand resting beneath his cheek. Street light filters through the bedroom window; a night bird sings, a single voice.

Glenn breathes deeply. He thinks of the beautiful birch tree that guarded the breezeway at Spikehorn. The carpenter from across the lake thought he was crazy, but he couldn't bring himself to cut it down. He ended up building the roof with a big zigzag in it, leaving plenty of room for the stately old tree to grow. He thinks of playing run-sheep-run and kick-the-can and gyp, playing trombone in the high school band, shaking hands with John Philip Sousa, listening to Stan Kenton on a superheterodyne radio. A Model T milk truck. A flapper in a beaver coat, dancing the Charleston. A thank-you note from Wendell Willkie. A letter from Bennett Cerf. Pounding nails into a scrap of two-by-four on the back porch while his mother snaps beans. Lucy in her square-dance outfit. Joan leaning against the radiator in his office in the collection department at the Mayo Clinic, drying her stockings on a cold, rainy day.

Water gurgles in an ornamental pond. The air conditioner kicks over, cycles up, begins to blow. Glenn sighs. He pushes his head deep into the feather pillow. It feels soft and cool. The clock radio on the night table whirs and vibrates; the number card flops: 10:35.

—SEPTEMBER 1998

# What Do You Think of Ted Williams Now?

RICHARD BEN CRAMER

Few men try for best ever, and Ted Williams is one of those. There's a story about him I think of now. This is not about baseball but fishing. He meant to be the best there, too. One day he says to a Boston writer: "Ain't no one in heaven or earth ever knew more about fishing."

"Sure there is," says the scribe.

"Oh, yeah? Who?"

"Well, God made the fish."

"Yeah, awright," Ted says. "But you had to go pretty far back."

It was forty-five years ago, when achievements with a bat first brought him to the nation's notice, that Ted Williams began work on his defense. He wanted fame, and wanted it with a pure, hot eagerness that would have been embarrassing in a smaller man. But he could not stand celebrity. This is a bitch of a line to draw in America's dust.

Ted was never the kind to quail. In this epic battle, as in the million smaller face-offs that are his history, his instinct called for exertion, for a show of force that would *shut those bastards up*. That was always his method as he fought opposing pitchers, and fielders who bunched up on him, eight on one half of the field; as he fought off the few fans who booed him and thousands who thought he ought to love them, too; as he fought through, alas, three marriages; as he fought to a bloody standoff a Boston press that covered, with comment, his every sneeze and snort. He meant to *dominate,* and to an amazing extent, he did. But he came to know, better than most men, the value of his time. So over the years, Ted Williams learned to avoid annoyance. Now in his seventh decade, he has girded his penchants for privacy and ease with a bristle of dos and don'ts that defeat casual intrusion. He is a hard man to meet.

This is not to paint him as a hermit or a shrinking flower, Garbo with a baseball bat. No, in his hometown of Islamorada, on the Florida Keys, Ted is not hard to *see.* He's out every day, out early and out loud. You might spot him at a coffee bar where the guides breakfast, quizzing them on their catches and telling them what *he* thinks of fishing here lately, which is, "IT'S HORSESHIT." Or you might notice him in a crowded but quiet tackle shop, poking at a reel that he's seen before, opining that it's not been sold because "THE PRICE IS TOO DAMN HIGH," after which Ted advises his friend, the proprietor, across the room: "YOU MIGHT AS WELL QUIT USING THAT HAIR DYE. YOU'RE GOING BALD ANYWAY."

He's always first, 8:00 A.M., at the tennis club. He's been up for hours, he's ready. He fidgets, awaiting appearance by some other, any other, man with a racket, whereupon Ted bellows, before the newcomer can say hello: "WELL, YOU WANNA PLAY?" Ted's voice normally emanates with gale force, even at close range. Apologists attribute this to the ear injury that sent him home from Korea and ended his combat flying career. But Ted can speak softly and hear himself fine, if it's only one friend around. The roar with which he speaks in a public place, or to anyone else, has nothing to do with his hearing. It's your hearing he's worried about.

Ted Williams can hush a room just by entering. There is a force that boils up from him and commands attention. This he has come to accept as his destiny and his due, just as he came to accept the maddening, if respectful, way that opponents pitched around him (he always seemed to be leading the league in bases on balls), or the way every fan in the ball park seemed always to watch (and comment upon) T. Williams's every move. It was often said Ted would rather play ball in a lab, where fans couldn't see. But he never blamed fans for watching him. His hate was for those who couldn't or wouldn't *feel* with him, his effort, his exultation, pride, rage, or sorrow. If they wouldn't share those, then there was his scorn, and he'd make them feel that, by God. These days, there are no crowds, but Ted is watched, and why not? What other match could draw a kibitzer's eye when Ted, on the near court, pounds toward the net, slashing the air with his big racket, laughing in triumphant derision as he scores with a killer drop shot, or smacking the ball twenty feet long and roaring, "SYPHILITIC SON OF A BITCH!" as he hurls his racket to the clay at his feet?

And who could say Ted does not mean to be seen when he stops in front of the kibitzers as he and his opponent change sides? "YOU OKAY?" Ted wheezes as he yells at his foe. "HOW D'YA FEEL? . . . HOW OLD ARE YOU? . . . JUST WORRIED ABOUT YOUR HEART HA HA HAW." Ted turns and winks, mops his face. A kibitzer says mildly: "How are you, Ted?" And Ted drops the towel, swells with Florida air, grins gloriously, and booms back:

"WELL, HOW DO I LOOK? . . . HUH? . . . *WHAT DO YOU THINK OF TED WILLIAMS NOW?"*

It is another matter, though, to interrupt his tour of life, and force yourself on his attention. This is where the dos and don'ts come in. The dos fall to you. They concern your conduct, habits, schedule, attitude, and grooming. It's too long a list to go into, but suffice it to recall the one thing Ted liked about managing the Washington Senators: "I was in a position where people had to by God *listen*."

The don'ts, on the other hand, pertain to Ted, and they are probably summed up best by Jimmy Albright, the famous fishing guide, Ted's friend since 1947 and Islamorada neighbor. "Ted don't do," Jimmy says, "mucha anything he don't want to."

He does not wait or bend his schedule: "I haven't got my whole career to screw around with you, bush!" He does not screw around with anything for long, unless it's hunting fish, and then he'll spend all day with perfect equanimity. He does not reminisce, except in rare moods of ease. He does not talk about his personal life. "Why the hell should I?"

His standing in the worlds of baseball and fishing would net him an invitation a night, but he does not go to dinners. One reason is he does not wear ties, and probably hasn't suffered one five times in a quarter century. Neither does he go to parties, where he'd have to stand around, with a drink in his hand, "listening to a lot of bullshit." No, he'd rather watch TV.

He does not go to restaurants, and the reasons are several: They make a fuss, and the owner or cook's on his neck like a gnat. Or worse, it's a stream of *sportsfans* (still Ted's worst epithet) with napkins to sign. At restaurants you wait, wait, *wait*. Restaurants have little chairs and tables, no place for elbows, arms, knees, feet. At restaurants there's never enough food. Lastly, restaurants charge a lot, and Ted doesn't toss money around. (A few years ago he decided $2.38 was top price for a pound of beef. For more than a year, he honed his technique on chuck roast and stew meat. Only an incipient boycott by his friends, frequent dinner guests, finally shook his resolve.)

The last reason is seized upon unkindly by restaurateurs in Islamorada and nearby Keys: "No, he doesn't come in. He's too cheap. He'd go all over town, sonofabitch, and he'd pay by check, hoping they wouldn't cash the check, they'd put it on the wall."

But this is resentment speaking, and it is Ted's lot in life to be misunderstood. Some are put off, for instance, by the unlisted phone, by the steel fence, the burglar alarm and KEEP OUT signs that stud his gates when he swings them shut with the carbon-steel chain and padlock. But friends think nothing of it. A few have his number, but they don't call, as they know he's got the phone off the hook. No, they'll cruise by; if the gates are unchained, if they see his faded blue truck with the bumper sign IF GUNS ARE OUTLAWED ONLY OUTLAWS WILL HAVE GUNS, if it's not mealtime and not too late and there's nothing they know of that's pissing Ted off, well, then . . . they drive right in.

And this is the way to meet Ted: by introduction of an old friend, like Jimmy Albright. It's Jimmy who knows where to park the car so it won't annoy Ted. It's Jimmy who cautions, as we throw away our cigarettes, that Ted won't allow any smoke in his house. It's Jimmy who starts the ball rolling, calls out "Hiya, Ted!" as the big guy launches himself from his chair and stalks across the living room, muttering in the stentorian growl that passes with him as sotto voce: "Now who the hell is THIS?"

He fills the door. "Awright, come on in. WELL, GET THE HELL IN HERE." He sticks out a hand, but his nose twitches, lip curls at a lingering scent of smoke. Ted's got my hand, now, but he says to Jimmy: "S'that you who stinks, or this other one, too? Jesus! Awright, sit down. Sit over there."

Ted wants to keep this short and sweet. He's in the kitchen, filling tumblers with fresh lemonade. Still, his voice rattles the living room: "D'YOU READ THE BOOK?" He means his memoir, *My Turn at Bat*. "Anything you're gonna ask, I guarantee it's in the goddamn book. . . . Yeah, awright. I only got one copy myself.

"Where's the BOOK?" he yells to Louise Kaufman, his mate. Ted thinks that Lou knows the location of everything he wants. "HEY SWEETIE, WHERE'S THAT GODDAMN BOOK?"

Lou has raised three sons, so no man, not even Ted, is going to fluster her. She comes downstairs bearing the book, which she hands to Ted, and which he throws to the floor at my feet. He growls: "Now, I want you to read that. And then I'm gonna ask you a *key question*."

I ask: "Tomorrow? Should I call?"

"HELL NO."

Jimmy says he'll arrange a meeting.

Ted says: "HOW'S THAT LEMONADE?"

"Good."

"HUH? IS IT? . . . WELL, WHAT DO YOU THINK OF ME?"

In the car, minutes later, Jimmy explains that Ted won't talk on the phone. "Ted gimme his number twenty-five years ago," Jimmy says. "And I never give it yet to any asshole." We both nod solemnly as this fact settles, and we muse on the subject of trust. I'm thinking of the fine camaraderie between sportsmen and . . . wait a minute. Jimmy and Ted have been friends for forty years now.

Does that make fifteen years Ted *didn't* give him the number?

*I'm glad it's over. Before anything else, understand that I am glad it's over. . . . I wouldn't go back to being eighteen or nineteen years*

> *old knowing what was in store, the sourness and the bitterness, knowing how I thought the weight of the damn world was always on my neck, grinding on me. I wouldn't go back to that for anything. I wouldn't* want *to go back. . . . I wanted to be the greatest hitter who ever lived. . . .*
>
> —TED WILLIAMS, with John Underwood: *My Turn at Bat*

San Diego was a small town, and the Williams house was a small box of wood, one story like the rest on Utah Street. It was a workingman's neighborhood, but at the bottom of the Great Depression a lot of men weren't working. Ted's father was a photographer with a little shop downtown. Later he got a U.S. marshal's job, in gratitude for some election favors he'd done for Governor Merriam, and that remained his claim to fame. Ted never saw much of him. His mother was the strength in the family, a small woman with a will of steel who gave her life to the Salvation Army. She was always out on the streets, San Diego or south of the border, the Angel of Tijuana, out fighting the devil drink, selling the *War Cry* or playing on a cornet, and God-blessing those who vouchsafed a nickel. Sometimes she'd take along her elder boy, and Ted hated it, but he didn't disobey. He was a scrawny kid and shy, and he tried to shrink behind the bass drum so none of his friends would see. There was school, but he wasn't much good there. History was the only part he liked. And then he'd come home, and his mother was out, and sometimes it was 10:00 at night, and Ted and his brother, Danny, were still on the porch on Utah Street, waiting for someone to let them in.

Soon home lost its place at the center of Ted's life. There wasn't much in the little house that could make him feel special. It wasn't the place where he could be the Ted Williams he wanted to be. North Park playground was a block away, and there, with one friend, a bat, and a ball, Ted could be the biggest man in the majors. The game he played was called Big League: one kid pitched, the other hit to a backstop screen. "Okay, here's the great Charlie Gehringer," Ted would announce, as he took his stance. Or sometimes it was Bill Terry, Hack Wilson, or another great man he'd never seen. "Last of the ninth, two men on, two out, here's the pitch . . . *Gehringer swings!*" Ted swung. *Crack*! Another game-winning shot for the great . . . *the Great Ted Williams.*

They were just the dreams of a kid, that's all. But Ted went back to the playground every day. First it was with a friend his own age, then the playground director, Rod Luscomb, a grown man, a two-hundred-pounder who'd made it to the Cal State League. Ted pitched to Luscomb, Luscomb to Ted. At first they'd always tell each other when they were going to throw a curve. But then Ted started calling out: "Don't tell me, just see if I can hit it." *Crack*! Ted could hit it. "Listen, Lusk," Ted used to say. "Someday I'm going to build myself a ball park with cardboard fences. Then, I'm going to knock 'em all down, every darn one, with home runs." But Ted wasn't hitting homers with his scrawny chest, those skinny arms. Luscomb set him to do push-ups, twenty, then forty, fifty, then a hundred, then fingertip push-ups. Ted did them at home on Utah Street. He picked his high school, Herbert Hoover High, because it was new and he'd have a better chance to make the team. When he made it, he came to school with his glove hung like a badge on his belt. He carried a bat to class. And after his last class (or before), it was back to the playground. Then in darkness, home for dinner, the push-ups, and the dreams.

There were no major leagues in San Diego. There was no TV. He had no more idea of the life he sought than we have of life on the moon. Maybe less, for we've seen the replays. Ted had to dream it all himself. And how could he measure what he'd give up? He wasn't interested in school, didn't care about cars, or money, or girls. He felt so awkward, except on the field. There, he'd show what Ted Williams could do. Now Hoover High went to the state tourney, traveled all the way to Pomona for a doubleheader, and Ted pitched the first game, played outfield in the second, and hit and hit, and Hoover won, and wasn't it great? There was an ice cream cart, and Ted ate eighteen Popsicles. His teammates started counting when he got to ten. But Ted didn't mind them making fun. That's how good he felt: him hitting, and Hoover winning, and the big crowd. Gee, that's the governor! And Ted found himself in the governor's path, the man who'd tossed his father a job, and he had to say something, and the awkwardness came flooding back, he felt the red in his face. So Ted grabbed tighter on his bat and he barked at Merriam: "HIYA, GOV!"

Of course people called him cocky. But he only wondered: Was he good enough? At seventeen, as high school closed, he signed with the local team, the Coast League Padres. They offered $150 a month and said they'd pay for the whole month of June, even though this was already June 20. So that was Ted's bonus—twenty days' pay. He didn't care: he was a step closer, and each day was a new wonder.

He rode the trains, farther from home than he'd ever been. He stayed in hotels with big mirrors, and Ted would stand at the mirror with a bat, or a rolled-up paper, anything—just to see his swing, how he looked: he had to look good. He got balls from the club, so many that his manager, Frank Shellenback, thought Ted must be selling them. No, Ted took them to his playground, got Lusk and maybe a kid to shag flies, and hit the covers off those balls.

Best of all, there were major leaguers, real ones, to see. They were old by the time they came to the Coast League, but Ted watched them, almost ate them with his eyes, measured himself against their size. Lefty O'Doul was managing the San Francisco Seals, and he was one of the greats. Ted stopped Lefty on the field one day. He had to know: "Mr. O'Doul, please . . . what should I do to be a good hitter? And Lefty said: "Kid, best advice I can give you is don't let anybody change you." Ted walked around on air. After that, in bad times, he'd hear O'Doul's voice telling him he'd be okay. The bad times were slumps. If Ted couldn't hit, the world went gray. In his second year with San Diego, Ted hit a stretch of oh-for-eighteen. He hung around the hotel in San Francisco, moping. He didn't know what to do with himself. He got a paper and turned to sports. There was an interview with O'Doul. The headline said: WILLIAMS GREATEST HITTER SINCE WANER. And Ted thought: I wonder who this Williams is?

It was a newspaper that told him, too, about Boston buying his contract. The Red Sox! Ted's heart sank. It was a fifth-place club and as far away as any team could be: cold, northerly, foreign. Still, it was big league, wasn't it?

He had to borrow $200 for the trip east; there were floods that spring, 1938. He got to Sarasota, Florida, about a week late. And when he walked into the clubhouse, all the players were on the field.

"Well, so you're the kid."

It was Johnny Orlando, clubhouse boy. The way Johnny told it, he'd been waiting for this Williams. "Then, one morning, this Li'l Abner walks into the clubhouse. He's got a red sweater on, his shirt open at the neck, a raggedy duffle bag. His hair's on end like he's attached to an electric switch . . . 'Where you been, Kid?' I asked him. 'Don't you know we been working out almost a whole week? Who you supposed to be, Ronald Colman or somebody you can't get here in time?'" Johnny gave Ted a uniform, the biggest he had in stock. But as Ted grabbed a couple of bats, his arms and legs stuck out, the shirttail wouldn't stay in the pants.

"Well, come on, Kid," Johnny said, and he led the bean pole out to the field. From the first-base stands, a voice yelled: "Hey, busher, tuck your shirt in! You're in the big leagues now."

Ted wheeled around, face red. "Who's that wise guy up in the stands?" Johnny told him: "That's Joe Cronin, Kid, your manager." Ted put his head down and made for the outfield. It wasn't the reception he'd expected, but at least he had his nickname. Everyone heard Johnny show him around: "Look here, Kid. Go over there, Kid." It stuck right away; it was a role, he knew. And soon Joe Cronin would fill the spot Rod Luscomb had held in Ted's life. Cronin was only thirty-one, but that was old enough. He was a hitter and a teacher, a manager, counselor, and Ted was ever the Kid.

Cronin had come from Washington, one of the Red Sox's imported stars. The owner, Tom Yawkey, was buying a contender. Along with Cronin, the Hall of Fame shortstop, Yawkey raided Washington for Ben Chapman, a speedy right fielder and .300 hitter. From the Browns, Yawkey got Joe Vosmik, a left fielder who would hit .324. From the A's, Yawkey bought two old greats, Lefty Grove and Jimmy Foxx, along with Doc Cramer, another .300 hitter, for center field.

These were the finest hitters Ted had seen. He couldn't take his eyes off the batter's box. But the presence of all those hitters in camp meant one thing of terrible import to Ted: no nineteen-year-old outfielder was breaking in, not that year, and the veterans let Ted know it. Vosmik, Chapman, and Cramer, rough old boys all of them, made sure he had his share of insults. He lasted about a week, until the club broke camp for the first game in Tampa.

Ted wasn't going to Tampa. He was headed to Daytona Beach, where the Minneapolis farm team trained. Ted saw the list and the shame welled up, turned to rage. He yelled to the veteran outfielders: *"I'll be back. And I'll make more money in this fucking game than all three of you combined."* When he walked to the bus stop with Johnny Orlando, he asked: "How much you think those guys make?" And Johnny said: "I don't know, maybe fifteen thousand apiece." Ted nodded, his mouth set in a grim line. He had his salary goal now. Then he borrowed $2.50 from Johnny for the bus trip to the minors.

In Minneapolis, Ted led the league in everything: average, home runs, runs batted in, screwball stunts. . . . There were tales of his conduct in the outfield, where he'd sit down between batters, or practice swinging an imaginary bat, watching his leg-stride, watching his wrist-break, watching everything except balls hit to him. If he did notice a fly ball, he'd gallop after it, slapping his ass and yelling, "HI HO SILVER!" He was nineteen, and fans loved him. But if there was one boo, the Kid would hear it, and he'd try to shut that sonofabitch up for good. Once, when a heckler got on him, Ted fired a ball into the stands—and hit the wrong guy. That was more than the manager, poor old Donie Bush, could stand. He went to the owner, Mike Kelley, and announced: "That's it. One of us goes. Him or me." Kelley replied, quick and firm: "Well, then, Donie, it'll have to be you."

By the time Ted came back to Sarasota, the Red Sox were banking on him, too. They traded Ben Chapman, the right fielder who'd hit .340 the year before. Ted told himself: "I guess that shows what they think of ME." It was like he had to convince himself he was really big league now. Even after a good day, three-for-four, he'd sit alone in the hotel with the canker of one failure eating at him. If he screwed up, or looked bad, the awkwardness turned to shame, the shame to rage. As the team headed north, Ted was hitting a ton, but it wasn't enough. At the first stop, Atlanta, Johnny Orlando pointed out the strange right-field wall—three parallel fences, one behind the other. Johnny said: "I saw Babe Ruth hit one over the last fence. . . ." Ted vowed right there he'd do it, too. But next day, he couldn't clear one fence. Worse still, he made an error. In the seventh, he put the Sox up with a three-run triple, but it wasn't enough. He had to show what Ted Williams could do! When he struck out in the eighth, he went to right field seething. Then a pop-up twisted toward his foul line. He ran and ran, dropped the ball, then booted it trying to pick it up. Rage was pounding in him. He grabbed the ball and fired it over those right-field walls. By the time the ball hit Ponce de Leon Avenue and bounced up at a Sears store, Cronin had yanked Ted out of the game.

Even Ted couldn't understand what that rage was to him, why he fed it, wouldn't let it go. He only knew that the next day in Atlanta, he smashed a ball over those three walls and trotted to the bench with a hard stare that asked Johnny Orlando, and anyone else who cared to look: Well, what do you think of the Kid now?

He had a great first year in the bigs. On his first Sunday at Fenway Park, he was four-for-five with his first home run, a shot to the bleachers in right-center, where only five balls had landed the whole year before. There were nine Boston dailies that vied in hyperbole on the new hero. TED WILLIAMS REVIVES FEATS OF BABE RUTH, said the *Globe* after Ted's fourth game.

From every town he wrote a letter to Rod Luscomb with a layout of the ball park and a proud X where his homer hit. He was always first to the stadium and last to leave after a game. He took his bats to the post office to make sure they were the proper weight. He quizzed the veterans mercilessly about the pitchers coming up. "What does Newsom throw in a jam? How about Ruffing's curve?" It was as if he meant to ingest the game. He only thought baseball. On trains, he'd never join the older guys in poker games or drinking bouts. At hotels, it was always room service, and Ted in his shorts, with a bat, at a mirror.

His roomie was Broadway Charlie Wagner, a pitcher with a taste for fancy suits and an occasional night on the town. One night, 4:00 A.M., Wagner was sleeping the sleep of the just when, *wham*,

**CRASH,** he's on the floor, with the bed around his ears, and he figures it's the end. He opens his eyes to see the bean-pole legs, then the shorts, and then the bat. Ted's been practicing and he hit the bedpost. Does he say he's sorry? No, doesn't say a damn thing to Wagner. He's got a little dream-child smile on his face and he murmurs to himself: "Boy, what power!"

He ended up hitting .327 and leading the league for runs batted in, the first time a rookie ever won that crown. He finished with thirty-one home runs, at least one in each American League park. There was no rookie of the year award, but Babe Ruth himself put the title on Ted, and that seemed good enough.

And after the season, he didn't go home. San Diego had lost its hold. His parents were getting a divorce, and that was pain he didn't want to face. He didn't want to see his troubled brother. He didn't want to see the crummy little house with the stained carpet and the chair with the hole where the mice ate through. He had a car now, a green Buick worth a thousand bucks. He went to Minnesota. There was a girl there he might want to see. Her dad was a hunting guide, and he could talk to her. And there was duck to hunt. As many as he wanted. And do what he wanted. He was twenty-one. And Big League.

Everyone knew 1940 would be a great year. Ted knew he'd be better: now he'd seen the pitchers, he knew he could do it. Tom Yawkey sent him a contract for $10,000, double his rookie pay. "I guess that shows what they think of ME."

No one thought about this, but pitchers had seen Ted, too. And this time around, no one was going to try to blow a fastball by him. Cronin was having an off year and Double-X Foxx was getting old and would never again be batting champ. So the pressure fell to Ted. If they pitched around him and he got a walk, that wasn't enough, the Sox needed hits. If he got a hit, it should have been a homer. A coven of bleacherites started riding Ted. And why not? They could always get a rise. Sometimes he'd yell back. Or he'd tell the writers: "I'm gonna take raw hamburger out to feed those wolves." The papers rode the story hard: O Unhappy Star! Then he told the writers: "Aw, Boston's a shitty town. Fans are lousy." Now the papers added commentary, pious truths about the Boston fans as the source of Ted's fine income. So Ted let them have it again: "My salary is peanuts. I'd rather be traded to New York." That did it. Now it wasn't just a left-field crowd riding Ted. It was civic sport: *He doesn't like Boston, huh? Who does he think he is?*

Writers worked the clubhouse, trying to *explain* the Kid. Big Jimmy Foxx, a hero to Ted, said: "Aw, he's just bein' a spoiled boy." The great Lefty Grove said if Williams didn't hustle, he'd punch him in the nose. Of course, all that made the papers. Now when writers came to his locker, Ted didn't wait for questions. "HEY, WHAT STINKS?" he'd yell in their faces. "HEY! SOMETHING STINK IN HERE? OH, IT'S YOU. WELL, NO WONDER WITH THAT SHIT YOU WROTE." So they made new nicknames for him: Terrible Ted, the Screwball, the Problem Child. Fans picked it up and gave him hell. It didn't seem to matter what he *did* anymore. And Ted read the stories in his hotel room and knew he was alone. Sure, he read the papers, though he always said he didn't. He read the stories twenty times, he'd recite them word for word. He'd pace the room and seethe, want to shut them up, want to hit them back. But he didn't know how.

And Ted would sit alone in the locker room, boning his bats, not just the handle, like other guys did, but the whole bat, grinding down on the wood, compressing the fiber tighter, making it tougher, harder, tighter. He would sting the ball, he'd show them. He'd shut them up. Jesus, he was trying. And he was hitting. Wasn't his average up? Wasn't he leading the league in runs? He was doing it like he'd taught himself, like he'd dreamed. Wasn't that enough? What the hell did they want him to be?

What else could he be? Some players tried to help, to ease him up a bit. Once, Ted gave Doc Cramer a ride, and they were talking hitting, as Ted always did. It was at Kenmore Square that Cramer said: "You know who's the best, don't you? You know who's the best in the league? You are." And Ted never forgot those words. But neither could he forget what was written, just as he couldn't forget one boo, just as he'd never forget the curve that struck him out a year before. Why didn't they understand? He could never forget.

And one day he made an error, and then struck out, and it

sounded like all of Fenway was booing, and he ran to the bench with his head down, the red rising in his face, the shame in his belly, and the rage. Ted thought: These are the ones who cheered, the fans I waved my cap to? Well, never again. He vowed to himself: Never again. And he could not forget that either.

Lou is in a Miami hospital for heart tests. Ted says I can drive up with him. He figures we'll talk, and he'll have me out of his hair. We start from his house and I wait for him on the porch, where a weary woman irons. The woman is trying to fill in for Lou and she's been ironing for hours. Ted may wear a T-shirt until it's half holes and no color at all, but he wants it just so. The woman casts a look of despair at the pile and announces: "She irons his *underpants*."

Ted blows through the back door and makes for the car, Lou's Ford, which he proclaims "a honey of a little car, boys!" When Ted puts his seal of judgment on a thing or person, by habit he alerts the whole dugout. We are out of Islamorada on the crowded highway, U.S. 1, the only road that perseveres to these islets off the corner of the country, when Ted springs his key question. "You read the book? Awright. Now we're going to see how smart YOU are. What would YOU do to start, I mean, the first goddamn thing now, the first thing you see when you're sitting in the seats and the lights go off, how would YOU start the movie?"

Ted is considering a film deal for *My Turn at Bat*. He is working the topic of moviedom, as he does anything he wants to know. Now as he pilots the Ford through Key Largo, he listens with a grave frown to some possible first scenes. "Awright. Now I'll tell you how it's supposed to start, I mean how the guy's doing it said. . . . It's in a fighter plane, see, flying, from the pilot's eye, over KOREA, Seoul. And it's flying, slow and sunny and then *bang* **WHAM** ***BOOOOMM*** *the biggest goddamn explosion ever on the screen,* I mean **BOOOOOMMM.** And the screen goes dark. DARK. For maybe ten seconds there's NOTHING. *NOTHING*. And then when it comes back there's the ball park and the crowd ROARING . . . and that's the beginning."

"Sounds great, Ted."

"Does it? LOOKIT THIS NOW. I wonder where he's goin'. Well,

okay, he's gonna do *that*. Well, okay—I'm passing too. Fuck it." Ted is pushing traffic hard to be at the hospital by 2:00, when Lou's doctors have promised results from the heart tests. He is trying to be helpful, but he's edgy.

"How long have you and Lou been together?"

"Oh, I've known Lou for thirty-five years. You shouldn't put any of that shit in there. Say I have a wonderful friend, that's all."

"Yeah, but it makes a difference in how a man lives, Ted, whether he's got a woman or not—"

"Boy, that Sylvester Stallone, he's really made something out of that Rocky, hasn't he? . . ."

"So Ted, let me ask you what—"

"LOOK, I don't wanta go through my personal life with YOU, for Christ's sake. I won't talk to you about Lou, I won't talk to you about any of it. You came down here and you're talkin' about me, as I'm supposed to be different and all that . . ."

"Do you think you're different?"

"NO, not a damn bit. I'm in a little bit different POSITION. I mean, I've had things happen to me that have, uh, made it possible for me to be different. DAMN DIFFERENT in some ways. Everybody's not a big league ballplayer, everybody doesn't have, uh, coupla hitches in the service, everybody hasn't had, uh, as much notoriety about 'em as I had ALL MY LIFE, so . . ."

"So . . ."

"I wanna go NORTH. I'm gonna go up here and go farther down. I made a mistake there, GODDAMIT, HOW THE HELL DO I GET ON THE FUCKIN' THING? I'll make a U-turn. . . ."

"Ted, I think you were more serious about living life on your own terms. . . ."

"Well, I wanted to be alone at times. It was the hustle and the bustle of the crowd for seven months a year. So sure, I wanted a little more privacy, a little more quiet, a little more tranquillity. This is the fucking left we wanted."

"Yeah, but it's not just privacy, Ted. I'm not trying to make it seem unnatural. But what you toss off as a little privacy led you *off* the continent, so far off in a corner that—"

"Well, lemme tell you about Koufax. He got through playin' baseball, he went to a fuckin' little shitty remote town in Maine, and that's where he was for five years. Everybody thought he was a recluse, he wasn't very popular just 'cause he wanted to be alone and he finally moved out. Lemme tell you about Sterling Hayward, Hayden. HELL of an actor. And still he wanted to be ALONE, he wanted to TRAVEL, he wanted to be on his BOAT GOIN' TO THE SOUTH SEAS. So, see that's not outa line! . . . I guess I'll take a right, that oughta do it. Eight seventy-four, do you see 874 anyplace? Go down here till I get to Gilliam Road, or some goddamn thing. . . .Fuck, 874's where I wanted to go, but looked like it was puttin' me back on the fuckin' turnpike, shit. So, you know, seeking privacy and, uh, seeking that kind of thing . . . what road is this?

"We're on Killian. . . .So privacy, you don't think that's what?"

"*Unusual*, for Christ's sake. Shit."

"I don't think it's unusual either."

"WELL, YOU'RE MAKIN' A PROJECT OUT OF IT!"

"No, I don't think it's unusual. . . .You don't think you're exceptionally combative?"

"Nahh, me? Not a bit. Hell, no. THAT SAY KENDALL? Does it? Well, I made a hell of a move here. HELL of a move! See, 874 is right off there, hospital's down here . . ."

"You're a half-hour early, too."

"Here it is, right here, too. Best hospital in Miami. Expensive sonofabitch, boy. Christ. I'm all for Medicare. And I've always thought that, ALWAYS thought that. Shit. WELL, WHERE ARE YOU GOING? Where ARE you going, lady? *Cunt*!" Ted takes the parking space vacated by the lady and tells me he'll be back in an hour.

When he comes back he has good news about Lou: all tests are negative, her heart is fine. "Gee, I met the big cardiovascular man, he came in and I met him." Ted sounds twenty years younger.

He's walking to the car when a nurse passes. "GEE, WASN'T IT A SHAME," Ted suddenly booms, "THAT ALLIGATOR BIT THAT LITTLE GIRL'S LEG OFF?" He casts a sly sideward glance at the nurse to see if she's fallen for his favorite joke.

"Honey of a little shittin' car!" he sings out as we hit the road. Now there is no fretting with traffic. Ted makes all the turns. Along the way, he sings forth a monologue about cars, this car, this road, this town of Homestead, that house, his house, the new house he's planning in central Florida, up on a hill, just about the highest point in the whole goddamn state, what a deal he's getting there, Citrus Hills, HELL of a deal; about his hopes for his kids, his daughter, Claudia, only fourteen, who lives in Vermont with her mother, Ted's third wife, who was too much of a pain in the ass to live with, but gee, she's done a hell of a job with those kids, HELL of a job, the little girl is an actress, she had the lead in the Christmas play and she was so good, the papers up there all said she bears watching, SHE BEARS WATCHING, and her brother, Ted's boy, John Henry, he's picking colleges now, he's a good boy and Ted's critical, but he can't see too much wrong with that boy, and even the big daughter, Bobby Jo, she's thirty-eight already, still can bust Ted's chops pretty good, boys, but she's straightening out now; and these islands, there's bonefish here, used to be wonderful, years ago, there was NOTHING, NOTHING, except a few of the best fishermen God ever made, and a narrow road between bay and sea, just a little shittin' road, and some women who weren't half bad on the water or off it either, and the world here was empty and the water was clear and you could have a few pops of rum, maybe get a little horny, go see friends, that's all there was here, a few friends, thirty, thirty-five years ago, when this place was young, when he first fished with Jimmy and he met Lou. . . ."

"Gee, I'm so fuckin' happy about Louise," Ted says. "Goddamn, she's a great person. Have more fun with her than . . . Goddamn."

THEY BOOED IN BOSTON? Well, not in Detroit, the 1941 All-Star Game, with all the nation listening in. Ted doubled in a run in the fourth, but the National League still led 5–3, going into the ninth. Then an infield hit, a single, a walk, a botched double play, and here it was: two out, two on, bottom of the ninth. *Here's the Great Ted Williams*. Claude Passeau, the Cubbie on the mound, sends a mean fastball in on his fists. *Williams swings*! When the ball made the seats, Ted started jumping on the base path. DiMaggio met him at home plate, Bob Feller ran out in street clothes, Cronin jumped the box-seat rail, the dugout emptied. The manager, Del Baker, kissed him on the forehead. They carried the Kid off the field.

He was showing them all now: after the All-Star break, Ted was still hitting more than .400. Sure, guys hit like that for a month, but then tailed off. No one in the league hit like that for a year, not since the Twenties, and each day the whole country watched. Writers from New York joined the Sox. *Life* brought its new strobe-light camera to photograph Ted in his shorts, swinging like he did in front of the mirror. Ted was on national radio: "Can you keep it up, Kid?" It was murderous pressure. By September, he was slipping, almost a point a day. On the last day, the Sox would have two games in Philadelphia. Ted had slipped to .39955. The way they round off averages, that's still .400. Cronin came to Ted on the eve of the twin bill and offered: "You could sit it out, Kid, have it made." But Ted said he'd play.

That night, he and Johnny Orlando walked Philadelphia. Ted stopped for milk shakes, Johnny for whiskey. Ten thousand people came to Shibe Park, though the games meant nothing. Connie Mack, the dour and penurious owner of the A's, threatened his men with fines if they eased up on Williams. But Ted didn't need help. First game, he got a single, then a home run, then two more singles. Second game, two more hits: one a screaming double that hit Mr. Mack's right-field loudspeaker so hard that the old man had to buy a new horn. In all, Ted went six-for-eight, and .406 for his third season. That night, he went out for chocolate ice cream.

Who could tell what he'd do the next year: maybe .450, the best *ever*, or break the Babe's record of sixty homers. He got a contract for $30,000, and he meant to fix up his mother's house. He'd have more money than he'd ever expected. He was the toast of the nation. But then the nation went to war.

Ted wanted to play. He'd read where some admiral said we'd kick the Japs back to Tokyo in six months. What was that compared to hitting? A lawyer in Minnesota drew up a plea for deferment, and Ted okayed the request: he was entitled, as his mother's support. When the local board refused deferment, the lawyer sent it up for review by the presidential board. That's when the papers got it. In headlines the size of howitzer shells, they said Ted didn't want to fight for his country. Teddy Ballgame just wanted to play.

Tom Yawkey called to say he could be making the mistake of his life. The league president told Ted to go ahead and play. Papers ran man-on-the-street polls. In Boston, Ted was bigger news than war in the Pacific. At spring training, Joe Cronin said he'd be on his own with fans. "To hell with them," Ted spat. "I've heard plenty of boos." Still, he remembered the venomous letters that said he was an ingrate or a traitor. The one that hurt most said nothing at all: it was just a blank sheet of paper, *yellow* paper.

Opening day in Boston, reporters sat in the left-field stands, out there with soldiers and sailors, to record reaction to Ted. The Kid treated the day as a personal challenge. His first time up, two on, two strikes, he got a waist-high fastball and drilled it into the bleachers. All the fans rose to cheer, servicemen among them. The Kid was back, and Fenway was with him. "Yeah, 98 percent were for me," Ted said later, as he scraped his bat. A writer said: "You mean 100 percent. I didn't hear a boo." Ted said: "Yeah, they were for me, except a couple of kids in the left-field stand, and a guy out in right. I could hear them."

In May, he enlisted for Navy wings and that shut up most of the hecklers. Still, he was always in a stew of contempt for some joker who said something unfair. It seemed Ted courted the rage now, used it to bone his own fiber. Now there was no awkwardness, no blushing before he blew. It was automatic, a switch in his gut that snapped on and then, watch out for the Kid. One day in July, a fan in left was riding Ted pretty hard. Ted came to bat in the fifth: he took a strange stance and swung late, hit a line drive, but well foul into the left-field seats. Next pitch, again he swung late, hit another liner, but this stayed fair—and Ted didn't run, barely made it to second. Cronin yanked him out of the game, fined him $250 for loafing. But Ted wasn't loafing, the hit caught him by surprise. He'd been trying to kill the heckler with a line drive foul.

• • •

Ted loved the service, its certainty and ease. He never had a problem with authority. It was drawing his own lines that gave him fits. He had his fears about the mathematics, navigation problems, and instrument work. But at Amherst College, where the Navy started training, he found his mind was able, and he was pleased. And he loved the feel of an airplane. He was good, right from the start. There was coordination in it, and care: those were natural to him. And he was a constant student, always learning in the air. But he was proudest of his gunnery, the way he could hold back until the last pass, then pour out the lead and shred the sleeve. That wasn't study, that was art. He got his wings near the top of his class and signed on as an instructor at Pensacola, Florida. He was happy, and good at his job. Strangely, in uniform, he was freer than before.

On the day he was commissioned (second lieutenant, U.S. Marines), he married that daughter of the hunting guide, Doris Soule from Minnesota. Now, for the first time, he'd have a house, a place on the coast near the base. And now, on off days, he'd scrape up some gas stamps, grab his fly rod, find a lonesome canal, and lose himself in a hunt for snook. Back at the base, Ted would grab a cadet and take him up in his SNJ, and the new guy of course was goggled-eyed, flying with *Ted Williams*, and Ted would make his plane dance over the coast, then he'd dive and point, and yell to the cadet: "*That's where the Kid fished yesterday.*"

Orders came through slowly for him. What base commander would give him up as ornament and outfielder? At last he got combat training and packed up for the Pacific. But Ted was just getting to Hawaii when Japan folded. So he packed up again for Boston, and now he felt he was going to war.

He came back like he owned the game. Opening day, Washington, after a three-year layoff: *crack*, a four-hundred-foot home run. And then another and another, all around the league. By the All-Star break in '46, he was hitting .365, with twenty-seven home runs. In the All-Star Game, Ted alone ruined the National League: four straight hits, two homers, and five runs batted in.

And the Red Sox were burying the American League. Tom Yawkey's millions were paying off. The team as a whole was hitting .300, and Ted was hammering the right-field walls. In the first game of two in Cleveland, he hit three homers, one a grand slam when the Sox were behind, the second with two on to tie, the third in the bottom of the ninth to win 11–10. As Ted came up in the second game, Cleveland's manager, Lou Boudreau, started moving men: the right fielder backed toward the corner, center fielder played the wall in right-center; the third baseman moved behind second, and Boudreau, the shortstop, played a deep second base; the second baseman stood in short right, the first baseman stood behind his bag. There were eight men on one half of the field (the left fielder was alone on the other) and Ted stood at home plate and laughed out loud.

There never had been anything like it. He had bent the nature of the game. But he would not bend his own, and slap the ball for singles to left. He hit into the teeth of the Shift (soon copied around the league), and when he slumped, and the Sox with him, the papers started hammering Ted again, his pride, his "attitude." At last, against the Shift in Cleveland, Ted sliced a drive to left-center field, and slid across the plate with an inside-the-park home run, first and last of his career. The Sox had their first pennant since 1918. But the headlines didn't say, SOX CLINCH. Instead, eight-column banners cried that Ted stayed away from the champagne party. "Ted Williams," Dave Egan wrote in the *Record*, "is not a team man." And when St. Louis pulled the Shift in the Series and held Ted to singles, five-for-twenty-five, a new banner read: WILLIAMS BUNTS. And the Red Sox lost the Series, first and last of his career, and after the seventh game, in St. Louis, Ted went to the train, closed his compartment, hung his head, and cried. When he looked up, he saw a crowd watching him through the window. The papers wrote: "Ted Williams cannot win the big ones." The Associated Press voted him number two in a poll for Flop of the Year.

It seemed like Ted couldn't laugh anymore, not in a ball park. He said he was going to Florida to fish. He didn't want to see a bat for months. Soon that was a pattern: one year, before spring training, he tucked in a week in the Everglades. Next year, it was a month. Year after that, longer. In early 1948, the papers discovered that Doris was in a Boston hospital to deliver Ted's first child. But where was the big guy? In Florida? FISHING? The mothers of Boston pelted the press with angry letters. "To hell with them," Ted said. He didn't come north for two days. And two days later, he was back fishing. In two years, he'd moved Doris and his daughter, Barbara Joyce, to a house in Miami, the first he'd ever owned. But he never stayed home there either. He heard about some men in the Keys catching bonefish with light fly tackle. When Ted tried this new sport, he found a love that would last longer than any of his marriages.

The Keys were empty, their railroad wrecked by a hurricane in 1935. There were only a few thousand souls on one road that ran for a hundred miles; the rest was just mangrove and mosquitoes, crushed coral islands, and shining water. In Islamorada—a town of one store, a bar, a restaurant, one gas pump—a few fishing guides, led by Jimmy Albright, were poling their skiffs over shallows that only they knew, hunting bonefish and inventing an art as they went along. These were Ted's kind of men, who'd sneer or scream at a chairman of the stock exchange if he made a lousy cast. Islamorada was a strange meritocracy: if you could not play a fish, tie a fly, cast a line through the wind, you were no one in this town.

Ted could do it all, brilliantly. The guides didn't make much fuss about his fame, but they loved his fishing. His meticulous detail work, always an oddity at Fenway Park, was respected here as the mark of a fine angler. Ted had the best tackle, best reels, best rods, the perfect line, his lures were impeccable. He'd work for hours at a bench in his house, implanting balsa plugs with lead so they'd sail off a spinning rod just so, then settle in the water slowly like a fly. He could stand on the bow of a skiff all day, watching the water for signs of fish, and soon he was seeing them before the guides. His casts were quick and long, his power was immense. He never seemed to snap a line, never tangled up, his knots were sure, his knowledge grew, and he always wanted to know *more*. He'd question Jimmy relentlessly and argue every point. But if you showed him something once, he never needed showing again. He fished with Jimmy week after week, and one afternoon as he stood on the bow, he asked without turning his head: "Who's the best you ever fished?" Jimmy said a name, Al Mathers. Ted nodded, "Uh-huh," and asked another question, but he vowed to himself: "He don't know it yet, but the best angler he's had is me."

Every winter, he'd fish the flats, then head north to make his appearance at the Boston Sportsmen's Show. He'd spend a few days doing fly-casting stunts and then take a couple of hours, at most, to tell Tom Yawkey what he wanted for a contract. His salary was enormous. He was the first to break Babe Ruth's $80,000. Ted didn't care for the money as much as the record. It was history now that was the burr on his back. The joy was gone, but not the dream.

Every day, every season, he was still first to the ball park, where he'd strip to shorts and bone his bats; still first out to the cage, where he'd bark his imaginary play-by-play: "Awright, Detroit, top of the ninth . . ." Then back to his locker for a clean shirt and up at a trot to the dugout, to clap a hostile eye on the pitcher warming up, to pick apart his delivery, hunting for any weakness. No, Ted would not give up on one game, one time at bat, a single pitch. No one since Ruth had hit so many home runs per times at bat. No one in the league hit like Ted, year after year: .342, .343, .369, .343. . . .It seemed he never broke a bat at the plate, but he broke a hundred in the clubhouse runway. If he failed at the plate he'd scream at himself, "YOU GODDAMN FOOL!" and bash the cement, while the Sox in the dugout stared ahead with mute smiles. Once, after a third strike, he smashed the water pipe to the cooler with his bare fists. No one could believe it until the flood began. And on each opening day, Ted would listen to the national anthem and he'd feel the hair rise on the back of his neck, and his hands would clench, and he'd vow to himself: "This year, the best *ever*."

In the 1950 All-Star Game, he crashed the outfield wall to catch a drive by Ralph Kiner. His elbow was broken, with thirteen chips off the radius. Surgeons thought he was through, but Ted returned in two months. His first game back, once again: home run, and four-for-four. But Ted could tell as weeks went by that the elbow was not the same. The ball didn't jump off his bat. So all next winter, Ted stayed in the Keys, where he poled a skiff, hunting bonefish and rebuilding his arm. He was pushing thirty-three now, just coming to know how short was his time. But then, after the '51 season, he was called back to the Marines, drafted for a two-year hitch in Korea. It seemed his time was up.

Ted's living room has a wide white armchair, into and out of which he heaves himself twenty times a day; the chair has a wide white ottoman onto which he'll flop, as whim dictates, one or both of his big legs. From this chair, he roars commands and inquiries, administering the house and grounds. Across the room, a big TV shows his *National Geographic* specials. At his side, a table holds his reading and correspondence. At the moment, these piles are topped by *Yeager: An Autobiography*, and teachers' reports on his son, John Henry. To Ted's right, ten feet away, there's a doorway to the kitchen, through which Lou can supply him and let him know who that was on the phone. To his left and behind, a grand window affords a view of a patio, his dock, some mangrove, and some Florida Bay. Finally, ahead and to the right, in a distant semicircle, there are chairs and a couch for visitors.

"NOW WE'RE GONNA SEE HOW MUCH *YOU* KNOW, SONOFABITCH," Ted is shouting at Jack Brothers. Jimmy Albright is there, too. The shouting is ritual.

"Ru-mer. R-U-M-E-R." Brothers contends he is spelling the name of the first spinning reel. But Ted has hurled himself up to fetch a fishing encyclopedia, and now he's back in the chair, digging through to the section on spinning. Just so things don't get dull, he says: "Where'd you get that HAIRCUT? D'you have to PAY FOR IT?"

Ted and Jimmy began this colloquy in the early Truman years. Jack helped heat it up when he drifted down from Brooklyn a few years after the war, before Islamorada got its second restaurant or first motel, not to mention the other ten motels, the condos, gift shops, Burger King, or the billboard to proclaim this place: SPORTFISHING CAPITAL OF THE WORLD. These elders are responsible for a lot of the history here, as they helped create flats fishing and turn it into a sport/industry (which they now quietly deplore). Jimmy and Jack were teachers of the first generation of saltwater anglers. Ted is the star of that generation, and its most ferocious pupil.

"Here. HERE! 'Mr. Brown began importing SPINNERS, starting with the LUXAR. . . .' THE *LUXAR*. WANNA SEE? GO AHEAD, SONOFABITCH!"

"Yeah, but that don't say the first spinning reel *manufactured*," Brothers grins in triumph. "Sonofabitch, with your books!"

"This is the goddamn HISTORY, Brothers. Not a FUCKING THING about RUMOR, RHEUMER, RHOOOMAN . . . I GUESS YOU DIDN'T KNOW MUCH ABOUT SPINNING REELS, DID YOU?"

Ted is always the one with the books. He wants *answers*, not a lot of bullshit. Ted is always reading history, biography, fact of all kinds. He doesn't like much made of this, as he's tender on the subject of his education. Once in a camp in Africa, while he and his coauthor, John Underwood, gazed at the night sky, Ted turned from the stars and sighed: "Jeez, I wish I was smart like you."

Now he reports to his friends on his college tours with his son, John Henry: "So we get to Babson and I like it. Babson's a pretty good school, boys. HELL of a school, but, uh, they got dorms, boys and girls all in one dorm, see, and I look on the walls and they're written all over, Fuck this and Fuck that, I'm thinking, Gee, right out there on the walls, it just seemed, you know . . ."

"Liberal?" Jimmy suggests.

"Well, I like to see a place with a little more standards than *that*. So we get to Bates. We got this German girl to show us around, see? And she was a smart little shit, two languages, and she's telling us what she's studying, *aw*, a smart little shit! She give us the tour, see, and John Henry loved Bates, LOVED it. We get back to the office and she goes out. I don't know, she musta told someone, told some of her friends, who she just showed around, see? Then somebody *told* her. She didn't know, see. . . .

"Well, a minute later, she's back with some kid and he says, OH, Mr. Williams! And OH this and OH that. And *then* we start talking. And how about *this*, how about *that*, and how would John Henry like to come for a *weekend*, get the feel of the place, you know. . . ."

Ted stops for a moment and thinks to himself. He doesn't really have to finish the thought for his friends, who can see him beaming in his big chair. So he just trails off, to himself:

". . . boy mighta thought the old man wasn't gonna . . . you know, around a college. . . .Well!"

THE MAYOR AND THE RED SOX held a day for Ted when he left for flight school. Three weeks into the '52 season, at Fenway, they gave him a Cadillac, and made a donation to the Jimmy Fund, a charity for sick children that Ted supported. They gave him a *Ted Williams Memory Book*, with signatures of four hundred thousand fans. For his last at bat, bottom of the seventh, he gave them a three-run homer to win the game 5–3. He threw a party that night, at his Boston hotel. The crowd was mostly cooks and firemen, bellhops, cabbies, ice cream men. Ted never liked a smart crowd. Smart people too often asked: "Oh, was your father a ballplayer?" "Oh, what did your mother do? Ted didn't like to talk about that.

He was just Captain Williams, U.S. Marines, at his flight base at Pohang, Korea. He had a shed for a home and a cot with inner-tube strips for springs. The base was a sea of mud, the air was misty and cold, and he was always sick. He was flying close air support, low strafing, and bombing runs. His plane was a jet now, an F-9 Panther, but he couldn't take much joy from flying. He was in and out of sick bay. Doctors called it a virus, then pneumonia, but his squadron was short of pilots, so he always flew.

On a bombing run, north of the 38th parallel, Ted lost sight of the plane ahead. He dropped through clouds, and when he came out, he was much too low. North Koreans sent up a hail of bullets. Ted's plane was hit and set afire. The stick stiffened and shook in his hand; his hydraulics were gone. Every warning light was red. The radio quit. A Marine in a nearby F-9 was pointing wildly at Ted's plane. He was trying to signal: "Fire! Bail out!" But Ted's biggest fear was ejecting; at six three, wedged in as he was, he'd leave his kneecaps under the gauges. So the other pilot led him to a base. Ted hauled his plane into a turn and he felt a shudder of explosion. One of his wheel doors had blown out. Now he was burning below, too. He made for a runway with fire streaming thirty feet behind. Koreans in a village saw his plane and ran for their lives. Only one wheel came down; he had no dive breaks, air flaps, nothing to slow the plane. He hit the concrete at 225 miles an hour and slid for almost a mile, while he mashed the useless brakes and screamed, "*STOP YOU DIRTY SONOFABITCH STOP STOP STOP.*" When the F-9 stopped skidding, he somersaulted out the hatch and slammed his helmet to the ground. Two Marines grabbed him on the tarmac, and walked him away as the plane burned to char.

He was flying the next day, and day after. There weren't enough pilots to rest a man. Ted was sicker, weak and gaunt. Soon his ears were so bad he couldn't hear the radio. He had flown thirty-seven missions and won three air medals when they sent him on to Hawaii and then to Bethesda, Maryland, where at last they gave him a discharge. His thirty-fifth birthday was coming up, he was tired and ill. He didn't want to do anything, much less suit up to play. But Ford Frick, the commissioner, asked him to the '53 All-Star Game, just to throw out the first ball.

So Ted went to Cincinnati, sat in a sport coat in the dugout. Players greeted him like a lost brother; even Ted couldn't hear a boo in the stands. Tom Yawkey was there and Joe Cronin; they worked on the Kid. The league president asked him to come back; the National League president, too. Branch Rickey sat him down for a talk; Casey Stengel put in a plea. Ted went to Bethesda to ask the doctor and then he told the waiting press to send a message to the fans at Fenway: warm up your lungs." He took ten days of batting practice and returned with the Red Sox to Boston. First game, Fenway Park, bottom of the seventh: pinch-hit home run.

Ted Williams was the greatest old hitter. In two months, upon return from Korea, he batted .407 and hit a home run once in every seven at bats. For the next two years, he led the league (.345 and .356), but injuries and walks robbed him of the titles: he didn't get the minimum four hundred at bats. In 1956, he lost the title in the season's last week to twenty-four-year-old Mickey Mantle (who finished with .353 to Ted's .345). The next year, Mantle had an even better season but Ted, at age thirty-nine, pulled away and won, at .388, more than twenty points ahead of Mantle, more than sixty points ahead of anyone else. With five more hits (say, the leg hits that a younger man would get), it would have been .400. As it was, it stood as the highest average since his own .406, sixteen years before. In 1958, Ted battled for the crown again, this time with a teammate, Peter Runnels. They were even in September, but then, once again, Ted pulled away to win at .328. For the final fifty-five games (including one on his fortieth birthday), he batted .403.

He accomplished these prodigies despite troubles that would have made most men quit. In 1954, he made spring training for the first time in three years, but he wasn't on the field a minute before he fell and broke his collarbone. He was out six weeks and had a steel bar wired into his clavicle. (First day back, twin bill in Detroit: two home runs, eight-for-nine, seven RBIs.) In 1955, Doris alleged in divorce court that he'd treated her with "extreme cruelty" and constant profane abuse. Boston papers ran the story under two-inch headlines: TED GETS DIVORCE, with a "box score" on the money, the house, the car, and "Mrs. Ted's" custody of Bobby Jo. In 1956, Ted came forth with his Great Expectorations. In a scoreless game with the Yankees, in front of Fenway's biggest crowd since World War II, he was booed for an error, and he let the fans know what he thought of them: he spat toward the right-field stands and spat toward the left, and when fans rained more boos on his head, he leaped out of the dugout and sprayed all around. "Oh, no, this is a bad scene," Curt Gowdy, the Sox broadcaster, mourned into his microphone. Tom Yawkey heard the game on radio, and Ted got a $5,000 fine (tying another Babe Ruth record). Boston writers said Ted ought to quit. But Ted was in the next game, Family Night, and at his appearance, fans gave him a five-minute ovation. (He then hit a home run in the bottom of the eighth and clapped his hand over his mouth as he scored the winning run.) In 1957, grippe knocked him flat and stuck him in his hotel for seventeen days in September. He came back to hit four consecutive home runs. In 1958, ptomaine from bad oysters wrecked opening day, then he injured an ankle, pulled a muscle in his side, and hurt his wrist twice. In September, after a called third strike, Ted threw his bat and watched in horror as it sailed to the stands and clonked a gray-haired lady on the head. Ted sat in tears in the dugout and had to be ordered to his place in left field. But over the next twenty at-bats, he hit .500.

Now the switch in his gut was always on. The Red Sox gave him a single room and barred the press from the clubhouse for two hours before each game. But it wasn't outside annoyance that was fueling Ted's rage. He'd wake up in the middle of the night, screaming obscenities in the dark. He kept himself alone and pushed away affection. There were plenty of women who would have loved to help. But Ted would say: "WOMEN?" and then he'd grab his crotch. "ALL THEY WANT IS WHAT I GOT RIGHT HERE." Now the press didn't cover just explosions on the field. The *American* wrote him up for shredding a telephone book all over the floor when a hotel maid failed to clean his room. "Now tell me some more," wrote Austen Lake, "about Ted's big, charitable, long-suffering spirit." Roger Kahn reported a scene when Ted was asked about Billy Klaus, the shortstop who was coming back after a bad year. "You're asking ME about a BAD YEAR? . . . OLD T.S.W., HE DON'T HAVE BAD YEARS."

But old Ted had a terrible year in 1959. A pain in his neck turned to stiffness, and he was in traction for three weeks. When he came out, he could barely look at the pitcher. His average languished below .300 for the first time in his career. For the first time, he was benched for not hitting. The sight of the Kid at the plate was pathetic; even the papers softened. They started summing up his career, treating him like an old building menaced by the wrecking ball. He finished at .254 and went to see Tom Yawkey. "Why don't you just wrap it up?" Yawkey said, and Ted started to boil. No one was going to make him retire. Ted said he meant to play, and Yawkey, who loved the Kid, offered to renew his contract: $125,000, the highest ever. No, Ted said, he'd had a lousy year and wanted a cut. So Ted signed for $90,000 and came back one more time.

Opening day, Washington: A five-hundred-foot home run. Next day, another. He slammed his five-hundredth in Cleveland, passed Lou Gehrig and then Mel Ott. Only Foxx and Ruth would top him on the all-time list. At forty-two, Ted finished his year with twenty-nine homers and .316. Talk revived that Ted might be back. But this was really quits. On his last day at Fenway, a headline cried: WHAT WILL WE DO WITHOUT TED? And though the day was dreary and the season without hope, ten thousand came out to cheer him and hear him say goodbye. There was another check for the Jimmy Fund and, this time, a silver bowl. And Ted made a speech that said, despite all, he felt lucky to play for these fans. And when he came up in the eighth and they stood to cheer, he showed them what Ted Williams could do. He hit a Jack Fisher fastball into the bullpen in right field. And he thought about tipping his cap as he rounded first but he couldn't, even then, couldn't forget, so he ran it straight into the dugout, and wouldn't come out for a bow. Now it was no hobby: Ted fished harder and fished more than any man around. After his divorce from Doris, he'd made his home in Islamorada, bought a little place on the ocean side, with no phone and just room for one man and gear. He'd wake before dawn and spend the day in his boat, then come in, maybe cook a steak, maybe drive off to a Cuban or Italian joint where they served big portions and left him alone. Then, back home, he'd tie a few flies and be in bed by 10:00. He kept it very spare. He didn't even have a TV. That's how he met Louise. He wanted to see a Joe Louis fight, so Jimmy took him to Lou's big house. Her husband was a businessman from Ohio, and they had a TV, they had everything. Lou had her five kids, the best home, best furniture, best car, and best guides. Though she wasn't a woman of leisure, she was a pretty good angler, too. She could talk fishing with Ted. Yes, they could talk. And soon, Lou would have a little money of her own, an inheritance that she'd use to buy a divorce. She wanted to do for herself, she said. And there was something else, too. "I met Ted Williams," Louise said. "And he was the most gorgeous thing I ever saw in my life."

Now Ted's life was his to make, too. He signed a six-figure deal with Sears, to lend his name to their line of tackle, hunting gear, and sporting goods. Now, when Hurricane Donna wrecked his little house on the ocean, he bought his three-bedroom place on the bay, near Louise's house. Now he bought a salmon pool on the Miramichi, in New Brunswick, Canada, and he fished in the summer season there. In Islamorada, he was out every day, fall, winter, spring. He wanted the most and the biggest—bonefish, tarpon, salmon—he called them the Big Three. He wanted a thousand of each, and kept books on his progress. He thought fishing and talked fishing and taught fishing at shows for Sears. He felt the joy of the sport, still. But now there was something else: the switch that clicked when he'd get a hot fish that ran and broke off his lure: Ted would slam his rod to the deck, or break it in half on the boat. "HERE, YOU LOUSY SONOFABITCH . . ." He'd hurl the rod into the bay. "TAKE THAT, TOO."

He married again in 1961, a tall blonde model from Chicago, Lee Howard. They'd both been divorced, and they thought they'd make a go. Ted brought her down to the Keys. But he still wasn't staying home: he'd be out at dawn without a word on where he'd go, or what he planned, and then he'd come home, sometimes still without words. Sometimes there was only rage and Lee found she was no match. After two years, she couldn't take it. She said: "I couldn't do anything right. If we went fishing, he would scream at me, call me a ---- and kick the tackle box."

So Ted found another woman, one to meet him, fire with fire. Her name was Dolores Wettach, a tall, large-eyed, former Miss Vermont. He spotted her across the aisle on a long plane flight. He was coming from fishing in New Zealand. Dolores had been in Australia, on a modeling assignment for *Vogue*. He wrote a note: "Who are you?" He wadded it up, tossed it at her. She looked him over, tossed one back: "Who are *you*? He tossed: "Mr. Williams, a fisherman," and later told her his first name was Sam. It wasn't until their third date that she found out he'd done anything but fish. When he found out she was a farm girl who loved the outdoors as much as he, he figured he'd met his match. In a way, he had. She learned to fish, she could hunt, could drink, could curse like a guide. And when they fought, it was toe to toe, and Ted who slammed out of the house. They had a son, John Henry, and daughter, Claudia. But that didn't stop the fights, just as it hadn't with Bobby Jo, the daughter he'd had with Doris. Ted would tell his friends he wasn't cut out for family. He was sick at heart when Bobby Jo left school and didn't go to college. He would seethe when any woman let him know that he'd have to change. What the hell did they want? When Dolores became his third divorce, Ted was through with marriage.

Ted made the Hall of Fame in 1966. His old enemies, the writers, gave him the largest vote ever. So Ted went north to Cooperstown, and gave a short speech outside the Hall. Then he went back to Florida. He never went inside. They gave him a copy of his plaque. It listed his .406 year, his batting titles, slugging titles, total bases, walks, home runs. It didn't say anything about the wars, the dream, the rage, the cost. But how much can a plaque say?

There are no statistics on fans, how they felt, what they took from the game. How many of their days did Ted turn around? How many days did he turn to occasions? And not just with hits: there was a special sound from a crowd when Ted got his pitch, turned on the ball, whipped his bat in that perfect arc—and missed. It was a murmurous rustle, as thousands at once let breath escape, gathered themselves, and leaned forward again. To see Ted suffer a *third* strike was an event four times more rare, and more remarkable, than seeing him get a hit. When Ted retired, some owners feared for attendance in the *league*. In Boston, where millions came through the years to cheer, to boo, to care what he did, there was an accretion of memory so bright, bittersweet, and strong that when he left, the light was gone. And Fenway was left with a lesser game.

And what was Ted left with? Well, there was pride. He'd done, he felt, the hardest thing in sport: by God, he hit the ball. And there was pride in his new life: he had his name on more rods and reels, hunting guns, tackle boxes, jackets, boots, and bats than any man in the world. He studied fishing like no other man, and lent to it his fame and grace, his discerning eye. He had his tournament wins and trophies, a fishing book and fishing movies, and he got his thousand of the Big Three. Jimmy Albright says to this day: "Best all around, the best is Ted." But soon there were scores of boats on the bay, and not so many fish. And even the Miramichi had no pools with salmon wall to wall. And Ted walked away from the tournaments. There wasn't the feeling of sport in them, or respect for the fish anymore. Somehow it had changed. Or maybe it was Ted.

Last year, Ted and Lou went up to Cooperstown together. This was for the unveiling of a statue of the Kid. There are many plaques in the Hall of Fame, but only two statues: just the Babe and him. And

Ted went into the Hall this time, pulled the sheet off his statue and looked at his young self in the finish of that perfect swing. He looked and he looked, while the crowd got quiet, and the strobes stopped flashing. And when he tried to speak, he wept.

"HEY, WHERE THE HELL IS HE?" It's after 4:00, and Ted's getting hungry. "I'M GONNA CALL HIM."

Lou says, "Don't be ugly."

"I'm not ugly," Ted insists, but quietly. He dials, and bends to look at me. "Hey, if this guy doesn't come, you can eat. You wanna eat here?" Then to the phone: "WHERE THE HELL ARE YOU?"

"Ted, don't be mean."

"I'm not. YEAH, TOMORROW? WELL, OKAY, BUDDY." Ted has had a successful phone conversation. Quick, and to the point.

"Awright, you can eat. Hey, sweetie, take him up so he can see."

There are no mementos in the living room, but Lou has put a few special things in a little room upstairs. Most of the pictures have to do with Ted, but the warmth of the room, and its character, have to do with Louise. This is no shrine. It is a room for right now, a room they walk through every day, and a handsome little place, too. Now it is filled with her quiet energy. "Here's Ted Williams when I met him," she says. "And if that isn't gorgeous, I'll eat my hat." And here's an old photo of Lou in shorts, with a fly rod, looking fragile next to a tarpon she pulled from Florida Bay. She does not seem fragile now. She is spry and able. She has been with Ted ten years straight, and that speaks volumes for her strength and agility. She gets angry sometimes that people do not credit Ted with tenderness—"You don't know him," she says, and her voice has a surprising edge—but she also knows he'll seldom show it. So here she shows a lonely young Ted with a little suitcase, off to flight school. Here's Ted and Tom Yawkey, and look: Mr. Yawkey has pictures of Ted behind him, too. "Here he is in Korea," says Louise. "You know, when he landed that plane, the blood was pouring from his ears. I have to tell people that . . . because he's *so* loud. Big, too." Lou picks up a cushion of a window seat. There are pictures beneath. "See, he's done so many things. . . ."

"Hey, you want a drink?" Ted is calling "TED WILLIAMS IS GONNA HAVE A DRINK."

Soon he flops into his chair with a tumbler, and hands over a videotape. He wants it in the VCR. He says: "This is the most wonderful guy. Hell of a guy. Bill Ziegler. I got him into the majors. . . ." That was when Ted came back in '69 to manage the Senators. Bill Ziegler was the trainer.

"So he had a son and he named him Ted Williams Ziegler. You're gonna see him now. IS IT IN? HEY, YOU LISTENING?" The tape shows Ziegler's two sons batting. Ziegler sends the tapes for analysis. The sound track sends out a steady percussion: *thwack . . . thwack . . . thwack*. Both boys get wood on the ball. "I'm gonna show you the first tape he sent, and I'm gonna ask what's the difference. See his kid, I told him his hips, he's got to get them OPEN."

From the kitchen, Lou protests: "Ted! Not now. Wait for me!"
"SEE? . . . *Thwack*. "Ground ball. A little slow with his hands."

From Lou: "Okay, okay, I don't know nothin'."

"HANDS THROUGH!" *Thwack*. "Center field, always to center, see where his hips are pointed? He's got to [*thwack*] OPEN 'EM UP."

From Lou, coming in, wiping her hands as she watches: "He doesn't step into it like Ted Williams."

Ted pretends he doesn't hear. "Hips come through OPEN. . . ."

"He doesn't bring his hands around like you do, honey."

"Yeah, he's got to, GROUND BALL!" See, when I'M up"—and now Ted takes his stance in the living room—"I'm grindin'. . . ." Now his hands are working. "I got the hands cocked. *COCKED!*" And here's the pitch. "*BAMMMM!*" says Ted, as he takes his cut and asks: "We got Bill Ziegler's number? WHERE'S HIS NUMBER?"

Ted is yelling on the phone in the kitchen, and Lou is in the living room, fitting her thoughts to small silences. "When Ted talks [*thwack*] it's always right now. . . ."

"BILL, I WANNA SEE HIM ON HIS FRONT FOOT MORE, AND THE HANDS QUICK, *QUICK*. . . ."

"You know, the baseball players . . . it's not macho, they're just . . . athletes, just beautiful boys. . . ."

Ted hangs up and throws himself into his chair: "AWRIGHT,

MAJOR LEAGUE! LET'S SET IT UP." That means dinner. Lou's cooking Chinese. Ted's still watching Ziegler's kids. "Ground ball. You don't make history hittin' 'em on the ground, boys." Now he pulls away from the TV. "Sweetie," he sings playfully. "We got any sake-o?" Lou sings: "Not tonight-eo." Ted sings: "Well, where's the wine-o?"

Lou says grace while all hold hands. Then we set to food, and Ted is major league. "It's good, huh?" he says between mouthfuls. "Well, isn't it? HEY! Aren't you gonna finish that rice?"

He's finished fast and back in his chair. "We got any sweets?"

A little album on the coffee table has pictures from Christmas. John Henry gave his letter of acceptance from Bates as his present to Ted. It's got Ted thinking now about the car he's got to buy so John Henry can take a car to school. "Got to have a car. . . ." He's thinking aloud so Louise can check this out. "Course, there's gonna have to be rules. . . ." He's working it over in his mind, and he muses: "Maybe say that other than school . . . he can't take the car if his mother says no. . . ." Lou is in a chair across the room. She's nodding. "HAVE to be rules," Ted says, "so he doesn't just slam out of the house . . . slam out and JUMP IN THE CAR. . . ."

Something has turned in his gut, and his face is working, growing harder. There's a mean glitter in his eye, and he's thinking of his elder daughter, walking away from him. . . .

"SLAM OUT . . . LIKE MY DAUGHTER USED TO . . ."

His teeth are clenched and the words are spat. It's like he's turned inward to face something we cannot see. It is a fearsome sight, this big man, forward, stiff in his chair, hurling ugly words at a vision of pain . . . I feel I should leave the room, but too late.

"*. . . THAT BURNED ME . . .*"

The switch is on. Lou calls it the Devil in him.

"*. . . A PAIN IN MY HAIRY RECTUM!*"

"Nice," says Lou. She is fighting for him. She has not flinched.

"Well, DID," he says through clenched teeth. "*AND MAKES YOU HATE BROADS! . . .*"

"Ted. Stop." But Ted is gone.

"*. . . HATE GOD! . . .*"

"TED!"

". . . *HATE LIFE!*"

"TED! . . . JUST . . . STOP!"

"DON'T YOU TELL ME TO STOP. DON'T YOU *EVER* TELL ME TO STOP."

Lou's mouth twists up slightly, and she snorts: "HAH!"

And that does it. They've beaten it, or Lou has, or it's just gone away. Ted sinks back in his chair. His jaw is unclenched. He grins shyly, "You know, I love this girl like I never . . ."

Lou sits back, too, and laughs.

"SHE'S IN TRAINING," Ted says. "I'M TEACHIN' HER . . ."

"He sure is," Lou says, like it's banter, but her voice is limp. She heads back to the kitchen, and Ted follows her with his eyes.

Then he finds me on his couch, and he tries to sneer through his grin: "WHEN ARE YOU LEAVING? HUH?"

". . . JESUS, YOU'RE LIKE THE GODDAMN RUSSIAN SECRET POLICE!

". . . OKAY, BYE! YEAH, SURE, GOODBYE!"

Ted walks me out to the driveway. As I start the car, Lou's face is a smile in the window, and Ted is bent at his belly, grabbing their new dalmatian puppy, tickling it with his big hands while the dog rolls and paws the air. And as I ease the car into gear, I hear Ted's voice behind, cooing, very quiet now: "Do I love this little dog, huh? . . . Yes, this little shittin' dog . . . Yes, yes I love you . . . Yes, I do."

—JUNE 1986

# AUTHOR BIOGRAPHIES

MARTIN AMIS (1949–) is the author of several novels, including *Money, London Fields,* and *The Information*; and works of criticism, including *The Moronic Inferno, Visiting Mrs. Nabokov,* and most recently, *The War Against Cliché.*

W. H. AUDEN (1907–1973) published many collections of poetry during his lifetime, including *Spain, Another Time,* and *Academic Graffiti.* In 1948, he was awarded the Pulitzer Prize in poetry for *The Age of Anxiety.*

JAMES BALDWIN (1924–1987), novelist and essayist, was the author of numerous books, including the novels, *Go Tell It on the Mountain, The Fire Next Time,* and *Another Country*; and the collections *Notes of a Native Son,* and *Nobody Knows My Name,* among others. He wrote several articles for *Esquire* during the Civil Rights era.

DONALD BARTHELME (1931–1989) was the author of four novels, including *Snow White,* over one hundred short stories, and the nonfiction collection, *Guilty Pleasures.*

JOHN BERRYMAN (1914–1972) is known for the erudition and originality of his poetry. His collections include *The Dispossessed, Homage to Mrs. Bradstreet,* and *77 Dream Songs,* for which he was awarded a Pulitzer Prize for poetry in 1965.

SVEN BIRKERTS (1952–) is the author of five books of essays and a memoir, *My Sky Blue Trades.* He edits the journal, *Agni,* based at Boston University.

HEINRICH BÖLL (1917–1985) was the author of *Billiards at Half-Past Nine, Group Portrait with Lady,* and *The Train Was on Time.* He won the Nobel Prize for literature in 1972.

CHIP BROWN (1953–) is a journalist and the author of *Afterwards You're a Genius: Faith, Medicine, and the Metaphysics of Healing* and *Good Morning Midnight: Life and Death in the Wild.* He was an *Esquire* contributing editor from 1989 to 1996.

PHILIP CAPUTO (1941–) is the author of several books, including *A Rumor of War,* a memoir of Vietnam. He shared the 1973 Pulitzer Prize in investigative reporting for his work at the *Chicago Tribune.*

TOM CARSON (1956–) writes *Esquire*'s "The Screen" column and is a contributing editor for the magazine. He is the author of *Gilligan's Wake*.

JOHN CHEEVER (1912–1982) is the author of *The Wapshot Chronicle*, for which he won a National Book Award, *Bullet Park*, and *Falconer*.

TOM CHIARELLA (1961–) is a Professor at DePauw University and the author of *Foley's Luck*, a book of short stories. He is an *Esquire* contributing editor.

RICHARD BEN CRAMER (1949–) is the author of *Ted Williams: The Season of the Kid* and most recently, *Joe DiMaggio: The Hero's Life*. In 1979 he won the Pulitzer Prize for international reporting.

SIMONE DE BEAUVOIR (1908–1986) is best known for that classic of feminist literature, *The Second Sex*. She was the author of many essays, novels, and autobiographical writings. Her novel, *The Mandarins*, won the Prix Goncourt in 1954.

PETE DEXTER (1943–) is the author of *Brotherly Love*, *The Paperboy*, and *Paris Trout*, which won the National Book Award for fiction in 1988. He wrote the "Sports Scenes" column for *Esquire* from 1984 to 1985.

JAMES DICKEY (1923–1997) was the author of *Deliverance*, *Helmets*, and *Buckdancer's Choice*, for which he received the 1966 National Book Award for poetry. He was the poetry editor of *Esquire* from 1971 to 1977.

JOAN DIDION (1934–) is the author of several essay collections and novels, including *Slouching Toward Bethlehem*, *The White Album*, *Play It as It Lays*, and most recently, *Political Fictions*. Didion and her husband, John Gregory Dunne, coauthored "The Coast" column for *Esquire* from 1976 to 1977.

DAVE EGGERS' (1970–) books include *A Heartbreaking Work of Staggering Genius* and *You Will Know Our Velocity*.

RALPH ELLISON (1914–1994) was the author of the novel, *Invisible Man*, and the essay collections, *Shadow and Act* and *Going to the Territory*. His novel, *Juneteenth*, was published posthumously.

NORA EPHRON (1941–) is best known for writing the romantic comedies, *Sleepless in Seattle* and *When Harry Met Sally*. She is also the author of two essay collections, *Crazy Salad* and *Scribble Scrabble*, and the novel, *Heartburn*.

M. F. K. FISHER (1908–1992) lived in Dijon, France, as a young woman and later became one of the most influential American writers on food and cooking. She is the author of *The Gastronomical Me*, *The Art of Eating*, and *Map of Another Town: A Memoir of Provence*.

F. Scott Fitzgerald (1896–1940) was the author of *The Great Gatsby*, and *Tender Is the Night*, among other books. His work appeared in the first issue of *Esquire* and in nearly every issue thereafter until his death. "The Crack-Up" has become a classic of confessional literature.

John Gardner (1933–1986) was the author of many books, including *Grendel*, *The Sunlight Dialogues*, *The Art of Living*, and *Mickelsson's Ghosts*.

Michael Herr (1940–) went to Vietnam for *Esquire* in 1967 and stayed for over a year. A decade later he published *Dispatches*, a collection of essays on the experience.

John Irving's (1942–) books include *The World According to Garp*, *The Hotel New Hampshire*, *The Cider House Rules*, and *A Prayer for Owen Meany*.

Tom Junod (1958–) has won two National Magazine Awards for feature writing. He has been an *Esquire* writer-at-large since 1997.

Robert Kurson (1963–) is a writer for the *Chicago Sun-Times* and has written two books about The Three Stooges. He was nominated for a National Magazine Award for "My Favorite Teacher."

Adrian Nicole LeBlanc (1964–) is a journalist and the author of *Random Family: Love, Drugs, Trouble and Coming of Age in the Bronx*.

John Leonard's (1939–) essay collections include *The Last Innocent White Man in America*, *When the Kissing Had to Stop*, and most recently, *Lonesome Rangers: Homeless Minds, Promised Lands, Fugitive Cultures*.

Norman Mailer (1923–) is the author of numerous books, including *The Naked and the Dead*, *Advertisements for Myself*, *Armies of the Night*, and most recently, *The Spooky Art: Thoughts on Writing*. He has written many articles for *Esquire*.

Greil Marcus (1945–) is the author of *Lipstick Traces*, *The Dustbin of History*, and most recently, *Double Trouble*. He wrote a column on culture for *Esquire* from 1998 to 1999.

Bucky McMahon (1955–) is an adventure writer. He has been a contributing editor at *Esquire* since 2001.

Claes Oldenburg (1929–) is known for such large-scale art projects as *Lipstick (Ascending) on Caterpillar Tracks* and *Clothespin*. He was one of a group of artists who developed the experimental performance art form of "The Happening" in the late 1950s.

Dorothy Parker (1893–1967) was the author of numerous poems, short stories, and critical essays. Her collections include *Lament for the Living*, *Death and Taxes*, and *The Constant Reader*. She wrote *Esquire*'s book review column from 1958 to 1962.

MICHAEL PATERNITI (1964–) is a journalist and the author of *Driving Mr. Albert.*

WALKER PERCY (1916–1990) was the author of several novels and books of nonfiction, including *Lost in the Cosmos, Signposts in a Strange Land,* and *The Moviegoer,* for which he won the 1962 National Book Award.

CHARLES P. PIERCE (1953–) is an *Esquire* contributing editor and the author of *Sports Guy* and *Hard to Forget: An Alzheimer's Story.*

DAWN POWELL (1896–1965), a figure in Greenwich Village's literary history, was the author of *Come Back to Sorrento, Angels on Toast,* and *My Home Is Far Away.*

SCOTT RAAB (1952–) is a graduate of the Iowa Writer's Workshop. He has been an *Esquire* writer-at-large since 1997.

JOHN H. RICHARDSON (1954–) is an *Esquire* writer-at-large, and has been writing for the magazine since 1997. A fiction writer and journalist, his most recent book was *In the Little World: A True Story of Dwarfs, Love and Trouble.*

MIKE SAGER (1956–) is an *Esquire* writer-at-large. He has written for the magazine for the past decade.

DAVID SEDARIS (1956–) is the author of *Me Talk Pretty One Day, Naked, Holidays on Ice,* and *Barrel Fever.* He is an *Esquire* contributing editor.

TERRY SOUTHERN (1924–1995) was the author of several novels, including *Candy* and *The Magic Christians*; nonfiction collections, including *Red Dirt Marijuana and Other Tastes*; and coauthor of several screenplays, including *Easy Rider* and *Dr. Strangelove.*

GLORIA STEINEM (1934–) is a cofounder of *Ms.* magazine. Her first major magazine story was published in *Esquire.*

GAY TALESE (1932–) is a literary journalist who wrote numerous articles for *Esquire* during the 1960s and 1970s. His books include *Fame and Obscurity, Honor Thy Father,* and *Unto the Sons.*

DYLAN THOMAS (1914–1953) was one of the most important and influential poets of the twentieth century.

FRANÇOIS TRUFFAUT (1932–1984) began his career as a critic for *Cahiers du Cinema,* although he is better known as a filmmaker of the French New Wave. A selection of his criticism was published as *The Films in My Life*; his films include *The 400 Blows, Jules and Jim,* and *Day for Night.*

GORE VIDAL (1925–), critic and novelist, is the author of many books, including *The City and the Pillar, Live from Golgotha,* and *The Golden Age,* the last in his "American Chronicles" series. He has written several articles for the magazine.

DANIEL VOLL's (1970–) short stories have appeared in many periodicals. He is an *Esquire* contributing editor, and was nominated for a National Magazine Award for "Nick Nolte Is Racing to Repair the Damage."

DAVID FOSTER WALLACE (1962–) is the author of the novels, *Infinite Jest* and *The Broom of the System*. He has also published the collections, *A Supposedly Fun Thing I'll Never Do Again*, *Brief Interviews with Hideous Men*, and *Girl with Hideous Hair*.

ORSON WELLES (1915–1985) directed, wrote, and starred in *Citizen Kane*, often hailed as the greatest film ever made. He went on to produce, direct, write, and act in numerous films, including *The Magnificent Ambersons*, *The Third Man*, and *Touch of Evil*. He received the Lifetime Achievement Award from the American Film Institute, and the D. W. Griffith Award from the Directors Guild of America.

ALEC WILKINSON (1952–) is the author of *Big Sugar*, *A Violent Act*, *Moonshine*, and *My Mentor: A Young Man's Friendship with William Maxwell*.

GARRY WILLS' (1934–) books include *A Necessary Evil: A History of American Distrust of Government*, *Papal Sin*, and *Why I Am a Catholic*. He won the 1993 Pulitzer Prize in nonfiction for *Lincoln at Gettysburg*.

TOM WOLFE (1931–) is perhaps the definitive writer of the sixties' New Journalism. He is the author of several books of nonfiction, including *The Pump House Gang* and *The Electric Kool-Aid Acid Test*, and novels, including *The Bonfire of the Vanities* and *A Man in Full*.

# CREDITS

Grateful acknowledgment is made to the following for permission to reprint copyrighted material:

The James Baldwin Estate: "Fifth Avenue, Uptown: A Letter from Harlem" by James Baldwin, collected in *Nobody Knows My Name*. © 1960 by James Baldwin, reprinted by arrangement with the James Baldwin Estate.

Sven Birkerts: "The Last Titan" by Sven Birkerts. © 2000 by Sven Birkerts, used by permission of the author.

Georges Borchardt, Inc.: "Do You Have What It Takes to Become a Novelist?" by John Gardner. © 1983 by John Gardner, reprinted by permission of Georges Borchardt, Inc.

Chip Brown: "The Transformation of Johnny Spain" by Chip Brown. © 1988 by Chip Brown, used by permission of the author.

Curtis Brown, Ltd.: "Hi, This Is Marcel Proust, Reporting from the Hamptons" by John Leonard. © 1976 by John Leonard, reprinted by permission of the author and Curtis Brown, Ltd.

Philip Caputo: "A Rumor of Resistance" by Philip Caputo. © 1980 by Philip Caputo, used by permission of the author.

Tom Carson: "And the Leni Riefenstahl Award for Rabid Nationalism Goes to . . . " by Tom Carson. © 1999 by Tom Carson, used by permission of the author.

Tom Chiarella: "The $20 Theory of the Universe" by Tom Chiarella. © 2003 by Tom Chiarella, used by permission of the author.

Don Congdon Associates, Inc.: "Repeat After Me" by David Sedaris. © 2002 by David Sedaris. "Is Truffaut the Happiest Man on Earth?" by François Truffaut. © 1970 by François Truffaut. Reprinted by permission of Don Congdon Associates, Inc.

Pete Dexter: "A Clean, Well-Lighted Gym" by Pete Dexter. © 1984 by Pete Dexter, used by permission of the author.

Donadio & Olson: "Hell Sucks" by Michael Herr from *Dispatches*. © 1977 by Michael Herr, used by permission of Donadio & Olson.

Éditions Gallimard: "Brigitte Bardot and the Lolita Syndrome" by Simone de Beauvoir from *Les écrits de Simone de Beauvoir*. © 1979 Éditions Gallimard, Paris, reprinted with permission of Éditions Gallimard.

Dave Eggers: "Long Live the Career Smoker" by Dave Eggers. © 1998, used by permission of the author.

Farrar, Straus & Giroux, LLC: "Tampa Stomp" from *Collected Poems 1937–1971* by John Berryman. © 1989 by Kate Donahue Berryman. "Why I Live Where I Live" from *Signposts in a Strange Land* by Walker Percy. © 1991 by Mary Bernice Percy. "That Kandy-Kolored Tangerine-Flake Streamline Baby" from *That Kandy-Kolored Tangerine-Flake Streamline Baby* by Tom Wolfe. © 1964 by Tom Wolfe, renewed in 1993 by Tom Wolfe. Reprinted by permission of Farrar, Straus & Giroux, LLC.

Garp Enterprises, Ltd.: "Gorgeous Dan" by John Irving. © 1973 by Garp Enterprises, Ltd., used by permission of Garp Enterprises, Ltd.

International Creative Management, Inc.: "A Few Words About Breasts" by Nora Ephron. © 1972 by Nora Ephron. "My Favorite Teacher" by Robert Kurson. © 2000 by Robert Kurson. "The Long Fall of One-Eleven Heavy" by Mike Paterniti. © 2000 by Mike Paterniti. "Nick Nolte is Racing the Clock to Repair the Damage" by Daniel Voll. © 1999 by Daniel Voll, reprinted by permission of International Creative Management, Inc.

Melanie Jackson Agency, LLC: "Staten Island, I Love You!" by Dawn Powell. © 1965 by Dawn Powell, reprinted by permission of Melanie Jackson Agency, LLC.

Janklow & Nesbit Associates: "Holy Water" by Joan Didion. © 1977 by Joan Didion. "Frank Sinatra Has a Cold" by Gay Talese. © 1966 by Gay Talese. "A Distasteful Encounter with William F. Buckley Jr." by Gore Vidal. © 1969 by Gore Vidal, reprinted by arrangement with Janklow & Nesbit Associates.

Tom Junod: "Can You Say . . . 'Hero'?" by Tom Junod. © 1998, used by permission of the author.

Adrian Nicole LeBlanc: "Falling" by Adrian Nicole LeBlanc. © 1995 Adrian Nicole LeBlanc, used by permission of the author.

Lescher & Lescher, Ltd.: "What Is the Difference Between This Photograph and a Real Frozen TV Dinner?" Copyright © 1970 by M. F. K. Fisher, reprinted by permission of Lescher & Lescher, Ltd.

Greil Marcus: "Bill Pullman's Face" by Greil Marcus. © 1998 by Greil Marcus, used by permission of the author.

Bucky McMahon: "Everest at the Bottom of the Sea" by Bucky McMahon. © 2000 by Bucky McMahon, used by permission of the author.

NAACP: "New York at 6:30 P.M." by Dorothy Parker. © 1964 by Dorothy Parker. The publisher wishes to thank the National Association for the Advancement of Colored People for the use of Dorothy Parker's work.

Bonnie Nadell: "Tennis Player Michael Joyce's Professional Artistry as a Paradigm of Certain Stuff about Choice, Freedom, Limitation, Joy, Grotesquerie, and Human Completeness" by David Foster Wallace, originally published in *Esquire* as "The String Theory." © 1996 by David Foster Wallace, reprinted by permission of the author and Frederick Hill and Bonnie Nadell, Inc.

New Directions Publishing Corporation: "The Crack-Up" by F. Scott Fitzgerald, from *The Crack-Up and Other Essays.* © 1945 by New Directions Publishing Corporation. "Fern Hill" by Dylan Thomas from *The Poems of Dylan Thomas.* © 1945 by The Trustees for the Copyrights of Dylan Thomas. "Lament" by Dylan Thomas, from

*The Poems of Dylan Thomas*, © 1952 by Dylan Thomas, reprinted with the permission of the New Directions Publishing Corporation.

Claes Oldenburg: "The Typewriter" by Claes Oldenburg, originally published as "My Very Last Happening." © 1969 by Claes Oldenburg, used by permission of the author.

Charles P. Pierce: "By Midnight" by Charles P. Pierce. © 1999 by Charles P. Pierce, used by permission of the author.

Scott Raab: "Zimmer" by Scott Raab. © 2001 by Scott Raab, used by permission of the author.

Random House, Inc.: "The More Loving One" from *The Collected Poems* by W. H. Auden. © 1957 by W. H. Auden. "The Golden Age/Time Past" by Ralph Ellison from *Shadow and Act*, © 1953, 1964 and renewed in 1981, 1992 by Ralph Ellison, used by permission of Random House, Inc.

John H. Richardson: "My Father, the Spy" by John H. Richardson. © 1999 by John H. Richardson, used by permission of the author.

Mike Sager: "Old" by Mike Sager. © 1998 by Mike Sager, used by permission of the author.

Susan Schulman, A Literary Agency: "Grooving in Chi" by Terry Southern. © 1968 by Terry Southern, reprinted by permission of the Terry Southern Literary Trust and Susan Schulman, A Literary Agency. All rights reserved.

Gloria Steinem: "Mrs. Kennedy at the Moment" by Gloria Steinem. © 1963 by Gloria Steinem, used by permission of the author.

Sterling Lord Literistic, Inc.: "What Do You Think of Ted Williams Now?" by Richard Ben Cramer. © 1986 by Richard Ben Cramer.

The Estate of Orson Welles: "Twilight in the Smog" by Orson Welles. © 1959 The Estate of Orson Welles. All rights reserved. Represented by Thomas A. White, Beverly Hills, California.

Alec Wilkinson: "Sam" by Alec Wilkinson. © 2002 by Alec Wilkinson, reprinted by permission of the author.

Wesleyan University Press: "For the Death of Vince Lombardi" by James Dickey from *The Central Motion: Poems 1968–1979*. © 1983 by James Dickey, reprinted with permission of Wesleyan University Press.

Writer's House, LLC: "Stichwort 1945" by Heinrich Böll. Copyright © 1965 by Heinrich Böll, collected in *Essayistiche Schriften und Reden*, Volume II, © 1979 by Verlag Kiepenheuer & Witsch Köln, reprinted by arrangement with Writer's House, LLC.

The Wylie Agency, Inc.: "Phantom of the Opera" (originally published in *Esquire* as "Ronnie and the Pacemakers"), by Martin Amis. © 1988 by Martin Amis. "And Now Let's Hear It for the Ed Sullivan Show!" by Donald Barthelme." © 1969 by Donald Barthelme. "Moving Out" by John Cheever. © 1960 by John Cheever. "Superman Comes to the Supermarket" by Norman Mailer. © 1960 by Norman Mailer. "What Makes the Newest Nixon Run?" by Garry Wills. © 1968 by Garry Wills. Reprinted with the permission of The Wylie Agency, Inc.

# ACKNOWLEDGMENTS

The editor gratefully acknowledges David Granger, Anna Godbersen, Lesley Bruynesteyn, Jackie Deval, Rachel Abramowitz, Peter Griffin, Mark Warren, Andrew Ward, Brendan Vaughan, and John Kenney. And to Arnold Gingrich and Harold Hayes, we can only offer our extreme gratitude.

# INDEX